FOUNDATIONS OF PROFESSIONAL COACHING

MODELS, METHODS, AND CORE COMPETENCIES

James Gavin, PhD, MCC

CONCORDIA UNIVERSITY

HUMAN KINETICS

Library of Congress Cataloging-in-Publication Data

Names: Gavin, James, 1942- author.

Title: Foundations of professional coaching : models, methods, and core competencies / James Gavin.

Description: Champaign, IL : Human Kinetics, 2022. | Includes bibliographical references and index.

Identifiers: LCCN 2021013690 (print) | LCCN 2021013691 (ebook) | ISBN 9781718200838 (paperback) | ISBN 9781718200845 (epub) | ISBN 9781718200852 (pdf)

Subjects: LCSH: Coaching (Athletics)

Classification: LCC GV711 .G29 2022 (print) | LCC GV711 (ebook) | DDC 796.07/7--dc23

LC record available at https://lccn.loc.gov/2021013690

LC ebook record available at https://lccn.loc.gov/2021013691

ISBN: 978-1-7182-0083-8 (print)

Senior Acquisitions Editor: Michelle Maloney; **Developmental Editor:** Anne Hall; **Managing Editor:** Hannah Werner; **Copyeditor:** Janet Kiefer; **Indexer:** Andrea J. Hepner; **Permissions Manager:** Dalene Reeder; **Graphic Designer:** Dawn Sills; **Cover Designer:** Keri Evans; **Cover Design Specialist:** Susan Rothermel Allen; **Photograph (cover):** Joe Klementovich / Getty Images; **Photo Production Manager:** Jason Allen; **Senior Art Manager:** Kelly Hendren; **Illustrations:** © Human Kinetics, unless otherwise noted; **Printer:** Sheridan Books

Printed in the United States of America   10 9 8 7 6 5 4 3 2 1

The paper in this book is certified under a sustainable forestry program.

Human Kinetics
1607 N. Market Street
Champaign, IL 61820
USA

United States and International
Website: **US.HumanKinetics.com**
Email: info@hkusa.com
Phone: 1-800-747-4457

Canada
Website: **Canada.HumanKinetics.com**
Email: info@hkcanada.com

E8207

Tell us what you think!
Human Kinetics would love to hear what we can do to improve the customer experience. Use this QR code to take our brief survey.

CONTENTS

PART II: GUIDING MODELS

PART III: THE COACH'S SKILL SET

ACCESSING THE HK*PROPEL* ONLINE CONTENT

INSTRUCTORS

If you received this book or ebook as a desk copy, you should use the access instructions provided by your sales representative instead of the access code printed on this page.

ALL OTHER USERS

Your purchase of the *Foundations of Professional Coaching* print book or ebook unlocks access to free HK*Propel* online content. The web resource includes several downloadable documents that will serve as practical tools for your successful coaching practice. We are certain you will enjoy this unique online learning experience.

Follow these steps to access the HK*Propel* online content. If you need help at any point in the process, you can contact us via email at HKPropelCustSer@hkusa.com.

If it's your first time using HK*Propel*:

1. Visit HKPropel.HumanKinetics.com.
2. Click the "New user? Register here" link on the opening screen.
3. Follow the onscreen prompts to create your HK*Propel* account.
4. Enter the access code exactly as shown below, including hyphens. You will not need to re-enter this access code on subsequent visits.
5. After your first visit, simply log in to HKPropel.HumanKinetics.com to access your digital product.

If you already have an HK*Propel* account:

1. Visit HKPropel.HumanKinetics.com and log in with your username (email address) and password.
2. Once you are logged in, navigate to Account in the top right corner.
3. Under "Add Access Code" enter the access code exactly as shown below, including hyphens.
4. Once your code is redeemed, navigate to your Library on the Dashboard to access your digital content.

Access code: GAVIN1E-B2AL-QP6J-TD9M

Once you have signed in to HK*Propel* and redeemed the access code, navigate to your Library to access your digital content. Your license to this digital product will expire seven years after the date you redeem the access code. You can check the expiration dates of all your HK*Propel* products at any time in My Account.

For technical support, contact us via email at HKPropelCustSer@hkusa.com. **Helpful tip:** You may reset your password from the log in screen at any time if you forget it.

PREFACE

WHAT'S YOUR RELATIONSHIP TO COACHING RIGHT NOW?

Are you a highly experienced practitioner, a beginner, someone who wants to learn core skills, or one who is somewhere else on a path of learning? As the title tells you, this book is foundational; it's not for everyone. Yet, foundational doesn't mean simple or basic. I think the word *core* also reflects its nature; it's must-know material, and there's a lot of it. It offers the essentials for becoming a competent coach practitioner.

WHY MIGHT YOU NEED THIS BOOK?

No matter where you are in your learning journey, my hunch is you will find much value in this book. It's not just for beginners. For experienced coaches, it offers opportunities to reground yourself in the cornerstones of your practice. This book provides practical wisdom derived from diverse sources relevant to coaching, learning, change, and helping relationships. Though there are so many approaches to coaching today, I believe there are central models that guide most practitioners around the globe. In this respect, the book's approach to and framing of essential competencies for coaching are fully aligned with those of the International Coaching Federation (ICF; formerly known as the International Coach Federation), making this work a critical read for those intending to pursue any level of coach certification.

Foundations of Professional Coaching provides historical and future perspectives about the coaching field. It identifies dominant roots of coaching knowledge. The ICF core competencies are deconstructed and reconstructed in a manner that makes their application more accessible. The coach's way of being is explored and aligned with a current appreciation of diversity, inclusion, and cultural humility. This book provides solidity and congruence to a field that is growing rapidly and in increasingly diverse directions.

WHY DID I WRITE THIS BOOK?

I direct and teach in an International Coaching Federation–accredited coach training program. Part of our curriculum requires participants to read extensively. As well, I know from former students and my coaching colleagues that the thirst for learning is never quenched. Fortunately, the literature on coaching is vast. Indeed, there are thousands of books and articles on coaching, yet there are only a few comprehensive texts. I thought I could make a contribution to the future of coaching by creating a strong foundational text. In my experience, no matter how intriguing and useful new methodologies have been in my career, I have always cycled back to foundational matters—how does change happen? What do my clients really need? What makes help helpful? How can I listen better? What is the quality of my relationships with my clients?

I had lots of other reasons for writing this book. Some were based on concerns and others were more inspirational. I'll begin with concerns. I have met magnificent, loving, and brilliant people working as coaches and as participants in various coach training programs. In my own coach training program, I have worked with community leaders, corporate officers, psychologists, social workers, human resources professionals, experienced consultants, and people with more letters after their names than I could count. These individuals had deep talent but generally little inherent comprehension of how coaching works. Becoming a coach isn't as easy as it is sometimes portrayed. I would hear my new students telling me, "I want to be an executive coach," "I want to be a life coach," "I want to empower women," "I want to coach young entrepreneurs," "I want to teach leaders all I know," and so on. Because of the explosion of coaching in our world, novice coaches can readily find books on almost any coaching topic or approach. If I think about the wonderful writings on narrative coaching, acceptance and commitment coaching, solution-focused coaching, or cognitive behavioral coaching, I say, "Wow, look how this amazing field is spreading its wings!" I also say, "I hope anyone reading these advanced books has first embodied the basics, the core essence of what coaching is and what it isn't. Do they appreciate the fundamental skills necessary to truly help people? Do they fully appreciate what partnering implies? Are they able to enter a coaching relationship while fully adhering to ethical guidelines?" Having made this book available comforts me. I feel good knowing that this resource is out in the world as a critical resource for those who want to achieve mastery in coaching practice.

As for inspiration, I have had the good fortune of studying with truly gifted teachers and inspirational human beings. My teachers came from diverse realms of this world. I don't think of just my academic or professional guides, because my list also includes people like my aikido sensei, Pierre Bohemier, who taught me so much about life and coaching. Indeed, my list is long and certainly includes many of my students who served as my awakeners. Over the decades of my life, I have gathered resources sufficient for me to say that I hold within me the collected wisdom of my teachers. I needed to share what I have learned.

WHAT THE BOOK IS AND ISN'T

There is simply too much going on in the world of coaching to be adequately embraced in even a very big book. There are countless approaches to coaching, schools of coaching, theories of coaching, techniques of coaching, and on and on. This book doesn't attempt to survey all that exists. It focuses on foundation.

Foundation consists of many things. This book is built around models, principles, competencies, and ethics. It reflects perspectives articulated by various coaching bodies and, in particular, the International Coaching Federation. What the ICF has put out in the world addresses the core of coaching. In dialogues with master practitioners, I have come to believe that one can never spend enough time emphasizing and exploring foundational matters, like what represents good listening? Or what makes a question useful? When can I offer advice? Or when is my voice too prominent? Whenever I sit with other ICF assessors evaluating candidates for coach certification, these and other fundamental questions consume our discussions. Did the coach candidate create safety? And how do we know for

sure? Was the coach leading the client or serving as a true partner?

This book is richly referenced with over 600 diverse sources of information—books, dissertations, journal articles, and opinion pieces. I might represent this work as an *evidence-based* treatise on coaching, but in truth it is more than that. It could equally be described as *practice-based* since so much wisdom from the field has been harvested here. I mostly consider it a richly researched and widely sourced text on coaching that includes a lot of evidence, an ocean of practical knowledge, and plenty of opinion. It contains vast resources necessary for practice as a coach as well as for those who mostly want to hold competent coach-like conversations. In addition, the accompanying online resources, which can be accessed by reading the HK*Propel* Access Code Page at the front of this book, provides additional downloadable tools to help you with your coaching practice.

WHAT'S UNIQUE ABOUT THIS BOOK?

Much in this text is unique. Let me pick a few aspects from the top of my list:

- It offers a powerful and original structure for navigating coaching conversations.
- It describes a metalevel model of the "dance" movements throughout a coaching relationship.
- It dives deeply into the processes of change, reflecting multiple overlapping perspectives.
- It fully articulates a coach's way of being as grounded in humility.
- It interweaves professional wisdom, practical guidance, and personal learnings.

Of course, another notable feature is that this book carefully deconstructs and reconstructs the International Coaching Federation's new framework for the eight core coaching competencies. In 2019, the ICF revised its original set of eleven core coaching competencies in a manner that simultaneously reduced the number to eight while increasing the scope and depth of these competencies. *This was not an easy feat!* From 2021 onward, the ICF will evaluate all candidates for certification according to criteria articulated in the new set of eight competencies. This book will be an essential guide for appreciating the deep structure of these coaching competencies.

Foundations of Professional Coaching goes well beyond definitions of core coaching competencies to help readers understand the microskills that are integral to effective coaching. It's my belief that this book makes more visible the connections between old and new sets of competencies, as well as between the unique language of coaching and the broader language of the helping professions, which include teaching, mentoring, counseling, advising, leading, consulting, and psychotherapy.

WHAT SHAPES MY APPROACH?

I do abide by Carl Rogers' belief that what is most personal is most general, and in this respect I try to be transparent about my perspectives throughout the chapters. This means that I name and own my slant on things, as much as that is possible in a writing of this sort. Let me identify a few of my slants represented in this work. The first is that I was deeply influenced by the person and writings of Carl Rogers, one of the founders of humanistic psychology and the originator of client-centered practice. I had the good fortune of working with him at the beginning of my career. He touched me at a core level in the way he showed up in such a genuine, caring, transparent, and human way. I continue to hold him as a model for how I strive to be in my daily presence on this planet. His voice comes through in different places in this book.

Another slant arises from the fact that I was trained as a psychologist. I began my practice long before the emergence of positive psychology, although I think in honoring Rogers' philosophy, I have generally experienced myself as inherently aligned with this field. I have always been drawn to the light in our existence while at the same time acknowledging the significance of our dark nights of the soul. I was a fully engaged participant in what was known as the human potential movement in the 1960s and beyond, and my work has been consistently directed toward growth and empowerment rather than rehabilitation. In this regard, I have never come to my work with a diagnostic or labeling perspective but rather one of respect, curiosity, and an offer to help in whatever ways seem appropriate. When coaching began to develop as a distinct

profession, I once again experienced a serendipitous alignment of purposes and practices. I can easily say, I think like a coach, I act like a coach, and I embody the way of coaching.

For decades, I have worked in a diversely constituted university department. It's not psychology, and, in fact, it's hard to capture in any simple way. Everyone in my department is a helping professional who intervenes to benefit the quality of our human existence. There are educators, social workers, family experts, leisure theorists, diversity professionals, Indigenous knowledge leaders, social innovation modelers, and more. My colleagues have been my teachers, and as a result very little of what I say seems solely sourced by any particular discipline.

In my writing, I rely on a fundamental microskills understanding of coach communication. The microskills perspective breaks down all the different kinds of interventions that helpers express in their work, whether they are coaching, interviewing, counseling, mentoring, consulting, or advising. This perspective allows us to get beneath some of the big ideas represented in coaching competencies, such as creating awareness. How do you do that with clients? Well, a number of microskills are especially designed to do exactly that. So, my slant is to break down core coaching competencies into their implicit microskills.

I have one other slant that I want to name, but it's a bit hard to frame. I'll try it this way. I believe we need to see beyond what we can see and that this requires help from others. We all have our limiting beliefs, our conditioned reflexes, and our blind spots. More than that, those around us are similarly hampered. I don't think coaches ever have the answers for anyone, but I do believe that in the human chemistry of a coaching conversation, wisdom is created. There's a common expression in the coaching field that clients have the answers to their own issues within them. I don't think this is entirely true. I think a lot of the answers that we are seeking to our complex human issues need to be *cocreated* in dialogues with sensitive listeners and deep thinkers. This is part of what I love about Otto Scharmer's (2016) work on the types of dialogues that lead us toward an emerging future that is not yet, that needs to be touched and brought into being. I do believe that good coaches are able to move efficiently into these dialogues to enable their clients to discover and then embody.

HOW TO READ THIS BOOK

The book builds knowledge and skill as it moves from chapter to chapter. In alignment with the title, each chapter serves as foundation for the next. Chapters 1 and 2 frame the field of coaching by delving into its origins and growth. Chapter 3 locates the approach to coaching advocated in this text by exploring the meaning and centrality of goals in this work. Chapter 4 describes three meaningful models of the change process, while chapter 5 offers three models to guide coaching interventions within sessions and throughout the relationship. Chapters 6 through 15 explore coaching competencies aligned with the ICF's new framing of eight core coaching competencies. These chapters represent deep dives into the skill structures required for effective coaching. The final chapter, chapter 15, reflects the ICF's second core competency, Embodies a Coaching Mindset, but it is much more than that. It illuminates the practice of coaching as a way of being and underpins that way with an exploration of humility as a suggested manner for how coaches might show up in the world.

Throughout this book there are illustrations of coaching that you will find in vignettes and examples. These are composites rather than actual stories. Yet, they capture core experiences of clients I have worked with over the years. So, please trust that confidentiality has in no way been betrayed in any of the descriptions you read.

I profoundly hope this book gives you what you need and that you come to cherish ideas gleaned from its pages. I trust that your work in coaching will serve both your personal evolution and some portion of the overwhelming needs of this world.

ACKNOWLEDGMENTS

A work of this nature is never a solitary expression. Its birth emerges from the confluence of so many energies. I will begin by thanking Human Kinetics Publishers for stepping forward in a new direction by welcoming this book, and in particular Michelle Maloney and Anne Hall, who served magnificently in enabling and guiding the birthing process.

A forerunner of this book was coauthored with my dear colleague, Dr. Madeleine Mcbrearty, who was forever present in my reflections on how and what to write. Madeleine and I have taught coaching together for almost two decades, and as I say each year, our relationship and work just seem to get better and better. I am deeply indebted to her.

I want to acknowledge all my clients, students, teachers, colleagues, and mentors whose voices live within me and are reflected in how I think about this amazing world of coaching. Thank you. In particular, I want to express my appreciation to Dr. Nicolò Francesco Bernardi, who had major input to the work on neuroscience and Dr. Monic Robillard who inspired me to include a new piece on the hero or heroine's journey of change. I am deeply grateful.

I have five children from two different marriages. I feel blessed by all the gifts I have received from my children and their mothers. They have magnified my appreciation of this world and how best I can contribute. All my children and my dear partner, Eva, shape the structures and meaning of my life. Words are inadequate. My oldest, Jessica, took on the daunting task of critiquing the original manuscript and did so with grace and wisdom.

My final thanks go to you, my readers. You inspire me. Your willingness to engage this work represents courage and an immense gift to our global community.

PART I

THE FIELD OF COACHING

CHAPTER 1

EVOLUTION OF A COACHING PROFESSION

You're off to great places! Today is your day!
Your mountain is waiting, so get on your way!

Dr. Seuss

MY STORY

I grew up in the heart of New York City before it was the safe tourist destination that we know today. Back then, even from my childhood vantage point, I remember feeling troubled about how people related to one another as well as how they were inside themselves. I thought a lot of people seemed robotic—just going through the motions of life. I knew then that when I grew up, I wanted to do something to better understand what I was seeing, and to perhaps help people become more authentic and joyful versions of themselves.

In my early teen years, I carried the nickname in my family of "The Fish." Indeed, I was a very happy member of my high school swim team, and, by the way, I had a great coach. As I recall, that's when I developed a clearer sense of a career intention. I thought someday I would become a coach. My coach, Joe Steady, not only helped me break a few swimming records here and there, but he was also a great person to talk to, especially during those early adolescent years.

Well, dreams do come true. I did become a coach, but the kind of coach I have become bears little semblance to what Joe Steady did in his role . . . except maybe for the exquisite listening part. I didn't fully leave behind the idea of being a swimming coach (in fact, I coached swimming off and on through my college years); rather I folded this aspiration into other ways of working with people in a helpful way. Notably, I became a psychologist in the 1970s, and when in the 1990s the field of coaching was relatively newborn, I envisioned a whole new pathway toward my dreams.

That was almost 30 years ago, and from today's perspective I want to tell you that this is truly an amazing young profession. Yet there has been such explosive growth in coaching that it is rather difficult to offer any simple description of the field or any clear forecast of where it's going. I do know that the growth of this field is only beginning and that we are nowhere near being able to identify all of the potential career paths that are likely to emerge. In this chapter, I want to offer a perspective about the coaching field and to capture key reasons why I believe it represents such promising and rewarding career opportunities.

How and when did coaching become such a positive force for human growth and development? What happened in the world that called forth this creative new profession and nourished its evolution? Where is the field now, and where is it going? Who are the coaches, and where might we find them? This chapter explores the various forces in society as well as in the helping professions that gave rise to the field of professional coaching. Here are some guiding questions to consider as you read:

- Is there a clear definition of professional coaching?
- Is coaching like therapy or consulting?
- Can anyone be a coach?
- When and where did coaching originate?
- Where is coaching going?

DEFINING COACHING

In most contexts of the modern world, you are likely to hear people using the word *coaching*. You may encounter it in a friend's offer to coach you on something that you want to learn, or you may have met people who present themselves as professional coaches. Schools, businesses, hospitals, social service agencies, and so many other settings either refer to styles of communicating as coaching or have people who occupy formal roles authorizing them to offer coaching services. In truth, the number of contexts in which you will hear the term *coaching* is likely to leave you wondering whether there is any coherence to it at all, or whether it is simply a generic way in which people talk about helping each other with whatever knowledge, skills, and intentions they may have.

Partly because the notion of coaching is embedded in so many historical roles like sport coaching or on-the-job coaching and training, it has been difficult for the profession of coaching to elevate the term to a level where it affords more clarity—like the terms *psychotherapy* or *consulting*. Sure, even these terms have some ambiguity, but it's improbable that someone would walk over to you in a casual way and say, "Would it be okay if I do some psychotherapy with you?" The fact is that a generic framing of coaching is unlikely to go away; nevertheless, a strong and well-identified profession of coaching is currently evolving. The bottom line here is that despite an untold number of definitions and applications of coaching in the world, a robust coaching profession has emerged in the past few decades.

According to the **International Coaching Federation** (ICF, 2020e), "Coaching is partnering with clients in a thought-provoking and creative process that inspires them to maximize their personal and professional potential." The ICF is the world's largest professional association of coaches, and its definition encompasses a commonly accepted understanding of coaching. There are innumerable alternative definitions, but I would like to work with this one to get closer to a starting point for our learning journey.

The ICF definition can be analyzed into four key components: *First*, it speaks of a way that coaches and clients are in relationship; namely, they are in a partnership where, as much as possible, responsibilities are shared and power dynamics are minimized. There is an effort to create equality and collaboration. *Second*, the definition describes the process of coaching as thought-provoking and creative. Here, you can imagine coaches working with clients in an out-of-the-box fashion to provoke deep thought about what matters most to them. *Third*, the impact of this process is identified as being intentionally inspirational. Coaches aim to breathe new life into their clients' musings and perspectives in order for them to find ample energy and motivation for forward movement. *Finally*, the definition asserts that the process of coaching is directed toward generating optimal outcomes, maximizing potential, and empowering clients to achieve their aspirations and goals.

DIVERSITY IN DEFINITIONS

As newcomers to the field of coaching, an initial task will be to identify the core characteristics of professional coaching. That's why I wanted you to begin with the ICF's widely acknowledged and respected definition (ICF, 2020e). As you broaden your review of coaching, you will inevitably come across many other ways in which coaching has been described. The sidebar (Definitions of Coaches and Coaching) provides a sampling.

You might notice in browsing through these definitions that terms are sometimes vague, or they could equally well apply to other ways of helping, including mentoring, counseling, and consulting. One author tried to make sense of the variety of definitions of coaching by reviewing 76 definitions of *life coaching*, which represents one of the principle applications of coaching methodologies. Jarosz's (2016) analysis of these definitions approximated the ICF expression of what coaching is. She summarized common threads running throughout the

Definitions of Coaches and Coaching

A few of the many definitions of coaches and coaching per se are referenced here:

- "A coach is a person who facilitates experiential learning that results in future-oriented abilities. . . . [A coach is] a person who is a trusted role model, adviser, wise person, friend, mensch, steward, or guide—a person who works with emerging human and organizational forces to tap new energy and purpose, to shape new vision and plans, and to generate desired results. A coach is someone trained in and devoted to guiding others into increased competence, commitment, and confidence" (Stober & Grant, 2006, p. 3).

- "Coaching is directly concerned with the immediate improvement of performance and development of skills by a form of tutoring or instruction" (Parsloe, 1995, p. 18).

- "Coaching is a catalyzing relationship that accelerates the process of great performance; it's about individuals and/or organizations identifying purpose and living out of that purpose" (Coach U, 2005, p. 10).

- "Masterful coaching is about inspiring, empowering, and enabling people to live deeply in the future while acting boldly in the present" (Hargrove, 2008, p. 2).

- "[Coaching] is a way of effectively empowering people to find their own answers, encouraging and supporting them on the path as they continue to make important choices" (Kimsey-House et al., 2018, p. xvi).

- "Coaching is . . . a developmental conversation and dialogue, a co-creative process between coach and coachee with the purpose of giving (especially) the coachee a space and an opportunity for immersing him/herself in reflection on and new understandings of (1) his or her own experiences in the specific context and (2) his or her interactions, relations and negotiations with others in specific contexts and situations. This coaching conversation should enable new possible ways of acting in the contexts that are the topic of the conversation" (Stelter, 2014, p. 9).

- "Coaching is unlocking a person's potential to maximize their own performance. It is helping them to learn rather than teaching them" (Whitmore, 1992, p. 8).

- Coaching is "that part of a relationship in which one person is primarily dedicated to serving the long-term development of effectiveness and self-generation in the other" (Silsbee, 2010, p. 4).

- Coaching is a "collaborative, solution-focused, result-oriented systematic process, used with normal, non-clinical populations, in which the coach facilitates the self-directed learning, personal growth, and goal attainment of the coachee" (Grant, 2003, p. 254).

- Coaching is a "systematic and collaborative helping intervention that is non-directive, goal oriented and performance-driven, intended to facilitate the more effective creation and pursuit of another's goals (Ives & Cox, 2012, p. 26).

- "Coaching is a human development process that involves structured, focused interaction and the use of appropriate strategies, tools and techniques to promote desirable and sustainable change for the benefit of the coachee and potentially for other stakeholders" (Cox et al., 2014, p. 1).

- "Life coaching is a long-term efficient relationship that allows clients to maximise their potential" (Jarosz, 2016, p. 40).

76 sources in this simple statement: "Life coaching is a long-term efficient relationship that allows clients to maximise their potential" (p. 40). Though largely similar, her conclusion differs in important ways from the ICF definition. For one, it doesn't specify the nature of the relationship, namely that of partnership, emphasized by the ICF, and it doesn't speak much about the process other than by saying that it is efficient, meaning that it endeavors to produce the greatest result for the client's investment of time, money, effort, and other resources. What may

come as a surprise to you is that Jarosz characterized coaching as a long-term relationship, stating that "it hardly ever brings about instantaneous changes" (p. 40).

Bear in mind that Jarosz's (2016) study was based only on definitions of one type of coaching, namely, life coaching. It is partly for this reason that some coaching experts entirely sidestep the task of defining coaching. They believe that no single definition is capable of capturing the diverse purposes, models, processes, clientele, and contexts that con-

---

Convergences in Perspectives About Coaching

There are some important agreements about what coaching is and what it isn't within the field. Distinguishing characteristics that seem common to most approaches to coaching include the following (Ives, 2008; Ives & Cox, 2012; Jarosz, 2016; Kimsey-House et al., 2018; Passmore & Fillery-Travis, 2011; Toogood, 2012; van Nieuwerburgh, 2017):

- Coaching is directed toward the realization of human potential. Its unwavering focus is toward growth and learning.
- Core values or principles in coaching posit that clients are creative, resilient, resourceful, and capable of reaching objectives they desire.
- Clients are considered to be experts in their own lives and, in this light, uniquely determine what agendas and outcomes they pursue.
- At its core, coaching is a nonhierarchical, collaborative, and client-centered experience based on mutual trust and respect.
- Coaching represents an appreciative stance that inspires both coach and client to search for resources and strengths rather than for weaknesses and deficits.
- Coaching focuses on solutions rather than on problems, with conversations that are centered more in the present and future than in the past.
- Coaches partner with clients in processes of inquiry, discovery, meaning making, strategizing, planning, and ensuring sustainability in goal pursuit.
- Coaching represents processes of deep reflection and open-minded curiosity.
- Coaching typically involves a flexible communication process encompassing modern technology (digital telecommunications) as well as more traditional forms of professional meetings.
- Accountability is two-sided; coaches are accountable for managing the process in a coach-like manner while clients hold themselves accountable for commitments they generate in coaching.

---

stitute the world of coaching today (Bachkirova et al., 2018). This speaks volumes about the extensive growth and diversification of the coaching field over the past few decades (see sidebar, Convergences in Perspectives About Coaching).

The more you explore the coaching world, the more you will realize its richness and multiplicity of structures and approaches. The next section will dive into a few practice-based matters you might want to understand.

PRACTICAL MATTERS

Who does what in coaching? Where and how does it happen? What kind of arrangements are involved in coaching?

As previously noted, lots of people may refer to a conversation they have with another person as a coaching conversation, and many may also list coaching on their business materials as one of the services they provide. In this book, I will consistently refer to coaching as a profession. As such,

coaches meet professional standards, they have undergone coach training, they draw up contracts with clients, they schedule sessions, they may have offices, they continue their education, and they do a myriad of other things that distinguish them from people who casually say, "Hey, can I coach you on that?"

We also have some relevant information about the clients who engage coaches for periods of time. The ICF's (2020a) most recent global study of coaching provides basic statistics about coaching clients. Around the globe, 57 percent of clients identify as female, with 5 percent of clients under 25 years, 19 percent between the ages of 26 and 34, 37 percent in the 35- to 44-year-old age category, 30 percent between ages 45 and 54, and only 9 percent above that age. Additionally, coaches in this study indicated that 27 percent of their clients were managers, 23 percent executives, 14 percent business owners, and 19 percent were seeking coaching for personal matters.

Of course, with all the variations of coaching styles, models, venues, and methods, you will find differences in many aspects of how coaches work.

What I will offer here are general perspectives about coaching practice.

Who Can Use the Title of Coach?

At present, almost anyone can use the title of coach. The title isn't regulated by government bodies or legal statutes. That said, professional associations like the ICF and the Europe-based Association for Coaching not only establish standards for the profession but also certify coaches who meet specific criteria. In its global coaching study, the ICF (2020a) indicated that 95 percent of practicing coaches had formal coach training ranging from 60 hours into the hundreds. Beyond hours of training, most people who refer to themselves as coaches have been certified by either a training institute or a professional association—or both. Coaches in the ICF study overwhelmingly agreed that potential clients screen coaches based on whether they are certified. The future is likely to be more exclusive. There is increasing pressure within and outside the coaching field to establish regulations concerning the practice of coaching and use of the title of coach.

Who Hires a Coach?

Both individual clients and organizations hire coaches. Within this professional field, people seeking coaching services are referred to as either coachees or clients, with no particular distinction between these terms. Throughout this book, I will use the term *client*, though in some of your other readings you are likely to come across the term *coachee*. They are interchangeable. Individuals may engage a coach to work with them on an identified agenda. Organizations may hire coaches to work with employees within their system in order to promote alignment, work motivation or well-being.

How Often and for How Long Do Coaches Meet With Their Clients?

There are some standards in the field pertaining to meeting duration, but wide variation is evident among coaches. The recent ICF (2020a) global study reported that about 27 percent of clients work with coaches for less than 3 months, 37 percent continue for more than 3 months and up to 6 months, 23 percent engage for between 7 to 12 months, and 13 percent continue beyond a year. A common practice is for coaches to propose an initial coaching contract of 3 months on a biweekly basis, which translates as six coaching sessions, before the coach and client pause to take stock of progress and renegotiate their work together. Of course, codes of ethics within the coaching field recommend that, no matter where you are in the process, when clients don't seem to be engaged or when desired results aren't forthcoming, coaches need to consider referring the client to another professional or otherwise terminate the relationship.

How Long Is a Typical Coaching Session?

The modal length of an individual session was found to be one hour by 43 percent of coaches, though an additional 32 percent reported their sessions lasting for between one and two hours according to the ICF (2020a) global study. A norm in the field is that coaching sessions are scheduled for roughly an hour on a biweekly basis, often with the coach's openness to clients communicating via web messaging or phone in between appointments.

Where Do Coaches Meet Clients?

The ICF (2020a) study found that coaches use multiple venues for meeting clients. Roughly 72 percent of coaches reported that they frequently coached clients in person, 48 percent frequently used audiovisual platforms, and 35 percent used the telephone frequently. Other forms of communication that were described as being frequently used included texts and emails. The global pandemic that was identified in 2020 will likely affect these statistics in favor of virtual communications.

While you may be concerned about the quality of engagement with telephone-based coaching, studies in the related area of psychotherapy suggest that high quality service can be provided by phone at a comparable level to face-to-face sessions (Andersson et al., 2014; Stiles-Shields et al., 2014). Given the need for coaching to fit the lifestyles of today's clients, it is likely that coaches will increasingly conduct their sessions in virtual ways, and when possible, they will meet in person. In times when appointments take place in person, it may well be that coaches travel to client offices or they might arrange to meet with them in their own private settings.

My hope is that clarification of these few details helps you fill out your emerging picture of the coach's work. We will spend time examining other matters like contracts with clients, cancellation policies, making referrals, and confidentiality in later sections of the book.

CRITICAL DISTINCTIONS

Another way to help you understand coaching is by describing *what it is not*. Here are some simple distinctions: Coaching is not about dwelling on the past to discover the root causes of a person's psychological and relational dysfunctions; it is not therapy. Likewise, coaching is not expert consulting—giving advice or proposing solutions to identified issues. Nor is it mentoring, which can be described as providing expert knowledge and practical guidance based on the mentor's experience. More generally speaking, coaching is not about giving advice, even though many people who are attracted to coaching may believe that the nature of coaching is centered in advice giving. Nothing could be further from the truth.

One of the thorniest distinctions to make is drawing a clear line between psychotherapy (or psychological counseling) and coaching. A number of writers argue that coaching clients enter a coaching relationship in a state of psychological health (Jordan & Livingstone, 2013; Stelter, 2014), though factual evidence about this is not readily available. It is clear that, as a profession, coaching is strongly oriented toward growth and development, rather than being focused on emotional and existential suffering (Stelter, 2014).

Throughout the literature on coaching, one finds unequivocal statements that coaches are neither trained nor authorized to engage in deep emotional or psychotherapeutic processes, yet the close relationship between the fields of therapy and coaching necessitates constant monitoring by practicing coaches (Grant & Green, 2018). Some coaching experts go a step further, asserting that coaches should not focus on emotional issues (Grant, 2012; Ives & Cox, 2012), though this is not a pervasive opinion in the field. In all of this, it is safe to say that coaching associations are doing their utmost to guide practitioners toward an application that remains solidly in the domain of accepted coaching interventions, offering referrals to those clients who may be better served by a psychotherapist or other helping professional.

What adds to the challenge of distinguishing coaching and therapy is the heavy reliance of coaching practice on psychological theories. Even though these theories and their recommended methods have been adapted for use by coaches, the fact is they were originally intended to guide therapeutic interventions. Examples of adaptations include psychodynamic coaching, narrative coaching, solution-focused coaching, and cognitive behavioral coaching, to mention just a few. The prevalence of psychological theories in the coaching literature raises major questions about what coaches may be doing in their sessions (Cox, 2013; Grant & Green, 2018). Coaching experts, in reflecting on the field's early reliance on psychologically based methods, have attempted to foster a greater appreciation of coaching's rootedness in learning theories and principles of human development. To that end, more recent coaching literature increasingly supports the position that the central foundation of coaching practice is far more aligned with learning and educational models than with psychotherapeutic perspectives (Cox, 2013; Ives & Cox, 2012; Stelter, 2014, 2018). Models of how humans learn, how they change, and how they develop over the life span offer profound guidance and insights into what clients might need in their journeys of self-initiated transformation.

Coaching, in its broadest conceptualization, reflects the wider trend that we see in the world of interdisciplinary fields of theory and practice. Increasingly, it has become difficult to say that particular ideas or practices belong exclusively to any one field of study. In this respect, it is entirely reasonable that coaching—as an interdisciplinary field—would identify its roots in an extensive range of established fields of study and practice such as education, psychology, communications, leadership, and systems thinking, among others. Even so, coaching experts will need to continue efforts to articulate exactly how coaching is a distinctive profession in its own right. One important focus of this work can be seen in coaching's strong philosophical stance about equality in the relationship of coach and client that allows for true dialogue in coaching sessions; this contrasts with a more traditional hierarchical process that typically involves someone with an identified problem being supported by an expert trained in a particular helping modality (e.g., medicine, psychotherapy, consulting, or social work).

I have taken time with you to draw your attention to how the coaching field positions itself in relation to psychotherapy for a couple reasons: The first is that with all of the ambiguity about what coaching is, newcomers to the field need to understand that coaching is not a synonym for something resembling therapy. A second reason is that as your career path in coaching matures, you will likely be part of continuing efforts ensuring that coach training rigorously transmits models and methods fostering coach-like rather than therapist-like behaviors.

I have not spent much time discussing how coaching differs from consulting. Here, the differences are clearer. Consultants are often positioned as experts who study issues and make recommendations. Generally speaking, consulting is not built around a premise of partnership. Of course, many coaches occasionally offer guidance and instruction to their clients, but their predominant style is not one of being the expert. Most coaches would acknowledge that if a coach's style is more about giving advice and information than listening and engaging in dialogue, it is more likely to reflect the norms of a consulting rather than a coaching role.

COACHING VERSUS COACHABLE MOMENTS

Another important distinction contrasts what happens with a coach and client in a professional coaching relationship and what occurs when a person who is not a professional coach offers to coach another person. Given the ubiquity of coaching in our modern world, you will hear people talking about either giving or receiving coaching in a wide range of contexts. A recent example emerged in a conversation with a close friend who told me how a colleague of hers was an excellent coach. She said,

"I didn't know how to structure a conversation with this guy who heads up an institute, and she told me exactly what to say. . . . She knows what works for him and the kinds of details he needs to make a decision." I appreciatively commented, "Oh great . . . I'm so glad you got what you needed . . . and just as a point of information, that's not how I understand coaching . . . maybe that's mentoring." We're not going to explore mentoring here other than to say it is more akin to consulting than it is to coaching. However, I do want to note that when people say they "coached" or were "coached by" somebody, often the meaning of what actually occurred is at odds with what professional coaches do. One area where this happens a lot today is in organizations. Vast numbers of managers attend daylong or multiple-day training sessions on coaching. It seems to be part of the mindset about managing in modern-day corporate cultures. The boss doesn't tell you what to do; she coaches you. Well, you know what I'm going to say: It really isn't coaching—although it may constitute what I would call a coaching conversation.

What's a **coaching conversation** (see table 1.1)? It's a conversation that arises in the moment to meet

Table 1.1   Coaching and Coachable Moments

	Professional coaching relationship	A coachable moment
Description	An ongoing professional relationship that is bounded by contractual terms and a professional code of conduct	Typically, an ad hoc conversation occurring in virtually any relationship (e.g., friendship, work, family, sports)
Context	A fee-for-service practice occurring by prearrangement either in a formal setting (office) or via electronic or phone contact	Occurring within another form of relationship in venues appropriate to that relationship (home, phone, office)
Assessments	Assessment of coachability, readiness to change, psychometric measurements, and other relevant indicators	Informal impressionistic observations, opinions, and perhaps prior knowledge
Focus	An explicit and consensually validated topic or subject of discussion along with exploration of its meaning, concrete goals, vision of success, and action plans	Focus on a current problem, with the intent of helping the person move from their current state to a more desirable state or outcome
Scope	Concerned with the whole person and intentionally aimed at immediate and long-term growth and development	Specific to aspects of the problem under discussion without focusing on extraneous elements
Process	A structured dialogue involving active listening, inquiry, feedback, and challenge to foster awareness, growth, action planning, and commitment	Informal and conversational in nature without clear structure or specific processes
Follow-up	The identification and development of support structures for client accountability to agreed-upon actions	Accountability not usually addressed

a particular need. It represents scenarios where one person expresses a problem or a dilemma and the other person, after listening, offers opinions or guidance. Maybe the manager who went to a one-day training session on coaching will have a little more finesse and try to partner with the problem presenter and help her come up with her own solution. Whatever shape it takes, once the discussion is finished, the coaching relationship typically ends or shifts into another kind of relationship. In the example here, the manager reverts to managing and directing.

The appeal of coaching is so widespread that you may hear people's stories about being coached by a seatmate during a flight or on the commute to work. In table 1.1, I offer a contrast between features of a coaching conversation and those of a professional coaching relationship. Though we haven't drilled into some of the features of professional coaching listed in this table, we will do so in upcoming chapters. However, there is one term in this table that may need clarification now. The term **coachability** refers to the coach's assessment of whether some attribute of the person being coached or the issue that the person is presenting suggests that coaching might not be a good fit. An example can be seen in a case in which a potential client wants to explore ideas but has no real motivation to change. The client's interest may make good sense, but this would not typically fall into the domain of coaching. Another example might occur when a client is primarily interested in getting other people to change but has no investment in personal change. Coaches don't normally work with clients to change other people, but rather to empower them to change themselves.

While coaching conversations are becoming increasingly common and, in organizational contexts, more aligned with the methods of professional coaches, they are immensely different from formal professional coaching relationships. As seen in table 1.1, these relationships are bounded by professional codes, they are structured, they have a clear focus, and they strive for meaningful and sustainable outcomes.

If we apply a wider lens to the current landscape, we need to ask ourselves what it is about this method of facilitating client development and the pursuit of life-changing initiatives that appeals to so many people and organizations. The answer partly lies in the way that coaching helps to efficiently identify directions for change and unrecognized resources to support appropriate actions. Coaching also enables clients to discover novel approaches and methods for goal attainment that lie outside their normal ways of understanding their worlds. A particularly important focus in coaching is on clients' **self-limiting beliefs**. We all have certain beliefs about who we are and who we are not, what we do well, and where we lack capacity. Most of these beliefs are experience based, but some are like personal myths that are formed from opinions and feedback offered at earlier moments in our lives. A self-limiting belief may sound like the following: "I'm just not good at (fill in the blank)," "I'm simply not an inspirational speaker," "I've always been a perfectionist—if I can't be the best, I don't even want to try," "I need to be in control at all times," "Putting my needs first is selfish," "Change is frightening," and so on. These beliefs aren't always wrong or harmful, but they can keep us spinning our wheels within artificial boundaries that block us from appreciating other ways of seeing, knowing, and doing. In other words, these beliefs can thwart forward movement toward more desirable lives.

Clients are often unaware of patterns that keep them stuck, and they may not choose the most promising paths to change. It is thought to be the case that clients engage coaches when their normal success strategies repeatedly fail to produce desired results (Hargrove, 2008) or when they feel trapped in a maze with no evident way out.

Professional coaches have a deep appreciation for the meandering course of change; they realize that linear thinking sooner or later leads us straight into a wall or to the edge of a cliff. No matter how small or big a client's goal, coaches embrace the whole person because even small changes need to be considered in the full context of a person's life. Coaches challenge clients to think outside the box and experiment with manageable steps toward desired outcomes. Coaches collaboratively address clients' challenges, substituting can-do ways for can't-do attitudes. They look beneath the surface; they access unrealized resources for generating a future that clients previously considered impossible. They ask powerful questions. They request that clients dream big and take that longed-for step toward sustainable change.

COACHING NICHES

Can a coach be effective for any agenda that clients might suggest? Not likely. While it is true that coaching involves a process that is relatively independent of the agendas presented by clients, it will probably be a more efficient process if the coach knows at least something about the subject matter pertaining to clients' agendas. Peterson (2018), in talking about the future of coaching, believes that coaches will have to become not only process experts but also significantly knowledgeable about the content of clients' issues. When coaches specialize, we refer to their focus as a **coaching niche**. To be clear, by being knowledgeable about the nature of issues that clients present, coaches aren't intending to position themselves as expert advisors or mentors. Rather, with knowledge about the subject matter that clients present, coaches are more likely to advance efficiently and less likely to ask innumerable questions simply to appreciate what their clients are describing.

The number of career tracks or niches in coaching is steadily growing. Just as helpers in other professions gravitate to areas where they have accumulated expertise and interest, so too professional coaches are quite likely to develop specialized practices (table 1.2). Even though coaches apply a general model to their work, clients' topics may require a certain knowledge or understanding beyond coaching fundamentals. In other words,

skill in the process of coaching is a necessary condition for effective coaching, but further training and experience may be required. For example, when a client is thinking about changing career tracks, altering lifestyle patterns, or developing a new set of leadership skills, being knowledgeable about various factors that might influence the design of relevant action plans is useful. There are so many coaching scenarios where coaches may need to possess content-specific knowledge or experience. Indeed, a coach's niche may be a central criterion when clients choose coaches.

Imagine that a woman wants to hire a coach to help her navigate organizational power dynamics in a large public bureaucracy with a patriarchal executive suite. Would she be best served by someone whose only organizational knowledge derives from tech industry startups, or would it be better for her to find a coach who has familiarity with large public and private sector organizations? Even though all coaches should have a solid grasp of how people go about changing behavioral patterns, this client

Table 1.2 Sample Professional Coaching Niches

Coaching type	Niche
Business coaching	• Career and career transition coaching • Entrepreneurship • Executive and leadership coaching • Managerial and supervisory coaching • Performance coaching • Team coaching • Work–life balance coaching • Workplace and organizational coaching
Personal or life coaching	• ADHD coaching • Conflict resolution coaching • Creativity coaching • Diversity and culture coaching • Emotional intelligence coaching • Environmental coaching • Family and parenting coaching • Financial coaching • Life skills coaching • Lifestyle fitness • Mindfulness coaching • Personal wellness coaching • Relationship coaching • Retirement coaching • Stress reduction coaching • Spiritual coaching • Transition coaching • Youth and at-risk youth coaching

might sensibly seek someone who has relevant knowledge for the agenda she is presenting.

In 2006, Brock (2006) reported on the distribution of coaching niches in her sample of over 1,300 professional coaches; they included business, leadership, career, relationships, wellness, and stress reduction. She concluded that about 50 percent of coaches focus on business, and another 50 percent on personal. The ICF (2020a) survey of 18,609 coaches found that the top five areas of coaching were leadership (30 percent), executive (16 percent), business (16 percent), life or vision (13 percent), and career (9 percent). Summating across all coaching niches identified in this study, approximately 74 percent had to do with work and career, while the remaining 26 percent reflected more personal matters, including personal growth, wellness, spirituality, and relationships. Though it's hard to compare these two studies directly, the implication seems to be that the coaching world is shifting more toward work, career, and organizational matters, even though client concerns could be seen as a mix of personal and professional, such as wanting to create more work–life balance or to manage stress.

While we are witnessing a trend toward specialization in coaching, it nonetheless remains true that coaching is generally defined as being about the whole person. To better understand this, let's consider something known as the **butterfly effect** that posits the question, "Does the flap of a butterfly's wings in Brazil set off a tornado in Texas" (Lorenz, 1972)? Put another way, will a change in one part of the world have ripple effects around the globe? This perspective is captured in the paradigm of systems thinking, which speaks to the interrelationships of all things and is often traced to the early works of Ludwig von Bertalanffy (1968), with present-day expressions in the writings of such theorists as Gregory Bateson (1979), Fritjof Capra (1997), and Peter Senge (2006). In the realm of coaching, if a client becomes more assertive in her work interactions, what ramifications might these changes have for other areas of her life? If someone successfully transitions from being an employee in a large organization to a self-employed entrepreneur, how might the structure and quality of his life outside work shift?

An invaluable implication of systems thinking shows up in our modern-day appreciation of the mind–body connection. When Hans Selye (1956), a medical doctor, began researching the concept of stress in the 1950s, his colleagues viewed him as eccentric. At the time, he argued that mental experiences could have profound effects on physical health, a premise that most of us now take for granted. Though evidence concerning the mind–body connection accumulated at an astonishing rate from the 1950s onward, mind–body medicine struggled to gain a foothold within the medical world throughout the second half of the 20th century. Today, physical scientists accept the relationship of mind and body and have come to describe health as the interaction of multiple dimensions of our personhood (Engel, 1977; Wilber et al., 2008). In the coaching world, it thus becomes necessary to appreciate that mental and emotional challenges that clients experience may also be manifest in the health and function of their bodies.

What might be the most relevant systemic impacts to consider when addressing coaching topics with clients? If you begin with the fact that your thoughts influence your emotions and vice versa, it's easy to extend this reasoning to the argument that your thoughts and feelings will influence your physical being—and, conversely, the state of your body will affect your mental and emotional health. Moving out from yourself, you can also acknowledge that how you act influences others. If you happen to be in a great mood, evidence shows that this affects the moods of those around you. Thus, your personal realities influence your social realities. In the language of causality, your emotional, physical, mental, social, and behavioral experiences influence one another. If you touch one part, you influence all other parts to a greater or lesser degree. If you touch one person, you touch untold numbers of others in a kind of ripple—or, if you will, butterfly effect.

This discussion reinforces a central matter in coaching—namely, that coaches are always working with the whole person. Many professions address specific realms of human existence. Lawyers deal with legal issues, accountants with financial issues, and so on. When a client hires a coach, there will be boundaries to this relationship. Obvious ones pertain to ethics and professional regulations that delimit the delivery of services for which the coach is trained and certified. If you consider the wide range of topics clients might bring to you in your professional role, how do you function as a systems thinker and yet intervene in ways that are within the boundaries of your profession? Take managing stress as a goal a client deeply desires. You may recognize that stress arises from a variety of sources. You may learn that family and friends have sabotaged the client's self-care intentions in the past. There might be genetic factors predisposing the person to heightened levels of stress. The client may also have particular beliefs ("I can't manage it") and knowledge ("A book I just read says . . .")

that may challenge progress. Your client might have a grueling commute, coupled with an exhausting travel schedule as a regular component of his work. How much will it help this client if he limits his change process to engaging in a guided meditation program or going to the gym three times a week? Surely, such actions can be beneficial, yet there is likely to be so much more that will be required to fully address this client's work and life stress.

A coaching approach is necessarily holistic in that it encompasses all that might be relevant and builds strategies for each area where there is a likelihood of impact. This means that even when coaches have specialties or niches, they need to be aware of all of the potential changes in clients' lives that are not part of the specific **coaching objective** and encompass these as well as possible in the strategies that clients develop for moving forward toward their desired futures.

FORCES AND FACTORS IN COACHING'S GROWTH STORY

It's hard to identify an exact birth date for this new profession, but a relevant time stamp in the history of coaching is 1995, when the International Coach Federation, a nonprofit association designed to guide the growth of the coaching profession, was established in North America. I will identify some of the seminal figures in the history of coaching in the next chapter, but here I want to offer you the big picture of coaching.

Presently, there are hundreds of professional schools of coaching, dozens of coaching journals and magazines, roughly 25 professional coaching associations, and an ever-expanding library of books on various aspects of the coaching field. Less than 50 years ago, there were only a handful of books on professional coaching, no formal schools, and ultimately no clear signs of a profession. While some experts debate whether coaching is a profession, a social movement, or perhaps just a unique set of techniques (Brock, 2016), the fact is that it is a multibillion-dollar global industry (ICF, 2020a).

Exploring some of the societal changes over the course of the 20th century helps us appreciate why coaching emerged with such immense positive momentum through the early years of the 21st century. A few things can be clearly identified as precursors to or stimulants for the growth of coaching; these include

- the growth of global awareness and an ever-increasing appreciation for the diversity of perspectives relevant to virtually every issue;
- monumental changes in the world of work propelled by technology and artificial intelligence;
- massive shifts in communication technologies and ways of relating;
- an ever-changing landscape of career and personal responsibilities calling for a virtual 24/7 availability;
- requirements for individuals to continually learn and even reinvent themselves as old careers disappear and entirely new ones are created;
- radical awareness of the deep structural inequalities that shape individuals' lived experiences and a global call to action in these matters; and
- the proliferation of high quality and accessible online and in-person learning experiences.

Indeed, this list can be considerably expanded, but hopefully in its limited form it offers some perspective. As we move closer to a scenario where a particular individual comes up with the idea that she needs help from a coach, rather than some other kind of helper, two other dynamics can be added to the equation that has generated phenomenal growth in the coaching field. The first has to do with stigma: the absence of stigma when seeking help from a coach contrasts markedly with the often-perceived stigma attached to help seeking from psychologists, psychiatrists, and social workers. The second derives from a modern-day paradox whereby individuals seem quite capable of explaining the reasons they do certain things but perhaps seem not as able to change those behaviors. Here, I am talking about the fact that with all the knowledge available through books, podcasts, and videos, lots of people seem reasonably aware of the root causes of their problems. By contrast, appreciation of what it really takes to generate effective designs for sustainable behavior change seems less widespread. As one client repeatedly said to me, "I understand what I'm doing wrong and why I'm doing it, but no matter what, I just keep doing it."

The bottom line in all this can be summarized in a projection that the 21st century's change trajectory is largely unimaginable even with all the wisdom of futurists articulating what life may be like in 100 years. Thus, we have the popular acronym VUCA, which is used to characterize the future: volatile, uncertain, complex, and ambiguous. It is my belief that the ever-evolving models and methods of coaching will be sufficiently agile and adaptive to meet people wherever they find themselves in order to offer them ways of developing that are uniquely aligned with the emerging futures they are facing. Coaching makes good sense for our times.

THE FUTURE OF COACHING

An appreciation of the roots of coaching provided in the next chapter will offer you a useful backdrop to the methodologies explored throughout this book, and what may be intriguing to consider in this moment is the future of coaching. Let's take a peek.

What seems to be true around the globe is that the topics clients bring to coaching sessions seem largely focused on career, work, leadership, relationship, and adaptation to life issues (Brock, 2006, 2015; ICF, 2020a). Based on future projections, the need for agile and adaptive assistance in these matters will accelerate because of the profound and continuous changes that will forevermore affect our work and personal lives. The renowned futurist Ray Kurzwell, tells us that progress in the 100 years of the 21st century will be the equivalent of 20,000 years of change (Ritacco & McGowan, 2017). We are in for a wild ride.

A study in Australia predicted that people entering the job market today will change jobs 17 times across five significantly different career sectors—and that most of their future jobs don't currently exist (Rainie & Anderson, 2017). No matter where we look in our future universe, the message is the same: People will need to continually reinvent themselves throughout their lives such that a lifelong commitment to continuous learning and adaptation will not be an option, but rather a necessary strategy for survival.

The more complex and intricate agendas of our lives involving deep human emotions, existential meaning, and freedom of choice will continue to require a skilled and compassionate coach who can help people navigate their emerging futures. To coach individuals in the midst of multifaceted change that affects their personal identity and understanding of themselves in the world requires much preparation and skill. Indeed, it requires ongoing learning, since, like your clients, your world will be changing rapidly as well.

For the present moment, coaches will continue to work with client agendas that are quite practical and manageable as well as ones that are more complex and multilayered. Learning about coaching right now affords you the opportunity to be challenged by reasonably straightforward client topics, to learn as you grow, and, as time passes, to open your practice to more challenging coaching objectives appropriate to your advancing levels of competence.

REFLECTIONS

It is no accident that the field of coaching arose with such presence at this particular point in history. Those who have studied or lived through the second half of the 20th century know the whiplash-like changes that increasingly emerged in the post–World War II era. From the somewhat placid 1950s, where the seeds of human revolution and evolution were slowly sprouting, through the turbulent and sometimes violent eruptions of the 1960s, deep structural changes have become increasingly manifest in the power dynamics of the world, the nature and ethics of business, the sociopolitical landscape, and the diversity of personal lifestyles and sexual mores. Turn-of-the-century scientific and technological innovations dramatically altered not only how we live but also who we are becoming. As Yuval Harari (2014, 2016, 2018) cautions us, we are moving into a completely uncharted realm of human existence where our own nature may be radically transformed through genetic engineering and the merger of human and artificial intelligence. There is no clear forecast for how this will turn out.

Coaching is fundamentally a learning process rather than a rehabilitative, therapeutic one. It is more deeply informed by learning theories than by psychotherapeutic ones, though there is a substantial overlap between some of these theoretical frameworks. The importance of this lies in the fact that as human beings we are on a steep and almost incomprehensible learning trajectory that will only intensify in the decades ahead. We will need sophisticated guides and coaches to help us learn, adapt, transform, and reenter the world for a period of time until we have to do that again.

You have hopefully gained some appreciation of what coaching is and some of its practical dimensions. In the final part of this chapter, I imagine you were able to appreciate the importance of this field and its relevance to the future of our world. Welcome to this journey. It will be a profoundly impactful one, where not only will you be asked to learn new methods and ways of being, but where you also will be required to transform yourself—to take a leap across an unclear chasm toward a new identity in the world.

CHAPTER 2

THE ROOTS OF COACHING

Humanity is now faced with a stark choice: Evolve or die—if the structures of the human mind remain unchanged, we will always end up re-creating the same world, the same evils, the same dysfunction.

Eckhart Tolle

MY STORY

I have lived much of the history surrounding the birth and development of the coaching field. I have had the good fortune of being exposed to many of the world's best theorists and practitioners who nourished the human potential movement, the field of organization development, the school of positive psychology, and now this multidisciplinary field of professional coaching. Coaching did not suddenly appear out of nowhere. Seminal thinkers from the 1920s on had hinted at what we now call coaching. Indeed, they had been creating the building blocks that have become foundational to this new field. In all of coaching's roots, I see the spirit of innovation and human evolution, the struggles to be more inclusive, the need to create a world of compassion, support, and opportunity for all people. To me the development of coaching is part of this whole process, not separate from it. It optimizes human development by applying knowledge from all relevant fields of study and practice in service of global well-being.

Coaching springs from many traditions, and in the present day it shows up in a variety of settings and styles. We will take a deep dive into the origins of coaching and some of the individuals who significantly influenced its growth. By seeing the richness of coaching's history, it should be easier for you to appreciate the predominant applications of coaching today. I will tie all of this together by offering an industry-wide model of coaching competencies that brings together the majority of the world's practitioners. Here are some guiding questions to consider as you read:

- Who were the main figures in coaching's growth story?
- What fields of study fed the development of coaching?
- How does the knowledge base of psychology intersect with different forms of coaching?
- How do areas of human development and learning play into the modern face of coaching?
- Does neuroscience have a place in coaching?
- How can various approaches to coaching be understood in a common framework?

A SKETCH OF THE FIELD

The word *coach* originally referred to a 16th-century wagon made in Kocs, a Hungarian city between Vienna and Budapest. In the 1800s, *coach* came to mean a tutor or someone who carries a student through a course of study to an exam. Later still, coaching became intricately linked to athletics and sport. Though the term still conjures up images of athletic training, this meaning constitutes only a part of the historical background of coaching (see sidebar, Historical Landmarks of the Coaching Profession).

At present, coaching is primarily a one-to-one helping modality. Yet, group and team coaching also represent an important application of coaching processes (Britton, 2010, 2013; Clutterbuck, 2010, 2020; Hackman & Wageman, 2005; Hawkins, 2014; O'Connor & Cavanagh, 2017). Though interest in group and team coaching is growing, the extrapolation of coaching methods from one-to-one to multiperson contexts is not straightforward. Group and team coaching involve the mastery of additional sets of skills related to group structure, interpersonal power, membership, group dynamics,

Historical Landmarks of the Coaching Profession

1974. W.T. Gallwey's *The Inner Game of Tennis* marked a major transition from a sport coaching model to what Werner Erhard (Erhard Seminars Training, known as est) and eventually Thomas Leonard developed into personal coaching.

1980s to 1990s. Graham Alexander, Alan Fine, and Sir John Whitmore developed the GROW model of goal setting (**g**oal, **r**eality, **o**bstacles and options, **w**ay forward).

1992. Thomas Leonard founded Coach University (Coach U), a virtual training program.

1992. Laura Whitworth and Henry and Karen Kimsey-House created the Coaches Training Institute (CTI).

1995. Thomas Leonard established the International Coach Federation (ICF) as a professional community for coaches.

2000. The Coaching Psychology Unit at the University of Sydney offered the world's first postgraduate degree in coaching psychology (initially master of arts, now doctorate of philosophy).

2002. The British Psychological Society and the Australian Psychological Society established coaching psychology interest groups.

2007. Oxford Brookes University in London established a doctoral program in coaching and mentoring.

2011. The ICF estimated the number of coaches worldwide to be around 48,000 (ICF, 2012).

2016. The ICF expanded the scope of coaching by including managers and leaders who apply a coaching approach in their work.

2020. International Coach Federation renamed International Coaching Federation.

2021 and beyond. Coaching continues to grow exponentially with increasing emphasis by consumers and professional associations alike on the need for rigorous credentialing processes.

and communications within groups. While I want to acknowledge such interests in multiperson coaching methods, my focus in this book is directed toward helping you master understanding and skills related to one-to-one coaching relationships.

The need for a coaching profession seems largely validated by its growth curve. In the 1990s, Coach U and the Coaches Training Institute (CTI), two leading training organizations at that time, agreed to create the International Coach Federation as a community for their graduates and as a regulatory and standards-setting association. Soon after, a number of other bodies appeared on the scene, notably, the Worldwide Association of Business Coaches in 1997; the Association for Coaching in 2002; the European Mentoring and Coaching Council in 2002; the Association for Supervision, Coaching and Consultancy of Australia and New Zealand in 2002; and the International Association of Coaching in 2003. Presently, the ICF appears to be the preeminent voice of the coaching world. With membership of only 200 coaches in 1995, the ICF currently lists over 39,352 members across 143 countries (ICF, 2020d). As well, there is an untold number of coaches aligned with other associations as well as unaffiliated coaches, who may or may not have formal coach training.

Certified professional coaches will have completed coach-specific training from coach-training organizations. It is likely they will also have engaged with mentor coaches to enhance their skills while accumulating the requisite number of coaching hours to obtain certification. The most recent ICF global survey (ICF, 2020a) indicates that 74 percent of the 18,609 participating coaches held credentials or certificates and that 99 percent reported coach-specific training.

TRACING THE ROOTS

Even if this book were entirely about the history of coaching, I would have difficulty fully representing the various contributions to the development of coaching over the past century. I will nonetheless do my best to acknowledge and describe some of the more significant individuals and schools of thought that gave rise to and currently feed the field of professional coaching. I will offer perspectives in the upcoming material in a way that hopefully will make it more immediately relevant and useful to you.

The core contributions I want to present derive largely from the fields of psychology, education, human development, and neuroscience. In Vikki Brock's (2006, 2012) study of the coaching field, a number of other professional areas were thought to contribute to the growth of coaching. These include but are not limited to philosophy, sociology and anthropology, management sciences, sport sciences, cybernetics, and the physical sciences. To some degree, the relevant perspectives of these other disciplines have been incorporated in the four fields mentioned previously. For instance, much of the contribution from sports and recreation speaks to issues of goal setting, performance, and motivation, which represent long-standing concerns in fields of psychology and education. Also, issues arising in the areas of organization development, leadership, and management have strong representation in the theories, models, and practices of counseling, social and organizational psychology. Again, this is not to imply that all relevant roots will be described, but rather that more central contributions will be identified in the upcoming material. Neuroscience represents a more recent contributor to thinking and perspectives within the coaching world. Its practical implications for human behavior are becoming ever clearer and are increasingly referenced in the works of modern-day coaching professionals.

As we begin our dive into the people and fields of study that contributed to the rise of coaching, you can get a snapshot of history in table 2.1. Here you will find a list of 20th-century theorists and practitioners whose work fed the principles and practices of coaching. Again, this is only a partial list ending with the 1990s, but it is based in the extensive research of Vikki Brock (2008), who is arguably the coaching field's most prominent historian.

CONTRIBUTIONS FROM THE FIELD OF PSYCHOLOGY

Early models of helping relationships in psychology and psychiatry relied heavily on a medical view of the person. One needed to be sick to request help. The *Diagnostic and Statistical Manual of Mental Disorders (DSM)*, originally published by the American Psychiatric Association (APA) in 1952, has consistently focused on the behavioral and psychological pathologies afflicting us as human beings. An ever-widening range of human behavior has been described as pathological through the progression of *DSM* revisions up to its current fifth edition (American Psychiatric Association, 2013). Not surprisingly, the broad-based pathologizing of human behavior has met with ongoing argument and debate as more sanguine views of our humanity have emerged.

Table 2.1   Major Influences on the Development of Coaching

Name	Discipline	Decade influence began
Alfred Adler	Psychology	1920s
Martin Heidegger	Philosophy	1930s
Napoleon Hill	Motivation	1930s
Dale Carnegie	Motivation	1940s
Abraham Maslow	Psychology	1950s
Albert Ellis	Psychology	1950s
Carl Jung	Psychology	1950s
Carl Rogers	Psychology	1950s
John Wooden	Sport	1950s
Milton Erickson	Psychology	1950s
Peter Drucker	Business	1950s
Red Auerbach	Sport	1950s
Chris Argyris	Psychology	1950s
Edgar Schein	Business	1960s
Fritz Perls	Psychology	1960s
Ken Blanchard	Business	1960s
Fernando Flores	Philosophy	1970s
John Grinder	Liberal arts	1970s
Peter Block	Business	1970s
Richard Bandler	Psychology	1970s
Werner Erhard	Business	1970s
Zig Ziglar	Motivation	1970s
Wayne Dyer	Motivation	1970s
Robert Dilts	Psychology	1980s
Stephen Covey	Business	1980s
Daniel Goleman	Psychology	1990s
David Cooperrider	Business	1990s
Ken Wilber	Psychology	1990s
Martin Seligman	Psychology	1990s
Mihaly Csikszentmihalyi	Psychology	1990s
Peter Senge	Business	1990s

Reprinted by permission from V.A. Brock, *Grounded Theory of the Roots and Emergence of Coaching*, Library of Professional Coaching (2008). https://libraryofprofessionalcoaching .com/concepts/best-practices-foundations/the-roots-and-emergence-of-coaching/.

Throughout the 20th century, methods and models of psychological assistance have been routinely adapted to the changing conditions of the lives and needs of the populations served. In the early 1900s, psychological treatment would best be described as elitist. For the most part, only the upper echelons of society could afford it. For the masses, the idea of lying on a couch talking endlessly about themselves to someone sitting behind them in a chair probably seemed indulgent and nonsensical. Not only did the general public raise questions about this approach, but increasing numbers of helping professionals expressed concerns about the practice as well. The fact that methods of treatment changed so vastly in the 20th century bears vibrant testimony to the commitment of all human service professionals to revisioning principles and practices to best benefit humanity.

As the fields of psychiatry and psychology developed, an emphasis on positive growth and the acknowledgment of **normative challenges** became increasingly evident in theories and applications, particularly from about 1950 onward. Even the classic Freudian model of psychoanalysis, known colloquially as the "talking cure," morphed dramatically in the works of innovative Neo-Freudian thinkers, among whom were Alfred Adler (1927), Carl Jung (1969), Karen Horney (1939), and Erik Erikson (1959), to name but a few. The much-parodied premises of the Oedipus complex and other archaic interpretations of psychic structures, such as the id, ego, and superego, were transformed into more lucid explanations for why we do what we do as human beings. We aren't all sick; sometimes life is hard, and we simply need a helping hand.

By the mid-20th century, B.F. Skinner's (1938, 1953) model of behaviorism had taken root in the Western world, supplanting Freudianism as the reigning paradigm from which to view human nature. This shift took humanity from a view where wildly erotic and violent internal forces ruled our lives to one positing that we were little more than stimulus–response machines. In this emerging, brave, new world (Huxley, 1932), there was little need to be concerned with what people thought. We might simply be manipulated with M&M-like rewards, or we could be controlled in a "clockwork orange" fashion of behavioral conditioning (Burgess, 1962). As happened to the Freudian model, the tide eventually turned against a rigid behavioral view such that by the early 1970s, human thoughts and feelings were welcomed back into the realm of psychology. Cognitive behavior therapy (CBT) increasingly integrated thoughts and feelings into the stark manipulations of behavioral psychology.

Prior to the 1970s, most psychological literature was inaccessible to the general public, largely due to its esoteric and jargon-filled writing style. George Albee (1970), who served as president of the American Psychological Association from 1969 to 1970, advocated that psychology needed to be given away, that is, made available in its presentation and format to everyone. An almost limitless literature on psychological issues is readily accessible today, partly as a consequence of the perspective of psychologists, psychiatrists, social workers, and others who believed that not only is knowledge power but that this power needs to be vested in the hands of every human being.

A number of more affirming and inclusive psychological perspectives emerged quite distinctly in the second half of the 20th century. Humanistic psychology, existential psychotherapy, and feminist approaches expanded our appreciation of the uniqueness and growth potential of every human being. Pioneers in the field of humanistic psychology were pivotal in reorienting psychological thinking toward self-realization (Maslow, 1962; Rogers, 1951, 1961). They believed that people were inherently wise, and that with a little guidance they could find their own answers. They argued against the notion that those who sought help were broken in some way, and they normalized many of the issues people face in life rather than considering them as reflections of pathology. Existential perspectives explored humanity's quest for meaning, purpose, and personal responsibility in our choices and actions (Frankl, 1969; May, 1996; Yalom, 1980). They embraced the normative challenges we experience as we search for meaning in our lives, as we confront a felt sense of being alone and of death, and as we grapple with what it means to be truly responsible. Of particular importance to coaching were feminist perspectives, which focused on social, gender, and political inequities in order to foster safety and balance within the inherent power structures of helping relationships (Chodorow, 1991; Gilligan, 1982; Horney, 1939; Walker, 1979). These works awakened us to the fact that most psychological theories of the 20th century had been written from a singular masculine viewpoint, which not only neglected a feminine perspective of reality but in many cases portrayed that view in a distorted and demeaning manner.

A more honoring vision of humanity grew from this richly fertilized ground. In the 1990s, the field of positive psychology began to emerge concurrently with the North American establishment of a coaching profession. Building on models that emerged in the late 20th century, Martin Seligman championed positive psychology as a strength-based approach to human development. His classic writings on learned helplessness (Seligman, 1975) and learned optimism (Seligman, 2006) shed light on the fact that we can learn new and more effective ways of being and that we have profound potential for growth. Seligman and Csikszentmihalyi (2000) described the approach as follows: "Positive psychology at the subjective level is about valued subjective experiences: well-being, contentment, and satisfaction (in the past); hope and optimism (for the future); and flow and happiness (in the present)" (p. 5). A major contribution to the coaching field is evident in positive psychology's emphasis on character strengths (see sidebar, Positive Psychology and Character Strengths).

Since the turn of the century, there have been even more profound shifts in psychological theories wherein Eastern and Western philosophies have merged to create a far greater concentration on the present or, as it is more popularly known, *the now* (Hanh, 2017; Kabat-Zinn, 2018; Kornfield, 2008, 2017; Tolle, 2003). A clear example of this blend is evident in transpersonal psychology, which provided a further thrust toward human potential and realization. Building on the works of Roberto Assagioli (1965), Stanislav Grof (1988), Abraham Maslow (1962), and Viktor Frankl (1969), transpersonal psychology asserted that such practices as spiritual rituals and meditation can create strong anchors in the present moment and enable people to move beyond compliance or resistance toward a transcendent consciousness about the normal human dilemmas we must confront (Davis, 2003). Perhaps the most prominent representation of this shift appears in the widespread application of mindfulness practices (Goldstein, 2016). See sidebar (Mindfulness).

One example of a mindfulness approach can be found in acceptance and commitment therapy, or ACT (Hayes et al., 2011; Luoma et al., 2017). As an offshoot of cognitive behavior therapy, ACT, along with other brief therapy modalities (Kim, 2014), solution-focused therapy (De Shazer, 1988) and narrative therapy (White, 2007), veers even further away from a pathological perspective of human beings in difficulty. Reflecting this trend, Ken Wilber (2000a, 2000b, 2006) assimilated research from arts and sciences to usher in a more holistic framing of human consciousness with his theory of everything. He and theorists such as Susan Cook-Greuter (2000, 2006) and Don Beck (Beck & Cowan, 1996) merged transpersonal psychology with Eastern practices to further promote human development. They articu-

---

Positive Psychology and Character Strengths

One of positive psychology's major contributions to coaching is its focus on character strengths and virtues associated with happiness (Seligman, 2002, 2012). Peterson and Seligman (2004) proposed that character strengths, if practiced consistently, could result in the good life. These were the strengths they identified:

Wisdom and knowledge. Cognitive strengths having to do with the acquisition and use of knowledge; these are seen in one's creativity, curiosity, love of learning, and perspective taking.

Courage. Emotional strength relating to the capacity to accomplish goals in the face of opposition; it involves bravery, persistence, integrity, and vitality.

Humanity. Interpersonal strength pertaining to how one cares for and relates to others with social intelligence, kindness, and love.

Justice. Civic strength demonstrated through active citizenship, social responsibility, loyalty, and leadership.

Temperance. Strength referring to self-regulation, prudence, humility, forgiveness, and mercy.

Transcendence. Strength in one's connection to the greater universe; includes a sense of gratitude, hope, playfulness, and faith (pp. 29-30).

The importance of positive psychology for the field of coaching shows up in its unparalleled focus on the promotion of health and happiness rather than on the treatment of mental illness and pathology. Positive psychology dwells less on what previously happened and more on what people can do now to move their lives forward. It acknowledges the unbounded resourcefulness of human beings with all their unrealized potential. Indeed, this shift toward identifying strengths and resources as a means to promote growth and wellness in individuals, families, workplaces, and communities is foundational to coaching.

Mindfulness

A number of traditions focus on cultivating mindfulness. For example, Buddhist mindfulness informs us that the goal "is to be mindful of the mind as it takes its own course" (Varela et al., 1992, p. 31). Jack Kornfield, a Western meditation teacher and cofounder of the Insight Meditation Society, explains mindfulness as "patient, receptive, non-judging awareness" (Kornfield, 2008, p. 99). Lama Surya Das (1997) describes it as "relaxed, open, lucid, moment-to-moment, present awareness" (p. 300), while Thich Nhat Hanh, a Vietnamese Buddhist Zen master, describes mindfulness as "the energy of attention. It is the capacity in each of us to be present one hundred percent to what is happening within and around us" (Seale, 2011, p. 36). Meditation (e.g., Zen, Vipassana, insight, yogic) is a practice associated with developing awareness and mindfulness. In the field of coaching, mindfulness is a core ingredient of presence. Silsbee (2010) likens the concept of mindfulness to that of flow (Csikszentmihalyi, 2008). He describes its manifestation as

> a surge of appreciation for our client, an insight about just the right question, or jointly discovering a new way of looking at the challenge she is facing. With this often comes a sense of connectedness and a delight in what is unfolding in the moment. (Silsbee, p. 44)

lated methodologies to accelerate personal growth and propel the evolution of human consciousness over the course of a lifetime.

Parenthetically, you might note that most of these modern approaches within the field of psychology were quickly adapted by coaching practitioners and offered as ways of working with coaching clients' issues. Coaching approaches that parallel the previously mentioned therapeutic modalities have appeared under such labels as acceptance and commitment coaching (Hill & Oliver, 2019), narrative coaching (Drake, 2018), presence-based coaching (Silsbee, 2008), transpersonal coaching (VanderPol, 2019), integral coaching (Hunt, 2009a), and mindfulness coaching (Chalmers, 2018). This phenomenon speaks to both the overlap of the fields of coaching and psychology as well as to the applicability of modern methodologies of helping to a wide range of human issues, whether they show up in therapeutic or coaching relationships.

This growing emphasis on awakening human consciousness and mindfulness blends well with the emerging societal imperative that we as human beings wake up to what is occurring in our world (Kabat-Zinn, 2018; Scharmer, 2016; Treace, 2019; Velandia, 2019). An important but slightly earlier representation of this concern can be found in the works of Daniel Goleman (1995, 2006) on social and emotional intelligence quotients (or SQ and EQ). His critical works allowed us to recognize and value intelligences beyond those encompassed by standard IQ tests (Albrecht, 2006). The core propositions of SQ and EQ emphasized awareness of our present emotional state, as well as that of others,

and the capacity to navigate these emotions in a mutually beneficial manner. Goleman linked this self-awareness with a state of mindfulness, which fosters greater accuracy in identifying our emotions in the moment and appreciating what our emotional tendencies might be across time and context. The accelerating attention to SQ and EQ in today's world reflects the critical importance of developing competencies in noticing, witnessing, and being with one's experience in the moment as a path to heightening self-awareness.

CONTRIBUTIONS FROM LEARNING AND HUMAN DEVELOPMENT MODELS

In Sir John Whitmore's (1992) observation that coaching is "helping clients learn rather than teaching them" (p. 8), the connection between coaching and adult learning seems quite evident. The art and science of facilitating adult learning is commonly known as **andragogy** (Knowles, 1980). In her scholarly effort to articulate what coaching is, Elaine Cox (2013) reasons that, at heart, coaching is a "facilitated, dialogic learning process" (p. 1). Cox also states that models of adult learning provide the theoretical basis for understanding a coach's actions. To gain a better appreciation of how embedded the principles of learning are in the foundations of coaching (Fazel, 2013), I will offer here some reflections on the social field of learning, types of learning, and detailed reviews of andragogy, experiential learning, and transformative learning.

The Social Field of Learning

Most learning theories deal only with the acquisition of knowledge, neglecting the social field in which learning takes place. Knud Illeris (2016, 2018) embraces a wide range of scholarly perspectives on how we change, including those of Jean Piaget (1952) and Carl Rogers (1961). He offers a definition of learning as "any process that in living organisms leads to permanent capacity change and which is not solely due to biological maturation or ageing" (Illeris, 2016, p. 3). This work is so helpful to a field like coaching because it positions learning in a social context—we learn through interaction with others.

Illeris (2016) describes two quite different processes in learning—an external one and an internal one. The external process involves the *interaction* of learners and their social, cultural, or material environment; this is essentially an interpersonal and social process. The second is an internal process of *acquisition* reflecting the psychological processing going on within individuals as they learn.

Referring to figure 2.1, you can see the interactive process represented by a vertical double arrow running between the individual and the environment. The double arrow reflects that both elements are always involved in an integrated way. Environment is located at the bottom of the arrow depicting the fact that it is the context in which everything else occurs. Individual learners are positioned at the top of the arrow since they are the focus of the learn-

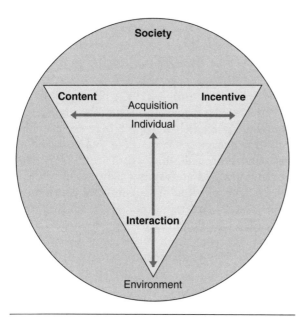

Figure 2.1 Knud Illeris's three dimensions of learning in a social field: content, incentive, and interaction.

Based on Illeris (2016).

ing process. Here's a quick example: During the pandemic, most learning experiences occurred in online formats—that's the environment of learning. How might this environment have affected learning compared to in-person learning?

Acquisition is shown by the horizontal double arrow; it describes a process occurring only for the learner. Related to acquisition, the model shows content of learning on the left and incentives for learning on the right. Content refers to what is being learned, whereas incentive references the mental energy required to engage the learning process.

What we have seen thus far is that three dimensions are involved in learning—namely, the *content* of learning, the *incentive* for learning, and the necessary social *interaction*. The *content* of learning would include knowledge, skills, understanding, insights, and social processes, including empathy. Illeris thinks of the content focus of learning as the individual's attempt to "construct meaning and ability to deal with the challenges of practical life" (Illeris, 2018, p. 3).

In coaching, learning is not likely to be about abstract understanding, but rather something practical and relevant to developing a new way of behaving. Imagine a client who has been unwillingly catapulted into a totally unexpected and overwhelming scenario like working remotely in the pandemic. The content of learning not only involves acquiring skill but also constructing meaning. Your coaching client not only has to skill up but also needs to construct new meaning for what she is doing.

What about the *incentive? Incentive* incorporates motivation, emotion, and volition that can mobilize mental energy for learning. What emotions might your coaching client who suddenly has to master whole new systems of working and living be experiencing? What would motivate your client to take on these massive adjustments? How much willpower would your client need? These three facets of *incentive*—motivation, emotion, and volition—result in varying degrees of "mental balance" (Illeris, 2018, p. 3) while someone is learning new content.

Go back to this fictional client who is feeling emotionally overwhelmed (incentive) and resistant to learning (incentive) yet has to master a bunch of new skills (content) that seem meaningless. Sound challenging? Now, let's add the *environment*. Not only does learning take place online, but your client has to learn in an uncomfortable corner of her house with noise all around and not much support from colearners (environment) because they are struggling, too! For this client, the challenging *environment* interacts with the meaningless *content* and a lack of mental balance owing to high emotionality, low motivation, and little willpower—in other words, not much *incentive*.

An important thing to realize is that the *content* of what you learn is forever associated with the conditions under which you learned it. Contrast these two scenarios: Inga, who is a recent immigrant, is required to take a physics course in a cold and uncomfortable classroom with classmates who shun her; she can't figure out why she needs this course for her life. Rachel, another recent immigrant, is welcomed into a different environment—a pleasant, open classroom, with other students who are receptive and helpful; she doesn't know why she is required to take this physics class, but the learning process encourages understanding physical principles in everyday life. Maybe both Inga and Rachel get *A*s in their courses, but their understanding of physics will be forever linked with the conditions under which they learned it. As Illeris (2016) tells us, all learning "takes place in a certain situation, a certain learning space, which both determines the learning possibilities and marks the learning process and the nature of the learning that takes place" (p. 91).

Let's connect this to coaching. Imagine two company-based coaching clients: Ola has been required to participate in 10 sessions of coaching by his boss to correct an interpersonal pattern that he does not see as problematic, while Warren is offered an opportunity to advance his leadership skills by participating in a coaching process oriented toward what he deems he most needs to learn. Let's add an environmental piece to these scenarios. Warren is also offered optional sessions with other high-profile learners to share and build upon his experiences, while Ola is quite isolated in his experience feeling almost shamed as he trudges into the coach's office located in the Human Resources department. Perhaps both Ola and Warren will focus on developing empathy for others as their coaching focus. Can you sense the likely impacts of interactions among *content* (making meaning), *incentive* (emotions, motivation, volition), and *environment* (the social context) on learning in these two scenarios?

Types of Learning

According to Illeris (2016), there are four distinct types of learning that have pivotal implications for coaching. Illeris uses the concept of *mental schemes* to help separate the types. As you know, when you have learned something, you are usually able to recall it quite quickly. Illeris describes what you

are remembering as a mental scheme. Our brains organize these schemes so they get triggered when we experience "situations that 'remind' us of earlier situations" (p. 6). In short, when you learn something new, it gets organized into schemes that may include combinations of facts, emotions, skills, and attitudes. How these schemes are formed and what happens with them once they are formed takes us into Illeris's four types of learning (cumulative learning, assimilative learning, accommodative learning, and transformative learning).

Cumulative Learning

This is the most basic type of learning, occurring when you learn something new that is unrelated to anything else. The mental scheme you create exists in isolation. It happens when you have no other mental schemes that you can associate with the new scheme or impression from the environment. Essentially, it has no personal meaning or significance at the time you learn it. For the most part, this kind of learning characterizes what happened during the early years of your life or when you had to learn something by heart, like a string of numbers, that had no inherent meaning to you. This is the essence of cumulative learning.

Think of the lists you memorized in grade school, including the alphabet when it was first presented or the dates of historical events that you could barely comprehend. Or you might remember when you first rode a bike and had no prior experience with anything like it. Nothing made sense in the moment of that first ride, and yet somehow you learned how to do it. In an adult world, you can imagine people working on an assembly line where they have to learn a sequence of meaningless steps in the manufacture of some complex product of which they only know a tiny, unintelligible part.

This is a rigid kind of learning. It applies to a fixed reality, and unless what you learned gets associated with other mental schemes, it has finite value helping you adapt to a changing world. For instance, how helpful to life's ever-shifting demands is the assembly line worker's job knowledge? Usually, when you form a new mental scheme, you try to relate it to something else, and that brings us to the second type of learning.

Assimilative Learning

The second type of learning happens when a new scheme is taken in and added to previously established mental schemes. Schemes get connected, describing the typical form of learning in most contexts of your life. As a child, you learned how to add and subtract, and then you applied these schemes to figuring out whether you had enough money to buy the different candies you wanted at the store.

You incorporate and extend mental schemes generated in earlier moments of life. You move from algebra to geometry to calculus. You may learn different languages like English, French, and Spanish, but you are likely to have to stretch to learn Mandarin or Arabic.

A problem with assimilative learning arises when it gets tightly bound to the contexts associated with the learning. Math skills that aren't applied to everyday life become less meaningful and helpful. With the world changing so rapidly, the more you connect your mental schemes, the more likely they will help you adapt to all the novel scenarios that you might confront in the future.

So far, both cumulative and assimilative learning don't seem likely to affect us deeply, even though the content can be challenging. Memorizing muscles and nerves in human anatomy can be taxing, but it's unlikely to affect your core nature or personality.

Accommodative Learning

The third type of learning takes us into the restructuring of previously established mental schemes. What happens when you try to apply what you already know to a situation in a new environment, and something doesn't fit? If you have moved from one culture to another culture, you might recall how habitual ways of interacting socially didn't always have the same result in the new culture. This can also apply to job settings, where a new role, a promotion, or a new company may present you with entirely different behavioral norms. All these situations compel you to adapt.

Accommodative learning forces you to take apart your old mental schemes and put them together in new ways. This is a more demanding learning type than either of the prior two. Demolishing your old schemes and then reorganizing and restructuring their components to form new ones takes effort and may affect not only how you see the world but how you see yourself in that world. When you change schools, jobs, or cultures, how do you take apart the old and create new schemes, and will your results be the same as someone else's? Contrast this with an assimilative learning process where in applications of math, 2 + 2 will always equal 4. In contexts that call for accommodative learning, the end results of learning are likely to differ from person to person.

Relating this to coaching, consider situations where people are faced with the challenge of taking on new roles or transitioning to different countries

where a company operates. A leader is likely to have a skill set built upon many mental schemes that have been assimilated over years of practice. There are mental schemes for decision making, personnel matters, and intracompany relations. All of these may change substantially, thus requiring the leader to deconstruct old schemes and piece together elements in forming new ways of understanding and acting. In this process, the leader may come to perceive herself and the world in significantly different ways. You might say that the leader has changed as a result. In this light, accommodative learning moves layers deeper into your core self.

Transformative Learning

The fourth type of learning emerges when multiple important schemes are involved in a learning process at the same time; such learning implicates the identity or self-understanding of the learner (Illeris, 2016, 2018). This kind of learning, called **transformative learning**, has long been understood in the field of psychotherapy, but only recently has it come into discussion in the world of adult learning. Carl Rogers was one of the first to speak about it in terms of a significant learning that evokes "a change in the organization of the self" (Rogers, 1951, p. 390). He described it as follows:

> By significant learning I mean learning which is more than an accumulation of facts. It is learning which makes a difference—in the individual's behavior, in the course of action he chooses in the future, in his attitudes and in his personality. It is a pervasive learning which is not just an accretion of knowledge, but which interpenetrates every portion of his existence. (Rogers, 1961, p. 280)

Illeris (2016) remarks that this kind of learning goes far beyond what is described in accommodative learning. Transformative learning involves a degree of pain, certain distress in giving up learnings that previously guided your life, and a period of turbulence throughout the undertaking. You feel confronted by challenges that seem to exceed your capacities, yet you must deal with them.

Illeris connects the rise in this kind of learning experience to global changes that are provoking breakdowns in traditional patterns of understanding and ways of being. People are more likely to find themselves "in a state of exile—sudden involuntary unemployment, divorce and other losses of close relations that create deep personal crises" (p. 43). Footnoting this discussion, Illeris comments that there is a strong societal push to resolve such setbacks quickly so individuals can rapidly resume their normal duties. In this assertion, you will find a clear role for current and future coaches.

The nature of transformative learning calls for a change in your core identity. Transformative experiences are not only challenging and difficult, but they evoke emotionality by needing to embrace learning that is not freely chosen. Optimistically, Illeris (2016) notes that at the end of this learning experience, there may be a sense of being "born again as a new and better person" (p. 45).

Hopefully, you can see why this typology is important. As a coach, you will engage with your clients in different types of learning processes. It is unlikely that people will hire you for basic *cumulative learning* agendas or even for *assimilative learning* ones that might be equally or even better served by artificial intelligence or virtual reality processes. As you move into more complex agendas involving accommodative and transformational learning, you will need to develop capacities to accompany your clients on uncharted journeys of change and adaptation so they can inhabit new worlds. I will offer more perspectives about transformative learning later in this chapter.

Andragogy

Coaching clients begin their work with an agenda to change some aspect of their lives, and this implies learning. Thus the question, how do we best work with adult learners? Malcolm Knowles (1980), a major voice in discussions on adult learning, believed that adult learners have a different set of needs than children do. Models for adult learning fall under the category of andragogy, as distinguished from traditional models of learning normally referred to as **pedagogy**. The difference isn't between children and adults per se but whether a person approaches learning as an adult or a nonadult (Cyr, 1999). Andragogy has ties to Piaget (1952) and the **constructivist theory of knowing**, which says that adults build on previous experiences when faced with new learning opportunities. Knowles described adult learners as being self-directed and moving toward increasing independence from their teachers over time.

Three key principles of andragogy are (1) adult learning is an active process with learners who possess innate curiosity about areas of interest and who are intrinsically motivated to learn; (2) adult learning is greatly influenced by the social environment; and (3) more often than not, adult learning is oriented toward performance rather than cognitive mastery of a topic (Cyr, 1999).

Knowles (1980) made some assumptions about the characteristics of adult learners that influence the way they learn. These characteristics as adapted for coaching can be expressed as follows (Bachkirova et al., 2010; Cox et al., 2014):

- Adults inherently need to know what they will be learning.
- Adults are self-directed and commence their learning journey with a wealth of prior experience.
- Adults choose the timing for learning; they learn when situations create a need to know.
- Adults are attracted to learn matters that have clear relevance to them.
- Adults' motivation to learn is often focused on problem solving.

Two more assumptions of adult learning theory are crucial for coaching: (1) Adults position themselves with their teachers as being mutually responsible for what they learn, how they learn, and what their learning goals are; and (2) criteria for learning include not only cognitive development but perhaps more importantly behavior change (Mezirow, 1994). These two assumptions take shape in coaching in the form of nonhierarchical partnerships and with strong emphasis on the learner's engagement in action and behavior change.

Experiential Learning

Coaching is not based in philosophical debate but rather in trying things out or putting new behaviors into practice. This action-oriented mandate of coaching is captured in the concept of **experiential learning**. In its simplest interpretation, it refers to learning by doing, but more typically it involves not only doing, but a process of reflecting on doing. David Kolb's (1984) four-stage experiential learning model has strong implications for how people continue to develop in their adult years and, therefore, is of great interest to coaches.

According to Kolb, experiential learning emerges through four stages. At the heart of his model is what he describes as concrete experiences (see figure 2.2). Such experiences allow people to reflect and observe, and then they may generalize their learning and sometimes form a new theory about how to act in future situations. This emerging **theory of action** influences new behaviors, which produce another set of concrete experiences. The cycle repeats itself

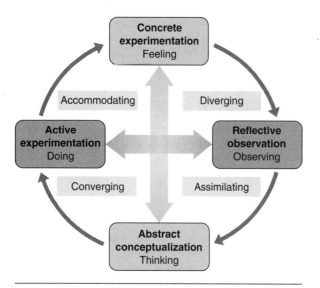

Figure 2.2   David Kolb's experiential learning cycle.
Based on Kolb (1984).

as people observe and reflect upon what they have just done.

As a simple example, suppose a man wants to get fit but has no idea what kind of exercise he wants to try. With some guidance at his fitness club, he tries a Zumba class (concrete experience). After the class, he reflects on his experience (reflective observation) and then comes up with some conclusions and general guidelines (abstract conceptualization) about exercising. Then, he puts all of this learning into a plan (active experimentation) for his next forays into the world of exercise and fitness.

Kolb and his colleague Roger Fry (1975) further defined ways they believe people absorb new information. They created the Learning Style Inventory (LSI) to help learners and educators—or coaches, in our case—understand how to present information so that it can be more readily processed when people apply their preferred **learning style** (see sidebar, Kolb and Fry's Learning Styles). According to Kolb and Fry, people navigate along two intersecting continua when they are confronted with new information (see figure 2.2): the *perception continuum* (how we think about things), which ranges from feeling to thinking, and the *processing continuum* (how we do things), which ranges from observing to doing. Depending on the learner's preferences, new information is absorbed in one of four ways. Kolb and Fry named their four learning styles as follows: **converging** (for those who learn best by thinking and doing), **diverging** (for those who learn best by feeling and observing), **assimilating** (for those who learn best by thinking and observing),

and **accommodating** (for those who learn best by feeling and doing). When coaches recognize their clients' preferences, they have an edge in helping them navigate the change process more easily.

Elaine Cox's (2013) important coaching contributions build on Kolb's model and integrate the things that clients experience through coaching with various thought processes and reflections. A critical addition that she brings to this model is the need that people have for dialogue when they are experiencing difficulty in navigating their way through a learning process. We will talk more about her work later, but for now I want to highlight the important role that coaches serve in experiential learning processes by helping clients make sense of new information and translating their recently acquired knowledge into action.

When clients reflect on experience, they increase the chances of learning. This potential learning allows them to acquire new ways of approaching their agendas and perhaps more effective strategies to reach their goals. Embedded in the philosophy of coaching are Kolb's suggestions that learners must be positioned at the center of the learning cycle and that they must assume ownership of their learning and development.

The Process of Transformation

In this section, I want to go back to the theme of transformation, which was raised earlier in relation to the four types of learning (Illeris, 2016, 2018). Transformative learning is likely to become a predominant focus of coaching work in the future, as more and more people are confronted by needs to reinvent themselves in order to sustain their livelihoods. The area of transformative learning traces back to the work of Jack Mezirow (1994) and has been described as "the social process of construing and appropriating a new or revised interpretation of the *meaning* [italics added] of one's experience as a guide to action" (1994, pp. 222-223). In other words, Mezirow thought that learning involves reframing your beliefs, principles, and feelings.

Mezirow said there are two dimensions in the structure of meaning that are involved in reframing. The first is described as *meaning perspectives*, or the lenses, most often acquired during childhood and youth, through which sensory perceptions, feelings, and thoughts are shaped and consequently limited. The second is called *meaning schemes*, or the set of concepts, beliefs, judgments, and feelings born out of our meaning perspectives that influence our interpretations. As you mature and become a more

Kolb and Fry's Learning Styles

Learning Style			
Converging	**Diverging**	**Assimilating**	**Accommodating**
Learning emphases: Abstract conceptualization (AC) + active experimentation (AE)	Learning emphases: Concrete experience (CE) + reflective observation (RO)	Learning emphases: Abstract conceptualization (AC) + reflective observation (RO)	Learning emphases: Concrete experience (CE) + active experimentation (AE)
• Great strength in practical applications of ideas. • Excels in situations where there is a single correct answer or solution to a question or problem. • Organizes knowledge through hypothetical-deductive reasoning. • Prefers working unemotionally with things rather than people. • Interests likely to be narrow with leaning toward the physical sciences.	• Great strength in idea generation and taking others' perspectives. • Views concrete situations through multiple lenses. • Creates meaning by seeing relationships among people and ideas. • Expresses keen interest in cultural matters. • Interests likely to be broadly framed in the fine arts, humanities and liberal arts.	• Great strength in the creation of theoretical models. • Skillful at inductive reasoning. • High interest in practical use of theories and relatively less interest in people. • Drawn toward the basic sciences and mathematics rather than the applied sciences. • Often gravitates toward work in research and planning areas.	• Great strength in doing things. • Likely to be a high risk-taker. • Highly adaptable in situations calling for flexibility in addressing situational demands. • Applies intuition and trial and error in problem solving. • Relies heavily on input from others rather than relying on own analytical ability.

Based on Tennant (2006).

autonomous thinker, transformation occurs as your perceptions shift and your worldviews change.

Transformative learning is facilitated by reflection on the rationale for your beliefs: *Why do you believe what you believe?* Only when you make explicit the assumptions that you have about your beliefs are you then able to challenge them. In this respect, you can probably see why reflection on your experience is so critical to transformative learning (Merriam, 2004). Mezirow (1994) says that reflection of this kind is usually awakened when you finally realize that your old ways of thinking are no longer working or serving you well. Most reflections of this sort are thought to be triggered by a disorienting dilemma in your life. Mezirow identifies three types of reflection that, along with self-reflection, might surface when you face difficult life situations: **content reflection, process reflection,** and **premise reflection**.

You generally do the first two types of reflection, content and process, on a daily basis as you solve problems or change your mind. For instance, you reflect on the *content* of an actual issue or on the way (or *process*) in which you went about solving a particular problem. An example would be when you think about all the data you might have in order to make a job change, and then identify what else may be needed (*content reflection*). Or you might realize that while you are going about determining whether to change jobs, you have left out the step of considering how such change might affect significant others in your life (*process reflection*).

The third type of reflection Mezirow (1994) identified (*premise reflection*) brings about a self-transformation in how you perceive your world. This is thought to be where the most significant learning takes place. In this type of reflection, you examine the basis upon which you defined the problem itself and explore the values, beliefs, and assumptions that gave rise to the issue in the first place. Imagine someone who is desperately upset with his weight and defines the problem as his chronic lack of motivation and the bad role modeling he witnessed with his parents. A *premise reflection* might bring this person to an awareness of cultural biases about body shape, the despair he feels about his career, the role he plays in his peer group as the lazy guy, and more.

Looking at the phases of *premise reflection* in the sidebar below (Mezirow, 1994), you might get the idea that the kickoff to this kind of reflection could be bumpy. Something abrupt, unexpected, or even undesired happens—and you are thrust into a difficult emotional place, often with feelings of guilt and shame. But then you dive deeper instead of looking for the first easy exit to your discomfort, and this choice leads you to a new world where you are no longer exactly who you were. Generally speaking, this is a far better place.

Premise reflection is no doubt at the core of most clients' work when they engage coaches to help them with profound personal shifts in their lives. As a coach, you will need to appreciate why and how change happens—and I will offer some useful models to guide your understanding in chapter 4. For now, I ask you to recognize that people who

decide to be coached usually don't show up with agendas that have a quick fix, even though that may be what they are hoping for. Seemingly simple agendas of changing diet, exercising regularly, managing stress, or gaining capacity in public speaking may represent the first doorway to transformation.

Models of Human Development

When Gail Sheehy (1976) first published her classic work, *Passages*, what her readers already knew but may not have articulated was that many of the things that once held the utmost value for them shifted in importance over the course of their lives. Agendas that were once nonnegotiable surprisingly dropped off the list. Sheehy wasn't the first to talk about stages of life; she was simply more successful than some others in popularizing the ideas. Early 20th-century thinking about development focused almost exclusively on childhood—to the point of telling us that by our 20s, we are relatively fixed for life. Fortunately, in the mid-20th century, Erik Erikson had very different thoughts about this matter.

Erikson (1902-1994), a developmental psychologist and psychoanalyst, is best known for his theory of psychosocial development, which details eight stages of life (table 2.2). Unlike Sigmund Freud, Erikson (1959, 1963, 1968) prioritized the social over the sexual aspects of the life span. He also went well beyond the first two decades of life in appreciating the critical themes and issues you need to confront as you age. Erikson believed that at each life stage, you have a pivotal conflict around which your life revolves. The way in which these conflicts are eventually resolved inevitably influences your life and character. In the *successful* resolution of stage-specific conflicts, you emerge with greater strength and potential for positive development.

Another framework that will help you gain appreciation for why clients present distinctly different concerns at varying points in their lives was described by Robert Kegan (1982, 1994), who built his model on Jean Piaget's pioneering studies of child development. Kegan reasoned that, to fully understand a person, it is important to discover where that person is in his or her evolution (Kegan, 1982; Lawrence, 2017). If a purpose of coaching is to enable individuals to maximize their potential, appreciating a client's developmental stage is crucial to a coaching conversation.

Kegan (1994) details five progressively "more complex systems of mind" (p. 9). These stages of development involve significant shifts in how we think, feel, and act—changes that may be both diffi-

Phases in Premise Reflection

- An event or experience (like job loss) creates disorientation.
- Feelings of guilt or shame may arise as a result.
- Assumptions about self and one's feelings are critically reviewed.
- A realization occurs that one is not alone—others have travelled this road.
- The learner explores new behaviors, actions, or roles.
- A plan for self-affirming actions begins to form.
- Necessary knowledge and skills for action are identified and pursued.
- The learner experiments with new roles.
- Confidence and competence in new behaviors and roles grows.
- New ways and perspectives are integrated into a transformed way of being.

Table 2.2   Erikson's Eight Stages of Development

Age	Stage	Central concern
Birth to 1 year	Trust vs. mistrust	Sensing that the world is safe and I can trust others
1-3 years	Autonomy vs. shame and doubt	Knowing that I can act on my own and be independent
3-6 years	Initiative vs. guilt	Planning and doing new things and managing my failures
6-12 years	Industry vs. inferiority	Learning basic competencies and comparing myself favorably with others
12-20 years	Identity vs. identity confusion	Integrating all my roles into a single, consistent identity
20-40 years	Intimacy vs. isolation	Sharing myself deeply without fear of losing my identity
40-65 years	Generativity vs. stagnation	Contributing to others and society through my offspring and productive work
65+ years	Integrity vs. despair	Appraising my life in a way that allows me to appreciate its significance and meaning

Based on Erickson (1963).

cult and painful (Kegan, 1982). The three stages most pertinent to adult development have been labeled as the *socialized mind*, the *self-authoring mind*, and the *self-transforming mind* (Kegan & Lahey, 2009). Individuals characterized as having evolved to the level of the *socialized mind* are aware of their feelings and able to think abstractly while also tending to be dependent on others for direction and understanding their own identity. Think of people whose self-image is tied to what their peers and authority figures think of them. Their internal framework for appreciating their talents and character seems loosely formed at best. In contrast, those reflecting the *self-authoring mind* know who they are. They recognize and own their internal authority and have a clearly formulated set of values and beliefs (Kegan & Lahey, 2001). As might be true of many midlife individuals, they seem to be independent, self-sufficient, and stable in their identities. Finally, in the infrequently attained stage of the *self-transforming mind*, individuals move beyond limiting definitions of their societally prescribed identities. They live with the multiplicity of identities within themselves. They not only recognize their inner states, but they are able to modify them to reflect other ways of orienting their thoughts, feelings, and actions to create more optimal social realities. They are visionaries who take the broadest perspectives of life, their purpose, and how best to contribute to the world. As you might imagine, in order to coach clients at different stages requires, first, that you

have awareness of where you seem to be in your own development, and secondly, that you have a solid capacity to shift from your own perspectives to those that govern your clients' thoughts, feelings, and actions.

None of the life-span development theories suggest that age is the sole determinant of movement from one stage to another. For instance, many 50-year-olds have been known to say, "I'm still trying to figure out what I want to do when I grow up," which is a statement that reflects the identity confusion of adolescence. Nonetheless, knowing someone's age allows us to explore client concerns that normatively might be awakened in this period of life. It also permits us to be sensitive to how we might want to enter the conversation with differently aged clients.

CONTRIBUTIONS FROM NEUROSCIENCE

Neuroscience offers countless ideas that serve to inform and inspire coaching practice. In this review, I can only sample some of the vast discoveries to show how they relate to coaching. Hopefully, this will whet your appetite to pursue these matters in greater depth. Many of the applications to coaching represent working hypotheses, waiting to be tested on the ground but plausible in light of what we know from basic science research.

Mind Activity Changes the Brain

You already know the brain is responsible for your ability to think, feel, and relate. Recent neuroscience research reveals that the opposite is also true: your thinking, feeling, and relating result in detectable changes in your brain, to the degree of actually changing its physical structure and chemical balance. The brain is constantly reorganizing itself based on your mental activity; brain and mind codetermine each other in a bidirectional and dynamic relationship. In neuroscience terms, a thought or an emotion can be described as the activation of a specific array of neurons. A key discovery is that any time a particular set of neurons is activated, it strengthens the connections among these neurons. Neuroscientists refer to this as *neuroplasticity*, capturing the idea in the expression, "neurons that fire together, survive together, and wire together" (Siegel, 1999, p. 219). Because of this strengthening, the same neural pattern is more likely to become active again in the future.

Illustrations

Imagine you have an important presentation to deliver tomorrow in front of a large group. As you rehearse the talk, several areas in your brain light up, such as the neurons that encode what you are going to say. At the same time, several other brain-based associations may become active due to your prior history with presentations. Imagine you have a habit of engaging in self-critical narratives when faced with public performances. Before you even know it, the brain networks responsible for generating negative self-talk kicks in. This happens regardless of whether you are well prepared for this particular presentation or not, because your history of brain activation simply shows up here. Your negative narratives will likely interfere with your rehearsal and may even trigger other associations with neural networks attempting to reduce the distress. Without realizing it, you might find yourself scrolling through your phone for your favorite newsfeeds as a patterned way of reducing discomfort.

Neural activation spreads across brain highways sculpted over the course of your life. Your construction of highways never ceases, and so they are constantly being updated based on your current state of mind. If you once again submit to your usual negative self-talk, you will further solidify the neural structure that holds it together, making it even more likely to outrun other possible competing brain programs. The good news is that you can also notice the negative narrative arising and make a conscious decision to ignore it and think of something positive instead. You might bring to mind your previous successful presentations. You might generate positive feelings toward the people you will be presenting to tomorrow. With these new patterns, you begin to strengthen different arrays of neurons. Repetition is key to the process. Whatever mental course you set, repeated activation of neural networks will generate an ever-growing automaticity in determining the actions you take.

Coaching Implications

You have seen how mental activity shapes your brain and determines the likelihood of future behaviors. This allows you to identify *awareness* of mental activity as a prime focus for development. When you encourage your clients to examine their patterns of thinking and feeling, you enable them to figure out how to interrupt automatic patterns of brain activation; this opens the way for new patterns to develop and gain traction. You have also seen how repetition is key in the development of new neural pathways. Engaging in deliberate awareness practices such as journaling, mindfulness, or mental preparation can be powerful aids in changing brain patterns. For instance, long-term practices of meditation remarkably alter the anatomy and physiology of practitioners' brains (Goleman & Davidson, 2017). Important for coaching is the fact that even short-term mental training can have significant behavioral effects. Studies show that a few weeks of daily mindfulness training results in a vast array of cognitive improvement, including improved attention, self-regulation, and working memory (Basso et al., 2019; Tang et al., 2007; Zeidan et al., 2010).

Outcomes of mental training depend on what specifically is being practiced. For example, a large study of different forms of mental training showed that attention abilities were maximally enhanced following attention training, whereas mental training focused on developing compassion increased participants' ability to deal with difficult emotions (Trautwein et al., 2020). It's wonderful to realize how much of what we know about physical training applies to mental development. This includes, first, the prime role of awareness, as well as the "what you practice, you develop" principle and its opposite, "use it or lose it." These parallels may seem less surprising when we consider the next topic: how mind and body are somewhat of a blur.

Mind Is All Over the Body

An old belief is that your mind is in your head, where the brain resides. There's some truth to this, but another way of looking at mind offers a different picture. The brain is one part of a system of communication referred to as the *nervous system*, which wires every part of your body, including skin, muscles, gut, and internal organs. The nervous system has two major divisions: the *central nervous system*, comprising brain and spinal cord, and the *peripheral nervous system*, comprising the somatic, autonomic, and enteric nervous systems. These textbook distinctions are useful for understanding anatomy of different body parts, but they don't reflect fundamental separations. If you examine the actual wiring in your body, you will see a continuous and multidirectional mesh of neurons that connect every fiber of your physical structure. Studies on nonhuman primates show precisely how neurons in several parts of the brain connect to internal organs such as the stomach and kidneys. There are as little as three neurons mediating the travel of an electric impulse from the surface of the brain to internal organs such as the stomach and the kidneys (Dum et al., 2019; Levinthal & Strick, 2020). These connections enable the many parts of your physical self, such as your brain and gut, to sync with each other, constantly adjusting to what is happening in the other parts.

Illustrations

Let's reexamine the example of your imagined presentation tomorrow, where you find yourself engaged in a self-critical narrative as you are preparing. The neural activation in your brain related to your negative story spreads down at a speed of about 120 meters per second and after just a couple stops reaches your stomach, heart, lungs, muscles, arteries, and kidneys. In a fraction of a second, your whole body has been notified that something bad is happening. The branch of the autonomic nervous system responsible for dealing with threats, called the *sympathetic nervous system*, kicks in. Your internal settings adjust to maximize chances for survival: several blood vessels constrict, causing blood pressure to rise; the heart accelerates its pumping; stress hormones flow in the blood; and digestion shuts down. You are ready for fight or flight. However, this is an enemy that can't be fought or escaped. You generated the threat yourself by engaging your uniquely human ability to remember and imagine. These faculties developed relatively recently in the evolution of our species and are made available through the most advanced portions of the brain. The rest of your nervous system evolved at a time when such sophisticated faculties didn't exist. The peripheral nervous system that wires most of your body doesn't fully get the difference between what's real and what's imagined. Adding to this, while threats in the environment are usually short-lived and allow for a rapid engagement and disengagement of the sympathetic nervous system, the subtle threats you create in your mind can continue indefinitely. As a result of neuroplasticity, as discussed earlier, feeling that you are under threat can even become your default way of functioning. You can easily trap yourself in a *chronic stress response* that undermines your ability to express your full potential, and that plays a major role in causing such diseases of our time as depression, anxiety, infertility, insomnia, stroke, diabetes, and irritable bowel syndrome, just to name a few. By the same token, however, you can leverage your nervous system to create conditions that are optimal for learning and development.

Imagine that as you notice the negative thoughts popping to mind, you take a few slow, deep breaths. The gentle stretch of the lungs stimulates specialized receptors that activate the *parasympathetic nervous system*, the branch of the autonomic nervous system that promotes several long-term maintenance functions including relaxation, healing, emotional regulation, and prosocial behaviors. Oxygen in the blood increases because of your slow and deep breathing, and this supports optimal functioning of all organs, including the brain. By leveraging these combined mechanisms, you have quickly turned what could have been an energy sinkhole into an optimal scenario for your brain to deal with this challenge.

Coaching Implications

Now you have seen how what we refer to as "mind" is the product of constant interactions among multiple layers of the nervous system. From this perspective, mind–body practices or ways of bringing together head, heart, and hand shouldn't be misjudged as new-age fantasies. These and similar metaphors point quite accurately to the way you are built. A neuroscience-based understanding of such metaphors can help you as a coach explain things with compelling clarity. When you encourage clients to pause their storytelling to examine their feelings, emotions, and bodily sensations, you are enabling them to integrate rich streams of neural data. Body-based information is often an entryway to breakthroughs and insights.

There are three interrelated mechanisms for why this may be the case. First, your body provides rich information about your emotional states (Critchley & Garfinkel, 2017). Studies show a correlation between how much people are aware of their body sensations and their ability to regulate emotions (Füstös et al., 2013). Additionally, you may think that in a given situation you are happy or anxious, or that a specific person makes you feel uncomfortable or in love. These framings are often language-based simplifications, and they may obscure what's really going on. However, focusing on the sensations in your body (rather than the verbal labels) may help you uncover more detailed layers of your experience that may be essential in approaching many complex human scenarios (Khalsa et al., 2018), for example, by discriminating whether the discomfort you are feeling is anger, sadness, or fear.

Second, information about your current state is an anchor for mindfulness, that is, the nonjudgmental awareness of your experience in the present moment. Peripheral sensory neurons all around your body that pick up sensory information (e.g., muscular tension, relaxation, heat) can only report on their current state. They have no built-in imagination function, nor by themselves can they provide judgments about whether a particular sensation is good or bad. Simply tuning into body sensations can quickly thin out a stream of rumination and bring you to a place of curious, receptive observation of what is happening in the present moment (Farb et al., 2007; Kerr et al., 2013). This type of mental shift is pivotal in any strategy aimed at reducing stress, both physical and mental, as well as for broadening the range of possible perspectives you can develop about a given situation (Killingsworth & Gilbert, 2010; Ottaviani et al., 2013).

Third, an important brain mechanism that promotes breakthroughs arises when you temporarily shut down your habitual patterns of thinking to enable nonobvious connections among distantly related information to be noticed (Salvi et al., 2020). Focusing purely on body sensations seems to have many ingredients that can facilitate "aha" moments and a decrease of negative mood (Basso et al., 2019; Ding et al., 2015; Kounios & Beeman, 2014). Beside the facilitation of insights, neuroscience findings on the mind–body connection suggest that the state of your body and your awareness of such states plays a crucial role in dealing with virtually any kind of coaching topic. Directly or indirectly, dimensions such as respiration (Ma et al., 2017), physical exercise (Heyman et al., 2012), physical pain (Moriarty et al., 2011), posture (Niedenthal, 2007), sleep (Killgore, 2010), and diet (Kennedy et al., 2017) all affect various aspects of cognitive functioning. These dimensions matter for your clients as they move toward their goals. For you as well, awareness and control of your body can contribute to shaping the quality of your presence and your ability to express empathy and support. Notably, increasing your body awareness will better enable you to detect an emotion that you begin to feel as a form of contagion from your clients' emotional states (Prochazkova & Kret, 2017). Indeed, the very fact that there seems to be some emotional permeability between you and other people warrants a further exploration of how your brain constructs your reality.

How the Brain Constructs Reality

Your conscious experience of the world has qualities of immediacy, continuity, and stability. You are likely to take for granted that what you see or touch is a direct rendition of something that in reality is exactly the way you perceive it. Neuroscience reveals a different story. The sheer amount of information coming from your senses is too much for your brain to compute and interpret. When clients speak to you, and you try to understand what they are saying, your brain is receiving at the same time sounds of speech and breathing, visuals of their moving face and hands, sensations in your own body, sounds of noise in the background, visuals of the surrounding environment, and a million other details. Add to that all the memories, emotions, and fantasies automatically activated by any one of these perceptions. How can you possibly function with such overwhelming information? To solve this problem, the brain uses mechanisms similar to filters that analyze the immense pool of available information and select just a few bits that *seem* to be the most relevant for a particular situation. What's more, the brain relies on a clever built-in mechanism that dramatically reduces the amount of information it needs to interpret; this mechanism is *prediction*. In most scenarios, the brain predicts what will happen next. If the prediction *seems to be* confirmed, the brain doesn't use energy in carefully analyzing what actually happened; it just assumes that everything went exactly as intended. The extra effort of careful examination is undertaken only if events seem to contradict the prediction. By combining attention (the ability to selectively concentrate on a discrete aspect of an experience), expectations (the ability to predict how something will unfold) and neural circuits that fill in the gaps, the brain successfully handles an otherwise unmanageable load of sensory inputs. The result is that smooth and snappy experience of being in the world that you take for reality.

Illustrations

What's the catch in all this? The brain is selecting and predicting information according to what was relevant in your *past*. Pitfalls in your reconstructions become evident when you encounter life changes. The neuroplasticity described earlier is at play here. Whatever has been significantly important at a given point in your life shapes your neural filters, so that you continue to be highly receptive to it. This, in turn, continues to make your filters more powerful and automatic, so that you see and predict more of the same. Over time, you may become very efficient at dealing with a certain scenario using a tried and true approach. But when that scenario changes, or when for whatever reason the approach you developed is no longer viable, the limitations are revealed. All of a sudden, what is happening around you or inside you no longer makes sense. No matter what you try, you keep running into obstacles, and you can't figure out why.

There are so many examples of what happens when some constant in your life disappears. Consider what might have happened to you when COVID-19 was declared a global pandemic by the World Health Organization in 2020. Multiple behavioral patterns or habits of living were severely disrupted. Other common examples can arise in long-term relationships when one of the partners significantly changes habits or when a family constellation suddenly shifts with the inclusion of new members or the departure of old members. Or consider what might happen should you have to adapt to a newly created professional role or to living in a very different environment.

Even though clues might be available to help you navigate new situations, you either don't see them, or you see them but don't think they are important. The attention and predictive filters you developed and that facilitated your past success are now among the causes of your struggles. In order to move forward, you need to develop new filters and new patterns of paying attention.

Let's focus on one class of filterlike mechanisms in the brain: attention to and predictions about other people. Humans have developed as a social species and rely on close, regular, and complex social interactions for survival. Accordingly, a lot of what you pay attention to and what you try to predict has to do with other people, such as understanding their emotions, knowing their intentions, and predicting their actions. These abilities are essential for any goal that involves more than you. Your brain has numerous specialized circuitries to help you with these tasks, some more automatic, some more under voluntary control. At the automatic end of the spectrum, for example, your brain can detect that another person is showing signs of fear without you even consciously realizing it (Tamietto & Gelder, 2010). It's easy to appreciate the survival value of sensing even the slightest signal of fear in another person: your brain and body need to prepare just in case you may be in danger, too. Readiness to act is not the only correlate of noticing emotions in others; you often end up feeling the same emotion too. Emotional contagion is a well-documented tendency whereby people unconsciously take on the sensory, motor, physiological, and affective states of others (Prochazkova & Kret, 2017).

Other mechanisms that help shape your social world are more under voluntary control. Emotional empathy is a particular form of paying attention to another person that enables you to feel the emotions they are feeling. It works by voluntarily activating parts of your brain that are similar to those that are active when you experience the same emotions yourself. In the well-studied example of seeing someone in pain (Fallon et al., 2020), emotional empathy activates your brain areas that signal pain, and you feel real pain yourself. Cognitive empathy, on the other hand, enables you to gain understanding about the situation from the other person's perspective, by predominantly activating areas involved in perspective taking, visuospatial processing, and working memory (De Waal & Preston, 2017). In the pain example, cognitive empathy helps you understand why a person is feeling pain without actually feeling it. Compassion is yet another form of directing attention to others that combines emotional and cognitive empathy with a positive intention to alleviate their suffering, and it recruits the neural circuitry for the feelings of love and affiliation (Singer & Klimecki, 2014).

Finally, let's look at the role of mirror neurons in this context. Discovered in 1992 in the monkey brain, this class of cells has the interesting property of becoming active both when the monkey performs an action toward a goal and when the animal observes someone else performing the same action (Gallese et al., 1996). Researchers who made the discovery hypothesized that mirror neurons enable us to *understand* the actions of others directly and without the need for complex semantic operations simply by activating the neurons that you use to perform those same actions. The process might be like this: I watch you—and without thinking, I know exactly what it is you are doing. The simplicity of the hypothesized mechanism and its apparent explanatory power brought enormous interest to the topic. Mirror neurons rose to fame among neuroscientists and the general public alike. They were quickly identified as the basis for prominent cognitive functions such as language, empathy, imitation, and self-awareness. Popular fascination surrounding this topic spread to wide-ranging areas of practice and research. Mirror neurons were used to explain behaviors related to schizophrenia, sexual orientation, self-awareness, cigarette smoking, music appreciation, political choice, obesity, and leadership. The coaching field was no exception: nearly every published coaching book that discusses the brain features mirror neurons among its prime explanatory mechanisms.

You may be wondering how a minute piece of brain tissue could be the foundation for such a wide variety of complex human endeavors. Many in the neuroscience field began to wonder the same. Speculations about mirror neurons became increasingly detached from scientific research. Often, they were employed as a convenient explanation for anything involving complex interpersonal functions that we simply didn't understand.

A growing volume of subsequent research is revealing that mirror neurons and the role they play are very likely to have been exaggerated and distorted (Hickok, 2014). Current scientific evidence suggests that mirror neurons may notify our brain of possible actions that you have learned through repeated association, and they do so not only when you encounter that context yourself, but also when someone else is encountering that context (Catmur et al., 2016). In this line of reasoning, mirror neurons may contribute to your ability to *predict* others' behaviors, based on your own bank of knowledge about your actions. This is a much humbler claim compared to the popular idea that mirror neurons constitute the basis for action *understanding*, an ability that seems to be founded on much more complex and distributed brain networks (Thompson et al., 2019).

Coaching Implications

Hopefully, you have a better idea about how what you perceive to be true is the result of an active filtering and reconstruction by our brain, and that such filtering is based on your previous experiences. What can you do with this as a coach? A clear implication is that you may want to invest seriously in discovering your own filters and the kinds of information you systematically tend to miss or ignore. Coach development exercises that

involve, for example, identifying your personality type, and then intentionally retraining yourself to attend to what you may ignore, will likely help you work with clients whose coaching issues implicate your blind spots.

This understanding may also raise your awareness of some potential pitfalls of jumping to conclusions and hastily giving advice. From a lifetime of accumulated practice, your brain has become great in solving your problems, doing so in the way that works for you. As you know, clients come with a wildly different set of filters, expectations, intentions, and past experiences. Your suggestions and interpretations, no matter how wonderful, may not make sense for them. In this light, an alternative might be to help clients become aware of the filters they are using. For example, clients can be invited to become aware of what they are paying attention to in relation to their topic, as well as to what they are not paying attention to, and what predictions they are making, wittingly or not. As clients explore beyond the edges of their usual reality, new options are likely to emerge organically from clients themselves.

The social wiring of your brain also alerts you to the fact that you are constantly picking up echoes of clients' emotions. To the degree this happens unconsciously, it can prompt in you a variety of reactions to regulate your own emotions, resulting in a muddling of the coaching process. A good example of this might occur when clients are experiencing intense discomfort, and coaches may begin to feel the discomfort themselves without fully realizing what is happening. In an unconscious attempt to regulate their own discomfort, coaches may hastily try to reassure and comfort clients, while a more helpful action might be to facilitate clients' exploration of this discomfort.

When you develop the capacity to resonate with your clients in full self-awareness, you may be able to appreciate what your clients are experiencing even though your clients may be largely unaware of their own feelings. Finally, understanding the differences between emotional empathy, cognitive empathy, and compassion, as well as how they are implemented in the brain, invites you to make conscious choices about which to rely on depending on the situation. Emotional empathy can provide a direct and powerful access to a client's emotional world. However, when negative emotions are at play, emotional empathy can provoke a stressful response in you as the coach, which in the long run may expose you to the risk of burnout. Cognitive empathy can provide key elements to better understand client situations. For example, it may be the basis for impactful **paraphrasing** and synthesizing of a lengthy client story. Yet, cognitive empathy alone may lack the degree of emotional connection and warmth that may be necessary for clients to experience trust in the process. Compassion leverages the understanding gained from cognitive empathy and can shift the negative emotions experienced through emotional empathy into a positive disposition to help and support the other person. As such, it doesn't expose you as a coach to the risk of burnout (Ricard, 2016). The expression of compassion in a coaching context still requires the nurturing of your deep self-awareness as a coach to prevent you from taking on a parental tone or offering help in a way that prevents clients from discovering how they can help themselves.

Applying Neuroscience

I have only scratched the surface here, and you are likely to want to know more. There are a number of coach-relevant neuroscience presentations in the current literature, including those by O'Connor and Lages (2019), Rock (2020), Brann (2017), and Cozolino (2017). Of course, the works of Siegel (2010, 2012, 2018) are likely to be quite helpful. I trust you will find other sources that will be equally valuable.

There is a caution in relation to incorporating the burgeoning knowledge base of neuroscience in your work as a coach. Even if you have a solid neuroscience education, the core work of coaching is not about teaching clients about how the brain works. Two of the most important implications of this review lie in its emphasis on increasing your self-awareness and delving into some of your automatic behaviors or ingrained ways of thinking and acting. Indeed, you can encourage these endeavors in your clients as well. Another conclusion one may draw from the neuroscience literature is that much of the wisdom of the helping professions developed over the last century seems to have solid scientific basis. For instance, we knew about the effectiveness of thought-stopping practices in helping clients deal with downward negative spirals of self-critical thinking long before neuroscience provided a more neurological explanation. No doubt, neuroscience will continue to refine and augment the knowledge available for coaching practice so you can function on firm ground in your interventions. In this respect, the future looks immensely exciting. Emerging neuroscience knowledge will serve to undergird your practices, to provide rationale for what you do, and to strengthen your own resolve to get on top of your own patterns. Yet, it does not, for the most part, suggest a need for you to embed neuroscience language in your interventions with clients. Their work is to move forward toward their goals, while your work rests in knowing how best to help them with the soundest principles and practices you can acquire from virtually any field.

COACHING AND COACHING PSYCHOLOGY— SAME OR DIFFERENT

In the early years of the coaching profession, a new branch of psychology known as coaching psychology emerged. Early estimates suggested that about 5 percent of practicing coaches described themselves as coaching psychologists (Grant & Zackon, 2004). The late Michael Grant, a pioneer in this subdivision of psychology, described coaching psychology as

> the systematic application of behavioral science to the enhancement of life experience, work performance and well-being for individuals who do not have clinically significant mental health issues or groups and organizations with no abnormal levels of distress. In broad terms, coaching psychology sits at the intersection of sports, counseling, clinical, and organizational and health psychology. (Grant, 2007, p. 23)

The work of coaching psychologists has often illuminated connections between practical applications in the coaching field and underlying psychological research. Palmer and Whybrow (2007) further suggested that "coaching psychology is for enhancing well-being and performance in personal life and work domains underpinned by models of coaching grounded in established adult and child learning or psychological approaches" (p. 3).

Even though these definitions provide some clarity about coaching psychology, they don't seem to sufficiently distinguish it from the broader realm of coaching practice. The coaching field also positions itself as a growth and development process rather than a rehabilitative one. And, like coaching psychology, it relies heavily upon the behavioral sciences and adult learning models. Clearly, psychologists have extensive educational requirements that go far beyond those required of coaching practitioners, but what would a coaching psychologist do that would be so distinctively different from what a certified coach might do? It just seems at this point that the exact relationship between coaching psychology and the broader coaching field needs further distinction. Though some might say that psychology, as a scientific endeavor, would be more likely than coaching, as a practice-based discipline, to contribute research knowledge to the field, but even that opinion can be readily questioned should one consider the hefty amount of research on coaching originating from nonpsychologists.

Nonetheless, efforts to distinguish psychological approaches from ones used in coaching seem necessary in articulating coaching's identity (Abravanel & Gavin, 2017; Price, 2009), particularly because so many coaching texts include adaptations of psychological methodology. For instance, when a therapy model such as cognitive behavior therapy forms the basis of a coaching model (Neenan, 2018), a reasonable question to ask is whether coaching practitioners using a therapy-like model will be skilled enough to use it well and sufficiently judicious to be able to figuratively draw a line in their work so that their interventions rest solidly within the domain of coaching. Earlier, you saw how other psychotherapeutic models had been adapted to fit coaching purposes, including works on narrative coaching (Drake, 2018), solution-focused coaching (Grant & Greene, 2003), and acceptance and commitment coaching (Hill & Oliver, 2019).

Grant and Cavanagh (2007), who helped establish the world's first doctoral program in coaching psychology, didn't think that all coaches should be psychologists. Rather, they recommended that coaches develop strong theoretical grounding. They further advised that coaches possess the necessary capacity to recognize clinical issues and act appropriately. According to them, only psychologically trained professionals should work with clients on issues involving significant emotional or cognitive development. Without such capacity to recognize clinical issues, coaches might unknowingly be involved with clients who are addressing such challenging agendas. I would agree that this needs to be an ongoing focus of attention in training and continuing education for coaches.

Concerns about whether coaches are addressing psychological issues in their work may partly result from a mindset wherein client issues get framed as psychological matters when, in fact, they could be described differently. For instance, it is a normal human experience for someone giving a speech to a large audience to feel anxiety. Anxiety is a core concept in psychology, but psychology doesn't have exclusive rights to addressing all manifestations of this common human experience. Educators, train-ers, and consultants will often refer to and address anxiety matters in their work. To repeat what was said earlier, the fields of learning and adult development may have at least as much or possibly more relevance in conceptualizing client issues and the processes of coaching (Bennett & Campone, 2017; Cox, 2013; Lawrence, 2017) than the field of psychology. We are complex beings, and as such, no single perspective or mode of working with clients can adequately address all the issues that arise in our lives.

From a multidisciplinary perspective, we can comfortably say that professional coaching, as a form of helping, is sufficiently distinct from any of its root elements (Abravanel & Gavin, 2017). Even so, as coaching becomes a more regulated field of professional endeavor, the capacity to concretely identify differences between coaches and coaching psychologists remains necessary.

A UNIFYING PERSPECTIVE

In this brief overview of contributions from the fields of psychology, learning, human development, and neuroscience, at least two things should be clear. First, the field of coaching has been strongly informed by developments in these areas, and relatedly, coaching needs to be appreciated not as an entirely new field but rather as a creative integration of the invaluable contributions of theorists and practitioners across a multitude of knowledge domains and human service professions. It is encouraging to see that the present-day coaching field has wholeheartedly embraced these frameworks and built its core around their grounded principles.

Different roots of coaching have guided the development of different approaches and schools of coaching. As Bachkirova, Cox, and Clutterbuck (2018) point out, each school or approach seems to operate with its own assumptions, knowledge sources, and styles of practice—and this can indeed be confusing. These authors try to bring order to all the varieties of coaching in the world by making a critical distinction between the theoretical perspectives underlying different approaches to coaching *and* the genres or contexts of coaching—that is, where coaching is applied or for what purposes. They identified 13 theoretical approaches and 12 different genres or contexts (see sidebar, Theoretical Traditions and Genres of Coaching). In their edited volume (Cox et al., 2018), these authors offer chapters describing each of these 25 traditions and genres. That's a lot to digest, particularly when you are just entering this field of work.

Theoretical Traditions and Genres of Coaching

Theoretical traditions	Genres or contexts
Psychodynamic	Skills and performance
Cognitive behavioral	Developmental
Solution-focused	Transformational
Person-centered	Executive and leadership
Gestalt approach	Manager as coach
Existential	Team and group
Ontological	Internal coaching
Narrative	Peer coaching
Adult psychological development	Life coaching
Transpersonal	Health and wellness coaching
Positive psychology	Career coaching
Transactional analysis	Cross-cultural coaching
Neurolinguistic programming	

Based on Bachkirova, Cox, and Clutterbuck (2018, p. xlvii).

So how can we make sense of all this without oversimplifying this diverse field? I think one of the best ways to do this is by referring to the practical manifestations of what coaches generally do in their work with clients. In 1995, the International Coach Federation (ICF, 2020c) presented a set of core competencies for coaching that was neither tied to particular theories nor limited by different coaching contexts. This set of competencies was thought to be robust enough to characterize the fundamental things that coaches do with their clients. In 2019, the ICF offered a revision to the original 11 core coaching competencies, subdividing the new set of eight competencies into four themes, namely, foundation, cocreating the relationship, communicating effectively, and cultivating learning and growth (see sidebar, ICF Core Coaching Competencies). While this revision was significant, it did not fundamentally shift the essential competencies required for coaches. Irrespective of the theoretical traditions or applications that inform different coaches, these eight competencies are about as universal as might be possible in the world of coaching (see sidebar, ICF Core Coaching Competencies).

In upcoming chapters, I will reference these competencies both to illustrate how ubiquitous they are as well as to drill down into coaching interventions that suggest their presence in a coaching dialogue.

To a large degree, these eight competencies as mirrored in specific behaviors must be evident in any professional coaching dialogue in order for it

to exemplify coaching practice. The first theme, *foundation*, reflects the fact that the coach needs to fully demonstrate personal integrity and honesty in all coach-related interactions. This ethical stance is evident not only in how the coach speaks but also in the nature and boundaries the coach establishes for the conversation. Before beginning a relationship, coaches will have clarified certain parameters for their work, which will necessarily include distinctions between what they do and what other helpers, like psychotherapists and consultants, might do. They will also adhere to limits set by their clients on what the focus is and what areas are out of bounds for discussion.

Foundation also encompasses a certain way of being for coaches. This includes how coaches regard their clients as self-directing and autonomous and how they are continuously engaged in a lifelong learning process enabling them to be more self-aware, sensitive to individual and cultural differences, mentally and emotionally prepared, capable of emotional self-regulation, and self-reflecting.

The second theme, *cocreating the relationship*, establishes that coaching is a contractual relationship wherein all parties involved are clear about the terms of the relationship, process, plans, and objectives. A professional agreement or contract is codetermined in either verbal or written form describing the conditions under which coach and client will work. Part of this codetermination centers on whether the context, focus, and dynamics of the

ICF Core Coaching Competencies

The following eight (8) core coaching competencies reflect the intent and much of the content of the original 11 competencies; they are identified as follows under four major themes:

Foundation

1. Demonstrates Ethical Practice

Definition: Understands and consistently applies coaching ethics and standards of coaching

2. Embodies a Coaching Mindset

Definition: Develops and maintains a mindset that is open, curious, flexible and client-centered

Co-Creating the Relationship

3. Establishes and Maintains Agreements

Definition: Partners with the client and relevant stakeholders to create clear agreements about the coaching relationship, process, plans and goals. Establishes agreements for the overall coaching engagement as well as those for each coaching session.

4. Cultivates Trust and Safety

Definition: Partners with the client to create a safe, supportive environment that allows the client to share freely. Maintains a relationship of mutual respect and trust.

5. Maintains Presence

Definition: Is fully conscious and present with the client, employing a style that is open, flexible, grounded and confident

Communicating Effectively

6. Listens Actively

Definition: Focuses on what the client is and is not saying to fully understand what is being communicated in the context of the client systems and to support client self-expression

7. Evokes Awareness

Definition: Facilitates client insight and learning by using tools and techniques such as powerful questioning, silence, metaphor or analogy

Learning and Growth

8. Facilitates Client Growth

Definition: Partners with the client to transform learning and insight into action. Promotes client autonomy in the coaching process.

Text content reprinted with permission from International Coach Federation (ICF) (2017). Available: https://coachfederation.org/core-competencies/.

coaching relationship are viable; this was partly suggested in chapter 1 in describing the term *coachability*. Where clients are sponsored by a third party (e.g., an organization), discussions and decisions related to the contract will appropriately include all relevant parties. The contract includes not only scheduling of sessions and fees, but also the main focus of the coaching work and the mutual responsibilities of the partners to the agreement. While this agreement is formed at the beginning of the relationship, it is also represented in how each session progresses. Coaches will typically begin with a question about what the client hopes to achieve in the current session—and how this focus relates to the overarching concern that the client expressed at the start of their relationship.

A core aspect of *cocreating the relationship* pertains to the coach's way of building a safe, trusting, and respectful connection with the client. An essential element in all coaching is that there must be a trusting and genuine relationship as a container for all that transpires. Throughout each coaching dialogue, one would need to witness ample evidence that both coach and client are present to each other and the dialogue. This calls for the coach's awareness and acknowledgment of clients' uniqueness, their appropriate expression of support and empathy, and their own transparency as a way of building trust. The manner in which a coach is present to the client should not vary based on the theoretical school to which a coach adheres, but rather should be observed in the coach's curiosity, focus, flexibility, and comfort in working with wide-ranging content and emotional expressions.

Within the third theme of *communicating effectively*, one not only sees the methodology of coaching but also a likely progression in how the coach moves with the client toward identified outcomes for their work together. The coach listens, asks questions, and at times may make suggestions or have other kinds of input. It is the artful flow of communication involving different types of skills that enables clients to progress efficiently and effectively from broad expressions of what concerns them toward viable strategies for addressing their concerns. At times coaches may challenge what their clients say, reframe perspectives, or share observations and insights.

In the fourth theme, *cultivating learning and growth*, we find the twin hallmarks of coaching—learning and results. Clients not only organize their thoughts and energies in formulating viable action strategies for change, but they also learn about themselves, their situations, and even new dimensions of their lives that they might want to explore and build. A final piece in this theme speaks about accountability, wherein one sees again the uniqueness of coaching. These are not philosophical discussions or abstract considerations alone; coaching conversations are intentionally designed to bring about change through some form of action to which clients are expected to hold themselves accountable. A client who considers changing interminably without ever putting words into action is not likely to be engaged in a *bona fide* coaching relationship. When clients are successful in their accomplishments, no matter how big or small, coaches join in the celebration through sincere acknowledgments of the road traveled and the destination reached.

REFLECTIONS

If you recall the distinction made in the first chapter between coaching as a profession and a one-off coaching conversation, you might now have a more thorough understanding of how much knowledge underlies the practice of coaching. The learning journey for coaches is lifelong. There will always be more to understand and new models for how best to serve your clients. This is not meant to discourage you but rather to inspire you to embrace all of the relevant fields of knowledge and practice that can help you be a better coach.

You might also have a better appreciation for why coaching is not entirely subsumed by any one field, such as psychology. Yes, there are psychologists who define their work as coaching related, but the vast majority of coaches are not psychologists—and more importantly, they don't need to be. In this chapter you became aware of how much psychological theory has been adapted within the practice of coaching, but that doesn't mean coaches are practicing psychology. I go back to the notion of multidisciplinarity. Knowledge in the modern world originates in the rich beds of diverse professional and academic domains. What becomes central is how and to what ends this knowledge is used.

I have been fortunate to have been able to work with thousands of individuals at fairly deep levels of their existence over the course of my career. The vast majority of these individuals showed exceptional signs of health, adaptation to life, and emotional well-being—but not all of the time. I consider these people to be normal, meaning that like you and me, most days are good, but there are challenges, struggles, downturns, upsets, and even devastating crashes. When these not-so-good things happen, we may need a really good doctor, lawyer, accountant, psychologist, or coach. We may even need all of these helpers at the same time. That's life. The accountant doesn't tell you how to deal with relationship difficulties, and the doctor doesn't tell you how to do your taxes. So, too, the coach has a defined role in the grand scheme of things.

Increasingly, as we encounter the projected shifts in our world that artificial intelligence, genetic engineering, and advanced technology will bring about, more and more of us will be on a unique learning journey, adapting to the sudden pivots in life direction. If coaches are anything, they are masterful guides to human change and evolution. As such, they may work in tandem with a client's doctor, lawyer, accountant, personal trainer, and who knows whom else. They will carry the big picture of where their clients want to go and help them identify the necessary steps they need to take to get there. This is the essence of coaching work.

CHAPTER 3

GOALS, GROWTH, AND TRANSFORMATION

Begin with the end in mind.

Stephen Covey

My parents were immigrants with almost no formal education. How I ended up with a doctor of philosophy (PhD) degree in my mid-20s remains one of the many curiosities of my life. After graduate school, I chose to work as a psychologist for a major airline but shortly thereafter made a clear decision to become a university professor. While in my first university job, I remember walking into a local studio looking for a tai chi class and found a modern dance class instead. Fast forward a year and I was dancing in a small, semiprofessional dance troupe. Later still, I emigrated from the United States to Canada. I also began studying the martial art of aikido, as well as initiating a regular practice of yoga. Why these choices? Where did they come from? I know that as a young boy, I had a number of intentions for my life.

Today, I feel as if I have lived a number of dreams even though they weren't always well articulated at the outset. There were times when I went madly off in pursuit of something whimsical. Do I think my life exemplifies goal-directed living? My answer is far more yes than no. I know my life was guided by some strong values and purposes that I identified at an early age. I was curious, I was experimenting with different interests, and I embraced learning. My love of physical activity shines through as a pillar of my life; kindness, equity, and caring have always been nonnegotiable qualities; helping others seemed to be my mission. In a way, whether I chose dance, aikido, or competing in triathlons wasn't critical. Whether I became a psychologist, a teacher, a sport coach, or a minister probably would have served similar purposes. Through the winding journey of my life, I believe I have achieved so many personally meaningful goals, and I am truly happy being where I am. All that said, I can really see how having a coach at various moments in my life would have been beneficial. As much as I enjoy wandering around in uncharted territories at times, having greater clarity in pivotal periods would have allowed me to pursue things with more focus and fewer detours.

Coaching is predominantly understood as a goal-centered process with goals emerging from clients in dialogue with their coaches. This chapter reviews relevant knowledge about the importance of goals, features of goal setting, and elements that need to be considered to foster goal attainment. Different ways of looking at goals and an appreciation of how the world around you affects the goals you set will also be examined. Here are some guiding questions to consider as you read:

- Is all coaching about the pursuit of goals?
- Can simply *being* be a goal?
- Are there different levels of goals?
- Are there different types of goals?
- Where does motivation fit into the pursuit of goals?
- How can clients set goals in such a turbulent world?

OUR GOAL-CENTRIC NATURE

Stephen Covey's (1989) profound advice to begin whatever you are pursuing with the end in mind underscores the centrality of goals in human behavior. It's likely that you have numerous goals or targets for yourself or at least that you can identify specific purposes and objectives you intend to pursue. Whether you habitually make New Year's resolutions or not, you probably guide your actions toward certain outcomes. You may even be in the habit of setting targets for each day's behavior—and tracking your success with an app on one of your devices.

Bringing this discussion into the world of coaching, I believe that the vast majority of clients who work with coaches have identifiable intentions for their engagements. Indeed, many clients decide to work with a coach after a number of unsatisfactory attempts to reach an important goal. As goal-driven beings, our well-being in life is likely to correlate with the effectiveness of our goal-pursuit efforts and strategies (Bandura, 2001; Locke & Latham, 1990).

You may have a dream about your life. The dream represents a kind of goal statement, and depending on how you work with that dream, it may remain forever elusive or, more optimistically, you may move ever closer to it over a period of time. A significant body of scientific knowledge has accumulated since about 1970 concerning what helps and what hinders goal attainment. It is this knowledge that underlies the field of coaching and that guides the way in which coaches work with their clients.

Maybe you are wondering, with solid science informing us about how to better achieve our goals, why aren't we all more successful—and in the perspective of coaching, why would anyone hire a coach to pursue his or her goals when science can show them how to do it? These are good questions. Answers partly lie in the fact that the process of identifying your goals takes a bit of creative effort that is often aided by an astute thought partner. Another element has to do with feedback. You may have 20/20 hindsight but not always see yourself clearly in the moment. Relatedly, you may not have articulated appropriate metrics related to progress toward your goal. Here is an example: You want to be happy. How do *you* measure happiness? Money? Friends? Possessions? Inner peace? All of these? There are other factors as well that summate in a proposition that as humans we do better when we work with an informed and sensitive guide who can help us foresee obstacles and identify critical variables along our path that may help or hinder our success.

What you will be exploring in this chapter is why goals are so central to the process of coaching. I will describe different types of goals, different levels of goals, and some factors you might want to consider when you set goals. You will also see how motivation is intricately related to the pursuit of goals. Before jumping in, let's take a moment to solidify the proposition that coaching is about the pursuit of goals.

How many times in the past 24 hours have goals played into your thoughts, actions, and feelings? Of course, I haven't defined what I mean by a goal, so let's just address this at a colloquial level. A goal can be a target, an objective, a standard, a purpose, an aim, an ambition, a resolution, a pursuit, or some other synonymous concept. Maybe you wanted to get up at a particular time and eat a healthy breakfast today. You might have set out a list of things to do. You might have made a commitment to go to the gym. Maybe you wanted to call a friend to stay in touch. Maybe it was time to give your dog a bath. You might have set a time limit to complete an assignment. Oh, yes, and then you had to get groceries. Some of these may not seem like goals, but as you read through this chapter, hopefully your goal-centric nature will become more evident.

It seems unlikely that you would describe yourself as a person without goals. That would be tantamount to saying your life is aimless. To the contrary, your life is probably replete with big, small, and medium-sized goals—and in all likelihood, your feelings about yourself have much to do with the degree to which you achieve your goals in a healthy fashion. Indeed, research clearly tells us that increases in positive (and decreases in negative) feelings correlate well with how much progress you make toward your goals (Koestner et al., 2002).

Let's return to the discussion of coaching. Coaching conversations are purposeful. Clients have intentions, desires, wishes, hopes, needs, and so much more. They want to accomplish or achieve something, even if it's figuring out an answer to a current life dilemma. Clients seek out coaching when they have an objective in mind. This doesn't mean that they always arrive with clarity about that objective. It may be fuzzy. It could be very tangled up and complicated. Whatever it looks or sounds like, clients probably believe that working with a coach will better enable them to reach their goals.

Maybe what I am saying here is all too evident to you. If so, that's great. My intention was to explicitly state that coaching work is not about aimless explorations of ideas, philosophies, or possibilities, but rather that coaches work with clients to help them achieve goals. For this reason, if a client experiences interesting dialogues with his or her coach about fascinating topics but never moves closer to desired states of being or toward concrete objectives, most professional coaches would say, "That's probably not a good example of coaching."

GOAL-CENTRIC COACHING

When we reflect on what clients do in a coaching relationship, two key realizations emerge: First, as clients begin their process of coaching, they tend to formulate a significant and overarching **coaching objective** that serves to inform their strategies and actions over time. Second, in pursuing this coaching objective, clients are likely to design multiple action plans with diverse subgoals that in combination form a matrix of outcomes underpinning their purpose for being in a coaching relationship.

The wide diversity in perspectives about what coaching is and what coaches do should be evident to you by now (Jarosz, 2016; Pappas & Jerman, 2015; Stelter, 2014; Williams, 2012). Even so, the predominant form of coaching worldwide is one that engages clients in processes enabling them to identify clear goals, explore their ramifications, design actions, and pursue their objectives. This can be seen in various definitions of coaching (Jarosz, 2016), as well as in the elaboration of core coaching

competencies by the International Coaching Federation (ICF, 2020c). Moreover, leading researchers and theorists in the coaching world seem to converge on a position asserting that coaching is about promoting action in relation to particular goals (Grant, 2012; Ives & Cox, 2012; Whitmore, 2017). Even when clients express interests in deeper explorations (Stelter, 2018), such depth does not preclude a concentration on the pursuit of goals (Reding & Collins, 2008).

Goal-centric coaching, or goal-focused coaching as it is otherwise described, identifies a broad category of coaching approaches that considers goal-directed activities to be a central pillar of coaching (Grant, 2012; Ives & Cox, 2012). Theories underpinning this approach derive largely from the pioneering efforts of such investigators as Locke and Latham (1990, 2002, 2006, 2009) and Bandura (1977, 1995, 1997, 2001) as well as from a foundational coaching framework advanced by Grant (2003, 2006).

Grant (2006) established the centrality of goals in coaching in his remark that "coaching is essentially about helping individuals regulate and direct their interpersonal and intrapersonal resources to better attain their goals" (p. 153). He and other goal-centric theorists believe that the work of coaching is to help clients reframe their challenges as practical problems for which various internal or external resources can be determined (Ives & Cox, 2012, p. 21). In this respect, they argue against a direct focus on psychological change (Grant, 2012), though such change may emerge as an indirect result of the coaching process. Bachkirova (2007) is even more explicit about this assertion in defining coaching as a process to improve performance rather than one intended to reduce psychological dysfunctions. In a goal-centric perspective, coaches assist clients in formulating well-designed goals that allow implementable action plans to be identified (Ives, 2008). This lends the whole experience of coach-client endeavors a deep sense of purposefulness (Grant, 2006).

Many clients who may come to you for coaching will have objectives that are strongly connected to unwanted emotionality. They may experience unpleasant reactions related to people or projects in their lives, or they may want to change patterns that arouse significant feelings of fear and anxiety. They may emphatically tell you, "I want to feel better about this." To contextualize this, think of individuals who complain about low job satisfaction, difficulties with a boss, stress related to workload, or unhappiness about health conditions. Other clients, who may be targeting higher levels of performance or wellness, might be less focused on moving away from uncomfortable emotions and more directed toward the pursuit of positive experiences of flow, happiness, or a sense of flourishing (Csikszentmihalyi, 2008; Seligman, 2012). When working with coaching clients in a goal-centric manner, you would probably want your work to result in more positive perspectives for your clients, yet the specific goals you help clients articulate are unlikely to be represented as states of emotional being. More explicitly, in a goal-centric coaching framework, a goal would not be to feel less sad, anxious, or fearful, but rather to pursue a more concrete outcome or behavioral change, which would likely have an associated benefit of positively affecting emotional states.

DOING AND BEING

In our sometimes frenetic, multitasking modern existence, it is important to consider whether we need more things to do, more mountains to climb, more seas to sail, and more and more to accomplish. Certainly, the mandate in coaching will be for clients to act on the issues they present to their coaches. Therefore, anyone entering a coaching relationship needs to be forewarned that this is not likely to be scripted as a sit-back-and-contemplate kind of experience; rather, clients will likely be expected to engage in significant efforts in between sessions with their coaches. Yet, with all of the doing that we are presently engaged in, isn't there something about simply being that might need to be cultivated for certain clients? If the answer to this question is yes, how does this fit with a goal-centric approach?

Goals are thought to provide direction for our lives (Latham et al., 2011; Latham & Locke, 2002). When we set goals, we initiate a process of action that focuses us on certain outcomes. In a sense, this becomes a cycle in our lives where we set goals, strive toward them, set other goals and do the same, in a seemingly endless fashion—because the end is just another place of beginning. One unintended result of this is the oft-heard complaint, "When am I going to get off the hamster wheel of my life?" I have had the experience in a number of coaching relationships where clients have groaned when contemplating yet another task they are about to construct for the period between our sessions. It's a kind of developmental fatigue—becoming ever better can be exhausting. You might be thinking, "Well this would be a good time *not* to focus on setting a goal."

Thinking this way reflects a fundamental misunderstanding about goals in our lives. We can have a goal to slow down, to balance work and family life, to reduce our stress, and to take time for relationships. All goals are not about doing more. Coaches work with clients who feel burned out, who are out of balance, who need to set limits and say no. The objectives (goals) that clients present in these scenarios may focus on doing less, relaxing more, meditating, or taking mini vacations. With such objectives, clients may create goals to redesign their lives and may commit to such actions as reading Tim Ferriss' (2009) *The 4-hour workweek*.

Coaches work with clients on their agendas—and many clients have goals targeting how to be rather than how to do more. While performing better is a key emphasis in some framings of goal-centric coaching (Grant, 2003, 2012; Ives & Cox, 2012; Whitmore, 2017), I want to encourage you to broaden the definition of performance to encompass a wide range of life-giving, joyful, and regenerative pursuits.

CLARIFYING GOALS AND GOAL TYPES

So much has been written about goals that it is difficult to present a simple definition. From their classic work on goal constructs in psychology, Austin and Vancouver (1996) proposed that goals be seen as "internal representations of desired states or outcomes" (p. 338). Goals are how we see what we want or the results we hope to experience. Imagine a coaching relationship has just begun and early in the first session the coach asks the client, "What are you hoping to achieve through our work together?" Clients could reply they want to become a partner in a law firm or a marathon runner; they might want to be a better leader or hope to live happily and healthily until age 110; they may want to be "more Zen" or to own their own business. Well, these are goals, aren't they? The broad answer is yes. They fit the definition of an internal representation of a state or outcome the client wants to achieve. A more detailed answer requires that we try to sort some of these potential answers into different levels and types of goals.

Levels of Goals

Goals can be thought of as existing in a hierarchical structure. The goal of becoming an effective leader would likely encompass such subordinate goals as working more collaboratively with staff or delegating in a timely manner. This can be represented in a diagram (figure 3.1) where at the top of the hierarchy of goals one might find purposes or values that guide our lives. Under these there are broad objectives or metagoals, and in turn these subsume more targeted objectives (Bandura, 1986; Cooper, 2018). There is no fixed number of goal levels in this hierarchy; rather, the graphic is intended to depict the fact that goals can be quite specific or limited in scope or they can be large, overarching purposes for our lives. Figure 3.2 provides a hypothetical example of how this might be described for a particular client.

When listening to clients as they express their goals for coaching, it is important to hear the level at which they are being articulated. Are they abstract like principles or concrete, representing specific actions? Either way, the task is to appreciate what is being said—and what information is missing. A client who says he she wants to complete her doctoral dissertation needs to be asked what this will serve; that is, what is the higher level goal that this achievement will support. Likewise, a client who says he wants to achieve a sense of balance in all aspects of life needs to be guided through an exploration that looks both up and down the hierarchy. More specifically, if the client had balance, what purpose would that serve (higher goal), and what more specific objectives (lower goals) would need to be designed into the different aspects of his life to create overall balance?

The point is that goals may range from broad to narrow or abstract to concrete. At a broad or abstract level, goals may be seen as fuzzy or somewhat ill defined (Cavanagh, 2013; Clutterbuck & Spence, 2017), whereas at a concrete level, you get a very specific idea of what someone intends. Consider a client whose stated goal is to become an accomplished pianist compared to another one who wants to master a particular musical score.

Paralleling this broad versus narrow notion of levels is a categorization of goals based on where they exist along a continuum of time, ranging from quite immediate in potential realization (proximal) to very much out in the future (distal). Reflecting on this temporal dimension, Ives and Cox (2012) suggest that the client's vision, or larger goal, may have to do with a principle of living (e.g., being in harmony with nature), whereas the implementable goals represent the means by which the principle can be realized. From a coaching perspective, the more distant, abstract, or broad a goal may be, the more work may be required to break it down into relevant, meaningful, and feasible elements.

I mentioned at the outset of this section the idea of a coaching objective. When a client enters coaching, what that person describes as his or her intention for the work is likely to be large or, in other words, a metagoal. This broadly framed objective may not be entirely clear to either the coach or the client who expresses it. Coaches would be ill advised to dive right into action planning with a new client who has expressed a rather ambitious goal (metagoal). Significant work may need to be done to clarify all the relevant dimensions of the desired objective before moving the client toward action (Dembkouski & Eldridge, 2008). Metagoals stated in the early phase of a coaching relationship need to be understood first for what they represent in themselves and only then deconstructed for their constituent elements. Ives and Cox (2012) offer an invaluable perspective in suggesting that the metagoals, dreams, or

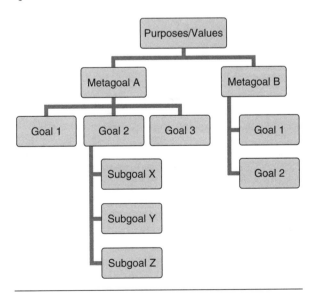

Figure 3.1 Hierarchy of goals.

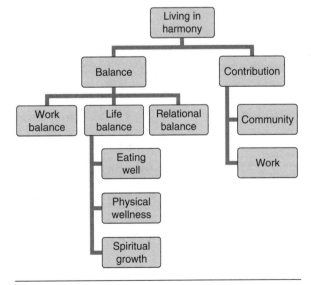

Figure 3.2 Hypothetical example of goal hierarchy.

intentions that clients may have at the outset tend to remain relatively constant, while the lower level goals they develop may be more changeable or substitutable. For instance, a client may want to be healthier, but this metagoal might be accomplished through changes in eating, increases in exercise, reductions in stress, work on relationships, or a combination of some of these subgoals.

As a final thought about levels of goals, it would seem that coaches need to engage in a kind of balancing act whereby they help clients move into action relatively quickly so they can experience a sense of success and increased self-efficacy (Bandura, 2001; Cox, 2013), yet pace the work such that clients are able to develop a sufficient appreciation of the grander purpose of their actions. Even when the driving force for a client's coaching engagement is an intention to achieve such specific objectives as preparing for a job interview, coordinating an upcoming business meeting, or training for a team triathlon, referencing these narrow goals to a larger vision or purpose can unleash invaluable sources of motivation.

Types of Goals

As we shift focus from levels to types of goals, there will be some overlap in ideas. There are big goals and little goals. There are goals that may be achieved in a single action and ones that take years. You are probably aware that many of the goals you set for yourself, like completing a certification program in coaching, take time and comprise a wide range of smaller goals, such as completing your reading of this book or engaging in a specified number of

coaching sessions. In this presentation of goal types, I want you to see how different writers describe goal types. This should give you a framework for translating types into different scenarios that might occur in your work as a coach (see table 3.1).

Originating in the field of exercise and sport psychology, three categories of goals have been identified: outcome, performance, and process (Weinberg & Gould, 2019). All three types play important roles in the change process. **Outcome goals** typically focus on the end result of some engagement, such as a final product or a target behavior. One client may aim to get a promotion, while another intends to lose a certain amount of weight. Both are outcome goals. **Performance goals** represent the achievement of certain standards of behavior, irrespective of others' actions. A client could have a performance goal of speaking up in business meetings at least once during a defined period of time while another may set a performance goal of going to a yoga class every day for the next 30 days as part of a fitness challenge. Performance goals may have a competitive component, such as when individuals are pitted against others (e.g., competing against others for a job promotion) or when one engages in races and contests, yet competition is not a necessary element of this goal type. Finally, **process goals** emphasize the qualities that one wishes to experience in certain behaviors. One client may have a process goal of feeling in flow at work while having another of experiencing a sense of balance in his or her life resulting from the management of work and personal time commitments.

From the coaching field, Kimsey-House and colleagues (2018) offered another way of distinguishing

Table 3.1   Types of Goals

Type of goal	Description
Outcome or fulfillment	Attaining an objective, realizing a specific result of action or creating a product
Performance	Realizing certain standards of behavior or maintaining behaviors according to specified criteria
Process or balance	Experiencing actions or events according to identified qualities of being
Approach or avoidance	Moving away from or toward something
Learning or performance	Demonstrating competence or pursuing mastery
Competing or complementary	Aligning or conflicting with other objectives
Unconscious	Arising and guiding behavior without full awareness or conscious intent
Self-concordant	Sourcing action based on intrinsic or extrinsic motivations

different types of goals. These authors conceived of three goal types—fulfillment, balance, and process—as a kind of progressive focus in long-term coaching relationships. When people first contract for coaching, they often have a specific objective in mind, such as completing a certification, earning a certain annual income, starting a business, or completing a marathon; these goals are known as **fulfillment goals**. After experiencing a number of successes, people may shift interest toward **balance goals**. Here, the emphasis is on creating a well-rounded life pattern of work, play, learning, and relationships. Finally, in what seems to be a more evolved focus, clients express a desire to alter their ways of being in the world so they might find harmony and peace. This is a process goal, where the way one lives moment to moment is what matters.

Also stated in the language of coaching, Grant (2012) suggested another framing of goal types. He, too, begins with what may be seen as the most prevalent form of goal in coaching, namely, outcome goals. Here, the client wants something that is more or less specific, and the coach works with the client to detail exactly what form this outcome would take (see A SuPeRSMART Structure for Setting Goals in chapter 14). A second type, known as an approach-avoidance goal, describes a continuum of behavior. What you will recognize here is how the objectives clients identify reflect movement away from or toward some state of being or experience (e.g., be less bored at work to feeling in flow at work). Based on the literature on goal setting (Locke & Latham, 2006), framing goals as aspirations or positive directions will likely be more motivating than articulating them as negative states to be avoided. Think of a client who states an avoidance goal of reducing time with certain irritating people at work, and then helping that client reframe the intention as an approach goal of spending more time with uplifting people at work.

Grant's (2012) third type of goal also represents a kind of continuum as he distinguishes between learning and performance goals (table 3.1). He notes that performance goals direct the client's work toward demonstrations of competence and abilities, whereas learning goals seem more associated with the pursuit of mastery than simply performing tasks. An individual may have a goal of engaging in a practice of meditation. If this goal is defined more from a performance perspective, it may be gauged by length of time and frequency, whereas from a learning angle, mastering meditation speaks more to the client's experience in the meditative state over and above time spent sitting on a meditation cushion.

A fourth goal type offered by Grant (2012) contrasts competing and complementary goals. In life there are always choices, and some of the things we choose conflict with other desired experiences. Training for a new career path takes time, and in our time-pressured lives that usually means something else has to give. Maybe that's sleep or time with family and friends. By contrast, some goals are well aligned with other objectives. Cessation of smoking coheres with creating a healthy and wholesome home environment. My sense is that this fourth type isn't really a different kind of goal so much as a facet of a goal that needs to be addressed in designing action, goal setting, and action planning. Many of the goals that clients set will cut across the grain of other life pursuits or patterns in living. A challenge for coaches is to surface potential conflicts and strategize for success.

Grant (2012) also has a category that he labels as unconscious goals. These are goals that we may not be fully aware of or that function at an unconscious level. We may behave in a way that limits the amount of attention we draw to ourselves at work or in other public venues. This might show up in how we dress, how quietly we speak, eye contact we seek or avoid, and so on. Grant suggests that goal-centric coaching calls on coaches to identify some of these unconscious goals in order to understand whether they support or interfere with clients' more consciously stated goals. This perspective has also been described by Kegan and Lahey (2009) as hidden competing commitments in their work on immunity to change. Whether we think of these potential saboteurs as unconscious goals or hidden commitments is less critical than recognizing the need for coaches to effectively identify these elements when working with clients' deep intentions. In this regard, an intriguing work by Chamine (2012) identifies 10 common saboteur types that many of us carry within us. These are labeled as the judge, the stickler, the pleaser, the hyper-achiever, the victim, the hyper-rational, the hyper-vigilant, the restless, the controller, and the sage. Each represents a behavior pattern that may interfere with our best intentions to succeed or change.

A final suggestion from Grant (2012) centers on what are known as **self-concordant goals**. These are goals that are aligned (or concordant) with what someone's intrinsic values or interests might be. The notion of concordance derives from the work of Sheldon and Elliot (1998, 1999), but it originated in an earlier work by Deci and Ryan (1985) on self-determination theory (see sidebar, What's the Nature of Your Motivation?). You have no doubt been in situations where the motivation you had

What's the Nature of Your Motivation?

Two important theories provide us with essential understandings about motivation. Both self-concordance theory (Sheldon & Elliot, 1998, 1999) and self-determination theory (Deci & Ryan, 1985, 2000, 2017) tell us that motivations for action have different sources of origination.

In different actions we take, our motivation may come more or less from inside us. Of course, there are cases where we don't act—where we experience no motivation. A representation of the different types or sources of motivation can be seen in figure 3.3, with the innermost circle representing motivation that is internalized or intrinsic (Deci & Ryan, 1985, Vallerand & Losier, 1999). Here are some key ideas to capture each:

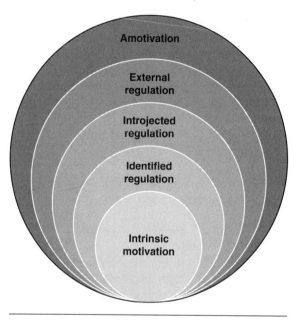

Figure 3.3   From exterior to interior—types of motivation derived from self-determination theory.

- **Amotivation.** This represents an absence of motivation or a lack of desire to act. Here you might say something like, "It's not worth doing."

- **External regulation.** This occurs when your reasons or motives for action come from outside of you, e.g., from external factors or people. Here you might say, "I really don't have a choice but to do this."

- **Introjected regulation.** This develops over time where values conveyed by others are accepted and internalized as your own. Here there's a quality of *ought* or *should* because it's the right thing to do. It may sound like, "I should do it because it's good for me."

- **Identified regulation.** This happens when you have come to value certain actions or behaviors, and you act accordingly to reach an important goal. This isn't yet a fully internalized motive and it may sound like this: "Doing this will help me reach my goal."

- **Intrinsic motivation.** This emerges when you feel fully aligned in values, interests, and needs with the action or goal; it feels as if it is part of who you are. Here you might say something like, "I just love doing this. I learn and grow so much from this."

Clearly, the more intrinsic or internalized the motivation for a goal, the more likely you will engage and enjoy what you are pursuing. It will feel rewarding in and of itself. By contrast, the more external or extrinsic the motivation is, the less sustainable it will be once the external source is removed.

to do something came from outside you—like from parents or others who essentially said, "You just have to do this." In contrast, I hope you are reading this book because you really want to—so it's wholly your choice. The first situation where you had to would be considered an example of extrinsic motivation, while your reading of this book would hopefully exemplify intrinsic motivation.

In general, these theorists make clear the power of intrinsic over extrinsic motivations and the importance of ensuring that clients are choosing goals that are well aligned with their values and needs. When clients identify and pursue objectives that originate in the needs of others, in external demands, or in introjected intentions, they are less likely to be successful in the long term. That said, I would see this less as a separate type of goal than as a quality or attribute of a goal that pertains to the client's reasons for engaging in action.

One last suggestion regarding types of goals derives more from the literature of counseling and psychotherapy. Cooper (2018) believed that many typologies of goals are too tied to content, such as goals related to work, family, leisure, and social life, among others. He recommended that we consider dimensions along which goals may vary. In his list of eight goal dimensions, you will find much overlap with previous typologies.

1. *Importance.* How important is this goal to the client?
2. *Challenge.* How difficult might this goal be to accomplish?
3. *Approach versus avoidance.* Is the client moving toward or away from something in relation to this goal?
4. *Intrinsic versus extrinsic.* Is this goal intrinsically or extrinsically motivated?
5. *Specificity.* How amorphous or vague is the goal—or is it specific and concrete?
6. *Temporal extension.* Is this a long-term or a short-term goal?
7. *Consciousness.* How conscious or aware is the client of this goal in driving behavior?
8. *Metalevel.* Is this more about an overarching purpose or is it something more basic?

Though you will have witnessed similarities across the typologies reviewed in this section, you will hopefully have come to appreciate how widely goals can vary in their nature and purpose. As you bring these frameworks into your coaching practice, you should be on more solid ground in working with clients to formulate robust goal statements.

GOAL COMPLEXITY AND THE ENVIRONMENT

All these different goal types can be dizzying. I personally think Weinberg and Gould's (2019) framework for goal types (outcome, performance, process) captures what coaching has been about in its initial decades. Most clients seem to pursue specific outcomes or increased performance, and over time they may want to create more of an internal state of harmony (process). Outcome and performance goals have a clear structure captured in the acronym **SMART** (Doran, 1981; Raia, 1965), which stands for specific, measurable, adjustable, realistic, and time specific. However, with ever-increasing complexities in change agendas confronting people today, you can easily imagine clients pursuing goals

that may not easily fit into a SMART formula. Think of a high-level executive parachuted into an organization following a hostile takeover. The acquired company employs radically new technologies and is located in a totally different culture with ill-defined norms about appropriate leadership behaviors. Trying to state in a SMART fashion the coaching objectives for this person would be extremely challenging.

Clutterbuck and Spence (2017) built on earlier works (Pryor & Bright, 2011) in differentiating conditions that might be conducive to the use of detailed SMART goal statements versus other ways of formulating goals. They identified two factors that play into the type of goals that might be appropriate for today's clients: The first describes the stability of the environment in which the client is embedded, and the second references whether the problem the client is presenting is relatively simple or complex.

Simple Problems, Stable Environment: *SMART Performance Goals*

Many issues that clients bring to coaching represent straightforward requests to shift a behavioral pattern within the context of a life that has a sufficient degree of predictability. A client might want to adhere to a consistent sleep regimen, attend a language class, make a straightforward change in eating habits, express appreciation to others more often, speak up in meetings, or integrate meditation into his or her lifestyle. Pryor and Bright (2011) suggest these conditions would work well for SMART goal structures.

Simple Problems, Rapidly Changing Environment: *Flexible Performance Goals*

Take the same kinds of objectives as those in the previous section but add the element of an unpredictable or rapidly changing environment. Here, Pryor and Bright (2011) suggest flexible performance goals, and this makes sense. To some degree, this was accounted for in a revision to the original SMART structure. The letter *A* in early renditions of SMART had been variously interpreted as meaning attainable, achievable, action oriented, or acceptable. In its present form, the letter *A* of SMART is interpreted as adjustable. The concept of adjustability reflects Gollwitzer's (1999) proposition that in formulating goal statements, we need to include contingency plans for occasions when the situation is different than normal. The more unstable the environment, the more goals need to have a certain flexibility in their design. Someone who travels often or has other spontaneously arising shifts in daily life schedules needs to have flexible performance goals. In this respect, clients' goal setting may need to factor in the kind of if-then structure Gollwitzer offers for these frequent environmental variations—if I can't go to the gym today, then I will walk home from work as my exercise commitment for the day.

Complex Problems, Stable Environment: *Learning Goals*

Imagine that a client desires greater work–life balance. How complex is this goal? The form balance would need to take and how readily it could be achieved depend on the person's work, life, and capacities. What we often see in coaching relationships is that clients are juggling many balls, and when they attempt to add another ball represented in the construction of a SMART goal, they freeze, panic, or resist. Even when their environments are reasonably stable, complex coaching topics often require multiple action strategies that can take their toll on the client's energy and motivation. Hitting precise performance targets may not be as appealing as setting learning goals with clients where they aim for takeaway lessons that can gradually add to their performance capacity and results. So in the case of the client desiring greater work–life balance, learning how to manage boundaries, how to delegate, or how to better recognize stress signals would be coaching targets, rather than an elusive intention of organizing life into a fixed and balanced state.

Complex Problems, Rapidly Changing Environment: *Fuzzy Goals*

Clutterbuck and Spence (2017) think of fuzzy goals as broad intentions that people have. Dyer (2010) spoke passionately about the positive effects of intentions on the changes we can realize in our lives. Given the perspective here that a client states a big-picture goal comprising many interacting elements while living in a turbulent and unpredictable

reality, generating a set of clear intentions may be an essential start point. In this regard, coaching may be designed to help individuals be as specific as possible about what they intend and then explore different parameters that would influence the expression of these intentions in different contexts. An example might be that a leader wishes to experience a quality of open-mindedness in all interactions throughout the day. This quality may not be entirely easy to gauge, yet this leader could include a self-reflective period at the end of each day to examine the degree to which he experienced open-mindedness in the day's interactions.

Clarity and specificity are essential in a goal-setting process and, of course, for action implementation. As a coach, you will need to recognize the range of projects clients might bring to you and be able to adapt your approach to their unique needs. Sometimes, you will be addressing issues at a macro level, while other times goals will be quite confined and delineable. The profession of coaching is growing exponentially, and it would be limiting to see the work of coaches as being restricted to only those matters that can be precisely identified and measured. That said, you nonetheless will want to remain vigilant about opportunities for helping clients articulate their wishes in ways that give them as much leverage on change as possible. The forecast is that more and more coaches will be working with clients who present complex issues occurring in rather turbulent environments (Einzig, 2017; Peterson, 2018).

THE COACH'S ROLE

We started this chapter with one of Stephen Covey's (1989) seven habits of highly effective people—namely, beginning with the end in mind. Concordant with this perspective, the coaching role has been largely framed as serving the goal intentions of clients, and thereby seems to clearly represent the tradition of goal-centric coaching.

Another reflection of the Covey habit can be found in the ICF's (2020c) newly framed 8th core coaching competency, which specifically addresses goals: The work of professional coaches is seen in the facilitation of conversations that enable clients to gain traction on deeply important goals. Of unique importance, however, is the fact that in reframing its original 11 competencies into the new set of 8, the ICF placed learning and insight on a plane comparable to that of concrete or practical results that have historically been the hallmark of coaching. It's not that the ICF discounted in any way the relevance of practical outcomes from coaching, but rather that it recognized the shifting ground in our coaching world. Clients, much as Clutterbuck and Spence (2017) highlighted, may need to learn new ways and perspectives as much as they need to achieve desired outcomes or performance improvements. In effect, the goals of coaching need to broaden to encompass growth in perspective and awareness along with quite tangible outcomes.

I trust that this chapter has given you a clearer appreciation of why I consider coaching to be a goal-centric process. In this regard, you have also seen that when coaches work with their clients, they initially begin by clarifying exactly what the client's big goals are, and following this, they help them set more specific goals, plan action, and implement their plans. What particular things do coaches do to help their clients in these matters? Although I have not yet presented the skills of coaching, you can probably imagine that coaches need to be highly competent in hearing what clients don't say as much as what they do. They also will inquire about issues that might be explored to better appreciate what clients desire and what motivates them to pursue their goals.

The material of this chapter certainly offers much information to assist you in understanding different levels and types of goals, as well as environmental influences on how best to frame client outcomes. As noted, I will need to circle back to the goal themes raised in this chapter from the ICF's wider perspective of cultivating learning and growth as the intention of coaching, as well as from the perspective of skills and processes that coaches need to employ when bringing a coaching dialogue to a concluding action plan (see chapter 14).

For now, what I hope you have clear sight of is that coaching occurs around clients' intentions to shift something in their lives. It is not an open discussion without explicit purpose. I have variously described these intentions as goals, purposes, and even dreams. The theory of goal setting tells us explicitly that unless goals reflect the parameters for effective goal setting identified in the research literature, people are less likely to succeed. The purpose of this chapter has been to make you aware of some of the things a coach needs to know about goals, goal setting, and action planning to work effectively with clients in a goal-centric coaching process. As you read on, you will find the skill sets underlying interventions that occur in coaching to bring clients to a point where they can fully express their ideas about where they are going, how best to get there, and what's needed to structure and implement action plans.

REFLECTIONS

Coaching is renowned for its capacity to help people move toward desired outcomes in their lives. Clients may want to pursue specific projects or shift patterns of thinking and behaving. Some experts in the field speak about the purpose of coaching as being strongly tied to performance enhancement, and this makes good sense particularly when the meaning is construed to encompass wide domains of performance, including such objectives as sustaining energy, maintaining health, creatively pursuing leisure activities, developing capacity to shut down the noise of life in order to relax, and so forth. In order for you to perform well in your life, you not only need to learn new skills, master certain information and knowledge, and act in ways that produce desired results, but you also have to replenish your energy, rejuvenate your spirit, nurture supportive relationships, and foster your health. These kinds of purposes fall into the realm of coaching as much as achieving excellence at work.

If someone were to come to coaching in order to think differently about herself, would you consider this to be a valid objective for goal-centric coaching? I would—depending on how the individual imagined that this process of self-change might unfold. If the prospective client said, "Well, we'll just talk about things and you can convince me to think differently," I would likely spend time describing the way that coaching works and determine whether this person could commit to a process that involves goal-directed activities outside of the session and whether she would buy into the principle that coaches are there to guide a process but not to provide answers. Depending on how this conversation went, we might begin, or we might say goodbye. Here's an example to make this quite concrete: A high-ranking military officer retires and takes up a job in a modern business company. She has lots of trouble managing her staff members, and turnover in her group is high. Her company offers her a coach to help her shift the way she works with people. She says to her coach in the first meeting, "I need to think differently about myself and how I manage in this new context." Is this a valid agenda? Most likely, yes, and the work will unfold with a clear coaching objective and lots of subgoals to be pursued while she remains in the coaching relationship.

The way you think and the way you act are highly interrelated. Psychotherapy in its early period focused almost exclusively on getting people to change the way they think. Coaching approaches facilitate change more through action or behavioral engagement with the intention that such change will also foster personal insights and learning. In truth, modern psychology focuses on behavior change as well, though the issues that therapists deal with can be distinguished from those that clients bring to coaches. Today's coaching world encompasses a far broader mix of goal objectives that clients bring to the process than was apparent in its earlier years, yet they all seem to reflect intentions to shift in positive ways clients' performance, learning, and ways of being.

PART II

GUIDING MODELS

CHAPTER 4

UNDERSTANDING CHANGE

Every great dream begins with a dreamer. Always remember, you have within you the strength, the patience, and the passion to reach for the stars to change the world.

Harriet Tubman

MY STORY

A few years back, I found a yellowed notebook page with a list of New Year's resolutions from 15 years earlier. I marveled at the fact that a number of the listed items were things I still wanted to change or accomplish. Once my embarrassment subsided, I wondered why I hadn't made these important changes long ago. I felt a bit of a jolt to my self-confidence in that moment. I know I have habits or preferred ways of being, but it seemed in looking at that list that I didn't have a great deal of willpower. Even though I have changed a lot of my habits and patterns, some change agendas seem to continually elude me. It's like those forever-nagging 5 or 10 pounds we say we want to lose, yet there they are year after year.

During my lifetime, I have repeatedly set myself up to change one or another of my behaviors. I usually succeeded, but when I didn't, failure was sometimes immediate, but more often it was a gradual process. Then, for a few of those things that I never seemed able to change, seemingly all of a sudden I found myself changed and felt as if it was a totally natural thing. Let me give you an example: I was attracted to the practice of meditation in my early 20s. I bought candles, books, recordings, incense, and cushions—you name it, I had it. But I could never stick with it. Bravely at one point, I signed up for a 10-day silent retreat, where participants are awakened at 4 a.m. for a full day of contemplative sitting. Aside from silent meals and silent breaks, I was in the meditation chapel for at least an hour at a time, session after session until bedtime at 10 p.m. This was hard core. I had made a clear commitment to this action. When it was over, I went home and began my daily practice. It lasted about 6 months until my "truancy" began to reappear. By the end of a year, I was meditating perhaps once a week. Fast forward multiple years to today, where I haven't missed a day in months. What made me stick with it? I am not entirely sure. Some of this change stuff is still a bit of a mystery.

As a field founded on humanity's aspirations and dreams, coaching requires practitioners to understand the journey of change through a multidimensional lens of thoughts, feelings, actions, and implications. Moreover, coaches need to appreciate the diverse targets for change that clients identify and the dynamics accompanying such objectives. You are about to read about some key models for how change is shaped and what might be implied for individuals who voluntarily embark on transformative journeys. Here are some guiding questions as you read:

- Why do people take on challenging change processes?
- What prevents individuals from being successful in changing behaviors?
- What phases do people go through in changing?
- How much of change is about willpower?
- How might past successes or failures in changing behavior affect a person?

MAPS FOR THE JOURNEY OF CHANGE

A number of years ago, the American Psychological Association (2012) conducted a survey in which participants were asked why they weren't able to follow through on commitments to lifestyle changes. Results showed that the lack of willpower was cited as the number one reason for not sticking to commitments. Consider your own life and occasions when you wanted to change a particular behavior. How easy was it—or are you still trying to change? Surely you have heard stories of people who decided seemingly in a moment to stop smoking or to start exercising, and to this day, they have been true to their resolve. If these stories underlie your understanding of change, you may believe that it's all a matter of willpower.

The fact is, the path to change is rarely straightforward, and steady progress toward goal achievement is usually the exception rather than the rule. Even in examples of instantaneous conversions, the individual's internal story will have more twists and turns than are externally evident. An example is my meditation story in the My Story sidebar! Experienced coaches will have numerous success stories as well as tales of dead ends and discouragement when it comes to accompanying clients through the change process. In this chapter, you will find perspectives about change that can benefit you both personally and professionally.

There are lots of theories and models that attempt to explain and predict changes in behaviors. By far the best known and most critically researched model of this sort is the **transtheoretical model (TTM)** (Painter et al., 2008; Prochaska & Velicer, 1997; Prochaska et al., 2008), sometimes referred to as the stages of change model. TTM is not explicitly a coaching model. It is a theoretical framework that describes six stages people seem to move through as they progressively discontinue an unhealthy behavior or adopt a healthy one. The model is relevant to coaching because it allows coaches to pinpoint where clients are situated in the stages of change and to then suggest potential strategies to propel them forward. Concepts embedded in TTM including those of **decisional balance**, **self-efficacy**, and **self-regulation** will be covered in upcoming discussions.

Another framework I will offer is Marilyn Taylor's (1986) learning-through-change (LTC) model, which provides a compassionate understanding of why some people spin interminably in indecision or insufficient commitment. Though not as widely researched as TTM, this model represents an insightful perspective of the inner world of clients in a change experience. The LTC model describes four distinct periods that are likened to seasonal changes. LTC deepens the way we might view the change process by suggesting beneficial patterns for navigating the sometimes-tumultuous cyclical shifts.

Both models tell us that what works for clients at the outset of a change process may be less effective later on. As clients advance toward their goals, they manifest different needs. Coaches who are aware of these dynamics can respond appropriately with varying kinds of support and guidance.

A third model reviewed in this chapter offers a very different map for clients' experiences in a change process. This model, the heroic journey model, derives from the work of Joseph Campbell and in particular from his book, *The Hero With 1000 Faces* (1949). In most stories and movie scripts involving a hero or heroine facing insurmountable odds, the trajectory of the plot involves an almost universal mythological structure or **monomyth**. As individuals embark on significant journeys of change, there are notable parallels between the stages of this monomyth and what clients must address in order to achieve a new order in their lives.

Certain concepts and change strategies appear to be common to virtually all change models. These ideas may be explicitly identified or implicitly described within a given framework. Following the review of the three models, I want to highlight these common approaches. They will be covered in two sections: The first identifies intervention strategies that largely derive from work on the transtheoretical model, while the second explores three central concepts in understanding change, namely, self-efficacy, self-regulation, and **relapse prevention**.

TRANSTHEORETICAL MODEL

How ready are your clients to make changes necessary to achieve their goals? The fact that someone has hired you as his coach would seem to indicate that he has moved beyond the starting gate. Even so, that person may not be sufficiently prepared to undertake more than talking about or considering necessary actions. TTM outlines a temporal sequence of stages pertaining to a particular behavior change (Prochaska & Norcross, 2018; Prochaska et al., 2002; Prochaska & Velicer, 1997). It offers practical guidelines for understanding a client's readiness for change.

Take a common change objective: smoking cessation. Surely, you know people who smoke tobacco and have little intention of changing (precontemplation stage). As well, you are likely to know people who were once smokers but haven't succumbed to temptation even once in years (maintenance and termination stages). In between these extremes are people who are thinking about changing (contemplation and preparation stages) and those who are actively wearing nicotine patches and practicing behavioral techniques to reduce their cravings (action stage). Equally, these stages would apply to such other change objectives as switching from private to public transportation, altering dietary habits, engaging in meaningful recreation, and shifting ingrained ways of communicating.

Though the stages of change represent a progression through a change process, TTM is dynamic in recognizing that clients sometimes relapse and need to be reenergized in their engagement. Movement toward a desired goal might be circuitous rather than linear. The model (see figure 4.1) describes a continuum of six stages through which people progress as they endeavor to change a current behavior (e.g., watching TV before bedtime) or adopt a new one (e.g., exercising daily). The six stages are sum-

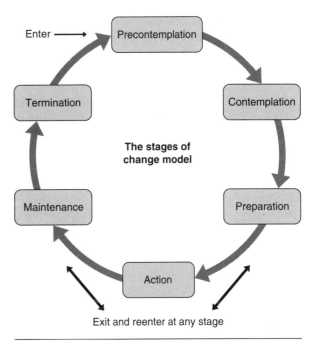

Figure 4.1 Transtheoretical model.

marized in the following sections with reference to coaching clients.

Stage 1: Precontemplation

Individuals in this stage have no current intention to change; they are not thinking about modifying their current behaviors to reach a certain goal. They are not swayed by the idea that the negative effects of their behavior likely outweigh the positive. Perhaps they have tried to change this behavior in the past and failed, maybe they are unaware that they have a problem, or maybe they completely deny that their current patterns could be harmful. Some people who have repeatedly failed in efforts to change a behavior will end up feeling demoralized and give up on the possibility of ever changing. It is unlikely that individuals in this stage would voluntarily enter a coaching relationship, though they might be mandated to attend coaching sessions, for example, by members of their work organization.

Stage 2: Contemplation

Those in the contemplation stage acknowledge that they are having a particular difficulty; they are willing to think about their need to modify their behaviors, yet they may be unable to initiate the desired change. They are considering the benefits of a different behavioral style, yet they are not quite ready to take concrete steps. Though they have not acted toward change, they are open to evaluating the pros and cons associated with their current problematic behavior. They are, in effect, mentally completing a decisional balance sheet, even at an unconscious level (see appendix A for a template and example). At this stage, an aggressively critical boss might be willing to acknowledge that he needs to change. Someone who continually consumes junk food whenever she experiences stress may readily concede a need to get on top of this behavior. People in contemplation are open to information and feedback. Though they speak as if they will act in the next six months, they can remain in this stage for years. Would individuals in this stage voluntarily enter a coaching relationship? It's possible, but their intention might not be to change per se; rather, they might want to clarify issues in order to advance toward a decision.

Stage 3: Preparation

Individuals in the preparation stage are on the verge of action. For them, change is imminent—maybe even within the next month! They are preparing for engagement by establishing priorities, setting goals, developing plans, and perhaps even making small changes. At this stage, people are pretty thoroughly convinced of the benefits of a behavioral change.

A large percentage of new coaching clients are likely to be in this stage. The act of contacting a coach to address a particular issue is a good indication that the client is prepared to change. In this perspective, the process of coaching is well suited to bolstering clients' intentions, reinforcing their self-efficacy beliefs, and enabling them to fully delineate what they want and how best to pursue it.

Stage 4: Action

People in this stage are actually doing it! They are following an action plan that they developed to modify their behavior and are keenly involved in the change process. The more they have prepared, the more successful they are likely to be in reaching desired goals. If they are in a coaching relationship at this stage, coaches may work with them on increasing their self-regulation and help boost their beliefs so they can successfully remain in action.

Stage 5: Maintenance

By definition, a person commences the maintenance stage only after consistently adhering to change commitments for at least six months. However, the maintenance stage itself can last indefinitely or until there is no temptation to revert to the original state. This stage is important to consider for at least two reasons: The first is that it takes at least six months of continuous engagement in a behavior change for people to be relatively solid in their new patterns. A second reason is that maintaining a behavior in no way implies that people can decrease their vigilance toward sustaining action. Although new behaviors or patterns may begin to feel natural, overconfidence and life stresses can lead to lapses or a full-blown relapse (Marlatt & Donovan, 2008; Marlatt & Gordon, 1985). From the perspective of TTM, the duration of a coaching relationship for clients addressing significant behavioral changes might need to be about a year or even more.

Stage 6: Termination

In this stage, the new behavior has become an integral part of daily life, and the likelihood of relapse is low or practically nonexistent. Some professionals question whether people ever reach this stage, although Prochaska and colleagues (2002) affirm that it is possible for a small percentage of people. Think of acquaintances who have successfully given up smoking or who have lost considerable weight through rigorous adherence to diets. Years of maintenance may give way to complete relapse in moments of laxity. Consequently, regular follow-ups by clients with their coaches can be invaluable in ensuring that they remain where they want to be. When clients take on major life changes, it is reasonable to consider check-ins or scheduled sessions every three to six months after the first year.

LEARNING-THROUGH-CHANGE MODEL

Changing long-term patterns is likely to involve deep restructuring of thoughts, feelings, and behaviors (Gollwitzer, 1999; Gollwitzer & Brandstätter, 1997; Mcbrearty, 2010). As an outside observer, you may only witness the results of long-term deliberations about change in a single moment when someone quits a job, uproots a family and moves elsewhere, enrolls in graduate school, smokes their last cigarette, or initiates a plant-based diet. Equally, you can observe sustained commitment to positive actions, such as participatory leadership, each time a person invites collaboration in meetings. Yet, a change process is more likely to unfold over time as individuals either choose or are propelled in a new direction. Virtually all models of change conceive of the modification of behaviors or the embodiment of new habits as a process that occurs through a series of phases.

To better understand the inside view of change, Taylor (1986) formulated the **learning-through-change (LTC) model** (see figure 4.2) that illuminates the internal world of those confronting transformation of their current realities. She believed that people in a change process face challenges to learn different things at different moments. In this respect, she framed change as a process of learning. Her metaphor for this undertaking is the four seasons of the year, reflecting distinctly different qualities of the change experience. Moreover, if you imagine areas of the world where there are four distinct seasons, you will readily acknowledge that there are also periods between seasons—transitional times that evidence their own characteristics. Where I live, for instance, between winter and spring there may be days of rain, then snow, and then warmth that suddenly drops to a deep freeze overnight. Taylor's LTC model therefore speaks of four distinct phases (seasons) and four phase transitions that serve to shift the person from one "season" to another.

The roots of change are not always predictable. Motivation may arise from an accumulation of experiences or from a single event. Someone grows weary of working in a job without passion while someone else is shocked into awareness when that person and her entire division have been outsourced. Regardless, it's unlikely that people randomly decide that today would be a good day to overhaul their lives. It is as if the dissonance between what their current

reality is and what their dreams represent reaches critical mass, causing people to tumble out of their comfortable worlds and enter a cycle of events that will eventually return them to a new equilibrium. It is important to note that this new state of equilibrium may or may not represent an improvement over their old way of being, depending on how the change process is managed.

The LTC model considers typical thoughts, feelings, and actions of clients as they move through the cycle of change. As orderly as this cyclical flow might appear, any change process can be easily derailed if certain conditions are not met. Human beings gravitate toward balance and a state of equilibrium (Sheldon et al., 2010), whatever shape that may take for each of us individually. You are unlikely to roll the dice with your life unless something has provoked you to pursue change. Even though modern life has been described as a kind of permanent white-water state (Cabana et al., 1995) where change is omnipresent, you can chart an intelligent course even while shooting the rapids. Change of the kind you are exploring throughout this book is different from the day-to-day adjustments of life. It represents a need or perhaps a demand for you to be different—to show up in your life with new perspectives, actions, values, styles, and other aspects of self-presentation.

Whether you choose to engage in change or are thrust into it involuntarily, the journey is one that will move you out of a state of equilibrium into a sometimes-chaotic world that you must confront and eventually manage in order to regain a new and hopefully more evolved sense of balance. Let's

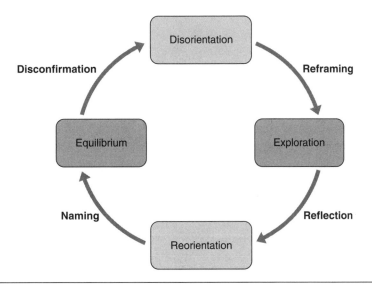

Figure 4.2   Taylor's learning-through-change model.

Adapted from M.M. Taylor, "Learning for Self-Direction in the Classroom: The Pattern of a Transition Process," *Studies in Higher Education* 11, no. 1 (1986): 55-72. By permission of Marilyn M. Taylor, PhD.

explore the LTC model within the framework of coaching relationships.

Transition 1: Disconfirmation

Clients who voluntarily commit themselves to a coaching process do so for significant reasons. Sometimes a big push comes from something like a job performance review. At other times a gradual accumulation of dissatisfactions breaks through all resistance to action. This first transition is called *disconfirmation* because some aspect of the client's old world no longer works or makes sense. There is inherent discomfort in disconfirmation. Feelings break through the surface and can't be pushed back down. The mind is drawn like a magnet to the emerging issue. Things don't seem right, and trying to meditate or medicate the issues away just doesn't work.

The idea that life crises open up possibilities for growth or decline is well documented (Ogden & Hills, 2008). This first transition is pivotal. There is real risk that another kind of transitional shift will occur—one that closes down clients' potential and narrows their perspectives of self, others, and the world. Think of people who have encountered traumatic injuries or losses. The risk exists for them to spiral downward into a despairing view of themselves and the world. They may inhabit a less capable self-identity long after the crisis has passed. In many instances, however, losses can open up possibilities for learning. The path of growth may require extraordinary effort, but in the end, is there really a better alternative?

Phase 1: Disorientation

When excuses seem lame or old solutions no longer work, people who are thrust into a process of change may feel defenseless. They can no longer justify their behaviors, and they cannot maintain their previous way of living. This first phase may be a highly emotional time. People may spin in confusion, anger, blame, sadness, frustration, or guilt. Taking a hard, cold look at themselves in the mirror of their lives, they may feel demoralized by what they seem to have created over years of inattention or convincing themselves that everything was just fine. They may blame someone else or perhaps feel badly for themselves. When clients drop the mask behind which they have hidden a certain truth, they may feel quite vulnerable. Although they may try to make light of this new awareness, there will be an inner voice continually reminding them of the way it really is. The first phase, disorientation, may last for days,

weeks, or even months, depending on the nature and extent of the disconfirmation. It is unlikely any individual will stay here too long, however, because it is just too uncomfortable. The critical question is whether they will address this emergence in a way that is constructive or destructive.

The disorientation phase generally corresponds to the stage of contemplation in TTM. Here's a simplified depiction of what happens: Imagine a client is dealing with a weight issue. The client's clothes are uncomfortably tight, and though he might grow accustomed to wearing clothes that are too small, it is more likely that over time he will either buy larger clothes or address the excess weight. From the perspective of TTM, the person who buys new clothes retreats to precontemplation or hovers on the boundary between precontemplation and contemplation. The LTC model identifies the risks that clients run throughout this phase as entering a downward spiral toward a new equilibrium where acceptance of a less desirable state is part of the new landscape. Of course, this may be accompanied by adopting a less positive self-identity. For instance, this overweight client who buys larger clothes might redefine himself as a large person, a lazy person, or simply an unmotivated person. In a completely different scenario where a client wishes to be more democratic in work habits but reverts to an autocratic style, the client might say, "Well, can't teach an old dog new tricks! I'm just a bossy person."

Within a coaching relationship, clients in disorientation will have strong support for upwardly spiraling movement. Coaches create ample space for emotional expression without allowing emotional relief to become the sole purpose of the sessions. The inner terrain of the client's world needs to be explored. Emotional support and the generation of first steps on a path forward would normally characterize the coach's emphasis at this time.

Imagine someone who lost her job without warning. This experience of disconfirmation (transition 1) would have pulled the person out of equilibrium and thrust her into disorientation (phase 1). This phase will normally last until the person is able to reframe what happened without blaming self or others. As long as the person spins in self-criticism and fails to gain a more sanguine perspective of this unsettling event, she will continue to ride the tumultuous waves of disorientation.

Transition 2: Reframing

Forward movement through the seasons of change requires gaining perspective about core issues. You might understand this as a movement toward acceptance, which is not to be mistaken for resignation. Though it may be that an out-of-shape, overweight client blames himself for creating whatever conditions he is now trying to address, the perspective that the client needs to develop in this second transition is one of acknowledgment of his present state—without blaming himself or projecting responsibility on others. When negative self-judgments and remorseful emotions are put aside through compassionate self-acceptance, the client will have a far easier time working toward healthier and self-supporting alternative behaviors.

Many people find motivation for action in the emotional charge of anger, resentment, blame, and disgust. However, the types of actions formed from these emotions are not likely to be generative and uplifting. Coaches will want to be attentive to the face of client pain, remaining ever attentive to the nature of energy—positive or negative—that clients rely on for change. Positive motivations are sought to replace negative ones. Life-giving perspectives are discovered to prevent a shriveling view of self and others. Effective coaching is not just about getting clients to do things differently; it involves grounding action in affirmations of self and others that breathes new life into their potential.

Phase 2: Exploration

As the spinning slows and the fog begins to lift, the way forward peeks out in the strangest places. Signposts appear everywhere. The challenge in this phase is to remain open minded and in an exploratory mode long enough to appreciate the value of all potential avenues before choosing one particular path. Imagine a client who has been in a particular line of work for 25 years that is disappearing due to artificial intelligence and automation. She is unemployed and unlikely to find a similar job in the future (transition 1). After she has framed issues without blaming herself (e.g., "I should have seen it coming a long time ago!"), she moves through the second transition and gradually begins to explore. Here, she starts to consider her options and sample the possibilities in a process of experimentation.

This phase is typically a more social time. People who are trying to figure out new skills, capacities, habits, or ways of functioning need other people, especially those who are in a similar phase of change or perhaps a step ahead. In this social context, they welcome knowledge and information from people, readings, and other sources. Clients signal to their coaches that they have entered this phase by their keen interest in facts and information, their need to talk about what they are doing, and their efforts to

socialize with others who are walking a similar path. Coaches will want to have appropriate resources at hand and perhaps be ready to schedule extra time to talk with clients in order to help them move efficiently through this phase.

The exploration phase generally coincides with the preparation stage in TTM. The LTC model adds an appreciation of the need to experiment, the relevance of like-minded others, and the importance of gathering valid information. Clients need to sample the options and discover the fit between possibilities they are discovering and their emerging new selves. The core work of coaching takes place in this stage when clients are progressively developing a new way of orienting themselves to the world; this requires significant adjustments in their processes of thinking, feeling, and behaving. Though this phase is highly active, it may take some time to move intentionally toward a single path. Depending on the nature and scope of the issue, sorting through the options could be relatively quick or it might be quite protracted.

Transition 3: Reflection

Deep and sometimes extended reflection marks the transition to the next phase in the cycle. The person may begin to withdraw to consolidate thoughts and feelings as well as to generate a coherent strategy for action. From the outside, the person may appear more introspective. This person may reduce requests for feedback and no longer ask for sources of information. As a coach, you will need to be sensitive to this shift by allowing clients space for reflection rather than continuing to offer ideas, suggestions, and encouragement for further experimentation.

Reflection does not come naturally to some people, and some may want to short-circuit this important transition. When clients go inward, coaches need to develop a keen awareness of the action-packed potential of this inner journey. In support of your clients' work, you may recommend such strategies as journaling, meditating, taking long walks, or recording one's thoughts to be listened to at a later point.

Phase 3: Reorientation

Clients generally enter the reorientation phase with a plan. The plan may be rudimentary, but they are usually committed to testing it out and determining how well it works. Maybe the plan is a particular strategy they will regularly employ when encountering certain work scenarios. Perhaps it is scheduling regular meetings with coworkers for feedback on projects and emphasizing listening rather than speaking. As a coach, your role in the reorientation phase may take the form of deep curiosity about what your client is trying, what results are being achieved, and what fine-tuning the plan might need. Since coaching is about co-creating action plans, you may even have ideas you want to offer—without attachment. Rather than facilitating a decision-making process as you might have in the exploration phase, you may now be engaged more in setting performance goals and managing progress. A kind of shakedown occurs in this phase; clients make final adjustments to plans before consolidating them into ongoing processes.

The reorientation phase parallels aspects of the action stage in TTM. What the LTC model adds to our understanding from TTM is the multidimensional shift that clients need to internalize during this phase. Consider a person who has committed to having a stronger voice and a clearer presence in meetings at work, as well as in social gatherings. If this client exemplified a pattern of reticence and nonassertiveness over a long period of time, shifts accompanying this change will not be limited to just speaking out. Emotionally, this client will be more aware of feelings and be required to effectively identify and manage them. Cognitively, she will experience her presence in the world differently; she will be more visible to others and may also need to cultivate skills in conflict management when her opinions run counter to others' opinions. As a coach, it's important for you to be attentive to this layered change process and guide your clients not only through external representations of behavior change but also along the lines of their evolving self-image, emotional realities, relationships, and mental models.

Transition 4: Naming

You have undoubtedly met people who recently succeeded in a smoking-cessation program or who have overcome long-standing patterns of procrastination. Usually, these people appreciate opportunities where they can tell others about their journey of change. Indeed, they may want to help others who have struggled with the same challenges they have overcome. Clients who have made it to this point are likely to be excited about their accomplishments and want others to feel as good as they do. Beyond the personal satisfaction they experience with their achievements, they may also need opportunities to articulate to others exactly what has changed

for them and how they managed to generate their successes.

This transition sometimes feels like an affirmation of an emerging identity shift—an affirmation of who the person is becoming through her journey. When this client speaks, you may notice the absence of doubt and vacillations in her reflections. Indeed, the cycle is almost complete, and clients realize their transformative work is nearing an end. As a coach, it's important for you to validate your clients' successes by acknowledging their achievements and making space for them to talk openly about their journeys. Creating opportunities for them to name publicly what they have learned and accomplished makes it more real for them and provides them with abundant opportunities to celebrate.

Phase 4: Equilibrium

The LTC model depicts a cycle that begins and ends in equilibrium, though the new equilibrium hopefully represents a more satisfying and beneficial way of being. It is characterized by the display of new patterns and orientations that have been tested and refined. It can be seen in the demeanor that clients present as a result of successfully challenging outmoded or unproductive ways of living. It shows up in transformed ways of thinking, feeling, and acting. At this point in the change process, the coach's role may be close to ending, at least until the next challenge knocks at a client's door.

The equilibrium phase corresponds to the TTM maintenance stage. LTC allows us to see the various facets of change that are represented in how clients orient themselves to the world. Consider what might happen to the hypothetical client referenced earlier who wanted to show up with greater voice and presence at work and in social settings. If this client successfully engaged the work of each season of change and responded to the agenda of seasonal transitions, you are likely to see someone who is more at ease with others and who expresses opinions with transparency and a willingness to dialogue without fear of conflict. What you may not be able to see is the inner self of this client that contains a more positive self-perception and a more centered feeling in social situations. Additionally, she is likely to perceive her inner emotional world as more manageable and calmer.

Applying Principles of the LTC Model

Understanding what motivates clients to address their change agendas enables coaches to appreciate how change processes may play out. If a client's coaching engagement arises in reaction to certain life events (e.g., forced career change, involuntary relocation to a different country, health crisis, family upheaval), you as coach need to be mindful that major life shifts that aren't personally chosen sometimes have complex ramifications for what individuals need to manage as they move forward. In these examples, there may be heightened emotionality (remorse, sadness, regret, anger) that can persist for extended periods of time. In other scenarios where engagement in a change process might represent a last-ditch effort on the heels of innumerable failures, coaches need to acknowledge and honor clients' persistence and courage in the face of defeat, as well as potential self-criticism for not having the wherewithal to have done it on their own. The LTC model offers guidance about the types of interventions or styles of coaching that would be most supportive for clients in specific seasons of change (see table 4.1 for a list of suggested interventions applied to each phase of the LTC model).

As clients move through LTC phases and transitions, certain cognitive, emotional, interpersonal, and behavioral patterns prevail. In particular, the nature of support will differ markedly in each phase: Clients in disorientation seek emotional support, those in exploration require guidance and encouragement, and those in reorientation need expert input and affirmation. Cognitively, clients in disorientation have difficulty thinking clearly, those in exploration need to work at remaining open minded, and those in reorientation need to be more analytical. Throughout the disorientation phase, clients are often unable to effectively address tasks that require strong shifts in perspective and action. Small steps oriented toward self-acceptance are likely to be helpful. In the exploration phase, clients will hopefully display a kind of playfulness as they experiment with new approaches and patterns. During the reorientation phase, clients need to be task focused and exhibit high levels of commitment to action.

The ways in which clients relate to their coaches may also shift over the cycle of change, from a sense of dependency to one of codirection and interdependence. The varying needs of clients and the styles they prefer in their coaching relationships are intimately related to their phases of learning and development. For example, as the exploration phase is ending, clients need to reflect more privately to create internal order of their thoughts, feelings, and actions. A client who has formerly been open and talkative may become more solitary and self-sufficient. Having a map of clients' internal worlds

during change demystifies so many of the alterations in patterns that coaches witness in their work.

As a final note about this model, clients who skip some of the essential work related to phases and transitions may arrive at a new but less functional equilibrium. They may make peace with certain self-perceptions that are ultimately disempowering, or they may have neglected exploration work that might have produced a more viable path. You probably realize that what we settle for when we try to recreate our comfort zones may be less than ideal. For this reason, clients who try to accelerate the process may find themselves reentering the LTC cycle sooner rather than later.

THE HEROIC JOURNEY

The third model I want to review emerges from the classic work of Joseph Campbell (1949), *The Hero With a Thousand Faces*. Campbell wrote about a presumably universal process that people go through as they encounter life experiences that call them forth from their current surroundings to embark on a journey of growth and self-discovery. He defined a hero as "someone who has given his or her life to something bigger than oneself" (Campbell, 1991, p. 123). You can probably identify moments in your own life when you were invited into a bigger realm of existence than the one in which you were living.

The hero's journey as originally described by Campbell progressed through 17 distinct moments or stages, though he also represented it more simply in three sections: The first is identified as *departure* or *separation*, where the hero or heroine is called to adventure, eventually accepts the call, and moves forward. The second is referred to as *initiation*, where the protagonist encounters the trials of the journey, is tested, experiences various ordeals, and then receives a boon or gift from the journey. The final section is described as *return* and depicts a kind of crossing back into the world from which the hero or heroine originated, but now this individual has a gift that empowers him or her to live more positively for self and others.

There have been numerous representations of Campbell's journey by other authors, as well as depictions of this type of journey from different perspectives. Notably, Robert Bly (1990) in his classic work on the men's movement, *Iron John: A Book About Men*, applied Campbell's monomyth of the hero's journey to the work of personal and spiritual growth. Relatedly, Maureen Murdock (1990) offered a feminine perspective in her definitive book, *The Heroine's Journey: Woman's Quest for Wholeness*.

Table 4.1   Guidance for Coaches According to the Transitions and Phases of the Learning-Through-Change Model

Transition/phase	Client's ways of being and internal states	Suggested coaching strategies and interventions
Transition: Disconfirmation	Shock Confusion Disruption Discomfort Sense of not coping	*This might be the moment when clients enter a coaching relationship.* Coaches need to create a safe space for expression, listen actively to what clients have experienced, and empathize with concerns that are expressed.
Phase: Disorientation	Dissatisfaction with current state Distress and high emotionality Difficulty in coping and managing realities Self-rejection Blame of self and others	In addition to listening actively and expressing empathy, coaches want to explore clients' current realities and concerns. They will also help review past influences on clients' current state with focus on positive change. Behaving in ways that generate trust and safety is essential.
Transition: Reframing	Acknowledgment of current state without blaming self or others Lessening of emotional turmoil Increasing self-acceptance and acceptance of reality	Coaches will want to express support for clients' self-affirmations. Reflecting thoughts and feelings pertaining to a reframed understanding also helps solidify shifts in perspective. Maintaining safe and supportive space will be critical.
Phase: Exploration	Search for new knowledge Pursuit of relevant social connections Attitude of experimentation Open-minded examination of thoughts, feelings, and possibilities	At this point, clients are willing to engage action. Coaches need to support creative ideas and experiments in new ways of being. Helping clients network with relevant others will be invaluable. Brainstorming and evaluating new avenues, new ways of being, and new beliefs will be part of the dialogue. Uncovering new sources of motivation will be helpful.
Transition: Reflection	Self-reflective and introspective periods Patience in absence of decision Need to turn inward in search of self-determination and consolidation	Coaches are likely to encourage clients to engage in self-reflective practices, including journaling, meditation, and dialogue with selected others. In the safe space of coaching, focus is on support for reflection rather than acting and for being more so than doing.
Phase: Reorientation	Analysis and evaluation of actions Making clear decisions Fine-tuning of intentions Clarification of emerging identity Positive emotionality	Here, coaches may emphasize providing feedback and sharing expert knowledge. Focus might be on ways for clients to increase self-efficacy and encouragement of self-monitoring and self-regulation. Reflective practices pertaining to emerging identity and new reality need to continue.
Transition: Naming	Self-affirmation Celebration Realization Appreciation of changes Supporting others in change processes Growth of self-efficacy	Coaches are likely to assist clients in conceptualizing the change process so as to derive learnings for the emerging reality and for future change processes. There will also be a movement toward closure of the coaching relationship in relation to the current agenda. Whenever possible, acknowledgment and celebration of the changes will be fostered.
Phase: Equilibrium	Ending the cycle of change and transformation Confidently incorporating new patterns	As the relationship is ending, coaches will encourage ways of fostering self-accountability, as well as the cocreation of processes for periodic review and renewal. When critical closure tasks have been addressed, the relationship comes to an end.

From a much earlier period and a different worldview, a psychoanalytic presentation of the hero's journey was offered by Otto Rank (1958), one of Sigmund Freud's most accomplished followers. More recently, the field of positive psychology has produced a work by Bruce Smith (2018) entitled, *Positive Psychology for Your Hero's Journey.*

One adaptation of Campbell's journey comes from the screenwriter Christopher Vogler (2007), who saw in Campbell's monomyth the structure of so many of our world stories, as well as what underlies a great number of screen scripts. If you examine such stories or screenplays as the Star Wars saga, the Harry Potter series, the Hunger Games series, *The Matrix*, and the *Lion King*, you will readily see how the main character moves through experiences identified in the stages that Vogler describes.

Vogler (2007) reduced Campbell's 17 stages to 12. From his perspective, the story begins in (1) the *ordinary world* of the hero or heroine up until she or he experiences (2) a *call to adventure*. Often, there is (3) a *refusal of the call* until (4) a *guide or mentor appears* to help the protagonist. Accepting the call, the protagonist (5) *steps across a threshold* from the old and familiar world to a very different reality, and here she or he (6) is *tested and encounters enemies and allies* along the path. Eventually, this hero or heroine (7) *approaches the significant challenge* that must be met alone or with allies, and then must endure (8) *the ordeal* that involves facing one's greatest fears or perhaps confronting death itself. Triumphant, the main character seizes (9) *the reward*, which could come in the form of wisdom or something more tangible. Even so, the journey is not over and there remain various threats on (10) *the road back*. At the climax of the story, the hero or heroine may be severely tested again as a prelude to (11) *resurrection*, where conflicts are resolved and a more complete integration occurs. Finally, the protagonist (12) *returns with an elixir* that not only is manifest in how he or she has changed but also in the power that is carried within to create a better world for others.

Now that you have a general orientation to this way of thinking about change, I want to take you through an even simpler model of the hero's journey crafted for the kinds of personal growth and transformational work that are at the heart of most coaching relationships. This perspective derives from the work of Gilligan and Dilts (2009), two forward-thinking writers, reflecting on the passages so many of us experience in a process of growth.

The Eight Stages of the Journey

Echoing the ideas of Joseph Campbell, Gilligan and Dilts (2009) remind us of the three life paths that you can take: the *village*, the *wasteland*, and the *journey*. When Campbell (1949) spoke about these, he said that the *village* reflected a path that has already been scripted for you by society and your culture. It is a life of living up to expectations that have been dictated to you by the context in which you live. It is a don't-rock-the-boat way of being that can result in a gold watch at the end of your days and a modicum of happiness. The *wasteland* depicts the way of the outlaw or rebel who lives life on the fringe. Here, you escape the *village*, but your life may be characterized by a certain denial of responsibility, isolation, and even patterns of neglect and addiction. Thirdly, your path may be the *journey*, where you follow your heart and listen intently to hear your calling. This calling may involve either an inner or outer journey—or perhaps both. Reflecting on Campbell's more detailed map of the journey, Gilligan and Dilts captured this transformative change in eight stages (see figure 4.3). As you read these, consider how well they reflect what you may have experienced in your own growth process over the years.

1. Awakening to the Call

More often than not, the kind of calling that you will experience in a heroic journey is one that touches your very identity. Something doesn't feel right in your world—and it's been like that for a long time. You know you need to get out of where you are and what you're doing—but nothing is entirely clear. So, you stay until that moment when you say, "Enough!"

As with the LTC model, clients experience a particular event or an internal shift that tells them that they can no longer stay where they are—they need to move out from the ordinary world, as Joseph Campbell (1949) described it. Clients are either thrust from their comfortable nests by life events or they choose to embark on the adventure of change because in some way staying where they are feels intolerable or perhaps impossible.

At this point in the journey, what occurs within the hero or heroine is a deep awareness that he or she is being called to adventure. The individual may not yet respond but is fully aware that something is pushing them out of the ordinary world.

2. Accepting the Call

You may have been called to change directions a number of times in your life, and maybe on at least one of those occasions you ignored the call. It's not as if you are waiting around for a signal, like the noble firefighters who jump onto the truck at the sound of a bell. I personally know I have hesitated, sometimes even for years—and when I

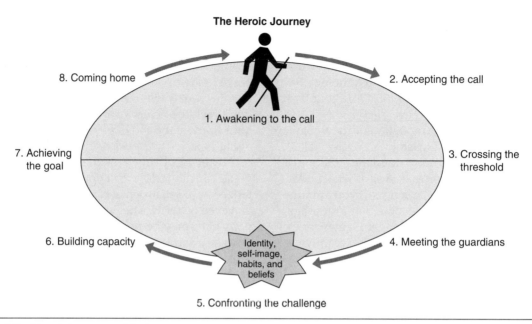

Figure 4.3   The eight stages of the heroic journey.

Based on Gilligan and Dilts (2009).

did so, it typically cost me in terms of additional unhappiness if not downright suffering. The kind of invitation to adventure that is under discussion here can be daunting. As noted, it means giving up part of your identity to be replaced by something as yet unknown. There is risk here. Are you certain you heard the call? Sometimes, it is crystal clear, and other times, the call can be faint.

Referring back to the transtheoretical model, people may be in the stage of contemplation or even preparation without fully committing to action. They seem to be forever contemplating and sometimes inching toward preparation. From the perspective of a heroic journey, you can more deeply appreciate why people may ignore, downplay, disguise, or even run away from such calls to action. This is not a walk-around-the block kind of adventure.

3. Crossing the Threshold

When Joseph Campbell spoke about this moment on the journey, he described a point of no return. In some journeys of this nature, the bridges have already been burned—and not necessarily by you. There is no option but to be in this new realm because the ordinary world no longer exists. This doesn't necessarily mean that you will successfully complete the journey, but rather that wherever you end up, you won't be in the same place—and you won't be the same.

Neither of the previous models (TTM and LTC) characterize the journey of change as a stepwise progression toward a positive ending. In fact, statistics related to the TTM suggest that people may remain interminably in stages of contemplation and preparation. Taylor's LTC model offers a more sophisticated perspective of what happens to people who are thrust from the ordinary world. The first phase of *disorientation* tends to be so uncomfortable that people cannot dwell there for long. They need some kind of resolution. The second transition of *reframing* is clearly the most beneficial type of resolution, whereby individuals move forward without blame or shame. However, an alternative path involves a resolution with persistent blame or shame that becomes incorporated into a new worldview that is less hopeful about self and life in general.

Once the threshold has been crossed, the ensuing heroic journey can be perilous. It requires unwavering vigilance coupled with help from others and the emerging new environment.

4. Meeting the Guardians

You and I are social beings. Our lives are richly supported by family, friends, and even strangers who assist us in invisible ways. No one travels the world alone; even when physically alone you can hear the voices of your internalized guardians. On a heroic journey you need help from others. You may refer to these helpers as guides, guardians, mentors, or protectors.

The LTC model speaks about the need for guides and companions particularly in the *exploration phase* of a change process. Similarly, in the heroic journey you simply may not know much about where you have landed after leaving the ordinary world. At this pivotal stage, it is important to find more resourceful and less perilous ways of proceeding than what you might choose from an uninformed place. Accessing help is essential. Adding complexity to this notion of help, you probably know from experience that when you have tried to make significant changes in your life, some members of your network supported you, while others actively resisted your efforts. Indeed, others are affected when you change—and they may not yet be ready to move out of their comfortable worlds. Campbell (1949) referred to the enemies and allies that one encounters on a heroic journey, again underscoring the social fabric of a change process as well as the need to be mindful of the choices you make about who your guides and companions will be on your journey.

5. Confronting the Challenge

Change involves challenge and learning. It means developing new muscles for unfamiliar tasks in a novel reality. To better appreciate this, take a couple of examples of seemingly simple—and probably not heroic—changes. Imagine moving to a different culture where your dress code is dramatically changed. This may sound superficial, yet for some reason you don't quite recognize yourself in this new garb. Perhaps your new outfits require you to move differently. As a result of all this, you begin to feel differently about yourself. Another example: What would it be like if, due to some organizational change, you were required to switch your working hours from 9 a.m.-5 p.m. to 9 p.m.-5 a.m. Consider all the adjustments that shift would likely influence in various realms of your life.

As significant as these two hypothetical challenges might be, they are not likely to be as deep and pervasive as some of the changes you might confront on a heroic journey. Think of this example: A 60-year-old director in a large organization was offered a choice of quitting his job or engaging in a year-long individual coaching program to deal with what was labeled as aggressive and abusive behavior. The precipitating incident revealed the director bumping his way through a throng of reporters who were covering a story about his company. He spoke roughly to one of the reporters and elbowed his way through the crowd. Of course, someone recorded the whole encounter and shared it on social media.

The next thing he knew he was faced with a choice. In truth, there had been other incidents indicating a particular style that was problematic. Needless to say, the challenge of change for someone who has lived a particular way for decades has multiple layers to it, and it touches deep components of identity, self-image, habits, and beliefs. Even though this seasoned executive may not have chosen this path of change voluntarily, there is no doubt that to successfully alter his patterns, he will need to embark on a hero's journey.

6. Building Capacity

You did not enter this world preprogrammed with all the skills and knowledge you need in your personal evolution over the course of your life. The degree to which you will be required to develop new skills or even reinvent yourself depends on so many factors. Think of places in the world where young adults toil away for years and perhaps decades doing some repetitive task in a manufacturing system. There's probably not much call for a heroic journey in their outer worlds. The same skills, mindset and behavior patterns will be continually evoked and reinforced. Yet, jobs like this will increasingly disappear with automation, and as a result, most future work will confront us with significant challenges to change. In parallel, shifts in our ecosystem will further provoke profound changes in how we live. Here are two simple facts to illustrate this: You probably know that the World Wide Web only became available around 1989, and reasonable proximities to our modern cell phones began proliferating just at the turn of the century. How much did these influence your life and the ecosystems around you? You don't have to be a futurist to know that this is only the beginning.

Let's return to the example of the director: What will need to shift for the director highlighted previously? Will it be superficial only, or will it affect his core character? Even when someone fakes a behavior change, over time I believe this person will change at deeper levels. As social psychologists have documented over the past century (Baumeister & Bushman, 2017), changing attitude changes behavior—and *changing behavior changes attitude!* More to the point, developing capacities on a heroic journey is often a requirement of survival. Either you adapt and learn, or you find yourself by the roadside as the world passes you by.

Coaching is increasingly thought of as a necessary support for the kinds of changes most of us will face in the not-too-distant future (Peterson, 2018).

When clients come to you with a sense of urgency or even desperation about the challenges they are facing, I hope you will have the tools and insights to enable them to discover not only beneficial paths forward but also life-giving motivations for change rather than fear or dread.

7. Achieving the Goal

At long last, the journey is coming to an end. New skills, perspectives, mindsets, and worldviews have been integrated into the hero or heroine's ways of functioning in the world. The ordinary world that the individual left no longer looks so desirable or comfortable, and perhaps this new and relatively foreign place makes more sense and offers more possibilities for the future.

It is somewhat of a misconception to think of this stage as a place of completion, where all is finished and finalized. Few things are ever that way. You are always on a path of change, though the rate of change required of you in certain moments may be more or less comfortable. So, after a year of intense work with a coach, our director will hopefully not only be able to acknowledge his prior worldview and behavior patterns, but also to be less captive to them. To survive, he will need to have grown new muscles for relationships with others and himself. In the best of all worlds, he will also be able to own and honor these changes as valued shifts in his understanding of the world and his capacity to function well within it.

8. Coming Home

Joseph Campbell (1949) reminds us that coming home is not always a seamless process of reentry. There may be refusals to return, along with difficulties of fitting in with formerly familiar company. I remember reading Peter Nichols' (2002) fascinating story, *A Voyage for Madmen*, about nine sailors who in 1968 set out on an incredible race to single-handedly circumnavigate the globe at a time when none of the modern aides of satellite communications were available. Only one finished, but another who could have won, after rounding Cape Horn, decided he wasn't ready to deal with real life quite yet. Instead of turning north for home, he kept on going, sailing round the world again—on yet another journey.

Maybe at some point in your life you took a trek somewhere for a month or more, and upon return, what was once so natural and familiar was difficult to comprehend. When you change, not only does the world look different, but the world regards you as somewhat foreign. There may be an uneasy tentativeness in relationships, your new behaviors

may seem odd to others or even unnatural to apply in old circumstances. The central point is that even homecoming represents a challenging space that requires learning and adaptation.

Another important feature of this homecoming from Campbell's perspective is that you return with certain tangible and intangible gifts. Not only have you yourself changed, but you carry within you the capacity to positively influence others through your way of being, through your way of working, and through talents you have mastered, which now become available to others.

Making Sense of the Heroic Journey

Adaptations of Joseph Campbell's heroic journey provide a beautiful metaphor for the shape, texture, and feel of transformative change. Though it is symbolically described, its structure is quite aligned with the other models you reviewed. TTM may not provide the richness of experience one finds in the heroic journey, but it does capture essential elements of the movements you go through in changing. Taylor's LTC model is perhaps better at detailing the social, emotional, interpersonal, and intellectual elements of a change journey, and in this respect can be more readily overlaid on the structure of Campbell's work.

As reflected in the final stage of the heroic journey, even homecoming can have its challenges. This helps us understand why when you get comfortable in some groove of life, it can be ever so difficult to muster all the motivations and energies to initiate and sustain a change journey. Also, in the final stage, you can find confirmation of the essence of being a hero or heroine. You return with a power that extends beyond yourself to the benefit of the world in which you live and to the people you touch in your daily expressions.

FUNDAMENTAL CHANGE STRATEGIES

While we have looked at different models of the change process, we haven't focused much on the strategies employed in promoting change. Though upcoming chapters will amplify your understanding of the skill sets involved in coaching, let's review some generic change strategies that have emerged from the works just considered. In particular, 10 strategies have grown out of the work of Prochaska and colleagues (Prochaska et al., 1994; Prochaska &

Velicer, 1997). These strategies include methods or techniques that can help people modify thoughts, feelings, and behaviors in the pursuit of desired change in diverse areas of their lives (Marshall & Biddle, 2001; Schumann et al., 2005). Some of these make sense in a coaching context, while others may not. The likelihood is that few people in the stage of precontemplation will seek out a coaching relationship. Similarly, when people are pretty solid in their new patterns after making a change (maintenance and termination stages), they are not likely to feel the need for coaching. The following section describes each strategy and associates it with the stages of change.

Strategy 1: Consciousness Raising

A client contacted me after reading a newspaper article on procrastination; it described some of the deeper psychological issues in patterns of procrastination (Steel, 2011). He told me the article prompted him to want to explore why he continued to procrastinate despite all the apps and time management techniques he had unsuccessfully employed in the past. He didn't intentionally seek out this news article, rather it happened almost by chance.

This example captures the essence of this strategy. Individuals come across information about themselves or their problematic behaviors through such means as lectures, discussion groups, readings, advertisements, films, or even unexpected life events (e.g., a health crisis). It happens often via chance encounters or unanticipated experiences, such as when a lifelong smoker goes to a movie where the main character seems to be killing himself by continuing to smoke. The moviegoer had no intention of exposing himself to this message; nonetheless he leaves the theater feeling motivated to explore his own smoking habits. Of course, we know that, even with strongly framed messages, such as the warnings on cigarette packs, people can turn a blind eye to the potential hazards they continually invite into their lives. A major limitation of this strategy is the fact that it often happens serendipitously. People don't choose to expose themselves to information or experiences that run counter to their beliefs—unless they are deliberately trying to change.

Strategy 2: Emotional Arousal

Emotional arousal usually accompanies consciousness raising. Films, books, dramatic media presenta-

tions, and fear-arousing experiences can generate strong emotions. This strategy is likely to be a side effect of other kinds of messages that people intentionally or unintentionally experience. Of course, there are ethical considerations regarding deliberate efforts to upset people about their behaviors or current status. I read lots of books and articles, and if clients ask what they might read that addresses changes they wish to make, I need to be mindful of the slant that I may represent in the choice of materials that I offer. Especially when films, books, or experiences may have a strong emotional impact, coaches need to carefully consider potential consequences as well as offering an explicit advisory about the nature of the content and possible effects.

Strategy 3: Social or Environmental Control

Your behavior is influenced by your social and physical environment—at least to a degree. Imagine you are in a meeting and feeling physically tense. It's unlikely you can just stand up and do a couple of yoga stretches to relax. Social and physical environments impose implicit or explicit constraints on behavior. Examples include nonsmoking areas, alcohol-free parties, and sanctions, such as social ostracism for behaving in certain ways. With the same reasoning, taxation or, in an obverse way, insurance rate reductions pertaining to certain habits can also influence behavior. Companies may have policies and programs that reinforce certain behaviors, such as exercising regularly. Even though people may have no expressed desire to address unhealthy behaviors, situations may support change.

Coaches are not likely to direct their professional efforts toward these kinds of interventions, though as private citizens they may encourage their application. On the other hand, knowing how much the surrounding environment influences us, coaches can work with clients to coconstruct ways of implementing their plans in supportive environments. For instance, a coach might help a client who wants to pursue a longevity-promoting lifestyle to choose restaurants with enticing healthy-option meals while traveling versus going to ones that resemble all-you-can-eat buffets.

Strategy 4: Environmental Assessment

Once, a client talked to me about how the stress from his work was affecting his interactions with his teenage son. He told me how he was bringing strong feelings of intolerance and impatience that were reinforced in his work role into his home where the exact opposite style would be beneficial. Applying the strategy of environmental assessment, individuals reflect on the impacts of their behaviors on their social and physical environments. In this example, the man would need to be more mindful of his emotionally charged entrance into family gatherings. Another way to see this is in the case of secondhand smoke. Using this strategy, smokers are encouraged to become aware of the effects of secondhand smoke on people around them. Better yet, they may strive to serve as role models for their children and those with whom they regularly interact. In work settings, leaders may want to better understand how much stress might be created in the lives of their staff members by some of their behaviors. Of course, for someone to initiate an assessment of this sort, they would need to feel some motivation to change.

Strategy 5: Personal Revisioning

This strategy involves looking toward the future by visioning life after you change problematic behaviors. Revisioning, or self-reevaluation, enables people to appreciate how their current behaviors may conflict with core personal values; such reevaluation would then help generate motivation to change. This type of intervention is well represented in the tool kits of professional coaches (see the 6 *whats* model in chapter 5). There are a number of ways coaches encourage their clients to create compelling visions of their desired future in order to drive current actions in that direction. People who are willing to imagine a more gratifying future are likely to open themselves to exploring new behavior patterns. As a caveat, you might want to be aware that people in the midst of enduring hardship may have difficulty imagining a more benign reality.

Strategy 6: Commitment

Choosing to change, accepting responsibility for change, and then publicly announcing one's commitment are core features of this strategy. It typically includes clear delineation of the intended change through a contract or other means of making the commitment explicit (see A SuPeRSMART Structure for Setting Goals in chapter 14). This strategy constitutes a core element in the coaching process. Even for small actions planned in individual coaching sessions, clients are typically asked how commit-

ted they are to engage in these change-promoting actions. Making overt commitments to their coaches is a form of public expression for which clients then are more likely to hold themselves accountable.

Strategy 7: Rewarding

This strategy relies on praise and other rewards to reinforce positive behavior change. Many of the changes that clients undertake in coaching relationships represent a significant challenge, so that building in some kind of reward schedule for milestones along the way can be beneficial. Rewards may be either tangible or intangible, or they may be earned for attaining particular levels of achievement or for adhering to commitments. Tangible rewards may take the form of small gifts, while intangible ones may be seen in enjoying time off or pleasurable pastimes. Of course, if people continue to rely on reward strategies after several months of sustained action, you may have legitimate concern about the degree to which the new behavior patterns are being internalized.

Strategy 8: Countering

In this strategy, people substitute supportive or positive behaviors for unsupportive ones, such as doing tai chi for five minutes instead of having a late-night snack or practicing a centering exercise rather than checking Twitter feeds. This approach relies on identifying and controlling internal reactions, such as being aware when an urge arises and then substituting a preplanned positive behavior. Coaches can help clients learn about their internal signals and make plans for countering potential challenges.

Strategy 9: Environmental Management or Stimulus Control

Similar to countering, environmental management involves intentionally controlling one's external environment. Individuals deliberately manipulate their surroundings to support change. For instance, the practice of meditation can be supported by reconfiguring your home environment so that there is a special spot that's set up for you to sit down on the cushion whenever you plan to meditate. When traveling, someone might only book hotels with fitness centers to support a practice of regular exercise. In another context, a person might rent a coworking space rather than trying to get important tasks done in coffee shops or at home. Planning for these kinds of strategic interventions is part of the normal dialogue in coaching relationships.

Strategy 10: Social Support

We are social animals. We flourish with support from others in the important works of our lives. Enlisting support from friends, families, colleagues, and professionals can help us advance through the stages of change. Of course, coaching relationships in themselves offer supportive guidance for clients as they encounter the challenges of change. A caveat is that coaching relationships are by definition temporary. In understanding clients' issues and the actions they pursue, ongoing and appropriate **social support** from others is helpful at all stages of change. Coaches encourage clients not only to explore the nature of their current relationships as a way to support change initiatives, but also to create new social networks that can reinforce commitments to action.

SELF-EFFICACY, SELF-REGULATION, AND RELAPSE PREVENTION

In the concluding section of this chapter, I want to move from specific strategies to broader concepts in changing behavior. Even though the theorists we reviewed earlier describe change in their own unique terminologies, the fact is the three concepts of *self-efficacy*, *self-regulation*, and *relapse prevention* are inherent in virtually all change processes, irrespective of theoretical perspective.

Self-Efficacy

What is self-efficacy? It represents a specific kind of confidence that people have or that they develop in relation to their ability to perform or execute particular behaviors (Bandura, 1995, 1997). It's not thought of as a generalizable concept like self-esteem or self-confidence, but rather one that is limited to a circumscribed set of tasks or activities. Having been a competitive swimmer for many years, I feel high self-efficacy about handling myself with confidence in pools, lakes, and oceans. My youngest son is really good at parkour, which roughly speaking is a thrilling form of urban gymnastics. I have low self-efficacy related to parkour, even though I consider myself to be reasonably athletic.

So, if coaching helps people perform better, then a predictable consequence of coaching is that it will enhance their self-efficacy in particular arenas by raising their performance (Green & Palmer, 2018). The influence of self-efficacy on the adoption, performance, and maintenance of a wide range of behaviors has been repeatedly validated (Allison & Keller, 2004; Bandura, 1998; Dallow & Anderson, 2003; Schwarzer, 1992).

Your self-efficacy beliefs will naturally differ from those of your friends and acquaintances. Albert Bandura, who studied this concept extensively, found that people with higher levels of self-efficacy set more challenging goals for themselves, consistently visualize successful outcomes, expend more effort, and persevere longer to achieve their goals. He also discovered that they are more resilient in the face of setbacks compared with those who have low confidence in their abilities. They also cope better with stress in difficult situations.

Four sources for developing self-efficacy described by Bandura (1998) are as follows:

1. *Mastery experiences or learning by successfully doing.* "I just gave a 10-minute speech in front of a small group; I think I'll be able to present a 10-minute piece in front of a larger audience."
2. *Vicarious experiences or learning by observing peers succeed through persistent effort.* "If my friends are able to do a night course while working, so can I."
3. *Social persuasion.* "My boss has a lot of confidence in me based on things I've done; I'm beginning to see my own potential in this area more clearly."
4. *Reframing psychophysiological states.* "Just because I'm feeling fatigued and have low energy right now doesn't mean that I can't succeed in the long run."

Let's look at self-efficacy beliefs through the lens of the transtheoretical model. Individuals' self-efficacy beliefs correlate with their stages of change. Typically, self-efficacy beliefs are low or nonexistent at the precontemplation stage and increase throughout the remaining stages of change. If self-efficacy is typically low at the beginning of a change process, how can coaching help? One way comes from the idea that there is a kind of self-efficacy about changing oneself that gets reinforced when someone is repeatedly successful at self-change (Luszczynska et al., 2005). Coaches who strategize for small wins will support their clients in fostering self-efficacy about their capacity to succeed in self-change efforts (preparation stage). Additionally, coaches who support clients in devising coping and recovery strategies will enable clients to form grounded beliefs in their capacity to maintain newly acquired behaviors (action and maintenance stages).

Self-Regulation

Another concept central to changing behavior is self-regulation, which reflects your ability and determination to control thoughts, emotions, impulses, or appetites in service of your ability to reach a desired goal (Carver & Scheier, 1998; Vohs & Baumeister, 2016). It speaks to your capacity to maintain focus and concentration on what you want to achieve by managing your resources as well as your attention (Baumeister & Vohs, 2007). If your capacity to self-regulate is low, old habits, personal inclinations, or even innate tendencies can impede your ability to achieve and sustain new and more desirable behavioral patterns (Baumeister et al., 1994).

If self-regulation pertains to your capacity to alter your own behaviors, then wouldn't you want to know what you can do to increase this capacity? The fact is, your ability to self-regulate can be enhanced in a number of ways. In the previous chapter, you learned about the importance of goals and how to structure them for optimal outcomes. Following goal-setting guidelines can be quite beneficial to outcomes you desire (Carver & Scheier, 1998). In addition, your capacity to keep track of your progress and get reliable and regular feedback about performance has also been shown to enhance self-regulation (Gregory et al., 2011).

Baumeister and Vohs (2007) further unpack the concept of self-regulation by suggesting that even if you have a goal, it's not enough to just manage the behaviors that you want to encourage—you also need to gain control over unwanted urges. Let's say you are trying to get on top of your tendency to dominate team discussions at work, and you aim to do so by listening more intently to what others have to say. As you can see, there are two things needed: promoting listening and controlling your contributions. These authors say there are four elements to the self-regulation process that you can develop; these can be found in (1) clarity about your standards, (2) how well you monitor your behavior, (3) your willpower, and (4) your motivation (See sidebar, Components of Self-Regulation).

Ives and Cox (2012) remind us that self-regulation is not about regulating the self; rather it is about the person (or the self) regulating their actions.

This distinction is critical. Imagine a client telling a coach, "I want to be a more open and transparent person." Surely, this broad intention makes sense, but unless it is translated into specific goals and standards for behavior (Vohs & Baumeister, 2011), a client might wander through her days in a state of wonder about what it means to be open and transparent, and whether she is showing up that way. Coaching helps clients identify and envision what change looks like only to them and to translate that idea into changes in their performance. As a result of these changes, the way clients experience themselves will likely shift in positive ways—even though this fundamental shift in the self is not the primary target of coaching objectives.

Preventing Relapse

Self-regulation helps you appreciate what you need to do to stay the course in a behavior change process, while the concept of relapse prevention speaks to what happens to either cause you to deviate from your intentions or to correct course and get back on track once you have deviated. As you might surmise, a relapse refers to a moment where you revert to a previous (and probably undesirable) behavior pattern instead of continuing on the path toward developing a more supportive one.

People seem unable to sustain behavior control over time for a wide variety of reasons (Baumeister & Heatherton, 1996; Heatherton & Wagner, 2011). Sustained progress in behavior change may be impeded when you are facing too many decisions (Vohs et al., 2014), when life becomes overwhelming, or simply when temptations to stray are strong (Heatherton & Wagner, 2011). In situations such as these, your capacity for self-regulation may be low.

Alan Marlatt and associates (Larimer et al., 1999; Marlatt & Donovan, 2008; Marlatt & Gordon, 1985) considered how each of us might deviate from our intentions. Their model was originally devised in the context of addictive behaviors such as substance abuse. It embraces many of the concepts I have already covered, including self-efficacy and self-regulation, but it introduces other useful ideas such as the identification of **trigger** situations where the probability of falling off track is more likely. Clients in coaching often experience setbacks when triggers distract them from pursuing their goals. In the context of a substance abuse issue, a **positive trigger** for an individual might be a big family celebration that calls for a few drinks, and as a result, the person abandons his change agenda. A **negative trigger** could be emotional states, such as anger, fatigue, or depression, that overshadow the determination to

Components of Self-Regulation

The concept of self-regulation may sound a bit mechanistic, but it really breaks down into four clear elements that will enable you to increase your success rate with your own behavior change intentions as well as those of your future clients. Here are the elements that Vohs and Baumeister (2011) believe are important in planning change:

1. *Standards.* If you want to change your behavior from one way to another or from not doing something to doing it, you need a well-defined standard for the behavior you want to manifest. Some standards may be easier to define than others. Think about counting calories in a dietary change plan, as compared to being more participative and less directive in staff meetings.

2. *Monitoring.* One of the wonderful things about setting an intention to change is that you become more aware of your behaviors relating to this intention. This awareness is key to monitoring the behavior you want to grow or diminish.

3. *Willpower.* This is akin to a strength or energy that enables you to self-regulate. If you are continually engaging in acts of self-regulation, your fuel can get depleted such that it becomes more challenging to continue controlling your behaviors. Think of the person who is trying to listen more in meetings instead of constantly speaking out. It takes energy to control speaking out behavior, as well as to listen. Willpower reflects not only how much of this kind of fuel you have but also what you need to do to replenish it.

4. *Motivation.* This is not the same as willpower. It speaks to how much you really care about making this change. Recall the earlier material (chapter 3) on types of motivation, and you will quickly recognize that some kinds of motivation (e.g., external regulation—doing something because you have to) effectively mean that you personally may not care very much about making the change.

What these four elements highlight is how helpful it can be to have a coach working with you while you are undertaking a significant behavior change. Figuring out what your standards are, how you can best monitor your behavior, how to replenish your fuel supply (willpower), and how to augment your motivation may be more complicated than you initially perceive. Coaches are experts in matters of this nature.

move forward. At other times, people might experience peer pressure to revert to habits they want to break. Similarly, they might let other priorities (e.g., work and family demands) interfere with desires to modify behaviors. Or they may get discouraged when they don't achieve results they want as quickly as expected. Relapses or setbacks can range from momentary lapses (the smoker who is trying to quit smokes a few cigarettes on a particularly stressful day) to a full-blown **relapse** (even though the smoker still wants to quit, he or she gives up all effort after experiencing too many lapses).

Most coaches don't deal with substance abuse issues unless they have specific training and certification in this area. Yet, the concepts of relapse and relapse prevention are entirely relevant to the coaching field. Take the example of a leader who defines his approach as autocratic and who dominates discussions in team meetings. He determines with a coach to increase his participatory behaviors by monitoring how much he speaks in meetings and by intentionally listening more carefully to what others are saying. As illustrated in figure 4.4, he has a goal, but then in a meeting about an important topic, he experiences a strong need to make sure that team members fully understand his perspective. As a result, he overcontributes in the meeting. A short while later in another team setting, he is feeling particularly anxious and fatigued and can't seem to concentrate on what others are saying or to manage his own participation. Again, he takes control of the room. Later, an important project is being reviewed and he believes it will look really bad if they don't get it right—so he takes over the meeting and tells team members what they are going to do. In this moment, he abandons—at least for a while—any intention of being more participatory.

To reiterate, whatever a particular theorist's way of describing components of a behavioral change process are, you can be certain that self-efficacy, self-regulation, and relapse prevention will be at least implicit in the discussion of how change occurs, what helps, and what hinders. These concepts don't in themselves describe a change model; rather, they highlight important dynamics in changing behavior.

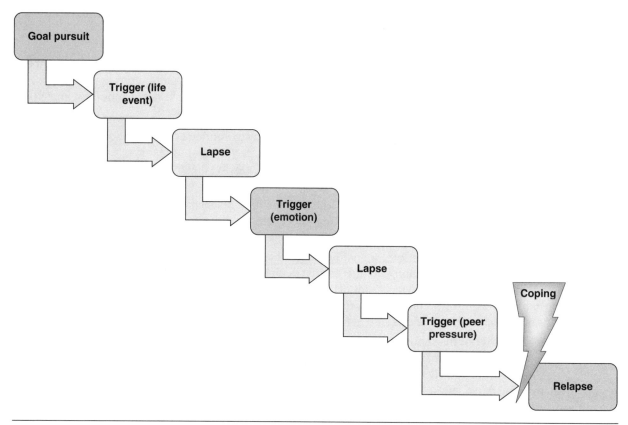

Figure 4.4   Relapse prevention model.

Based on Larimer, Palmer, and Marlatt (1999).

REFLECTIONS

Change models are core to the practice of coaching. You will want to grasp the inner and outer experiences of individuals as they initiate significant changes and as they persist in the face of unanticipated obstacles and requirements.

Throughout my career as a coach and psychologist, I have met thousands of people seeking change of one sort or another. I can't remember a single person who ever said something like, "Everything's fine. I just thought I would start making big changes in my life today to see what happens." Sure, you might be curious at different moments about trying something new, but that's not the same as investing significant resources and jumping into the abyss, not knowing where you will land and how safe you will be once you touch solid ground. All of this reminds me of a kind of precept that I have heard numerous times and in varying forms throughout my career: *People are motivated to change by experiences of crisis or calamity.* The first time I heard this I felt concerned. It sounded like bad things needed to happen before someone got moving. Well, after all these years, I don't know about the bad things aspect, but I do know that you and I aren't likely to change just for the sake of it.

Recently, I found myself in some powerful discussions about whether we can change as human beings without discomfort or even downright suffering. Again, I would take issue with the necessity of a suffering dimension in change; this really depends on so many factors, including the impetus for and magnitude of the change agenda, as well as the individual's patterns and competencies in navigating change. On the other hand, I don't take much issue with the idea of discomfort, since that is almost by definition part of a significant change experience. There is at least an awkwardness or anxiety about the unknown, as well as other emotional and mental states that collectively you may describe as discomfort. Fortunately, our world offers us so many resources for help when we are in the midst of change. Coaching happens to be one of these resources that individuals can access as they embark on these journeys in order to generate a greater sense of flow, optimism, and success.

CHAPTER 5

COACHING MODELS

*You cannot understand a system
until you try to change it.*

Kurt Lewin

MY STORY

Having lived through a few revolutions of theory and practice in the helping professions, I know that models of practice and their associated rationales continue to evolve in order to better serve client needs and lifestyles. As a young psychologist, I understood that a counseling relationship could continue for years, but later on while working in a community-based mental health center, I was required to wrap things up in 10 sessions or fewer. Fortunately, I learned the structures that went along with that kind of process. Then, in the 1990s, coaching entered the scene. In one of the first training programs I attended, a highly seasoned coach demonstrated how to hold a 5-minute coaching session. Wow! The idea that you could create something valuable in 5 minutes seemed radical. Fast forward 20 years, and I believe quite firmly that it typically takes more than 5 minutes to cocreate sustainable change with clients. Even so, I recognize that what that coach did in 5 minutes had a very clear structure that led to a clear outcome.

I have been training coaches for many years now and the model I use has evolved. I think it's comprehensive yet uncomplicated. Even so, I have had participants with deep talent and wisdom in my training programs, and rarely has any participant been able to *immediately* grasp and apply this "simple" model. While the structure of a coaching conversation may be crystal clear, the beauty and complexity of the human condition requires of the coach not just an understanding of a framework, but also an ability to travel with clients on their sometimes circuitous, but always unique paths. Things don't unfold in a lockstep fashion like when we follow the instructions for building IKEA furniture. I guess this is my way of saying that the material you are about to read may seem easy if not self-evident at times; however, putting it into an evolving and seamless conversational flow might take years to master. Please be patient with yourself.

Coaching conversations have a unique structure that generates meaningful outcomes for clients. They are not open discussions where coaches follow clients wherever they want to go, nor are they so tightly designed that clients have no say in how the dialogue unfolds. When you consider the structure of coaching, keep in mind at least two types of framework: The first describes what happens in an individual session between coach and client, and the second is what transpires across the entire coaching relationship. This chapter offers both practical and theoretical perspectives about the coaching process identifying pivotal moments in both a single session and during the entire coaching relationship. Here are some guiding questions as you read:

- How does a coaching relationship progress over time?
- Is coaching solely about the specific issues clients identify?
- Is coaching only focused on the present and future, and never on the past?
- What is the structure of an individual coaching session?
- Is the structure of a session always the same?
- Do all coaching sessions culminate in some kind of action plan?

THE *GROW* MODEL OF COACHING

Let's begin our exploration with a classic coaching model originating in the 1980s. At some point or other in most coaching programs around the globe, participants are likely to learn about the *GROW model*, which was formulated by Graham Alexander, Alan Fine, and Sir John Whitmore (Whitmore, 2017), founding figures in the coaching field. GROW is an acronym representing the following concepts:

- *Goal.* What is the client striving for in her or his work in coaching?
- *Current reality.* How does the client describe the current status of experiences, life circumstances, and behaviors relevant to her or his goal?
- *Obstacles (or options).* What seems to stand in the way of goal attainment for the client (obstacles) and what are the different ways of addressing them (options)?

- *Way forward (or will).* What will the client do to address the obstacles and move toward the goal?

From this, you might imagine a conversation where over a period of time a coach asks a client what his or her goal is, how things are now, what stands in the way, and what actions he or she is prepared to take in order to advance toward the *goal.* Does this seem simple? Well, you probably remember from chapter 3 that clients aren't always clear about their goals. It usually takes effort to sort through various wants and needs for the client to get to the heart of the matter. Similarly, *reality* can be framed as much in perceptions as in concrete facts. A client may describe his or her status and conditions with an uncertain degree of accuracy, thereby necessitating a sensitive questioning process where the coach tries to determine how things may actually be as contrasted with how they are described. In this process, the coach isn't doubting the client's veracity but rather discovering aspects of the current situation that may unwittingly have been misunderstood and those that have been overlooked. The same kind of exploratory process is required to identify *obstacles*, real and perceived, along with *options* that may be proposed for overcoming roadblocks. Finally, the *way forward* can be a challenging discovery process where actions are suggested, reviewed, rejected, resisted, and maybe redesigned repeatedly. Doing all of this will certainly take more than five minutes and could in fact take multiple meetings before the client is even ready to step forward onto a path directly related to goal attainment.

Client Stories

With the GROW framework in mind, let's anchor your understanding of the structure of coaching by applying what you have learned to five constructed examples of clients based on an amalgam of typical coaching themes. Though none of the examples describes an actual client, each captures important dynamics that I have seen repeatedly in coaching relationships.

Your task for each example is to imagine what the goal is, where the client is now, and what obstacles and options might show up in moving toward the goal. Then, consider what concrete actions you might cocreate with your client. Finally, in doing all this, give some thought to how your answers for these clients might be shaped by your own filters and worldview. It is often surprising in coaching relationships how differently clients construct their paths based on their own perspectives when compared to ours.

Tolerance for Risk

Zhi Ruo immigrated to North America as a teenager with her family. Having learned English as a child, she rapidly adapted to her new world and excelled in school. After graduating from medical school and working at a large hospital for a few years, she turned toward research in the pharmaceutical industry, where her sharp mind and creative talents led to an accelerated climb through her company's hierarchy. Then, her meteoric rise slowed and eventually stalled for almost a decade. A glass ceiling, she thought. Work lost its luster. While she continued to gain skills and technical know-how, she yearned for something else. She felt the dulling impact of too many bosses, too many layers of approval, overly bureaucratic processes, and a major lack of imagination in the world around her. Friends and family encouraged her to go out on her own and start her own company. She had friends who had tried, and a small percentage had major success. Her finances were in good shape, but she had two children inching their way toward their college years. Through all this, she continued to hear the call, and it was becoming more insistent. Earlier in her tenure with this company, she had heard a faint version of this call and embarked on an MBA degree at a local university. Now she had the letters *MD* and *MBA* after her name, but her job remained the same.

Recently, she participated in a human resources–sponsored 360-degree performance evaluation. She was disappointed by the results. Feedback about her technical competencies was stellar, but her soft skills seemed more problematic. Moreover, she was stunned to hear feedback about her risk tolerance; she was seen as hypercautious and conservative. How would she ever start her own business with that profile? Even with this new data, the call was becoming incessant. She needed help, and though her family and friends were always there for her, she wanted an outside opinion. Zhi Ruo decided to engage an executive coach.

A Paralyzing Thought

Malik had always seen himself as an entrepreneur. While in college, he began a student-run house painting business, which was wildly successful and led to multiple franchises. In his early 20s, he built a ride-share app with some techy friends that got snapped up by a notable tech company. Then, he looked into Internet dating sites and created a platform that got good traction before it was mimicked by another company that had a much better funding model. Things continued like this for more than a decade—imagine, create, build, and sell. Of course, there was more to it than that. Malik worked around the clock, never thinking of the toll it was taking on him.

Then, life beckoned to him from a different direction. He fell in love. He was 32, between gigs and contemplating fatherhood. He and his fiancée decided to take a world backpacking tour—the last window before settling down. One of the biggest surprises of this trip was that it awakened visions of other ways of living, yearnings for social contribution, questioning of the primacy of money, and a fear-fueled angst about whether he could ever go back and get on that entrepreneurial ride again.

Baby came bouncing into his world and he fell in love again in a very different way. At about the same time, business opportunities emerged. New venture possibilities proliferated in conversations with friends, as did offers from late-stage start-ups for him to take over as chief operating officer or chief executive officer. He even got scouted by some established information technology companies offering glittering compensation packages, benefits, and perks. Malik was only 34 now but began wondering whether he would be selling out his identity as an entrepreneur by going after the secure opportunities that would allow him more time at home with his child. Jenny, his talented partner, knew this had to be Malik's call. She suggested he hire a coach.

Life in the Pandemic

If you weren't hit too hard by all the life and work changes occasioned by the pandemic, then you might actually have had time to consider whether you wanted to stay on the road you had been traveling for so long. Well, Naira thought she was pretty lucky, but she wasn't having an easy time. She worried about her elderly parents in South America and her unemployed brother in London. In her corner of the world, she felt lonely, bored, and unstimulated, all the while feeling grateful that she was still employed in a job she just happened to fall into about 10 years ago. She was good at it, but she would often tell friends, "I just took it. You know, I needed to work and it was okay, paid well, good benefits, nothing special, but it's okay." Cut off from virtually all her usual contacts in the pandemic, Naira felt she was living Groundhog Day every day, and she was seriously struggling to find meaning in her existence. She didn't think she was depressed, but she felt she was living on a very flat terrain. She continually reminded herself of all the things she had wanted to do when life was normal, but her wish list only got longer over the many months of the pandemic. She should meditate, take up a hobby, start exercising, connect more with friends, write poetry, cook exciting meals, paint her apartment, and on and on. She rarely got excited about things and knew she wasn't much of a self-starter, but this inertia felt totally ridiculous to her. After a few months, she admitted that she was stuck. "Big picture: life's okay," she said. "I'm healthy. I have work. I haven't lost anyone in my family. I have a nice place to live." And then she added, "But I am in one heck of a rut." Naira knew enough to hold up her hand and ask for help, so in the fifth month of on and off lockdowns and doomy forecasts, she found herself a coach.

The Hijacked Sabbatical

Sophia didn't surprise anyone nearly as much as she surprised herself. She had succeeded in a very tough business that played to her managerial brilliance but that allowed scant air for her suffocating creative talents. Over her 20 years at work, her talents yielded solid results culminating in her chief operating officer position in a prestigious global manufacturing company. In her late 30s, she and her partner, Alex, agreed to have children, despite all the worries about balancing work and family time. Alex carried the lion's share of home and childcare responsibilities, which was cool with him, except for the fact that the more time he made for Sophia to work, the more she seemed to need. Quality time seemed to be the solution, so precious days off or brief vacations were adventure-filled and fun-packed extravaganzas.

Pushing into her early-40s, the psychic and physical wear began to fray her world more noticeably. It wasn't her success that was the surprise, it was her quitting without a plan that stunned those around her. She told everyone she was taking a sabbatical—time to reflect, refuel, and restart. As life would have it, that's exactly when everything really fell apart. Her younger son got really sick with one of those undiagnosed but nonetheless disturbing kinds of illnesses. Then her husband had a disabling work accident. He was down for the count. Sophia was now 24/7 at home, caring for her family. The idea of having time to creatively imagine next steps vanished.

In her first few months at home with her young son, she wrote a children's book about living with some strange and painful thing going on inside. She got a friend to illustrate it, and soon was selling it on Amazon. She had always been a voracious reader and as a child was a prodigious writer of prose and poetry. She did not have much time for reading these days, but sitting quietly with her loved ones nearby for hours on end did stir her muse. Her ever-present tablet was smoking from her fingertip strokes.

Sophia knew the manufacturing world, she knew marketing, she knew lots of things about getting products to market. Now, however, she had a new product idea—her writing. What should she do about it? And what about the mortgage? "Hmmm," she thought, "maybe I should hire a coach."

A New Start

Getting a master's degree in engineering (ME) was going to give Sandra a whole new start. After Sandra got her undergraduate degree, it had taken her a while to wander through a few dream jobs that ultimately disappointed before she saw the truth: Sandra needed better credentials to enter the job market at a different level. She learned a lot in her ME program, yet her biggest learnings weren't what she expected. Unlike her undergraduate program, the ME program required a lot of team assignments. She was really sharp and wondered why her classmates were always so slow to catch on to things. Frequently, she would just take the ball and run with it, brilliantly completing team projects on her own. Of course, she expected her teammates to be grateful, but more often than not they weren't.

Sandra's first job after her ME gave her exactly what she was hoping for: a midlevel management role in charge of a team. It came with a great salary, nice perks, and a significant mandate to create new products. In the first couple of months, she was bewildered by all of the antiquated methods her company was using. Given all that she had learned in her master's program, she wanted colleagues to have the benefits of her knowledge. She was dumbfounded when people would say things like, "This is the way we always did it here, and it's worked for us so far." What were they thinking? The world was changing, and it was changing fast. She thought, "Get with it or get out of the way."

Results from her team in the first few months were also disappointing. They were way below her targets for them and some of them had a work ethic that she simply couldn't grasp. In her mind, they were professionals, and professionals don't work 9 to 5 jobs. They needed to be hungrier and to take the next step without having to be asked. She was glad when some of them quit or requested transfers to other teams, but her boss wasn't at all pleased.

It was time for her six-month review, and, in spite of all the obstacles and poor staff support, Sandra had made things happen. She felt proud of her accomplishments and entered her boss's office with a spring in her step. As the meeting started, Sandra sensed tension in Michele's tone, and when Michele described her serious concerns about Sandra's leadership style, Sandra's mind flooded with defensive retorts. She managed to keep quiet up to the point that her boss said, "Sandra, if you want to continue with us, I need you to begin working on a regular basis with one of our professional coaches." She started to say something, but then remembered what one of her ME professors told her at graduation. He had said, "Sandra, you are no doubt one of the brightest students I have taught, *and* I think you have some real work to do in how you relate to people. This could really hinder your career if you don't get on top of it."

FLOW MODEL OF COACHING

These scenarios suggest how clients come to coaching. When reflecting on the five examples, you want to be able to identify what gave rise to their intentions to be coached. Many clients enter coaching with a need to get out of their habitual mindsets, especially when old patterns continually drive them into familiar yet frustrating walls. Each individual profiled in the previous sections experienced a certain calling and a need to redirect energy and indeed life itself. Of course, some experiences that give rise to client intentions feel more like something they have to do or something that is necessary for survival. Consider Sandra in this regard. Her story is not unique. Recent history reveals innumerable stories of people who are mandated to change—suddenly unemployed, confronting mountainous debts, displaced geographically, suffering unimaginable losses of family and friends, or confronting other spectacularly disturbing new realities.

Thinking back to the GROW model, you can probably see in each of the five stories an emerging *goal* and parts of the current *reality*. You might also be able to imagine the *obstacles*, as well as some of the *options* that could emerge. Probably what is most out of sight is the *way forward*, since this requires a fair amount of exploration, reflection, and planning before any of these individuals would be fully equipped to articulate possible actions.

The work of coaching as sketched in the GROW model breaks into two separate types of processes, each requiring distinct mindsets (Ives & Cox, 2012). The first is goal setting, and the second is planning. Considerable exploration and analysis about the goal or objective of the coaching relationship is required before coach and client can get down to the business of planning. Ives and Cox (2012) think of goal setting as a more "abstract and conscious" activity, while planning is thought to be more "concrete and automated" (p. 37). The goal that the client lands on tends to be less negotiable than the types of plans the client might generate in working toward the goal. Another way of saying this is that there may be many means to the same end, but the desired end is likely to remain constant.

Years ago, a colleague and I were imagining how best to describe the process of coaching. We came up with a metaphorical description of it and named it the **flow model of coaching** (Gavin & Mcbrearty, 2018). We expressed it as a metaphor capturing essential features of a change journey.

Flow Metaphor

Imagine a mountaintop lake sitting at a high altitude in a pristine wilderness area. This lake is the source for innumerable rivers and streams coursing down to the sea. As seasons come and go, the rivers and streams fluctuate in their force and volume of flow. Heavy rain may overfill this lake, giving rise to new streams that chart unique paths toward the sea. So, too, times of drought may cause some streams to dry up—at least until the next heavy rainfall.

Each new stream has to make its way down the mountainside. Sometimes there isn't enough flow to sustain its coursing path, so it diminishes, and its waters get absorbed into the earth—it never makes it to the sea. Other times, a stream may encounter barriers that block its flow. It may become a pond and once again never reach its destination. With heavy rainfalls, new streams may suddenly burst forth over steep cliffs, giving rise to spectacular waterfalls. With such volume and power, these streams rush relentlessly toward the sea.

How many rivers and streams can this lake feed? Which ones will continue to flow even in the dry seasons? What kind of landscape allows a new stream to carve its bed down the mountainside toward the sea? How might natural occurrences or human interventions help or hinder a flowing stream?

Deconstructing the Metaphor

How do coaches work so that clients experience a sustained flow of energy and other resources to achieve their dreams? Clients enter a coaching relationship with varying levels of energy and resources for change. They may want change, but much like the mountaintop lake, they may be in the midst of a personal drought. It may well be that the first task of coaching is to address the energy levels and resources available to clients at the onset of coaching. Once the change process is initiated, clients may fluctuate over time in their energy flow. By clarifying clients' intentions, small actions may be planned. If they are well constructed, these actions can enhance the energy available for future actions. As noted in goal theory research, strategizing for early wins in coaching through codesigning significant yet achievable tasks can propel clients forward in their efforts (McLean, 2012). Of course, disruptions and obstacles may occur along the way to diminish flow. No matter how well intended clients are, unexpected events may arise and redirect energy flow into other streams. Change also requires energy not only in the moment but in a sustained manner over time.

When someone charts a course of change, it may not always be the most direct path. Sometimes it meanders, hopefully giving rise to rich growth along the way. What will augment flow when source waters are low or a winding path curves uphill? Even though water naturally seeks the lowest ground, intentional action may nevertheless be needed to ensure that obstacles preventing natural gravitation are managed.

Coaching represents a partnership between coaches and clients that purposefully increases clients' resources for change. Coaches are temporary members of clients' support systems, and they cocreate novel routes around seemingly insurmountable obstacles. They help clients discover new resources; they also lend a hand so that clients can furrow through blockages in their flow to reach desired destinations. In the long term, clients need to become self-sustaining in their commitments, but as the path is being created, they are likely to require support from a variety of sources including from their coaches.

The flow model of coaching characterizes a client's journey as one of flowing toward the sea from a high source above the clouds. When people announce intentions for coaching, you will want to appreciate the source of their desires. Beyond gaining awareness of the origins of client dreams,

coaches seek to understand whether initial levels of motivation are sufficient to sustain the journey over time. What if clients have many wishes and dreams? What if these aspirations arrive during a dry season?

In the previous chapter, you learned that the initiation of a change process is not a random or whimsical event. It derives from places of deep desire and intentionality that may have been more or less present for a long while. Clients arrive with an objective in mind; they rarely show up with a wish as vague as the desire to do better or be happier. Before the first conversation occurs, it is likely that clients have identified a preferred direction and potential outcomes. These initial intentions are often transformed through the process of coaching into even clearer articulations of the dream, of the desired state of being that has manifest and measurable benchmarks.

In the broad realm of coaching, client dreams may be as concrete as buying a new house, losing weight, or finishing a doctoral degree. Equally so, clients may wish to sustain an ongoing commitment to a course of action, such as balancing career and personal agendas, managing stress effectively, or continuing to behave in alignment with one's most important values. In all cases, the interior and exterior worlds of the client will change throughout a coaching process.

The flow model is divided into two major phases: engagement and goal pursuit (see figure 5.1).

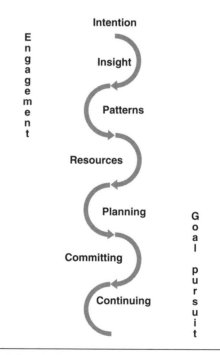

Figure 5.1 The flow model of coaching.

Within each phase are three critical areas of focus. In the engagement phase, the areas are *insight*, *patterns*, and *resources*. In the goal-pursuit phase, the areas are *planning, committing,* and *continuing*. During the engagement phase, areas of focus may occur more or less simultaneously; in the goal-pursuit phase, areas tend to be more sequential. Let's explore this model to understand how coaches can cocreate with their clients an experience of flow toward the realization of dreams and visions.

Flow Model: Engagement Phase

The waters spill over in a new direction today! What has happened to create this shift? What is it about today that is different from yesterday? A client may have had your name for months or just heard about you today. A call is made. A connection begins.

How does a coaching relationship start? Among other things, the first session of a coaching relationship includes discussions of fees, meeting structures, time frames, and mutual expectations. It is also important to ask what clients know about coaching to ensure that they understand what coaching is and what it is not. In particular, clients need to recognize that it is action oriented rather than a protracted analysis of issues. They need to know that coaching requires them to arrive at each session with a targeted topic for discussion. During the session, they will explore the many layers of that topic and then develop a plan for action that they will initiate and potentially complete before their next session. (See appendix C, The First Session, for more information about the initial conversation in coaching.)

As a coach, you need to determine if the client's topic is appropriate for coaching and whether you are the right coach to work with this specific client. You will want to assess the client's expectations. Are her desires appropriate for a coaching relationship? Are the two of you a good match? Because the success of coaching often hinges on the strength of the relationship, a good fit between coach and client is essential. Positively answering questions such as, "Can I see myself working with this particular client?" and "Is there good chemistry between us?" will increase the chances for successful outcomes.

In the beginning, terms and conditions are carefully reviewed until an agreement is reached (see appendix B). Assuming all aspects of business contracting and role expectations are agreed upon, you can now legitimately engage your client in the work of coaching. You begin to focus your attention on creating insight, uncovering patterns, and discover-

ing resources. Through these explorations, clients gain new appreciations of themselves in relation to their aspirations. Unique solutions may spontaneously emerge. The goal itself may evolve so that it is both more easily achieved and more fulfilling.

1. Focus on Insight

What are clients' larger stories? Who are they in the fabric of their lives? How do their intentions mesh with their realities and other dreams they may have? What exactly is motivating this intention? Where else are their life energies being directed? How well do they understand themselves at this juncture in life?

Each client begins with a wish or intention. It may be broad or circumscribed, short or long term, concrete or abstract. This intention cannot be separated from the rest of the client's existence, and as a coach, your role is to understand this desire in context. The gift of this phase of the flow model is that as the coach expresses genuine curiosity in deepening her understanding of the client, awareness is also created within the client. In the safe space of a coaching relationship, clients begin to put together the pieces of their own puzzles. Reflect upon Naira's story during the pandemic. She acknowledges she is in a rut, but where's the focus? You have some clues from her story that she has trouble getting started and that she "fell into her job" and has been there for 10 years without much excitement. Should coaching focus narrowly on finding a hobby, or is

---

Insight: What's the Focus?

In fostering insight, coaches guide clients to focus on the following:

- Understanding oneself in the context of this change
- Perceiving oneself clearly and accurately
- Mapping "all of me" in the world
- Seeing the interactions of all the forces at play
- Understanding the sources and depth of one's motivation
- Appreciating the larger picture of other visions, dreams, needs, and realities
- Exploring the likelihood of intended and unintended changes over the long term
- Identifying the deeper wants and needs that will be met by this pursuit

there something larger that she needs to awaken in herself?

A focus on insight is about generating awareness and access to sustainable motivation. It is meant to provide strength and clarity for the journey. However, it is not an end in itself. This stage is intended to ground clients' dreams in the practical realities they will likely face. When the distance to a goal seems far, more immediately attainable goals can be created to feed motivation along the path. Helping clients appreciate their intentions within the broader frame of their lives facilitates action planning to account for all relevant elements. For instance, in the story of The Hijacked Sabbatical, Sophia clearly had a deep passion for writing, but she mused about paying the mortgage especially under the present conditions of her life. Reality interfaces with dreams in this story, and awareness of this dynamic promotes thoughtful planning.

Creating insight does not mean finding out all the areas where clients are unconscious or asleep, but it does involve exploring critical beliefs that could interfere with success. In the Tolerance for Risk scenario, Zhi Ruo was surprised by how colleagues assessed her risk-taking tolerance. Was this an artifact of her role in the organization or something embedded in her character? Coaches need to awaken insight in appropriate domains through sensitive reflections and questioning.

2. Focus on Patterns

Each of us flows in different ways. What are clients' unique patterns of engaging their worlds and getting things done? What styles do they prefer? What are their habits of mind, body, and spirit? What makes them tick? What are their needs, inclinations, and sources of energy? How do they go about pursuing their dreams and daily lives?

Take something as common as your waking rituals. What do you do first? When do you eat? What's your preferred way of starting your day? These patterns are uniquely yours, and that's simply the way it is. You developed your ways of doing things over many years. They are habitual—so much so that when some of the steps are out of sequence, you feel slightly off. Think of the subtle shifts you experience in yourself when, for example, you stay overnight in a hotel for one reason or another. Remember the story of A Paralyzing Thought, where Malik woke to another vision of his life that ran counter to all of his patterns while taking a much-needed break from work. In Life in the Pandemic, Naira seemed to have been living on autopilot until she was sequestered with herself for a long period of time during the pandemic.

Another gift of a coaching relationship is how it enables people to be mindful of their habitual behaviors when they are trying to approach things in novel ways. Coaching often involves implementing unfamiliar approaches to action. Your chronic patterns may urge you to go back to the tried and true, rather than chance uncertainty. Coaches need to know how clients go about change and what happens when things don't work as planned. Some aspects of clients' patterns may have fostered success; others may have resulted in less desirable outcomes when applied in certain situations. Think of Sandra in the story of A New Start. She was bright and competent, yet her team behaviors were problematic. Imagine a client who has a habit of making jokes when life gets too serious. This can be helpful in reducing stress, but it may be problematic in certain professional situations or when others are not quite in the mood for laughter. The implication is not that the person has to become stern and somber, but rather that he or she needs to discriminate between times when it's okay to be funny and when a more focused attitude is more beneficial.

Exploring clients' patterns means uncovering how they make decisions, how they plan, how they implement actions, and how they energize themselves. While identifying relevant sources of motivation represents part of the insight focus, the emphasis here is on clients' patterns in calling upon certain motivations. For instance, when a client is falling down in his commitments, he may typically prod himself to action by self-labeling his behavior as "lazy." Through such explorations, clients might discover more beneficial motivational strategies that can be readily applied to their coaching agendas. At other times, they might glimpse how old ways of being prevent progress toward outcomes they desire. You may have noted in Sophia's Hijacked Sabbatical story that she had impressive skills in getting products to market and making sure that they were profitable. If you overlay that skill set on what might be required in today's publishing world, there are likely to be strong reasons for her to be hopeful.

A focus on patterns is not entirely separate from the previous focus on insights. Throughout, you are trying to understand your clients—how they function, what they value, how they know, what helps them start, and what hinders them. After learning about these things, coaches develop a sense of where clients will leap forward and what might stop them in their tracks.

Patterns: What's the Focus?

Coaches enable clients to explore and reveal the following patterns:

- Habits and patterns of daily life
- Preferred ways of organizing or scheduling life events
- Criteria by which clients prioritize life agendas
- Characteristic modes of thinking and feeling
- Habitual ways of generating motivation for action
- Go-to places or defaults when they are stuck or under stress
- Bodily patterns of movement or inactivity
- Preferred modes of sensing—auditory, visual, or kinesthetic
- Strong attractions and aversions

Patterns are usually ingrained ways of being or habitual manners of thinking, feeling, and acting. There is a sequencing that is represented in patterns of behavior, feeling, or thought. One thing leads to another, and then a certain, perhaps predictable, outcome occurs. It's likely that when people hire coaches, one of their dominant patterns for creating success in their lives is no longer working. They may have experienced a number of disappointments in relying on their tried-and-true ways. If that's not the case, it may be that they don't yet see how their old patterns are misaligned with their new intentions. A new path has not yet been taken.

3. Focus on Resources

In a change process, clients encounter challenges, opportunities, and a need for resources. What are your clients' assets and capacities? What are their supports? Who's there for them? What opportunities are opening for them? What skills will they need for their journey?

Your clients will have traveled the roads of change before, and they probably know that other people may offer critical support along the path. Resources show up in Zhi Ruo's Tolerance for Risk story not only in the support of family but also in her old colleagues who pursued entrepreneurial interests. Whether they succeeded or not in their ventures, her colleagues might offer relevant experiences for her consideration.

Resources may appear in the strangest forms and places: reading an old diary, bumping into a long-lost acquaintance, being invited to a community gathering. Beyond social support, clients may need certain skills and capacities to achieve desired goals. Do they already have these competencies, or will they need to be developed? Similarly, the practicalities of concrete resources, such as physical tools, books, weather conditions, finances, or access to facilities may need to be factored into the client's emerging plans for change.

Focusing on resources occurs concurrently with fostering insight and uncovering patterns. Coaches elicit information and listen carefully; they then sort what they have sensed into various lenses and reflect back relevant elements to their clients. In exploring resources, coaches want to enhance clients' awareness about the social fabric of their lives. You and I have networks that are likely to be more extensive than we realize at any given moment. Clients may not have intimate contact with key people who can help them in their quest, yet friends of friends might be invaluable.

Just as there are likely to be strong supporters of clients' intentions, there may be others who are less enthusiastic or even obstructive. Mapping strategies to address how clients deal with unsupportive people may make the difference between success and yet another failed attempt. For instance, family members may be ambivalent about a client's intended changes because these changes might affect them personally; they may worry that if the client changes, they may have to change too.

The robustness of action planning relies on the depth of consideration given to all the elements that can augment or diminish flow. Coaches encourage clients to explore the obvious, the possible, and the yet-to-be-discovered resources that will enable them to successfully move toward goal realization.

It's not always clear how resources differ from patterns; in fact, they may overlap. Resources pertain to what clients can bring forward to support and sustain action toward goal fulfillment. Areas for inquiry might include the following: What do they know about their topics? What would pursuing their goals require of them? Whom do they know who can help, and who might try to block their progress? What skills will they need in order to do what they wish, and do they have them? If skills are lacking, what will it take to acquire them? What practical resources might be required for clients' agendas? What kinds of unrecognized opportunities are currently available for their agendas? What else may be occurring in the near future that could

Resources: What's the Focus?

Coaches support client explorations of resources by asking the following questions:

- What are clients' unique skills and abilities?
- Where are their social support networks? Which ones have they not yet tapped?
- What opportunities are opening up for them in their worlds?
- Which ones seem to be closing down?
- What other kinds of resources might be available? What can they create?
- What obstacles might appear, and who or what can help the client with them?
- Who will oppose or resist clients' efforts to change?
- What capacities and resources will be needed to address resistance from others or their environment?

influence their plans? Are there any obstacles that need to be acknowledged and addressed?

By comparison, patterns have more to do with ingrained ways of thinking, feeling, or acting. They refer to your habits. Someone can be habitually easygoing, and that might serve certain goals but not others. When viewed from a resource perspective, habits like this one might be considered as a capacity to get along well with others.

Flow Model: Goal-Pursuit Phase

Has the flow of energy grown or diminished through the engagement phase? Did the client retreat into doubt, or did she find new sources of strength and motivation? It may take one or more sessions to move through the various explorations encompassed in the engagement phase, yet the process is anything but linear. If there have been multiple sessions, the client will have left each session with a plan of action—to gather information, investigate possibilities, talk to particular people, or accomplish tasks that create foundation and momentum. Just as a new stream must make its way around boulders and through flatlands or even create underground passageways, so too clients must find creative ways to address matters that will facilitate their journeys.

A coaching relationship develops throughout the work of the engagement phase. Clients learn first-

hand what coaching is about and what is required for progress. Moreover, they gain trust in their coaches as reliable sounding boards and guides for the journey. A way of partnering in discovery and action evolves through the sessions. Coaches perceive how clients like to work and what challenges them. Clients understand what coaches' tasks are and what they can expect when working together.

Although action occurs throughout the engagement period, a clearer emphasis on tasks directly pertinent to the goal now takes shape. This phase is about taking steps into the dream so clients can begin experiencing at least part of what they are yearning for. In most cases, the dream represents a complex construction requiring a sequence of steps, each of which brings clients closer to a complete realization of their desires.

In the engagement phase, there may be a multidirectional exploration across the three main areas of focus. In goal pursuit, the focus areas have more of a consecutive flow. Clients must first plan, then commit, and finally take action on a continuing basis.

1. Focus on Planning

Wishing alone won't make things happen. How will clients reach their goals? What's the overall strategy? What's the immediate plan? Does the plan address all the elements of who, what, when, where, and how? How robust is it? Do clients understand what will be required each step of the way? Is the plan fixed, or will it evolve based on what happens at each new point on the journey?

Planning happens in every session, and hopefully a kind of master plan will emerge soon. In early sessions, clients may be gathering data and experimenting. Planning for these kinds of actions is articulated in the coaching sessions. In some cases, the goal of coaching is so straightforward and there is only one path of action. Even here, the client may not be ready to take it. She may need to build competencies, obtain further resources, develop support structures, and so on. Planning for these preparatory actions can occupy a significant portion of the coaching dialogue. In time, the groundwork will be laid, and planning becomes more squarely situated in actions reflecting elements of the client's dream. Returning to Sophia's story of The Hijacked Sabbatical, how many preliminary steps do you imagine she would need to be in a position to commit herself to a new and financially rewarding career in writing and publishing?

As you know from the earlier discussion of the TTM and the LTC model, when clients are moving through a change process, adaptation to their new

Planning: What's the Focus?

When coaches help clients with planning, attention focuses on the following:

- Determining the overall strategy or coaching plan
- Identifying the subtasks of the coaching plan
- Understanding the sequencing of actions as building blocks
- Estimating a timeline for different aspects of the plan
- Identifying who, what, when, where, and how for each action plan
- Using well-defined action goals and plans

---

way of being is fragile and sometimes awkward—it has yet to be integrated into their lifestyle. Planning in the latter stages of a coaching relationship represents a kind of fine-tuning or adjustment process wherein clients explore how well they are sitting in the new lives they have created.

Planning is about the big and the small, the immediate and the long range, the preparatory and the final steps. It is an integral part of each coaching session, though early planning is often exploratory or directed toward building a foundation. Planning hopefully results in clear actions, which then produce new data and insights about clients' intentions and possibilities. Just as a new stream may branch out in many directions until it finds the one pathway that allows it to continue flowing, so too clients may investigate a variety of options in the beginning of their coaching relationships. In this respect, even though planning may not always chart a direct path to the desired goal, it generates momentum that motivates clients through the learning they derive and the concrete samplings of their dreams.

2. Focus on Committing

When the plan has been fully detailed, there remains the doing. How strongly committed are clients to engage in positive actions? What's their level of determination? How can they commit themselves without traces of hesitancy? What's required to ensure that commitment doesn't dissolve between coaching sessions?

Determining commitment often means listening for the hesitancy in clients' resolutions or the qualifications they make about committing. "I'll try" is a classic red flag for commitment. The coach responds, "What would it take to move that 'I'll try' to 'I'll do'"? Remember the scenario of A New Start? Sandra might be reluctant to change, given that it wasn't her idea that she needed to work with a coach. This type of scenario replays itself increasingly in the world of coaching. Organizations often direct individuals to coaching due to performance or behavioral concerns. Resistance may permeate the coaching relationship for much of its duration.

Relatedly, sometimes clients take on projects for which they have little enthusiasm. People who have lost jobs or otherwise been unwillingly thrust into situations where they have to adapt may recognize the need to change but struggle with motivation and commitment. Coaches may need to stretch clients to engage in more demanding action objectives than the comfortable ones that clients appear halfheartedly committed to trying. The strategy here is that by working toward higher client engagement, there will hopefully be a clearer and more satisfying payoff. In addition, through engaging in action, excitement is more likely to grow. When clients continually lag on their engagements, the coach will probably sense a degree of resistance to the coaching process. Coaches don't always know in advance how things will go, even though the coaching contract may speak about clients needing to experiment with new behaviors.

When clients look for loopholes or a way out of commitment, coaches don't revert to cheerleading or manipulation. Coaching involves a genuine inquiry into aspects of the plan that haven't generated solid resolve to move forward. In this respect, it's not just about changing "I'll try" to "I'll do." It may be that in creating the plan, the coach's enthusiasm overshadowed the client's reluctance for a particular action objective. Clients have to own their plans, and that may take some redesign. Also, when coaches continually stretch clients to do more than they choose, uninspired engagement may result.

There are countless examples of people who encourage others to do things with rhetorical questions such as, "You're really going to do this, aren't you?" Relationships between coaches and their clients are intentionally egalitarian; the coach doesn't have special powers over clients to make them comply. Yet as social beings, there may often be a people-pleasing element to requests from others, including thoughts like, "The coach wants only the best for me, so who am I to deny her simple requests?" Indeed, this dynamic may be stronger than you realize in coaching relationships. For this reason, you need to be extra sensitive to the qualifying commitments that clients offer, such as "I'm

Committing: What's the Focus?

Coaches demonstrate attention to commitment when they are engaged in the following:

- Listening carefully for the ways in which clients express commitments
- Recognizing hesitancies and fine-tuning plans for stronger commitment
- Helping clients identify resistance and ways to transform it into a positive resource
- Reflecting on their own actions to detect whether they may be more invested in action plans than their clients are
- Checking for client commitment with some type of scaling (e.g., scale of 1-10)

going to do my best," "You can count on me," or "I'll do it [for you] for sure!"

Many times, clients will try their best, and that may be good enough. Each coaching session ends with a commitment to action, and sometimes the client may simply not get as far as anticipated during the interval between sessions. Life happens. What a coach looks for are patterns of behavior related to commitments that clients make. A once-in-a-while lapse in follow-through is different from a string of excuses over several months.

Committing is a process, not a single action. It represents a discussion rather than a yes-or-no answer. It should generate exploration and dialogue in order to lead to closure. A coach's question about commitment has to be presented on an open hand, to be accepted or refused without judgment. It needs to be offered with compassion and understanding, no matter how much time has been spent detailing the action plan for which the question is being asked.

3. Focus on Continuing

A good start is just that. What do clients need to stay the course? How will they deal with setbacks? What will keep them going when the end seems so far away? What happens when the anticipated end represents a new beginning on the journey? How do your clients solidify and nurture what they have gained?

As noted in the discussion of the TTM, continuing action for at least six months brings a person to the stage of maintenance—and maintenance can go on for a lifetime. Within the coaching relationship, a focus on continuity is about ensuring that the

desired changes and new patterns are sufficiently established, and that the client has awareness and skills to address relapses and setbacks. In essence, the achievement of a goal is just a marker along the way.

The focus on continuity may become more or less central in coaching, depending on the degree to which clients struggle with follow-through. Clients may enter coaching with a far-reaching agenda. A necessary engagement in innumerable tasks may be embedded in these agendas. Based on client skill sets and resources with which they begin their journeys, the process may be more or less prolonged. When clients struggle, coaches need to be proactive. They explore the sources of difficulty, examine other paths to the same objectives, uncover hidden resources and opportunities, and search for deeper meaning and motivation.

Some clients have clear, well-articulated goals at the outset of the relationship. Even so, they are likely to realize that strong, habitual patterns are resistant to change. Deconstructing these habits and the motives they serve is often an important element in coaching (Kegan & Lahey, 2009). Moreover, the more clients unpack habitual ways of being that interfere with their desired changes, the more likely they are to discover deeply transformative paths forward. Imagine once again in Naira's story of Life in the Pandemic how different her days might look and feel if she were to really take charge of crafting her best life.

Continuing: What's the Focus?

As clients' actions take hold, coaches direct attention to clients' continuity of engagement through the following actions:

- Helping clients articulate in concrete ways the ongoing standards for actions
- Identifying with clients what they have to do to achieve their standards today, tomorrow, and next month
- Generating ways for clients to monitor their actions and hold themselves accountable
- Emphasizing discussions around adjustments and contingency plans
- Enabling clients' designs of reliable ways to get back on track should lapses occur
- Developing clients' self-efficacy related to relapse prevention

Coaches focus on how clients are engaging in demonstrable actions and continuing toward their goals over time. Clients plan action, commit, and then engage in various processes between meetings with their coach. At some point in most sessions, a review of progress is likely to take place. When a client's actions are inconsistent or chronically absent, the coach may question whether coaching is a viable approach for this client. More fundamental matters may need to be addressed before the client can wholeheartedly pursue significant change efforts. Put differently, coaching does not intentionally work on core personality change processes. Though personal transformations often emerge through coaching, these changes are not typical coaching objectives. They are more common in the practices of counseling and psychotherapy. Referring clients to other helping professionals does not imply failure or that clients don't want to change. There are building blocks to change processes, and sometimes the deep structures of how clients show up in their worlds need to be more firmly established.

At some point, coaching relationships end, and if the work has taken root, clients will continue on their path with skills to address predictable and unpredictable experiences that may derail them on their journeys. Over time, whatever it is they are pursuing or have achieved may need adjustment—or perhaps a new intention signaling a new journey will arise. The waters spill over in a new direction.

Principles for Applying the Flow Model

Clients begin coaching with intentions to change aspects of their lives. We already considered the idea that clients are unlikely to be capable of fully articulating their goals at the outset of coaching. Also, the overarching objective that clients eventually identify usually breaks down into lots of interrelated subgoals (see chapter 3). A client may want to be an effective leader, which may involve shifting how she interacts with others, how she manages her boundaries, how well she copes with stress, how decisive she is, and so on. Another client may want to stand strong in the midst of conflict, which may require him to know his values, regulate his emotionality, cultivate a more open mindset, and so much more.

The flow model identifies major tasks in a coaching relationship as it evolves over time. Each area of focus helps to gather a set of understandings about clients: What are the insights that arise? What relevant patterns are evident? How available are

resources? How do they move through the process of planning? How easily do they commit? What do they need to continue? Think of each of these as areas of appreciation and knowledge that you are developing over time in order to efficiently work with your clients toward their dreams and visions.

This model represents a mindset that coaches need to have about areas of continuing focus from session to session. An important message within the flow model speaks to the legitimacy of knowing about aspects of clients' past experiences in order to empower them to move into their desired futures. The emphasis on patterns in the flow model highlights an obvious fact that clients enter coaching with ingrained ways of being that may either contribute to or detract from their success. Sometimes coaching work involves actions to deconstruct and reconstruct these patterns or habits, so they better serve clients' emerging needs. Once patterns are appreciated, coaches move forward rather than remain in historical excavations. Referencing the metaphor, flowing streams and rivers move relentlessly forward.

THE 6 *WHATS* MODEL

The flow model applies to the entire coaching relationship and allows you to see how core elements in coaching play into a continuing process. Now I would like to offer a model that frames a single coaching session. The *6 whats model* (Gavin & Mcbrearty, 2018) describes the shifting focus of a coach from beginning to end of each session (see figure 5.2). While each session focuses on a specific purpose, a particular subgoal, or a different exploration, discussions in the coaching relationship are typically aligned with the overarching **coaching objective**. It is only by being mindful of the more encompassing objective of a coaching relationship that coaches can detect the connective tissue that unites these conversations over a series of sessions.

The 6 *whats* model relies on the eight core coaching competencies proposed by the International Coaching Federation (ICF, 2020c); these will be detailed in upcoming chapters. In this reliance, the model captures best practices for professional coaching as proposed by the ICF. Each *what* in the model represents an area of focus in a coaching session. They are sequenced according to where they are likely to occur as a session advances. Though it's possible to arrive at the final *what*, namely, *what's the learning?*, without covering all the prior *whats*, results are likely to be less robust when any area of focus is overlooked.

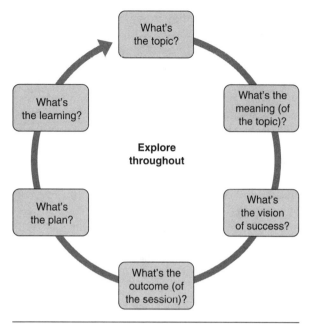

Figure 5.2 *6 whats* model.

This does not imply that the model is linear. There may be a lot of recursive, back-and-forth movement among the *whats*. As clients disclose new information and hear their own words, they may revise expressions made earlier in the session. Or the coach may hear something and wonder aloud whether what was just said shifts ever so slightly the meaning of something said before, such as the client's intent for the current session.

There is nothing mechanical about this model. It doesn't direct coaches to robotically ask a series of questions in order. Indeed, clients will often answer one of the *what* questions before being asked, or they may imply an answer in something they say when responding to another question. Coaches assimilate this information in a manner that allows them to determine whether each focus area of the 6 *whats* model has been adequately addressed irrespective of whether they asked directly.

Finally, the model does not imply a question-and-answer process wherein whatever the client says in response to a *what* question is accepted as sufficient. Coaches not only ask *what* questions, they also explore clients' replies. For each *what*, the coach may need to ask questions, reflect, offer impressions, or even provide feedback. Coach and client work jointly to discover what needs to be understood or determined so that meaningful plans can be generated to guide client actions between sessions.

The upcoming sections provide descriptions of each area of focus. You will hopefully see that each *what* represents an area of inquiry and exploration rather than a single question.

First *What*—What's the Topic?

Beyond the practical agendas incorporated in the initial session of a coaching relationship, the first order of business in any coaching session is for coaches to explore clients' intentions or focus for the session. Generally speaking, this is what is meant by the term *topic*. Coaching clients are encouraged to arrive at each session with a concern, interest, agenda, or topic they want to address. Usually, the focus that a client identifies for a session represents a facet of the coaching objective, which will have been articulated during early coaching sessions. Of course, the coaching objective will also be represented in what coach and client have indicated in their coaching agreement (see appendix B for a sample coaching agreement).

In any given session, clients may arrive with issues that appear unrelated to the coaching objective. The issue may arise from recent events that clients want to debrief, from an unexpected turn of events, or perhaps from a whimsical interest that seems worthy of discussion. Whenever this occurs, coaches need to allow clients sufficient space to express this seemingly unrelated topic. Through careful listening, coaches may come to appreciate how the new topic relates to the coaching objective. Equally, they may surmise that the client is moving in a new direction, distinctly different from that captured in the original coaching objective. Coaches remain mindful of the alignment of each session's coaching topic with the overarching coaching objective to ensure coherence within the coaching relationship. If each session has an ad hoc focus with little apparent connection to the original purpose, it will be hard to gauge benchmarks of progress or to assess the overall results.

Exploration pertaining to the first *what* includes a determination of whether the client's topic is one that can be appropriately or effectively addressed through coaching. In his book *The 7 Habits of Highly Effective People*, Stephen Covey (1989) wrote about things in our lives that are under our control as well as areas where our actions have little or no impact. He used the term *circle of concern* for the many things you care about and *circle of influence* for matters that you can influence. Your circle of concern would probably include a wide mixture of things you deem important, such as your health, family and friends, career, and finances, as well as perhaps larger concerns including global warming, politics, overpopulation, armed conflicts, or natural disasters. Something within your circle of concern may not be within your circle of influence. Covey believed that proactive people focus their energies on changing matters that reside within their circle of influence. This does not mean that because you are personally unable to end world hunger that you simply ignore the issue. To the contrary, if world hunger is within your circle of concern, you might focus on the role you can play to lessen human suffering. However, from a coaching perspective, topics that are outside clients' circles of influence may be more challenging to address and measure impact.

In a related sense, coaching topics that involve making other people change to accommodate the client's desires will probably need to be reframed so they represent changes in the client's own behaviors that potentially could affect others. For instance, a client might arrive with a topic related to a colleague's anger issues or her child's behaviors or a friend's neglect of her health. Valid coaching objectives and session topics pertain to matters within the client's control. Concerns about a colleague's anger can be reframed to focus on how the client can respond when anger occurs in her work environment. A client's desire for a child to get serious about his studies may be refocused to emphasize client strategies pertaining to her parenting style. Getting a friend to take better care of her health may be articulated as finding ways for the client to express concern for her friend irrespective of the outcome.

What kinds of questions do coaches ask to identify a session's topic? You might think it's as simple as, "What's the topic?" Fundamentally, it is; yet the fuller expression of this simple question might sound like this: "In our time together, what's important for you to explore so you can appreciate it better and hopefully come up with some meaningful steps that you will implement in the near future with a deep sense of commitment?" That's a lot more than, "What's the topic?" Clients learn what coaching is about over time so that shorter versions of this question may sound more like the following questions:

- What are you bringing for us to work on today?
- What's the topic you would like to move forward today?

- Would you tell me about the issue you want us to delve into today?
- How would you headline what you want to address today?
- What's your focus for our time together today?
- What are you invested in learning more about so we can craft action steps you might take?

Suggestions for Coaching the First *What*—What's the Topic?

Coaches need to continue exploring until the client has sufficiently clarified the topic to the degree that both coach and client can readily articulate what the focus for this session is. Here are a few helpful tips:

- Request that clients explain words or expressions that are ambiguous or that may have multiple interpretations.
- When clients present lengthy descriptions of what they want to work on in the session, request that they capture the essence of their topics in a short expression.
- Even when you think you have a good understanding of what a client wants to address, invite the client to succinctly restate the topic.
- Continue to explore ideas the client presents until there is an unequivocal phrasing of the topic. In brief, don't proceed in your work until you have clarified and confirmed the topic that the client wants to address.
- If clients repeatedly struggle to find a focus each session or if they continue to say they didn't come with a topic to address, remind them of the way coaching works and then ask what their intention is for your time together.
- If you sense a drift in the topic as the session progresses, invite the client to restate what the topic seems to be now based on their recent remarks.
- If you hear another topic emerging in the session, check it out! Offer to describe to the client what you are hearing and ask for their response to what you have offered.

Second *What*—What's the Meaning of the Topic?

Once clients identify their session topic, coaches will want to move toward the second *what:* What is so important or meaningful about this topic at this time? Exploration of the meaning and significance of the topic serves not only to increase awareness but may also surface additional sources of motivation. Coaches guide the conversation toward meaning so clients can access insights about the deeper importance and implications embedded in their topics. Clients may come to sessions with ideas that have to be unpacked before they can be fully appreciated and framed in ways that are actionable. Asking a man who is in the midst of a divorce and working 70 or more hours a week why finding balance (his topic) is important to him may seem redundant. Yet this kind of question is essential to revealing how the client perceives himself in the world, what his needs are, and what deeper purposes he wants to pursue in this coaching relationship.

Let me be clearer about the meaning of *meaning* in the second *what.* If a client says, "I want more balance and serenity in my life," you might want to know how this client interprets the words *balance* and *serenity.* Inquiring about the meaning of these words is critical in coaching, but it's not what's intended in the second *what.* A useful synonym is *importance*—as in "What's the importance of the topic?" When my colleague, Madeleine Mcbrearty, and I first created this model, we had a lengthy rationale for why the word *meaning* was at the heart of this question. One of the things guiding our choice was the belief that human beings are meaning-making creatures (Brown & Augusta-Scott, 2006; Frankl, 1969; Novak, 1993). As such, we tend to ask the big questions from time to time: What's life all about? What's the meaning of my existence? Why is this so deeply meaningful in my life? The bottom line is that when you are asking your clients about the meaning of their words, you are trying to understand your client's language better. My interpretation of serenity may be different from yours, for instance. When you ask about meaning in the framework of the second *what,* you are taking a deep dive into the core importance of this topic to your client. *You are going beyond linguistics into existential importance.* Of course, your client may not always be able or willing to go there, but it's key for you to know that this is the reason you are asking the question.

Goals are neither devised nor pursued in isolation. Issues rooted in the client's current topic are tied to other factors in this person's life. Exploration around the second *what* helps clients pinpoint the prominence of the topic in their lives and how addressing it will affect other dimensions of their worlds. When coaches inquire "What is it about this that so deeply matters to you?" clients may be challenged to consider the roots of their concern. A client who wants to become more assertive in social and work contexts may have to confront the implications of his more passive way of being on important elements of his life, including success, happiness, self-esteem, and more. Sometimes when coaches hear clients name session topics, it may be tempting to think, "Of course, I understand why he wants to change that!" Even if the coach is right, the value of having clients articulate their motivations is inestimable.

What kinds of questions might coaches ask to get at the meaning of the topic? You already know that

---

Suggestions for Coaching the Second *What*— What's the Meaning?

While clients' statements of their topics or session goals may seem to have transparent value, as a coach it is essential that you explore the meaning clients associate with their change objectives. Often, clients express the importance or meaning of their topics without being asked. In these instances, it's likely to be beneficial to request a deeper exploration of the stated meanings. Here are some guides to your exploration of the second *what:*

- When you haven't heard your client voicing why the topic is important, express your curiosity without offering your guesses. That is, ask your client to explicitly name the various motives or reasons why this topic came forth today.

- When the client clearly states (without you asking) why the topic is important, reflect the reasons back to the client asking for clarification where you think it might be important. Then ask if there are other reasons why it may be important.

- As the session progresses, be mindful of other reasons that seem to emerge and, in a timely manner, reflect them to the client as a way of building motivation for change.

this question seeks answers beyond clients' unique interpretations of the words they use, so clarifying questions might include the following:

- What is so deeply meaningful to you about this topic?
- In what ways is this issue important to you?
- What is motivating you to address this topic now?
- What led you to bring up this topic today (why now)?
- Of all that's going on for you, why did this topic show up as being so important today?
- What do you imagine effectively dealing with this topic might bring you?
- What personal values does this goal represent for you?

Third *What*—What's the Vision of Success?

Whatever the client brings to the session will be brightly illuminated when you inquire about the client's vision of success—that is, what life will be like once this topic has been fully addressed and realized. Exploring the third *what* guides attention toward the world clients want to create. Examining a positive future resulting from successfully mastering issues related to a topic often reveals actionable steps. When clients dive into visions of success, they often see the things they need to do to achieve their goals. Moreover, they more fully recognize the myriad of implications that changing one particular thing has for the rest of their experiences. There are systemic relationships between even minor changes in clients' lives and the larger whole of their lives. Not only does modifying one behavior affect other behavioral patterns, but it also can affect significant relationships, including those at home, work, play, and within the community.

The purpose of exploration in the third *what* is to elaborate a picture of what the client is yearning for. The vision statement acts as a beacon that guides goal pursuit and strengthens clients' determination. At this moment in the session, coaches encourage clients to describe a future vision that is both challenging and attainable. It works well when coaches help clients to "time travel" into the future and, from that imagined future, to describe the realities they hope to have created through their change processes. Future projections can be situated at more or less specific points in the future depending on what the goal is. It may be months or years, but regardless

---

Suggestions for Coaching the Third *What*—What's the Vision?

The more complete the vision of goal attainment, the more powerful its influence on the client's determination to succeed. Here are some guiding ideas related to this *what*:

- Ask clients to use the present tense when describing their future world. Reframe their descriptions from "I will be . . ." to "I am . . ."
- Encourage a dreamlike quality to this part of the session. Invite your clients to fast forward beyond all the steps they might need to take and to situate themselves solidly in a satisfying future world.
- When clients focus on reasons they can't do what they desire, encourage them to take a leap of faith and just imagine that somehow all of their problems and obstacles have magically disappeared. Treat it as an exercise in fantasy and imagination.
- When speaking from a future voice is too difficult for clients, work with them to articulate concrete benchmarks of what success would look like.

---

of where in time that future is projected, the more concrete and comprehensive the vision, the more motivating it will be for the client.

How might coaches stimulate the elaboration of a future vision? Coaches may need to structure these future explorations carefully and creatively, especially when clients experience difficulty imagining anything other than their present realities. Clients may feel they are in a deep hole in the ground and the coach is asking them to describe a panoramic vista that they can only see from a vantage point outside of their pit. Coaches need to be sensitive to the potential difficulty clients might have when they are invited into the future by questions such as these:

- How do you imagine you (or your life) will be when you have done all that is necessary to realize your goal?
- Would you paint me a picture of what success would look like X months from now when you have achieved your goal?
- What changes will you experience or bear witness to once you have achieved your goal?

- What will the changes you anticipate allow you to do differently?
- How will the changes you hope for affect your life?
- What effect will reaching your goal have on you personally? On your relationships? On your world?
- What are the benchmarks that will clearly tell you that you have succeeded?

Fourth *What*—What's the Desired Outcome of the Session?

Once the future vision has been thoroughly explored, the client will likely have generated an implicit road map requiring various actions. Imagine that this person's coaching objective centers around career change and, after a number of coaching conversations, she states her topic for the current session as a desire to become an independent consultant in her area of expertise. The client's vision of success two years hence may sound like this:

I am a full-time certified consultant. I work with companies as well as providing my services to individuals needing my expertise. It took me about a year after quitting my former job to match my previous income level, but in my second year, I've almost doubled that. For sure, I have a thriving practice. I work from a beautiful office space with all the resources I need to provide excellent services. My partner and other family members support my professional endeavors. I am exactly where I want to be, doing what I want to be doing. I even have that much-needed self-care time that I could never find in my old job. Even though my reputation keeps growing, I know the risks of taking on too much. I've learned how to say "no" when things aren't aligned with my vision and when I simply have too much on my plate!

What might be her starting point for reaching her ultimate goal? Given that most coaching sessions range around 60 minutes in length, what can realistically be accomplished in this current session to get the client on the road toward the goal? Does the client need to concentrate on getting certified, designing a marketing plan, finding a suitable space, having a conversation with her partner, or doing web searches to see how other consultants profile themselves? The list is long, but the client will point the arrow in some direction because she will likely realize this is a big project with innumerable interlocking steps. The essential focus in explorations concerning the fourth *what* is on what the client chooses to explore for the remainder of this session. What outcome does she want to leave with?

Implicit in the fourth *what* is the likelihood that whatever clients bring to sessions will entail extensive exploration. Yet, given the limited time in a session, only so much work can be done. I think of this as a request for the client to identify a bite-size piece of the bigger topic that stands a good chance of leading to an actionable agenda for the period between this session and the next. Occasionally, the topic framed in the first *what* may be concise enough so that all of it can be explored and brought to an actionable plan within a single session. This is infrequently the case and so the fourth *what* serves to bring sharp focus to the remainder of the session by identifying an aspect of the topic that can be adequately dealt with in the time remaining.

Hopefully, the conversation related to the fourth *what* will begin within the first half of the session, thereby allowing ample time to create an action plan. Working on this *what* opens the door to creating a concrete statement of the client's desired outcome for the session. The task in addressing this *what* also includes detailing markers or benchmarks for the session so both client and coach can know whether the desired outcome for the session has been achieved. Though the coach has a voice in this conversation, responsibility for identifying the session outcome rests squarely on the client's shoulders. When a client fully addresses the previous *whats* related to the topic, importance, and vision, the coach should have sufficient cues about what might need to be dealt with first and what could have the greatest immediate effect. Since coaching is a partnership, coaches can offer perspectives and thoughtfully challenge client proposals that seem too broad or unfocused for the time remaining in the session.

Let's go back to the example of the woman who wants to quit her job and become a full-time consultant. Imagine that her desired session outcome is to fully map out and schedule all the tasks she will need to complete over the next year to effectively make this transition. Based on experience, the coach may think this is too large of an agenda for the short time remaining in this session. Perhaps the coach has an idea that what's feasible in the time remaining is for the client to scope out what a map would need to contain and then to have her schedule times in her calendar over the next two weeks to fill in the map with target dates. If this were the case, the coach might offer her perspectives about what seems doable in this session. Though the targeted focus for the session is the client's choice, the coach needs to act responsibly—as a partner—in helping the client frame an achievable outcome

Suggestions for Coaching the Fourth *What*—
What's the Session Outcome?

In the first few sessions of a coaching relationship, clients are unlikely to have much of an idea about what they can accomplish in the allotted time. Understandably, they will want to have as many of their issues resolved as possible, which could result in unreasonably high expectations for the time available. It's a bit of a learning curve for the client. Here are some thoughts about navigating the fourth *what*:

- There are two fundamental parts to the fourth *what*: First, the identification of a clear objective for the remainder of the session that will lead to an action step, and, second, the articulation of benchmarks for the achievement of this objective. So, it's not only "What do you want to leave with?" but also, "What will you have concretely realized or experienced that will tell you that you have it?"

- Remember that the more thorough the work on the vision question, the more readily your client will be able to identify an exciting focus for action.

- Be mindful of abstract outcomes. A client wants to gain insight or understanding. Another client hopes to make a decision or reach some kind of resolution. Maybe a client wants to feel more at peace with an issue. These outcomes are not necessarily out of reach, but they might be either unrealistic in terms of their achievement within a session or require a process other than coaching for their attainment.

- Continue working on this *what* until you feel there is a high likelihood that your client has landed on an objective that can be realized in the time remaining.

- Check your assumptions, especially when what the client is targeting sounds like something familiar to you, for instance, "I want a plan," "I'd like to understand . . . ," or "I want a strategy . . ." Common vernacular phrases may slip right by your filters so you say to yourself, "Sure, I know what that is." Maybe you do, but maybe you don't. The bottom line is whatever a client states as the desired outcome needs to have the same shared meaning.

- Sometimes clients have difficulty identifying the *one thing* they want to start with. If discussions related to the fourth *what* consume more time than you thought, negotiate a shift in focus to how the client can continue exploring the necessary delineation of where to focus after the session ends. In other words, the action plan resulting from a session like this might be a structured plan for the client to continue identifying what is needed for progress.

for the remaining time. Keep in mind that most of the work in a coaching relationship takes place between sessions. In this light, session time is spent on identifying work to be completed in the period between now and the next meeting rather than on doing all that work in the session.

In addressing the fourth *what*, coaches need to be mindful of their assumptions. When a client says in response to the coach's question regarding a benchmark of success for the session itself, "I want to leave with a list," the coach might think she knows what a list is, yet she may need to ask, "What would a list look like?" A client may want to leave the session with more insight about why he or she behaves in a particular way; the coach needs to inquire, "What does it mean to have insight about this?" and "How will you know you have gained insight?" No matter how obvious the statement of a desired session outcome appears to be, coaches

need to pursue a clear definition of the desired end articulated in the client's words, along with measurable markers of its achievement within the session.

What are some of the questions that coaches might ask to identify the specific outcome of a session? Here are some examples:

- Reflecting on what we've been talking about, what aspect of your goal do you think we can address in a way that will result in some concrete actions today?

- What specifically would you like to explore in the remainder of our time together?

- Of all that you have said, what do you want to walk out of this session with today?

- What would you like to leave with today that you can work on further in the time between now and when we next meet?

- What concretely will tell you that you've gotten what you need from this session to move forward?

- Project yourself to the end of our session today. You're ready to go and feeling happy with the session. What exactly are you leaving with?

- What's your benchmark for success in this session?

Fifth *What*—What's the Action Plan?

Hopefully by this point in a coaching session, clients have expressed where they are in relation to their goal compared to where they want to be. Without a baseline, it's impossible to know where to start codesigning action. Among other things, exploration related to the fifth *what* is intended to further promote clients' awareness about themselves. At some point in the current session or perhaps based on prior conversations, coaches will have developed knowledge about their clients pertinent to action

planning; this knowledge might include an appreciation of clients'

- strengths and challenges,
- beliefs about what they are able to accomplish in relation to their topic (self-efficacy),
- patterns that show up when they are engaged in goal pursuit,
- current capacities that would promote sustained engagement, and
- resources available and roadblocks that might be encountered.

Inquiry pertaining to all these elements is essential to complete the tasks of the fifth *what*. Coach and client partner to transform understandings and insights that have emerged in their discussions into actionable steps. Their work in this moment is to identify and design action plans, determine commitment, and cocreate ways in which clients will hold themselves accountable for the actions to which they commit.

What are some of the questions that coaches may ask clients to promote robust action planning, a

---

Suggestions for Coaching the Fifth *What*—What's the Plan?

There is a unique sweet spot for action plans that work best for each of your clients. There is a level of challenge that's not too much and not too little. As coaches explore action plans, they are fully mindful of the need to encourage client self-determination in decision making about plans. They also listen for limiting beliefs that may weaken the client's sense of self-efficacy. Clients cannot achieve desired results without confidence that they are capable of engaging in goal pursuit. Here are some suggestions for effectively addressing the fifth *what* in a coaching conversation:

- Partner with clients regarding how they want to approach the planning process.
- When clients seem stuck, suggest methods like brainstorming to access creative thinking.
- Continue exploring options for action until clients resonate with the ideas they have put forth.
- Sense where clients' energy is and what might be the most beneficial step at this time.
- Remember that the first idea put forth is not necessarily the best. Explore until there is a sense of *yes* that resonates.
- Hold in mind the structure of SMART goals so that you can inquire about elements of the plan that are not explicitly identified.
- With all the necessary details described, invite clients into a conversation about resources and potential obstacles.
- Be sure to discuss clients' sense of commitment to action—even when you think it's solid!
- Remember that clients themselves are accountable for their commitments. You are not a monitor or overseer of their actions.
- Help clients establish clear strategies for evaluating their progress and ways of assessing whether they are on track.

sense of autonomy and strong commitment? Some examples of questions include the following:

- How can we work together to create options for the outcome you have identified for this session?
- What ideas come to mind when you think about the (session) outcome that you have just described?
- How can we plan together for the (session) outcome you have identified?
- What have you done in the past or more recently related to this?
- What might be some aspects of the plan that you are contemplating now (what, when, how, etc.)?
- How do you envision that particular plan taking form in your life over the next few weeks?
- Projecting yourself forward over the next couple weeks where you fully comply with your plan, what would you be saying to me when we next meet about what happened?
- What would help you carry out your plans? What could stand in your way?
- What resources would be important to consider? What resources are you aware of now?
- Who else might be involved in this plan? Who can help or support you?
- How would you describe your level of commitment to this plan?
- How might you hold yourself accountable for doing what you plan to do?
- What measures might help you know that you are being accountable to yourself for the plan you've described?

Sixth *What*—What Learning Comes from the Session?

What helps sustain progress for clients is the learning they gain from the work they do within and outside sessions. Individuals may normally continue doing things that bring them little satisfaction because they feel obliged, they are unaware of options, they don't believe they are free to choose, or they fear the unknown. When clients take steps forward in a coaching relationship, they are likely to learn a lot about themselves—their patterns, their beliefs, their dreams, and so much more. In the course of each session, clients may have "light-bulb" moments where they see something perhaps for the first time.

Awareness can be generated when clients gain deeper understanding of what is so meaningful to them, when they are able to recognize their ingrained patterns of thinking and behaving, or when they address their underlying emotions (hope, excitement, joy) that promote goal attainment. Coaching might enhance clients' awareness of limiting beliefs that impede forward movement, personal strengths, and available resources to support success, or unique new ways to achieve desired results. Coaches partner with clients in developing insight through in-depth exploration during sessions as well as through the plans clients implement between sessions.

To help anchor insights and new learning and to make them more available to clients in future situations, coaches invite clients to voice what they have learned in each session—that is, the awareness and understanding they have gained about themselves and their topic. You may want to note here that learning can roughly be sorted into two categories: Insights and learning pertaining to who the client is and those related to what content or agenda the client has been addressing in the session. Coaches facilitate the expression of learning by inquiring about clients' takeaways from sessions. Also, in the spirit of true partnership, coaches may share some of their observations or inklings about clients' learning, along with any personal lightbulb moments they have experienced.

Unlike action planning, which normally arises in the second half of the session, learning moments may permeate a coaching session. Whenever clients offer evidence of insight or learning, coaches mark these moments either through reflecting to the client the learning expressed or inviting the client to explore them a bit further. As the session draws to a close, elevating learning and insights to conscious awareness and integration is supported by requesting that clients reflect on the session from the perspective of what they have learned.

What questions might coaches ask that can illuminate learning achieved in the session? These inquiries might include the following:

- From all we have discussed today, what might be some things that you learned about yourself today? About your topic?
- What if any new perspectives have emerged today about yourself? About your topic?
- What are some things that you learned today that you might be able to relate to other aspects of your life?

Suggestions for Coaching the Sixth *What*—What Learning Occurs?

There's a difference between what clients learn about goal setting and action planning and the deeper, more personal awareness that arises through an in-depth coaching session. When coaches ask certain questions, clients may reply, "That's a good question," as they pause to reflect on something they hadn't previously considered. This is the kind of material you want to highlight throughout the session so clients can appreciate the profound nature of the discussions taking place and then put this new learning into action. If clients are simply engaging in actions without extracting the broader implications for their lives, they will not benefit as much from the coaching experience. Unlike in the early years of the coaching profession when "action, action, action" was the hallmark of the field, in its maturity, coaching has fully embraced learning and growth as the purposes of the coaching relationship. Here are some ideas for navigating the sixth *what* of a coaching session:

- Invite clients to connect the dots, to make sense of what they have expressed in the session.
- Allow ample time for the sixth *what*. It should not be an afterthought, but rather a *bona fide* and dedicated period of the coaching session.
- Ask a question about learning, which may lead the client to reiterate his or her action plan. Be sure to inquire about the *who* and the *what*—personal learnings as well as situationally relevant insights.
- Remind clients of any aha moments that you witnessed in the session.
- If time permits, ask questions about the *so whats* of your clients' learning—what can they do with the insights they derived?
- When clients are highly focused on their action plans, insights may take a back seat—trust that they will come in time.

- How might you apply the learning and insights from today to this and other situations?
- Stepping back from the work we've just done, what broader messages can you extract from our time together?
- In a sentence, what's your biggest aha about yourself from this session?

Principles of Application for the 6 *Whats* Model

The 6 *whats* model will be an invaluable aid to your practice. It offers a map of a session's structure and can guide your explorations from goal identification toward learning and action planning. What I am about to say may seem obvious: You know this model, but your clients don't. Over time, as you repeatedly guide them through this process, they will learn it. However, at the outset they may think that coaching is just about them talking or answering your questions. They don't have a script for the session.

Can you share the model with your clients? Frankly, that can work. There is nothing to prevent you from showing them a graphic of the process and letting them know that this structure will help

guide your conversation. Since coaching is a partnership, it may empower clients to feel a sense of responsibility for moving the process along its path toward fruitful outcomes.

There are a couple of things to be mindful of when using the 6 *whats* model: The first is an awareness of the client's agenda, and the second is the realization that sessions don't always move in a linear fashion from one *what* to the next.

When clients begin their sessions, they hopefully will have a topic in mind. Even so, they may have competing intentions for their time with you. Something big may have just occurred and they may need support through an active listening process. If you attempt to push them through the 6 *whats* model, you may notice they are lagging behind. Rather than force fit a process on the session, you might inquire about what they most need for this session. Should clients tell you they just need you to listen, you would be wise to recontract with them in the moment for the outcome of the session. You might say something like, "Okay, I hear you; you need to talk and for me just to listen. Am I correct then that our goal for this session is primarily for me to be a sounding board for you, and for you not to pursue the development of some action from the session?" By saying this, you appropriately place responsibility for the session outcome on the client's shoulders.

Should this become a pattern in a particular coaching relationship, you may need to restate what coaching is and possibly suggest another avenue for the client's needs other than coaching.

The second consideration speaks to the fact that the 6 *whats* model is a guide, not a rigid structure. It isn't a set of steps you always follow in lockstep fashion. Sometimes you will find that you can't quite work your way through all six *whats* in a session. The client may become fascinated with exploring what a desirable future might look like. Or as a client begins to talk about what she thinks the topic is, another more salient topic emerges. Here, you have to rapidly switch tracks and move toward considering the emerging new topic. Obviously, in either of these scenarios, you would not want to impose the six *whats* structure. Throughout the remainder of this book, you will learn how to address variations in the way coaching sessions might unfold. The principle point here is that as invaluable as this model is, it must be applied with sensitivity and flexibility according to what the client needs most and what you can appropriately offer in your role as coach.

REFLECTIONS

Coaching conversations address significant matters in clients' lives; they are rarely focused on trivial concerns. Clients want something badly enough to go through the effort of finding a coach, telling their story, and challenging old habits and beliefs. You want to honor your clients' courage throughout their journeys in a coaching relationship.

Sometimes people live in a world of wishful thinking. Their hopes and aspirations come and go without evidence of realization. We know of the inestimable capacity of human beings to make dreams come true, and we also know that the dreams-into-reality process is rarely fed by idle thought alone. Actions are needed. But what actions are best?

At the beginning of the relationship, clients often express energy and enthusiasm. They have taken the first step, or at least an important new step. Coaches need time to understand their clients, what their intentions are, how their lives are configured, what resources they have, and how actions need to be sequenced to best facilitate the realization of their wishes in a fashion that endures over time. Gaining insight, understanding patterns, and identifying resources provide the basis for action planning. Without them, there are limits to the energy and resources clients can bring forth, how long they can endure, and how many setbacks they can sustain before they stop, turn back, or sit down in bewilderment.

The flow model of coaching provides both a useful metaphor and practical guidance for working with clients as they apply intelligent action to the pursuit of their dreams. While the flow model provides overall guidance for your work throughout the course of the relationship, you also need a structure that can help you navigate each individual coaching session. Without such a structure, clients may wander through thought processes or stories in a conversational manner, believing that this is what coaching is about. As a result, sessions may be rudderless, drifting from story to story without a sense of purpose or connection. The 6 *whats* model is inherently collaborative in nature, facilitating a partnered experience that empowers clients to chart their own course toward the goals they identify. The coach sensitively guides the process; the client generates the material for discussion.

PART III

THE COACH'S SKILL SET

CHAPTER 6

THE ETHICAL COACH

*The first step in the evolution of ethics is a sense
of solidarity with other human beings.*

Albert Schweitzer

MY STORY

Here's a story you may think is strange. Earlier in my professional training as a psychologist, I was undergoing a process known as psychoanalysis. It's based on Freudian psychology. One day, during the period when I was participating in that world of lying on a couch multiple times a week and talking to someone sitting behind me in a comfortable chair, I happened to attend a dance performance at a center for the performing arts near where I lived. I saw my psychoanalyst, and he saw me, but we didn't say hello. A few days after this when I showed up for my next appointment, he informed me that he had given up his season tickets to the dance series to reduce the possibility of seeing me in this venue (he knew I liked dance). I was astounded. He said it was part of the professional distance required in psychoanalysis.

Social contact outside of scheduled meetings takes on varying levels of significance in different professions. Coaches don't have the kinds of professional boundaries that psychoanalysts do, yet they are expected to be mindful of the implications of any contact or relationship they have with clients outside of their sessions. That, of course, is just one of many aspects of a coach's ethical stance.

Here's another not-so-unusual part of my history as a helper. When you help people, they often tell their friends how good you are. Not surprisingly, I have found myself coaching people who represent maybe only one or two degrees of separation from each other: relatives, best friends, and work associates. Sometimes, clients referred by those I have previously helped talk about the referring client almost as a mutual friend about whom we share knowledge of various kinds. I navigate these moments mostly in silence or sometimes with a gentle reminder that all my conversations are entirely confidential. This is not always easy, but it is necessary.

The more experience I have gained over the decades as a coach, the more I have come to appreciate the subtle ways in which ethical issues arise in my practice. Yes, there are right-and-wrong matters—like not developing intimate friendships with clients while you are working in a professional relationship—but most of the things I puzzle about are the gray zone questions, like when to end a relationship that doesn't seem to be producing much movement or what to do when a client offers me a small gift.

et's discuss first things first, and in that perspective, our review of competencies begins with an exploration of ethical behavior in coaching. What does it mean to be an ethical coach? It isn't about following a bunch of rules; rather it reflects a way of seeing, feeling, thinking, behaving, and comprehending the world. An ethical coach deeply and explicitly honors all individuals in their uniqueness. In capturing ethics in coaching, other core constructs are necessarily implied; these include values, virtues, and morals. Since there are innumerable ethical codes situated in different helping professions, we will look at some of the fundamental principles tying all of them together. This review will paradoxically offer you both the clarity and ambiguity represented in professional ethical codes. Here are some guiding questions as you read:

- How do constructs such as ethics, morals, values, and virtues relate to one another?

- Is there anything like a universal code of ethics, or are ethics more specific to cultures and communities?

- Are ethical principles absolute, or are they open to interpretation?

- Does my unique character or personality play a role in my morals and values?

- Are coaching ethics similar to other codes of professional conduct?

- When do ethics interface with legal issues?

ROOTS OF ETHICAL CONCERNS

Let me begin with a wonderful parable about a monk traveling back to his monastery. As the monk crossed an open field, a fierce samurai warrior suddenly confronted him. The samurai blocked the monk's path with his hand menacingly poised above the hilt of his sword. In a threatening voice, he asked the monk three questions in staccato fashion: "Who are you? Where are you going? Why are you going there?" At first speechless by this unexpected turn of events, the monk regained his composure and responded with a question of his own: "How much does your shogun pay you to stand on guard here and ask these questions of all travelers?" The samurai, slightly taken aback by the question, replied, "A bag of rice each month." The monk smiled and said to the samurai, "I will

pay you two bags of rice a month if you will ask me these same three questions every day."

The relevance of these three questions is reflected in the literature of other helping professions such as counseling and psychotherapy (Kottler, 2008). In coaching, clients are likely to explore their answers to these three questions—*Who are you? Where are you going?* and *Why are you going there?*—over and over again with the help of their coaches. What the parable of the monk and samurai brilliantly illuminates is the interrelationship of goals, motivations, and personal identity. Though coaching is ultimately a goal-driven, action-oriented methodology, effective coaches continually strive to appreciate who their clients are in the context of their yearnings and dreams.

When contrasted with some other forms of helping, such as counseling and psychotherapy, coaching clients typically begin the relationship with identifiable goals. In this respect, they are likely to have at least a preliminary answer to the question, *Where are you going?* However, a requisite understanding of self and the underlying motivations for client goals may require sensitive inquiry by coaches. Coaching does not rely on a generic or formulaic method of analysis but rather on a deep appreciation of who the client is, what boundaries there might be to inquiry, and whether the coach is competent to help a client with the particular agenda being presented.

When individuals find themselves amidst the multiple challenges of living and growing, the list of potential helpers can be perplexingly long: psychoanalyst, psychotherapist, counselor, social worker, mentor, member of the clergy, consultant, naturopath, psychic healer, coach, personal trainer, and so on. By analogy, if your car breaks down, you know immediately that you need to find an auto mechanic. In coaching, the responsibility for determining whether the person seeking help is in the right place rests squarely on the coach's shoulders. This brings ethics down to some very practical questions; for instance, how do coaches know they are able to address clients' issues competently and efficiently?

When you imagine a professional code of conduct, you may picture a list of dos and don'ts. This would imply an unequivocal right-and-wrong perspective. As previously noted, there are things that are clearly right and wrong, but ethical codes are more often framed as broad guidelines for responsible professional engagement. Coaches need to understand the nature of their role—what they can do, what they cannot do, and what their process of working with clients looks like. Moreover, they must be able to articulate these ideas so that clients' potential misunderstandings are minimized to the greatest degree possible at the outset.

DISTINGUISHING VALUES, VIRTUES, MORALS, AND ETHICS

You probably have your own idea of what ethics means, and you are likely to realize that other concepts can seem very close in meaning to ethics. Three such concepts are values, virtues, and morals. Only a fine line differentiates these terms, yet these distinctions may at times have perplexing or even contradictory implications. **Values** are individually held ideals that provide direction for everyday life (Maio, 2017), whereas **virtues** are character strengths that act as the basis on which individuals make ethical decisions (Vainio, 2016). **Morality** implies perspectives of right and wrong wherein actions are evaluated on the basis of broader cultural contexts or religious standards (Gert & Gert, 2017). Finally, **ethics** pertain to beliefs about what constitutes right or wrong conduct. More specifically, ethics represent moral principles adopted by an individual or a group to inform rules for behavior. Often, ethics are presented in codes outlining accepted standards of practice for a profession (Corey et al., 2014). The upcoming material is intended to strengthen your understanding of what it means to respect ethical standards of conduct as a coach.

Values

Values are core personal principles that are not necessarily about right or wrong. Viktor Frankl (1969), a prominent psychiatrist who wrote about his experiences as a prisoner in a Nazi concentration camp, argued that human behavior constantly raises issues of values. One definition offered by Williams (1979) suggests that values serve as "criteria for selection in action . . . criteria for judgment, preference and choice" (p. 16). Life is about choice. As you express your choices, your values become evident.

Personal and social factors shape your values (Maio, 2017). Among these factors are your genetics, upbringing, and age. Socially, your culture, religious beliefs, education, and peers have a marked effect on the values you develop (Bano et al., 2016; Maio,

2017). You can add to these factors the effects of traumas, such as accidents, wars, and personal violations. Of course, let's not minimize the influence of the media.

You might on occasion hear a remark such as "Wow, I like her values!" The framing of this comment suggests that values imply judgment (Kirschenbaum, 2013, p. 177). The remark could be heard as "this person has good values," which makes room for the possibility that someone could have bad values. But good or bad according to whom? If individuals place a high value on wealth, they may direct great effort toward earning money, and this value may serve to justify any means for obtaining it. Judgment of good or bad isn't inherent in the valuing of wealth—it's a matter of perspective.

People's alignment of their actions with their values is closely correlated with their levels of happiness (Hefferon & Boniwell, 2011; Kavedzija & Walker, 2017). Part of a coach's work is to help clients clarify their values so they can align their actions accordingly. Of course, when you ask people what they value, they may recite such things as freedom, safety, happiness, achievement, respect, equality, or world peace, among others (Schwartz, 2012). Yet, the best indicators of a person's values are likely to be the things the person chooses, the ways the person acts, and their behavior toward others.

Interestingly, client values may present serious challenges for helping professionals (Ivey et al., 2018). What if clients pursue goals that ignore the values of significant others at home or at work? What if they want to achieve objectives through methods you don't value? What if they want your help to do something that you personally think is wrong?

Values have implications for ethical behavior, but they are not exactly the same thing as ethics. You can have substantially different values than your clients' values and yet work with them toward goal attainment in an entirely ethical manner. For instance, suppose a client wants to be in the top one percent of wage earners in the country, but you personally are content with a more modest income. Sometimes, differences in values between coach and client will affect the harmony of the working relationship. A client may show total disregard for the environment while his coach is fully invested in preserving the earth's ecosystems. In such cases, the coach might refer the client to another coach whose values may be more aligned.

Nothing guarantees that clients will be perceptive enough to fully comprehend the coach's values early in their relationship, though they are within their rights to inquire about the coach's values (Silsbee, 2010). In this light, coaches need to remain alert to value differences that may negatively affect the effectiveness of the coaching relationship.

A question that arises here is, can a coach be value free? The simple answer is no! In fact, I don't think you or I ever engage with others without expressing our values. Similarly, it's improbable that you can be totally without judgments of another person. It's what you do with your value-laden judgments that matters. The critical point here is that you need to become aware of your values and how they may motivate your actions as a coach. If you're not aware of your values, you may be blind to how they influence the questions you ask, the assumptions you make, and the choices you promote. Awareness of values also raises the question of whether and how you might reveal your values to your clients. Answering this question moves us closer to ethics, especially if you consider attempts to influence clients toward your own value system (Ivey et al., 2018).

Being effective as a coach means cultivating awareness of beliefs, thoughts, judgments, habits, and blind spots that are detrimental to effective human relationships. Knowing your values doesn't mean that you are able to impose them on your clients (Ivey et al., 2018; Silsbee, 2010). Ideally, your value-guided actions as a coach will reflect growth-promoting values. For instance, a coach who manages her stress, nurtures her physical and emotional well-being, and communicates in an open and collaborative manner will serve as a supportive role model for clients working on personal and professional development issues.

You might also be interested to know that your values are related to your personality. The link can be framed as follows: Personality influences behavior and behavior shapes values (Bano et al., 2016). Together, personality and values influence your outlook on life, the way you interact with others, and how you approach the tasks of coaching (see Five-Factor Model of Personality sidebar).

A particularly important consideration in coaching pertains to the client's preferences for extroversion and introversion. Based on the work of Carl Jung (1971), Isabel Briggs Myers and her mother, Katharine Cook Briggs, developed the Myers-Briggs Type Indicator (Briggs Myers et al., 2009; Quenck, 2009). A premise of this type indicator is that extroversion and introversion identify the direction of people's attention—how they process information. Extroverted types relate to the outer world of people and things, whereas introverted types relate more to the inner world of ideas and impressions (Briggs Myers et al., 2009). Clients who evidence a preference for extroversion might speak enthusiastically and quickly about their agendas as a way of thinking about their topic. A coach who prefers introversion might find it challenging to interrupt a highly extroverted client from wandering into more and more unrelated topics. Conversely, clients who demonstrate a preference for introversion might at times appear unresponsive to a coach's questions since they need time to process all the information internally. In this situation, if the coach prefers extroversion, he may be inclined to continue asking and talking, even though he will likely serve this client better by leaving time for the client to process in silence rather than continuing to ask questions.

Values and personality preferences are like a pair of glasses through which you see the world. Self-reflective practitioners (Mezirow, 1994, 2000; Schön, 2003) devote time and effort to understanding their values as well as any personality traits that may affect their work with others. This requires a kind of dedication to increasing their self-awareness (Silsbee, 2010). Reflective professionals cultivate a keen sense of who they are, what makes them tick, and why they do what they do in the world.

Virtues

Aristotle wrote that virtue is learned through habit and practice and that moral behavior is what a virtuous person does by choice (Bartlett & Collins, 2011). For someone to consistently exhibit ethical behavior requires strength of character or moral excellence in order to remain true to self when faced with challenging situations. Typically, virtue and morality are intricately linked to such a degree that the words virtue and character strengths are often used interchangeably (Seligman, 2002, 2012).

A research team of positive psychologists (Seligman, 2002) surveyed philosophical and religious writings generated throughout history. This team identified six virtues, which they believed were endorsed universally. According to them, the virtues that "capture the notion of good character" (p. 133) are (1) wisdom and knowledge, (2) courage, (3) love and humanity, (4) justice, (5) temperance, and (6) spirituality and transcendence (p. 132). Further work on these six universal values by Peterson and Seligman (2004) subdivided them into 24 character strengths that can be cultivated and maximized throughout life. According to these authors, you and I are likely to possess "three to seven 'signa-

Five-Factor Model of Personality

There are lots of theories of personality, but one that has a lot of traction in psychological and educational research is known as the five-factor model of personality. This model is presented so that you can reflect on how individuals' values might relate to their scores on these five traits.

The five factors, often identified by the acronym OCEAN, are (1) **o**penness versus closedness to experiences, (2) **c**onscientiousness (high versus low), (3) **e**xtroversion versus introversion, (4) **a**greeableness versus antagonism, and (5) **n**euroticism versus emotional stability.

The five-factor model of personality conceives of each personality trait as spanning a continuum from one end of a spectrum to the opposite end. Just as attention to a client's learning style (discussed in chapter 2) helps coaches adjust to the uniqueness of each client, awareness of personality orientations can be invaluable in your ability to communicate with your clients.

Here's a little more detail on OCEAN to enrich your understanding:

1. *Openness versus closedness.* This factor refers to interest in culture and openness to new ideas and novel experiences. At the open end, scores imply high degrees of creativity, curiosity, and the pursuit of new experiences, whereas scores toward the closed end suggest that one is more traditional, practical, and reluctant to try new things.

2. *High conscientiousness versus low conscientiousness.* This factor refers to how people engage in goal pursuit. High scores reflect strict self-discipline, organization, and extreme goal orientation, whereas low scores point to patterns of being more laid back, disorganized, and indifferent to achievement.

3. *Extroversion versus introversion.* This factor refers to preferences for how one engages in social situations. One end of the range, extroversion, identifies people who thrive on social interactions, whereas introversion characterizes people who are more reserved and deliberate in expression.

4. *Agreeableness versus antagonism.* This factor refers to the manner in which people interact with others. One end represents characteristics of being good-natured, forgiving, and trusting, whereas the other end suggests a pattern of unfriendliness, skepticism. and a highly competitive style.

5. *Neuroticism versus emotional stability*. This factor refers to thought patterns and ways of experiencing emotions. One end suggests a pattern of nervousness and insecurity with a propensity to experience negative thoughts and emotions, and the other end reflects a manner of being calm, relaxed, and secure.

For further information, Widiger (2017) provides a review of the literature on the five factor model, while McCrae and Allik (2002) offer a cultural perspective.

---

ture' strengths of character that we own, celebrate and exercise frequently" (p. 18). An online survey is available to help you discover your signature strengths (viacharacter.org).

Character strengths are often correlated with resilience and overall life satisfaction (Martinez-Marti & Ruch, 2014, 2017). The good news is that one's character strengths can be developed through practice (Biswas-Diener, 2010). Since coaching is often understood as a strength-based approach, it is entirely fitting for coaches to direct energy toward helping clients identify and develop their character strengths in change processes.

Morals

Morality has been described as "principles of right and wrong actions and judgments" (Vozzola, 2014,

p. 3) with the sense that these principles are embedded in the moral norms of society. If you search for a deeper understanding of morality, theories of moral development represent an important source of insight. One example is Lawrence Kohlberg's (1981) moral stage theory, which describes a fixed sequence of moral reasoning. Kohlberg believed that moral judgment evolves from strict adherence to rules, authority, and conventions toward universal ideals of fairness, equality, and reciprocity (Lapsley, 2006). In the early years of life, the *preconventional level* prevails. At this level, morality is largely influenced externally, for example, by authority figures, including parents and teachers. In adolescence and adult years, a *conventional level* emerges. At this level, one adheres to a somewhat rigid and societally determined identification of right and wrong. Adherence to this form of morality ensures positive relationships and a degree of societal harmony. Finally, in the most evolved stage, the *postconventional level*, one's own sense of principles takes precedence over static societal morality. Different perspectives are appreciated, and morals can be more fluid and contingent on unique circumstances.

Carol Gilligan (1982), a student of Kohlberg, believed that many of her mentor's methods and conclusions were male centric. Kohlberg had built his theory from research with boys and men, and he thought that women seemed to have an inferior stage of moral development. Gilligan's work tapped into girls' and women's experience and, as a result, strongly questioned the universality and invariability of Kohlberg's hierarchical stage theory. She believed that the essence of morality is based in human relationships and in what she termed the "ethics of care" (Gilligan & Richards, 2008). Her theory promoted women's equality in the sphere of moral reasoning. Noddings (1984), another pivotal figure in the realm of feminist ethics, viewed the ethics of care as an innate human condition. In the framework of care ethics, a person's morality is expressed through a focus on care—care of self and care for others (Noddings, 1984, p. 99). It's important to know that Gilligan's perspective doesn't negate the idea that moral capacity is developed through social experiences (Docety & Howard, 2014).

Just as you can acknowledge various factors that contributed to your values, so too you can appreciate all the experiences that shaped your moral reasoning, not the least of which is your culture (Hofstede, 2001). Moral codes underlie the values you see expressed in different communities and cultures. Even so, moral principles remain reasonably constant across various helping professions. At root, they speak to the need to do what is right, anticipate and prevent potentially harmful actions, be honest, be fair, respect clients, and actively prepare them for independent action.

When it comes to appropriate behavior in your work as a coach, the necessity of remaining alert to all aspects of diversity is paramount (Passmore, 2013). Language that is appropriate to millennials or Gen Zers might be unsuitable for older adults; forms of greeting acceptable in North America might be construed as disrespectful to someone from another culture. Even the use of the pronouns *she* or *he* may upset individuals who identify their gender as nonbinary. While it is important to recognize the manner in which your preconceived ideas, assumptions, and judgments influence your behavior toward others, you don't want to be constantly walking on eggshells or second guessing your every move so as not to offend clients. Rather than regarding

differences as "barriers, threats or irrelevancies" (Rosinski & Abbott, 2016, p. 209), you want to learn about your clients' preferences. Express curiosity and be open to how they want to be treated; invite them to let you know when your speech and action might feel insensitive.

Ethics

There are many helping professions and innumerable forms of one-to-one professional relationships. Commonalities in these professions are likely to include deep compassion for others and profound desire to be supportive. In this light, wouldn't it seem that ethical behavior would come naturally? Helpers want to be helpful. Yet wanting to help isn't enough. Being a good and moral person isn't enough. Having fabulous communication skills isn't enough. Even when you put all these things together, there is much to learn to ensure that good intentions are fully respectful of the character and perspectives of each unique individual we encounter.

Merriam-Webster defines ethics as a theory or system of moral values and as the principles of conduct governing an individual or a group. Whereas morality pertains to how you should or should not treat others (Appiah, 2008), ethics refers to a set of moral principles that affects the way you make decisions and lead your life (Passmore, 2011; Passmore et al., 2019). Indeed, ethics is inseparable from issues of morality (De Jong, 2016). In the helping fields, professional ethics focus on your conduct and moral decisions in the context of your work relationships and transactions.

Nagy (2011) identifies a number of principles for professional behavior that commonly appear in the ethical codes of most North American professional societies (e.g., coaching, psychology, law, medicine). These principles include beneficence and nonmaleficence, fidelity to professional responsibility, justice, and respect for people's rights and dignity or autonomy. Let's consider these in light of the work that coaches do.

Beneficence and Nonmaleficence

Beneficence, or doing good, refers to promoting the welfare of clients. **Nonmaleficence**, or doing no harm, means actively avoiding identifiable risks or damaging actions. Though coaches intend to help their clients within the context of an egalitarian professional relationship, it may become evident that they either cannot help a particular person or the actions a client is contemplating will not enable him or her to reach a goal. Additionally, clients may not be aware of the potential effects of certain actions and may not realize what embedded emotional triggers might surface in discussions of goals and objectives. Coaches can't foresee all possibilities, but they need to be mindful of risks and potential negative consequences. Beneficence and nonmaleficence require that coaches assess, to the best of their abilities, their competence to help clients. These principles press upon coaches a responsibility for ongoing monitoring of the benefits of the relationship.

Fidelity to Professional Responsibility

This principle is about making honest promises and honoring commitments. It speaks to truth in advertising and ensuring that clients know what to expect as they enter a coaching relationship. In particular, clients must be informed about fees, cancellation policies, and limitations to the relationship at the outset. Coaches need to be proactive in informing clients about dimensions of the coaching relationship where clients may not have full knowledge. In this regard, they should discuss the limits of confidentiality and spell out what coaching is and what it is not. For instance, coaching is not therapy, and clients—not their coaches—are responsible for the results they achieve.

Fidelity also means ensuring that your qualifications and areas of competence are marketed accurately. It asserts that coaches will have received the credentials they advertise and are trained to do what they do in sessions. Moreover, fidelity means that coaches are trustworthy and strictly abide by the code of ethics in all professional activities. The principle of fidelity requires that coaches consistently have the best interests of clients at heart. Coaches shouldn't take advantage of their relationships with clients, and they need to make full disclosure where potential conflicts of interest may arise (e.g., being a shareholder in a client's business). Responsibility rests with the coach when he or she deems that another professional would be more helpful.

Justice

Justice refers to providing equal treatment to all clients. This concept does not mean that coaches have to be equally skilled in working with all types of people or in all issues that clients might bring them, but rather that within the range of their expertise they treat all clients fairly, without discrimination, and with sensitivity to their individual backgrounds and issues. Where feasible, this principle also carries an expectation that methods and processes will be adapted to the particular needs and characteristics of the client.

Respect for People's Rights and Dignity or Autonomy

This principle requires that clients' privacy be respected through strict adherence to confidentiality. It also implies that coaches recognize the uniqueness of their clients and fully respect their cultural norms, values, and beliefs. As previously mentioned, coaches are expected to cultivate self-awareness of their potential biases and prejudices that could affect their coaching and work diligently to minimize them. This principle necessitates the promotion of clients' independence and self-determination through the practice of coaching. Paradoxically, dependency may be evident in the beginning phases of the coaching relationship, yet as the relationship develops, greater self-sufficiency should emerge.

The core of ethical responsibility is that professional helpers do nothing that will harm the client, the community, or society in general (Nagy, 2011). Clients who seek help may be vulnerable and susceptible to undue influence. My experience is that people who train to be coaches want to do what is right. In building ethical competency, coaches will want to get beneath the somewhat abstruse language of ethical codes to concretely identify what it means to be competent to help another person with a specific concern or desire.

ETHICAL CODES

Professional societies typically have ethical codes offering guidelines for conduct based on moral principles and critical values. Ethical codes are agreed-upon standards of conduct that guide practice (Corey et al., 2014; Passmore et al., 2019). Though legal considerations are certainly relevant to codes, laws are different from morality and ethics—laws are the "agreed-upon rules of a society that set forth the basic principles for living together as a group" (Remley & Herlihy, 2015, p. 4). Ethical codes speak more to ideal standards—to the highest aspirations of a professional group for member conduct and relationships with clients.

All codes of ethics presume that practitioners will act in accordance with relevant governmental statutes and regulations. Occasionally, ethics and the law may be in conflict (Johnson, 2013). For instance, what occurs in helping relationships is often bound by a client's right to confidentiality, yet some circumstances may require a professional to breach this ethical principle. Ethical guidelines require professionals to inform clients of conditions under which rights to confidentiality are inapplicable.

Associations With Ethical Codes Relevant to Coaching

Organizations, such as the International Coaching Federation (ICF), have made significant efforts to formalize certification requirements for professional coaches. Becoming an ICF-certified coach carries the requirement of adherence to its code of ethics. A number of other organizations related to coaching have detailed standards of conduct that are well worth reviewing. The following organizations or associations may provide guidance:

- American Association for Marriage and Family Therapy: www.aamft.org/
- American Counseling Association: www.counseling.org/
- American Psychological Association: www.apa.org/
- Association for Counselor Education and Supervision: www.acesonline.net/
- National Board for Certified Counselors: www.nbcc.org/
- Worldwide Association of Business Coaches: www.wabccoaches.com/

Ethical dilemmas usually arise in situations where a decision must be made that involves conflicting ethical standards that are relevant to the same situation or where there is a conflict between personal values, ethics, and laws (Allen, 2012). An example of such a dilemma might appear when a client with whom you have been working for several months consistently lies to his employer to reduce his workload as a means to manage stress. You have a personal value of honesty, and it really bothers you that this person repeatedly describes lying to his boss. Another example arises in a scenario where you become increasingly aware that the issues your client presents might be served by another kind of professional, yet your client strongly believes that she is gaining a great deal from your sessions. A third example occurs when a client is mandated by his organization to work with a coach on performance issues, but he wants to use the time with you to prepare for pursuing job opportunities elsewhere. To guide your future work, please take a moment to review the ACTION ethical decision-making model (see sidebar).

ACTION Ethical Decision-Making Model for Coaching

Duffy and Passmore (2010) developed an evidence-based ACTION ethical decision-making model for coaching. The authors suggest that ethical dilemmas stem from four main areas: (1) issues with the coach, (2) issues with the client, (3) issues with boundaries, and (4) issues arising from dual relationships.

The ACTION ethical decision-making model for coaching can be summarized as follows:

- *Maintain **a**wareness.* What's your knowledge of the ethical code governing your profession (e.g., the ICF *Code of Ethics*), and how aware are you of your own personal values and beliefs in this situation?
- ***C**lassify.* What do you identify as the dilemma and what are the conflicting issues?
- ***T**ake time for reflection, support, and advice.* Have you spent time reflecting on the issue? Who else can support you? Might you speak to a supervisor, mentor, or peer?
- ***I**nitiate.* What's the best way for you to brainstorm potential solutions?
- *Assess the different **o**ptions.* How does each option look through the lens of a cost–benefit analysis? How does each solution seem when examined against personal and professional codes applicable to the situation?
- ***N**ovate.* How can you best apply your chosen approach (adopted solution) to the dilemma? How would you shift your practice to apply your learning to future dilemmas?

Adapted from Duffy and Passmore (2010).

THE ETHICAL COACH IN THE ICF CORE COMPETENCIES

How might the material you have just read relate to what the International Coaching Federation describes in its core coaching competencies? Let's initiate this discussion by considering first the ICF's code of ethics.

The ICF (2020b) recently revised its code of ethics to make it more applicable to issues coaches currently confront in their work. In so doing, the ICF acknowledged the fluid realities of the coaching world. A careful examination of the new code (see appendix D) reveals, first, how well it addresses the core concerns of universal significance in professional codes of ethics and, second, how shifts in client populations and the contexts of coaching work have been appropriately identified in this revised code. More specifically, the ICF code explicitly extends its coverage beyond individuals engaged in coaching to include those who may be involved as coach supervisors, mentors, coach trainers, students of coaching, support staff, and ICF staff members themselves. Another noteworthy emphasis in the revised code acknowledges the contexts in which coaching takes place by speaking about those who happen to work within organizations as internal coaches and identifying some of the particular elements of these roles that need to be navigated. In a similar vein, the new code addresses the matter of sponsors, defined as entities (e.g., organizations) and their representatives (e.g., human resources personnel) who pay for coaching services for identified members of their systems. Sensitivity to these tripartite coaching contexts (coach–client–sponsor) is critically relevant in the emerging world of coaching. Finally, and perhaps most importantly, the ICF explicitly addresses issues of equality and inclusivity in a pervasive manner throughout its code, speaking to matters of human differences and the need for diligence in how coaches regard and engage with such rich diversity in our worlds. It is essential in your training and ongoing participation in the world of coaching to regularly review this code of ethics and discussions pertaining to it.

It is not by chance that the ICF (2020c) listed as its first core coaching competency the requirement that a coach "demonstrates ethical practice" (see sidebar, ICF Core Coaching Competency 1: Demonstrates Ethical Practice). The centrality of embodying an ethical stance in coaching practice is beyond question. This core competency speaks to a number of issues. First, it addresses coaches' personal integration of ethical principles in their way of being in the world. Coaches need to embody such core values as integrity and honesty, taking time to reflect on their own thoughts, feelings, and behaviors that may or may not represent an ethical way in the world. Beyond this more internal focus, a second matter this competency addresses is the need for coaches to interact with clients and others in ways that are respectful and sensitive to their unique-

---

ICF Core Coaching Competency 1: Demonstrates Ethical Practice

Definition: Understands and consistently applies coaching ethics and standards of coaching

1. Demonstrates personal integrity and honesty in interactions with clients, sponsors and relevant stakeholders
2. Is sensitive to clients' identity, environment, experiences, values and beliefs
3. Uses language that is appropriate and respectful to clients, sponsors and relevant stakeholders
4. Abides by the ICF *Code of Ethics* and upholds the core values
5. Maintains confidentiality with client information per stakeholder agreements and pertinent laws
6. Maintains the distinctions between coaching, consulting, psychotherapy and other support professions
7. Refers clients to other support professionals, as appropriate

---

ness. A third aspect positions the ICF *Code of Ethics* as a necessary guideline for action. Coaches need to have examined in depth the ICF ethical code to fully comprehend how ethical issues might play out in their own practice. Indeed, such exploration of ethical matters may call for engagement in different forms of professional conversations about dilemmas that might arise in the practice of coaching.

PRACTICAL MATTERS

There are a number of practical matters that warrant your attention and ongoing mindfulness in your capacity as a professional coach. It's likely that your interest in coaching arises in good part from your deep caring for others, and this can at times represent a delicate balancing act. Another issue that we have touched upon is confidentiality. Here, it's important for you to have clear appreciation for when conditions of confidentiality may not apply. A third matter arising in practice is what to do when it becomes clear that the person you are working with needs a different form of assistance. A further issue in this short list of practical matters concerns boundaries—what they are and where you might find yourself on a slippery slope. Finally, as a coach you will need to acknowledge the possibility that you may face a charge of malpractice. Increasing your understanding of malpractice and the steps you might need to take in safeguarding yourself and your clients is critical.

How Much Caring?

At times, caring for someone within a coaching relationship slips into more intimate feelings from the perspective of either the client or the helper. Caring is always viewed in relation to the contract and the nature of the work occurring between coach and client. Coaches may become concerned about clients' health or well-being, especially if they see clients intentionally putting themselves at risk. Yet to intervene in such cases, coaches need to frame their actions within the legitimate bounds of the profession and the contractual nature of the relationship. Of course, the ICF, like other professional bodies, stipulates that when caring becomes too intimate, ethical issues may arise. Clearly, sexual or romantic relationships with current clients are inappropriate.

Exceptions to Rules of Confidentiality

Certainly, coaches need to assure clients of their rights to privacy and the confidential nature of the coaching relationship, and therein lies a responsibility for coaches to inform clients fully of all matters pertaining to their agreements, actions, and aspirations. Common sense would tell you that in a life-and-death emergency or in the event a coach has information that might save a client's life, the coach would have reason to breach confidentiality agreements. This principle extends to such unlikely situations as clients' revelations that they are intending to end their life or plan to harm someone else. Similarly, if there is clear evidence that clients are abusing or neglecting minors, elderly people, or disabled people, coaches must assume their civic and legal responsibilities and breach the confidentiality agreement. Legal statutes also stipulate other conditions under which a coach must make records and conversations with clients available to the courts.

Referrals

Coaches may find reason to consider referring clients to other professionals or services. Two forms of referral can be identified. In the first, the coach completely ends the relationship with a client and refers all matters to another professional that the client chooses. In the second, the coach retains an overseeing or facilitative role with the client and cocreates topic-specific referrals that will advance the client's objectives. To illustrate the first type of referral, a coach may recommend that a client who manifests significant impairment by virtue of a substance abuse problem seek help from an appropriately trained professional. The coaching relationship would then officially end even though the client may not have reached the intended objectives. In the second type of referral, a client may need help on certain topics that are out of the coach's area of expertise. In such instances, the client might be referred to qualified helpers, such as medical doctors, lawyers, real estate agents, or financial planners while continuing to work with the coach. Of course, the way in which referrals are made would incorporate principles of free and informed choice. In practice, this might involve encouraging clients to look for a service provider on their own or offering a list and suggesting how they might obtain independent assessments of these professionals.

Boundaries

Ethical behavior is intricately related to the concept of boundaries. Boundaries serve as guides for making calls about what is within limits and what is out of bounds. In sport as in life, the rules of the game are intended to be clear. Subjective elements related to boundaries can be problematic. The more effort you invest in clarifying role and relational boundaries, the more readily you can identify out-of-bounds behaviors.

Professional boundaries stem from definitions of your role, job skills, and responsibilities. Professional boundaries help guide actions in a wide array of situations, but they can never cover all events you are likely to encounter in your coaching practice. In discussions of boundaries, a useful distinction has been made between a boundary crossing and a boundary violation (Zur, 2009).

Boundary Crossing

Boundary crossings refer to behaviors that may lead to professional misconduct but are less serious than boundary violations (Gabbard, 2016). Examples of such behaviors include accepting a token gift from a client, giving a client a hug after an achievement, or regularly attending social events or community organizations that your client normally attends. It is important to remain attentive to matters of diversity and cultural differences here; what may seem to be a completely innocent expression on the part of one person may assume meaning of far greater proportion by another. The ICF holds coaches responsible for "being aware of and setting clear, appropriate and culturally sensitive boundaries that govern interactions, physical or otherwise" (ICF, 2020b, part 4, section III, no. 23).

Boundary Violations

The more serious matter of **boundary violations** is universally understood to be unethical (Gabbard, 2016). Overstepping these boundaries is problematic in most helping relationships because it blurs professional role definitions (Welfel, 2012). An obvious example of a boundary violation is having sexual relations with a current client. If you think of boundaries as limitations to thought, action, or even the expression of feeling, three aspects of your work provide a framework for the establishment of limits; these include your role, your resources, and the situation itself.

Your Role   In addition to your coach training, you are likely to have prior educational and professional training and experience, which may qualify you to focus on a particular domain of practice (niche) with full confidence. Your contracts with clients help define your scope of work. Moreover, although you may be competent to administer a certain service, legal limitations relevant to professional groups serve to restrict the activities of members. As a coach, you may be an insightful and skilled communicator with a graduate degree in psychology and extensive knowledge of psychological issues, yet it would be unethical for you to switch into a psychotherapeutic role with a client even though you might consider yourself able to do it well.

Your Resources   Even with clearly established boundaries, at times you will have to make a judgment call. When your personal resources are at a low ebb, you may not have the capacity to take on the scope of work that might be required by a potential client's agenda. Another example might occur when you are offered a coaching mandate that you know will seriously impede all the self-care practices that are essential to maintaining the quality of your work.

The Situation   At times, situational dynamics may supersede normal boundary limitations and require intervention. Most rules have exceptions that apply in unusual circumstances. Imagine that a client breaks down and cries uncontrollably in the midst of a session because he or she has just experienced the ending of a long-term intimate relationship. This issue may not be part of your contractual agreement, but because of the sensitivity of the matter, it would seem to be appropriate to listen with great empathy. However, it might be that your actions reinforce or encourage the occurrence of such exceptional moments. For instance, you may actively encourage clients to delve deeply into emotional content when it begins to arise in coaching sessions. If this is happening, it would be prudent to talk things over with a coaching supervisor.

Malpractice

Even when you believe you are fully adhering to the ethical code for coaches, things can go seriously wrong. Clients may believe that you have harmed them through your coaching and may accuse you of malpractice. Malpractice is a legal term that involves unethical conduct and negligence resulting in injury or loss to the client. Evidence pertinent to malpractice appears when coaches fail to render appropriate professional services or fail to exercise the degree of skill or expertise that would ordinarily be expected of similar professionals in the same situation. As summarized by Corey and associates (2014), malpractice generally falls into six categories, which have been modified here for professional coaches:

1. The coach engaged in a procedure not considered within the realm of accepted coaching practice.
2. The coach used a technique or method for which he or she was not properly or adequately trained.
3. The coach failed to use a technique or procedure that would have been more beneficial to the client.
4. The coach failed to warn others about a violent client and thereby did not act to protect these people.
5. The coach failed to obtain or properly document the client's informed consent about coaching activities.
6. The coach failed to explain to the client the possible consequences of coaching interventions.

In malpractice cases, the burden of proof generally rests with the client. Four elements must be demonstrated to prove that a coach is guilty of malpractice: (1) A bona fide professional relationship existed between the coach and the client, (2) the coach acted in a negligent or improper manner or deviated significantly from the usual standards of care in the coaching profession, (3) the client suffered harm or injury from acting on the coach's recommendations, and (4) a causal linkage exists between the coach's negligence or breach of conduct and the actual injury or damage presumably experienced.

Discussions of malpractice may seem more pertinent to medicine or psychiatry, yet all professionals must be vigilant about these matters. In isolated cases, practitioners consciously engage in harmful behaviors with clients. In most instances, harm or injury results from some oversight, a moment of inattention, or unconscious neglect. Coaching is still an unregulated profession, and many coaches do not believe that they need professional liability insurance to cover malpractice lawsuits. I advocate that, just as for any other service provider in the helping professions, you acquire liability insurance that will cover legal fees and compensatory damages in the event of such unexpected occurrences.

REFLECTIONS

There is much to explore in relation to the themes raised in this chapter. Your good intentions are likely evident in the generous way you relate to people and how you care for them in your day-to-day interactions. Yet, a professional practice in coaching asks even more of us than good intentions.

Each client you meet will have a unique history shaped by diverse experiences, some good and others mixed in nature. They will have values that may seem more or less similar to yours, but they will rarely be identical. As a coach, you will have to work hard to grow your sensitivity pertaining to diversity and inclusion and to ensure as much as it is ever possible to communicate in ways that honor and respect your clients' ways of being and approaches to understanding.

As I reflect on the growth of the coaching profession, I am aware of the high levels of social and emotional intelligence that guide the behaviors of my colleagues. This isn't just a matter of the quality of individuals who are drawn to the coaching profession, but perhaps more so an indication of their dedication to lifelong learning. Coaches are curious beings, and that curiosity shows up in how they are willing to explore what they don't know or what seems to be shifting in the world around them. Beliefs, values, and morals have a highly fluid nature in our times. What seemed normal a decade ago may be problematic today.

As you think about your own ethics of practice, you are likely to experience ambiguity at least as often as you feel certainty. That is perhaps the nature of ethics—we are provoked to ponder and explore. In so doing, it's good to stay in touch with peers, supervisors, mentors, and programs of professional training. We need to remain awake to all that might be out of our lens of awareness. As noted previously, our good intentions are necessary but are probably not sufficient for sustaining a wholly ethical practice in coaching.

CHAPTER 7
PARTNERING IN AGREEMENTS

Do not agree, if you do not agree with it.

Gift Gugu Mona

MY STORY

My best friend in my tween years was Johnny. We lived in an area of New York City that was pretty rock 'n' roll—gangs, crime, lots of sketchy stuff. We had a way of navigating our way from West 85th Street and Amsterdam Avenue to Riverside Park that zigzagged north, south, east, and west to avoid going through certain neighborhoods. Sometimes we didn't quite make it. Surrounded by some local "little league" gang, I would look over my shoulder for Johnny. He was nowhere to be found. Despite the fact that we often talked about always having each other's back, he had a talent for skipping out at just the right moment—for him! Obviously, I survived—and Johnny and I continued our adventures, although I would yell at him for deserting me in those moments.

Years later, living in Colorado, I bought a used motorcycle. I called it "Johnny." Why? Well, a few times when I was in full throttle down some back road, the rear wheel mysteriously locked and I went skidding precariously to a stop. I couldn't really trust that motorcycle. I guess back then I hadn't fully gotten over Johnny bailing on me in those dicey moments on Manhattan's west side.

I'm a big fan of Don Miguel Ruiz's (2001) *Four Agreements,* and in particular, the first agreement: "Be impeccable with your word." It's a nonnegotiable for me, though I come up short more often than I want to admit on some of the lighter agreements like being on time, reliably doing my chores, and keeping in touch with friends. But in truth, I don't really consider any of these as light agreements. I am still a work in progress, and I hope I continue to get better at this. And I forgive Johnny, though if we had remained in contact over the years, I probably would have needed some new experiences with him on which to rebuild my trust.

We make agreements all the time. Some we consider soft and others hard. There are legal agreements and agreements to get groceries on the way home. Agreements differ in so many ways, including in the consequences for noncompliance. Yet, there are threads of confluence running through all of them. Our work as coaches is articulated within the framework of written and verbal agreements. In this light, the connection between ethics and coaching agreements becomes evident. A coach's ability to determine with a client the terms, logistics, processes, and objectives of the working relationship needs to be founded on an ethical examination of what the coach and the client can reasonably do together to advance action toward agreed-upon outcomes in ways that are appropriate to the roles of the coach and the client. Here are some guiding questions as you read:

- What distinguishes contracts from agreements?
- Why would coaches need written agreements with their clients?
- What is a psychological contract?
- How does action science help our understanding of agreements?
- What are the critical elements of agreements?
- How do coaching plans and objectives differ?
- What is coachability all about?

THE BIG PICTURE

An experience common to most of us is working in teams. Throughout your school years, you may have been in classes working on group projects. All of you got the same grade, but there were those times when some members didn't pull their weight. Maybe the group talked about it or maybe everyone just skirted the issue. When someone got blamed, that person might have thought the agreement had been unclear, unfair, or arbitrarily determined. Perhaps it was.

Now consider a car you may have bought in your earlier years. Perhaps it turned out to be a lemon, and you tried to take it back, but the agreement had this fine print that you hadn't read. Or maybe once you had a lease on an apartment and the place was cold throughout the winter or it wasn't kept up—and maybe you bailed on the rent.

"See you at 5; don't be late" is an example of the kind of agreement you probably make every day—sometimes with others and even with yourself. Think of your to-do list that you periodically make; it's a kind of promise to yourself. What's your experience of how you and others live up to these kinds of agreements? Let's take it up a notch. Think of some of your early jobs. You got paid to do certain tasks. There was an agreement. It may or may not have been written. In some of your early work experiences, you may have heard what the boss told you and then during your first week on the job, you watched what others did. Then, you may have said to yourself, "My boss told me to do this, but the way it works around here is that you don't exactly have to do it that way."

Let's move this discussion into coaching. Normally, your clients choose to work with you as their coach because they want to achieve something. They have one or more goals in mind, of which they may be only partly conscious. As we now know, clients aren't always clear about what they really want and some of what they really want may only emerge midstream in your relationship. Now think about the fact that as you begin your work with clients, you will be tasked with the responsibility of articulating a coaching agreement—that is, a mutually determined understanding of commitments based on objectives and other considerations. Does this give you an inkling of any challenges you might have in navigating agreements in your work as a coach?

Coaching involves a contractual and partnered agreement about lots of things, including what the objectives of your work together are. You are probably wondering, "How can I draw up a contract for working together if my clients aren't clear at the beginning or change their mind over time?" It may take a fair amount of exploration to get to the real topic that clients want to address. Initial statements of goals could be objectives such as enhancing leadership skills, changing careers, or managing stress. As topics are explored, something else may surface as the overarching purpose that clients want to realize. The reframed goal may not be leadership talent as much as it is sharing power in management team sessions. Perhaps an initial goal of work–life balance evolves into an objective of becoming more assertive about one's personal needs at work. Likewise, changing careers may morph into finding greater opportunity for self-expression in one's present employment.

Whether initial intentions or derivatives of these intentions become the coaching objective, clients have something they want to get from their investments of time, money, and effort (Ives, 2008; Ives & Cox, 2012; van Nieuwerburgh, 2017). Coaches need to clarify what the client truly wants and then determine whether they can help. Assuming a clear topic is identified and the coach believes she or he is competent to help this client reach this goal, the discussion will eventually turn to the specifics of the agreement: How will coach and client work together? What will the coach do, and what won't she or he do? What is expected of the client? What happens if the coach or client doesn't live up to the terms of the agreement? Who else might be involved? How confidential is the relationship? How long will the relationship continue? How much will it cost?

The process of articulating an agreement is two sided. Both coach and client are engaged in determining its elements; they are both involved in reviewing expectations and assessing whether the coach's methods are appropriately suited to the stated goals. A client may have an objective pertaining to an area where the coach is richly experienced and knowledgeable. Based on her background, the coach believes she can help. But perhaps the client has expectations that the work will take a particular shape. For instance, the client may believe the coach will give him answers to pressing problems. Such difficulties in establishing agreements may arise from current ambiguities about what coaching is. However, even when coaching evolves into a more commonly understood professional field, clients will continue to arrive with expectations that may not align with a coaching model.

There are also questions of match or fit. Will this client work well with that coach toward the achievement of this particular goal? Will using that method of coaching be effective? Will this coach be able to work with that client who has this particular style of behavior and set of expectations toward a specific outcome within a defined time frame? The question of fit is sometimes framed as, "Is there good chemistry between coach and client?" but it's so much more than that.

Written Agreements

The concepts of contract and agreement are sometimes used interchangeably, though contracts may have more formal or legal implications. While a written agreement in coaching allows for mutually determined modifications, such documents provide a formality that calls for both coach and client to pay full attention to what they are committing to do. The act of creating a written agreement serves to specify elements of the coaching relationship and give it direction; moreover, agreements protect the rights, roles, and obligations of both parties and thereby increase the probability of a successful relationship (Gladding, 2013). It's also important to

bear in mind that the ICF *Code of Ethics* stipulates that client records must comply with the law and be maintained, stored, and disposed of in a manner that "promotes confidentiality, security and privacy" (see section 1, item 7 in appendix D).

Clients will generally benefit more from the structure of a written rather than a verbal agreement. Such agreements give clients an opportunity to revisit their commitments and review the terms of the work they are undertaking with the coach. Written agreements remove the element of doubt or question about what was said at the outset. In the first coaching session, when agreements are typically determined, clients may be preoccupied with the issues they are presenting and less so with the processes and terms the coach is describing as part of their contractual working relationship. Later on, it may come as an unwelcome surprise when they are informed, for instance, that they have to pay for a missed session. The prevailing wisdom is that the terms and conditions of helping relationships should be agreed upon in writing as early as possible—either before, during or shortly after the first session (Wilson, 2007).

A written agreement serves as a road map providing general directions for getting from one point to another and confirming that both coach and client have explicit intentions to move in the same direction (Shebib, 2020). Contracts add to the clients' sense of ownership of and responsibility for agreed-upon objectives and methods. An often-overlooked value of signing an agreement pertains to the specification of terms and conditions for ending the relationship. Coaching relationships may often be time limited rather than open ended. Having agreements concerning how and when the relationship might end focuses both coach and client on benchmarks of progress and the identification of probable moments for closure.

Psychological Contracts

The concept of **psychological contracts**, first suggested by Levinson (1976), has profound bearing on how coaching relationships evolve. A psychological contract isn't an actual written or verbal agreement, but rather an implicit or assumed agreement that emerges in professional relationships. Clients have rich histories with all kinds of professionals. Based on these histories, they enter new professional relationships with certain expectations. For example, when you make a doctor's appointment, do you expect to be seen at the precise time of your appointment? Maybe you do, but my experience is that I am likely to wait for an indeterminate period of time. Your expectations develop through experience.

What complicates matters a bit more is that psychological contracts represent two-way streets. Both coach and client initially meet with separate sets of assumptions. Clients may believe that coaches have the answers or that coaches should make them feel better each time they come for a session. Novice coaches in particular may expect that clients are fully committed and able to take on the challenging engagements of a change process. Coaches may also assume that they can enable clients to succeed no matter what. Similarly, clients may believe that seeing a coach guarantees results.

The fewer unexpressed assumptions there are in a coaching relationship, the better off both parties will be. Even when coach and client establish clear terms for their relationship at the outset, actions by either party may suggest that the contract has been implicitly renegotiated. That is, the psychological contract may evolve differently from the written agreement. Let's look at a few situations where this may happen:

- The client repeatedly shows up 5 to 10 minutes late for appointments, and the coach always gives her the contracted 45-minute session. Might the client not assume that she is entitled to the full session no matter when she shows up?

- A coach starts off each session with a bit of chitchat about current events or the weather and then eases into the session. Similarly, at the end of the session, the coach switches style and becomes more conversational. What might the client come to assume is part of the coaching process?

- A client answers his phone during sessions without comment from the coach. Even if sessions end at the established time, what is the implied agreement about calls during the session? Might they not be seen as taking precedence over the coaching agenda?

All these situations have one thing in common: People observe behavior and infer the rules or agreements. Regardless of what you say, actions often speak louder than words. Each time a deviation from an agreement occurs without comment or discussion, it holds the possibility for altering what was formally agreed upon. Over time, both coach and client may come to assume that their agreement is different from what was originally stated. This is not to say that agreements should remain fixed; rather, the parties need to acknowledge variations or changes explicitly and either define them as exceptions or incorporate them in a revised agreement that is confirmed by both parties.

I have listened to hundreds of recorded coaching sessions, and I find myself making up stories about the psychological contracts coaches and clients have made with each other. Here's a common one: The coaching session begins with some friendly conversation. Depending on how much of this happens at the beginning, I develop a sense of how the coach is going to work. If there's a lot of mutual sharing, I expect there will be a quality of two friends having a helpful conversation. In contrast, when there's virtually no chitchat, I imagine the coach will sound more formal and perhaps a bit distant. In a sense, the psychological contract in the chatty relationship is one where coach and client are sort of friends, while in the nonchatty one, the contract is strictly business. So what? Well, one client might call up his sort-of friend late one night when he is feeling stressed, while the other client would be less likely to impose herself on a coach who has a more restrained approach.

A critical skill for effective coaching is the ability to surface unexpressed assumptions and expectations that clients might have about the professional relationship and its objectives. Embedded elements of the client's unexpressed psychological contract may take time to identify. You will want to remain alert to the possibility of misalignments between client expectations and the realities of the coaching experience. When patterns begin to emerge suggesting that assumptions may be at the root, it might be prudent to present your impressions so they can be mutually explored.

PERSPECTIVES FROM ACTION SCIENCE

A model that might help you better appreciate the values underlying robust and ethical agreements derives from an area known as action science. In brief, action science concerns the attitudes and logic underpinning human action. In their work, Chris Argyris and colleagues (Argyris, 1970; Argyris & Schön, 1974, 1978, 1995) developed two sets of values that can be interpreted from the ways in which people engage in action (see Argyris and Schön's Value Models That Guide Action sidebar).

Works by Argyris and Schön (1974, 1978, 1995) have a lot to do with agreements. Imagine what values might govern the behaviors of competing organizations when one company is trying to reach

Argyris and Schön's Value Models That Guide Action

Our actions are guided by underlying values. Sometimes, how we act doesn't reflect the values we believe we hold. Chris Argyris and Donald Schön (1974, 1978, 1995) initiated a field of action science oriented toward helping people generate personal knowledge about their actions that could serve to improve their professional and personal behaviors (see table 7.1).

Table 7.1   Values in Action

Model 1	Model 2
1. Unilaterally control goals that are set and the ways to achieve them 2. Continually strive to maximize my winnings and minimize losings 3. Suppress the expression of negative emotions 4. Act or at least appear to be entirely rational	1. Strive for and generate valid information 2. Promote free and informed choice 3. Seek internal commitment to choices 4. Continually monitor actions so as to appropriately adapt

They discovered two sets of guiding values that, in many ways, are polar opposites. Their research revealed that a great many people believe that they are operating by model 2 values, when in fact their actions more clearly reflect model 1 values. The relevance of this work to the topic of agreements is best understood in comparisons of what people agree to do vis-à-vis how they actually behave. For instance, a coach may believe she is quite collaborative in coaching processes while behaviorally manifesting a high degree of controlling behavior.

an agreement to buy out the other company. Or think about an individual with a unique skill set negotiating the best employment agreement with an organization. Considering the two models, you might hope that the behaviors of the actors in the above two scenarios would ideally reflect model 2 values. The actors would seek valid information, promote free and informed choice, and engender internal commitment; but it's possible their conduct would borrow heavily from the values in model 1. Why? In many contexts, people want to negotiate the best deal for themselves and strategize to emerge with outcomes most beneficial to them. Throughout the process of negotiations, they might maintain a rational and nonemotional demeanor so as to appear thoroughly professional while strategizing to win. This is what model 1 looks like. And maybe this is perfectly fine. Not all professional relationships are intentionally collaborative, but surprisingly even ones that are—that implicitly or explicitly subscribe to the values of model 2—may manifest more of the values of model 1 than the actors might even realize.

Let's now look at these models in the context of coaching. Intentionally, agreements in coaching would be guided by efforts to generate valid information, promote free choice, foster internal

commitment, and monitor any decisions that are made. As you know, a core element in coaching is partnership in the relationship. Coach and client have different roles, yet they collaborate and cooperate in a way that purposefully represents model 2 values. When coaches describe in their agreements what coaching is and what it isn't, they are offering valid information that will aid clients in making informed choices about whether this is the kind of relationship they most need. Open communication processes in coaching foster not only the exploration of client commitment, but also an ongoing dialogue to determine whether the way in which sessions and the relationship itself are unfolding meet clients' needs. Can you see the connections to a model 2 perspective, as well as how a model 1 approach would entirely contradict the underlying principles of coaching?

With all this in mind, we come to perhaps the most important contribution of Argyris and Schön's work: Agreements are lived experiences, represented in the actions of parties involved. What coach, client, and stakeholders agree to at the outset constitutes a template for action, a kind of behavioral script for how the parties intend to engage with one another. Argyris and Schön (1974) think of this as the model someone espouses, or how people believe they are going to act. However, what someone fully intends may not show up as robustly in their actions. A coach may say he promotes free and informed choice, yet, if you observed the coach, you might think that he continually tries to convince clients of the validity of his recommendations. Similarly, a sponsor may say unequivocally that what goes on between coach and client is confidential, while calling the coach into her office to subtly find out how things are *really* going with the client. Given that agreements are lived experiences, coaches and sponsors need to remain mindful of the degree to which their actions are aligned with what they espouse. Argyris and Schön (1974) remind us that too often what we say and what we do are different.

Having awareness of differences between what you espouse as your guiding values and how you actually and perhaps unwittingly behave (Argyris & Schön, 1974) is essential to an understanding of agreements as lived documents. The intersection of ethics and agreements emerges in how well your behaviors adhere to the principles and practices described in your agreements. You not only need to develop the capacity to generate fair and clear agreements with clients but also to monitor the process so that you are living in alignment with your agreement as well as honoring the core values and principles of the coaching profession.

CRITICAL ELEMENTS OF AGREEMENTS

Agreements detail the *what* and *how* of a coaching relationship—the coaching objective and the coaching plan. Also, objectives and plans may evolve, and thus agreements may need to be modified as the relationship progresses. In one sense, the initial agreement needs to be general enough to allow minor shifts (e.g., meeting on Tuesdays rather than Thursdays), but not so broad as to be largely ambiguous. A key point to recognize is that agreements are not commitments to goal attainment within specified time limits. You wouldn't want to write a contract with clients stating that by a certain time they will have achieved their goal. Agreements need to indicate the direction of the work (coaching objective) and the way of working together (coaching plan) without promising results.

Intentions of Agreements

What are the intentions of agreements? Think about your experiences with both formal and informal agreements you have made. Imagine making plans with a group of friends for a picnic. What would you imagine your agreement would encompass? More formally, you might agree to take on a piece of work with a colleague. Again, what's the ground you intend to cover in the terms of your agreement? Here are some intentions that I believe are important to be addressed in coaching agreements:

- The agreement would clearly identify goals and processes for the coaching relationship, including benchmarks of progress and success.

- The agreement would explicitly describe what coaching is and what it is not, distinguishing this process from other ways of working.

- The agreement would delineate roles and responsibilities of all parties to the agreement, including coach, client, sponsors, and other relevant stakeholders. An agreement would incorporate any special considerations arising from the unique nature, circumstances, or conditions of individual parties to the agreement.

- The agreement would meet the legitimate needs of coach, client, and other stakeholders where appropriate; all parties need to perceive the agreement as valid and fair.

- The agreement would clearly stipulate essential details and exchanges of resources, materials, and fees. These exchanges should be based on objectively justifiable principles. For example, fees, meeting schedules, terms of working together, and limits of the working relationship should be based on principles of professional expertise, industry norms, mutual respect, and scientific evidence, among others.

- The agreement would describe arrangements for reviews of how the agreement is working and how terms and conditions can be renegotiated when necessary.

- The agreement would address duration of the relationship and the ways in which the agreement may be terminated.

- The agreement would speak thoroughly about confidentiality, including limits to confidentiality in this relationship.

- The agreement would adhere fully to relevant laws and government regulations pertaining to such relationships.

This list is extensive, but not exhaustive. There may be other intentions one would hope to have addressed in agreements that are unique in nature. Overall, you probably have a sense now that an agreement requires attention to both small and large matters. Despite their detailed nature, agreements nonetheless can energize the relationship by providing clients with solid ground for their work. They can serve as relationship-building engagements that support the capacities of coach and client to work collaboratively and come to fruitful resolutions of differences.

Details of Agreements

The coaching agreement details rights, responsibilities, and understandings of coach, client, and stakeholders in various elements of the agreement, as well as in its implementation. A useful framework for understanding the elements of coaching agreements can be found in the questions *who? what? when? where? how? how much?* and *why?*

You may have been involved in home renovation projects where you signed a contract with a company for the work. There was a *what* in the contract, and ideally there was a *how.* My experience is that the *how* in that kind of contract isn't always highly detailed. Let's say it was a kitchen renovation. The *what* was a new kitchen! Hurray—at long last! The contract might have detailed different parts of the *what*, such as removing and replacing the old floor, installing new lighting, etc. What about the *how*? Maybe there were parts of the contract where time frames and progress benchmarks were indicated, where midpoint checks for decision making were detailed, where plumbing and electric work subcontracting were described, where the arrival and departure times of work teams were stipulated, and where cleanup details were outlined. These are all part of the contract!

In the next section, I will review some of these critical elements in agreements. However, it's important to know that because of the unique scenarios that can present themselves in the world of coaching, it will always be the coach's responsibility to reflect on the comprehensiveness of the contracts they detail with their clients.

Who?

Who is the client? And who else is involved in this coaching relationship? Much of the time, coaching involves an agreement with an individual who seeks coaching and who will be financially responsible for payment of services. However, a significant number of coaching clients are supported in their coaching relationships by their organizations. The ICF (2020a) global survey indicates that according to the participating coaches, approximately 52% of their clients receive financial support for their coaching experiences from their organizations. Sometimes these clients find their own coaches and get organizational approval, while in other instances, coaches are hired by the organization and assigned to members. When an organization is sponsoring the coach, not only will the organization pay for the services, but members of that organization may have a significant voice in the determination of the coaching objective and the planning of the coaching process.

Here's a common example: An organization determines that all managers at a certain level or above should participate in a six-session coaching process, which begins with a 360-degree feedback review and proceeds through the discussion of reports on psychometric tests. Coaching is structured so that the first two sessions are about feedback from the 360-degree review and the tests, the third session involves a determination of a target area for leadership development, and the final three sessions are centered on the creation and implementation of an action plan to address this goal. The client's choice of the coaching objective is circumscribed to the area of leadership development.

Another application of coaching in organizations arises in cases where employees are transitioning in their careers to either higher levels of responsibility, significantly different roles, or new locations—perhaps in different countries. This type of coaching is intended to assist individuals in their transitions, so again the coaching objective is predefined as having to do with adjustment and adaptation issues.

One more important example concerns the use of coaching to address performance or behavioral issues. Organizational members may have acted in inappropriate ways with other members of the organization or the public, for example, by demonstrating gender or cultural insensitivity, and as a result are required as a condition of employment to spend a certain number of sessions addressing these behaviors through coaching processes intended to augment awareness, sensitivity, and appropriate behaviors.

These are just some of the examples of coaching in organizations. As you can imagine, the initial contracting for the coaching relationship might not only involve coach and client but also one or more members of the organization. Typically, the organizational members who are directly involved in the coaching agreement are described as sponsors or representatives of the sponsoring organization. There will typically be responsibilities related to the sponsors, which might include the initial setting of the coaching objective, terms of the relationship, fee and payment structures, and reporting activities at specified points in the coaching relationship.

In the context of sponsored coaching relationships, there may be other stakeholders who would need to be included in the coaching agreement. Imagine a scenario where an organizational leader has created conflictual relationships with another department in the company. It may well be that the leader of that other unit is party to the agreement and to the initiation of the coaching relationship in terms of expectations of behavioral changes; moreover, the agreement may contain requirements regarding periodic conversations between the two leaders that validate the effectiveness of the coaching sessions.

Other scenarios can be imagined where the intended process and behavioral outcome of coaching calls for involvement of external (to the coaching relationship *per se*) individuals who would likely benefit from the results of coaching for the client. Consider a case where a leader engages in coaching to improve interactions with his or her team members. Let's say that this leader knows that he or she tends to be domineering in meetings and at times dismissive of team members' opinions. Though the leader is well liked, he or she nonetheless stifles creativity and open discussion in meetings. The leader and the coach may think it advisable to involve team members in both assessments and conversations related to the client's competency development. For instance, the coach may involve staff by periodically observing their meetings with the leader. These colleagues would be identified as stakeholders to the agreement and would need to consent to all terms related to their participation. Think back to the discussion of guiding values in models 1 and 2. Stakeholders, defined here as the team members reporting to the client, would certainly need valid information about their involvement and free and informed choice regarding their participation.

I hope you can now see some of the variations of who might be involved in a coaching agreement. Mostly, you will be contracting with an individual; however, as your career in coaching evolves, you may need to familiarize yourself with multiparty agreements, especially those involving members of a sponsoring organization.

Why?

Why is the client here, and what's his or her objective? This question goes together with who the client is. In reviewing the question of *who* in the previous section, I have already offered a number of scenarios where the *why* of coaching is largely prescribed by sponsors or stakeholders, rather than exclusively by the client. In my experience, however, the vast majority of clients I have worked with have been the sole authors of their coaching objectives. In the initial session of a coaching relationship or even before, in a preappointment interview, clients will give you a sense of why they want to engage you and what they are hoping to achieve through the coaching work. Again remembering that what clients initially describe as their reasons for hiring a coach may change, you will want to remain ever alert to how the topic for the coaching work may shift in such a way that you might consider the need to renegotiate your agreement. You may also want to evaluate whether you are the appropriate person to work with this client on their emerging identification of *why*.

The *why* of coaching largely pertains to the objective, and this is where good judgment is required. The ICF (2020a) global study identifies a wide range of topics that clients bring to their coaching engagements. However, a frequently asked question is whether coaches are able to work with any agenda clients present. Can you imagine topics that you think would be outside the realm of coaching? Maybe someone wants to know if he should get divorced. Someone else may want to learn how better to manipulate people to her own ends. Another person may want to figure out how to get his parents to move into an assisted living facility.

Topics like these may reflect a number of things—a misconception of what coaching is, a significant value misalignment between the coach and client, or perhaps a requirement that the coach have knowledge relevant to the topic. The question of topic appropriateness is separate from ones about client readiness, motivation, or capacity to address the topics they bring (Ciuchta et al., 2014; Guttman, 2007; Shannahan et al., 2013). So, how do coaches know whether the why of coaching is something they can address?

Research based on highly experienced coaches says the answer partly rests in coaches' self-perceived capabilities (Sime & Jacob, 2018). A person seeking coaching on a spiritual matter may need to find a coach who has studied and worked in that domain (Belf, 2002; Schreckhise, 2015; Esquer, 2014).

A coach interviewing a potential client who wants to be coached on spirituality would be best to have solid and verifiable competence in this domain before accepting this task. Even though both parties to the agreement need to have their eyes open, responsibility for saying yes or no to particular coaching requests rests with the coach.

There is yet another way to answer a potential conundrum when a client asks you to work on something about which you know relatively little. Sime and Jacob (2018) found that seasoned coaches largely focused on the *role* they were being asked to take when deciding about a potential coaching relationship. For instance, you already know that being asked to serve in a role resembling that of a psychotherapist would be out of the question. However, as reflected in chapter 1, there are so many ways in which coaches define their roles that a coach may decide to take on a coaching topic about which she knows very little based on how she defines her coaching role. In their review of the coaching literature, Sime and Jacob found that some coaches readily accept such roles as teacher, guide, conscience, facilitator, sounding board, and professional friend, among others.

From a goal-centric coaching perspective, it's unlikely that you would serve as a teacher other than for perhaps specific moments in the relationship, and it's questionable that you would sign on as the client's conscience. As a coach, you would check with yourself to determine whether the topics that potential clients present are ones you justifiably feel confident in being able to address. Sometimes this sense of justifiable confidence may need to be validated by documented knowledge, skills, and experience.

What?

What is and what is not coaching? What is the work that is being contracted for? Exactly what services are provided and not provided? For example, coaching is not counseling, consulting, training, or the communication of strictly factual information. What are the boundaries of the relationship? What are the coach's responsibilities? What are the client's responsibilities? What do sponsors and stakeholders do? What are all parties expected to do to live up to their responsibilities?

This set of questions references multiple issues. First, you need to make sure your potential clients understand what coaching is and what it isn't. Not only does this pertain to the differentiation of a coaching approach from educational, consulting, or counseling styles, but it also speaks to the necessity of describing your methodology and action focus. When you are describing this, you will inevitably need to articulate what the roles and responsibilities of coach, client, and, where appropriate, stakeholder and sponsor are and what is required of each to function effectively in this kind of work.

All professional relationships have boundaries, and thus in your agreement you will reference boundaries to the relationship partly by emphasizing your dedication to the agreed-upon coaching objective rather than to emergent themes that clients may want to discuss just to get your opinion. Indicating your adherence to a code of ethics further clarifies for the client that this is not something like a friendship relationship or one that might gravitate toward either a business partnership or a more intimate relationship.

As noted earlier, agreements are alive. They are expressed and reconfirmed in each session of the relationship, not just at the outset. Here's an example pertaining to the boundaries of the relationship:

A client states as his objective a desire to take a particular entrepreneurial project through to completion, given that he has consistently stopped short of delivery on previous projects. In the fourth meeting, you begin by asking what the client wants to focus on in the session, and he tells you about an argument with himself about buying a new house and wants to figure that out. You might wonder in this moment what this has to do with the coaching objective the client originally determined. A topic having to do with buying a new house shifts the focus of what you had originally agreed upon. Maybe the client says it's a one-off topic—something he really needs to resolve. Assuming you feel competent in guiding a coaching process around this agenda and that the client takes responsibility for the choice, the two of you might agree to this as the goal-centric purpose of this session. However, if the same kind of thing happens repeatedly, you will likely need to take time with this client to clarify your role and the nature of coaching work.

When clients ask you to teach them a technique or to give them advice or to make decisions for them, you might have an easier job reorienting your client, especially when you have spent adequate time at the beginning of your relationship ensuring that your clients know what coaching is. Indeed, there may be times when you teach a technique or give advice, but these aren't your predominant patterns. They may be contextually justified in the moment and relatively rare in occurrence. It's when these kinds of interventions (giving advice, teaching, telling) become the norm that you have moved out of the coaching role and have potentially invalidated your agreement with your client.

When?

When will coaching take place and for how long? Coaches vary in how long their sessions are and how often they meet (ICF, 2020a). Moreover, the duration of the relationship itself will vary all the way from one session to many years. After exploring what clients want to achieve and what time frames they have in mind for the work, an agreement is usually made that determines a reasonable number of sessions before coach and client pause to take stock of where they are and where they may still want to go. A typical beginning framework for coaching might be about six 45- to 60-minute sessions spaced on a biweekly schedule, resulting in a three-month contract. You will also remember that sometimes in sponsored coaching processes, the organization will stipulate that sessions are to be scheduled weekly or biweekly for, let's say, exactly six sessions. This is a kind of semiscripted process of coaching, where the design has been formulated to achieve particular organizational objectives.

Another facet of the *when* question pertains to coach–client contact outside the agreed-upon sessions. Coaches may check in via email with clients on a regular or ad hoc basis. Clients may have any number of unanticipated needs to contact coaches for quick checks or requests for an unscheduled session. Working with the unknowns of how the relationship will unfold and needs that may arise during this process surfaces another kind of boundary. What are the terms of agreement about contact between coach and client beyond scheduled sessions?

You might imagine a scenario where a client bumps into her coach at a community event and begins to fill the coach in on what has been happening. This can be sort of an awkward moment. I don't know of any coaching contracts that stipulate that if coaches happen to see their clients in public places, they won't talk to them, yet it's likely to be understood that you don't engage your coach in professional conversations outside of the office. But, then, we are in a global village and different individuals may have different norms about this kind of situation. In considering this situation, bring back to mind two ideas: first, your understanding of a psychological contract and, second, the idea that agreements are living documents. The notion of psychological contracts tells you that if you engage this

client in this unexpected encounter, you may set a precedent and implicitly add a line to your contract saying that if you happen to bump into me, feel free to talk about our coaching work. The second piece is about agreements as lived experience. So, instead of accommodating your client's interest in talking to you about her coaching in the moment, you might politely interrupt and suggest that she hold this for your next session or call you for an interim appointment. In addition, when you eventually meet, it's probably important to acknowledge what happened and to set clear expectations about this kind of chance encounter. In this way, the agreement grows to be even more explicit about the *when* of coaching.

The question of *when* implicitly speaks to the matter of termination of a coaching relationship. When is it time to end, and how does this unfold? This is a significant matter in most coaching relationships. When coaches function within defined parameters of, for instance, a six-session coaching plan, the end is in the beginning. Coach and client are continually mindful of the finite nature of the contract and orient their work to accomplish as much of the coaching objective as possible in this period of time.

In other contexts, clients may enter with a quick-fix mindset about coaching, which implies a relatively expedient process of a few sessions. Again, the ending is implicit in its beginning. There are, however, long-term coaching relationships that endure for many months and even years. My sense is that both coach and client who are functioning in a clear coaching process that hasn't morphed into some other arrangement (e.g., friendly helper, confidant, advisor, teacher) will experience a growing sense of the timeliness of the ending. In my own experience, a session or two at the end of longer coaching relationships may be devoted to bringing closure to the work.

Quite often, clients end coaching by canceling an appointment and not rescheduling or perhaps by concluding a session with a statement like, "Let me see how this goes, and I'll get back to you to reschedule." With abrupt endings, coaches may want to communicate with these clients either in suggesting a concluding session or in requesting any feedback that might be informative. In such cases, coaches will typically let clients know that the door is open to continuing, should the need arise.

It's unlikely you can cover all aspects of *when* in your agreement, but as much as possible you want to be clear about your preferences. You might let the client know that, to the degree possible, you will normally get back to any emails or phone calls within a specified period (e.g., 24-48 hours), that you schedule sessions between, say, 8 a.m. and 6 p.m., and that you don't meet or correspond on weekends. In essence, you set the parameters for your work as a professional as part of your terms of agreement.

Where?

Where does coaching take place? Coaching is a relatively new profession and, as such, it has evolved during an era where virtual communications are increasingly the norm. The ICF (2020a) global study showed that a large percentage of professional coaches hold sessions on telephone and web-based platforms such as FaceTime and Zoom. Up to this point, in-person sessions have been the most common way of communicating in coaching, yet that may shift dramatically in coming years as online platforms become more user-friendly and as individuals become more accustomed to communicating virtually.

My reflections on the changing venues for coaching are that indeed there may be a bit of a learning curve for both coach and client in mastering virtual communication on different platforms, but with all of the online communications required during the pandemic, people seem more and more comfortable working this way. A significant upside of the shift to virtual coaching sessions is that clients who might otherwise be impeded by travel requirements for coaching sessions would have easier access, thereby increasing the reliability of their participation.

Where do *in-person* sessions take place? You might imagine that in sponsored coaching mandates, sessions are likely to take place in clients' offices. Otherwise, coaches may have their own offices or shared office spaces. While in the early years of coaching, sessions might have taken place in coffee shops or other public venues, presently coaching in such environments would, at the least, be questionable and possibly even unethical. The unethical aspect of meeting in public venues is not only about confidentiality risks but also about the kinds of distractions that might occur that could reduce the coach's capacities.

How?

How does coaching occur, or what do the processes of coaching look like? Definitions of coaching attempt to give some idea of what the process looks like. The ICF (2020e) defines coaching as "partnering with clients in a thought-provoking and cre-

ative process that inspires them to maximize their personal and professional potential." This definition doesn't tell you that coaching is a structured conversation, that coaches ask a lot of questions, that they may share ideas with clients in creative discussions, or that a lot of the work in the session focuses on the development of an action plan for the intervening period between sessions and often beyond. These parts of the *how* begin to identify the process of coaching, which may be difficult to fully articulate in a coaching agreement. Nonetheless, when clients ask, "How does this work?" coaches need to provide some information. Remember the value of valid information in Argyris and Schön's (1974) model 2? To make a free choice and to commit to the process, clients need to know how coaching happens. You have read about this particularly in the description of the 6 *whats* model. You may not include this kind of information in the written agreement you develop with your client, but you want to be mindful of the information that clients need to fully agree to this way of working.

There are other aspects of the *how* answer depending on the way you work. Some coaches like to use assessment tools, others normally use a presession preparation form, and so on. If a particular technique or approach is a significant part of the way you work, you will want to inform clients of this methodology again so they can be fully informed and are able to choose based on valid information.

I haven't spoken about confidentiality as a core feature of the *how* of coaching since we covered this previously. Even so, it bears repeating that coaches need to incorporate details about the nature of confidentiality and its exclusionary conditions in the agreement.

The *how* is also a living process that adapts within its boundaries of coaching to the unique nature and needs of your clients. Being sensitive to the diversity of clients with whom you work, you may want to periodically ask, "How is this process working for you?" The *how* isn't rigid but rather fluid and adaptable within the parameters of coaching. You can request feedback regularly. Some coaches have a practice of concluding sessions with a question to their clients about whether anything in the process was particularly helpful or unhelpful. I think it's a nice piece to include so that we can continuously learn from our teachers—namely, our clients.

How Much (and Other Details)?

How is payment handled? When you are learning coaching, most professional schools of coaching require that your services be offered *pro bono* or without cost to your clients. Upon completion of training, you begin charging for coaching. How do you do this? Many coaches contract for a number of sessions at the outset. Coaching agreements explicitly stipulate clients' financial responsibilities. These include how much each coaching session costs (or the total cost of a set of sessions), when payment is expected (e.g., at the beginning of the month or at the conclusion of each session), which payment method is preferred (check, credit card, e-transfer), what the client's obligations are in terms of canceling appointments (e.g., 24 or 48 hours), when sessions can be made up, and what happens if the coach needs to cancel a meeting. Specifying these details reduces risks of misunderstanding. When working through a sponsoring organization, billing and payment details are also clearly defined with the same set of parameters.

Two issues that coaches struggle with are how much to charge and what to do when clients cancel or fail to show. Typically, there are normative rates within geographical regions and even within professional contexts. Coaches who serve the general public in areas such as life or wellness coaching may develop sliding scales, citing a fee range for clients with different capacities to pay. Coaches who work in organizational contexts may have responded to a call for coaches, which often stipulates a fee-for-service rate. As you develop your practice, it will help to join professional coaching groups where information on fee structures can be shared.

Agreements need to speak to the exact financial consequences of acceptable cancellations, late cancellations, lateness for sessions, and failure to show for a session. For instance, many coaches permit a no-consequence rescheduling if the notice of change comes one or two days before the appointment. Beyond that, change in scheduling is referred to as a late cancellation, carrying with it consequences of some percentage of the fee that would be charged. No shows might be charged at full rate. Then comes the complication. Your client sends you a text saying, "I forgot," "There was an emergency meeting at work," "I got stuck in traffic," "I had a family emergency," "I had the flu," etc. Each reason has to be considered and reasonably judged.

Think back to the issue of *psychological contracts.* Imagine that a coach says to the forgetful client, "Oh, I understand, I forget things, too! So, this time I won't charge." What do you imagine the implicit agreement between coach and client becomes? Your time is finite, and it is your vehicle for professional practice and your own economic well-being. Once

again, through your professional networks, you may want to initiate clinics of peer supervision around these types of questions.

To give you an idea of a coaching agreement, please refer to appendix B. You can adapt this agreement with more or less detail depending on your personal style and the nature of your practice.

COACHING AGREEMENTS IN THE ICF CORE COMPETENCIES

Let's now connect what you have been learning about agreements with what the International Coaching Federation offers in its articulation of competencies associated with coaching agreements (see sidebar, ICF Core Coaching Competency 3: Establishes and Maintains Agreements). As you review this competency, you are likely to see different facets of agreements from the ICF perspective. Passmore and Sinclair (2020), in their consideration of this competency, delineated three distinct "levels of agreement" (p. 107): agreements related to (1) the coaching plan and goals, (2) the coaching relationship, and (3) a session's goals and objectives. In effect, the ICF (2020c) focuses its attention not just on competencies related to what coaches need to do in setting the stage for the coaching relationship, but also what they need to do in individual sessions.

It is evident, for instance, that coaches need significant capacity in facilitating conversations that enable clients to articulate their objectives or goals for coaching. They also need to partner with their clients as they work toward agreements on the nature of the work, parameters for coaching, responsibilities, and processes. These broader agreements form the container for the coaching work. Yet, competency in collaboratively shaping agreements within individual coaching sessions toward goals and outcomes is also necessary. These matters have been amply addressed in the material we have just covered. However, I want to delve into three important themes relevant to agreements that gain significance from the way in which the ICF expresses this competency; these are partnering in agreements; distinguishing goals, objectives, and plans; and client–coach compatibility.

Partnering in Agreements

The ICF framing of agreements references the larger context of agreement elements for the entire

ICF Core Coaching Competency 3: Establishes and Maintains Agreements

Definition: Partners with the client and relevant stakeholders to create clear agreements about the coaching relationship, process, plans and goals. Establishes agreements for the overall coaching engagement as well as those for each coaching session.

1. Explains what coaching is and is not and describes the process to the client and relevant stakeholders
2. Reaches agreement about what is and is not appropriate in the relationship, what is and is not being offered, and the responsibilities of the client and relevant stakeholders
3. Reaches agreement about the guidelines and specific parameters of the coaching relationship such as logistics, fees, scheduling, duration, termination, confidentiality and inclusion of others
4. Partners with the client and relevant stakeholders to establish an overall coaching plan and goals
5. Partners with the client to determine client–coach compatibility
6. Partners with the client to identify or reconfirm what they want to accomplish in the session
7. Partners with the client to define what the client believes they need to address or resolve to achieve what they want to accomplish in the session
8. Partners with the client to define or reconfirm measures of success for what the client wants to accomplish in the coaching engagement or individual session
9. Partners with the client to manage the time and focus of the session
10. Continues coaching in the direction of the client's desired outcome unless the client indicates otherwise
11. Partners with the client to end the coaching relationship in a way that honors the experience

relationship, as well as what happens in individual sessions. You will recognize that some points of this ICF competency reflect coaching competencies articulated in the 6 *whats* model. While clients may set out an ambitious coaching objective, each session represents a kind of microcosm of the larger agreement. Coaches begin a session establishing what the focus of work will be for today, knowing that it may more or less reflect the explicit language of the overall coaching objective. Part of the coach's work is to determine how the part relates to the whole.

The language of this competency brings into clear view the salience of partnering in the relationship. The ICF refers to a collaborative and nonhierarchical way of working with clients wherein both coach and client have voices. Though the focus of the work always derives from the client, the coach is fully able to explore and contribute to the evolution of thought and action regarding what the client wants to achieve. It is often said that the client is the expert in the subject of the coaching session, while the coach is the expert in the process. The expertise of both participants in coaching coalesces in a flowing dialogue that advances in a fashion that is mutually determined and agreed upon.

In this partnered way of working, coaches explore their current understandings of agreements with clients to ensure full alignment. They fluidly comanage with their clients coaching structures and processes that can benefit objectives of the work. Agreements to explore further, to redirect conversation, to advance to a planning process, and other essential transitions in the flow of a coaching dialogue are never dictated but rather agreed upon in partnership.

Distinguishing Goals, Objectives, and Plans

This core competency indicates a need for coaches to partner with the client in establishing "an overall coaching plan and goals" (ICF, 2020c). The ICF's reference to goals seems aligned with what you know as the **coaching objective.** Based on the framework of goal-centric coaching, you will remember that there are overarching goals that may be at the level of life purposes, and there are perhaps multiple levels of subgoals beneath that highest level objective. Clients may describe a coaching objective in their early sessions that is broad or narrow, abstract or concrete. No matter how that overarching objective or goal is stated, it will typically subdivide into a number of subgoals. So in this ICF competency, you might be aware that there is reference to the overall goals of the coaching relationship, which compare to our construct of the coaching objective, and there are goals or intentions for individual sessions. Agreements are shaped around the *big goals* or coaching objectives, and they are also formed around *small goals* or objectives that clients identify within individual sessions.

The ICF speaks of goals rather than a singular goal, suggesting that at the very outset of coaching, clients may have many goals they want to pursue. For example, a client may say he wants to feel less stressed, to be better organized in work habits and to have more work–life balance. In exploring these three seemingly different objectives with this client, you might ask the client at some point whether it would be useful for him to capture the three intentions in one statement. In reply, he could say something like, "I want to be more effective at organizing and managing my life." In that statement, the client would have shaped a more comprehensive goal or coaching objective. So, at times the coaching objective, in our terms, could be presented in a number of separate parts (or goals), while at other times, you and your client may be able to unite all the different parts (or goals) that are presented under a higher level goal, which then becomes the coaching objective.

With the term **coaching plan**, the ICF seems to be referencing structures and processes for the work of the coaching relationship. You have already reviewed aspects of the coaching plan in the Critical Elements of Agreements section of this chapter. When coaches stipulate the *who*, *what*, *when*, *where*, *why*, and *how* of coaching, they are specifying ways in which coaching will intentionally unfold, who will be involved and why, what the conditions of coaching will be, its duration and meeting frequency, and so forth. Plan and objective are related but separate, as when someone says, "This is my objective, and here's my plan for achieving it."

One important distinction to bear in mind is that a coaching plan isn't the same as an action plan that clients generate in their sessions. Action plans refer to a more or less detailed description of what clients will enact in the period following a session.

Client–Coach Compatibility

The notion of compatibility is hard to define in its specifics. Another expression that is equally difficult to concretely explain is *chemistry*—in this case, the sensed chemistry between coach and client. It often comes down to a matter of personal judgment and preference. Thinking back to Argyris and Schön's (1974) models, when coaches operate from a value stance of creating valid information, free and informed choice, and internal commitment to decisions and actions, it is more likely that coach or client might decide after some preliminary contact that there isn't a good fit in the coaching relationship.

An earlier term applied to situations where the coach evaluated the viability of a coaching relationship was **coachability**. It has been defined as a client's "willingness to enter one's discomfort zone to change behavior" (Guttman, 2007, p. 14), although I think this is only partially descriptive of how this term has evolved in the coaching field. In previous discussions, you have encountered a number of matters relating to the viability of a coaching relationship. For instance, we considered the issue of topic appropriateness and then pointed to other questions such as client readiness and client motivation or capacity to adequately address their agendas (Kretzschmar, 2010).

I appreciate the fact that the ICF has steered away from using the term *coachability* in its recent updating of the code of ethics and core coaching competencies. My own sense is that this term is fraught with judgments, mostly pointing to the client. I'd like to share a short story: During the final residential session in a coach training program I was leading, a student coach was having a particularly difficult time getting anywhere with her approach to coaching her student client. In an exasperated tone, she threw up her hands, looked at the mentor for the session, and said, "He's just not coachable." Rather than viewing her difficulty as a complex combination of factors, she blamed the client.

This vignette exemplifies some of the apprehension I have about supporting the use of the term *coachability* in our work. There may well be times when clients want to address issues in their lives, but their capacity happens to be limited by a number of factors at this particular moment. Other times, a client wants to achieve a particular objective but hasn't dealt with some of the foundational pieces required to begin addressing this objective. Imagine someone who hasn't learned to swim but aspires to complete a triathlon. Then there's the matter of compatibility as pointed to by the ICF. On either side of the relationship, coach or client may not have a strong enough connection with the other. Of course, another factor that we addressed earlier is whether the topic a client is presenting is something that a given coach is able and willing to competently engage.

So, it feels far more respectful for coaches to say, "I just don't feel that I can do my very best with this client and her topic at this time and under these conditions. Maybe someone else can be more helpful, and the client deserves the very best coach she can have working with her on this matter of deep importance." Wrapping this up, we can at the very least acknowledge the following:

- There are topics that don't fit the scope and processes of coaching.
- There are clients who have expectations that don't match the ways of coaching.
- There are coaches and clients who for one reason or another aren't willing or able to work together.
- There are clients who discover they have some basic groundwork to complete before they take on a coaching relationship.
- There are conditions in the lives of coaches and clients that impede or prevent a successful coaching relationship from evolving.

I wouldn't try to lump all these under a rubric like coachability or compatibility but rather stick with a more fundamental appreciation that the necessary and sufficient conditions for a viable coaching relationship simply aren't present. Another pairing of coach–client, another time, another set of conditions, or other shifts might make the difference.

REFLECTIONS

We have traveled a fair distance in reviewing competencies related to coaching agreements. There are so many elements to be considered and monitored as the relationship evolves. We need things to be explicit so we can say yes or no with full awareness and commitment. We don't want important matters left to assumption or guesswork. If you reflect on some of the challenges you have had in business and personal relations, can you identify how perhaps unclear agreements were at root? In a big way, agreements speak to a theme of trust and trustworthiness. I can give you my word, but what if I don't live up to my word? How does that affect our relationship? I mentioned Don Miguel Ruiz's (2001) *Four Agreements* at the beginning of the chapter. As coaches, we strive to be impeccable with our word, and that is essential to the nature of agreements. When you think of it this way, you may begin to realize what the competency challenge is here. Sometimes you may not be sure what the implicit agreements are in the relationships you have. What do people expect of you? How did they develop those expectations? What do you expect of others? It might be beneficial to sit with the task of exploring how agreements—implicit and explicit—have played out in your life in order to harvest the knowledge of your own experiences about agreements.

CHAPTER 8

CULTIVATING TRUST AND SAFETY

Trust is the bridge from yesterday to tomorrow,
built with planks of thanks.

Ann Voskamp

MY STORY

Throughout my professional career, I have been amazed at the courage of my clients as they unfold their stories during the hours of our relationship. I try to ease into the conversation, so they feel they are fully in control of what and how much they say, and then I am almost equally surprised when I realize we have come to the end of our time and yet there is so much more to be said.

I think that humans have an inborn need for intimate connection and when a deep sense of safety has been offered, profound personal meanings and understandings are easily expressed. The curious thing that I have begun to acknowledge more fully is that at any moment something I say can stop the flow of a vulnerable self-disclosure. So, it is a dance of sorts—stepping on your partner's foot has an immediate impact on movement.

Working with clients as I have over the decades has been a profound and humbling privilege. How do I merit such trust that often shows up in the first moment of contact? What do I do consciously or unconsciously to continue to warrant that trust? I am acutely aware that the trust that my clients bestow upon me is fragile and never to be taken for granted. When I open my door to a client or click the link for a web connection, I have cleared the space in me to receive them—wherever they are in that moment in their fullness of being, with all their stories and dreams.

Coaching is based in relationship, and the qualities of this relationship influence the effectiveness of the process and its outcomes. Building on seminal understandings of the working alliance between client and helper, the nature of trust in relational dynamics will be explored in this chapter along with factors that contribute to a client's capacity to experience trust and a coach's trustworthiness. Issues surrounding power and influence, as well as the filters through which coach and client perceive one another, are examined for their potential impact on the working alliance. Here are some guiding questions as you read:

- How important is the relationship to the outcome clients realize from coaching?
- What are the key factors in creating a trusting and safe coaching relationship?
- How do social and emotional intelligences play into relationship dynamics?
- What is the meaning of the working alliance?
- How do power dynamics play out in coaching?
- Does transference really happen in coaching?

A UNIQUE RELATIONSHIP

I rely a lot on the words of Carl Rogers, founder of humanistic psychology and of client-centered relationship work. He knew the deep importance of relationships and what was at risk when you open yourself to another person's world. As he said, "If I let myself really understand another person, I might be changed by that understanding. And we all fear change. So as I say, it is not an easy thing to permit oneself to understand an individual" (Rogers, 1961, p. 18). Each client is unique, and you will form a unique bond with each of your clients. You will shape yourself in that relationship so as to honor all that this client is now and all that is in a process of becoming. So too, you will be changed by this partnership to the degree that you open yourself to all its potential.

Relationships are what help define our humanity (Johnson, 2014). You were born from relationship, and you need relationships to survive. Whether as a professional, friend, family member, or citizen, you are shaped by your social existence. To some degree, you know who you are through others' impressions of you. Coaching is first and foremost about relationship. The bottom line is that without relationship, there can be no coaching.

The strength of relationships between helpers and clients has been thoroughly examined as a major factor in creating positive outcomes (Lambert & Barley, 2001; Zilcha-Mano, 2017). Coaching represents a distinctive form of helping in terms of the relationship qualities it nourishes. For instance, consider the affiliation that might exist between a surgeon and patient. Though bedside manners may be relevant, most patients are more concerned with the doctor's surgical skills and track record than with their interpersonal skills. Viewed from another angle, the surgeon isn't primarily engaged in dialogue as the form of treatment, whereas in coaching the outcome is heavily affected by the coach's communication acumen and capacity to invite clients into safe discussion about personal matters. A coach's expertise is founded in relationship dynamics, and her value relies greatly on a capacity to connect in ways that build trust and create realistic hope for meaningful change.

Let me qualify this before we continue: Compared to a therapeutic dynamic, some coaching experts believe that the relationship may not be as salient a factor in successful outcomes based on the belief that the subject matter is likely to be less sensitive in coaching than it is in therapy (Ives & Cox, 2012). In their work on goal-focused coaching, Ives and Cox (p. 55) suggest "that it is not the relationship with the coach, but with the (need for) coaching that makes the difference." It's not that they minimize the coach–client relationship but rather that they underscore the client's relationship with the process of coaching itself. This seems an important point.

I assume that each of us is involved in helping relationships every day; some of these relationships occur informally, whereas others are more formal. Accordingly, expectations of helpers vary based on whether the person is a family member, friend, or professional. You might expect certain types of support and advice when you share concerns with friends, whereas professional helping carries other expectations. In general, professionals bear greater responsibility throughout the helping process and are expected to be objective, purposeful, and skilled in their domains.

TOWARD TRUSTING AND SAFE COMMUNICATIONS

Relationships constitute a fluid, complex, and powerful realm in our lives. Trust—as evidenced in clients' willingness to engage in coaching, self-disclose, and fully explore their topics—is the very fabric of the coaching connection. In fact, trust is a *sine qua non* (without which, nothing) for successful coaching. When searching for a coach who will facilitate their goal attainment, clients look for someone who gets them and is honest, sincere, and trustworthy. From the very first encounter with their coaches, clients want to experience a special connection, a feeling that they click and that they can work with the coach. Establishing trust and safety is foundational to healthy helping relationships. It allows clients to believe that their decision to engage in a coaching partnership will work for them.

Of course, coaches also decide whether they wholeheartedly choose to work with a client. You will remember this from the previous chapter's consideration of the concept of client–coach compatibility. When coaches are deciding to work with a particular client, there are at least two core ingredients that factor into their decision: Does the coach believe the client can engage productively within the structures of a coaching relationship, and is there a sense that this client will faithfully engage in the required work of coaching? Think of these two ingredients as the ability and willingness to be coached rather than as indicators of coachability, which can imply an ingrained characteristic of the person. The ability piece becomes questionable when clients continually expect coaches to tell them what to do, to act as therapists, or to address needs that are beyond the boundaries of coaching. On the other hand, the willingness aspect comes down to the clients' motivation and commitment to reliably follow through on their agreements to act since the nature of coaching relies on clients' engaging in actions to which they commit in sessions.

So we come back to trust. To what degree does the coach trust in the client's willingness and capacity? As you can see, that's one sided. The coach's ability and willingness also factor into how they enter this relationship: *Do I have the ability to work with this client, on this agenda, in his or her context, and in light of everything else going on for me at this time? And do I sense a strong desire or willingness to work with this client with an open mind, heart, and will?*

When the answer to these questions is clear and affirmative, then the coach will need to show up in ways that are consistently trustworthy. Though there isn't a precise formula for being perceived as trustworthy, the concepts of social and emotional intelligence are relevant to this matter. Belsten (2013) writes that "social and emotional intelligence is the ability to be aware of our own emotions and those of others, in the moment, and to use that information to manage ourselves and manage our relationships."

Consider an initial contact between coach and client. How does a client sense that this relationship will work, that he or she can trust this person

and feel safe? While I wouldn't discount intuitive knowing on the part of the client, it is perhaps more useful to reflect on the coach's behavior that induces the client to experience his or her trustworthiness. If social and emotional intelligence references capacities, and one has to sensitively navigate emerging relationships, then you can probably see how building trust relies on skill sets embedded in this kind of intelligence. A new client says, "I've come here to address something that I have been working on for years without any success." The coach replies, in the absence of any other information, "I am sure I can help you with that." What do you think the client's perception of this coach's trustworthiness might be? The coach doesn't really know this client or the depth of the issue being presented. How can he or she promise results?

Trust is built over time on big and small actions, words and silences, questions and offers, and numerous other barely perceptible communications. When a coach has a high level of social and emotional intelligence, the client leaves that initial encounter thinking and feeling that the coach is trustworthy.

Social and Emotional Intelligence

Social and emotional intelligence (S+EQ) is essential to effective relationships. Unlike an intelligence quotient, which is considered to be consistent over time, this intelligence is not thought to be static. It comprises sets of skills that can be developed. Core elements of S+EQ are awareness of your own emotional states (i.e., becoming emotionally literate) and accurate perception of the feelings of others accompanied by an empathic and caring response. It also involves the ability to tap into emotional awareness for managing yourself and your relationships with others (Belsten, 2013).

In other words, those with high S+EQ cultivate the capacity to become aware of their feelings in the present moment; they nurture their ability to identify their emotions and feelings accurately in order to express them appropriately. For instance, if you realize that your muscles are tense and you have a pain in the pit of your stomach, you might know this sensation as a feeling of irritation. In naming the emotion, you can then use proven strategies to deal with your feelings without provoking negative responses.

The ability to accurately perceive the emotions and feelings of another person implies that one might be capable of experiencing and expressing empathy, an indispensable element for connecting positively with others. Social and emotional intelligence is crucial in coaching because it provides evidence of how competent one is in creating an atmosphere where trust can flourish.

There is a fine distinction between emotions and feelings even though the words are often used interchangeably. Emotions are your brain's reactions to physiological sensations and physical actions (Barrett & Fischer, 2017). According to Cavanagh (2006), "emotions can be a source of data to inform the coaching conversation" (p. 333). There are thought to be six universal emotions, which are often considered automatic: anger, disgust, fear, happiness, sadness, and surprise (Damasio, 2000). Referencing Damasio, Elaine Cox describes feelings as the "initial mechanisms through which understanding [of your emotional state] is achieved" (Cox, 2013, p. 17). There are many types of feelings (e.g., happy, sad, angry, content, proud, grateful, anxious), which are experienced at different levels of intensity. While emotions may be expressed verbally, they are also likely to show up strongly in nonverbal communications. This fact raises the importance of coaches' S+EQ in being able to appropriately perceive and interpret nonverbal cues as a way of knowing what emotions clients may be experiencing. By more accurately perceiving the client's world, the coach creates the conditions to be seen in the relationship as trustworthy.

Understanding Trust

Trust is a quality that is more or less present at any moment in a relationship. It is not static—it ebbs and flows. Your ability to trust others may be challenged by events that rightly or wrongly imply that someone is not entirely trustworthy. To a large degree, trust derives from your *perceptions* of another person's trustworthiness (Johnson, 2014). A coach's capacity to build trust and intimacy stems from awareness of how to show up in relationships in ways that are likely to be perceived as trustworthy. In upcoming sections, key elements that foster trust in coaching relationships will be highlighted. These include intimacy, genuine concern, empathy, congruence, personal integrity, and respecting diversity.

Understanding Intimacy

Intimacy represents a kind of emotional bond between coach and client; as such, it is one of the necessary conditions for engaging in effective communication processes with clients to address their dreams and visions. The term intimacy in the context of professional relationships may seem misplaced. You can better interpret it as psychological intimacy, which has been defined as openness and honesty in "talking with a partner about personal thoughts and feelings not usually expressed in other relationships" (Mackey & Diemer, 2000, p. 201). Though you might think this definition applies only to deep personal relationships, coaches have to establish an appropriate level of intimacy to work effectively with clients. They need to ask questions and discuss information that goes beyond superficial exchanges. When you reveal personal details, you are likely to feel vulnerable. Correspondingly, it's easier to express intimate matters when you feel the other is trustworthy. To encourage clients and develop the relationship, coaches sometimes self-disclose details about themselves to create the grounds for trust. Suitable self-disclosure (see chapter 12) can reduce clients' uneasiness and allow positive connections to evolve (Ruddle & Dilks, 2015).

What's the level of intimacy in coaching relationships? That may be hard to define, but it certainly stops far short of physical contact and does not encompass wide-ranging disclosures unrelated to the coaching topic. However, that still leaves a fair amount of leeway. Problems may arise when coaches either push for too much intimacy or, conversely, come across as distant. A coach with strong needs for intimacy may probe deeper than necessary to address the contracted agenda. On the flip side, if a coach is tentative about emotions, she may behave in a manner that precludes clients from talking about their own emotionality. For example, to avoid strong emotional content in sessions, a coach may subtly discourage the client from expressing such emotions as anger and sadness by redirecting conversations when she notices the client is becoming upset.

Deep fears of intimacy or strong emotionality can be a liability for coaches. A coach who remains consistently objective and aloof may dampen clients' emotional expressions or their willingness to confront personal vulnerabilities. As a result, the coach may feel safe, but the value of the coaching experience will be limited to the degree that critical emotional themes are constrained.

Genuine Concern

Carl Rogers (1961) expressed the belief that people are always in a process of becoming. In other words, no matter what age, people are able to change—

they are not bound by their past. Rogers' position represented a dramatic shift in beliefs about human nature derived from an earlier Freudian perspective (Freud, 1964). Rather than treating people as products of their past and incapable of continued growth, Rogers and his followers, Carkhuff and Truax (Carkhuff, 1969; Truax & Carkhuff, 1967), urged helpers to appreciate clients as having strength, potential, inner resilience, and the capacity for self-realization. In a Rogerian perspective, coaches' attitudes and genuine concern toward clients are as important in determining outcomes as their technical skills or theoretical knowledge.

A classic tale of helping that Rogers (1961) described was of a man who successfully completed counseling after having previously had an unsuccessful experience with another counselor. When the second counselor inquired why the client was able to work through his issues so successfully this time, he responded that this second practitioner had done essentially the same things as the first but that in working together, the client felt that this counselor really cared about him. Rogers' (1957) profound concern for the client and the quality of the helping relationship might be framed in simple questions that coaches can ask themselves.

- How can I act so my clients perceive me as trustworthy?
- How can I cultivate attitudes of caring and interest toward my clients?
- How do I demonstrate deep empathy for my clients' feelings and their perspectives?

The quality of the coach–client relationship has been identified as a key success factor across different forms of coaching (Baron & Morin, 2009; de Haan et al., 2013). Coaching has been described as a collaborative process of learning and behavioral change (Sonesh et al., 2015). It is noteworthy in this regard that helpers who are effective in facilitating learning and change have also been found to exhibit trust, flexibility, and empathy in their coaching relationships (Ackerman & Hilsenroth, 2003).

Empathy

Empathy is considered to be a fundamental element of prosocial behavior—behavior intended to help others (Eisenberg & Miller, 1987; Telle & Pfister, 2016). Whether demonstrating positive or negative empathy (i.e., empathizing with others' positive or negative emotions), a coach needs to be able to express awareness of the other person's reality (Andreychik & Lewis, 2017). Once again, I call upon the wisdom of Carl Rogers, whose definition of empathy has gone virtually unchanged for more than 70 years; he described it as "the concept of the 'as if'" while identifying the empathic helper as someone who takes on "insofar as he is able, the internal frame of reference of the client" (Rogers, 1951, p. 129). This is often understood as seeing the world through the eyes of the other.

To further clarify the concept of empathy, take a look at two hypothetical client statements and corresponding coach responses. Each response has been critiqued to highlight differences in empathy (see Examples of Empathic and Nonempathic Responses sidebar).

In the tradition of Rogers' work, three levels of empathy have been identified within helping relationships (Carkhuff, 1969; Rogers, 1961; Truax & Carkhuff, 1967); the first two are likely to be helpful, while the third can be quite problematic:

1. *Basic empathy.* A helper's responses carry roughly the same meaning and are essentially interchangeable with those of the client. When this is done well, it creates the sense of a conversation with strong focus on what the client is saying.

2. *Additive empathy.* A helper's responses acknowledge aspects of the client's communications that were perhaps implied, communicated nonverbally, or inferable from other things the client said; these elements are then added to a basic empathic response. Here, the helper integrates both verbal and nonverbal messages as well as hunches about what the client may not yet have expressed. It deepens the conversation.

3. *Subtractive empathy.* A helper's responses omit significant elements of the client's communications or even distort their meaning. While this is likely unintentional, the effect can be a gradual erosion of trust. Having left out or forgotten something deemed important, the helper might be perceived as expressing her own interests over those of the client.

Empathy sometimes gets confused with the concept of sympathy, though the two are quite different in nature and effect. Sympathy is more about feeling sorry for or pitying someone who is going through a hard time, whereas empathy requires that a helper allow the client's thoughts and emotions to be personally experienced and then reflected (Carré et al., 2013). Helping professionals are sometimes

---

Examples of Empathic and Nonempathic Responses

Client Statement Concerning Public Speaking

Client: I'm not very good at public speaking. I've never been able to stand up in a group and express myself without feelings of total panic.

Response from coach A: Well, I think you have everything it takes to be a great public speaker!

Response from coach B: I can sense how deeply this upsets you—wanting to feel comfortable speaking up in groups yet being gripped by fear.

Critique of Responses

The first response is like cheerleading; it asserts something that may or may not be true, but more importantly that might cause the client to wonder how the coach could possibly know that.

The second response shows acceptance and understanding of the client's reality yet allows opportunity for further exploration should the client choose.

Client Statement Regarding a Sense of Failure

Client: Ugh, these past weeks have been so difficult. I really tried to follow the plan, but I couldn't do it. It was a good plan—I simply failed.

Response from coach A: Don't say you failed! You tried! You'll do it! Cut yourself some slack! It happens— sometimes you just need to back off, regroup, and then try again.

Response from coach B: I hear you. It's been difficult, you believe that you failed, and you don't see a clear reason for this. How might we explore this so you can understand it better?

Critique of Responses

The first coach's comments are intended to be encouraging, but they attempt to mollify the client's intense feelings and reactions, substituting what the coach wants the client to think and feel. Exploration and insight are largely blocked by this response.

The second coach captures the core messages and connects with the client's inner world, as unsettled as it may be. The coach reflects the client's belief that there was no solid reason for what happened and then opens the door to exploration.

---

reluctant to fully allow themselves to experience empathy since it entails getting close to the emotional world of their clients. It takes a strong sense of self to enter another person's reality with assurance that you won't get trapped there. This may be much more likely to occur when coaches themselves are in personal turmoil.

Another concept that gets mixed up with the meaning of empathy is identification. When a situation is too close to a helper's own, the helper might identify with the client's difficulties rather than expressing empathy. When empathically engaged, one retains one's separateness, whereas identification means that one person takes on the feelings and reality experienced by the other as if they were his or her own. An empathic response requires an ability to recognize other people's emotions with the knowledge that these emotions belong to the other (Carré et al., 2013; Siegel, 2018). When a coach identifies with his or her client, there is no separate-

ness. The coach has become the client, and there is a kind of symbiotic quality to the relationship; whereas when empathizing, the coach is able to verbalize his or her understanding of clients' inner worlds so they experience a caring reflection of the realities they live.

Consider a simple example. A coach says to the client, "I know exactly what you're feeling," and thinks to himself, "This is the same stuff I've been going through for years!" In this awareness, the coach is caught up in either reliving his own experiences or projecting himself onto the client's situation. Either way, the coach is no longer present or listening. The coach may be revisiting his own story and unconsciously force fitting the client's reality to his own. At a certain level, the coach becomes the client and then projects his own experiences, feelings, and solutions onto the client. This is the essence of identification; it is not what is meant by the term *empathy*.

Congruence and Personal Integrity

Coaching is a partnership—an agreement to collaborate in working on an agenda defined by the client. Coaching requires personal integrity and consistent behavior. When you experience another person as communicating through filters or from behind a mask, your willingness to be open and trusting with that person diminishes. Of course, a coach's actions with clients would not be expected to be the same as with intimate friends and family, even though core qualities of his or her presence may be virtually indistinguishable. It is therefore important for you to know how to navigate the boundaries between private and professional areas of your life in a safe and seamless manner. Professionals who show caring, empathy, and sensitivity with clients but then switch off these qualities when sessions end will invariably reveal leakage between their disparate ways of being.

The quality of congruence refers to the coach's personal integrity and not simply to the match between what is expected of the coach's role and what the coach actually does. Congruent coaches understand their own values and motivations; they know when they are aligned at all levels of their being. The coach's nonverbal messages are consistent with their verbal ones. What the coach says is an accurate reflection of their inner values and beliefs.

People easily sense insincerity. When someone smiles because it is a programmed role response, you are likely to recognize it as insincere. Consistently demonstrating integrity, congruence, and sincerity means that clients know they can expect honesty even in difficult matters.

Respecting Diversity

Respecting diversity merits consideration as a wholly separate theme, though it is fully integral to the creation of trusting and safe relationships. It pertains to valuing others and holding them in positive regard simply because they are human. Embedded in this concept is a capacity to minimize judgmental attitudes. Not only is it nearly impossible to remain without judgment, but certain types of judgments are essential. You need to assess situations and use judgment to evaluate people, circumstances, and conditions to determine whether they will support you or threaten your well-being. Making these kinds of judgments is different from being judgmental, which has a negative connotation implying a quality of being disparaging or disapproving. Coaches are expected to hold positive beliefs about clients and humanity in general. No matter who your clients are, what they have experienced, or what patterns they might present, effective coaches remain confident that there is much unrealized potential and capability in every person with whom they work.

Respecting diversity requires that rather than acting on assumptions and biases, you strive to approach people and situations with an open mind and heart. Along with empathy, respecting diversity means communicating a deep sense of appreciation and regard for clients irrespective of differences. The world is increasingly diverse. Diversity encompasses such aspects as race and ethnicity; sex; gender identification; sexual orientation; age; physical attributes; religious affiliation; language; education; civil, social, and economic status; intellectual capacity; state of mental health; beliefs; values; preferences; and so much more. As you have previously learned, diversity also includes learning styles and personality traits.

Unfortunately, there is still stigma attached to many faces of diversity, and some more so than others. Eliminating stigma requires a willingness to value differences and a commitment to foster awareness of your own biases, negative judgments, and prejudicial thoughts. To remain in integrity as an empathic and respectful individual who appreciates diversity requires that you consistently make the choice to embrace differences rather than act on fear-based negative judgments of others. Appreciating and respecting diverse others calls for learning about people with traditions and preferences that vary from your own.

Honoring diversity also speaks to a stance of activism. It means speaking up when you hear disparaging comments pertaining to diversity from those around us, as well as proactively engaging in processes that address systemic bias within society. What it does not mean, however, is constantly walking on eggshells because you aren't sure how to address aspects of a person's diversity. When in doubt about something, it is better to be up-front rather than suppress your confusion to avoid offending someone. Simply ask others respectfully for guidelines regarding how they would prefer you address a particular situation that puzzles you. We will return to this subject in the book's final chapter.

THE WORKING ALLIANCE

The relationship is the principal medium through which clients bring forth significant ideas and feelings that constitute the agenda of coaching (Lambert

& Barley, 2001). Though there is some debate on this issue (Ives & Cox, 2012), an early work by Bluckert (2005) asserted that the coaching relationship is "not just a critical success factor, but *the* [italics added] critical success factor in successful coaching outcomes" (p. 336). Research has documented that the strength of the coaching relationship "as rated by the client, correlates with client-rated coaching outcome to a considerable degree" (de Haan et al., 2013, p. 52). One might say that the **working alliance** empowers clients to identify, explore, and achieve objectives they so deeply desire.

In the coaching literature as well as in the broader works of helping and counseling, the term *working alliance* provides perspective for understanding what needs to happen between coach and client to maximize trust and safety, and thereby appreciating the effectiveness of a supportive relationship (Horvath & Greenberg, 1994). A coaching relationship in which the coach dedicates time and energy to establishing rapport, building trust (Du Toit, 2014), and demonstrating commitment leads to better coaching outcomes and behavioral change (Boyce et al., 2010). While coaches may have a certain level of expertise relevant to their clients' topics, it will ultimately be the quality of the working alliance that most strongly influences outcomes (de Haan et al., 2013, 2016; Rogers, 1961; Sonesh et al., 2015).

Three necessary elements of the working alliance have been identified as (1) agreements on goals, (2) agreements on tasks, and (3) the emotional bond between coach and client (Bordin, 1979). Essential elements of agreements were reviewed in the previous chapter, so here I will look more closely at the emotional bond that fosters trust and safety in the relationship.

When you imagine professional behavior, do you have an anticipation of warmth or of emotional distance? Expressing emotional warmth in professional relationships is usually based on the valuing of clients as individuals of equal worth (Mehr & Kanwischer, 2011). Clients are likely to express greater willingness to try new behaviors and risk failing because of the openness and acceptance they experience from their coaches. In simple words, warmth sends a message of trustworthiness. Warmth and caring, overtly expressed, communicate that it is safe for clients to be vulnerable, just as coaches need to allow themselves to be vulnerable in their expressions with clients. Demonstrating warmth in no way precludes dealing with difficult issues or confronting clients when needed. In fact, confrontation (see chapter 12) becomes more productive when clients sense their coaches' genuine warmth toward them.

You probably realize that whenever two people meet, each party's history in relationships influences what evolves between them. So, it's not surprising that there are identifiable patterns in helpers' behaviors that can signal difficulties in their professional relationships (Brems, 2001). Coaches may have intimacy needs that are either excessive or insufficient to form effective alliances with clients. Relatedly, they may have strong needs for approval causing them to look to clients for validation. In building rapport with clients, they may be over- or underdisclosing of personal information with clients who, by way of contrast, are expected to reveal significant aspects of their private lives. Finally, coaches may have patterns of emotional dependency. As the relationship develops, coaches may become dependent on clients for a sense of accomplishment or they may foster dependency in clients by presenting themselves as indispensable to their welfare and growth.

There are no simple guides to knowing what clients will evoke in you as they present intimate details of their lives. There is, however, one clear requirement, which is to be awake to all that is happening in these powerful helping relationships. No training program or teacher can tell you what you will experience personally when you begin coaching. You will learn from your own practice by becoming a self-reflective practitioner (Johns, 2017; Schön, 2003). Two dynamics that are often present in the working alliance pertain to our needs for competence and power (Brown, 2007; DeVaris, 1994; Norcross, 2002; Weiner & Bornstein, 2009). In truth, these needs factor into all your relationships. For now, let's see how the needs for competence and power might play out in coaching.

Competence and Trusting Your Inner Knowing

No matter how many degrees or certifications you have, the career path of a coach places you on a never-ending learning journey. Part of the experience of being a coach involves sitting with uncertainty and ambiguity about how best to help. For many of us, when we are in moments like these, we may doubt ourselves and our capacities.

Coaches sometimes rely on different tools and formulas to demystify what might be happening in a coaching relationship. You might imagine that if your client took a particular psychometric test, you would know more about why he shows up the way he does. Not knowing and not feeling competent can be uncomfortable. The more you experience yourself in a place of not knowing or ambiguity, the more you might want to search for facts or concrete data in the hope that this kind of information will enable you to reduce your uncertainty. Indeed, you may pressure yourself to dive deeply for details and to mechanically ask questions that might bring you, perhaps prematurely, to actionable targets even though you might still feel a bit lost as to what is really needed. What can help in these moments?

One critical strategy in moments such as these is to strengthen your capacities for self-awareness and mindfulness. The fact is, you don't need to know all the facts or all the details. Uncertainty and lack of clarity are inherent in certain aspects of coaching work. With self-awareness, you can rest calmly in a state of curiosity, allowing yourself to ask out loud what your clients most need to tell you to help you partner with them in the process. Another core strategy relies on having internalized the structures of a coaching session (e.g., 6 *whats* model). Knowing how a session proceeds, you can mindfully open yourself to not knowing while being fully conscious of the process. Trusting your inner wisdom and intuition, you can clear your mind to hear what seems to be most important in your clients' stories. When you sense you have what is essential, you can check your understanding with your client and move seamlessly to subsequent parts of the process that you know so well. Your ability to be fully conscious, alert, and available will allow you and your clients to explore unfamiliar territory, generate new insights, and discover novel avenues for action even when the complexity of client issues seems difficult to comprehend at the outset.

Developing your capacity to reflect and to be mindfully aware allows you to better appreciate your own vulnerability to self-doubt, negative self-beliefs, and self-criticism (Johns, 2017). You may have strong needs to know and to appear competent even when these needs interfere with your presence and your capacity to comprehend what is right in front of you. When doubt and self-questioning continually disrupt your capacity to be open and transparent in the moment with your client, you may need to find help through readings and conversations with peers, mentors, or supervisors. If you are challenged by feelings of inadequacy and doubt in some of your sessions, strategies of denial, minimization or projection of responsibility are likely to be counterproductive. Acknowledging how you respond in moments when you experience less-than-stellar results allows you to devise supportive practices and options. How you manage these moments in your career will affect the degree to which you thrive in this challenging line of work and how compassionately you are able to assist others. After all, if you are not a good coach to yourself, how beneficial can you be to others?

Power and Influence

One thing is certain—there is a clear difference between the power bases of coaches and their clients. Clients may be highly successful in many domains of life, yet in the particular topic for which they are seeking your help, they are likely to feel puzzled, confused, or even inept. They look to you for knowledge and guidance, and in this regard, you are likely to be seen as having power. Power isn't a bad thing or something to be denied. Indeed, power differences exist in virtually all relationships. When acknowledged and appropriately understood, they facilitate the achievement of objectives and the cohesion of the people involved.

Ideally, a coaching relationship evolves so that clients experience a sense of equality with their coaches. Even so, there will be differences in power. Take, for example, the matter of asking questions (see chapter 11). Coaches need to ask questions, some of which can be very personal. Within a short time, they obtain a lot of information about their clients, but clients know far less about them. If knowledge is power, as the dictum goes, do coaches offer to tell clients as much about themselves to balance the power in the relationship? For the most part, the answer is no. However, creating opportunities for clients to ask what they need to know often makes sense. Wisdom lies in determining what constitutes a need to know.

Your life is embedded in different contexts permeated by power dynamics. You are likely to have had experiences where you felt you had too much, too little, or maybe just the right amount of influence over another person and vice versa. Discomfort with exercising power may lead coaches to minimize attempts to influence clients or perhaps hold back from intervening even when such actions could help. At the opposite extreme, power can be misused as when coaches reflexively use the power inherent in their role to influence client behavior. This may occur when a coach invites a client to consider an option for change and expects the client to comply. Without awareness, reflection, and self-monitoring, coaches who assume they know what is right for their clients are likely to misuse their power. It is crucial that coaches respect the boundaries of coaching (i.e., use approaches and techniques that are within the purview of coaching and for which they are qualified) and partner with clients in such a way that clients are fully empowered to accept or refuse the coach's suggestions.

Social scientists readily acknowledge that most communication is about influence (Johnson, 2014; Knapp & Daly, 2002). When it comes to your own ability to influence or willingness to be influenced, you probably know there are a lot of different factors to be considered: Who is doing the influencing? What is the intention? How much do you already agree with what you are being influenced toward? How much will you benefit? What are the collateral impacts? There are many more factors than these examples.

You may know people who are very effective at influencing others and others who are characteristically easy to influence. What elements of personality, presence, or relationship allow one person to be more influential than another? If a particular person can easily influence you, does that mean she will be equally influential with others? You might want to explore your understanding of the dynamics of influence and how you feel about either being the influencer or the one being influenced.

In accord with principles of adult learning, the agenda for coaching derives from the client (Bennett & Campone, 2017). Another principle speaks to the importance of clients willingly embracing actions they codesign with their coaches to reach self-determined goals (Gessnitzer & Kauffeld, 2015). So where do the concepts of power and influence come in?

Clients are motivated to change or to pursue a goal, and they seek help unearthing the reasons, values, needs, and personal dynamics that pertain to their wishes. They may require assistance in formulating plans that are robust and realistic. Once engaged in action, clients typically benefit from support, and although coaches should not be the sole source of support, they can provide invaluable assistance in creating support systems. If clients could do everything on their own, they probably wouldn't need a coach. This doesn't imply fault or deficiency. Most coaching professionals regard their clients as individuals who are well functioning, psychologically healthy, successful, and strongly motivated to pursue their goals (Auerbach, 2003; Biswas-Diener, 2009; Grant, 2003). From this perspective, power and influence are often straightforward and appropriate in coach–client relationships. Simply put, coaches act in full partnership to positively influence their clients in alignment with clients' requests, intentions, and preferences for ways of working together.

In their exhaustive analysis of helping skills, Ivey and colleagues (Ivey et al., 2018) identify two major classes: One is defined as attending and the other as influencing. The interweaving of these skills in helping relationships is evident in the structure of coaching where the coach first seeks to understand the client and then to intervene to influence change. The coach relies on different attending and influencing skills throughout the process. Clients may require clear guidance (influencing) in telling their stories yet need an attentive listener (attending) as they explore their own initiatives for change. Applications of coaches' attending and influencing skills are generally shaped by input and feedback from clients. A common recommendation is to continue building foundational trust and safety in the relationship through a strong reliance on attending skills until two conditions have been met: (1) the coach has sufficient information to begin the process of influencing the client, and (2) the coach has an adequate basis of rapport. That is, the **core relationship conditions** of trust and safety along with the attainment of sufficient knowledge pertinent to clients and their agendas must be sufficiently realized before coaches attempt to influence client behaviors.

Let's work to remove any remaining confusion about power differences in coaching. Both coach and client choose to work together and adhere to certain definitions and responsibilities of their roles. Clients do their job by answering questions and exploring their inner worlds and dreams, while coaches do so by asking questions, cocreating meaning, and forming a foundation for forward movement. Both parties contribute, and throughout the relationship, each retains the right to consider a renegotiation of how they work together. As long as such considerations safeguard the boundaries of the coaching contract and relationship, all is well. At certain moments, coaches may intentionally try to influence their clients, and the clients may willingly open themselves to this influence. In this process, everything remains on track. There is a sharing of power even though the expressions of power differ for coaches and clients. Clients show power by cooperating, resisting, or requesting information; coaches demonstrate power in what they say, the questions they ask, the feedback they give, and so forth.

Power expressions might disturb the relationship's equilibrium when one or both partners have problematic histories with power dynamics. For instance, even though clients hire coaches to help, they may nonetheless express strong resistance to any kind of feedback due to a history of unconstructive feedback experiences. If both parties were totally conscious and completely evolved beings, we probably wouldn't have to worry about any of this.

But, after all, we are all in the process of becoming; we are all human.

DEMYSTIFYING TRANSFERENCE

Did you ever meet someone for the first time and find yourself having strong positive or negative feelings without knowing why? Nothing the person did warranted the strength of your reactions, yet you felt them! You might call this a sixth sense, or you could call it **transference**. Maybe you know something about the concept of transference and think it pertains to some mysterious element of intense psychotherapeutic relationships. Well, it's true that the concept of transference derives from original studies in psychotherapy (Freud, 1949; Jung, 1969), but it's also extremely common in everyday life. While we may tend to associate transference with something negative or possibly pathological, the fact is, virtually all social behavior is influenced by past experiences. When you meet someone, you enter the relationship with the fullness of your personal history. For many, this history is exactly what allows us to be trusting and open, and this predisposition represents a form of transference.

Transference

Transference shows up in many contexts such as, for example, when you meet someone who reminds you of another person from your past. From the outset of this new relationship, you may need to be conscious about how your previous relationship affects the development of the current one. Appearances, mannerisms, or some other aspect of the new acquaintance may continue to trigger associations to an older relationship. Recognizing physical similarities is easier than identifying a resemblance that occurs at a less visible psychological level.

Transference in coaching is a process whereby clients project onto their coaches the thoughts, feelings, or attributes that they experienced in relation to other significant people in their lives. Kahn (2005) suggests that it is extremely common in helping relationships. He sees it as a natural reaction to the stress that people experience as they explore issues. A more practical way of looking at transference is that clients focus more on their helpers than on themselves (Young, 2017) and thereby amplify the meaning of helpers' behaviors beyond their actual intentions.

Watkins (1986) discussed five patterns of transference that seem common to helping relationships.

These patterns have been reframed for your work as a professional coach. It's important to note that the way these patterns are described represents a less conscious and rational interpretation of the reality the client is experiencing. Think of these as internal fantasies that clients may have, with little or no awareness.

1. *The perfect coach.* Because you are perceived as being perfect, the client begins to imitate your behavior, including modes of dress and manners of speech. He or she is complimentary of anything you do or say. Although flattery and imitation may be gratifying to the ego, a signal of transference is that you begin to worry about the excessive influence you have on the person's attitudes and behaviors.

2. *The great wizard coach.* The client sees you as having all the answers, as being all knowing and flawless in judgment. Conversely, he or she behaves in a self-minimizing manner, questioning his or her own judgment and knowledge. If you continually receive such high praise, you may begin to worry about the potential of failing and focus on the possibility of making mistakes. Usually, this transference process can be felt in the client's excessive positive feedback.

3. *The divinely caring coach.* The client sees you as a totally loving and nurturing person with whom he or she feels entirely safe and secure. The coaching relationship becomes a private haven where the client can open himself or herself to all feelings; however, he or she confides that this all-embracing nurturance happens mostly with you. This kind of response may encourage you to give excessively out of a desire to be even more helpful. Over time, however, you might begin to feel depleted, experiencing an energy drain occasioned by the client's seeming neediness.

4. *The obstructive coach.* The client acts as if you are standing in the way of his or her progress either through questioning, planning, or requesting action. The client sets up various tests and expresses a thinly veiled mistrust. Here, you can become caught in a kind of self-fulfilling prophecy in which the more the client questions you, the more uneasy and cautious you become. Invariably, this exacting awareness may cause you to trip, thereby proving the client's misgivings about you.

5. *The irrelevant coach.* The client uses the coaching session in an aimless and unmotivated manner. Although physically present, he or she prevents progress by somehow negating your efforts to focus conversations or direct action. Because you are being committed *and* being paid, you may begin to feel useless and come to doubt your own competency. You may experience growing annoyance as the client continues to thwart your intentionally helpful efforts.

Although it may never be entirely clear whether clients' strong emotional reactions to coaches represent transference or honest and appropriate responses to perceptions of their behavior, there are constructive ways of addressing possible transference phenomena (see the Moving Clients Through Transference Experiences sidebar).

When you believe that you carry no conscious bias toward a client, have behaved compassionately and supportively, and have lived up to your end of agreements, then persistent client concerns about your behavior may represent unresolved issues emanating from their past relationships (Kahn, 2005). With some of the skills that we will review in upcoming chapters, you can caringly discuss these matters, always with the client's agenda and welfare in mind. Of course, you need not confront all transference projections; some of them may

Moving Clients Through Transference Experiences

So many expressions of transference are benign and nonproblematic. In cases where transference seems to be interfering with your work as a coach, some helpful steps you might take have been suggested to increase the likelihood of a positive coaching relationship (Young, 2017).

Step 1. Express acceptance. When clients experience significant transference reactions, they are likely to direct strong emotions toward their coaches. Especially when these expressions are unwarranted, coaches need to communicate empathy and a genuine appreciation for the reality of the feelings experienced.

Client: This is feeling like a poor investment of time and money. I'm not sure where we're going with all this. Most of the things we come up with haven't been very helpful. I'm still stuck.

Coach: I'm sensing that you're pretty upset right now, and at the same time I'm glad you're talking about this. Now that you've brought this up, I think it would be useful to explore this further. Would this be okay with you?

Step 2. Explore the client's thoughts and feelings. In the face of the coach's accepting behavior, the client may be less likely to retreat into feelings of shame, hurt, or fear of retaliation. The coach's role at this point is to encourage further expression and clarification of the sources of emotion.

Client: I just don't think this is working out. Though I keep coming here, my lack of progress is becoming one more way I get to criticize myself.

Coach: Thanks for telling me this. Are you aware of any messages coming from me that sound like I'm criticizing you or blaming you for what's happening?

Step 3. Work to find new patterns for expressing feelings and getting needs met. By maintaining a reassuring, accepting attitude throughout the dialogue, the client is likely to feel an increased sense of safety in expressing emotions and working through complaints without having to wait until an emotional buildup has reached unmanageable proportions. Even when clients have legitimate issues, their manner of expression can be the focus of new learning. If coaches at any point turn to self-justification or efforts to prove their effectiveness, this learning opportunity will likely be lost.

Client: No, I think it's me feeling like I'm not doing enough, and I guess I'm blaming you and the work we're doing.

Coach: That sounds like an important awareness. No matter how it came out, I'm glad we've reached this understanding. . . . I have a couple ideas about things we might discuss: The first is about exploring your feeling that you're not doing enough, and the second is about cocreating ways that you can feel more comfortable expressing feelings about our work in the future. Would you be open to that discussion now?

simply be information that you note for potential future conversations. Moreover, not every concern voiced by clients will be evidence of transference; not every feeling will be a projection. We do form new relationships. We do like some people a lot and have difficulty with others simply because of our experiences with them.

Countertransference

Of course, relationships are two-way streets; coaches may also project attitudes, feelings, or thoughts onto their clients. This phenomenon is known as **countertransference**. Gelso and Hayes (2007) articulate how, when mismanaged, these projections negatively influence the helping relationship. Alternatively, when helpers take time to consider the feelings and attitudes behind these projections, they can learn a great deal about themselves and their clients that they would otherwise miss (Luborsky & Barrett, 2006).

All intimate helping relationships include both overt and covert personal dynamics that play out at varying levels of conscious awareness (Horton, 1996). For instance, you may work with a client who is extremely conscientious about his program, never tardy, and always takes your advice without resistance; yet he irks you for some inexplicable reason. A common way of reacting to this might be to discount it or attribute it to some quirk of your own. You certainly don't want to tell this outstanding client how irritating you find him! If you have behaved professionally and compassionately, an irritation that keeps surfacing is a signal that something deeper may be occurring. Let's assume you have no conscious issue with this client, yet you often feel triggered by what you describe as his perfectionist ways. Exploring your own history might reveal stories of being in school with classmates who were always prepared and got things right while you struggled to stay afloat, for example. Realizing this piece about yourself could help you name your countertransference and get on top of it. As a result, you would increase your capacity to be present and appreciative of your client's efforts rather than hold back or feel mildly annoyed.

The bottom line is that when you have done your personal work to be a clear receiver and thoroughly professional, your awareness of clients and your reactions to them may be fed by an ability to tune into a different frequency of interpersonal communications. Before you toss out the data, spend a little more time exploring their potential meanings.

CREATING A SAFE SPACE

Has someone ever approached you with a perplexing human drama or an all-consuming problem? Most of us have been present for friends, family, or even relative strangers who simply needed to talk about their experiences and wanted nothing more than for us to listen. In reflecting on such experiences, you might remember how you wanted to say something—the right words to make the person feel better—yet you realized that nothing you could say would achieve this result and, in fact, there was little that anyone could say to resolve the drama or emotions expressed. So you simply listened with all your heart and soul. At the end of this encounter, the person probably thanked you profusely for being there, and you might have felt bewildered, thinking to yourself, "But I really didn't do anything."

To understand the structure of helping and, thereby, the function of a coach, one needs to grasp the significance of creating a safe space, which is sometimes referred to as a **holding environment** (Winnicott, 1958). Experts such as Kohut (1984) and Hendrix (2008) offer insight into the healing capacity of safe spaces we create for others to express their realities. In a world of action and doing, it is important to recognize the power of simply being—without compulsion to do something. Just as day makes sense in relation to night, doing gains significance in its connection to being. When someone comes to us for help, our immediate thought is often about doing, such as "What can I do that will be helpful?" Maybe the question is more like, "How can I hold this person in a safe space so she can access her inner wisdom about *what she needs to do*?"

Though coaching is intended to facilitate forward movement, it begins with compassionate and empathic understanding of the client's story. To promote storytelling, a coach wants to be as inviting and supportive as possible. To reveal all the critical elements of their stories, clients need a safe environment where their thoughts, feelings, and behaviors can be welcomed without judgment. Creating such an environment is not always easy. When people feel unsafe, the story that gets told may be replete with distortions, deletions, and misinformation (Dilts & DeLozier, 2000).

To hold and support another person's story requires full presence and openness to that person's felt meanings. It also requires empathy to experience what it might be like to have lived this story. This task implies not only a readiness to listen but also an ability to convey to the person a message that acknowledges and honors the journey he has been on.

This discussion of safe spaces highlights two important issues: The first is the matter of how you can create the conditions whereby clients believe it is safe to disclose information. The material previously discussed on trust and intimacy was intended to help with this. The next chapter on coaching presence will add more to your understanding of how to create safety for your clients. The second issue pertains to your inner state and the work that you personally undertake to create space for your clients' stories with awareness of how your own story may pull you toward distracting connections. You spent time in this chapter appreciating the importance of such processes as identification and transference. In my experience training coaches, I see these processes happening quite frequently.

Consider these examples. A young stay-at-home dad who once was quite physically active but now is managing a household with young children complains to you about a lack of support from his partner for pursuing his creative passions. A busy executive talks to you about feeling so stretched by work that she neglects friends, family, and even her own needs. It's possible that one or more elements in these stories causes you to reflect about your own story. The closer the client's story is to your reality, the greater the probability that you will experience personal emotions. How do you create a safe space for your clients when you are caught up in your own internal examination of your life? This happens, and it reminds us of the need for coaches to continually engage in their own work through reflective practices, supervision, and ongoing training.

So now imagine this: You are sitting across from your new client and listening intently to his story. You are fully present—mind, body, and spirit. You have no agenda other than to be there. You have no need to change him; it's the client's own need to change that you are committed to following. Your deep desire is for your client to experience trust and safety in unfolding his story and determining where he wants to go from here. How wonderful and rich this moment is!

CULTIVATING TRUST AND SAFETY IN THE ICF CORE COMPETENCIES

In relation to how the International Coaching Federation has articulated its core coaching competency pertaining to trust and safety (see sidebar, ICF Core Coaching Competency 4: Cultivates Trust and Safety), the material presented in this chapter seems to track quite well. Clients need to experience the coaching space as a safe one for discussion and exploration. No matter what their reason for working with a coach, clients want to feel appreciated for their strengths and capacities; they don't want to be problematized. They want to be understood for the gifts of their uniqueness rather than stigmatized for differences. These presenting desires of clients require a psychological space that fully welcomes and honors them.

ICF Core Coaching Competency 4: Cultivates Trust and Safety

Definition: Partners with the client to create a safe, supportive environment that allows the client to share freely. Maintains a relationship of mutual respect and trust.

1. Seeks to understand the client within their context, which may include their identity, environment, experiences, values and beliefs
2. Demonstrates respect for the client's identity, perceptions, style and language and adapts one's coaching to the client
3. Acknowledges and respects the client's unique talents, insights and work in the coaching process
4. Shows support, empathy and concern for the client
5. Acknowledges and supports the client's expression of feelings, perceptions, concerns, beliefs and suggestions
6. Demonstrates openness and transparency as a way to display vulnerability and build trust with the client

It's noteworthy that in the previous version of its core competencies, the ICF described this focus as "establishing trust and intimacy with the client" (ICF, 2020c). The shift in language from intimacy to safety makes good sense in terms of what coaches need to do. While both client and coach may experience their relationship as an intimate one, this is by no means universal. However, feeling safe does seem to be an essential quality to be nurtured in every coaching relationship. The juxtaposition of the terms *intimacy* and *safety* relates back to the idea that the coach–client relationship may not be as pivotal to success as would be the therapist–client relationship developed in counseling (Ives & Cox, 2012). Further, the point was made that what could be more central is a client's relationship to the work of coaching itself. You might see this clearly in considering clients who have been mandated by their organizations to work with a coach to address problematic behaviors. These clients may be more focused on making sense of their relationship to coaching *per se* than on forming a bond with the coach.

A particular element of this competency that warrants underlining centers around a coach's capacity to acknowledge clients for their efforts and accomplishments. This implies saying what you are seeing in client efforts, especially when clients take their own behaviors for granted. The practice of shining a light on big and small accomplishments needs to become part of a coach's way of being.

The various aspects of this competency emphasize what coaches need to do to create a welcoming, trusting, and safe environment for clients, and in so doing, the ICF has captured the essence of extensive human development and psychological research regarding what people need most to grow. In a way it comes back to the core values honored in the coaching profession (Coach U, 2005; Gavin & Mcbrearty, 2018; Jarosz, 2016; Stelter, 2014). Coaches promote human growth and development by nurturing their own capacities to show up in ways that clients can perceive as being safe and trustworthy.

REFLECTIONS

We are relational beings (Gergen, 2009). We live and thrive in relationships with others. Yet coaching differs from friendships and family connections. For you to work effectively with your clients, something unique is asked of you: You need to step out of your skin, at least temporarily. You need to see the world through your clients' eyes, understand it through their mental filters, and feel it through their senses. This is not easy, and it doesn't come naturally to most of us. You and I have to work at it continually.

You already know how subtle human communication can be and how powerful nonverbal messaging is. This supports your work in being as conscious as you possibly can, in reflecting on your behavior so that you can learn, and in showing up fully—mind, body, and spirit—in all your relationships. Being trustworthy and creating safety through your presence with others is indeed a high aspirational goal. Some days are better than others in this regard, yet you want to set your sights high and continue striving toward this goal. How do you ideally want to be as a coach? You might say welcoming, awake, consciously aware, supportive, trustworthy, or one of several other adjectives. In moving toward these aspirational goals, you can then relax more into your deepest source, from which you can draw the necessary capacities for compassionate and effective work with clients. In so doing, you will create the conditions for your clients to tap into their inner knowing.

It may be comforting to know that in many of my conversations with highly experienced coaches, I hear how committed they are to their own learning and evolution. They question themselves; they fret about whether they could have done more with certain clients; they step into the lives of complete strangers (their clients) and awaken disquieting feelings in themselves. Indeed, as one good friend said to me after a day of back-to-back coaching appointments, "You know, what we do isn't easy." Yet, it is worthwhile, and it is our chosen path to growth.

CHAPTER 9

COACHING PRESENCE

Be here now.

Ram Dass

MY STORY

I think I have been more of an expert in absence than presence in many moments of my life. I'm not talking about traveling or leaving places or even things like missing school or ghosting appointments. Yes, I've done those things as well, but what I am reflecting on here is how many ways I know to not be fully present in this moment. Along the line, I decided to understand this topic better. Some of my explorations took place during a period in my career when I was deeply interested in the psychology of sports and exercise—that was natural enough since I love movement experiences. Experts in that field often debated the comparative value of associative and dissociative cognitive strategies in exercise (Masters & Ogles, 1998), that is, whether it's better to focus on your immediate experience in exercising or allow yourself to be distracted by listening to music and podcasts or watching the scenery. This was one of those scientific areas that offered no clear answers but rather led to other questions. In my physical training, sometimes I listened to music, and other times I meditated on my body in motion. My core training in high school and university was as a competitive swimmer, and in those experiences, I couldn't really listen to music, the scenery wasn't very interesting, and counting laps was usually necessary. So, to some degree, I learned to pay attention. Later on, I gravitated to triathlon training, yoga, tai chi, dance, and aikido. Since I struggled with sitting meditation, I thought of my training as meditation in motion. I loved the idea and I thought it helped me be present in other settings.

My truth in all of this became more clearly known to me when I finally developed a regular meditation practice. I realized that my meditation in motion was great and really helpful, but it didn't quite offer me what I got from sitting meditation. When I am listening deeply to another person, I need to feel a stillness within me—mind and body, and sitting meditation made that experience come more easily. Even so, I think both the still kind and the moving kind of meditation both have value for me. I guess I am still learning what helps me be fully present—especially in everyday moments.

Coaching presence assumes a central position in the skill set of professional coaches. Not that any of the core competencies can ever be identified as most important, but presence is nonetheless foundational. Most models of communication recognize not only the inner noise in our minds that accompanies our best intentions to be present for another person, but also the habitual filters through which we take in the world outside us. Presence speaks to the quality of attention that coaches are able to create within themselves in order to focus as purely as possible on what they are receiving through words and other ways of communicating. Cultivating presence as a coach requires of us a dedication to practices of mind and body that strengthen capacity to sit in inner stillness while dancing with another human being through all our senses and intelligences. Here are some guiding questions as you read:

- What does coaching presence mean?
- What are the roots of this concept of presence?
- Is coaching presence similar to other ideas about presence?
- Where is our attention when we are fully present?
- Are there specific ways to cultivate presence?

PRESENCE VERSUS ABSENCE

How can you coach if you aren't present to your client? You might think, "Well, of course, I would be present. I'm not sure what you're getting at." Pay attention to your mind in this moment. How many thoughts are streaming through your consciousness? You might also have various physical sensations, whether an itch, hunger, or some discomfort in the way you are sitting. The more you tune in to your experience, the more you might feel as if you are in a crowded space with lots of fragmented parts of your awareness vying for attention. Sure, if there's a fire in the house, all those other mini yous get shut down so that the survivalist firefighter you can function without distraction.

In the previous chapter, you read how coaches sometimes identify with the topics that clients bring to sessions, and other times they get triggered by some characteristic or behavior of their clients that throws them back in time to another place, another relationship. If you take to heart the essence of presence in coaching as identified by the ICF (2020c), namely, being "fully conscious and present with the client, "how present can you be when you are revisiting past moments in your life or when you have identified with the client's topic as if it were your own or when physiological sensations such as hunger break through to your consciousness?

The heading for this section, presence versus absence, may now seem not so much an either-or but rather a more-or-less phenomenon—that is, your presence can be gauged on a continuum. I would suspect that you can identify a long list of moments when you were almost off the scale in your presence—and then there were times you were fully absent. Think back to your school years when you may have been caught daydreaming by a teacher. Think about a pivotal moment playing a game or sport when you were totally focused on the task at hand.

Let's get closer to coaching. Remember a conversation you had with someone recently where you were interested in the discussion. At some point, something that the person said triggered an internal thought. Maybe there was a question you wanted to ask or something you wanted to say. But you were polite and attentive—or at least you tried to be—until there was an opportune moment for you to say what was on your mind. The question is, how attentive were you really from the time this idea or question came to mind until the moment when you were able to express it?

When you are fully present to another, you are able to open yourself to the other while emptying yourself of your own experience and thought processes (Clarkson, 1997). From another perspective, you are able to suspend whatever preconceptions or views you have of the other so that you can appreciate the unique nature of this other person purely and not through conceptual or attitudinal filters (Hycner, 1993).

I want to refer again to the seminal writing of Carl Rogers (1980) as he describes the experience of the listener who is fully present:

> I hear the words, the thoughts, the feeling tones, the personal meaning, even the meaning that is below the conscious intent of the speaker. Sometimes too, in a message which superficially is not very important, I hear a deep human cry that lies buried and unknown far below the surface of the person. So I have learned to ask myself, can I hear the sounds and sense the shape of this other person's inner world? Can I resonate to what he is saying so deeply that I sense the meanings he is afraid of, yet would like to communicate, as well as those he knows? (p. 8)

For me, this way of being represents an aspirational goal that I only sometimes touch after all these years. I have a busy mind and I need to continually cultivate presence in order to be of utmost service to my clients.

THE COMPLEXITY OF PRESENCE

Given the centrality of presence to coaching practice (Virgili, 2013), it is not surprising that there are so many understandings of what this competency is all about. To help situate you in a deeper appreciation of presence, I want to review some of the core perspectives about presence and then try to draw all of this together so that you have a practical framework for your own pursuit of greater presence in relationships with clients and others in your world. Before diving into what the coaching field has to say about presence, I want to highlight three fields of work that have contributed significantly to our understanding of coaching presence: Eastern traditions, philosophical perspectives, and psychological viewpoints.

Eastern Traditions

Tracing coaching's focus on presence to earlier traditions most likely takes us back at least six or seven centuries to the Eastern philosophical roots of Taoism and Buddhism. Most conceptualizations of coaching presence seem to implicitly or explicitly reference these and other Eastern approaches (Cox, 2013). If you consider the recurrent references to mindfulness practice in everyday conversations, you will have some hint of how the Buddhist mindfulness tradition has permeated Western culture over the past few decades. It has been brought forth through the teachings of such practitioner-writers as Tara Brach (2016), Jon Kabat-Zinn (1994, 2005), Jack Kornfield (2008, 2017) and Pema Chodron (2019), among others.

In the Buddhist tradition, the sense of awakening is likened to mindfulness in daily life. To achieve such mindfulness, one needs to practice in order to calm the mind with all of its desires. Describing ancient Buddhist texts, Wallis (2004, p. 40) contrasts the fully awakened state of mindfulness with a lesser state of craving where one is trapped in constant distractions of the senses. Modern practitioner-writers (Brach, 2016; Chodron, 2019; Kabat-Zinn, 2018; Kornfield, 2017) make clear the need for mindfulness practices in order to create the possibility for embodied awareness and presence.

In the origins of Zen meditation, there is another root of present-day practice fostering mindful presence. The word *Zen* derives from Sanskrit and roughly translates as "meditation, contemplation, pondering" (Schloegl, 1976, p. 3). Though Zen practices usually emphasize sitting meditation, there is also an emphasis on awakened presence in everyday actions, which describes applying mindfulness as you engage in the world as well as when you are sitting on a cushion. Ancient Zen writings reference a way of meditating in spontaneous activities, which we can easily equate to the objectives of presence in coaching relationships (Dumoulin, 2005).

From the ancient tradition of Taoism, you can discover another useful connection to the coaching concept of presence in the notion of *wu wei*, which represents a flowing engagement in natural activity while conserving energy (Xing & Sims, 2011). This almost effortless quality of doing represents a kind of paradoxical action without action (Smith, 1991) such that a focused ease and awareness is evident in an individual's presence. In the words of religious scholar Huston Smith (1991), *wu wei* represents a kind of simplicity and freedom that "flows from us, or rather through us, when our private egos and conscious efforts yield to a power not their own" (p. 208).

Philosophical Perspectives

Though philosophical perspectives will likely have indirect influence on practices for developing coaching presence, they nonetheless provide a framework for appreciating the centrality of this competency to a coach's way of being in the world. These perspectives reflect how one shows up in daily actions as well as a way of understanding relationships you have with others.

I want to focus primarily on the work of Martin Buber (1878-1965) as he explored our way of relating in the world. He characterized two fundamental ways of being as I–thou and I–it (Buber, 2004; Kohanski, 1975). There is much complexity to Buber's work that requires a full reading of his writings, yet the substance of the relationships he describes can be captured in the idea that sometimes relationships you have in the world are between you as the subject and something outside of you as the object. Think of driving a car. You, the subject, drive the car, the object. It's a kind of I–it relationship. Other times, the relationships you have in the world are between you as the subject and another who also is the subject. Here, there is a unity between the two of you; that is, there is no separation. To help clarify this, think of yourself in a total love experience with another. You may experience a oneness, an absence of barriers, a kind of spiritual union. This is an example of what Buber meant by an I–thou relationship. Indeed, he believed you can have this kind of relation with physical objects, elements in nature, and with other human beings.

Fundamentally, when you are having an I–it relationship, you (or I) feel separate from the object (or it). The object is something you might experience or use for some purpose, like the car or perhaps a cashier in a supermarket. In contrast, there is no sense of separation from the other in an I–thou relationship. In no way do you objectify the other. In this respect, you can have this kind of relationship with complete strangers simply—even with the cashier—by your perspective of unity. I don't know if you have ever been in a choir or on a team in some intense effort where there seemed to be harmony or a union in your experience; the boundaries melted, drawing you together in an intersubjective relationship. There is full presence in an I–thou moment and an absence of present centeredness in an I–it one (Buber, 2004). Indeed, Buber's perspective implied far more than a sense of unity; he thought of an I–thou relationship as a deeply spiritual connection.

Buber saw our existence in this world as being composed of experiences we have with objects and relationships that we inhabit (Kohanski, 1975). As you connect his perspectives to what coaching is all about, you might imagine the ideal wherein coach and client are united in an I–thou relationship, yet you might also be able to appreciate that there will be times when coach and client are very much in an I–it transactional or functional connection. Both may be valid at different points in the context of coaching, though the ideal is certainly something you would want to strive for in the deeper dialogues of your coaching work.

When your relation with a client largely has an I–thou quality, your work would likely represent what is referred to as **coaching the person**. This means that even though your client has a topic or issue that the two of you are engaged in discussing, the primary focus is on your relationship with the wholeness of your client. By contrast, there is another way that is often described as **coaching the topic** and this more closely represents the quality of an I–it relationship. The sense in this experience is that as a coach you are tinkering with the client's topic as if you are trying to repair or improve the thing that you are working on. In this coaching process, the being of the client is less present in you.

Another important philosophical connection to the current expression of presence derives from the work of Martin Heidegger (1889-1976), a contemporary of Buber. Heidegger's (1962) classic work, *Being and Time*, represents an existential perspective, which in his description of the term *Dasein*, or being-in-the-world, moved away from more rationalist perspectives of human existence (Descartes, 1998) where thinking was at the core of our experience. He rejected the notion of dualism that separated mind and body or self and the world. He believed that human beings are embedded in the world, and the world is here and now. In other words, he emphasized the present and very physical context of human experience. His sense of being-in-the-world speaks about each moment of existence: how and who I am at this moment in the world. He focused on the question, "What does it mean to be?" rather than the question emphasized by the rationalists, "What does it mean to know?"

Heidegger's insistence on appreciating each person as being immersed in the practical realities of everyday life reflects the image of a coach's presence in the moment to what is happening, both within oneself and in relation to the client. The concept of *Dasein* carries with it an experience of reflective self-awareness that is also quite central to the concept of presence. It emphasizes understanding the world of possibilities present in the moment, not just the facts pertaining to current experience. You can recognize traces of Heidegger's thinking in the coach's focus not on the facts of a client's reality as much as on felt experience and emergent possibilities.

Neither Buber's nor Heidegger's works can be easily summarized, yet from these brief descriptions, you can hopefully see how they differ from objectifications of others and purely rational and logical interpretations of reality. Moreover, you can probably appreciate the sense of being with the other not as someone totally separate and outside yourself and of moving beyond the merely factual to the realm of incipient possibilities.

Psychological Viewpoints

The concept of presence is thought to be foundational in the field of psychotherapy (Hycner, 1993; Rogers, 1986). Schneider (2015) offers this definition: "Presence is defined as a complex mix of appreciative openness, concerted engagement, support, and expressiveness, and it both holds and illuminates that which is palpably significant within the client and between client and therapist" (p. 304). Seen as one of the contextual or common factors in the healing process of psychotherapy, presence is believed to significantly contribute to positive outcomes (Erskine, 2015; Wampold, 2015).

Although opinions about presence in psychotherapy are plentiful, research is scant. Geller and Greenberg (2002) provided one of the most useful investigations of this topic. Through interviews with highly experienced therapists, they derived a definition of presence as "the state of having one's whole self in the encounter with a client by being completely in the moment on a multiplicity of levels—physically, emotionally, cognitively, and spiritually" (p. 7). From their evolving work, they believed that therapeutic presence was composed of three aspects: (1) being open and receptive to the client's experience, (2) inwardly attending to one's bodily resonance with the client's experience, and (3) extending and connecting with the client from this place of receptivity and inward contact (Geller, 2013). In their model of presence, Geller and Greenberg described three separate categories or moments in helpers' expressions of presence, namely, preparation, process, and experience (see sidebar, Preparation, Process, and Experience in Presence).

In ongoing reflections about presence, Geller (2013) explored the connection between Rogers' (1975, 2007) three necessary conditions for change (empathy, congruence, and unconditional positive regard) and therapeutic presence. She believed that presence was "a distinct quality that provides a foundation for these [three] qualities." Later in his life, Rogers similarly described presence as an embodiment of these necessary conditions for therapeutic change (Baldwin, 2000).

In sum, one might say that in the field of psychotherapy, there are many critical elements encompassed in the concept of presence. These include an appreciation of the uniqueness of the client; a suspension of expectations, preconceptions, and theoretical lenses; an openness to all aspects of the client; a full willingness to be present to the client; and a nonjudgmental stance from which the helper can spontaneously respond.

What you may also want to know is how helpers can develop a greater capacity for presence. In the writings of Geller and Greenberg (Geller, 2013; Geller & Greenberg, 2012), a number of ideas were presented, ranging from inner work to self-care and promoting healthy relationships. Mindfulness practices are especially noted, along with deliberate pauses, breathing deeply into the moment, clearing a space, centering, and grounding, among others.

Preparation, Process, and Experience in Presence

Geller and Greenberg fully understood that presence doesn't simply emerge in the instant of contact with clients in a helping relationship (Geller, 2013; Geller & Greenberg, 2012). They conceived of therapeutic presence as being expressed in three ways: preparation, process, and experience.

1. *Preparation.* Helpers need to prepare for their sessions by bringing their whole selves into the moment prior to the session. For Geller and Greenberg, presence involves both intention and commitment to being in the moment, along with a capacity to set aside expectations, preconceptions, and theoretical perspectives so that helpers can show up as fully open, accepting and without judgment.

2. *Process.* Presence is a process wherein the helper experiences "being receptive to the client's experience, inwardly attending to their own ongoing flow of experience, and extending and contact with the client" (Geller, 2013, p. 216). The helper is attuned to the whole of the client's experience and guided by what is most immediate in each moment.

3. *Experience.* Three facets of the experience of presence were highlighted by Geller and Greenberg; these begin with the helper "feeling grounded in themselves," which then allows them to be "fully immersed in the moment with their client" which is experienced as a sense of "inner expansion or spaciousness" (Geller, 2013, p. 216).

These research-based perspectives about presence are likely as applicable to the work of coaches as they are to the practice of therapists.

Geller also describes an eight-step process captured in the acronym, PRESENCE (see the Cultivating Presence sidebar).

Reading all this may give you rich impressions of what presence is about, as well as some general directions for cultivating greater presence. However, there is no one best way for developing competencies related to presence. Indeed, if presence is fed by having better relationships, good self-care routines, rituals of grounding, and meditation practices, you might come to realize that fostering presence is more than a simple skill and perhaps more like a way of living and being in the world. In this light, presence ties into the ICF core competency of embodying a coaching mindset, which we will review in the final chapter.

Cultivating Presence

Based on their extensive work on presence, Geller and Greenberg (Geller, 2013; Geller & Greenberg, 2012) offered a model for cultivating presence involving eight steps. The first letters of the eight steps form the acronym *PRESENCE*:

1. **p**ause—take a moment to stop what you are doing;
2. **r**elax by taking a deep breath;
3. **e**mpty yourself of judgments, thoughts, distractions, agendas, and preconceptions;
4. **s**ense your inner body and emotions;
5. **e**xpand your sensory awareness outward;
6. **n**otice what is true in this moment and notice the relationship between what is within you and around you;
7. **c**enter and ground yourself and your body; and
8. **e**xtend and make contact with your client.

PRESENCE FROM A COACHING PERSPECTIVE

The concept of presence is centrally located in models and methods of coaching. A number of definitions have been offered, including the ICF's framing of presence in its list of core competencies as a way of being "fully conscious and present with the client, employing a style that is open, flexible, grounded, and confident" (ICF, 2020c) (see sidebar, A Sampling of Coaching Perspectives on Presence).

A Sampling of Coaching Perspectives on Presence

- "A state of awareness, in the moment, characterized by the felt experience of timelessness, connectedness, and a larger truth" (Silsbee, 2008, p. 21)
- "a way of being . . . creating an enabling space . . . focusing all your attention on this coaching relationship . . . You notice the nuances, and you wonder about what you notice" (Iliffe-Wood, 2014, p. 1)
- "staying present and attentive to our conversational partner, which means in practice returning ourselves from self-conscious inner worries, or self-criticism, or wild speculations about what might happen next in the conversation" (Flaherty, 2010, p. 101)
- "one's quality of relating to the here and now, or present moment" (Topp, 2006, p. 3)
- "our presence needs to be transformed into action, so that not only does it encompass our mindfulness, but it also involves interaction with the client, the coaching alliance and the setting of the coaching" (Cox, 2013, p. 134)

Similar to what was noted in psychologically based framings of presence, the concept seems far broader than a simple skill. It is variously defined as a capacity to stay "present and attentive" (Flaherty, 2010, p.101), a "quality of relating" (Topp, 2006, p. 3), a "state of awareness" (Silsbee, 2010, p.21), or a way of being (Iliffe-Wood, 2014, p. 1). I want to take you through a deeper examination of some of the perspectives of coaches about presence, and then give special attention to Iliffe-Woods' typology related to coaching presence.

Different Voices

As you saw, the concept of presence is not easily captured in a brief definition. Coaching presence reflects the way a coach engages in relationships, including physical posture, openness, spontaneity, flexibility, and creativity. Coaching presence seems strongly tied to trust as one of the ways in which coaches communicate their trustworthiness. It also links to our previous discussion about emotional intelligence, which includes capacities to work confidently with strong emotions, to engage deeply without becoming enmeshed with clients' feelings, and to manage oneself with grace and compassion amidst the sometimes tumultuous moments of change experiences. Also, it is intricately linked to other coaching competencies, such as active listening (see chapter 10) since deep listening is only made possible by full presence.

Coaching experts apply different lenses to their perspectives about presence. Elizabeth Topp (2006), through her doctoral research, came up with a presence-based coaching model, which was informed by principles and methods of mindfulness meditation, flow, and Taoist literature. She offered a four-step process to facilitate presence; the steps were stop, observe, align, and allow. Informed by the perspectives of integral coaching (Divine, 2009b; Hunt, 2009b; Wilber, 2000b), Deborah Kennedy (2013) relied on the construct of self as instrument to position coaching presence more globally as a way of being. Based on the construct of flow (Csikszentmihalyi, 2008), McBride (2014) devised a model for enhancing presence by facilitating coaches' experience of flow during sessions.

An interesting fact is that much of the research on coaching presence is based on clients' experiences rather than on those of the coach. Studies emphasize ways of enhancing clients' coaching outcomes through the inclusion of different forms of meditation or mindfulness focus (Collard & Walsh, 2008; Linger, 2016; Spence et al., 2008; Topp, 2006). This raises an important consideration: Is it just the coach who needs to be fully present for effective coaching to occur? Abravanel (2018) identified three ways of positioning presence: presence of the coach, presence of the client, and presence in the relationship between coach and client. Of course, in considering coaching competencies, the focus needs to be on *your ability* as a coach to be fully present to your client. At the same time, it's good to be aware that your clients' presence is also relevant, as is the degree to which you and your client are present to the relationship.

Modes of Coaching Presence

A fascinating way of considering coaching presence was developed by Maria Iliffe-Wood (2014), who described four purposeful and deliberate *modes* of coaching presence. Each mode represents a way in which the coach shows up in the relationship. Intentionally, each of her four modes acts as a catalyst for clients to access what she identifies as the four levels of awareness or channels of perception.

Here's a brief description of Iliffe-Wood's approach to consciousness and awareness building through different modes of presence in coaching.

Level One: Invisible Coach Mode

In this mode of presence, coaches are very much in the background, and their interventions are brief and simple; they neither interrupt nor challenge the client. The invisible mode is intended to facilitate the emergence of the client's inner coach. Coaches focus on the use of attending skills, such as listening, silence, and minimal encouragement (see chapter 10). They fully trust in the resourcefulness of clients to explore what they want to explore in the way they choose. Coaches' presence invites clients to tell their story in its entirety, self-reflect, access their own inner wisdom, and discover what is obvious and readily available about themselves and their topics. By intentionally showing curiosity, listening to the whole person, and noticing patterns, the coach gathers data that might be used subsequently to help further the client's agenda.

Level Two: Emergent Coach Mode

In the emergent mode of presence, coaches become more visible partners in exploration. Without going as far as sharing expertise and knowledge, coaches deliberately intervene to help clients access what they know at a deeper level. Coaches use creativity and consciously apply influencing skills, tools, and techniques to support clients in discovering new perspectives. In this mode, coaches endeavor to broaden the scope of exploration and facilitate connections with information that is not readily accessible to clients. The aim of the emergent mode of presence is to help clients delve into the fullness of their topics, gain new insights, and consider ways of being and perceiving that are not within their usual purview.

Level Three: Evident Coach Mode

In this mode of presence, coaches intentionally show up in all that they are, as active partners in clients' explorations. Though clients still choose the direction of sessions, coaches in evident mode tap into their own intuition to further client learning and change. They share hunches, knowledge, emotions, and somatic senses so clients can access their own "invisible coach," which then allows them to access what they either don't know they know or what they are consciously avoiding. Here, coaches challenge limiting beliefs and self-imposed limitations. They ask powerful questions to help clients explore values, needs, and wants as a means to expand thinking about themselves and their topics.

Level Four: Visible Coach Mode

This mode of presence supports clients in accessing what they really don't know or are unconsciously avoiding. It needs to be used judiciously since it is almost contrary to what we believe about coaching. Visible coach mode supports transformational learning. In full partnership with clients, coaches liberally use influencing skills, interrupting, challenging, offering suggestions, and even steering clients in a direction deemed by the coach to be most generative of transformational learning and sustainable change.

Iliffe-Wood (2014) believed that all modes of coaching presence serve to guide clients toward higher levels of consciousness where their own inner coach resides. In essence, her work reflects the purpose of coaching as a means of generating greater capacity for autonomy and self-direction in all clients.

TOWARD A SYNTHESIS

The varied perspectives about presence have likely increased your appreciation of coaching presence, yet the diversity of ideas may cause your understanding to remain a bit out of focus. My intention in this section is to offer you a more complete map of what coaching presence is and how you can develop it. To set the stage for this synthesis, I want to raise four questions that you may have been asking.

1. What do you think it would be like to have a coach who focuses all her or his attention on remaining solidly attuned to her or his own deep internal experiences in the moment?

2. What might happen in a situation where a coach concentrates all her or his attention on techniques, questions, and ensuring that the client has a well-detailed action plan in a coaching session?

3. What do you imagine it would be like to have a coach who is solely attending to the moment-by-moment relationship she or he feels with the client in the session?

4. How do you think it would be if the coach was listening and probing to uncover all the details of opportunities, obstacles, external dynamics, situational characteristics, and the likely effectiveness of various strategies of action?

In each of these four scenarios, you might realize that the coach is present—but present to what? The coach is fully present to (1) her or his inner world, (2) her or his actions, (3) the relationship, or (4) the system of elements affecting the client in this moment and in her or his chosen topic. Doesn't it seem that presence isn't just one but rather all four of these areas of attention?

Quadrants of Focus

A model that helps us synthesize what goes into creating full presence was described by the integral theorist Ken Wilber (2000a, 2000b, 2006), who identified four areas of attention or focus that each person may have. These areas of attention roughly reflect the four synthesis questions. He portrayed this as a quadrant model varying along two continua: The horizontal continuum reflects attention moving from *inside of you,* which isn't publicly visible, to *outside of you* or to more external manifestations, which are fully observable by others. The vertical continuum of attention varies from the *individual* level—that is, pertaining only to you personally—to the *collective* level, reflecting all that is around you—near and far—including yourself.

Let's go through Wilber's four quadrants one at a time (figure 9.1).

1. *Upper left (UL).* In the upper left quadrant, the focus is internal and self-oriented. If this is your most dominant focus, you are highly aware of and attentive to your internal subjective feelings, desires, thoughts, needs, and so forth. To appreciate this, imagine yourself sitting in a contemplative state with your eyes closed, wondering what you want, what you need, how you feel, and what your thoughts are about.

2. *Upper right (UR).* In the upper right quadrant, the focus remains self-oriented, but it is visible not only to yourself but to others as well. If this is your most dominant focus, you emphasize and remain attentive to what you do, what actions you are taking, the motions and physical sensations of your body, and the manifest efforts you are expressing. To appreciate this, imagine yourself concentrating on checking items off your to do list, moving about, getting things done, experiencing the physicality of your body as you continue to engage in action.

	Inside Me	Outside Me
Individual	**Upper left (UL)** **Inside myself** I focus on my needs, wants, thoughts, feelings, perspectives, etc. I concentrate on my awareness of my inner states and thoughts. In my coaching, I am highly self-aware.	**Upper right (UR)** **Myself in action** I focus on my actions, my physicality, getting things done, making things happen, moving, expressing myself in accomplishing things. In my coaching, I concentrate on my actions and interventions.
Collective	**Lower left (LL)** **My relational self** I focus on my connections to others – how aligned I am with their values, beliefs, and needs. I experience my world through my sense of belonging and how well I serve others. In my coaching, I focus intensively on my relationship with my client.	**Lower right (LR)** **My systems self** I focus on the big picture, on how things happen, on the systemic relationships in the world, what causes what, and what outcomes result. I am interested in performance, measuring things, understanding impacts. In my coaching, I analyze, measure, and try to see the relevant systems in motion.

Figure 9.1   The four quadrants of integral theory adapted to the work of professional coaching.

Adapted from by S. Esbjorn-Hargens, *An Overview of Integral Theory: An All-Inclusive Framework for the 21st Century* (Metalintegral Foundation, 2015), 3.

3. *Lower left (LL).* Now attention is internal, but it shifts to the collective—that is, to yourself in the context of others. Imagine yourself working in a group. Your awareness is on how your thoughts and actions might be aligned with those of the group. You pay attention to how group members are getting along, whether someone is feeling left out, and whether you or someone else might not be respecting the values of the group. Internally, you think about how to better serve the group and what might be needed so everyone feels good and included. No one can really see your thought process, though someone could infer by your behaviors that you are being deeply mindful of your identity with the group. This quadrant of attentional focus also applies to such collectives as families and social groups, where one's internal state is guided by what the collective believes, wants, or advocates. The group can be small, as in a tight group of lifelong friends, or large, as in membership in a culture or a country. For instance, think of someone raised in a family with strong cultural and religious identities. Assuming that person fully embraces all those familial, cultural, and religious values and norms, you might realize how this person's capacity to think and choose freely would be heavily influenced by the collectivities in which he or she is embedded.

4. *Lower right (LR).* Finally, attention shifts to the external realities and observables, to all that affects what is happening, all the possible outcomes of what is going on, and how things and people interact with one another. So, here you would often find yourself hovering in situations, focusing on how things happen, what causes what, what the outcomes are, how things can be measured, the availability of resources, and so many other elements. You focus on the big picture so much so that you zoom out from the immediate experience to encompass broader factors, projections of results, and people and systems in interaction.

Before translating this model into the world of coaching, you might want to know that each person you meet tends to see and experience their world predominantly through one of the four quadrants. Each of us has a preferred quadrant that we rely on heavily to interpret and respond to our realities. Yes, you can shift your focus so that you look at experience through any of the four lenses or quadrants, but Wilber's point is that most of us tend to orient ourselves to experience through one quadrant more than through the others. For instance, you may mostly look at life through your actions, what you do, what you accomplish, and how much you get done. You may have lots of to do lists and projects on the go. You may also be impatient with inaction so much so that friends and colleagues often hear you saying, "Okay, so what can we *do* about this?" Alternatively, you may focus a lot on the collective, on what *we* want, on how *we* feel, on how *we* are getting along, on what *we* share in common, on how *we* can better serve each other.

The point is that as a coach you need to take into account all four perspectives. You need to consider what you are thinking and feeling, how the relationship seems, what actions are occurring, and what's the big picture of you and your client in this context, including the measurable outcomes of your time together. It hasn't always been clear in the coaching field that presence involves all four of these perspectives. You might remember from the definitions before that some coaches seem to emphasize one or two quadrants but make little explicit reference to the others. Topp (2006, p. 3), for instance, stresses "one's quality of relating to the here and now, or present moment", and similarly Silsbee (2010, p. 21) emphasizes the "state of awareness, in the moment." By way of contrast, Cox (2013, p. 134) speaks about how presence needs to be "transformed into action" so that it moves beyond mindfulness to involve "interaction with the client, the coaching alliance and the setting of coaching." In this regard, she seems to reference all four of the quadrants, the self (mindfulness), the relationship (the coaching alliance), action, and the big picture (the setting of coaching). In fairness to all of these coaching experts, my remarks about their views derive from their definitions and may misrepresent the fullness of their perspectives.

A Quadrant Study of Coaching Presence

Michael Abravanel (2018) completed an impressive study for his doctoral thesis on coaching presence. He conducted in-depth interviews with 16 highly experienced coaches on the topic of coaching presence. Employing a qualitative research design, he transcribed and coded these interviews, exploring major convergences in their comments. Six themes seemed evident; these were named mindful self-awareness, authentic connection, deep attunement, embodied engagement, holding outcomes, and structural alignment. While these labels only hint at fuller explanations, the exciting finding in his research was that the six themes could be easily

located in the four quadrants described by Wilber (2000a, 2000b, 2006). From this research, it is even more evident that coaching presence is a multidimensional construct. It's more than mindfulness, it's more than focusing on the relationship or the coaching alliance, it's more than the observable interventions that coaches make, and it's more than attending to all the factors in and around the client and her topic. In fact, it's all of these pretty much at the same time—as much as that is ever possible.

Abravanel's (2018) study helps us appreciate what good coaches need to do to be fully present: They are attuned to their inner states and mindful of themselves moment by moment (upper left focus); they move their inner awareness into action and embodied engagement with their clients (upper right focus); they are keenly aware of the relationship they currently have and the one they want to foster with their clients (lower left focus); they have a big-picture awareness of the present context of their coaching conversation, namely, the environment in which it occurs, and the larger context of their clients and how the work they are trying to move forward is situated in a very complex life space (Lewin, 1935).

You probably want to know how a coach can comfortably maintain presence in all four quadrants simultaneously. Part of the answer lies in what was just described—that is, knowing that there are four major areas of attention. By reflecting on your practice, by continuing in peer or supervisory reviews of your sessions, and by engaging in personal development to enhance your capacities in the realm of presence, you will gradually nurture a natural habit of being able to maintain presence and focus in all four quadrants while working with your clients. I want to be more specific about how to develop presence according to this model, so the next section offers some ideas.

Building Capacity for Presence

Maybe you already have a solid meditation or mindfulness practice, and in this moment as you read about the field of professional coaching, you are becoming better informed about the wide range of client issues. Also, earlier chapters on change processes, models of coaching, ethics, and relationship issues might motivate you to remain vigilant about how the context of your coaching relationship and the broader framework of your clients' issues affect the processes and outcomes of your work.

Part of Abravanel's (2018) research delved into the practicalities of what coaches do to enhance their capacity for presence. As we move through the upcoming material, please bear in mind that coaching is often thought as a way of being (see chapter 15) rather than as a circumscribed skill set. Developing your capacity for presence relies not only on presence-focused practices that you rehearse, but in how you live your life moment-by-moment.

Developing Presence in Self

A critical presence theme that emerged in Abravanel's (2018) study was named mindful self-awareness; he located this focus in the upper left quadrant. Some of the ways in which coaches might engender self-attunement may already be evident to you. Abravanel's research identified a few dominant methods that coaches described, including meditation, journaling, and self-presence pauses.

There are so many techniques of meditation that it may be difficult to choose. The good news is that evidence doesn't identify any one as better than another. However, adherence to a practice on a regular basis is key. Whether one engages in a mindfulness meditation practice (Kabat-Zinn, 2018), self-compassion meditation (Neff & Germer, 2018), or a breath-based method such as Vipassana (Hart, 2011) will not be as critical as engaging in one's chosen practice regularly.

Journaling is another method that coaches rely on to enhance self-awareness. The practice of journaling is often described as a spiritual practice (Banks, 2014), though there is also a long tradition of reflection as a critical habit for helping professionals (Schön, 2003). Just as a regular mindfulness practice draws your attention to experience of the present moment, so too journaling as a regular activity increases your capacity to be aware of yourself in action. A particular style of journaling arises from Julia Cameron's (2002) well-known work, *The Artist's Way*, which describes a process of writing "morning pages," an exercise that initiates your entry into each day with awareness.

A third category of practice that surfaced in Abravanel's (2018) research focuses on what he labeled self-presence pauses. These are demonstrated when coaches deliberately take time out (sometimes less than a minute) to center and focus intentionally (Brown, 2010). When coaches engage in such self-presence pauses on a regular basis, the likelihood is that they increase their capacity to call forth greater presence with their clients while coaching.

Developing Presence in Action

Abravanel (2018) described a category of presence that he called embodied action, which he located in the upper right quadrant or self-in-action (Wilber, 2000a, 2000b, 2006). Becoming aware of yourself while acting, speaking, moving, intervening, or engaging in physical activities takes practice. It is perhaps easier to sit on a cushion and meditate than to walk down a crowded street with intentional presence and focus. Indeed, if you observe people exercising in fitness centers, the likelihood is that many of them will be wearing headsets and listening to podcasts or music. Attention to one's body in motion is challenged by the competing awareness of sounds and music (Gavin, 1988).

In the field of coaching, the approach of somatic coaching (Strozzi-Heckler, 2014) offers a pathway to developing practices that enhance body awareness through bodywork and other physical methods. Strozzi-Heckler, the founder of this approach, describes how in modern life we have become disturbingly distanced from our bodies. He provides helpful guidance for ways of reconnecting to our bodies, including awareness of sensations, bodywork to release tensions, and specific types of movement experiences. Indeed, this perspective of developing awareness in movement or action has a long history in the fields of dance, physical rehabilitation, and sports (Chaiklin & Wengrower, 2015; Feldenkrais, 2009).

Research conducted by Abravanel (2018) revealed other ways in which coaches can develop embodied presence. As you might suspect, many coaches referred to ongoing practices of yoga and qigong. Also, coaches discussed how being in nature fosters an enhanced sense of their physical beings. It seems there are many ways in which you can bring greater awareness of yourself in action, and indeed a more expansive perspective of mindfulness practice offers exactly that—an enhanced capacity to be in the moment with awareness no matter what you are doing.

Developing Presence in Relationships

The coaches in Abravanel's (2018) study suggested two strong themes in their discussions about presence; one was identified as authentic connection and the second as deep attunement. These speak to Wilber's (2000a, 2000b, 2006) lower left quadrant. In that coaching is embedded in a relationship between coach and client, the importance of presence while being with another person is paramount. In discussing how coaches enhance their capacities in relation to these two themes, a number of ideas were offered; these included such practices as cultivating gratitude and loving kindness, fostering open hearted relationships, and being more intentional in communicating by practicing active listening in all relationships.

There's a connection between these themes pertaining to relational presence and what Goleman (2006) described in his concept of social intelligence as well as in Gergen's (2009) construct of the relational self. These and other writings emphasize a perspective where the center of our world is not *I* but rather *we*. Siegel (2010) also captures this in demonstrating how, from the stance of neuroscience, we are highly interconnected in our emotionality. Work on this competency seems quite complex because it largely addresses the whole of our human nature as social beings. From a coaching perspective, what does it take to be fully present to another without identifying or becoming part of the other's story? Conversely, how do you listen in a way that is both objective and subjective in a coaching relationship?

Divine (2009b) captures this well from an integral coaching perspective when she differentiates between *looking at* and *looking as* the client. What she means here is that coaches need to at times be fully outside their client's experience to observe and understand what is being presented, while at other times they need to inhabit the experiences of their clients to gather necessary appreciation. In fact, it isn't an either-or proposition, but rather her perspective asks that coaches develop the capacity to seamlessly navigate the looking at and looking as stances in order to be of utmost service to their clients.

Sometimes clients tell stories that provoke in me an initial sense of surprise or incomprehension of how they can view situations in the way they describe. It takes effort to put these looking at judgments aside, and indeed some of my ongoing practices in meditation have helped me sit more openly in such experiences. This discussion brings to mind the lyrics from a Bob Dylan song, *Love Minus Zero/ No Limit*: "My love winks, she does not bother, She knows too much to argue or to judge."

Developing Presence to the System

Two of the themes emerging in Abravanel's (2018) study suggest aspects of the lower right quadrant focus on systems; these themes were holding outcomes and structural alignment. Coaches in this study talked how they created a "container" for the sessions and intentionally held the emerging network of outcomes in perspective as they worked with their clients. Further, they indicated an awareness of the larger environment and how it affects the evolution of the coaching relationship. Focusing

on these matters represented a kind of presence to the context in which the coaching relationship was developing.

As a coach, you want to be able to see the system (Meadows, 2008; Oshry, 2009) in which clients are embedded. Unlike classical psychoanalytic work where the focus remains almost exclusively on the interior experiences and fantasies of clients, coaching is grounded in all of the realities interfacing with your clients' objectives. Coaches need to be present to all the elements in the client's life space (Lewin, 1935) while simultaneously attending to all of the ways the client is showing up in this moment—words, feelings, expressions, implied meanings, and more.

Abravanel (2018) describes how coaches in his study tried to strengthen their capacity to see the big picture or the system through reading, research, and the mindset of a lifelong learner. When their clients would present unfamiliar ideas to them, these coaches talked about investigating this material through reading and web searches. Sometimes they mentioned their focus on a particular niche they preferred in their work so that when clients mentioned esoteric concepts, they would understand and not be distracted by internal thought processes to determine whether they knew what their clients were saying.

There is no clear curriculum for building competency in this quadrant, though you probably can recognize a need to become a systems thinker for change (Rutherford, 2019; Stroh, 2015). Surely with what the world has experienced in the recent pandemic and all of its sequelae, you will have a much greater appreciation of the interconnection of absolutely everything. Narrowing down the focus from everything to what you need to know partly entails gaining clarity about where you want to focus your coaching practice. As much as some coaches may say they can coach anyone, I would condition this answer with an awareness that coaching most clients requires more than a basic understanding of the contexts in which they live and the nature of the issues they are addressing. Futurists speaking about the field of coaching argue that in coming decades, coaches may have to become content experts as much as they are now required to be process experts (Einzig, 2017; Peterson, 2018).

Putting this in a more concrete frame, what if you have an international practice with clients from diverse cultures who may be addressing a similar theme, such as leadership competency. You would likely know that leadership will imply some similar but other more distinctive competencies across cultures. Based on your practice niche, you will come to realize what the big picture is that you need to understand for the kinds of clients you want to attract. By grasping more fully this aspect of the lower right quadrant, you will be capable of remaining present to all the other ways in which clients may be wrestling with their stories.

The Sum of It All

Most coaches acknowledge the centrality of coaching presence to their practice. While I believe each competency is uniquely essential to coaching practice, I also recognize that coaching presence is more complex than has generally been acknowledged. Further, I would say that through the lens of quadrants, no quadrant is more important than another—you will need to develop competency in each to become the best coach you can possibly be. By all means build your capacity by meditating, practicing yoga, taking up archery, extending your active listening to more than your clients, journaling, engaging in gratitude practices, or nourishing your curiosity by reading about things your clients discuss. All of this will help build your multidimensional capacity to be more present to your clients and in your life.

COACHING PRESENCE IN THE ICF CORE COMPETENCIES

The ICF's definition of presence highlights key indicators of this competency in coaching (see sidebar, ICF Core Coaching Competency 5: Maintains Presence). As in meditation, presence involves a highly awakened state of being. The ability to be fully present is an intricate part of the coach's personal foundation. Presence implies that the coach tunes in on all channels—sights, sounds, emotions, intuitions, and beyond. As in a state of flow (Csikszentmihalyi, 2008), the coach is open to all that is present to her, including her own special ways of knowing. Even though there is an intention to assist the client in moving forward, the process is never scripted in advance. Effective coaching interventions are highly responsive to all that a client is bringing forth in the moment and over time. As Cox (2013) so aptly remarked, "there is no such thing as absence-based coaching, there is only presence-based coaching" (p. 133).

ICF Core Coaching Competency 5: Maintains Presence

Definition: Is fully conscious and present with the client, employing a style that is open, flexible, grounded and confident.

1. Remains focused, observant, empathetic and responsive to the client
2. Demonstrates curiosity during the coaching process
3. Manages one's emotions to stay present with the client
4. Demonstrates confidence in working with strong client emotions during the coaching process
5. Is comfortable working in a space of not knowing
6. Creates or allows space for silence, pause or reflection

There is a clear emphasis on maintaining focused attention and connection to clients in this ICF competency. In the material you have just reviewed, I have broadened the framework for presence, but perhaps have not adequately underscored some aspects of this competency as articulated by the International Coaching Federation. In particular, I want to draw your attention to two manifestations of presence that the ICF highlights. The first points to the coach's capacity to self-regulate their emotionality and the second speaks about curiosity.

When clients are caught up in strong emotions, coaches need to confidently hold the space for them with empathy. To do so, coaches need to manage their own emotionality, which may be associated with their clients' stories or with their own issues. Another facet of presence relevant here speaks to coaches' capacities to remain grounded when they aren't sure what is happening or where to go or when clients lapse into long reflective silences.

Curiosity is emphasized in this competency seemingly as an outgrowth of open-minded and responsive witnessing. From a quadrant perspective, if you have quieted your inner chatter and maintained focus on what is emerging in the relationship and in the client's story, you may quite spontaneously express thoughts and questions from a place of innocent wonder. I go back to Divine's (2009b) distinction between looking as and looking at as I think about the curiosity I have sometimes expressed in sessions. In the looking as frame, I feel as if I am inside the client wondering about something that perhaps in that same moment the client is contemplating as well. I speak almost as if I am speaking to myself. Other times, in more of a looking at frame, my mind is unwittingly putting together a kind of puzzle and needs a piece that currently does not appear on the "table" of this discussion. So I ask. I have no investment in being right, but only a hope that my curiosity might be helpful.

The different aspects of this ICF presence competency don't explicitly reference presence in the four quadrants as previously discussed. However, in order to manifest presence as defined by the ICF, you can easily imagine that the emphasis on being fully conscious while remaining open, flexible, grounded, and confident would require that coaches have mastered being present to self and others, acting with full awareness, and keeping perspective of all of the factors that may be influencing the conversation itself and clients in the context of their topics.

REFLECTIONS

In an awareness of how a career path in coaching will stretch each of us in ways that at times will ground us and other times unsettle us, I am reminded of the words of Otto Scharmer (2016) when he speaks of the three challenges to deep presence—or presencing as he labels it. He identifies these as the voice of judgment, the voice of cynicism, and the voice of fear. If you have ever tried to sit for prolonged periods in silent, unguided meditation, you will know well the mind's chatter and how incessantly it intrudes on the silence you are trying to cultivate. Your thoughts are rarely just random fluffy ideas, but more likely they come loaded with judgments, speculations, and emotions. This complex chatter happens readily when you are alone with yourself, doing your utmost to center and quiet your mind. With a client who values you enough to choose you and whom you are doing your utmost to serve, the mind and emotional chatter may amplify exponentially.

Practices of traditional meditation and mindfulness have swept the world in popularity for good reason. Our minds are increasingly stimulated and rarely still. We can't listen well to others when we are busy sorting out the noise in our minds. Even when we think we are serving our clients by analyzing their situations and structuring our words to align with their purposes, there may be more of our attention on the formation of our responses than there is on the actual stories of our clients. Scharmer (2016) tells us to move into stillness to launch the creativity required for significant shifts in our lives. This is easier said than done. Our intelligence and all the knowledge and experience packed inside us wants to find a place in the dialogue with our clients and thus sometimes what we already know is our greatest impediment to being fully present to what our clients are offering. Appropriately now, the next chapter moves us into the realm of active listening.

CHAPTER 10
LISTENING ACTIVELY

*When we listen, we hear
someone into existence.*

Laurie Buchanan

MY STORY

Maybe you've played some variant of the game *broken telephone*, where people sit in a circle and one person begins by whispering a message to the person next to him or her. That person then whispers the message to the next person and so on until the original message travels all the way around the circle to the originator. In all the times I have played this game, the message delivered at the end to the originator was never the same as the one this person sent. I mention this game because it makes a point about listening: Most of us think we are good listeners, yet evidence often contradicts this belief. One of the greatest testing grounds for our capacity to listen is in intimate relationships. I have listened to couples for decades in their efforts to accurately hear what the other is saying. Sadly, there's often too much interpretation and misrepresentation in what is understood. When asked to repeat what one's partner said, statements presented as accurate reflections of what was expressed are sometimes even more distorted than what comes back to the originator in the game of broken telephone.

What causes this common if not universal phenomenon? I am aware that I have a busy mind. Even when I am totally focused on what someone is saying, my mind is often making up stories or translating the words I am hearing into my own ways of expressing these ideas. I may then sit contentedly thinking I have really understood the other person and perhaps offer some suggestions based on what I interpreted. Well, when my understanding is a composite of what the speaker said plus my own internal musings, whatever I offer back stands a chance of taking the conversation on a new course that may be more mine than the other's original trajectory. Of course, my mind isn't the only culprit in this drama; I am also an emotional being. Sometimes I get triggered or I may get thrown by the content of someone's story into some happy or not-so-happy memory, and I add the emotional flavor of my personal recollections to my understanding of the other person's message. "Wow, that sounds like a real fun time!" I say, but maybe it wasn't for the storyteller. It seems to me that the longer I live and the more people I talk with, the more I need to practice the basics of active listening. The frequency of comments like, "Been there, done that"; "I understand exactly what you mean"; and "Yeah, me too!" highlight our assumptions of understanding. So, in this sense we are all in this together: Trying to get it right without inserting our own musings and emotions into someone else's story.

How do we listen, and what exactly do we listen for? This chapter moves the locus of listening from the ears to the mind, heart, and body. It distinguishes between hearing what another is saying and communicating to that person expressions confirming the depth and sensitivity of your listening. Hearing words and repeating them is not enough because, as you know, most of our communication is nonverbal. The upcoming material takes you on a voyage about what listening really means, how empathy plays into the listening process, what authentic listening represents, and how all of those nonverbal messages need to be appreciated in understanding what the real messages are. Beyond such knowledge, there is practice. This chapter offers clear guidance pertaining to methods coaches rely on to listen well. Here are some guiding questions as you read:

- What does active listening really mean?
- What needs to happen in order for coaches to listen well?
- Is listening one-sided in a coaching relationship?
- Are there different types of listening?
- Where do nonverbal communications fit into listening?
- What are the methods coaches use to listen to their clients?

HOW IS LISTENING ACTIVE?

You probably have had experiences where people seemed to be listening to you, showing all the right nonverbal attending signals, only to then say something that either misses or distorts the content and intention of your message. Depending on the context, this can be really problematic. Listening actively doesn't always come easily. It involves an expression of the core content of the speaker's words and implicit emotionality in a succinct and timely manner. Words are sometimes repeated verbatim and other times captured in synonymous expressions that hopefully mirror meanings without distortion. Active listening involves reflecting back what is expressed by the speaker through their words, actions, manner of speaking, and implied or expressed emotional qualities.

Listening actively in coaching has a delicate and distinctive rhythm deriving from the unique dynamics of who the client is, who the coach is, what the context is, and the nature and content of agendas they are addressing together. Clients begin from varying places of trust and openness and then unfold into the relationship at different rates and intensities. An extensive body of literature documents the centrality of active listening in helping relationships (Brew & Kottler, 2008; Cox, 2013; Egan, 2014; Ivey et al., 2018; Smith, 2007). Maintaining focus on clients' agendas requires that you show up in all the ways that coaching presence entails (see chapter 9). It necessitates listening and responding in a manner that doesn't draw the client's attention to your world or toward things you think are important. As Carl Rogers demonstrated throughout his career, there is profound power in listening well (Rogers, 1961, 1980; Rogers & Farson, 1995).

Stephen Covey (1989) once said, "most people do not listen with the intent to understand, they listen with the intent to reply" (p. 239). Listening actively is a highly engaged process of attending to the client's words and behaviors with exquisite awareness and then expressing back in a timely manner the messages received so the client feels understood. It can be tricky when someone's communication is met with replies such as "Got it!" "Understood!" or the more classic, "I hear you." If you are the speaker, you may have little certainty that what you said was received with the same meaning as you intended. Indeed, it may only be when someone verbally reflects what you have said that you realize that what you said wasn't understood. Interestingly, when your words are accurately reflected, you are offered so many gifts, one of them being the opportunity to gauge whether what you said is what you truly feel. Relationships are bilateral. Each party plays a role in what is expressed and what is received.

I want to tell a brief story before we dive into some useful frameworks for active listening: I was coaching an executive who was wondering why one particular staff member didn't follow through on his directives. In a team meeting that I was facilitating, the executive told this staff member what was on his mind. He said, "Harry, I'm baffled by the fact that when I ask you to take care of situations, you sometimes do, and you sometimes don't. Aren't I being clear enough with you about what I want?" The somewhat stunned staff member replied, "John, most of the time when we get together, you say things like, 'It might be good to look into X,' or 'I'm wondering what might happen if we tried Y.' I can hardly ever remember you telling me directly to just do something!" So, Harry heard John through his personal understanding of words and their meanings to him. John felt frustrated because some of his directives were being ignored. I suggested a practice of active listening. It helped a lot.

THEORY *U*

More than a decade ago, Otto Scharmer (2007) presented his first edition of a model that he called *Theory U* partly because the form of the letter *U* represented for him the flow of movement in a change process toward an emerging future. Today, hundreds of thousands of people involved in personal, organizational, and social change processes are likely to be familiar with this seminal model. Although it is largely thought of as a model for fostering social innovation, it is at the same time a profoundly meaningful framework for appreciating how individuals can foster the kinds of personal transformations that are typically embraced in coaching relationships. A pertinent question here is *how can this model help coaches better grasp what active listening is all about?*

Scharmer's (2016) model references various kinds of dialogue that you may have, including ones with yourself. For our purposes, I want to concentrate on conversations occurring between a coach and client. The notion of dialogue denotes an invitation for all parties to listen at deeper levels, but in the realities of a coaching relationship, clients may not always be able to adequately hear themselves—never mind hearing someone else. Thus, coaches try to model processes of listening at deeper levels, although their own capacities in listening will be influenced by the degree to which they have adequately addressed what Scharmer refers to as the enemies of listening. In upcoming sections, I will review these enemies as well as describing the four levels of listening that Scharmer identifies (see figure 10.1).

Voices of Judgment, Cynicism, and Fear

As you are reading this material now, you may be aware of an inner dialogue you are having with yourself. You may be evaluating, critiquing, or even having some emotional response to ideas being presented. This is a pretty natural process. So, too, when you are listening to someone, you might similarly be aware of your internal discourse, which sometimes gets so loud that it blocks out the external voice to which you are attending.

When Scharmer (2007) put forth his model of transformative and innovative change, he considered the qualities of one's presence that nourish deeper listening. He spoke about the need to have an open mind, heart, and will; this is how he expressed these ideas:

> An open mind is the capacity to suspend old habits of judgment—to see with fresh eyes. An open heart is the capacity to empathize and to look at a situation through the eyes of somebody else. An open will is the capacity to "let go of the old and let come" the new. (Scharmer, 2018, p. 25)

In reflecting on your own experiences in listening, you might recognize how suspending judgment, empathizing, and letting go into the unknown

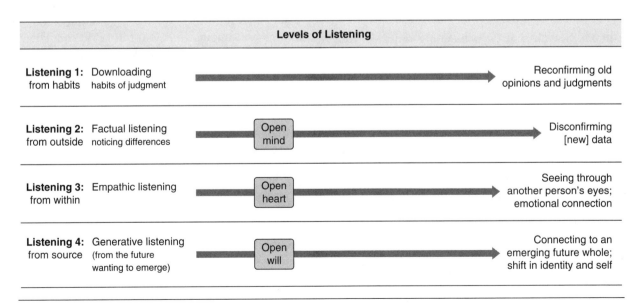

Figure 10.1   *Theory U* and the four levels of listening.

to allow new possibilities to arise are crucial in any creative venture. Indeed, being able to bring forth such openness in a coaching relationship fosters conditions for the kinds of outcomes that most clients desire.

Openness may be consciously or unconsciously resisted in your coaching and other relationships when one or more of the voices of judgment, cynicism and fear arise. Scharmer (2018) labels these voices as enemies or "inner voices of resistance" (p. 28).

Voice of Judgment

Each of us has a history packed with knowledge, experiences, and so many other elements. Your brain is designed to detect patterns and to predict outcomes for both survival and success. I am reminded of the adage that past behavior is the best predictor of future behavior, a quote most often associated with B.F. Skinner, the founder of behavioral psychology (Albarracín & Wyer, 2000; Skinner, 1953). It tells us that knowing how someone has acted in the past allows high probability predictions of how that person will behave in future situations. Coaching clients are at least implicitly aware of this, and that's one of the reasons they have chosen the coaching option—to break away from old patterns. Even so, as you listen to your clients' stories, an enemy of your openness of mind will be the voice of judgment, which will direct you toward old habits of thinking and close off new ways of seeing and understanding. This voice is driven in part by your need to confirm your personal worldview and the mental models you have generated over time.

Voice of Cynicism

You know well that deep listening requires you to open your heart—to allow not only a cognitive understanding of what someone is experiencing but to create an inner space to receive what your client is actually experiencing in the moment or in his or her story. This might be scary. A fear arises that we may begin to feel the other's emotions as if they are our own. Neuroscientist and psychiatrist Dan Siegel (2007, 2012) also described how our neurobiology connects us to others in ways that can arouse disquieting feelings as we identify with what they are experiencing. In this sense, the inclination to distance ourselves emotionally from what another person is describing makes sense, even though it limits the degree to which we can fully comprehend what they are going through (De Llosa, 2011). The voice of cynicism in Scharmer's perspective speaks to all the ways we close our hearts to the experiences of others. In not wanting to feel another's suffering, we keep our understanding of the other at a more rational—and manageable—level, so that we can perhaps feel more in control and logically dissect or analyze what we are hearing. As a coach, you will need to cultivate a capacity to keep your heart open in your work in order to facilitate deeper listening. In a sense, you will need to become even more vulnerable than you might have ever imagined possible.

Voice of Fear

No doubt by this point in your life you have formed a reasonably coherent definition of yourself. You move through the world with a certain assuredness of what you know and who you are. As much as you see yourself on a lifelong trajectory of change, you might also recognize that some change agendas require a galloping leap of faith that you will arrive in a new reality that isn't unsettling.

As you listen to your clients' experiences, you may be challenged to let go of many ideas and even long-held beliefs about yourself, others, and the world at large. You may not realize this fully if you are at the beginning of your career as a helper, but coaching changes coaches, too! You may be shaken out of your worldview, your beliefs about how the world works, and even your sense of who you are. The implicit coaching mandate is for you as a coach to let go in order to let come. This isn't always easy or comfortable. You may feel a degree of fear when confronted at a core level because some belief or aspect of your identity no longer feels valid.

It can be as basic as questioning the importance of success as you have understood it over the course of your lifetime—or realizing you are not as open minded and unbiased as you think. When a client presents you with a radically different perspective on life that challenges values you have clung to for decades, it can shake you to the ground. Listening in moments like these requires a fierce faith that allows you to move through the fire and burn off whatever you don't need for creating your own future and for facilitating your client's capacity to grow in unpredictably wonderful ways.

The Four Levels of Listening

In Scharmer's (2018) words, "changing how you listen means that you change how you experience relationships and the world" (p. 26). In effect, changing how you listen changes everything. Deeper levels of listening become available to you the more you are able to manage the three voices just described. There may be times when you can open your mind, but not your heart—or when you can open both mind and heart, but not be able to let go of your precious beliefs. In this sense, it's not an all-or-nothing capacity but a fluid one that hopefully evolves and grows with practice and the work you do on yourself. Let's look at Scharmer's four listening levels.

Downloading

If you enter a dialogue or conversation holding tightly to all you know, you will likely listen so as to confirm what you already believe. If something is expressed that doesn't fit your templates for understanding, it's possible you won't even hear it. Your focus in listening is predominantly on what you already know through your habitual frameworks and judgment patterns. Listening in this fashion serves largely to confirm what you presently believe to be true.

Maybe you think it's improbable you would ever listen this way. My sense is we all listen this way more often than we know. Imagine being in a rush and wanting a certain piece of information from someone like a family member, friend, or colleague. Somewhere embedded in a lengthy reply to your question is the nugget you needed. You hear it, but most everything else flits away without awareness. Put this in another context: A person with a long-standing chronic condition is having a periodic exam with a family physician who is habitually overscheduled and pressed for time. The doctor asks a bunch of questions but doesn't really have the capacity to take everything in. The doctor just needs to find the right answers. Whatever information fits the preset categories is registered, and not so much anything else. The requisite boxes are checked, but what is unattended to may have critical bearing on a diagnosis.

Factual Listening

How is listening affected when the mind is open? When you suspend judgment and allow the data to speak for itself, you have progressed to the level of factual listening. This is akin to what happens in the scientific world—emphasizing what is evident and factual as well as attending to what might be different or novel about the messages or experience. While this kind of listening requires an open mind, it ignores the complex social and internal realities of the speaker. It gives almost exclusive attention to facts and data. In a more likely representation of the doctor–patient conversation, an examining physi-cian would be like a scientist trying to confirm or disconfirm evidence of various physical concerns.

In the coaching world, what does it mean to suspend judgment? Clients very often want to create new realities for themselves. They may want to change careers, write a book, complete a triathlon, run their own business, flip an autocratic leadership style to a fully collaborative one, and so on. If your mind is flashing back on B.F. Skinner's idea that past behavior is the best predictor of future behavior, might you be in a place of judgment in listening to such agendas when your clients' past experiences offer little evidence of capacity to achieve such objectives?

Take Scharmer's (2007) words to heart: Factual listening means that "you begin to focus on information that differs from what you already know" (p. 11). This is harder than you might imagine. Even in science, there have been untold numbers of experiments that disproved the experimenters' hypotheses but were somehow unseen, unrecognized, or ignored. What does it take to release all of your judgments while listening to another?

Empathic Listening

What happens in your listening when you open your heart? It may be evident, but I will say it anyway: Opening your heart rests on the foundation of an open mind. You can't really have an open heart without an open mind. An open heart means that I let myself feel your reality—I take in your experience to the extent that I can fully empathize with what you are saying. I am reminded of Victor Frankl's (1969; 1988) expression that there is no hierarchy to pain. My suffering is not better or worse, bigger or smaller than someone else's. When you listen to someone describing a situation with obvious discomfort and you find yourself thinking, "What's so upsetting about that?" you know that in this moment you are struggling to fully open your heart.

I have already discussed the challenge to your own equilibrium that you welcome when you allow yourself to enter emotionally into another's world. Cognitively, you may be able to understand what is happening, but when you empathically connect to others' realities, you may experience the pain they are carrying in a disquieting way. Though coaching is not therapy, we are nonetheless emotional beings and our stories are imbued with feelings we have experienced in living certain events. It is likely to feel safer to emotionally distance ourselves from some stories. They may touch too closely our own stories, or they may convey an intensity that is hard for us to contain.

Novice coaches often tell me about their struggles carrying the emotions they bear witness to in conversations with their clients. Your work is not about creating a kind of immunity to the emotionality of clients' stories, but rather it is about building capacity to hold these emotions without attaching yourself to or identifying with them. Indeed, there is an uplifting face of empathic listening in that you come to realize at a profound level the resilience and triumphant qualities of humanity. Surfacing client strengths in their stories is part of our work, and even so, you will need to learn how to ride the emotional waves without being continually swept under.

Generative Listening

Can you recall a conversation with someone in your life that changed you? I am not asking about the outcome that might have resulted from this conversation, like being offered a new opportunity in life. Rather, I want to know if, in the process of the dialogue, you felt the ground under you shift so much so that when you stepped out from this encounter, you felt ever so slightly different—and better in some way.

When you release fear and embrace simultaneously the unknown and the expansive realm of possibility, you will find yourself listening with wide-eyed curiosity and openness to something yet unseen that might emerge. Generative listening rests on the openness of your mind and heart and then asks that you loosen your grip on the known world within and around you to allow totally novel possibilities to emerge. In this way of listening, you may experience your voice differently, ideas may surface that pleasantly surprise you, and though the dialogue may seem to challenge understandings of yourself and broader realities, you experience a kind of lightness of being. It is akin to a state of flow (Csikszentmihalyi, 2008) where you are awake to all that is evolving in you as you embrace that which is evolving in the other. This type of listening requires that you release things you normally rely on to anchor your understanding so you can open to possibilities in your client that you might not normally allow. As you listen from this place, something may awaken in you that gives birth to new ideas and ways of being with this client.

When Scharmer (2007) describes generative listening, he speaks of it as "listening from the emerging field of future possibility" (p. 54). It is a form of listening that moves beyond the deeply empathic connection with your client to a sense of union with the broader field of reality that both of you exist in at the moment of your conversation. As Scharmer says, you may experience in some way at the end of this dialogue that you are not exactly the same person you were at its beginning. In my own practice, I don't often experience this level of listening, but I do know it reasonably well. It speaks to me of moments when I say something in response to my client that is largely surprising to me but so apt to the theme and direction of the conversation. In times like this, clients sometimes ask me where this idea came from, as if it was a well-known principle or prescription. If I were to answer coherently in those moments, I would probably say, "It came from us."

You may wish to discover more about developing this capacity for generative listening, and to this end, Miriam Subirana's (2016) work on appreciative coaching would be useful. Also, a similar idea identified as *generative empathic listening* was described by Hawkins and Schwenk (2010). As a final reference before leaving this review, I would like to offer you the seminal words of Carl Rogers (1980, p. 129) as he might describe a generative moment, in his words:

> When I can relax, and be close to the transcendental core of me, then I may behave in strange and impulsive ways in the relationship, ways I cannot justify rationally, which have nothing to do with my thought processes. But these strange behaviors turn out to be right in some odd way. At these moments it seems that my inner spirit has reached out and touched the inner spirit of the other. Our relationship transcends itself and has become something larger.

Clearly, this way of being and way of listening may be challenging to achieve in most situations, yet it offers us a vision of the listening process that we can cultivate through our work with clients and with ourselves.

COACHING FRAMEWORKS

Scharmer's perspectives derive more from the field of dialogue (Bohm, 2004; Isaacs, 1999) than from coaching per se. Yet, recent developments in coaching largely reflected in what is known as *third generation coaching* (Stelter, 2013, 2018) seem strongly aligned with Scharmer's representation of generative listening. Some of the core works on listening within the field of coaching also speak of listening in a manner that resembles a more generative listening stance. In the upcoming sections, I will review two coaching models that describe levels of listening (Hawkins & Schwenk, 2010; Kimsey-House et al., 2018; Whitworth et al., 2007), and a third that provides an invaluable perspective regarding authentic listening (Cox, 2013).

A Classic Analysis of Levels

Within the coaching field, the writings of Whitworth and colleagues (Kimsey-House et al., 2018; Whitworth et al., 2007) have been hugely influential. In considering the core competency of active listening, they observed that, "Most people do not listen at a very deep level. . . . Conversations skim along the surface" (Kimsey-House et al., 2018, p. 37). In their listening model, three levels are described; they range from an internal process, which is largely listening to oneself, to one that approximates some of the meanings suggested in Scharmer's generative listening.

Level I. Internal Listening

Awareness in this form of listening is largely about yourself. Even though you may register the words of the other person, Whitworth and colleagues suggest that the only question of pertinence in this type of listening is what someone else's words might mean to you personally. You tend to focus on content that you deem important. In many ways, this characterizes everyday listening experiences, as well as some coaching experiences where coaches attend largely to information that might inform their next comment or question; they are listening in order to respond. Even though this type of listening may not characterize an entire conversation, when a client says something to you that throws you into an internal dialogue about your own experiences and understanding, at this moment you may be in a level I listening mode.

Level II. Focused Listening

This way of listening requires a clear focus on the other person. It involves greater empathy and connection with the other such that your own mental noise virtually disappears as you allow yourself to become more fully aware of the other, mirroring messages and being conscious of how your listening might be affecting this person. Listening to understand is less typical of daily conversations and more representative of a coach's level of listening. The scope of listening not only embraces what is said but what is not said as well. You are listening for values, visions, and even subtle energy shifts. The authors describe it as a "wired connection" (Kimsey-House et al., 2018, p. 43) between coach and client.

Level III. Global Listening

The authors liken level III to listening where coach and client are "at the center of the universe, receiving information from everywhere at once" (Kimsey-House et al., 2018, p. 45). Listening is not just auditory but through all sensory intakes. It opens up access to your intuition, which might also be understood as the almost infinite elements of perception that weave together to provide understanding and insight. Level III listening takes in all elements of your experience, including the environment, temperature, and subtle shifting energies that you and your client might experience. There is a heightened sensitivity at this level to emotion and mood, yet you experience a certain lightness in your attentiveness. Much as generative listening represents a desired way, so, too, listening at this level is what you as a coach would aspire to in your sessions with clients.

From Another Angle

The model described by Whitworth and colleagues (Kimsey-House et al., 2018; Whitworth et al., 2007) is probably the most widely known depiction of levels of listening in the coaching literature, but there are others. In particular, Hawkins and Schwenk (2010) identified four levels of listening that even at the most fundamental level represent a positive coach-like listening process. Here is a brief description of their four levels:

1. *Attending.* The coach is attentive to what the client is saying, employing both verbal and nonverbal signals to reflect to the client how they are closely following the dialogue.

2. *Accurate listening.* Here the coach adds to attending behaviors an active reflection or paraphrasing of what the client is saying. Through such actions, coach and client can better align the emerging story and its understanding.

3. *Empathic listening.* Building on the foundation of attending and accurate listening processes, the coach now uses more advanced ways of expressing a deeper understanding of what the client is saying. For instance, this may be through the use of metaphors to capture the underlying implications of client expressions in a unique perspective.

4. *Generative empathic listening.* In this highest level, the coach engages with the client in helping to shape the narrative that the client is exploring. The coach partners with the client in a kind of reimagining of the story through the addition of other ideas and elements.

Though the final level described by Hawkins and Schwenk bears similarities to Scharmer's (2016) generative listening, my sense is that these two conceptualizations are quite distinct. At a minimum, Scharmer's framing suggests a wider awareness of the field in which coach and client are situated as well as a more detailed description of what it means as a coach to release attention to one's own voice of fear.

Authentic Listening

Elaine Cox (2013), in her enlightening treatise, *Coaching Understood*, examines various ways in which listening has been described in the coaching literature. She sadly notes that, "No research has been carried out to explore the function of listening in coaching" (p. 57), thus forcing a reliance on other disciplines for our appreciation of this key element in a coaching process. She also expresses concern about the hierarchical implications of levels of listening, where higher is thought to be better. Preferring to focus on the experience of being heard rather than listening *per se*, Cox expresses the belief that for all individuals "there is a yearning for 'witnessed significance' which is satisfied when someone listens to us" (p. 42).

With solid rationale, Cox (2013) reframes levels as modes of listening since each mode may be appropriate and useful at different moments in a coaching dialogue. Moreover, she speculates that the much-revered level of empathic (or generative empathic) listening might have less significance in coaching than in therapy relationships. While potentially important early in the formation of a coaching relationship, Cox thinks that something more is needed. Empathic listening does not permit the coach to introduce elements of judgment and analysis. She suggests that coaches need to do more than attune themselves to their clients—they need to engage with their clients in the construction of new understandings, paradigms, and models for action.

Cox (2013) proposes the idea of authentic listening, which offers more than a coach's reproduction of the clients' feelings and thoughts through reflective and empathic processes of listening. As she states, "coaching is a co-construction; it is a production rather than a reproduction" (p. 52). Tying her perspective closely to Heidegger's (1962) expression of "being with" (see chapter 9), Cox believes that coaches need to help clients explore their values and beliefs, and even "knock holes in them, shake them up and reform them" (Cox, 2013, p. 56). What is required in authentic listening is not that the coach be without bias or judgment, but rather that such elements be transparently expressed as such. She notes that a coach's bias or prejudice can be positive or negative, and by making them explicit, the coach provokes a search for understanding in the dialogue. Citing Hyde (1994), she points to the paradox occurring when coaches attempt to hide their personal views in service of appearing unbiased. This she sees as a kind of fundamental deception. Cox captures the requisite process for authentic listening in the following statement: "The authentic coach uses his/her prejudices openly and productively in service of the client, seeking the support of a supervisor to help with the kind of candid self-reflection necessary in this process" (p. 56).

What Seems Simple

As you can see from this lengthy review, a deeper appreciation of active listening brings us into more complex considerations. There is indeed a solid place for competent listening skills in coaching, but coaching is more than just listening. My sense is that the cocreative processes of coaching, such as authentic listening as described by Cox (2013), speak more of other competencies than what is intended in the active listening skill set that the International Coaching Federation (ICF, 2020c), along with other coaching bodies, have advocated. We will cover these other competencies in upcoming chapters. For now, I want to reiterate that skillful listening is more often assumed than demonstrated in our world. To build capacity for skillful listening, the next sections will delve into some of the well-established methods that coaches employ to listen actively.

UNSPOKEN COMMUNICATIONS

Active listening encompasses both what is and is not said. According to Mezirow (2000), effective communication "requires that we assess the meanings behind the words; the coherence, truth, and appropriateness of what is being communicated; the truthfulness and qualifications of the speaker;

and the authenticity of expressions of feeling" (p. 9). Of course, what is not said might simply be at clients' unconscious level, or there may be particular aspects of their stories that they deliberately protect. Perceiving what is not openly spoken often relies on communications that are transmitted nonverbally.

Nonverbal communication holds a prominent place in coaching. It has been formally defined as "communication effected by means other than words" (Knapp et al., 2014, p. 8). Early research in this area estimated that nonverbal behavior conveys from 65% to 93% of the meaning of a message (Birdwhistell, 1970; Mehrabian, 1972, 1981). Based on his research, Mehrabian proposed a ratio of 55:38:7, representing the proposition that 55% of a communication comes from body language, 38% from tone of voice, and only 7% from the actual words. Indeed, before client and coach exchange their first words, nonverbal communication may have fed judgments and impressions. In some cultures, nonverbal messages are thought to outweigh the significance of verbal content (Sue et al., 2019). Another important feature of nonverbal messaging is that it operates at a more unconscious level than verbal remarks.

As a coach, increased awareness of and sensitivity to nonverbal communications is crucial. You may notice various nonverbal expressions and interpret their meanings. These working hypotheses about meanings can be verified either through direct questioning or further observation. In the early stages of the coaching relationship, you may choose simply to remain alert to nonverbal cues. As the relationship develops, you may be able to discuss hunches developed from clients' nonverbal behaviors and thereby add depth to the coaching experience. In most cases, you might want to tread lightly when interpreting nonverbal messages, avoiding strong attachment to the meanings you attribute to them.

Five dimensions pertaining to the nonverbal domain have been identified: kinesics, paralinguistics, proxemics, environmental factors, and time (Cormier et al., 2017). Let's explore how these dimensions can guide your appreciation of clients' messages.

Kinesics

Kinesics refers to body motions and includes facial expressions, eye movements, gestures, posture, touch, and body movements (Cormier et al., 2017). According to some experts (Birdwhistell, 1970), kinesics may also include unchanging aspects of the body, such as height, weight, and physical appearance. In isolation, a single observation of kinesics may have limited value. Over time, however, patterns that seem correlated with certain subject matter or emotional content may emerge. Though kinesics can add new dimensions to someone's verbal messages, nonverbal gestures—just like words—often have more than one meaning (e.g., smiling at a wedding vis-à-vis at a funeral). Let's consider some selected areas of focus concerning body messaging.

Eye Movements

Much of what you might sense about another person comes from their eyes. The way someone's eyes appear when you engage in conversation offers hints about her or his inner state. Do they look at you when speaking? Is there meaning in a raised eyebrow or furrowed brow? Does the person blink often, or is her or his gaze more of a stare? Being aware of subtle eye movements offers clues about how best to respond to client needs.

If a client easily reciprocates your attentive eye contact throughout the coaching conversation, it makes sense to interpret this as an expression of interest and interpersonal comfort. However, when your client shifts her or his eyes from side to side or looks down rather than directly at you, the client is not necessarily conveying avoidance or disinterest. In some instances, this could reflect cultural norms; for example, lowering the eyes while speaking may be a way that members of certain cultural groups show respect and deference in conversations. Although many white North Americans might equate eye contact with listening, people from other cultures may interpret eye contact as bold and confronting (Knapp et al., 2014; Sue et al., 2019).

Communication experts in the area of **neurolinguistic programming** (NLP) (Andreas & Faulkner, 1996; Bandler & Grinder, 1979, 2005; Grinder & Bandler, 1976) believe that eye movements correspond to neural thought processing (see figure 10.2). They suggest that whether a speaker's eyes move up, down, or side to side can indicate how information is being processed and what types of internal experiences the person may be having.

For instance, when a person's eyes move on a horizontal level from side to side, neurolinguistic programming theory suggests that she or he is accessing verbal information. A movement that is horizontal and to his or her left indicates the person is trying to remember the words of past conversations, while one that is horizontal and to the right means she or he is constructing new sentences in her or his head. Eye movements up and to one side or

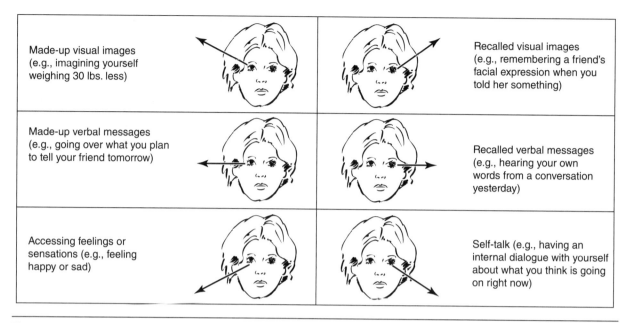

Made-up visual images (e.g., imagining yourself weighing 30 lbs. less)		Recalled visual images (e.g., remembering a friend's facial expression when you told her something)
Made-up verbal messages (e.g., going over what you plan to tell your friend tomorrow)		Recalled verbal messages (e.g., hearing your own words from a conversation yesterday)
Accessing feelings or sensations (e.g., feeling happy or sad)		Self-talk (e.g., having an internal dialogue with yourself about what you think is going on right now)

Figure 10.2   Neurolinguistic programming representation of eye movements

the other mean she or he is either accessing visual images from the past (left) or creating new images in the moment (right). Eye movements down and to one side or the other reflect either an internal dialogue in which the person is talking to herself or himself (left) or the experience of a significant emotion, such as joy or sadness (right).

A straightforward implication of this theory is that clients may move their eyes to access internal information. For instance, if you ask someone to imagine herself or himself participating in a sport, the person may create a visual image (eyes up and to her or his right) or remember a time when she or he participated in this activity (eyes up and left). In either case, NLP would argue that this person's eye movements parallel the kinds of information being accessed.

Facial Expressions

Scientific studies of facial expressions and emotion (Cohn & Ekman, 2008; Ekman, 1993, 2003) confirm much of what you may intuitively sense when looking at another person. Although the face is a body area that people usually learn to control, in unguarded moments all of us may reveal more than we want. Specific facial areas tend to convey certain emotions. You can usually see anger in the brows and lower face, for instance, while fear appears more in the eyes. The mouth and jaw tend to display surprise, happiness, and disgust. For the most part, cultural differences are not thought to influence basic emotional responses shown in the face.

When a client is not speaking, expressions of the lips and mouth may communicate a great deal. A person who is tight-lipped may be conveying experiences of control, anger, frustration, or repression. Biting the lips may express tension, and when the edges of someone's mouth turn down, you might be witnessing sadness or disappointment (Ekman, 2003; Ekman & Rosenberg, 2005).

Head

What does it mean when clients tilt their heads or play with their hair? Playing with one's hair has been linked to nervousness (Woods et al., 1996), while some believe that angling one's head to the side suggests a questioning or doubting attitude about the matter in discussion—or it could simply indicate that the client has a hearing impairment (Fast, 2002). A rigidly held head can reflect anger or tension, whereas hanging one's head may imply disappointment or sadness. In Western cultures, nodding one's head typically implies agreement or compliance while shaking the head from side to side is likely to suggest disagreement. Interestingly, people often make these movements without awareness.

Upper Body

Your client opens the door and walks toward you. As you greet one another, you have already learned a lot about that person from the way she or he stands. Posture reflects attitudes of assurance, rigidity, dependency, or self-esteem (Briñol et al., 2009).

A slouched posture with a protruding abdomen may indicate dependency or lack of assertiveness, whereas a rigidly erect posture could convey defensiveness and a controlling attitude. A rounded spine may imply lack of confidence and low self-esteem (Dychtwald, 1977; Kurz & Prestera, 1976).

From a seated position, leaning into the conversation may express interest and attention, while leaning too far forward could convey aggression. How does the person occupy the chair? Is the person sitting on the edge of the chair? Is she or he crumpled into it with a look of resignation? Or is the person bolt upright, as if readying for action?

Shoulder positioning may also tell you something about your client. Shoulders that slope downward may indicate disappointment or depression, whereas shoulders turned inward toward the chest may represent nonreceptivity. Shoulders elevated toward the ears may indicate fear or anxiety, and a shrug of the shoulders could convey doubt, uncertainty, or indecision (Dychtwald, 1977).

Clients will also communicate a great deal with their hands. Though some cultures use hand gestures as a normal way of punctuating speech, tension or anger may also be evident in hands that are tightly held or clenched into fists. Fidgeting motions may indicate anxiety or worry, while arms tightly folded across the chest generally represent a self-protective or closed attitude. Easy arm movements could signify openness and involvement, whereas rigidly held arms and hands may be a sign of anxiety or self-restraint (Dychtwald, 1977; Kurz & Prestera, 1976).

Upper body posture becomes relevant in context. Comparing body posture with spoken words allows you to understand whether the same message is being conveyed in both languages—or whether there is a potential double message being expressed in this communication.

Total-Body Movement

The degree to which your body movements are synchronized with those of your client may often be out of your immediate awareness. When your body moves easily in an unconscious mimicking pattern in relation to your client's movements, you are likely to sense greater connection and flow in the relationship. Equally, when both bodies display different shapes and speeds of total-body movements, you may feel a kind of disharmony with your client. Moreover, research suggests that power dynamics may be at play such that in a two-party or dyadic interaction, the more mobile body may be conveying greater discomfort (and less power) than the body that exhibits limited and steady movement (Rainie & Anderson, 2008; Talley & Temple, 2015).

Ekman (1993) discussed how people's overall body movements describe their current internal experiences. Body touching, scratching, rubbing, or other repetitive motions can also reflect the person's psychological state. You may observe someone stroking her or his arm when describing a difficult situation, suggesting that the person may be soothing herself or himself while talking.

Touch

A final dimension of kinesics is the extent and manner of touching that occurs between helper and client. In depth-oriented helping relationships, such as counseling and psychotherapy, most forms of touching are likely to be problematic, but professional coaches may choose to engage in appropriate forms of touching, perhaps as a show of support or as a spontaneous expression in a moment of celebration.

While rules about physical contact with clients may have some flexibility in the coaching field, touch can have so many connotations, especially when we factor considerations of diversity into the mix. It is wise to remain vigilant about any form of physical contact with clients. Clients who like to give you a full embrace at the beginning and end of each session may simply be expressing themselves the way they do with most people. However, as coach, you need to be attuned to how this affects you and whether it crosses any of your boundaries. You also need to consider how this may influence your ability to work with these clients in a manner that competently addresses their agendas.

Paralinguistics

When you listen to people, you not only focus on their gestures and words, but you also hear the music of their speech. How loudly do they speak? Where are their intonations? What words or expressions do they emphasize? Is their speech fluid, staccato, or monotonic? Does their voice quaver? Although these aspects of **paralinguistics** may characterize a person's general speech pattern, they may also vary depending on the topic or emotional shifts in the relationship. The flow of conversation in any relationship mirrors the styles and internal experiences of the speakers. Some people have a rapid-fire conversational style, while others speak more slowly or in a measured manner. Perhaps this comes from cultural background or personality. You will need to identify your clients' patterns so you can recognize fluctuations in how they speak. Changes in paralinguistics may signal a shift in their internal world, and noticing these shifts can help you better understand their messages.

Silence or pauses in speech also convey much meaning. A refusal to answer, hesitation before responding, or a reflective silence may communicate much more than words. Clients hesitating before answering sensitive questions may reveal the truth before they speak. Silence may also be a means of control or an indication of a need to reflect.

Each culture has norms about silence (Sue et al., 2019). In general, North Americans interpret a pause in the conversation as disruptive or indicative of discomfort. It is common to avoid the gap and fill the space; we disallow a pregnant pause. To effectively use silence, it is important to be comfortable in the absence of verbal communication and to learn how to use conversational pauses to deepen the communication and help clients shift perspectives. Novice coaches often describe their discomfort with silence. In the early phases of a coaching relationship, too much silence can unduly spike client anxiety. Later on, when rapport and trust have been established, clients may welcome a pause as an opportunity to gather insights.

Proxemics

How big is your body bubble? When is close too close? You know intuitively at what physical distance from another you feel most comfortable. When someone moves into your personal space, you may experience anxiety, fear, a desire for greater intimacy, or a need to keep conversation informal (Hall, 1966, 1976; Sommer & Iachini, 2017). In a North American helping relationship, physical distance of 3 to 4 feet (90-120 cm) between helper and client tends to be experienced as comfortable (Trenholm et al., 2010; Young, 2017).

Proxemics pertain to the way in which you perceive and use social and personal space (Knapp et al., 2014). When you meet clients in person rather than on a web platform or over the phone, you need to be intentional in how you arrange the space in which you coach. You may place chairs face-to-face with no obstructions in between or you may work at tables or desks either side by side or across from one another. There is no such thing as a neutral environment. Everything in your office offers itself to interpretation, and your clients will glean messages from your coaching environment. It is important to take care in preparing your space before each session. Create an environment that is most likely to facilitate transition from the world outside to this unique world of opportunity—and bear in mind such diversity issues as culture, gender, age, and personality that may hold implications for spacing and other elements in the physical environment (Cormier et al., 2017; Sue et al., 2019).

Environmental Factors

While proxemics addresses the arrangement of your coaching space, environment refers to where that space is located. Some of the available spaces for coaching may be shared or have multiple uses. Where you meet your clients has meaning and conveys intended or unintended messages. As a professional coach, you may choose to base your practice in allied health or professional centers, a home office, a shared office space, or clients' office spaces. Wherever you coach, you need to ensure safety and confidentiality given the sensitive nature of coaching conversations.

Coaching sometimes takes place in clients' environments. Some conditions may need to be negotiated for these venues to be viable. Imagine that you meet your clients in their offices, but they tend to allow interruptions by coworkers or answer phone calls during the session. Sometimes, this needs to happen, though in general you want to create clear boundaries about how you will work together in this space to maximize the effectiveness of the coaching relationship.

The growth of coaching can be partly attributed to the versatility in possible environments where sessions can take place. Web-based and phone coaching significantly increase accessibility. Internet options further propel communication through the transmission of materials and the availability of quick updates and check-ins. Though there are pros and cons to each coaching context, the ability to readily adapt environments to circumstances is a hallmark of the industry. If coaching sessions take place by phone or online, a clear agreement stipulates boundaries for times of contact and the inviolability of the session. If a client is multitasking (e.g., working on a computer, driving a car, sorting through papers) while talking with you, the effectiveness of the session will be adversely affected. If you hold virtual sessions, the physical environment where the session takes place remains important. You may want to ask yourself ahead of time what your client will see on and around you during the video call. Is this the message you want to convey as a coach?

Novice coaches may have some concerns about the limitations of phone coaching when contrasted with the richness of face-to-face communications. Allaying such concerns, research suggests that phone sessions can be highly effective (Kraus, 2017). To some degree, it may be a matter of preference and practicality.

Time

The nonverbal dimension of time has at least three relevant interpretations, and its meaning varies significantly across cultures (Gielen et al., 2008; Sue et al., 2019). Time can reference things like when and for how long coach and client meet. It may also be seen as a boundary that is respected or violated. Lastly, it may be understood in terms of where coaching conversations are located—in the present, past, or future. Each of these meanings of time offers a unique lens to understanding clients beyond the spoken word.

Let's look at something as straightforward as scheduling preferences. How often do your clients want to meet? What do they imagine the expected duration of a coaching relationship to be—weeks, months, or even years? Can clients schedule well in advance, or are their lives so unpredictable that sessions can be set for only the near future?

The second sense of time is about honoring agreed-upon meeting schedules. Is the client habitually punctual or consistently late? Does the client push to end early, or does she or he want to extend the session by bringing up significant topics in the last few minutes? How about cancellations? Whatever the reason, how often does your client cancel?

You may wonder, what if your client gets highly engaged or emotional toward the end of a session? Should you allow the session to go over? Although rigidly enforced time boundaries may adversely affect client perceptions of the coach's care and support, lax boundaries are problematic in other ways. One interpretation of a relaxed attitude toward session length is that the relationship is more like a friendship than a professional engagement. As a rule, coach and client may consensually agree to end the session early when the following conditions have been met: the topic has been thoroughly explored, the client is satisfied with the robustness of the action plan, modes of accountability have been established, the learning from the session has been made explicit, and the client appears ready to jump into action. What about the opposite scenario where a session runs over the agreed-upon time limit? In such situations, you might acknowledge the time issue and ask the client's permission to pursue the session for another few minutes. Though clients might feel concerned when their sessions consistently end early, they might also experience annoyance with the coach's inability to effectively manage sessions when they always end late.

A final consideration of time centers on the point in time coaches and clients locate their discussions—in the present, past, or future. A hallmark of coaching is its emphasis on the present and future rather than on the past, although knowing what a person has experienced before the coaching relationship or what has previously worked well for that person can be critical for successful goal pursuit. However, as alluded to during our discussion about the differences between coaching and therapy, it is important to move efficiently from historical analysis toward future-focused planning.

You may wonder, "What if my client likes to tell long stories?" For some clients, historical narratives need to be expressed in order for them to gain momentum toward change (Gielen et al., 2008). You will need to be sensitive to how this need varies from client to client. Yet, in a coaching model, you are responsible for a process that results in some form of goal setting and action planning. There is a kind of learning curve for clients as they come to understand what the process of coaching is all about. If clients' stylistic patterns of meandering storytelling or disconnected reflections continue without feedback from coaches, clients may assume that this is the way coaching works. Keep in mind that fact that clients don't know the form of coaching conversations, so what you may unwittingly allow with a client's unfocused narrative may be interpreted as the way it should be. Backing up from a pattern that gets set over a series of early sessions can be difficult.

In general, appreciating your clients' relationships to time—in its multiple meanings—can offer invaluable insights. Similarly, you may want to be conscious of your own habitual ways of relating to time: What are your patterns linked to scheduling? How punctual and reliable are you? In which "time zone" (past, present, or future) do you prefer to locate conversations?

The Gift of Nonverbal Awareness

It is rare that in an interpersonal context you are not communicating something. In all likelihood, you have your own set of algorithms for interpreting nonverbal behaviors. You probably form impressions without ever having spoken to someone.

While you may hold these impressions lightly as working hypotheses, they nonetheless may shape your behavior in conscious and unconscious ways. This section was not intended as an exhaustive coverage of nonverbal messaging, but more as a stimulus to self-reflection. When you are feeling a particular way about a client, yet can't track your feelings to any particular words that were expressed, you might shift your analysis to what you experienced nonverbally. The more thought you give to this, the faster you will learn to translate between the verbal and nonverbal realms and the more you will be able to appreciate the degree of accuracy of assumptions you make based on nonverbal signals.

A METHODOLOGY FOR ACTIVE LISTENING

Active listening is often distinguished from other skills by its unwavering respect for following and feeding the flow of the client's story without deliberate efforts to provoke shifts in direction. Coaches listen with a kind of map—not one of the content of what the person is saying but of the range and robustness of the story as it is told. Human experience is composed of thoughts, feelings, desires, values, actions, morals, and a myriad of other elements. Knowing what might be missing in clients' stories requires that you appreciate what needs to be there not out of personal curiosity but from awareness of elements that will elevate the tale from a simple recitation of facts to an expression that can nourish transformation.

It's quite challenging to support clients in telling their stories without subtly influencing the emergence of their unfolding narratives. Earlier in this chapter we looked at different types and levels of listening, but we didn't drill into the actual process or methodology of active listening. In the upcoming material, I want to contain the methods for active listening to those interventions made by coaches that actively follow—without unduly influencing—clients' flow of expression as they describe their thoughts and feelings about issues raised in a coaching session. I said "without unduly influencing" because I believe it is virtually impossible to have zero influence in the communication processes of a coaching relationship. You can sit stone silent, and that will influence your client. You can be animated and supportive, and that will influence your client. You can simply nod your head, and that will influence your client. Whatever you do or don't do

has potential and likely unknown impact on your clients and how they tell their stories.

In my descriptions, I will borrow four skill designations adapted from the domain of communication (Evans et al., 2017; Ivey et al., 2018; Young, 2017). While these skills largely derive from the field of psychology, I believe they have sufficient generalizability to apply to any listening process. The four skills are commonly referred to as minimal encouragement, reflection of content, reflection of feeling, and summarization. There is another type of reflection, reflection of meaning, which I will discuss in chapter 13 related to how coaches create awareness in clients.

Minimal Encouragement

As active listeners, coaches need to clearly communicate to their clients that they are attending to their expressions. One way of doing this without interrupting the conversational flow or guiding clients toward other matters is by using minimal encouragers. A **minimal encourager** has been defined as a verbalization that echoes "the exact words" of the client or provides "some notable indication that [they] should continue" (Ladany et al., 2008, p. 226). Encouragers have also been identified as "brief interventions to kindle the fire of self-expression" (Young, 2017, p. 73). You may find yourself using minimal encouragers without realizing it when you are listening to someone's story. Almost under your breath, you utter "Mm-hmm." With more awareness, you might respond with expressions such as "Yes, I hear you," "Right," or "Okay." A nonverbal body posture that reflects attention or a nodding head may be accompanied by your repetition of key words expressed by the client. Minimal encouragement has the magical effect of supporting clients without unduly redirecting their flow, thereby allowing them to express their topic in greater detail (Sharpley et al., 2000).

Coaches know when they are listening, but clients may not know that they are being heard. Perhaps more importantly, they may not know *how* they are being heard—that is, whether the coach is listening critically, judgmentally, or empathically. In an effort to be nonjudgmental, your face may appear mask-like, and paradoxically, this may convey an impression opposite to that intended. Although you might believe that your quiet, nonverbal presence adequately demonstrates your interest, clients who feel uncertain in disclosing intimate details often need overt signs of support and encouragement. In this sense, you want to bear in mind paralinguistic qualities (e.g., tonality, volume, and pacing) that accompany the verbal expression of your minimal encouragers.

Some people use minimal encouragement liberally and without much forethought or awareness. Coaches, however, need to be aware of their perhaps unconscious way of encouraging clients to speak. For example, the timing of minimal encouragers may have a pattern. A coach may say, "Mm-hmm" multiple times in rapid succession, almost conveying a message of, "Hurry up and finish." Minimal encouragers may more often coincide with certain content areas of client stories than with others. For instance, a coach may show keen interest through the use of minimal encouragers whenever clients talk about uplifting events or success experiences. If the coach exhibits an evident pattern of responding with enthusiastic "Mm-hmms" to happy experiences while otherwise remaining relatively silent, what might a client interpret from this communication? Might the client come to believe that the coach only wants to hear about happy events and is disinterested in problem-saturated stories?

If we take behavioral conditioning to heart, a coach's pattern of using encouragers may unintentionally reinforce presentations of particular themes or types of content (Skinner, 1938, 1953). If, for example, the coach responds to key words connected to success with minimal encouragement, clients may begin to dredge up any remotely connected story of achievement in their histories to get the reward of that acknowledgment. Another point to bear in mind is that because minimal encouragers act as behavioral reinforcements, they can influence not only the direction of a conversation but its depth as well. A client's conversation can be driven into deep terrain by encouraging self-disclosures that are more intimate or emotional. Incidentally, a nonverbal behavior, such as nodding or smiling, can have an effect similar to a verbal reinforcer.

There are a few caveats to bear in mind regarding how you express your active listening through minimal encouragers in coaching. The first is to be mindful of where and when in a session you tend to use minimal encouragers. By listening to your recorded sessions, you may gain insight into some of your unconscious reinforcements of certain topics or themes in client stories. A second caveat is that paralinguistic qualities can significantly affect the meaning of minimal encouragers. In listening to coaching sessions, my colleagues and I often hear coaches using the same encouragers multiple times as a signal to clients that they have something they want to tell them (Gavin et al., 2021). An example

here might be a coach saying, "Okay, okay, okay" in rapid succession or saying, "Mm-hmm" with a kind of judgmental inflection. A third caveat references the words you use in your habitual patterns of encouragement. I have particularly noted when coaches use words like "Right!" or "Okay!" or even "I understand," each of which can potentially convey more meaning or judgment than the coach intended.

Since virtually everything you do influences your clients, a central issue to explore is whether the direction of influence results in shifting clients' stories from their organic expression to adapted forms of these stories intended to please or gain the approval of their coaches. In this regard, it may be simplistic to say that the use of minimal encouragement only demonstrates listening; encouragers may also communicate to your clients *what* you are listening to as well as *how* you are listening.

Reflection of Content or Paraphrasing

Imagine yourself standing in front of a mirror. What do you see? The mirror reflects only the part of you that you present. It doesn't afford a 360-degree view of your physical exterior and certainly doesn't reveal what is on the inside. Client messages are complex constructions. At one level, content is expressed through the words your client uses; additionally, there may be emotional elements that are conveyed nonverbally. At another level, there may be connected thoughts and feelings your client is trying to express but hasn't yet figured out exactly how to do so.

Paraphrasing (Weger et al., 2010), sometimes referred to as mirroring (Geldard & Geldard, 2008), is an essential process in active listening. Ivey and colleagues go as far as saying that it is "the most important cognitive empathic listening skill" (Ivey et al., 2018, p. 137). Paraphrasing is feedback "that restates, in your own words, the message you thought the speaker sent" (Adler et al., 2004, p. 154). Though the term *paraphrase* is widely used, **reflection of content** is perhaps more precise because it identifies the focus of feedback as being specifically related to the content of a message. Another communication skill I will discuss later, reflection of feeling, addresses the emotional dimension of the message. Together, these two types of reflection create a more complete mirroring of client messages. A third form of reflection, reflection of meaning, offers an inside mirror of what the person might

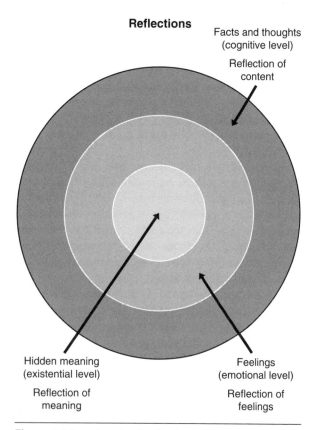

Reflections

Facts and thoughts
(cognitive level)

Reflection of
content

Hidden meaning
(existential level)

Reflection of
meaning

Feelings
(emotional level)

Reflection of
feelings

Figure 10.3   Three levels of reflection.

be expressing. Figure 10.3 depicts how these three reflections are understood in terms of the depth of content. Emotions are deemed to be deeper than the verbal content, and the core meaning of a message represents the deepest level of the message.

A reflection of content is not a word-for-word reiteration; rather, as a coach you are hoping to express a kind of synopsis of key elements just put forth by your client. Your reflection of content captures the essence of your client's message in a natural manner (Evans et al., 2017; Ivey et al., 2018). Good reflections are the antithesis of formulaic repetitions of words (see sidebar, Effective and Ineffective Reflections of Content). They are offered with ease, and as a result the client is likely to experience an attitude of caring attention.

Rationale for Reflections of Content

Strange as it may sound, clients don't always comprehend what they are saying. In some ways, until they express what they are thinking, their thoughts remain ghost-like. Through their expression, words become real especially when someone is listening intently. When you reflect their words to them, clients not only feel like they are being heard but

they also experience more deeply the impact of what they have just said. In a sense, your reflections offer clients opportunities to weigh and evaluate their words. So many times, I have had clients say, "That's not what I meant!" and even "Did I really say that?" Reflections provide an avenue for further exploration of their ideas.

I also believe there is risk when coaches assume they know what clients mean, partly because clients themselves may not know exactly what they mean and also because we as coaches are imperfect mirrors. We automatically translate language into what we believe to be synonymous expressions, and if we don't verify our interpretations, we may generate a somewhat slanted view of what the client is saying (see sidebar: Vignette: A Significant Misunderstanding). When we transparently express what we are understanding from what clients are telling us, we allow for the possibility that we have misunderstood, that clients may have misrepresented their realities, and that a new awareness can emerge through the process of reflection.

Another rationale for employing reflections of content arises whenever you might experience an emerging conflict with your client. Typically, in conflict situations, someone says something with which you disagree—so you express your disagreement. The cycle repeats. The other disagrees with your disagreement and so on. Verbal exchanges of this nature tend to accelerate at the expense of listening. Even when you may be factually correct, it is generally wiser to focus on listening rather than on proving your case. Fully hearing your client and reflecting content can deescalate arguments while also creating space for clients to hear their own words. By listening nondefensively, you nourish your capacity to empathize while detaching from personal needs to prove your point.

Practicalities in Reflections of Content

Reflections of content are generally far shorter than the words expressed by your client. When some of the words used by your client aren't entirely clear to you in their meaning, it's best to use them exactly in your reflection rather than offering what you imagine to be synonyms. You will want to intervene with this kind of reflection sparingly, so you don't sound as if you are parroting your client. Moreover, you might include some lead in words to your reflections, like "sounds like you . . ." or "I'm hearing that . . .," so the clients don't mistakenly assume that the words you are expressing are your own ideas. Consider, for example, a client says, "I think I should quit my job" and your reflection is "You

Effective and Ineffective Reflections of Content

What the client says	How the coach reflects content
I'll never be able to stop smoking! I've tried so many times but never lasted more than a week. I'm addicted! I come to the end of a meal, and I have to have a cigarette. There are other times, too, when I automatically reach out and light up. It's just something I do. I also smoke when I'm stressed. . . . I can't deal with stress without a cigarette.	*Effective reflection.* I'm hearing how hard it is for you to believe you can ever stop smoking. Even with small successes in the past, smoking feels like an addiction . . . so many triggers . . . quitting seems unimaginable. Is this right? *Ineffective reflection.* You don't believe you will ever be able to stop smoking. You've tried so many times but never lasted more than a week. You think you're addicted. You smoke automatically at the end of meals and there are other times, too, when you automatically reach out and light up. It's just something you do. You also smoke when you're stressed. In fact, you can't deal with stress without smoking.
I've lost my compass; I don't know where I'm going in my career . . . I'm on automatic pilot most of the time. . . . Even in my personal life, I seem to be drifting without purpose . . . I don't know how to pull myself out of this state of mind.	*Effective reflection.* I'm getting how you've lost your compass and seem to be on automatic pilot . . . and you don't know what to do about it. *Ineffective reflection.* You are on automatic pilot because you've lost your compass and you don't know what to do in your career. You also feel this way about your personal life. You said you were drifting without purpose. In this situation presently, you don't know what to do to get yourself out of this situation.
I'm thrilled! I've done what I said I'd do last time we were together. I completed my project on time without stressing myself or my team. I really didn't think I could do it.	*Effective reflection.* Sounds like you're both pleased and surprised to have achieved the goals you set last time. *Ineffective reflection.* You are happy, and you have done what you planned to do the last time we were together. You were able to complete your project on time without stressing yourself or your team even though you didn't think you could do it.

Vignette: A Significant Misunderstanding

I recall an experience with a high-level professional who had taken a year-long sabbatical in his career to ground himself in his life's purpose. During this sabbatical he built a solid practice of meditation and gradually created a mindful reentry into the next phase of his life's work. A couple years after his sabbatical, he expressed an emerging need to reconnect with himself. As good as his life was, he told me he was feeling disconnected and often depleted at the end of each workweek.

When this issue came up, I remembered his stories about training for and completing numerous Ironman Triathlons. He had told me that he learned to disconnect his mind from his body in order to shut down awareness of discomfort at various points in these grueling endurance events. But that was a long time ago. My current understanding of him was more related to how hard he had worked to develop a daily practice of meditation, which he reinforced through periodic meditation retreats. Based on this more recent behavior pattern, I had made a translation (read: assumption) that all of his meditation practice and his frequent referencing of mindfulness in his life equated to living with awareness in the moment—even at work! So, I was a bit surprised by his state of mind at this time. I needed to unpack some of my assumptions about how he was applying his mindfulness practices to his day-to-day behavior at work. Through some delicate questioning, we were able to discover that his mindfulness at work more closely resembled his triathlon experiences than his mindful meditation practice. He told me clearly in one particular session that his expression of being mindful at work translated as tuning out his inner experience for large portions of every workday. He put it this way: "I'm fully focused on the task, but minimally self-aware."

should quit your job." Your client might think you are giving her or him your expert opinion. Finally, you might sometimes conclude your reflections with a question to validate your understanding. This might sound like, "Is this what you're saying?" or "Did I understand you correctly?"

Reflection of Feeling

Whereas reflection of content pertains to the details and information contained in a client's message, **reflection of feeling** is an expression of the emotional, often nonverbal part of the story (Evans et al., 2017; Ivey et al., 2018). In coaching, a distinction can be made between emotions that are conveyed as part of clients' past experiences (historical accounts of emotional states) and those they are sensing in the moment (account of present emotional states). An historical account of emotional states may be accompanied by descriptive details that minimize their importance (e.g., "I was so angry at the time, but that was just a silly reaction.") or distance the person from the emotion (e.g., "Well, that was a long time ago—it doesn't bother me at all now."). In these cases, the reflection of feeling may be more akin to reflecting content than to capturing the client's present emotional state. Consider this example:

Client: I used to feel embarrassed about my weight, but I'm not sensitive about it anymore. Even so, I would like to lose about 30 pounds just for health reasons.

Coach: What I understand is that your motivation to lose weight is for health concerns, though at one point you felt embarrassed about your weight. Is that right?

By way of contrast, present emotional states are verbally expressed when the client describes a current feeling. This might happen as follows:

Client: My desire to lose weight is primarily driven by health concerns, but ever since I can remember *(blushes, shows obvious discomfort)* I have been really uncomfortable about the size of my body.

Coach: I hear your concern and sense your discomfort even as you talk about it now.

In reflections of feeling, emotionality in an experience may be highlighted with or without reflections of content.

Your clients' capacities to appreciate their own emotionality in the moment and your own awareness of feelings and emotional content capture the theme of emotional intelligence (Belsten, 2013; Goleman, 1995), which we reviewed in chapter 8. Clients may experience emotions in coaching sessions without stating exactly what their feelings are. Even when their words suggest feeling states, they may mask their genuine feelings by putting up a kind of verbal smokescreen, as illustrated in table 10.1. Feelings are just that, yet when people continually repress, deny, rationalize, or otherwise contain them, they may take on proportions far larger than the realities they represent. Growth and development may rely on the capacity to give voice to emotional experiences to inform and motivate appropriate action.

Rationale for Reflections of Feeling

A rationale for reflecting feelings may be that by addressing the emotional content of client experi-

Table 10.1   Pseudo and Real Expressions of Feelings

Pseudo expressions of feelings	may indicate ...	real expressions of feelings.
I'm feeling that you aren't really listening.	→	I'm feeling lonely. I'm annoyed.
I'm really feeling that you don't care about me.	→	I'm feeling sad. I feel rejected.
I feel like you're not going to help me.	→	I'm disappointed. I'm frightened.
I'm feeling that I'm never going to reach my goals.	→	I'm worried. I feel hopeless.
I feel that everyone here is in a great mood.	→	I'm happy. I'm enjoying being here.

ences, clients may be better able to appreciate their issues, generate new sources of motivation, and find purpose for the actions they need to engage throughout a coaching process. In a broader perspective, I would say that emotionality is simply another dimension of our human experience and of the stories we tell about our lives and our dreams. As such, it is just as important to acknowledge these emotions as it is to reflect the details and content of clients' conversations.

Let's examine this more closely. I would like to capture four principal reasons why coaches might choose to highlight the emotional component of client communications by reflecting feelings (Cormier et al., 2017). First, a reflection of feeling can help clients identify their emotional experience (positive or negative) in a certain situation, with a particular person, or about a specific topic. Emotions are key sources of energy for movement. When they become more aware of their emotional responses, clients are likely to be able to make clearer choices concerning change initiatives.

A second purpose is to increase clients' capacity to manage emotions. When clients believe they can't handle certain emotional states, they may avoid critical actions out of fear of the emotions that might surface. Imagine your client feels distressed about speaking up in meetings or confronting coworkers about their performance. Reflecting these feelings becomes an important first step in strategizing how to initiate relevant changes in behavior. While coaching is not therapy, it shares the objective of empowering clients through acknowledging and validating their experiences. When clients express emotions in a coaching process, they are likely to experience a sense of relief in this safe environment and over time may feel less controlled by their emotions.

A third purpose relates to the coaching relationship itself. At various times, clients may have reactions to the coaching experience or to the coach. Think of instances where clients have been required to participate in coaching by their organization. Emotionality and resistance may be prevalent in the early sessions of this kind of coaching relationship. Behaviors such as lateness, skipped sessions or even subtle criticisms of the coach might show up. By respectfully and supportively naming such emotional signals, coaches can enhance clients' capacities to appreciate and manage their emotional world. When feelings related to the coaching experience remain unexpressed, clients may block themselves from addressing more salient issues standing in the way of growth and learning.

The fourth purpose of reflection of feeling is similar to one for reflection of content, namely, to convey empathy and understanding. Think of norms for everyday greetings. You may typically respond to the question "How are you today?" with the response, "Fine. How are you?" Expressing real emotion allows others to see your inner reality; it is an intimate act. Even when you take the risk to expose your feelings, the response you get in everyday life may be minimizing or rationalizing. For example, you might say, "Actually, I'm feeling off today" and hear "Yeah, must be the weather" or "Don't worry; it will pass" in reply. To be heard with empathy when you reveal emotions can be validating and enable you to move beyond present feeling states.

We can characterize feelings in a variety of ways (Hutchins & Vaught, 1997; Lazarus & Lazarus, 1994; McLaren, 2010; Puglisi & Ackerman, 2019). For our purposes, I have extracted four major categories: glad, sad, mad, and distressed. Within each category are levels and words representing degrees of emotional experiences (see table 10.2). For instance, a person might express a low level of sadness as feeling disappointed. The person might show a moderate level of sadness in words such as *dejected* or *down*. Words such as *hopeless* or *crushed* might communicate a strong level of sadness.

Some clients may not even have a vocabulary for emotion, and they simply remain in undifferentiated states of feeling without knowing what the implications might be or how to shift out of those feelings. Although the coaching agenda is not necessarily about developing emotional intelligence as an end in itself, increased self-awareness may be a means to goal attainment. For instance, a client may need to be able to concretely identify feelings about her or his experiences in various professional activities (means), whereas another client may wish to become more assertive in team meetings and as part of that work become able to differentiate emotions such as anxiety, fear, and excitement (ends).

A question that coaches often ask their clients at the outset of a session may be something like, "How are you coming into the session today?" In listening to coaching sessions, I am sometimes surprised when clients indicate they are troubled or unsettled by some experience only to be ignored by their coaches, who move right to the next question, "What do you want to work on today?" as if the client had said, "Everything is just fine." This brings me to one final perspective on this topic.

In some discussions of goal-centric coaching theory, the legitimacy of emotional agendas in the

Table 10.2   Types and Levels of Feelings

Level/type	Glad	Sad	Mad	Distressed
Strong	Ecstatic Overjoyed Delirious Blissful	Depressed Crushed Disconsolate Stricken Tearful Hopeless	Furious Outraged Enraged Livid Infuriated Boiling	Frightened Terrified Scared Dreading Panicky
Moderate	Cheerful Happy Delighted Joyful	Dejected Cheerless Sad Down Blue	Mad Stormy Angry Antagonized Incensed	Agitated Frustrated Upset Flustered Rattled
Low	Pleased Glad Content Cheery	Low Bored Disappointed Dour	Upset Ticked Displeased Ruffled Vexed Disgruntled	Anxious Apprehensive Confused Dismayed Uneasy Bothered

field of coaching has been questioned (Grant, 2003, 2006; Ives & Cox, 2012). Many novice coaches seem to interpret this as an injunction against addressing any emotional material in their work. I think this is a misconception. Emotionality in coaching processes needs to be acknowledged and addressed when it arises. This doesn't mean that coaches take on coaching objectives of helping clients become less anxious, less depressed, or happier. In brief, coaches don't take on emotional or psychological improvement agendas as the focus of their work. Even though such improvements may result from coaching work, these wouldn't normally represent the contracted agenda for the relationship. Keeping this in mind, coaches often strategize with their clients to create processes and actions that have a secondary effect of improving emotional states.

Practicalities in Reflections of Feeling

Reflections of feeling make clients' emotions explicit. As a coach, you will need to develop the capacity to identify emotions at both verbal and nonverbal levels. You then need to determine whether it is appropriate to reflect feelings for the purposes of your work in the moment.

The language of emotion is complex. Not only can we describe various types and levels of emotional experience (see table 10.2), but we also have to recognize that each individual has her or his own framework for identifying and labeling emotions.

My happiness may not have the same definition as yours. For this reason, in focusing on emotional experience in coaching sessions, it may be safer to acknowledge emotionality without labeling it precisely. You might say "I'm sensing how talking about this brings up some emotions" or "It seems this topic touches you deeply."

I have often experienced clients in coaching sessions moving seamlessly in and out of emotional experiences as they discussed significant issues in their lives. I hope it is true that at least nonverbally I acknowledged their emotional experiences through something as subtle as a softening of my presence. Yet, I am also aware that frequently the value of interrupting the clients' flow by verbally reflecting their emotional states isn't sufficient to justify such action. My judgment may derive in part from knowledge of my clients' patterns and how they prefer to express themselves, as well as from a consideration of whether overt recognition of their emotions will be of value to them at this particular moment of the dialogue (see Vignette: A Curious Emotional Experience).

Summarizing

Sometimes you listen to a client for quite a while with the occasional interjection of a minimal encourager or a reflection. At a certain point, you begin to sense that the person needs to shift focus or both of

Vignette:
A Curious Emotional Experience

I had been working with a client who was addressing a significant career change. She had quit a high level leadership position and was exploring new pathways in life. Somewhere in the middle of this work, her daughter was tragically killed in a car accident. We stopped our work together but unexpectedly my client called to resume coaching less than three months later. As I sat with her in the opening session, I bore witness to a highly contained and rational analysis of pros and cons of different career opportunities. My client was thoughtful and detailed. She also seemed quite detached. Surprisingly, I found my eyes beginning to water. My nascent tears weren't evident enough to draw attention, but I did feel a deep sense of sadness and loss. Whose feelings were these? I truly didn't know if I was picking up the repressed emotions of my client or whether it was just my stuff. I stayed with my client's dialogue and we were able to achieve some degree of traction on her topic in this and subsequent sessions. To this day, I am still unable to answer the question about the source of my emotionality, but I do know that I would have been out of line raising my emotional sensing in this session.

you need to step back and review all that has been said up to that point. Summarizing the conversation that has taken place will help you do just that.

Summarizing can be described as a kind of reflection that occurs over a longer conversational period (Evans et al., 2017). It relies on the methods of reflection of content and feeling in that it is not intended to unduly influence the direction and flow of clients' own processes, even though you already know that everything you do as a coach has more or less potential to influence your clients. Clearly, summaries need to be succinct and thus you might recognize the skill required to offer unbiased summaries to your clients.

Rationale for Summarizing

Summarizing parts of sessions or recurrent themes across sessions can create new energy and understanding in coaching relationships. The effective application of summaries not only builds trust but can also motivate change. Three reasons for summarizing described in the literature (Evans et al.,

2017; Kratcoski, 2004) have been reframed in the context of coaching.

The first reason you would choose to summarize is to confirm general understandings or validate assumptions during a session. Given that clients may present a range of information, providing a timely review of issues or themes not only demonstrates that you have grasped their core messages but also validates that you are accurately tracking them. At the same time, summarizing affords clients an opportunity to reflect on the whole of their communications and perhaps realize that an important element is missing. Additionally, clients who express diverse ideas may have little clarity about their relative importance. By summarizing, you offer them an opportunity to consider and then continue the discussion with greater clarity.

A second reason for summarizing is to shine a light on a particular theme your client has repeatedly mentioned either in one or a number of sessions. When a statement or issue continues to emerge, you are likely to attribute additional weight to that topic. At an appropriate point, you may summarize the various references to this single theme and thereby enable your client to weigh its significance and its relationship to their objectives. For instance, a client who has repeatedly mentioned the need for a more supportive work environment may need to explore this issue further. Summarizing the repeated mention of this issue allows your client to grasp its significance more fully.

A third reason for summarizing is to bring all the themes and issues of a session together toward the end. A closing summary serves as a confirmation of what has been discussed as a progress review and as an opportunity to launch the next step from this platform. Clients need to experience forward movement in coaching. A summary at the end of the session will likely reflect progress and thereby reinforce commitment to action.

Practicalities in Summarizing

Summaries can be significant moments in coaching dialogues. They often are longer than reflections of content or feeling, and as a result they bring your clients to a place of silence where they can consider the key points they have been expressing. While summaries can occur at any point in a session, they will tend to serve different purposes depending on where and how you employ them. A critical characteristic of effective summaries is that they need to be perceived as accurate and representative by your clients. That is, as succinct as they may be, they need to capture all the core elements encompassed by the type of summary you are offering. To this end, you may want to invite your client to participate in the process of summarizing by asking for their input and things they remember. Depending on what you are summarizing, these interventions may or may not include emotional content.

LISTENING ACTIVELY IN THE ICF CORE COMPETENCIES

This essential core competency as identified by the ICF (2020c) captures the complexity of listening skills. Notably, in its definition, the ICF references the coach's awareness of what is and what is not being said. This speaks to multiple issues in listening: It references the need for coaches to master the language of nonverbal communication. It strongly asserts a requisite awareness of the systemic contexts in which clients are embedded; verbal and nonverbal communications are best understood in the larger frameworks of clients' lives rather than in the more limited scope of what happens in this one-to-one conversation. The ICF definition also points to the necessity for coaches to encourage and support client expression, which brings back awareness of other competencies including how present coaches are and how they cultivate trust and safety (see sidebar, ICF Core Coaching Competency 6: Listens Actively).

Earlier in this chapter, listening was examined according to various levels and types. Three forms of listening were highlighted—empathic, authentic, and generative (Cox, 2013; Rogers, 1961, 1980; Scharmer, 2007). It is clear that empathic listening is fully reflected in the ICF framing of active listening. As for authentic and generative listening, there also seems to be some evidence of these perspectives in the ICF's articulation of active listening. The coach is not only reflecting but also exploring for meaning and to understand themes, patterns, values, and beliefs. This more encompassing perspective of listening is key to generative listening. Finally, the idea that coaches need to sense when there is more that needs to surface in client communications encourages a deep listening process that moves well below a surface level of content.

Surely there is more complexity to the ICF's delineation of this competency than is represented in the methodologies of minimal encouragement, reflections, and summarizations as reviewed in this chapter. As noted, the ICF framing mentions exploration as well as invitations to inquire about meanings and themes. In the ICF's perspective,

---

ICF Core Coaching Competency 6: Listens Actively

Definition: Focuses on what the client is and is not saying to fully understand what is being communicated in the context of the client systems and to support client self-expression

1. Considers the client's context, identity, environment, experiences, values and beliefs to enhance understanding of what the client is communicating
2. Reflects or summarizes what the client communicated to ensure clarity and understanding
3. Recognizes and inquires when there is more to what the client is communicating
4. Notices, acknowledges and explores the client's emotions, energy shifts, non-verbal cues or other behaviors
5. Integrates the client's words, tone of voice and body language to determine the full meaning of what is being communicated
6. Notices trends in the client's behaviors and emotions across sessions to discern themes and patterns

---

active listening can be demonstrated by the questions that coaches ask their clients. The idea is that when coaches listen well, their questions are strongly aligned with clients' emerging thoughts, feelings, and directions.

In the perspectives that I offered in this chapter, active listening isn't exemplified by sentences ending with question marks. That is, inquiry and questioning are thought to represent different skill sets than those identified in this chapter. I fully acknowledge that good questions can communicate to clients that you are listening well, but I prefer to locate any questioning process in other coaching skill sets like inquiry (see chapter 11). I don't think this is just splitting hairs. It seems important to me because when I ask questions, I feel as if I am expressing a greater degree of influence than when I am accurately reflecting. Even though a question may be beneficial, it nonetheless represents me taking the lead in the dialogue. Positioning active listening the way I have seems to make it clearer, while at the same being restrictive. Concepts such as Cox's (2013) authentic listening and Scharmer's

(2018) generative listening wouldn't fit the way I am defining active listening, and I think that's just fine. When coaches put their own perspectives into their dialogues with clients as they would in an authentic or generative listening process, they are influencing—they figuratively have their hands in the clay along with their clients' in comolding stories and emerging directions.

Whichever way we choose to conceptualize active listening, one thing we know for sure is that the competency of listening is tightly interwoven with other skills that, in combination, constitute the requisite skill set of professional coaches. In the ICF perspective, a well-framed question that reflects what a client has been presenting could offer evidence of coaching presence, inquiry, creating trust and safety, and listening actively. Indeed, it is challenging to parse out the exact implications or impacts of a single coaching intervention from the rich context and meanings in which it occurs in order to say that it represents only one thing, such as active listening.

REFLECTIONS

The ideas you have just reviewed elevate listening to a whole new realm of meaning and understanding. In so many life experiences, you may find yourself multitasking and perhaps even attending to multiple conversations at the same time. Consider driving a car and listening to a friend telling you a story. Where's your attention? A bit divided I would imagine.

In the coaching world, even when you are as present as you can be, words spoken by another stimulate your mind, and they may even spike your emotions. You find your mind conjuring up ideas and images. You may be busy connecting the dots of this conversation with previous conversations with this same client, and you may feel various bodily sensations and emotional energies all at the same time. You may even find yourself waiting for an answer to a question that you haven't yet asked. So, what do you do with all that is arising within you as you listen? In my sense of active listening, you do your best to stay with what has been expressed by your client and mirror it without distortion or interpretation. Of course, you may want to ask a question or to offer some insight that arises about what you believe the client is really saying but has not explicitly expressed. Are these parts of listening? In order to ask good questions or to offer impactful observations, you have to be listening deeply, but these interventions are not, purely speaking, reflections of what was expressed by your client either in words or nonverbal behaviors. Since the material I offered in this chapter encompasses far more than this purified reflective process, I want to underscore in these final words the immense value of just doing the pure listening piece from time to time. That is, I want to honor how significant clear, accurate, and concise reflections can be for your clients' growth, for the validation of their experiences, and for enhancing the trustworthiness of your relationship with them.

CHAPTER 11
THE ART OF INQUIRY

Keep yourself away from the answers,
but alive in the middle of the questions.

Colum McCann

MY STORY

I was thinking about the role that questions play in casual conversations I have with friends and family. A dear friend who has a unique way of engaging in the process of inquiry came to mind. It goes like this: When we are catching up with one another, Kate asks me in a most enthusiastic manner one question after another. All of her probing seems relevant and tracks with what I want to talk about. There is an exhilarating energy that develops between us. Then, almost when I am beginning to tire of answering questions, Kate says, "Okay, now it's my turn. You ask the questions." So, we switch roles. The first time this happened, I was a bit confused, but even then I realized I had been getting all the attention, and it felt right to share the space. Besides, I do wear down when I am questioned at length. It may not feel like an interrogation, but I don't experience it as entirely relaxing.

Kate is masterful in knowing how to catch up quickly after long absences, and I like how we do it in such a balanced way. Of course, questioning differs from friend to friend and with members of my family. I also recall my sister and how she would deal with catch-ups. She would ask nonstop questions until I was exhausted, and she rarely opened herself to reciprocation. Of course, she was my big sister who was forever watchful of her little brother. When I think about questions in my professional world, the process shifts dramatically. My clients ask considerably fewer questions than I ask, and I would only rarely say to them, "Hey, it's my turn. Now you ask me questions."

t is hard to imagine most interactions without some kind of inquiry or questioning. Coaches rely on inquiry to serve so many purposes, and they are ever mindful of the need for artistry in their questioning process. There is great variation in style among coaches in the extent to which they use inquiry in their sessions, ranging from almost always to relatively infrequently. Having just reviewed the chapter on active listening, you know that reflections without questions can feed the flow of a coaching conversation, but you may wonder in what direction will sessions flow when unguided by questions. This gives rise to an awareness that questions tend to be more directive than listening processes. In this chapter we will move through material that situates inquiry or questioning in the coaching relationship and then explore different types of questions. Here are some guiding questions as you read:

- What functions does inquiry serve?
- What are the areas of inquiry in coaching?
- What makes for a good question?
- When might inquiry be problematic?
- What are the limits of questioning in coaching?

INQUIRY IN CONTEXT

When you think about inquiry or asking questions, you probably sense how it functions differently in different contexts. Certain questions can be asked in some contexts but not in others. Sometimes your only role is to answer questions—there is no chance for reciprocity. Also, you come to expect questions in some situations but not in others. Think about questions in your family when you were growing up and how they were phrased. Then consider what happened in grade school all the way up to your final years of formal education. What about at work? Who asks whom what questions?

There are not only the questions being asked but also a set of expectations about how you might answer. Are you always expected to answer the whole truth, or are your answers shaped by some kind of social conventions? Consider here a star basketball player being interviewed before the big game. The interviewer asks, "So who's going to win tonight?" Or imagine a sales presentation before a major client. The client asks, "Do you foresee any problems with this new product?" There are levels of candor that are called for in different situations. You will typically ask yourself, how real can I be in my answers, how safe is it, and what does the questioner really want to know, anyway?

Inquiry is one of the ways we express interest in others. Where do you live? What do you do? What's your favorite food? What makes you happy? The way you express your curiosity through questioning can fuel connection and learning or shut down communication completely (Cormier et al., 2017; Strachan, 2007). Just as there are great questions and unique ways of framing them, there are also ways of inquiring that are problematic. As Antoine de Saint-Exupéry (1943) tells us through his characters in *The Little Prince*, people often seem to ask the wrong questions, or they may ask the right question at the wrong time. The narrator in his story, the little prince, says this about adults:

> When you tell them that you have made a new friend, they never ask you any questions about essential matters. They never say to you, "What does his voice sound like? What games does he love best? Does he collect butterflies?" Instead, they demand: "How old is he? How many brothers has he? How much does he weigh? How much money does his father make?" Only from these figures do they think they have learned anything about him (p. 8).

In the coaching conversation, inquiry has many purposes and forms. It's a means of fostering rapport, understanding the client's perspective, and deepening the relationship. Asking questions is a potent way to develop insight and guide change. Although questions are essential to coaching, as Kottler (2008) remarks, "asking questions is a mixed blessing. It does get you the information you want in the most direct fashion, but often at a price" (p. 77). He advises that if you can't get the information you need some other way, then, as a last resort, ask a question.

If you have had a job interview recently, you might recall how frequently interviewers ask questions and how it feels to be questioned. You may also have memories of being cross-examined, grilled, interrogated, or otherwise required to answer a seemingly endless list of pointed questions. As a result, you might have developed extreme sensitivity to being questioned. Interviewers may gather a great deal of information with their questions but with what effect on the relationship? They might use forced-choice questions, leading questions, biased questions, closed questions, or questions to which they already know the answer. When a person asks you a leading question (e.g., "You like this job, don't you?" or "Isn't this wonderful?"), you are likely to assume that the questioner already has her or his mind made up, that she or he expects a certain answer, or perhaps that the situation is a bit unfriendly. In this light, how can questioning serve as a supportive, trust-building, awareness-generating, action-promoting empathic skill?

Coaching clients expect you to ask questions; they recognize questioning as part of the process and more or less open themselves to it. Yet the experience of being questioned can move the client in so many directions—some of them beneficial and others not. No doubt, you want to be helpful, and surely you intend to probe delicately and caringly. If you commence your relationship by asking lots of questions, some clients may assume that this is the way it should be, so they will await your direction through questioning. Occasionally, when you ask a particular question, your client may say, "Ouch," and you may retreat a step or two. Sometimes, even when your client says, "Ouch," you make a judgment that it would be beneficial to the client to inquire further. Questioning is an art! The job interviewer referred to earlier may have it easy by comparison. She or he typically will have a preset list of questions and areas to cover and isn't necessarily interested in building a relationship. In coaching, however, you are an explorer in an uncharted world. Asking the wrong question can bring you to the edge of a precipice; asking the right one can reveal new worlds.

AREAS OF INQUIRY IN COACHING

What are the areas of inquiry most often pursued by coaches? In a broad sense, questioning in coaching is bound by the contracted agenda between coach and client—you can't ask any question you want. You don't need to know about their hobbies or intimate relationships, unless they are part of the contracted agenda.

Over the past few years, I have been trying to answer the question, "What do coaches really do?" My research team has come up with a reasonably inclusive list of the kinds of things coaches verbally express in their sessions. Listening multiple times to hundreds of recorded coaching sessions, we came up with a list of 37 different categories of verbal expressions by coaches in their sessions (Gavin et al., 2021). We didn't analyze what clients were saying, other than to understand some of the context for how the coaches intervened. Almost half of these expressions (17 out of 37) represented different areas of inquiry. Let's go through these so that you can more fully comprehend what the typical areas of questioning are in coaching relationships. They have been grouped into five categories representing the following broad themes of inquiry: structure and process, actions and learning, narrative inquiry, systemic relations, and meaning and values.

Structure and Process

In these types of inquiries, coaches are exploring questions with their clients related to the structure, processes, assessments, or immediate experiences within coaching sessions or pertinent to the coaching relationship as a whole.

Coaching Structure Inquiry

At the beginning of coaching relationships, coaches may focus questions on the pragmatics of the engagement, including scheduling, structuring, roles, fees, attendance, and other matters. Also, issues related to roles and responsibilities in the coaching process may arise to the degree that coaches need to delineate various aspects of how coach and client collaborate in their work.

Progress Inquiry

It is typical in coaching relationships for coaches to inquire about clients' sense of movement and progress, either in the current session or over a span of time. Such inquiries would include exploration of how clients measure or benchmark their success in the experience, as well as the degree to which they think they are progressing.

Immediacy Inquiry

Coaches need to understand not only how clients feel about their success, but also how they might be experiencing particular moments in sessions. Especially in light of their intention to partner with clients, coaches check from time to time with questions that might focus on what's happening now (e.g., "How are you feeling in this moment?"). Given the importance of cultivating trust and safety in the relationship, coaches may need to explore the quality of the working alliance by inquiring about how the client perceives it (e.g., "How well do you think we're working together?").

Assessment Inquiry

Coaches may employ psychometric measurements or other types of assessment tools to help clients better appreciate various personal or systemic dynamics. Some coaching processes are structured to include a series of assessments, including 360-degree evaluations or diagnostic measurements. When the coach might be exploring understandings and implications related to various measurements, the conversation becomes centered in inquiry related to this kind of external information.

Actions and Learning

Coaching is about facilitating client growth through the attainment of valued objectives and relevant learning. In pursuing these kinds of outcomes, coaches will explore with their clients the design and pursuit of actions, as well as learning processes.

Outcome Inquiry

Whenever coaches direct attention to outcomes clients desire from their work together, inquiry may center around intentions, goals, or objectives. Discovering the metagoal and its component subgoals often requires some investigation, and coaches help clients articulate specific target objectives for each session through processes of inquiry.

Learning Inquiry

As the field of coaching has matured, attention has gravitated as much to learning outcomes as to more concrete manifestations of success. Learning may pertain to insights about oneself, others, or situations. To stimulate awareness of learning, coaches often inquire about emergent learnings in coaching sessions.

Design and Planning Inquiry

When clients have articulated various objectives for their work in coaching relationships, attention will gradually shift to considerations of designs and plans related to these objectives. The question of what clients will do to move toward their goals becomes paramount, and to this end coaches inquire about how clients can turn dreams into reality.

Commitment and Accountability Inquiry

Another fundamental aspect of coaching conversations focuses on clients' commitment to their plans and ways in which they intend to hold themselves accountable. This isn't simply about asking clients how committed they are but rather a process of inquiry related to identifying and enhancing commitment, as well as exploring ways that clients can track their commitment as they enact plans.

Narrative Inquiry

If you think of coaching as a process of clients telling a story that they would like to refashion so that it has different or more positive outcomes (Drake, 2018), then you can better appreciate how coaches might work to comprehend more fully all essential elements of what clients describe, as well as inquiring about parts that are not entirely clear or that might be implied but not overtly stated.

Content Inquiry

As coaches are navigating their way through parts of the dialogue with their clients, they may not know immediately what the client's focus is or whether they themselves fully comprehend what the client is talking about. In a general way, they may ask a question such as, "What else is important for you to say about this?" or "What other details might you want to express about this subject?" Content questions are typically open invitations for clients to say more about issues they are presently discussing.

Language Inquiry

Each person has unique associations to many of the words they use. I recently heard a client say, "I am mostly satisfied with what's going on." I asked what does *mostly* mean. She said about 95 percent; I had thought *mostly* meant somewhere around 65 percent. I was glad I asked. Coaches need to make sure they are understanding the exact meanings that clients attach to the words they use. You can't ask about every word, but some words jump out as begging for definition.

Emotion Inquiry

Similar to a language inquiry, coaches sometimes need to better appreciate what clients mean when they say they are happy, sad, glad, mad, irritated, elated, and so on. Bandler and Grinder (1979, 2005) used the term *complex equivalence* to reference instances in which the same word, phrase, or experience has different meanings for different people. When a client says, "I was upset," you don't want to assume that you know what that person means. So, coaches ask, "Would you be willing to tell me more about what upset means?" Other times, body language suggests that clients are experiencing a certain emotionality, and even if the coach has a good guess, a question such as "What emotions, if any, are arising for you in this moment as you talk about this topic?" might be asked.

Nonverbal Inquiry

Given Mehrabian's (1972, 1981) ratio of 55:38:7, representing the proposition that 55 percent of a communication comes from body language, 38 percent from tone of voice, and only 7 percent from the actual words, coaches often need to inquire to appreciate what certain expressions or vocal qualities might add to the meaning that coaches are hearing in client stories (e.g., "I'm aware that you are speaking more slowly in this moment. Would you help me understand what, if anything, might have shifted inside you?").

Systemic Relations

In a sense, inquiry to better understand the systemic relationships pertinent to clients' stories may represent a subset of the previous category of narrative inquiry. Clients are imbedded in a context that has significant bearing on what they want to achieve through their coaching work. Inquiry to examine more fully the systems relevant to their coaching objectives is essential.

Ecosystem Inquiry

Within the confines of the boundaries suggested by clients' topics, coaches are likely to explore external environmental and systemic influences on clients and their intentions. These inquiries might encompass but not be limited to questions about their organizations, family, culture, history, regulations, networks, and so much more.

Interpersonal Inquiry

Other people are certainly part of clients' ecosystems, but as coaches move beyond the factual (e.g., Who is your boss? How many people are on your team?) to appreciate the quality, nature, and dynamics of relationships, they are engaging in an inquiry that is deeper than a kind of mapping of interpersonal networks.

Resource Inquiry

In coaching conversations, understanding resources and opportunities along with obstacles and constraints is critical to the process. Not only may clients be unaware of all the resources and possibilities available to them in service of their goals, but they may also articulate certain resources as obstacles when a slightly different angle of analysis reveals how they can be helpful. Thorough inquiry in this realm is a hallmark of coaching.

Meaning and Values

In some framings of goal-centric coaching (Grant, 2012; Ives & Cox, 2012), values are situated as the metagoal that constitutes clients' aspirations and intentions in their coaching work. Not only might coaches need to explore client values, but they may also need to delve into their belief systems and the meanings they attach to various aspects of their stories.

Values and Beliefs Inquiry

At different moments in their dialogues, coaches may deem it important to explore underlying beliefs, assumptions, worldviews, mindsets, and values that may serve to rationalize or motivate patterns of behavior and intended directions for change. Furthermore, self-limiting beliefs often emerge as critical areas for examination in coaching conversations.

Meaning and Importance Inquiry

A key question that coaches ask in virtually every session is framed as some variation of "What makes this (goal or topic) so important to you now?" A significant variation of this question is something akin to "What is so deeply meaningful about this?" Inquiry about the existential level of meaning in clients' intentions and actions often reveals powerful sources of inspiration and motivation. To be clear, this type of inquiry is far deeper than the kind of definitional inquiry represented in language inquiry, described earlier in this section.

No doubt there are other areas of inquiry that coaches pursue in their work. This extensive list is by no means exhaustive of all the possible avenues that coaches might pursue through their questions and in service of facilitating client growth. What is important to understand here is that these categories of inquiry emerged from an in-depth analysis of what coaches actually do in their sessions.

GENERIC QUESTIONS

Having a better appreciation of the areas of inquiry in coaching, I think it makes sense for us to focus now on the form or structure of questions. The two most prevalent forms of questions are typically identified as closed and open questions. A third type, indirect questions, occurs when people make statements that imply a need for response.

Closed Questions

Closed questions invite clients to respond in a word or short phrase rather than giving an expansive answer. They are typically used to obtain facts, verify information, close off lengthy explanations, or control the flow of the interview (Sommers-Flanagan & Sommers-Flanagan, 2015). They may begin with such words as *do*, *is*, *are*, or *have*. Their form is best recognized by the implicit demand of the question to answer directly and briefly. Here are some examples of closed questions:

- Can we begin now?
- Is this the book you were talking about?
- Do you agree?
- Are you interested?
- Do you want to continue talking about this?

Open Questions

Open questions invite exploration and conversation; they help create clarity and generate new learning. An open question may direct the client to a theme of discussion, yet it allows ample latitude to explore thoughts and feelings (Evans et al., 2017; Ivey et al., 2018). When asking open questions, you may receive lengthy responses that you may choose to paraphrase or summarize to ensure understanding. Open questions might begin with words such as *how*, *what*, *would*, *could*, or *why*. Some examples of open questions include the following:

- How are you coming into our session today?
- What would you like to explore today?
- What results are you hoping to achieve through this coaching relationship?
- What have you learned about yourself in this session?
- How do you imagine life would be if you were able to make that change?

Indirect Questions

Indirect questions are actually statements, rather than questions, that imply a need for response. They represent a less intrusive way of seeking information and can often unlock a deep understanding of issues (Shebib, 2020). Especially when the coach has just asked a long series of questions, the use of an indirect question may break the pattern and ease the pressure of questioning for the client. Here are some examples of indirect questions:

- It would help me to understand your perspective if you said more about this.
- I am curious to hear how you reacted.
- It seems you want to say something else about this.
- I don't know exactly what you mean by that last statement.

Clients' Answers

No matter how well you phrase your questions, clients often answer with things they have on their minds even though their replies may seem unrelated to what you have asked. No doubt you have had exchanges similar to the following in which the question requires a certain kind of answer but the respondent uses the question as an opportunity to offer something completely different.

> *Person A:* Where were you last night?
>
> *Person B:* Oh, I've been having a rough time in general. Things simply haven't been going well. Yesterday, I tried to . . .

Here's another example:

> *Person A:* What time is it?
>
> *Person B:* I think it's late. I'd better get moving. I have an appointment this evening.

Neurolinguistic programming theorists (Bandler & Grinder, 1979, 2005) propose that the meaning of your communication—or question, in this case—can be discovered in the response you receive from your client. You may ask about your client's progress on a project, and she or he may tell you about relationship difficulties at work. When clients are highly motivated to discuss certain things, the question you ask them is almost a signal for them to say what's on their minds.

Careful structuring of questions is essential for effective coaching. If you ask a client a confusing question, the client might give a seemingly irrelevant reply. In this case, you can't be sure whether the response results from a poorly constructed question or something unique about the client. By contrast, if a client responds with a tangential remark to a well-formed question, the coach will have gained significant, though unexpected, information.

Depending on the purpose of your inquiry, one form of question may serve your purpose better than another. Do you want to moderate the pace of the session, refocus the conversation, explore an issue, confirm your perception, or obtain a simple answer about something? Asking open questions facilitates client expression. Closed questions likely generate short, specific answers. Indirect questions can lead to either short or long answers but generally have less of a mandate to reply.

PROBLEMATIC QUESTIONS

Research indicates that a lengthy questioning process may weaken rapport in addition to reinforcing unproductive power and dependency dynamics in the relationship (Evans et al., 2017; Kottler, 2008; Shebib, 2020; Young, 2017). Moreover, the framing of a question may in itself be problematic. Let's consider some examples.

Leading Questions

A question is said to be leading when the way it is phrased most likely suggests the expected response (Shebib, 2020). Leading questions can be laden with assumptions that may simply be wrong (Hargie, 2017). To provide an answer, the respondent has to embrace the assumptions you embedded in the question as if they were true. Typically, leading questions elicit defensiveness. Sometimes, these questions are phrased as negations, making it difficult for the client to disagree with or deny the question's premise. Here are examples:

- Wouldn't you like to try this?
- Is this so difficult that you won't even consider it?
- Don't you think it would be a good idea to have your brother join you?
- Why is this always so hard for you to do?
- What has to happen for you to stop making excuses?
- Why are you resisting any kind of positive change?

Limited-Option Questions

A question of this sort not only contains embedded assumptions but also limits responses to the options provided even though these do not represent all possibilities. In some forms, it is a forced choice in which all answers are potentially incorrect. Examples include the following:

- So, are you going to quit your job or just keep getting passed over for promotion?
- Would you rather be a winner or a loser?

- You have to choose now—which proposal can you live with?
- Do you want to meet Tuesday or Thursday?
- Whose plan is this —yours or your team's?

Stacked Questions

This style of questioning is not so much leading or biased as it is confusing. The coach asks several questions at the same time even though they may be unrelated to one another (Cormier et al., 2017). Your client may not know which question to answer first, or she or he may answer one and get so involved in the answer that the second question gets lost. Some examples include the following:

- Why do you think you need a coach, and what have you tried in the past to reach your goal?
- What are your main goals, and what is your time frame for achieving them?
- What I'd like to know from you is what motivates you most, what turns you off, what's the longest you've ever stayed with a plan, and what is your vision for the future?

Why Questions

Why questions may evoke a sense of interrogation. Parents ask their children, "Why did you do that?" Teachers might use *why* questions in trying to get to the bottom of things. For instance, they might ask, "Why are your assignments always late?" By the time you reach your adult years, you may be overly sensitive to *why* questions and react defensively even though a questioner's intent may be to help. Mindfulness about the potential impact of this kind of question is important. Of course, defensiveness in response to a *why* question may reflect the level of rapport between coach and client as much as it does the question's wording (Ivey et al., 2018). A safe approach would be to avoid using *why* questions as much as possible. Here are examples of *why* questions and possible alternatives:

- Why do you want to leave your job? *Alternative*: What do you imagine the pros and cons of leaving your job might be?
- Why do you want to work with me? *Alternative*: Help me understand your reasons for wanting to work with me.
- Why did you say that? *Alternative*: I'm curious about what brought you to say what you just said.

STRATEGIC QUESTIONS

Coaches often struggle to find the best question they can ask in the moment. This has led to a quest to identify powerful questions (Berger, 2018; Stoltzfus, 2008; Wise & Littlefield, 2017). Indeed, it can be useful to have a repertoire of concise and purposeful questions for moments when you are wrestling with how to move a coaching conversation into more fruitful territory.

At the beginning of your coaching career, the idea of consistently asking great questions may seem to be an overwhelming challenge. What makes a question great, anyway? It may come as a surprise, but a great question could sound as simple as "How will you do that?" or "What do you want to do?" Isolated from the rich texture of a coaching conversation, such questions seem anything but amazing. However, within the weave of words, the precise timing and sensitive delivery of a simple question can send shock waves through carefully constructed walls of doubt or resistance. Great questions are generated in the moment from foundations of your coaching presence and listening skills. Maintaining aware-

---

Useful Questions

The questions in this sidebar represent commonly used kinds of inquiries in coaching. How useful or powerful they are depends on their context and timing. You might reflect on them, noticing their simplicity and also appreciating that the wording itself may not be as magical as the way in which you ask them at an appropriate time and in clear relationship to what your client is addressing in that moment.

What deeply matters to you?

Where are you going?

When can you do that?

What experience would you most like to create?

Who's there *just* for you?

What are you passionate about?

What's your purpose in this precious life of yours?

What's your biggest learning from this?

If you had an extra hour each day, what would you do with it?

How did you make that happen?

How can you make this happen?

What advice would you give yourself in this situation?

What makes sense to you about this?

What's stopping you from getting what you want?

How are you feeling right now?

What keeps you going?

How can you set that boundary?

What beliefs hold you back?

What is under your control in this situation?

How can you let that go?

How are *you* taking care of *you*?

How might you deal with that feeling?

How can you ask for this?

What's the one thing you want most from this?

Who can partner with you in making this happen?

If your body had a voice, what would it tell you?

---

ness of how your questions are structured is necessary since few of us have had much instruction on questioning skills, particularly in the framework of a partnered and appreciative coaching relationship. In essence, a near infinite number of questions might be deemed powerful in the context of a particular coaching moment, even though in isolation from the dialogue they may appear somewhat mundane (see sidebar, Useful Questions).

When you open your mind, heart, and will in the listening process (Scharmer, 2016), you might gain an inspiring awareness of your client's world. Add to this your own sensitivity, knowledge, and insight, and you have substantial support for generating great questions. When clients tell you they are thrilled with their jobs yet continue to express themes of dissatisfaction, it's easy to imagine a question that confronts this apparent contradiction. What might make your questioning more powerful, however, is knowing how to ask your question in a timely and supportive manner that fully respects the client's world and invites creativity.

Certain types of questions can have strategic value in coaching sessions. Let's examine seven types of strategic questions (Carpetto, 2008; Cormier et al., 2017; De Jong & Berg, 2013; De Shazer, 1988; Kimsey-House et al., 2018).

Miracle Questions

Clients can get stuck in their thinking and become unable to see a way out. If you ask them what they can do to move forward, they repeatedly blank out or offer options they know won't work. A miracle question is a way of getting beyond this impasse by making a grand assumption that the obstacle has magically dissolved or disappeared. It jettisons clients from their current state into a desired future where they have reached their goals. Miracle questions focus clients not on the road ahead but on a mountain peak they have summited in their imagination, allowing them a better vantage point from which to see the road taken, which they could not previously envision. This question is shaped into a dreamlike journey with a scenario and question such as this, "Imagine that while you were sleeping, a miracle happened and magically removed all barriers and obstacles, and, because you were sleeping, you were unaware of this happening. When you awoke, you realized that you made the leap and reached your goal. Your world is different. I invite you to be there now. What do you notice that's different?"

As your clients begin to describe an altered reality, they will likely see glimmers of how they got to where they see themselves now. Projecting clients forward gives them a new perspective from which to observe the obstacles that they currently perceive to be in the way. As you continue to explore with clients, they may gain a heightened capacity to look back over their journey to this new reality and appreciate what they need to do to get there.

Exception Questions

When you hear the words *never* or *always*, you might wonder what the exception to that pattern or belief is. Generally speaking, there are exceptions to most patterns and rules. A client says, "I've never been able to stick with a diet." You reply, "Never?" The client pauses and adds, "Well, there was this one time . . ." When clients describe what they have tried in the past to achieve their goals, there may be a sense of inevitability and incapacity. Nothing has ever worked, no matter how hard they tried. Exception questions bring into focus the times when something did in fact work!

Clients may perceive themselves as incapable of doing certain things. "I could never stand up in front of a group and speak my mind," a client may say. The coach asks, "Has there ever been a time when you were with a group of people and you talked to them about your ideas?" The client answers, "Well, if you put it that way, of course I've done that! Just last week . . ." It's true that you do some things better than others and that your talents are not equally distributed. Yet this is not the same as saying you have zero capacity in certain areas. You may not have run a marathon, but that doesn't mean you can't.

What Else Questions

The answer clients offer to a question about actions they might take often represents their automatic, first response: "I could try talking to my colleague to iron things out!" Then you ask, "What else could you do?" Even when the person produces a lengthy list of alternatives, you may continue to stimulate creativity by asking, "What else comes to mind?" The first answer isn't always the best, and the most promising answer may not emerge if the client stops generating ideas too early in the process.

Sometimes clients seem to be wearing blinders when it comes to seeing alternative explanations for why things happened in their lives. Over time, they tell the same stories about their experiences and why things turned out as they did. This becomes their personal mythology. When clients lose out on prized opportunities, they may cement a rationale for why things went wrong. In another context, clients may have heard certain words as devasting criticism such that they never wanted to try again. Well, what if their interpretations were wrong? They might have to revamp the story of their lives. Asking questions such as "What else could have explained that happening?" or "What else could you have done?" may break open locked-in self-beliefs to the degree that clients start experiencing hopefulness and competency for the first time in a particular area.

A special use of the *what else* question occurs in brainstorming, which may be useful as a creative problem-solving method. Brainstorming is a technique that helps individuals or groups generate novel ideas and produce new methods to answer a question or address important issues (see sidebar, An Example of Brainstorming). Here are a few rules that govern the technique of brainstorming:

- Define the question and the time frame (e.g., "I'm suggesting we take five minutes and generate answers to the question, "What can I do to reduce my stress?").
- Create a relevant sentence stem targeted to the area of interest (e.g., I can reduce my stress by . . .).
- Generate as many answers and ideas as possible in the given time frame.
- Keep asking, "What else?"
- Welcome all ideas and record them (no matter how unusual or seemingly unrelated).

An Example of Brainstorming

Jamal wants to find new motivations to exercise every day. Both he and his coach engage in a brainstorming activity with the coach asking *what else* questions.

Coach: Jamal, if it's okay with you, let's take five minutes in which I'm going to ask you to generate as many answers as you can to this sentence stem: "I would want to exercise if . . ."

Jamal: I would want to exercise if . . . I had a friend to go with me.

I would want to exercise if . . . my partner came with me.

I would want to exercise if . . . I could see it as time just for me.

I would want to exercise if . . . I got results.

Coach: What else?

Jamal: I would want to exercise if . . . I had great exercise gear.

I would want to exercise if . . . I could go on a weekend away as a reward.

I would want to exercise if . . . I could do it at lunch.

I would want to exercise if . . . I had a little more time in the morning.

I would want to exercise if . . . my days weren't so stressful.

Coach: What else?

Jamal: I would want to exercise if . . . my supper was ready when I came back.

I would want to exercise if . . . I had a trainer.

I would want to exercise if . . . I could join that new gym.

I would want to exercise if . . . I had fun doing it.

Coach: What else?

This exercise could go on until Jamal completely runs out of new options or the agreed-upon time frame has elapsed. Once the brainstorming is over, the coach might then move into an exploration of the possibilities generated.

For further reading on brainstorming, see www.mindtools.com/brainstm.html.

- Withhold all comments that imply evaluation or judgment.
- When there are no new ideas or the time is over, review all the ideas that have emerged.

Scaling Questions

You might be accustomed to being asked a question that begins with the words, "On a scale of 1 to 10 . . ." In coaching, it's important to appreciate the relative strength of clients' beliefs and experiences. One special application of a scaling question is likely to arise at the end of a session: "On a scale of 1 to 10, how committed are you to completing your action plan this week with 1 being absolutely not committed—will not do it, and 10 representing I'm psyched—I can't wait to get out of here to start?" Of course, there are other types of scales. You can ask whether your clients strongly agree, strongly disagree, or hold an opinion in the middle. You can ask where they would place themselves on an undefined scale between the words *clear* and *unclear*.

Over a series of sessions, if you ask the same scaling question, you might develop a progress chart. Here is an example: "On a scale of 1 to 10, how satisfied are you with what you've accomplished in our session today, with 1 being totally dissatisfied and 10 being extremely satisfied?" Of course, using this type of question to chart progress needs to be made explicit; otherwise, asking the same scaling question time and again can sound mechanical or pointless.

Resourcefulness Questions

As individuals, we are often our own worst critics. Some clients may have a bias toward perceiving where they weren't successful rather than acknowledging their strengths and capacities even in failed efforts. Suppose a woman tells a story of perseverance against insurmountable odds and focuses on her lack of success. You ask, "What enabled you to continue putting effort into doing this time and time again?" She feels a bit stunned and stammers, "Well, I guess, I, uh . . ." Coaching empowers people to persevere partly by surfacing unrecognized assets and resources. Asking the following kinds of questions allows clients to see their deep capacities in spite of the undesired outcomes of their efforts:

- How did you keep going despite all the opposition you were facing from friends and family?
- What did you do that prevented this situation from getting so much worse than it did?

- How in the world do you manage to cope with all that's on your plate?

Relationship Questions

When clients are being hard on themselves, it can be helpful to ask what other people in their world would say about the situation or behavior. Coaches learn over time what their clients' social networks look like and where there is reliable support for a change process. They develop impressions of how others would see their clients in action and can call upon these voices to help clients through tough moments. For instance, you might ask, "What do you think your brother would say about your progress to date?" Even when clients hang on tightly to limiting beliefs, they are likely to acknowledge that others may have a more objective or fair-minded assessment of the situation. In some cases, you might bring yourself into the picture as the observer. A question such as the following might be asked: "If I had been a fly on the wall while you were learning how to tango, what do you think I would have seen?"

Presumptive Questions

It's reasonable to assume that after a few sessions, you will have mapped your clients' belief systems to a degree where you can anticipate how they will respond to certain questions. For instance, you are likely to know whether they have an optimistic or pessimistic bias toward themselves and their capacities. A presumptive question bears some similarity to a resourcefulness question, except that it consistently skips a step in order to project clients beyond their limiting beliefs. A woman may habitually describe ways in which she doesn't live up to her own standards. Yet, as her coach, you readily see all the ways in which she generates positive outcomes in her life. So, you ask, "What's your personal success formula for making things happen?" The question presumes—without making the presumption explicit—that she has been successful. A variation of this question might be "What personal qualities have enabled you to recommit yourself time after time?" Here, the coach presumes not only that the client has some specific assets but also that she perseveres no matter what. Of course, the use of presumptive questioning requires careful consideration. If you can predict that the woman will challenge any implication that she is better than she thinks she is, you may need to use another approach.

PRACTICALITIES IN INQUIRY

Implicitly or explicitly, you want to let your client know that you will be asking questions. Yet that's not all you do. A good practice is to ask, listen, and reflect before you repeat the cycle. You also want to be aware of how clients respond to a process of inquiry. I think of a client who typically responds to my question and then waits for the next one. I learned with this client that I needed to be a bit more patient than usual to allow him to find his own next question.

Silence is a critical element in processes of inquiry. Using silence after a period of questioning can be helpful in that it offers clients a chance to reflect on what they have been saying. If I am caught up in my mind trying to figure out the next question, I may miss the fact that the client would benefit most from a moment of silence. If I am anxious about making sure we develop a robust action plan and feel the clock ticking, I may push forward with more inquiry even when the client needs time to collect her or his thoughts. There is a graceful balance in coaching conversations of doing and being, and the being part is honored in the timely silences that we allow in the midst of dialogue.

Another important awareness here is that clients who prefer introversion may have a more measured response rate than those who are extroverted (Cain, 2013; Quenck, 2009). Your reaction to these patterns will depend on your own preference, that is, introversion or extroversion. Those who tend more toward introversion generally like to reflect and engage in internal self-talk before expressing their opinions; in this respect, their answers to probing questions may come after lengthy pauses. Those who are more extroverted, on the other hand, are likely to respond quickly while thinking aloud. Their responses will probably be more immediate. If as a coach you prefer extroversion, you may occasionally need to slow down your questioning process. Your own tendency to think aloud and to speak without extensive reflection could run counter to the needs of your clients. If you prefer introversion, you may have a pattern of reflecting internally on what the person has just said before asking the next question. When working with extroverts, however, you may need to process your thoughts aloud so these clients can experience continuous engagement in the coaching process.

Inquiry can be experienced by clients as a show of interest, and it can feel intrusive at times (Anderson & Killenberg, 2009; Cormier et al., 2017; Evans et al., 2017; Ivey et al., 2018). As a coach, you are guiding the conversation through your inquiry. In this sense, you are exercising a degree of control over the flow and direction of your clients' disclosures. You want to remain alert to the power dynamics that are inherent in questioning, which suggests that from time to time you might want to check with your clients about how they are experiencing themselves and the relationship itself.

Related to this idea is a caveat regarding the depth of the dialogue you can legitimately pursue in your coaching. The boundaries for inquiry are at least implicit in the agenda that the client determines for the coaching relationship. You may be very curious about so many aspects of your clients' experiences, yet you don't have carte blanche to explore whatever you wish. With the best of intentions, you may believe that the more you know about your client, the more helpful you can be. Smith (2007) and Williams and Davis (2007) offer sage advice for those who might want to explore deeper levels of the client's world. According to them, effective and ethical helpers gather necessary information to inform their actions with clients while guarding against pursuing deeper understanding for its own sake.

If you refer back to Cox's (2013) discussion of authentic listening, you might remember that she was suggesting something more akin to a bilateral dialogue of inquiry and discovery. I think this is the direction we want to move toward as coaches so that clients are increasingly able to ask themselves powerful questions.

INQUIRY IN THE ICF CORE COMPETENCIES

When the ICF revised its set of coaching core competencies, it subsumed some previously separate competencies under the broad framework of *evoking awareness*. This new competency integrated the previously distinct competencies of powerful questioning, direct communication, and creating awareness. I want to highlight here some of the obvious and perhaps not-so-obvious references that the ICF (2020c) makes to questioning so you can better appreciate inquiry from the ICF perspective and see how it relates to material in this chapter.

As described earlier, there are multiple areas of inquiry appropriate to coaching (Gavin et al., 2021). In the elements listed under the ICF's definition of this competency (see sidebar, ICF Core Coaching Competency 7: Evokes Awareness), there are explicit mentions of asking questions, and there

ICF Core Coaching Competency 7: Evokes Awareness

Definition: Facilitates client insight and learning by using tools and techniques such as powerful questioning, silence, metaphor or analogy

1. Considers client experience when deciding what might be most useful
2. Challenges the client as a way to evoke awareness or insight
3. Asks questions about the client, such as their way of thinking, values, needs, wants and beliefs
4. Asks questions that help the client explore beyond current thinking
5. Invites the client to share more about their experience in the moment
6. Notices what is working to enhance client progress
7. Adjusts the coaching approach in response to the client's needs
8. Helps the client identify factors that influence current and future patterns of behavior, thinking or emotion
9. Invites the client to generate ideas about how they can move forward and what they are willing or able to do
10. Supports the client in reframing perspectives
11. Shares observations, insights and feelings, without attachment, that have the potential to create new learning for the client

are other points where inquiry may not be as obviously indicated. The ICF highlights questioning pertaining to ways of thinking, values, needs, wants, and beliefs. It references inquiry that helps clients explore beyond current thinking. However, it's my sense that inquiry is implicit in virtually all the elements under this definition. For instance, how can a coach support the client in reframing perspectives without perhaps inquiring about those perspectives beforehand and then verifying through questioning how the coach's reframing may have resonated? As noted in its definition, the ICF identifies powerful questioning as one of the tools to facilitate client insight and learning.

We discussed the importance of silence earlier, as well as in chapter 10. In this competency, silence represents a powerful means of evoking awareness. For a coach to live well in silence during a coaching session requires much self-awareness coupled with acute sensitivity to where your clients are in the moment and what would serve them most. It's helpful to remind yourself in these precious silences that you can have all the insight in the world, but that it's the client who needs to source her or his own wisdom and insight. Silence is the client's ally in this process.

The ICF competency described here speaks of other competencies beyond questioning. These will be taken up in chapters 12 and 13.

REFLECTIONS

I am hoping that by now you have ample appreciation for two key competencies—active listening and inquiry. When I think about these competencies, I am aware that they are central to the work I do with clients. Of course, there are moments in a coaching dialogue when coaches will have their own voices, expressing their ideas, beliefs, perceptions, and stories. These kinds of interventions seem to better illustrate the concept of partnership in coaching. When you add your piece as a coach, in effect, you are comolding the clay that shapes clients' futures. Yet inquiry also signifies partnering in so many ways. By the questions you ask, you reflect to clients whether you are outside their experience looking in or whether you are inside, pondering about the same questions that they are beginning to ask themselves. Some questions you ask won't always have immediate answers. They can initiate a process of search or exploration. They represent invitations to craft a new way, a new vision, a new world. When you are truly partnering with your client, you are likely to feel united in a joint inquiry without much of a road map but with great heart and courage for exploration and discovery.

CHAPTER 12

THE COACH'S VOICE

*Alone, we can do so little;
together we can do so much.*

Helen Keller

MY STORY

My relationship with offering opinions or giving advice has assumed a kind of bell-shaped curve over the trajectory of my life. In my early years . . . well, what did I know? How could I tell anyone anything, especially since a lot of my clients were older than me? Later on, I went through a period where I thought I knew a lot, but I assiduously avoided offering my opinions because I believed it was pretty much against the rules. Even so, I think I must have conveyed to some clients that I really knew what they needed to do, but they just had to find that out for themselves! Where I am now is pretty much feeling as if I don't have a whole lot to offer, because I'm not living anyone else's life other than my own. This doesn't prevent me from telling stories and saying how things land for me, but it feels different from figuratively sitting on the mountain awaiting the seekers of wisdom to ask me questions.

In my coaching practice, there's one request for an opinion that I often hear; it comes up in words such as this: "Is this normal?" The question may be about reactions clients are having or perceptions they hold. Another question is framed as follows: "You must have seen this before. What do people usually do in this kind of situation?"

I have to make a confession. There was a time when I thought it would be helpful to normalize a client's experience by saying things like, "Sure, lots of people have that kind of reaction." I don't do that very much anymore. More likely, I might say: "Well, it seems that it's pretty normal for you given what you're going through right now." I'm not sure there's a right or best answer to these requests. I do believe that lots of things, when abstracted from the specific context of someone's life, may appear odd, but when examined in context, they seem to make perfect sense.

Coaches listen and ask questions, and they also have their own voice. This chapter brings to life the multiple ways in which coaches express their ideas, opinions, insights, hunches, and information. In expressing themselves, coaches are cautioned to tread lightly, acknowledging the power of their position and the centrality of fostering clients' creativity. The uses of feedback, confrontation (or challenge), self-disclosure, and immediacy are explored for what they might generate in a coaching dialogue. In addition, offerings of information, instructions and suggestions are described in terms of their necessity, their limitations, and alternative ways of accomplishing the same objectives in the dialogue. Here are some guiding questions as you read:

- What's the best way to offer feedback?
- How do I challenge clients in a supportive way?
- How much should I talk about myself?
- How do I address issues that arise in the moment?
- Can I tell clients what to do?
- What do I do when clients ask for my advice or opinions?

DILEMMAS IN HAVING VOICE

The gift of coaching arises from the synergy of two people cocreating a new and more desirable future from old stories that might no longer be useful. Your clients enter the coaching relationship with strong desires to change, and you as coach serve as a catalyst in this process of transformation. A rich chemistry emerges when both you and your client wholeheartedly combine energies in service of change.

Unlike some other processes of helping, coaching represents a relationship where the coach neither dominates nor disappears (Iliffe-Wood, 2014). Coaches do not unilaterally dictate actions or interventions, nor do they passively observe their clients wandering in a fog. As a coach, you have your own rich history, wisdom, and personal insights that will differ from those of your clients. In the upcoming material, I want you to join me as we enter a more complex domain where the coach becomes more visible. **Direct communication** represents a broad range of interventions that is evident when coaches voice their ideas, percep-

tions, knowledge, and insights. In contrast to active listening and inquiry, the coach's character and style may take the foreground in these kinds of interventions. In part, direct communication is premised on an assumption that coaching clients are robust enough to accept or reject ideas and perspectives that coaches might offer.

Moving From Reflection to Influence

In the lexicon of the helping professions, direct communication unquestionably situates itself in what has traditionally been described as the realm of influencing skills (Cormier et al., 2017; Ivey et al., 2018). A distinguishing characteristic of all forms of direct communication is that messages originate in the beliefs, values, observations, and perspectives of the coach; the coach is transparently expressive in these communications. Direct communication implies speaking directly to issues arising in clients' stories from a stance that is well thought out and tailored to clients' needs and experiences. There is a quality of telling or informing clients about something that may be outside their consciousness with the intention of moving them toward their objectives. Since coaching is a partnership, direct communication is never dogmatic. Different forms of direct communication may, however, shift the dynamics of the relationship as when coaches offer their opinions, ideas, or observations; doing so represents far more than reflecting or mirroring what the client has said.

Direct communication may intentionally attempt to deconstruct clients' old views and perceptions of reality to create the foundation for a more viable and satisfying future. Given this intention, coaches need to mindfully express their ideas through critical discernment and skillful application. As is true of all coaching processes, direct communication relies on the coach's capacity to use language that is respectful of the unique nature, heritage, and coaching agendas of their clients.

Coaching as a Social Construction

Your clients describe their realities in words. Their words may have special meanings for you, yet your meanings may differ from those of your clients. You may more or less concur with your clients' perspectives of reality because many of the words they use align with your understandings. Sometimes you may believe that there is something that your clients aren't clearly seeing, and you decide to help them perceive more accurately in order to traverse the course of change implied in their coaching agendas.

Direct communication references a number of coaching skills wherein you as coach speak your truth in the hope that your words will be understood in the way you intended. Whether you listen, question, or present your own thoughts, you ideally position yourself as a collaborator—a partner—in the change process even though you base your work on the principle that agendas for change derive entirely from your clients. Or do they?

As your clients express their stories, their stories become yours in a certain way. You are likely to have your own thoughts and feelings about their stories, which you may choose to express. As a result, there will now be a new story that is jointly authored. This new story is what you work on session after session, generating plans and implementation processes.

From the way I have just expressed this, how much of what happens do you think belongs exclusively to the client, and how much of it is a synergistic product of your relationship that has emerged through dialogue? This describes the essence of the theory of social constructionism (Gergen, 1985, 1991, 1999).

Theoretical Premises

Social constructionism argues that realities don't exist independent of observers and the language systems these observers apply to their stories. Moreover, this theory tells us that the knowledge each of us has about reality is socially constructed. That is, what clients understand about reality is based in part on the language they use and the situations in which they live. Culture and context amidst a myriad of other factors shape their perceptions and languages and, indeed, their self-definitions and identities.

In the perspective of social constructionism, the language you use in telling your story creates meaning. From this premise, there will be as many meanings derived from stories as there are storytellers, and each of these versions of meaning represents truth for the individual expressing it. It may be comforting to know that there won't be an infinite range of possible stories simply because there are limited contexts that inform storytelling; these contexts include all relevant historical events, language, and predominant cultural perspectives.

When your clients tell their stories and you reflect their words to them, you may, by virtue of your way of capturing their stories, end up cocreating a new social reality and new meanings! Even though you fully intend to be helpful and likely think of yourself as capable of accurate reflections and objective observations of clients' situations, a social constructionist would say that the coach and client are simply collaborating on the construction of a new truth, which hopefully will be more beneficial to the client (see sidebar, Vignette: A Mix of Meanings).

Your values are transmitted through your language so much so that in the course of communicating with your clients, you may unwittingly influence your client simply by showing up the way you are, with your unique greetings, expressions, inflections, and choice of words. This is simply the way it is. It reminds us to be ever mindful of the degree to which our words mingle with our clients'

Vignette: A Mix of Meanings

Some years ago, I was working away from home over a long period with a team of people. We were quite close with one another since our travels caused us to have to rely on each other for so many reasons. Mornings were typically gatherings around a table where we would eat, drink coffee, and begin our days with various ways of connecting.

On a particular occasion, I had been away from the team for a week and reunited with them again at the breakfast table. I began describing a dream I had the night before to one of my colleagues and noticed that all the other conversations had stopped and everyone was listening. My dream was situated in my home city where I had suddenly arrived, and upon opening the door to my home, I discovered that no one was there! I ran frantically from room to room, calling out the names of my children and my partner, only to be met with a deafening silence. I became more and more panicky and ended up sitting in a small room with my head in my hands. I concluded with the line, "Wow! I have just been away from home for far too long!" Laughter erupted and a team member said, "Go on . . . That's not it; you missed us. You were missing us. You can't stay away from us for long; we're your family." He wasn't wrong, but that's not the interpretation I had in mind when I reflected on my dream. Their joyous welcoming and reframing of my dream brought up some new realizations about how close we had grown over our time together.

expressions in giving birth to something new that emerges from both parties, rather than being solely created by our clients.

Cox (2013) captures the dilemma for coaches when she juxtaposes the relatively recent emphasis on clean coaching (Dunbar, 2017) with more traditional perspectives about how coaches reflect and paraphrase their clients' words. Clean coaching derives from a perspective about clean language introduced in the 1980s (Grove & Panzer, 1989). In this perspective, coaches assist clients in uncovering their personal meanings and metaphors without contaminating client worldviews with their beliefs, values, interpretations, and meanings. Clean coaching assumes that coaches need to get out of the way of their clients by asking questions and accurately reflecting so as to introduce no new meanings or metaphors to what the client is trying to discover. A big question here is whether this is really possible! In normal dialogue, our words mingle, metaphors mix together, and new perspectives emerge. Clean coaching would argue that this kind of process interferes with clients' own processes and leads them in directions that may not be uniquely their own.

The counterargument to clean coaching easily arises from the question, *What if the client's views are wrong—or ill informed?* Or maybe it's just that the clients' perspectives may be insufficient to get them where they want to go. From this angle, Cox (2013) suggests that the coach might then need to move to a more authentic process of exploration, where the coach's worldview, assumptions, values, and beliefs become more relevant. I agree with Cox's perspective in this regard. It is my sense that we are, indeed, relational beings (Gergen, 2009); our lives are socially constructed, and we grow through our human connectedness. Accordingly, it makes good sense to acknowledge that coaching is a social experience wherein the process of dialogue merges the wisdom and experiences of both coach and client.

So how does this help you with the dilemmas arising from having voice as the coach in your sessions? Paradoxically, it both frees and restrains you. It legitimizes your input in the coaching process and cautions you to be ever mindful of what you say and how you say it. You don't just offer advice because you happen to know something. You don't simply give instruction because you can. You are as fully aware as you can be in the moment of what you are adding to the mix, how you are potentially shifting or supporting a particular perspective, and how you are a true partner to your clients in the best sense of that term.

With this theoretical perspective in mind, it's time to move into the methodology related to direct communication. I will first address the process of giving feedback. Then, I will explore the matter of challenge and how this intervention has the potential to motivate change. Next, I will review self-disclosure, where coaches reveal aspects of their stories in service of clients' topics. I will then unpack the methodology related to immediacy, or here-and-now dialogue, that focuses on what is happening in the moment within the coaching relationship. Finally, I will consider direct input in the forms of instruction, information, and advice.

FEEDBACK

Feedback is thought of as an effective way of increasing clients' awareness of their behaviors and motivating them toward desired change. It is intended to provide clients with specific data about how they behave as well as how you might experience them.

Rationale for Feedback

The term *feedback* can be linked to the field of cybernetics where information is fed into a system to ensure the correction of processes directed toward achieving certain outcomes (Fradkov, 2007). With the advance of technology, most systems have built-in autoregulating devices so that when undesirable deviations from ideal performance occur, a feedback-initiated, self-correcting process begins. Think of a thermostat attached to a furnace or cooling system. In the realm of human behavior (Carver & Scheier, 2001, 2002), feedback is thought of as an essential means of bringing behaviors to others' awareness so they might consider making important changes. It also serves to reinforce behaviors that are effective or promote growth. With all its potential values, it can nonetheless be challenging to optimize the processes of feedback. Consider job performance evaluations. A manager may ignore important behaviors for a long time before suddenly confronting an employee with overwhelming evidence of ineffective performance. The outcome of that conversation may be less than ideal. Among other things, timeliness and content of feedback are critical to success in most contexts.

Practicalities in Feedback

The literature in the helping professions shows a strong consensus regarding considerations in offering feedback (Brammer & MacDonald, 2003; DeForest et al., 2005; Hargie, 2017; Ivey et al., 2018; Young, 2017). Let's take time to review these guidelines from the perspective of coaching.

1. Feedback is to be offered when, and only when, it can be rationalized in terms of its association to the client's coaching agenda. There may be many areas where you, as a coach, might see benefit in offering clients feedback. It's critical to remember that you and your clients set clear boundaries for the *what* and *how* of working together, and these boundaries delimit the kinds of feedback you are sanctioned to offer. Of course, ethical considerations (see chapter 6) may dictate other considerations in offering feedback.

2. Feedback needs to fully respect and be framed in consideration of the client's unique nature and background. Coaches need to consider who their clients are when offering feedback. Based on a wide range of individual differences, including cultural heritage, gender preference, age, and character, feedback needs to be shaped and offered in a manner that acknowledges and respects clients' individuality.

3. Feedback is about the behavior, not the person. Especially when feedback highlights problematic behaviors, it is never framed as a personality characterization. Character assessments such as "You just don't seem motivated" are inappropriate and potentially damaging. Imagine an executive who has difficulty making presentations to groups. An effective coach focuses feedback on the behavior rather than, for example, labeling the client as shy. Saying that someone is smart, lazy, kind, or generous represents personality characterizations inferred from behaviors. Instead of generalizing an observation and making it into a personality trait, you want to focus on specific behavior. For example, feedback to the executive with presentation difficulties might sound like, "When you were just speaking, I could barely hear you, and as you were speaking, you were looking up toward the ceiling. I wonder whether my observation has any bearing on how you behave when you are speaking to groups in your organization."

4. Feedback is most effective when the client asks for it or, at a minimum, consents to it. When clients ask for feedback, they are more likely to accept responsibility for what they hear, even though they may not entirely agree with it. Clients may be emotionally unprepared when they are surprised by the delivery of feedback in a session; consequently, they may resist your messages even when they are accurate. Practically speaking, it's not always advisable to await clients' invitations to offer feedback. In some cases, you want to request permission to offer feedback so as to foster positive outcomes. For example, you might say, "I wonder if we can take a few minutes so I can offer you some feedback that seems pertinent to your agenda."

5. Feedback needs to focus on what clients can control. There are things you can change and things you can't. Feedback is more useful when it addresses issues that clients perceive as being under their control—that is, matters that are changeable and relevant to their goals. A man may be able to alter his daily routine, but he cannot change his history. A woman may be able to modify her dietary intake, but she cannot change her genetic composition.

6. Feedback must not imply judgment. When offering feedback, you might sometimes be motivated by a certain disappointment with your client. Indeed, when you invest yourself heavily in your coaching relationships, you might take client behaviors personally. When your emotions become caught up in your feedback, words and nonverbal messages might convey disapproval or rejection. As much as possible, evaluative words, such as good, bad, right, or wrong, need to be avoided. If you find it difficult to contain your feelings and judgments, you may wish to work with a supervisor or mentor who can help you defuse any emotional charge about your client so you can recapture your compassionate and empathic presence.

7. Feedback is best when it is focused and limited in scope. Even with praise, human beings seem to have a limited capacity to absorb feedback effectively. For this reason, organize feedback to address the most critical issues in a timely manner

and offer it in portions that the client can digest. Often, in feedback discussions, one of the parties may try to capitalize on the conversation by broadening the agenda, saying, "Well, since I'm telling you about this, I might as well tell you about that." Alternately, a client receiving your feedback may use this opening to voice unexpressed concerns with you. Making a clear contract for the boundaries of feedback can control reactions that could easily snowball into an all-out defensive argument. In agreeing to a feedback dialogue, you and your client need to delineate terms so you will address only an identified agenda—a specific issue—and thoroughly debrief it. You may acknowledge other topics arising during the feedback and schedule them for a future time.

8. Feedback takes time. Guidelines about having adequate time for feedback generally don't pertain to celebratory moments—giving someone praise usually doesn't take much time. Feedback involving behaviors that seem to be derailing clients from the path of progress will likely take more time. You need to allow time for clients to consider and validate what you are offering and then to respond as they feel appropriate. Normally, your decision to offer feedback should take into account whether sufficient time in the session remains to address client responses.

There are other guidelines that may be pertinent to unique feedback exchanges, but those listed represent some key considerations. Indeed, there are often moments of spontaneous feedback that may represent the coach's sharing of an immediate response of joy or concern. Even in instances where a coach says something like "That represents such an achievement" or "That might be a challenge for you," coaches need to be mindful that their clients will likely hear an evaluative quality to these remarks and, thus, leaving space for client response may be important. We will look into this a bit more in upcoming sections, since these examples may not only represent a kind of feedback but also a form of self-disclosure and direct input.

CHALLENGE

Challenge is thought of as a coaching intervention where discrepancies, distortions, mixed messages, or incongruities are identified and then explored with the client (Cormier et al., 2017; Ivey et al., 2018). Challenge is akin to the skill of confrontation, which may sound harsher because it implies conflict and emotionally charged encounters. Young (2017) views challenge as a broader skill that encompasses both feedback and confrontation, while Cormier and colleagues (2017) look at confrontation and challenge as being interchangeable. Whether certain coaching interventions are described as a confrontation or challenge is less relevant than is the coach's intention, which is to foster greater client awareness in service of positive change. Of course, bringing messages of incongruity or distortion to a client's attention requires sensitivity to the individual's readiness to address these matters. Young correlates the amount of support provided by the helper with the degree of challenge. He suggests that when support is low and challenge high, the client is likely to perceive input as criticism, whereas with strong support and moderate challenge, not only would the coach be perceived as helpful but change is more probable.

Challenge as a coaching skill is likely to differ from a more common interpretation of this term. Being challenged often implies that someone or something is presenting you with a task or experience that requires significant effort. Think of contests or competitions where individuals are challenged to perform against others. One way in which a coaching challenge matches this meaning is in the case where coaches challenge clients positively by noting the discrepancy between their potential and actual behaviors. In so doing, this type of confrontation may motivate clients to perform at higher levels (Gladding, 2013).

Rationale for Challenge

Challenge may be one of the more demanding skills to master in coaching. It is based on keen observation of client communications over time. When important discrepancies or inconsistencies are evident, coaches may choose to use challenge to explore aspects of thinking, emotions, or behaviors that clients might otherwise overlook (Adler & Myerson, 1991). Challenges can build trust rather than breach rapport (James & Gilliland, 2003). Indeed, confronting issues is often necessary to foster progress. Yet, this must be done with care and empathy and in a manner that steers clear of judgment.

Challenge needs to be aligned with the goals of the relationship. Evidence suggests that it can help people "see more clearly what is happening, what the consequences are, and how they can assume responsibility for taking action to change in ways that can lead to a more effective life and better and fairer relationships with others" (Tamminen & Smaby, 1981, p. 42). Failing to confront clients on important issues may impede their success.

Challenge also enables clients to see themselves differently and come to greater self-acceptance (Kottler, 2008; Prochaska & Norcross, 2018). Egan (2014) associates this type of communication with helping people gain greater awareness of blind spots. Clients may be missing certain pieces of information about their behavior or thought processes, and through a challenge they may become more cognizant of their way of being in the world. For example, clients with body-image issues may choose goals based on distorted perceptions of themselves. Other clients may have inaccurate views of their competencies; they may underestimate their abilities and consequently refrain from engaging in potentially rewarding experiences.

A number of theorists consider the identification of discrepancies as paramount in challenge (Chang et al., 2013; Gladding, 2013; Kottler & Shepard, 2015). Clients may show inconsistencies in words and actions; that is, their words may differ either from their actions or from other words they express. Studies of human behavior (Argyris, 1970; Argyris & Schön, 1974) suggest that people tend to be inconsistent partly because of lack of feedback. As described in chapter 7, Argyris and Schön point to discrepancies between what people might believe they do and how they actually behave. According to their perspective, when individuals are well functioning, they respond appropriately to feedback about their inconsistencies. They act in order to bring behaviors in line with their values and beliefs. Coaching relationships are premised on the assumption that people who seek coaching are both able and willing to function in mature, responsible, and healthy ways. Confronting coaching clients with incongruities, discrepancies, distortions, or other forms of inconsistency may seem difficult, but when done skillfully, these challenges will most likely yield positive results.

Practicalities in Challenge

In order to better equip you to apply this skill in your coaching practice, it might help to appreciate the different types of challenges that might be offered by a coach. Once you have this in mind, I will offer some guidelines for applying challenge as a coaching skill.

Types of Challenge

Distortions and incongruities in communication can be seen in the mismatch of one part of a communication with another. Let's examine five types of mixed messages and how they can be addressed through the skill of challenge (Cormier et al., 2017; Egan, 2014; Ivey et al., 2018).

Inconsistencies Between Verbal and Nonverbal Messages   Suppose a client describes certain reactions or feelings, yet nonverbal communications suggest other meanings.

Client example: A client describes his job as challenging and fun, yet the more he talks about it, the more he bites his lips, furrows his brow, and clenches his fists—potential signs of discomfort and anxiety.

Coach's challenge: "You say your job is fun and challenging, yet the more you talk about it, the more I see tightness in your face and your fists clenching."

Inconsistencies Between Two or More Verbal Messages   In this type of mixed message, a client makes one statement at one time and a contradictory statement at another.

Client example: In the first session, the client says that his family totally supports his commitment to a time-consuming project at work, but in the third session, he mentions that his partner has been complaining about the time he spends at work.

Coach's challenge: "When we began our work, I remember you saying that your family totally supported your new work commitment, and now I'm hearing that your partner is complaining about the time you spend at work. Would you be willing to explore this with me?"

Inconsistencies Between What the Client Describes and Circumstances   In the next example, a client expresses certain thoughts, wishes, or aspirations, yet her circumstances represent either insurmountable obstacles or conditions that contradict her words.

Client example: A client who is planning to make a big leap into self-employment says she is going to buy an expensive new car in anticipation of her future success. You know that the job transition will involve at least a temporary reduction in earnings and that she currently worries about her modest savings and lack of discretionary funds.

Coach's challenge: "I hear your excitement about your future and the idea of buying a new car. Based on other things you've said, I am wondering how the new car idea fits into your present financial worry and the projected decline in your earnings as you make this job transition."

Inconsistencies Between Words and Actions

In this scenario, what the client says differs significantly from how he acts.

Client example: A client says he simply doesn't have time to cook the meals he agreed to prepare, yet he keeps talking about all the sports he watches on TV every night.

Coach's challenge: "May I check out something that I've heard? (Pauses for agreement) You just told me that you don't have enough time to prepare the meals you agreed to cook for yourself, yet each day you said you watch about three hours of TV. Can you help me understand how these statements fit together?"

Inconsistencies Between Two or More Nonverbal Messages

Here, the client exhibits two contradictory or opposite nonverbal communications.

Client example: A client laughs loudly while sitting rigidly with hands tensed into fists as he describes getting another rejection letter regarding employment.

Coach's challenge: "I would like to check something with you. I'm hearing you laugh and at the same time clenching your hands as you describe this most recent rejection. Would you help me understand what you are experiencing right now?"

These interventions can be quite sensitive. Coaches need to find the right moment and the right words to bring to awareness relevant discrepancies in clients' behaviors. It's not that coaches are trying to catch clients in moments of incongruity, but rather they are softly shining a light on the kind of tension that their clients may be holding in these self-discrepancies.

Guiding Ideas

Pointing out discrepancies when evidence suggests clients are doing better than they say is likely easier than highlighting discrepancies of the opposite nature. For instance, indicating that a client's progress is much better than she perceives is likely to generate positive feelings and renewed commitment. On the other hand, some of the challenges previously exemplified could generate emotional discomfort. More optimistically, even when challenges address difficult matters, they can awaken clients to new sources of energy.

Young's (2017) correlation of support and the use of challenge bears repeating. Pointing out discrepant behaviors to clients works best when clients feel strongly supported by their coaches. In difficult relationship moments, coaches might want to refrain from offering sensitive challenges. This is more a matter of timing than whether to challenge or not. The identification of key behavioral discrepancies can open the floodgates to positive change. Avoidance of such confrontations may represent a kind of collusion with clients' self-defeating patterns. Coaches need to intervene from a place of compassion when bringing clients from states of confusion into the light.

It's also true that clients are likely to do better when they discover their own inconsistencies than having them identified by their coaches. When they hear themselves verbalizing inconsistent thoughts or feelings, chances are they will become more mindful of their discrepant messages. The active listening skills reviewed in chapter 10 offer nonconfrontational ways of helping clients become aware of incongruities. In many respects, a delicately delivered challenge might sound like a simple reflection of content or a summarizing response, and clients may not even realize they have been confronted. Instead, they get to discover, through the coach's paraphrasing, their self-contradictions.

SELF-DISCLOSURE

Research tells us that transparency and authentic behavior are linked to positive well-being and health (Kernis & Goldman, 2005; Palmer, 2000; Sheldon & Kasser, 1995). Such behaviors involve showing up in a genuine way, unafraid to be seen for who we are (Rogers, 1961). In coaching, it may come down to this: clients need to experience their coaches as real people in order to fully engage the relationship (Raines, 1996). For this to occur, a certain degree of **self-disclosure** can be invaluable. Clients are likely to feel a greater sense of hope and connection through shared experiences that self-disclosures reveal, yet self-disclosure can represent a double-edged sword (Henretty & Levitt, 2010).

Rationale for Self-Disclosure

What information can you share as a coach? What wouldn't you talk about? More generally, why would you say anything about yourself during coaching sessions? These are complicated questions. Generally speaking, literature tells us that clients are likely to perceive self-disclosing helpers as more caring than those who disclose little (Capuzzi & Gross, 2017). Yet, the complexity of knowing what and how helpers might self-disclose was recently highlighted in a study of therapists (Levitt et al., 2016). One implication of this study is that when helpers self-disclose their personal appreciation for their clients, it may not be as effective as when they say and do things that humanize them—that is, make the helpers seem less perfect or idealized. Also, clients seem to be more appreciative of moments when helpers express ways in which they are similar to their clients more so than how they might be different. Overall, this well-done study underscores the fact that engaging in self-disclosure as a professional helper can be quite tricky in terms of its impact.

Johnson (2014) provides a useful analysis of self-disclosure within an interpersonal, nonprofessional context. He defines it as "revealing to another person how you perceive and are reacting to the present situation and giving any information about yourself and your past that is relevant to an understanding of your perceptions and reactions to the present" (p. 48). This definition of self-disclosure reveals how it can be supportive in interpersonal relationships. Johnson emphasizes that to be most beneficial, self-disclosure should be structured to (1) focus on present reality rather than history; (2) include references to feelings as well as facts; (3) cover a wide range of topics; (4) have depth in terms of personal revelations, and (5) be reciprocal, especially in the formative stages of a relationship.

These specifications for appropriate self-disclosure in everyday life stand in sharp contrast to the emerging wisdom about self-disclosure as a skill in professional helping relationships. For the most part, self-disclosure in a professional context refers to "a conscious, intentional technique by which the helper strategically shares personal information in order to achieve a specific benefit to the relationship or for the client" (Simone et al., 1998, p. 174). Coaching differs from psychotherapy by taking a more favorable view of self-disclosure, partly due to the nature of coaching work as a partnered experience as well as the belief that coaching clients are resilient (Biswas-Diener, 2009; Kimsey-House et al., 2018; Martin, 2001; Williams & Davis, 2007).

Regardless of its benefits, using self-disclosure in any professional relationship requires a high degree of self-awareness. Coaches need to understand their own needs and issues and how these might pertain to the client in the moment. Effective self-disclosure also relies on a strong sense of self-acceptance. Coaches who risk exposing their vulnerabilities need to have accepted their own behaviors and imperfections, particularly as they might be portrayed in the stories they tell. Coaches who expect acceptance or approval for their self-disclosures might react poorly when clients respond with indifference or negativity.

Practicalities in Self-Disclosure

Earlier, you had an opportunity to consider the relevance of a social constructionist's perspective to coaching, wherein coach and client work collaboratively in sharing ideas and possibilities toward the generation of a better future. In a collaborative, partnered experience, coaches need to be transparent and authentic, and this means sharing some aspects of your own thoughts, feelings, and experiences. Let's look at some types of self-disclosure relevant to coaching and then consider guidelines for intervening through self-disclosure.

Types of Self-Disclosure

Not all self-disclosures carry the same weight or meaning. Four types of self-disclosure seem relevant to coaching relationships. They include disclosures of professional information, disclosures of personal information, content-congruent self-disclosures, and thematic stories.

Professional Information   Clients need to know that their coaches are qualified to provide the services for which they have been hired. It is therefore necessary for coaches to disclose the nature of their training and credentialing. This information can be shared in a straightforward manner, perhaps through a brief professional résumé or on a website.

Personal Information   Different cultures have their own norms about sharing information (Pedersen et al., 2008). In some cultures, it is deemed inappropriate to expect professionals to reveal personal information such as age, relationship status, or number of children. However, inquiries about some of these details may be quite normal in other cultural contexts. In this light, coaches need to be aware of the potential meanings that sharing information may have for clients. Individuals inquiring about a coach's age may be asking, in an indirect manner, whether they can trust the coach because they might equate age with wisdom.

Content-Congruent Self-Disclosures   Think of social conversations in which a person uses some aspect of the speaker's remarks to launch into her or his own story. People share stories and disclose personal information to pass time and establish a sense of commonality. For instance, upon hearing about someone's recent travels, you decide to describe your recent travel adventures. However, when coaches tell stories having similar content to those related by their clients, they would need a credible reason for chiming in. Such sharing would ideally serve a strategic purpose of enhancing clients' capacities, fostering their goal attainment, or building trust and safety. For example, if a client is struggling in a new job, the coach might mention she or he also had difficulties in the first months of a job transition, and the coach might further describe actions that were helpful.

Thematic Stories   Embedded in each story is a theme—one of victory or defeat, hope or despair, love or loss. Coaches are unlikely to always have stories with content that corresponds well to their clients' stories, yet they may have had experiences with similar themes. For instance, if someone tells a story about being discouraged and not being able to find the resolve to overcome obstacles, the coach may choose to speak about a personal experience containing the same themes or dynamic to help the client in the process. Usually, when telling this kind of story, the coach would want to have her or his story conclude with a hopeful resolution; that is, coaches will avoid sharing stories that end up in the same puddles as those of their clients. The strategic part here is to connect through the theme of the story and then offer a ray of inspiration or a useful perspective through a relevant self-disclosure.

Guiding Ideas

Why would you share your story? As a coach, you need to have a solid reason for bringing your personal experience into the dialogue. What is your intention in doing so and what do you hope the effect will be? Your personal experience might be shared as a means of instilling hope or clarity or perhaps as a way of encouraging your client to develop new perspectives about certain dilemmas (Egan, 2014). Your intention would not be to show identification by matching experiences or to counter clients' perspectives.

Here are some questions that offer cautionary guidance about whether it might be helpful to share parts of your story (Simone et al., 1998):

- Will your sharing diminish the significance of your client's experiences?
- Will the act of your sharing reduce the amount of attention your client experiences?
- Will the boundaries of your coaching relationship remain intact?
- If your story depicts your vulnerability, might this cause your client some concern?
- Will your client perceive you as less capable because of your self-disclosure?

When you decide to tell a story about yourself, you might want to be succinct and to the point. Lengthy storytelling can take focus away from the client's desires and intentions for the session. As brief as you are, you still want to model transparency and authenticity in how you reveal your own experience. By being vulnerable, you allow clients to experience your humanity and thereby foster greater openness on their part.

IMMEDIACY

Imagine a sticky issue arising in the middle of a conversation that might feel akin to trying to dance with glue on your shoes. These kinds of moments happen in coaching where something begs to be focused on immediately! If you sense something is sufficiently important, it's best if you address it. Importance is gauged by the degree to which the issue has clear relevance to either the client's topic or the coaching relationship. When coaches step into this kind of process, they will most likely be employing the skill of **immediacy**.

Immediacy is based in the coach's sensitivity to the present situation within the relationship; sometimes it is described as relationship immediacy (Young, 2017). Immediacy is thought of as an important skill, as well as a means of strengthening helping relationships (Shebib, 2020). Immediacy requires perception of what is happening in the moment and willingness to explore the here and now openly and directly. Immediacy may also involve expressions of the coach's desires, needs, or wants in the moment (Hargie, 2017).

Rationale for Immediacy

Immediacy often relies on core skills of challenge, feedback, and self-disclosure, but what merits its separate consideration is that immediacy is about addressing something arising in the present moment. Immediacy may be more complex because it often requires that you as the coach discuss your own feelings and reactions (Capuzzi & Gross, 2017; Turock, 1980). It derives from a pervasive moment-by-moment awareness of the subtle shifts and communications during coaching sessions. That is, you see or feel something in the moment and then comment on it. Immediacy calls for transparency;

the client is likely to feel seen, and you will also be quite visible. In these perspectives, it is thought of as one of the most difficult and demanding helping skills (Egan, 2014).

Immediacy isn't always about major moments in coaching. Sometimes, an intervention involving the skill of immediacy reflects something simple and direct. Here are a few examples of immediacy interventions by a coach:

- I am so happy to see you right now!
- I heard that deep sigh. It makes me so curious to know what just happened!
- I, too, feel excited about all your great results!

Associating immediacy with any particular stage of coaching is difficult because it may be applied at various points depending on what needs to occur to foster client trust and progress. Immediacy is positioned as a tool for exploring, evaluating, and deepening the relationship (Shebib, 2020). It represents a form of direct communication because it derives from the coach's perceptions rather than representing a reflection of the client's expressions. Potentially, it can also be a way of creating awareness (see chapter 13) since bringing what seems so obvious in the moment to a client's attention may be a kind of wake-up call.

Practicalities in Immediacy

There are different types of immediacy that you might want to understand. I will cover these before describing guidelines for this kind of intervention.

Types of Immediacy

Immediacy is always about what is happening right here, right now with the coach, with the client, or in the relationship (Cormier et al., 2017; Evans et al., 2017; Gladding, 2013). It might occur when coaches consciously choose to express their own thoughts and feelings. Another instance might be when coaches direct comments to something related to the client that's happening in the present moment. A third occurrence might emerge when something pops up in the relationship that provokes an immediate response.

Coach-Centered Immediacy   Immediacy can be heard whenever coaches express their immediate thoughts or feelings in the exact moment when they occur. Expressions of this nature may range from simple statements of welcome, such as, "I'm happy to see you," to admissions of personal feelings, like, "I'm flattered by your feedback." Deeper expres-

sions might sound like, "I'm feeling concerned" or "I'm feeling a bit off today." Though these examples of immediacy pertain to the coach, the comment is always intended to serve the goals of the coaching relationship. You might notice how these also resemble examples of self-disclosure.

Client-Centered Immediacy   A second form of immediacy is akin to giving feedback. It involves sharing your perceptions about your client as they occur in the moment. Here, immediacy may serve multiple purposes, including increasing client self-awareness, acknowledging the client, or pursuing an issue. A coach, noticing nonverbal signals, may say to a client, "Seems like you're struggling to understand what I'm saying." Or, when a coach detects a certain discomfort, an immediate response might be, "I sense in this moment you're upset with yourself." You may notice that in these examples, the coach's inner world becomes visible since the coach's words describe a degree of interpretation.

Relationship-Centered Immediacy   A third form of immediacy addresses the relationship itself. What is the climate of the working relationship? How well are coach and client functioning together? Shebib (2020) writes about relationship immediacy as a way of focusing on how the relationship is developing. Coaches can use immediacy to explore both their own and their clients' feelings, hopes, or annoyances as a way of assessing the strengths and needs of the relationship. Relationship immediacy might be called for when difficult feelings and resistance to coaching are adversely affecting progress. With a here-and-now focus, this kind of intervention arises quite spontaneously. Imagine a woman who tells you her friends complain that she is always distracted and listens poorly. As the coach, you had just described something to the client, but she continued speaking as if you had said nothing. Relationship-centered immediacy might sound like this: "You've been saying your friends complain about your lack of listening; I believe that I just experienced that with you. I said something and got no response. Would you be open to talking about this?"

One way to distinguish immediacy interventions from other forms of direct communication can be found in the purpose of the intervention. When the intent is to focus on the relationship per se, it is more likely that you will use immediacy. A client says something, and you respond quite spontaneously with something you feel deeply. As the coach, you are not trying to represent your remarks as a reflection; rather, you own them fully as your own. You are showing up with your own humanity, with your own needs and worldview. Although your intention as a coach is always to serve the goals of the relationship, sometimes the way you might do that is by acknowledging your own experiences in the moment.

Guiding Ideas

The effective use of immediacy relies on the relational foundation of trust and safety. It also depends on the quality of your presence in the moment. Immediacy arises from an awareness that something is happening in the relationship that pertains to the coaching agenda. This speaks to the importance of cultivating your self-awareness through personal practices, which might include mindfulness meditation, dedicated periods for self-reflection, and ongoing coaching supervision. These kinds of practices lessen the chances that you might project your own issues on clients or use the relationship to meet your own needs.

Immediacy is applied when you as coach can clearly see the value of this type of intervention for the client. What is your intention of using immediacy in this moment? Sometimes your own feelings in sessions need to remain private. It's also true that many relationship dynamics can be irrelevant to a particular coaching agenda at a particular time. Finally, even when clients may seem reactive to aspects of the dialogue, you don't need to call attention to all of these moments.

Immediacy interventions in coaching may feel quite gratifying to both coach and client, and this may represent an area of risk. Engaging in here-and-now dialogue about how you are feeling, how your client is feeling, and how the two of you are working together may be satisfying, but do these conversational elements serve the purposes of coaching? You might want to reflect on whether you feel drawn to these kinds of interventions or whether you tend to avoid them even when they might be relevant.

DIRECT INPUT

Sometimes coaches may choose to offer their clients particular kinds of information. Coaches may want to instruct their clients, for example, in certain relaxation or centering processes. Occasionally, clients may wish to solicit their coaches' advice or suggestions on topics of interest. From my experience, these kinds of moments are relatively common in coaching. They are grouped under the heading of **direct input** in that they all involve interventions where coaches offer methods, data, or perspectives based on their education, training, professional practice, and life experience.

The act of informing, instructing, or advising clients is at least partly based on the idea that the coach actually knows or is presumed to know something that could be useful to the client. This fits with the construct of authentic communication (Cox, 2013), which I reviewed in chapter 10. If coaches have information, why wouldn't they share it? Isn't this what partnering implies? Maybe you are thinking, "Yes, but I didn't think coaching was about telling clients what to do. Clients need to figure things out for themselves." Well, yes and no.

Sometimes, it saves a lot of effort offering a piece of information or instructing a client to do a simple breathing exercise or providing a suggestion. This is pretty harmless, don't you think? Hopefully, you said, "maybe." Imagine scenarios where you might offer clients information, instruction, or advice. What would allow you to feel okay about informing, instructing, or advising a client? On the flip side, what might create the conditions under which your clients would ask you to do these kinds of things, as well as considering you to have credible expertise?

If we refer to the discussion in chapter 7 of Argyris and Schön's (1974) value models that guide action, you will remember that in matters of interpersonal influence, you want certain conditions to prevail. In a coaching context, you want the client to be able to validate the information offered, to experience informed and free choice in accepting and applying that information, and to feel a sense of internal commitment about whatever they do with what is offered. So, these probably represent necessary conditions for coaches who intervene in this manner. But are they enough? Do they provide sufficient rationale for coaches to give advice, offer information, or instruct their clients?

You already know that coaching represents a collaboration between coach and client in service of the client's agenda. How might interventions of providing information, instruction, and advice shift the degree to which clients see themselves as capable and autonomous? Coaches work to empower clients or, more precisely, to have them become more self-reliant and autonomous agents of change in their own lives. If a pattern emerges in a coaching relationship where a client continually relies on the coach for answers, advice, or instruction, at what point does this relationship stop being coaching and shift into something more like mentoring, consulting, or teaching?

There is no simple answer to the questions I just raised. Different coaches and different schools of coaching will take widely varying positions on the matter of direct input. Some will say you should almost never engage in direct input around the coaching topic, while others will say as long as you adhere to principles such as those suggested by Argyris and Schön (1974), you can judiciously provide these kinds of interventions in a coaching context. This brief review has hopefully primed you for consideration of the different types of direct input that coaches might offer in coaching sessions.

Instruction

Instruction may look like teaching a client how to do something or guiding them through an experience, such as imagining a more desirable future state. Normally, coaches would request permission for engaging in such instructional moments within a coaching session. Another way in which instruction shows up in coaching is in brief interventions. Coaches may indicate to clients what to do at particular moments in the dialogue in terms of ways of thinking, feeling, or acting (Evans et al., 2017; Ivey et al., 2018). Consider the simplicity of these instructional interventions by coaches:

Instructions Related to Thoughts

- Think about it this way: . . .
- Focus your mind on your breath.
- Imagine your boss as someone who wants you to excel.

Instructions Related to Feelings

- Feel what's happening inside your body right now.
- Sense the energy in your center radiating out through your arms and legs.
- Smile inwardly just as you are about to speak.

Instructions Related to Action

- Please say that again.
- Write this down.
- Sit comfortably in your chair.

Hopefully, these examples normalize the idea of instructions in coaching. I would imagine you can think of scenarios where such instructions would seamlessly enter a coaching dialogue. Even though these kinds of interventions have a place in coaching, concern arises regarding the way in which these instructions might be delivered and regarding their frequency!

Some conditions for using more extended instructional interventions, such as guided imagery or a role-playing exercise, are as follows (Shebib, 2020; Young, 2017):

- You have expert knowledge or training specifically related to the client's agenda.
- You have extensive experience in assisting clients with the approach you are using.
- You are aware of the limitations of the approach and advise your client about potential benefits and liabilities.
- You have adequate understanding of the client's background, needs, capabilities, and limitations.
- You are able to adapt instructions to fit the client and the circumstances.

These are likely to sound like commonsensical guidelines, yet when coaches in their lifelong quest for personal and professional development learn exciting new techniques in workshops and seminars, they may want to try them out without sufficient appreciation of potential ramifications.

Information

Offering information usually means providing data that you believe can help clients better pursue their goals (Young, 2017). Information might include ideas about how to accomplish something or to challenge problematic understandings. As a general guideline, information would be offered sparingly since too much information might shift the nature of the relationship from coaching to something more like consulting or mentoring.

Providing information can be a crucial intervention when coaches perceive that clients are potentially putting themselves at risk out of ignorance or misunderstanding. Conveying information takes a multitude of forms, from verbal descriptions to recommending readings, podcasts, videos, or websites. Offering clients information is largely appropriate when it relates to their goals and their overall well-being. Coaches can assess the appropriateness of this kind of intervention by answering three questions (Young, 2017): (1) What does the client need to know? (2) When does the client need this information? and (3) What's the best way of finding or delivering this information to achieve optimal results?

Information is seldom unbiased or value free. When you inform your clients about options or activities, you are typically presenting your own knowledge about a topic or referring them to resources you know. It's unlikely you have fully scoped the available information on an issue, yet you would likely strive to be representative in what you offer. The more diverse your clientele is, the more attention you will have to pay to your clients' unique backgrounds, capabilities, limitations, values, needs, and interests. Especially when you might present information as a way of influencing clients' thoughts and actions, you will need to be vigilant about the sources of your data, as well as their accuracy and credibility.

Advice

Of the three forms of direct input, giving advice or suggestions is the most problematic and likely the most widely used (Brammer & MacDonald, 2003; Young, 2017). In relationships with friends and family, advice is one of the most common responses that people offer each other (Johnson, 2014).

Cultural differences may affect the degree to which clients solicit or accept advice from coaches based on a presumption that they are apparent experts (Corey, 2017; Corey et al., 2014). Novice coaches may be especially vulnerable to the expectation that when requested, they should offer their clients advice. Yet, as Kleinke (1994) notes about giving advice in therapy, "Clients can get all the advice they want from acquaintances, friends, and family members" (p. 9). An even stronger admonition about advice giving suggests that coaches who offer advice may be motivated by a need to bolster their authority more so than supporting their clients' own inner wisdom and self-determination (Steele, 2011).

Coaching is about supporting clients in generating alternatives for themselves, choosing among alternatives, and pursuing their choices. The bottom line seems to be that coaches need to focus more on helping clients think and decide than on providing them with answers. The question then becomes this: In which circumstances would giving advice be appropriate? Guidance from arguments in the broader helping professions (Brammer & Mac-Donald, 2003; Shebib, 2020; Young, 2017) indicate that coaches might be on solid ground in offering clients advice when one or more of the following conditions applies:

- Clients seem largely unaware of problematic implications of their actions.

- Clients may be at risk of harm or injury.
- Clients may not know about or might have overlooked critical elements.
- Suggestions derive from extensive experience, knowledge, research, or valid data.
- Advice pertains to strategies for dealing with issues rather than solutions.
- Suggestions relate to valid communication processes pertaining to the topic.

When clients ask for advice, it might make sense to turn the request back to them. You might say, "What advice would you give yourself in this situation?"

Practicalities in Direct Input

Why does your client need your input in this moment? Though you may optimistically believe that clients have all the resources they need to resolve their own difficulties (Kimsey-House et al., 2018; Martin, 2001; Williams & Davis, 2007), it's possible clients don't have the necessary information or the requisite skills. They may also lack confidence in their own solutions and, as a result, want to rely on your input to strengthen their conclusions. Even though interventions of this nature may be a last resort, you will encounter many situations where it is appropriate to provide instruction and information; other times, the use of feedback, challenge, or immediacy might be more beneficial.

Some creative alternatives to direct input that might draw out the client's inherent wisdom include questions such as the following:

- How do you think you might approach this situation?
- What do you think your options are?
- What resources come to mind when you think about this matter?
- What would your best friend tell you?
- What advice would you expect me to give you?

The dilemma for coaches comes down to the question of how to maintain a sense of equality and collaboration in the relationship while freely offering input at appropriate moments in the session. Navigating this dilemma requires ongoing awareness of the nature and quality of your relationship with your client and reflection about your own needs and rationale for providing answers and input. As a coach, you want to have voice, but you don't want that voice to diminish your client's involvement. You also want to be mindful of the reality that when your input is guiding client action, whose ideas will your clients be testing? Maybe they will have internalized a sense of commitment to plans informed by your advice, but will they feel the same degree of ownership and responsibility as when their ideas and plans are self-determined?

DIRECT COMMUNICATION IN THE ICF CORE COMPETENCIES

In the previous chapter, we looked at this competency from the angle of inquiry. Here, we want to see how it relates to material described in this chapter concerning direct communication. Elements of this newly revised ICF competency include challenging clients, noticing what is occurring in the relationship, adjusting the coaching process in response to client needs, and sharing perceptions and observations. You might notice how these elements relate to such skills as giving feedback, challenge, self-disclosure, direct input, and immediacy. When coaches share observations, insights, and feelings, they may self-disclose or provide facets of direct input in the form of information or suggestions. They may evoke awareness by challenging clients to reconcile an apparent dissonance in things they have expressed verbally or nonverbally. When they notice what is working, there is an aspect of feedback as well as immediacy in communication. In the ICF's previous 11 core competencies model, direct communication spoke more explicitly about feedback while presently the model seems to reference it in more indirect ways. Yet we can still imagine how feedback is critical to evoking awareness in clients.

It is also noteworthy that explicit reference to providing instruction, information, or advice in coaching sessions seems mostly absent from this competency. What might be inferred? Though my research (Gavin et al., 2021) clearly shows that coaches employ these kinds of interventions, it makes sense that the ICF would not highlight these methods as dominant modes of intervention in coaching. In terms of competency development, do coaches need to learn how to give advice and instruct people? It's more likely that they need to learn how to work as thoroughly as possible without a telling or informing style of intervention. Build-

ing client autonomy relies on a coaching approach that continually accesses the inherent wisdom of our clients, rather than demonstrating our own knowledge and expertise.

REFLECTIONS

By this time, I hope you are accruing significant awareness of different coaching interventions that, in their manner of delivery, share common principles of promoting collaboration, self-reliance, and self-determination. You likely know that these interventions rely on extensive training, experience, and self-awareness.

There are multiple elements of a coach's makeup that are implicated in interventions based on direct communication. They concern your current level of self-esteem that can be at stake in presenting your own ideas to clients who may or may not be receptive. Secondly, values come into play as you clarify whether your motivation to offer input is based solidly in an intention to serve the relationship rather than something more personally motivated. A third and no doubt essential element is your capacity to be appropriately assertive in bringing forth potentially sensitive matters. It takes courage to confront relationship dynamics or aspects of clients' stories. Being assertive implies a certain equanimity in how interventions are made. You don't need to force awareness. Your purpose isn't to open clients' eyes to the truth. Assertiveness is about bringing forth what needs to be said in a manner that is likely to be heard and received positively—without attachment. It is not shying away from saying difficult things or saying them with such ambiguity that client benefit is diminished.

I know that the approaches reviewed in this chapter become more natural and effective through ongoing practice and reflection on your coaching experiences. What strikes me from my work in developing competencies in new coaches is how deeply ingrained our tendencies to be directive and to offer advice and information can be. We don't always know we are being directive. You may have a client who says in a follow-up session, "That was great advice you gave me a couple weeks ago." Scratching your head, you struggle to recall whether you ever gave this client advice. This is another reason why, as much as possible, I would advocate that you regularly record and listen to your sessions.

CHAPTER 13
STIMULATING NEW PERSPECTIVES

*The human spirit lives on creativity
and dies in conformity and routine.*

Vilayat Inayat Khan

MY STORY

As far back as I can remember, I wanted to write. Earlier in life, I thought about writing novels—but I ended up writing a whole lot of research monographs based on various personal growth and psychological ideas. I've written a number of books, but sometimes I don't see this as the kind of writing I imagined as a young man. I dabble in poetry, and that gets a bit closer. What I have come to realize over time is that I love the creativity I experience in my own and others' writings. I think of myself as a slow reader, partly for this reason. I can dwell on a sentence for a long time, feeling it and living the reality it expresses as best I can. These are amazing moments. I've had periods of immersion in different genres of literature and popular writings. No matter what I read, I find myself at times hypnotized by a phrase or a sentence.

The secret I have only recently let myself in on is that I do this with the spoken word as well. I listen to people, and I am spellbound. I have to tell you this simple story: A client expressed a dilemma she was experiencing in a metaphor; she said, "It's like being a kid in a candy store and you can have anything you want—but you can only have *one* thing." It was a powerful image thanks to her tonality, emotionality, and the history of this story. I immediately saw that kid. I saw all the candy. I could feel her wanting almost everything. The clock was ticking. Her father's hand was going to tug her toward the cashier with or without candy in hand. She simply couldn't decide. Then, I heard my client say, "So, I left the store without getting any candy." My heart ached.

Coaches intervene at times to stimulate insight and deepen awareness of matters related to the coaching agenda. While coaching is premised on the belief that it is best that clients discover answers for themselves, coaches need to have ways of fostering learning and creativity. Inquiry processes are key to evoking awareness, although at times clients will derive significant value when coaches offer interpretations, metaphors, or a reframing of the way they see their realities. These are other representations of the coach's voice. As powerful as these methods can be, coaches are cautioned to be judicious in the ways they might foster insight and awareness in their coaching approach. Here are some guiding questions as you read:

- How do you know where best to direct your explorations?
- Are there frameworks for exploration?
- How might you help clients appreciate their motivations?
- Should you ever interpret what clients are saying?
- How can you create useful metaphors for clients?
- Does a reframing always depict a better reality?

AWAKENING

You no doubt know the expression, "Ignorance is bliss!" It makes sense sometimes, and other times not so much. For the most part, clients need new perspectives to achieve their goals. Coaching fully embraces the centrality of generating insight and awareness in the service of personal and professional change. Coaching processes create learning cycles where clients experiment with new behaviors and ways of engaging their worlds and then reflect on what they have learned (see David Kolb's four-stage process of experiential learning in chapter 2). Rather than puzzle interminably over what to do, they are encouraged to make changes. Changes at the outset may be limited to small steps from which clients can learn and then plan their next move.

Coaching is less focused on the retelling of old stories than on creating new stories from which awareness and action can grow (Drake, 2018). It's true that some clients come to coaching with clear goals and a beginning sketch of the path forward. In such cases, the coach's work might largely be to sharpen the focus on objectives and then through a structured goal-setting approach to help clients design action processes. More likely scenarios are ones where clients have a desired destination and rather than an identifiable path forward, they might have a history of routes they have taken that haven't worked out particularly well (Hargrove, 2008). Some kind of awakening may be required.

You personally have vast amounts of information about yourself. Even with your awareness, you may have blind spots as well as parts of your story that you generally keep private. Moreover, you may have certain misconceptions about yourself or things that you believe but which others see differently. How much you are willing to share your story will depend on a number of factors, including the reasons you are telling your story, your relationship with the listener, how private you are, as well as your capacity to fully identify your thoughts, internal states, and processes.

One way of representing what I have just described can be seen in a simple yet enduring model of the interrelationships of self-disclosure, feedback, and self-awareness. Joe Luft and Harry Ingham (Luft, 1969) described an awareness matrix known as the **Johari window** (Get it? Joe and Harry?). It can help frame clients' self-knowledge and identify areas they may want to explore (see table 13.1). Let's take a closer look at the four quadrants of this matrix.

Table 13.1   The Johari Window: An Awareness Model for Coaching

	What I know	**What I don't know**
Others know	**Public self** What I know about myself and am willing to make public	**Blind spot** What I don't know about myself but others know about me
Others don't know	**Private self** What I choose to keep private and others don't know	**Unconscious self** What I and others don't know about me

Adapted from Luft (1969).

Public Self

What clients share with their coaches is part of the public self. They may not discuss this information with everyone, but by describing it to their coaches, they make these aspects of themselves public. Coaches may use all forms of active listening, questioning, and other skills to broaden the dimensions of this quadrant of awareness for clients.

Private Self

This area represents self-knowledge that clients have not yet disclosed. Because they need to share only what is necessary to assist coaches in their collaborative efforts, large areas of their lives may remain private. Coaches may inquire about personal matters they deem important. However, if clients hold back, chances of success diminish proportionately to the importance of the information to their stated agenda. If, for instance, a man is considering new career options but doesn't tell the coach that he has difficulty working in teams, much time may be wasted considering possibilities that ultimately the client will reject. Sometimes the deliberate withholding of pertinent information can undermine the viability of the coaching process.

Blind Self

You sometimes see things in others that they don't see in themselves. This is called the blind spot—you and others may know it, but the person in question doesn't. In the coaching process, the task is to help clients become aware of relevant aspects of themselves that may show up in their actions or unconscious communications. Curiously, it's not always helpful to disclose this information. Timing is critical, as is a regard for the legitimate agenda of the relationship. If the information is pertinent to the coaching process, then, at an appropriate time, the coach may sensitively communicate what he or she has observed. When the information is irrelevant to the coaching agenda, it may well be left unsaid.

Unconscious Self

Much of the early work in psychoanalytic theory (Freud, 1949) was premised on the belief that we all have significant areas of unconscious experience, and this information remains virtually unknown to us or to anyone else until pivotal events surface previously hidden material. *This unconscious domain is never the focus of direct intervention in coaching.*

As a rule, coaches do not deliberately attempt to unveil aspects of clients' unconscious. This does not mean, however, that the person's unconscious self is irrelevant to coaching. I think that the more individuals work on themselves, the more they come to understand some of the unknown reasons they strive for certain things and avoid others. I believe it's quite likely that transformational coaching agendas will awaken in clients' sources of motivation in their lives that have heretofore gone unrecognized or which, in their shrouded presence, drove them toward goals they didn't inherently desire. Not all coaching has a transformational agenda, but even so you might be mindful of how embedded patterns of behavior in your clients tend to persist in spite of negative outcomes. When you keep bumping up against this kind of experience with a client, it may well be that there is a deeper issue that needs to be explored, and this might entail referring your client to someone qualified to do deeper work.

Before concluding this review of the Johari window (Luft, 1969), here are a few practical implications for applying this model in your own coaching practice:

- When critical knowledge for coaching resides in the client's blind self, coaches might help generate awareness of this information in a sensitive manner that promotes trust and safety.

- Should the client be withholding pertinent information (private self), coaches might create comfort and safety for the client to discuss these matters.

- When the client continually deviates into commentaries about life issues that evidence no clear relationship to the coaching agenda (public self), coaches might help clients either clarify the relevance of these disclosures or engage in discussion about the coaching agreement and the boundaries of coaching conversations.

- Should problematic patterns occur or if troubling memories are triggered in the coaching dialogue (unconscious self), coaches might sensitively acknowledge these occurrences and open a conversation about a possible referral to professionals more qualified to constructively manage these experiences.

Some methods are more potent than others for creating awareness. Even so, the fact remains that people sometimes gain insights simply by telling their stories to an attentive and concerned coach.

The kinds of interventions that coaches employ offer multiple lenses through which clients can explore their stories. Each lens may foster awareness by helping clients appreciate experiences through a novel perspective. Coaches may focus clients' attention on particular aspects of life events, they may search for deeper meaning, they may reframe how clients experience things, or they may offer various kinds of interpretations and imagery. Let's explore these well-tested ways of creating awareness: focusing; reflection of meaning; and interpretation, metaphors, and reframing.

FOCUSING

A classic interpretation of **focusing** derives from the work of Eugene Gendlin (1981) who represented it as a type of awareness enhancement. In his view, focusing encourages clients to direct their attention toward a specific theme or, at times, on their felt experience, almost as a meditative act. However, the perspective of focusing represented in this chapter derives more from the work of Jean Baker Miller (Baker Miller, 1991; Baker Miller & Stiver, 1997). Applying her approach, coaches take a variety of angles for listening and responding to clients' stories. Let's examine a hypothetical expression by a client that you have coached for the last two years. See how many different angles for exploration you are aware of in this story. The client is a young entrepreneur who has come through a four-year process of building and selling a software development company and is now looking for his next step.

> *Ben's story:* You know what a grueling gauntlet the last six months have been for me. I thought I would never have a good night's sleep again. I'm really struggling with the question of what to do next, but I'm not even sure if I've recovered enough to throw myself back into the game. My partner wants to start a family, I want to travel the world, and a bunch of my investors are pushing for me to find another business for them. I know these are my prime years, so I don't want to waste time, and yet, I'm having doubts about why I'm driving myself so hard. Isn't there more to life than making money? And the family agenda has been pushed off once too often. I keep making excuses. I'm scared, and I don't know how to talk to my partner about it. I really don't know if my 24/7, type A workaholic lifestyle is really compatible with having a family. I really need to think all this stuff through, but there's

this clock in my head and it keeps telling me to stop wasting time and do something. Get back in! Find a company! Build it! Meanwhile, I think back to when my father died—he was only 42. Massive heart attack. I'm turning 33 next year. What do I really want to do with my life?

You could respond to this client with a comprehensive reflection encompassing all elements of his message, yet if you had been working with this person for a while, you might have a hunch about the most productive lead to follow. What areas of focus jump out of this story for you?

Maybe you heard something about life purpose. You may have also been aware of some ambivalence about family, a need for a time-out, emotional wear and tear, pressure from external sources, internal pressure, self-definitions, and possibly others. What would give you reason to prefer one focus over another? Your experience with this client likely informs you of where there is fertile ground for exploration. It's unlikely that with a long-term client, any of these issues would represent new material.

Focusing is one path to creating awareness in that it acknowledges the multiple lenses through which clients can reexamine their stories. It opens avenues for exploration that might not be at the forefront of their minds. It brings under the microscope key elements for generating insight and directions for growth.

Identifying Areas of Focus

One way to think about relevant areas of focus comes from the perspective that clients often need to develop new skills, capacities, and perspectives in order to attain their objectives. The goal of coaching is rarely a static event or a solitary achievement like winning a race or getting a job. More likely, it represents an enhanced or even different way of being in the world. To show up differently, clients may need to develop new competencies and to thoroughly shift their perspectives so their behavior can be informed by new kinds of input.

When you listen to clients' stories, you hear different categories of things. You may hear things about their personal and professional relationships; their emotionality; what they do and don't know; their beliefs, values, and morals; whether and how they nurture themselves; and other facets of their experience. How aware is Ben of different career options? Does he take good care of his health? Does he nourish transparency in his relationships? Does he know his values? Can he competently manage his emotionality? What's his skill set—what does he do well and what does he need to learn?

To help identify relevant areas of focus, I want to borrow from the seminal work of Howard Gardner (1983, 2006) on multiple intelligences. Gardner originally described six areas of human intelligence. Later theorists expanded these areas into other frameworks (Armstrong, 2003; Cook-Greuter, 2000; Ellison, 2001; Wilber, 2000b). Given that coaching is more about development than a static interpretation of intelligence, I would suggest a slight shift in language here, substituting the term *competency* for that of *intelligence* because it denotes a course of development more readily than does the construct of intelligence, which might suggest something fixed or a function of our DNA.

In the world of coaching, competency development can be seen quite clearly in the integral coaching approach of Joanne Hunt (2009a) and Laura Divine (2009a), which articulates a philosophy and methodology for addressing the wholeness of clients. Sourced from the work of Ken Wilber (2000a) and his integral theory, Hunt and Divine propose that the clients' agendas be framed in the complex nature of who clients are and their ways of being in the world. Within this framework, clients' agendas are viewed through multiple lenses of knowledge, relationships, emotions, morality, and values, among other elements.

When considering where you might want to inspire greater awareness through a process of focusing, a finite set of lenses or areas of focus can be beneficial. In service of client growth and development, these lenses would hopefully shed light on what capacities clients already have and which ones they might want to develop. Referring to the brief description of Ben's agenda, it's unlikely that you have enough information to gauge his competencies, although you should have some information about what needs to be explored.

Focus on Six Competencies

Building from the work in integral theory (Wilber, 2000a) and integral coaching (Hunt, 2009a), I want to suggest six areas of focus when exploring client stories for pathways to growth and development. Each focus represents a potential area for competency development that may be pertinent to what clients need in order to remold their ways of thinking, behaving, feeling, valuing, and being with others. In combination, these areas of focus represent a holistic perspective of clients and their needs; the areas are labeled as follows: general knowledge competency, self-knowledge competency, emotional competency, somatic competency, interpersonal competency, and moral competency.

General Knowledge Competency

What do clients know about the issues related to their agendas? This knowledge could be information and data or scientific evidence and opinion. Beyond this, you might also consider their degrees of competency in converting knowledge into strategies. How capable are they of applying relevant knowledge to their agendas? In working with someone whose goal is to reduce stress, you might inquire what the person knows about stress, its causes, and strategies for managing it. For this client to be autonomous and self-directing in the future, what knowledge would they need? Where can they find reliable information? Once the gaps in their general knowledge pertaining to stress have been identified, designing and planning action becomes more realizable.

Self-Knowledge Competency

How accurately do clients know themselves in relation to their agendas? How well do they understand their values and beliefs pertaining to their goals and the processes that might be required in reaching them? To what degree do they know and appreciate their personal preferences and styles of behaving that might relate to their agendas? If a client's goal centers on stress management, how well do they understand the ways in which they generate and manage stress? Do they recognize their triggers and sensitivities? Do they know about their optimal stress levels for performance? What are their mental models of stress? How readily can they translate self-knowledge into practical strategies for stress reduction? The difference between self-knowledge and general knowledge can be explained as follows: Knowing about one's specific triggers for stress is self-knowledge, whereas understanding what stress is and the fact that it involves triggering situations or stimuli is general knowledge. When clients need to develop self-knowledge, then interventions to augment their recognition of how they experience stress and what they normally do in response might be avenues to pursue.

Emotional Competency

What are clients' emotional capacities related to their agendas? It's important for you to know that most coaching agendas incorporate a variety of emotional experiences. Are clients able to identify emotional experiences—their own as well as others'—with a high degree of accuracy? Can they differentiate levels of emotional experience, especially as they arise in the context of their coaching topics? This competency is comparable to Goleman's (1995) proposal of emotional intelligence. If a woman's desired goal is smoking cessation, for example, how attuned is she to her emotional world as it relates to this behavior? What are her competencies in emotional self-management in general? How does she deal with emotions other than through smoking? What feelings arise in regard to her self-concept pertaining to her agenda (e.g., embarrassment)? Do these feelings overwhelm her, or does she have perspective about them? What are her strengths in appreciating and managing her emotional world? Awareness of emotional competency related to clients' coaching topics may direct attention to the design of actions related to emotional development or regulation.

Somatic Competency

What is the client's knowledge of her body as it relates to her agenda? Attunement to your physical being can be critically relevant to your understanding of what happens in different situations. Do you know how your posture shifts in different contexts, how your body signals impending illness, what deep fatigue feels like, or what your body needs to relax or reenergize? Your body is a great source of data about your experiences, so focusing on somatic awareness can be highly instructive regarding what's happening for you in the moment as well as what you might to do to change (Strozzi-Heckler, 2014). A wealth of literature informs us about the relevance of somatic awareness to our overall well-being (Dychtwald, 1977; Fogel, 2013; Kurz & Prestera, 1976; Tonkov, 2019). Think of clients who are working on topics like assertiveness, work–life balance, job transitions, or reinventing themselves. Can you imagine how their somatic selves would be implicated? If so, how might a focus on their somatic awareness provide insights related to successful adaptation?

Interpersonal Competency

Similar to Goleman's (2006) concept of social intelligence, this competency addresses clients' competencies in relationships with others. Do they have an accurate and useful social map of their world as related to their agendas for coaching? Who and how do others influence them? How do they influence others? What is the quality of their relationships with people critically related to their topics? How well are they able to navigate elements implicated in their coaching plans with friends, colleagues, family, and strangers? If a client's intention is to develop greater self-confidence at work, how do others play into his experiences and self-presentation? How aware is the client of these interpersonal influences? How effective is he in dealing with conflicts? Focusing on the interpersonal aspects of clients' agendas may boost awareness of resources, challenges, and partnerships.

Moral Competency

Borrowing from various propositions regarding moral development (Gilligan, 1982; Kohlberg, 1981), this competency examines clients' judgment processes related to their agendas. How capable are they of understanding their goals and the path toward these objectives in ways that are fair and compassionate toward self and others? What's their capacity to minimize blame, shame, or guilt and to transform such judgmental experiences into more empowering perceptions? When strong self-judgments arise, how able are they to move toward more accepting and self-compassionate ways so as to avoid stalling in change processes? Consider a client who unexpectedly loses his job and spins in judgment either blaming himself or his organization for what happened. Imagine a leader whose style involves categorizing colleagues as good or bad based on their adherence to his work ethic. Moral judgments may be so deeply rooted in topics that unless coaches intentionally focus on the client's story through a moral lens, clients may lack awareness to acknowledge limiting beliefs.

Practicalities in Focusing

As clients tell their stories, you may have a sense that some elements are more present than others. There may be a rich texture to what they know, but the story seems relatively devoid of people or emotion. The story may sound factual, yet you may sense underlying judgments feeding the choice of facts presented. As the story is being told, you may notice different body parts tensing or relaxing. The more you get to know your clients, the more you will appreciate which areas of focus might be most fruitful.

If we go back to Ben's story, there is ample reason for focusing on self-knowledge based on statements such as, "What do I really want to do with my life?" You might also see a possible focus on interpersonal competency in his remark that, in the midst of his struggle, "I don't know how to talk to my partner about it." Similarly, a moral theme arises in his remark, "There's this clock in my head and it keeps telling me to stop wasting time and do something." Again, based on prior understanding of this client amidst his topic, you might have a hunch of which focus to pursue—of course, checking your assumptions with him.

An important consideration in identifying focus is that it may emerge as much from what isn't said as from what is. If you were to only reflect what clients say, you could miss elements of clients' stories that are consistently avoided or deleted. Interventions involving focusing intentionally target areas that you believe to be important for clients to explore, even when they don't mention them very much. As with other matters, the choice of focus needs to be justified within the contractual agreement and the client's delineation of the coaching objective.

The six areas of focus represent a map of areas for exploration that is reasonably comprehensive. Yet, there may be something unique—beyond these areas—to a client's story that warrants attention. Focusing as an intervention directs clients toward discovery of thoughts, feelings, or experiences by intentionally shining a light on a particular facet of a story. Through your intervention, you as coach may be implicitly suggesting that you believe there is something relevant and potentially helpful in this area of inquiry.

REFLECTION OF MEANING

You may remember from chapter 10 that three types of reflection were identified: reflection of content, reflection of feeling, and **reflection of meaning**. A discussion of meaning reflection was delayed until this chapter because it typically isn't an intervention where the coach is paraphrasing to clients what they have just expressed. Rather, it is more likely a process of inquiry and discovery where coaches probe with a variety of interventions to understand what is beneath the surface.

One of the early questions that you will ask your clients is what they want to get from the coaching experience. Once you have a reasonably good grasp of what that is, you will typically move to a questioning process around the importance or meaning of the agenda they have identified. You will remember this from the 6 *whats* model in chapter 5. Here, you potentially move into the existential level of understanding what your client is all about. What is known as third-generation coaching (Stelter, 2013)

reflects a strong emphasis on understanding the deeper meanings in client issues.

Human beings are meaning-making creatures (Frankl, 1969; Stringer, 2007). Others may not ask you the somewhat taboo *why* question, although you may often ask it of yourself: Why did I do that? Why is this so important to me? Why do I want to be with this person? Why do I keep doing this? Why am I here? Existential psychologists suggest that crisis and tragedy prompt people to search for meaning (Binswanger, 1963; Bugental, 1965; Frankl, 1969; May, 1996; Yalom, 1980). An accomplished CEO muses about why she continues working in a toxic job while repeatedly telling friends that she wants to go off and explore the other side of life. A wildly successful entrepreneur wonders why he always chooses work over fun, while continuing a punishing work schedule from year to year.

Commenting on the existential perspective, Prochaska and Norcross (2018) offer this sense of our humanity: "We create meanings in our lives by the lives we create. We are not born with intrinsic meaning in our existence, but we are born with a creative self who can fashion intrinsic meaning from our existence" (p. 63). Coaching involves appreciating the meaning clients are creating from their experiences and what new meanings they are yearning for. As a coach, you want to be acutely attuned to discovering the meanings embedded in your clients' stories (see sidebar, Weaving Skills in Reflecting Meaning).

The search for meaning can run deep. Yet, your role is to explore just enough to surface clients' more potent motivations and to discover how these might be integrated into their lives. Occasionally you may find that the reasons justifying a client's pursuit of a particular objective are more related to fear and avoidance than to inspirational and life-giving intentions. The quest for such vitalizing sources of action underpins much of the thinking of positive psychology (Biswas-Diener, 2009; Biswas-Diener & Dean, 2007; Green & Palmer, 2018; Ivtzan et al., 2016). For instance, a client whose apparent motivation for running a marathon is to counter his fears and self-doubts may through an exploration of meaning uncover other reasons for pursuing this goal that are not as fear driven.

Practicalities in Reflections of Meaning

As noted, reflections of meaning rely on such fundamental methods as inquiry, active listening,

Weaving Skills in Reflecting Meaning

A reflection of meaning represents a focus of attention rather than a single intervention by a coach. It shows up through a concerted exploration surrounding the underlying or existential meaning that drives client intentions and dreams. In the following hypothetical dialogue, you will see how a coach weaves a number of coaching skills in the process of reflecting meaning.

Background Information

Elijah, a 62-year-old man in good health, recently retired from a well-paid position as a research scientist. He feels he has denied himself opportunities to follow many of his dreams throughout life, but he now has the time and financial security to pursue them. Many of these dreams involve high-risk pursuits. As a wise and cautious person, he wants to make sure that he's in the best condition to embark on these adventures. After three sessions, his coach wants to address a theme she has heard several times.

Coach: (Asking permission and preparing for a thematic summary) Elijah, would you be willing to allow time today for me to frame a theme I think I'm hearing from you—and for us to discuss it together?

Elijah: Sure, sounds intriguing!

Coach: (Using reflection of content) The picture you have drawn of yourself is of a highly successful scientist who got where he did by being careful, conservative, and never taking chances. Is this part accurate?

Elijah: Yes, that certainly was the old me.

Coach: (Using reflection of content and a gentle confrontation) Now I'm hearing that you want to engage in some pretty rugged and even risky activities because although you've often dreamed about them, you never took the time for them. This seems to be a shift in the way you have lived your life. (Using an indirect question directed toward meaning) I'd like to understand more about what you are seeing in this new direction, especially when you contrast it with your previous patterns.

Elijah: Frankly, I'm not 100% sure about this, but I think I lost an important part of myself being the responsible scientist all these years, and now I want to start having fun. I had fun discovering things but not like the fun I think I could have had sailing the globe. I've been a good scientist, but I had to suppress my wilder side all these years.

Coach: (Using interpretation to evoke meaning) I hear you . . . and you imagine that sailing the globe or something like that would allow you to get to know that wilder side better.

Elijah: I think so. I would be careful, but I need to break out of the mold that I've created all these years (emotion evident in tone).

Coach: (Using reflection of feeling) I'm sensing you have strong feelings about this.

Elijah: For sure. Though I've had a good life, it has been one-dimensional. It's time to change that. I'm still young enough and healthy enough to push it a bit, so why not?

Coach: (Using powerful questioning) So why not?

Elijah: Yeah, why not? I'm looking to you to help me keep things in perspective because this isn't just about doing wild things. It's about all of me—it's about more than that one dimension—it's about a fuller identity, and I want to start by getting reacquainted with that spirited teenager I once was. I was a great student, but I also knew how to have fun.

Coach: (Using a blend of skills) This seems really important to you. I hear that all of this is about being your whole self, the way you have always seen yourself but have not always allowed yourself to be. It's about bringing more excitement into your life in a thoughtful way, even though it looks a lot riskier than what you've been doing for the past 30 years.

Elijah: Absolutely—that captures it. I'm going to think about this some more because having talked about it, I can see it better, and I feel a bit more in charge of it. Sometimes, I've felt an urge to just rush right into it, but now I have a better sense of where this is coming from.

challenge, immediacy, interpretation, and focusing. Sometimes the deliberate intention of your interventions will be to uncover meaning; other times, meaning just seems to pop out of what clients are telling you. In short-term coaching relationships, you will ask questions about the meaning and importance of clients' coaching objectives though you may not delve too deeply into this exploration. However, when clients continue their work with you over longer periods, it's likely you will need to inquire more often about the meanings they attribute to a wide variety of their choices and actions (see sidebar, Stimulating Reflection of Meaning).

Even with reasonably concrete objectives, the quest for meaning is justified. Imagine a client says, "I want a new car and I'd love to have a summer cottage." You might immediately identify with these interests because you, too, would like to have those things. What's important to realize is that the same objective phenomenon, whether it is a car, a house, or a new job, is likely to have substantially different meanings for different people. It might be problematic assuming that objective things represent the same internal motivations as your own. Using reflection of meaning allows you to discover what clients' experiences, desires, or goals mean to them. When someone tells you a story about certain life experiences, you may say something like, "I can certainly relate to that." But can you really? Curiosity is essential in coaching (Kimsey-House et al., 2018; Martin, 2001). Only by probing for meaning in clients' stories can you begin to assist clients in making sense of their own stories.

In a goal-centric approach to coaching, meaning explorations are never an end in themselves. However, some emerging models of coaching (Stelter, 2013, 2018) place existential objectives of purpose and identity as the goal of the coaching dialogue. While these models are not common, it is quite likely that in coming decades they will become more prevalent. In a world where individuals are living significantly longer, where they are required by technological advances to periodically reinvent themselves, and where ways of working and relating continue to evolve, questions of purpose and identity may become a more central coaching focus.

INTERPRETATION, METAPHORS, AND REFRAMING

Of the three terms—*interpretation*, *metaphors*, and *reframing*—interpretation is likely to be the most challenging to wrap your mind around. In training coaches over many years, I often find myself giving novice coaches feedback that goes something like this: "It seems you were interpreting what your client said rather than reflecting. What's your sense of that?" Usually, they would tell me that they were only repeating back what their clients told them. Herein lies the issue. When you don't use the exact words a client used, when you combine pieces of information from different parts of the dialogue, when you express something that you thought was clearly implied by your client, you will sometimes be perceived as interpreting their remarks—which means that what you say back to them is understood as your opinion rather than what they said.

This represents a dilemma. You don't want to parrot your clients' words, you do want to put the pieces together from all you know, and you may want to raise awareness of things that your clients imply. Moreover, you want them to experience you as listening to them carefully and not always interpreting what they say. Coaching conversations are subtle dances. The bottom line is that many of the ways that coaches express themselves to their clients may represent one form or another of interpretation.

Stimulating Reflection of Meaning

These questions offer some ideas about how you might move into explorations of meaning by stimulating your clients to reflect.

- What are you yearning for?
- What do you want to create?
- Which of your values are most represented here?
- What is your deepest intention in this?
- What will this mean to you if you are able to achieve this?
- What makes this so important to you at this point?
- Tell me how this makes sense to you.
- If you were to put this all together, what would it represent to you?
- Who will you become if you achieve this?
- Why do you want to do this?
- Who do you want to be in this situation?
- Why this goal and not that one?
- What motives might lie under this story?

Interpretation is one of the oldest interventions in the helping professions (Clark, 1995) and one of the most widely misunderstood. Interpretation is often associated with the highly complex and esoteric work of psychoanalysis (Freud, 1964). However, according to Frank and Frank (1993), virtually all professional helpers interpret their clients' behaviors according to the theoretical frameworks in which they were educated. In coaching, the term *interpretation* continues to be widely used (Kimsey-House et al., 2018; Neenan & Dryden, 2002; Williams & Davis, 2007), although it is often associated with concepts such as reframing and the use of metaphors.

Ivey and colleagues (Ivey et al., 2018) use the term *interpretation* almost synonymously with *reframing*. They define interpretation as providing

> the client with a new perspective, frame of reference, or way of thinking about issues. Interpretations/reframes may come from your observations; they may be based on varying theoretical orientations to the helping field; or they may link critical ideas together. (p. 259)

Kimsey-House and colleagues (2018) refer to interpretation, or reframing, as a hunch or intuition that a coach has about the client's situation. In this view, interpretation is not a judgment or even something definite. Coaches develop a sense about what is going on and, in their own words, try to communicate their hunches to their clients. Borrowing more from the concept of reframing, Williams and Davis (2007) believe that what coaches do is find other words or descriptors for something that appears to be a challenge, problem, or deficiency in the client's view. Placing the behavior or perception, as articulated by the client, in a new context or frame "allows the client to see whatever the situation or concern is in a new way. Rather than viewing the problem as a weakness, it can be seen as an opportunity for learning" (pp. 107-108).

Interpretations that one might expect in psychotherapy include significant reframing of a client's reality. For instance, a person struggling with addiction may be told that his addiction represents a defense against feelings of inadequacy. Coaches typically aren't trained to make these types of interpretations, and it's unlikely that contracts for coaching would ever legitimize such reframes. Coaching involves more transparent interpretations where the language used by the coach makes clear sense to the client and the practicality of the information surfaced by the reframe has evident connection to the client's goal.

Types of Interpretation

Examining different types of interpretation might remove any remaining beliefs that this skill belongs more to counseling and psychotherapy than to coaching. To some degree, the following types might be seen as occurring along a continuum of depth (see sidebar, An Illustration of Types of Interpretation).

Interpretations That Add Implied Messages

Interpretations can be seen as an advanced form of empathy. The coach includes aspects of the client's message that are seemingly implied through nonverbal or verbal cues but not stated directly (Egan, 2014). Clients may look sad or elated when describing experiences but never label their feelings. Were the coach to reflect the content of the client's messages as well as the unspoken element of feelings, it would represent an interpretation. In this form of interpretation, the coach rather than the client voices unstated feelings or meanings that are often interpreted from nonverbal indicators.

Interpretations That Connect Messages and Add Implications or Conclusions

In chapter 10 you learned that the methodology of summarizing involves bringing together various messages that a client has delivered over time. When coaches summarize a number of client messages and then add something that may be implied or even something they infer (a hunch) from the information, this process is more accurately described as interpretation. It's important to be aware of when you are accurately reflecting client messages and when you are adding something that has been unspoken to these reflections. Coaches may think that what they are sensing in a situation must be obvious to the client. Possibly it is, yet making the implicit explicit can be unsettling—and illuminating. When what seems obvious to the coach isn't obvious to the client, the coach will have brought to awareness something in the individual's blind spot that may foster learning.

Interpretations That Reframe the Client's Issue

This form of interpretation has sometimes been described as looking on the bright side of things (Kimsey-House et al., 2018), but it is much more than that. When clients are struggling with issues, they may be unaware of strengths they are exhibiting or

An Illustration of Types of Interpretation

This dialogue illustrates the different types of interpretations that can be derived from a client's statements. Some may be more potent than others, although all have the purpose of moving the client forward rather than diving into analysis.

Background Information

Jenna, a 27-year-old financial analyst, has been working with a coach for six months on a multifaceted program to build confidence at work and compete successfully in an amateur tennis tournament. In tennis, she performs well in training but invariably makes errors in competition that she almost never does in practice sessions. Over the past few sessions, Jenna made these remarks, which the coach noted:

Comment 1: Even at work I seem to clutch whenever I feel someone is watching. I don't like people looking over my shoulder.

Comment 2: I want to win so badly that I make stupid mistakes because I'm trying too hard.

Comment 3: I hate competition.

In this session, Jenna wants to focus on a recent loss in a tennis competition against an opponent whom she always defeats in practice.

Comment 4: I can't believe it. I threw the game away. She can't play anywhere near my level, yet she trounced me yesterday. I'm such a loser.

Adding Implied Messages

Coach: Jenna, it sounds as if you're feeling frustrated with yourself, like someone who is determined to lose.

Connecting Messages and Adding Implications or Conclusions

Coach: Jenna, I can really hear how disappointed you feel with yourself, and I sense from other things you've said—like about work and about trying too hard—that when the spotlight shines on you in competition, you "clutch" and make stupid mistakes. There seems to be something in this about not being able to perform well when it counts the most.

Reframing

Coach: Jenna, I hear you . . . how disappointed you feel with yourself . . . like you set yourself up for failure. Yet maybe there's another message in this. I remember your telling me one time that you hate competition. Perhaps some part of you is trying to get through to you that how you are engaging in this game doesn't work for you. You do well in practice because you're having fun. As soon as you define the situation as competition, the fun exits—and this overaggressive, angry competitor that you don't want to be comes roaring out. How might you come to experience competition as fun?

Theory-Based Interpretation

Coach: Jenna, I can see how upset you are and how you're blaming yourself for all this. Things you've said to me over the past few weeks make me wonder whether this all might be about a fear of success. You know that your inherent skills are far better than what you demonstrate when you're competing, and you've also said that you hate competition. Yet you continue to place yourself in the limelight at these kinds of events. You do what you don't like or even hate under conditions that you normally find upsetting, like having people watch you. Then, no surprise, you fail, almost as if you set it up to happen that way. I guess the unknown in this little theory is what it would mean to you if you were to be successful at something that you wanted so badly.

Metaphorical Interpretation

Coach: Ouch . . . it seems like you're really hurting and upset about this. I have an image of you tying your shoes together before you go out on the tennis court and saying to everyone watching, "Look at me. I'm going to make it as difficult as I can for myself to win." It reminds me of that children's story, *The Little Engine That Could*, except you're saying, "I know I can't. I know I can't. I know I can't."

the vast potential in their dilemmas. Walking in a fog, you may not realize what lies just beyond your range of vision. To the client involved, a situation may seem hopeless, whereas to the coach who isn't immersed in the dilemma, possibilities may abound. The notion of reframing refers to a way of taking what people are describing and presenting a more adaptive view for them to consider as an alternative. As noted, reframing generally provides perspectives with greater potentiality and hopefulness, although not always. A reframe could also present the dangers or negative implications of a scenario with the intention of alerting the client to unforeseen consequences that might be best to avoid.

Theory-Based Interpretations

When a particular theory informs a coach's work, interpreting a client's thoughts, feelings, or behaviors within this framework can provide an entirely new way of understanding. Chapter 4 describes the transtheoretical model. If you were to describe to your clients where they are in the change process using the language of TTM, you would be offering a theoretical interpretation. Similarly, if you use certain inventories or profiling tests and communicate meanings extracted from these measures, you would be employing theoretical interpretations. Many coaches ask their clients to take such psychometric tests as the Myers-Briggs Type Inventory or MBTI (Quenck, 2009) or they may employ such measures as the enneagram (Riso & Hudson, 1999). Discussing clients' ways of being in terms of concepts central to these measures is a clear form of interpretation. As noted previously, psychiatrists and psychologists may use quite complex theoretical expressions, but these expressions would rarely represent the kinds of interpretations that coaches offer in their work.

Metaphorical Interpretations

So much has been written about metaphors and their applications (Atkinson, 2014; Lakoff & Johnson, 1980; Stoddard et al., 2014; Torneke & Hayes, 2017). Metaphors may be simple or complex. "You seem to be rising above it all now and seeing your situation for what it truly is" is a metaphorical expression implying that the client is extricating herself from a situation to gain perspective. This simple metaphor captures in visual imagery some aspect of an experience; however, the description comes from the coach rather than from the client. Metaphors that are more complex may take the form of stories that illuminate certain dynamics of what the client has been expressing. Fables and fairy tales

are elegant metaphors from which coaches hope their clients will draw a useful moral (see sidebar, Common Metaphors in Everyday Speech).

As Robert Kegan (1994) puts it, "A metaphor is interpretive, but it is an interpretation made in soft clay rather than cold analysis. It invites the clients to put their hands on it and reshape it into something more fitting to them" (p. 260). Metaphors seem to transcend clients' conscious way of seeing the world, and potentially bring forward something that is out of their view. This, in turn, allows for the creation of novel possibilities for change and action. A beautiful expression of the power of metaphor comes from Hildebrandt and colleagues (2007) who offered the following: "Metaphors intentionally disorient clients so that they must discover what works and what doesn't based on their experience rather than on literal, linear rules" (p. 59).

Common Metaphors in Everyday Speech

Metaphors permeate your daily language so much so that you may be unaware of how pervasive this way of expressing yourself might be. Many of them come in the form of common proverbs. They represent a kind of shorthand that captures the obvious, the unobvious, and the potentially insightful perspectives when applied in a particular context.

- I feel blue today; I feel on top of the world; I feel flighty; I've been turned inside out; I am blown away.

- Life's a beach; life's a bowl of cherries; life's a roller coaster; life's just a dream; life's a hard road to travel; life's a gift.

- Your friend/partner/colleague has a heart of gold; is like a cat with nine lives; is as cold as ice; is a rock (a snake, a pig, a diamond in the rough).

- Time is money; a stitch in time saves nine; don't cry over spilled milk; make hay while the sun shines; a bird in the hand is better than two in the bush; a penny saved is a penny earned; absence makes the heart grow fonder.

- A chain is only as strong as its weakest link; actions speak louder than words; a journey of a thousand miles begins with a single step; a picture is worth a thousand words.

Practicalities in Interpretations, Metaphors, and Reframing

The first thing to realize is that you are likely to use metaphors, reframed statements, and interpretations in life as well as your coaching practice almost unwittingly. These ways of expressing yourself just seem to slip out at times. If this is so, then it may be possible when you are listening deeply to your clients and reflecting their own words back to them that your interpretations may be seeping into what you say. In this respect, you may be influencing them more than you realize at moments when you believe you are just following them.

A second thing to be aware of are the natural expressions of interpretations, metaphors, and reframed statements that your client may be using. What metaphors do they use when speaking about their experiences? What kinds of interpretations are they making? As you listen carefully to these, you might become aware of ways they are articulating experiences that contain certain elements, that if they are adjusted or shifted slightly, might provide a wholly different perspective of their behavior. To give an example, remember the story of the woman imagining herself as a little girl in a candy shop leaving empty handed? You might ask her to reimagine that story in a way where the little girl realizes she loves almost everything in that store so that any choice is a happy choice. As she walks toward the cashier, she sings to herself a little jingle: "One, two, three—and what do I see? This candy here is just for me." And then she picks! Of course, you need to consider whether this is the appropriate time to offer your insights about what clients have expressed. They may be so caught in the dynamics of their own metaphors that shifting perspective might meet with considerable resistance. So timing is key.

A third awareness is more internal to you. What arises in you as you imagine your clients' stories, as you listen to what is or isn't being expressed? Are there metaphors, stories, conceptual frameworks, or other imaginal associations that are taking shape inside you as you listen and explore with your client? Whatever emerges represents an important part of your process but isn't necessarily something you need to share with your client. Some of your personal thoughts and images may require further reflection before you bring them into the coaching dialogue. There is certainly space for spontaneous intuitive offerings in coaching. As you gain experience in your practice, you will come to know what's likely to be beneficial, offer it easily, and graciously accept whatever your client's response may be.

STIMULATING NEW PERSPECTIVES IN THE ICF CORE COMPETENCIES

I concluded the last two chapters with reflections on how the new ICF core coaching competency of evoking awareness captures inquiry and direct communication. Here, I want to offer perspectives about how this competency speaks to the methods explored in this chapter. Interestingly, this competency addresses ways of evoking awareness through explorations of current experiences as well as by stimulating projective processes about the future. In identifying elements that may influence clients' patterns and realities, insights may emerge when coaches draw attention to particular aspects of their experiences, as well as through inquiries related to the deeper meanings embedded in the stories that clients tell. In these respects, the methods of focusing and reflection of meaning seem to find a valid place in the skill sets of coaches as they evoke awareness in their clients.

Equally, as coaches explore beyond the client's current thinking or feeling to new or expanded ways of thinking or feeling about themselves and their situations, a variety of methods may be inferred. The ICF explicitly references reframing as a means of evoking awareness, and, as noted earlier, reframing is thought of as somewhat synonymous to interpretations in the coaching literature. Moreover, metaphor and analogy are referenced in the definition of this competency. What might be harder to see is the methodology of offering interpretations. Perhaps this may reflect some of the historical connotations of interpretation that would limit its inclusion as a valid method of intervening for coaches. However, as I have described here, interpretative remarks are commonplace—and they are generally quite different from interpretations occurring in a psychotherapeutic context.

Cautions that are clearly articulated in this competency support coaches in offering their insight-provoking interventions without attachment to their value or correctness and with the utmost sensitivity to client experiences. A stance of nonattachment, open-mindedness, and supportiveness needs to frame these offerings.

REFLECTIONS

A basic premise in coaching is that your clients are creative, resourceful, and whole. Sometimes you just need to get out of their way to let that brilliance shine through; other times, you need to stimulate their internal processes so they can better access their own wisdom. The questions you want to ask in awakening insight and creativity may be simpler than you realize. The quest for meaning comes down to a question like, "What makes this so deeply important to you in this moment?" Metaphors may be quite fundamental and straightforward: "In all your comments, I sense a lightness of being—almost as if you are preparing to fly."

What I struggle with in my own practice is balancing expressions arising from my own inner process with efforts to deeply connect with what is growing within my client. It's true that sometimes, maybe in the best of times, I feel my client and I are one mind, almost taking turns in imagining possibilities. Yet, coaching sessions are about the client's brilliance, not mine. Keeping this in mind frees me from working too hard, which may result in me taking up more airspace than is perhaps optimal for my client. So, I don't have to search for the perfect metaphor or to craft the most incisive reframe. I can trust that remaining fully present to all that is happening will provide me with what is most important to say. I also know that when I am not coaching, I need to nourish my imagination in a deliberate way through things I choose to read or see, being with people who stimulate my creativity, and accessing experiences that open my mind, heart, and spirit.

CHAPTER 14

COACHING ACTION AND LEARNING

> *To exist is to change, to change is to mature,*
> *to mature is to go on creating oneself endlessly.*
>
> *Henri Bergson*

MY STORY

It seems so long ago that I was visiting my hometown, New York City, and consulting with a movement therapist, Dr. Ellen Goldman, who had written a book that linked body movements to mental processes—an all-time favorite topic of mine. Being an experiential learner, I asked Ellen to do a movement and personality analysis for me. Her process required me to sit with her and answer a number of pretty reasonable questions about my life. She video recorded the session and asked me to come back the next day so she could give me her analysis. I remember being so excited yet wondering how she could get anything out of the tame questions she asked me.

This was a long time ago, but what I remember most from her debrief was this deep sense of being seen and understood. Her analysis the following day named a pattern that I inherently knew but was never able to coherently describe. Not recognizing this pattern really put me at risk of repeating ways of acting that really didn't serve me well.

Here's an interesting part of this story. At the beginning of the debrief, she told me that to create her analysis, she watched my video recording with the volume turned off—she only considered how I moved in the interview. When she said that, I wondered internally, "How useful is this going to be?" Then, she laid it all out. Her system was called action profiling, and it essentially looked at how someone moves from contemplation into action. Her core message was that my pattern was one of getting an idea, jumping into action, and later on thinking about whether it was a good idea or not. Ready, fire, aim! It wasn't exactly about being impulsive, but it had the scary dynamic of something like, "I wonder if I can fly. Let me jump out of the plane and find out." I never did anything that drastic, but I did act a bit too quickly with not-very-benign consequences a number of times in my life.

What's the relevance of this story? Coaching is not just about action. It's also about reflection, learning, resources, capabilities, the big picture, and a myriad of other things. Coaches don't simply drive conversations to actionable conclusions by asking things like, "Oh, you're unhappy with your job? Let's do something about that! How would you find a new job?" Sorry if that example seems silly, but I have experienced far too many people, including many of my coaches-in-training, running madly toward solutions for other people's lives. Having been involved in the evolution of the coaching field over the past quarter century, I feel ecstatic about the way in which coaches today embrace learning and insight as companions to action in their practices.

The coaching field today embraces a more expansive range of purposes and outcomes than in its formative years. Cocreating clear commitments to action in sessions remains a hallmark of coaching. Yet, coaching is not only about the pursuit of action; it increasingly encompasses significant learning and growth objectives. In an evolved perspective, coaching may be seen to focus on learning how to learn, which then drives client capacity for self-directed and self-managed change. This chapter circles back to the topic of goals, but from a pragmatic perspective. It then widens the lens to explore coaches' focus on learning and growth as outcomes of the coaching relationship. It also considers what coaches do in harvesting clients' lessons, learnings, and commitments. Finally, it addresses the matter of closure or endings of coaching relationships.

Here are some guiding questions as you read:

- How are action and learning related?
- Are clear goals always possible in coaching?
- What's the necessary structure for coaching goals?
- What are the important tasks as coaching relationships are ending?

ACTION AND LEARNING

As weeks pass within a coaching relationship, clients will increasingly experience the changes they have created. Not only will their actions, learning, and reflections pave the way, but they will sense a growing confidence—a conviction that they can keep going. They may find themselves awakening to an ever-expanding and increasingly satisfying new world. Their learnings feed new actions, and these actions in turn stimulate new awareness. That process reflects the experiential learning cycle (Kolb, 1984) as discussed earlier (see chapter 2).

In looking forward to the upcoming decades, you probably know that people will be on a lifelong journey of learning and change, based on the need to continually reinvent themselves for jobs and realities that presently don't exist (Boston Consulting Group, 2018; Einzig, 2017; Forbes Coaches Council, 2018). Forecasts are that most people will need coaches—and that these coaching relationships may endure over extended periods of time. In the future, the outcomes of coaching engagements may not be as univocally expressed in terms of concrete actions as they were in the early period of the coaching field. Though change is typically reflected in

behavior, sometimes early phases of change may be internally manifested in altered ways of perceiving, thinking, and feeling. For instance, shifting one's perspective may be cultivated through behavioral commitments to targeted readings, periods of reflection, and practical engagements. Being able to work effectively in a different culture or to nurture a more inclusive perspective about society might represent coaching objectives, yet their benchmarks of success are unlikely to be as clear cut as those related to outcomes like getting a new job, buying a house, exercising regularly, or making partner in a law firm. No matter what the objective, learning, growth, and self-directed change do not occur without concerted action.

You can look at a coaching relationship through the lens of its overall purpose or through a more limited lens of what happens in each session. Both lenses tell us that action and learning are pursued in the process, with coaches facilitating the design of actions and stimulating reflections on learning and growth in the process. There may be an overarching goal or purpose to the relationship, but it is realized only through ongoing engagement by clients in well-crafted experiments, deliberate actions, and structured processes of reflection that propel movement not only within coaching sessions but in the in between spaces.

When you learned about coaching goals earlier in this book (chapter 3), the discussion was theoretical. Here, I want to reexamine goals in a pragmatic way that describes what coaches need to bear in mind as they help clients structure their learning and change agendas in each coaching session. Recall the discussion of the 6 *whats* model. The last two areas of focus concerned planning and learning. In effect, each session draws toward a conclusion as clients and coaches work toward commitments to processes and actions that are intentionally aligned with an aspect of the larger coaching objective that clients have identified. Throughout each session, coaches partner with their clients to extract and explore various insights and learnings that emerge from their dialogue. These learnings are not limited to the scope of the coaching objective. At times, clients become aware of personal patterns that are pervasively present in their lives.

In the upcoming sections, you will learn about the structures of goals so that you can systematically work with your clients to create robust actions plans, and then you will get a chance to dive into the spacious realm of what clients learn in their coaching conversations. As clients realize their objectives, coaching relationships draw to an end. The final segment of this chapter will offer perspectives of how coaching relationships come to closure.

COCREATING CLEAR GOALS

What does a coach need to be aware of when developing goals with clients? Ives and Cox (2012) offered critical advice on this matter when they divided the task of goal construction into three components or, in their shorthand, the 3Ws: goal setting, action planning, and motivation (p. 93). The 3Ws refer to the understanding that goal setting is about *what*, action planning is about *when and how*, and motivation relates to the *why* of the goal. All three components are deemed critical to successful goal attainment.

When coaches work to clarify what the goal is, they need to bear in mind the matter of levels (see chapter 3). While it is true that some clients come to coaching for a quick fix or for the answer to a very specific question, the vast majority of coaching clients have rather broad objectives—either seen as a purpose they have for their lives, a value they are trying to attain, or a complex agenda that while being relatively specific contains multiple subgoals. Examples here might include moving into a different line of work, advancing to a higher level within a hierarchical organization, adapting to a new culture and geographical location, managing one's life in a recently blended family environment, initiating an entrepreneurial venture, or drastically altering one's lifestyle habits. Sometimes these big goals are thought of as metagoals (Carver & Scheier, 1998), while a more common phrasing within the coaching field identifies them as coaching objectives; they invariably contain numerous subtasks or subgoals. Ives and Cox remind us that the larger goals that clients present are likely to remain reasonably constant, while some of their subgoals may not only shift but also be interchangeable with equally appropriate other subgoals. For instance, a goal of adapting to a new culture can be addressed in part by a subgoal of engaging in social groups attached to a language school or by joining community interest groups.

Regardless of the goals that clients propose, seeking clarity is essential. Goals guide actions (Senge, 2006). Goal statements also elucidate the boundaries of the coaching relationship—what needs to be intentionally pursued and what is off limits. In this regard, Cormier and colleagues (2017) suggest that clear goals allow helpers to determine whether they have the skills, experience, and credentials to effectively work with certain client agendas. Moreover,

clear goals inform coaches about relevant strategies and interventions to assist clients' goal attainment. Finally, they enable coaches and clients to structure concrete frameworks for evaluation and assessment of progress (Smith, 2007; Stober, 2006).

Once again referencing Ives and Cox's (2012) 3Ws, coaches need to be mindful of the distinctly different processes involved in the *what* versus the *when and how* efforts in coaching. In their words, "Setting a goal and planning its implementation are two quite separate, even disparate activities. The former is more abstract and conscious, the latter more concrete and automated" (p. 37). There is a dialogue quality to the exploration around what goal a client really feels committed to pursuing. Coaches engage clients in a robust review of matters related to the client's intention in order to move it toward greater clarity and commitment. With a clear goal in sight, the planning process related to goal attainment becomes more practical and grounded in actionable possibilities.

The value of all these efforts to clarify goals and to move abstract ideas toward implementable action is underscored by research. Locke and associates (Latham et al., 2011; Locke et al., 1981; Locke & Latham, 1985, 1990) have consistently shown that goal setting has a powerful effect on behavior. Their extensive research indicates how goals need to be formed so as to optimize chances of success. Building on previous research, Ives and Cox (2012) proposed three main factors deemed essential for framing coaching goals; these are goal difficulty, goal specificity, and goal proximity (p. 95). The following guidelines derive from these and other perspectives about goals and activities intended to realize them.

Set Goals at Moderate Levels of Difficulty

Evidence supports the idea that the difficulty of attaining goals should represent a level of intermediate challenge—not too hard, not too easy. Grant (2006) suggests that this is a matter of attainability; that is, whatever goal is established must be realizable. In the field of coaching, the concept of stretch goals is often invoked (Hargrove, 2008; Kellogg et al., 2015). Admirable as the idea of increasing goal challenge may be, there is inherent risk in setting goals that are too difficult. A literature review on coaching goals by Clutterbuck and Spence (2017) advises that coaches need to be thoughtful about goal difficulty levels they cocreate with their clients. Framing goals that are appropriately difficult rather than too easily attained or too difficult to reach can be a delicate matter. Though the idea of getting behind clients' intentions to dream outside the box and aim for the stars is laudable, goals need to be set with achievable targets. As people reach intermediate goals, they tend to build confidence and eventually attain what was previously considered to be unreachable (Bandura, 1997).

As a general principle, frame short-term goals so they are challenging enough without increasing the probability of failure. A corollary to this point is that setting goals that are too easy may reduce satisfaction and future motivation. Coaches may land on an action plan toward the end of a session where the person says, "Great. I can do that. In fact, I've already been doing something like that for months." If clients agree to do what they have already been doing, they will probably believe that coaching adds little value to their goal pursuit. In cases like this, actions need to be designed so they are more challenging.

Strive for Goal Specificity

Goal specificity is deemed essential in goal setting (Bandura, 2001). As much as goal specificity has been emphasized in the literature, a considerable gap continues to exist between what clients think are clearly stated goals and how detailed these goals actually need to be to make progress. Coaches may seem to be overly granular when they ask questions such as, "When are you going to do that?" or "What will it look like?" or "How will you know you have done what you said you were going to do?" These questions may seem too detailed, yet they are often necessary. Indeed, this is one place where the magic of coaching can be readily demystified. Clients might be ready to end a session with what they think is a clear goal to pursue in the period between sessions. But then coaches may take one additional step by asking their clients to imagine themselves engaging in their designed actions, almost like a behavioral rehearsal (Suinn, 1986). This allows clients to go through a trial run of their commitment to further define its nature and possible impediments. Through this process, coach and client may come to realize that the action plan is missing critical elements for success.

Amorphous, ambiguous, or generic goal statements are not characteristic in coaching. It is the coach's responsibility to ensure that whatever goals are established in a coaching session conform to a significant degree to the elements of SuPeRSMART (Donatelle & Kolen Thompson, 2011), which will

be reviewed shortly. All the good will and well-meaning intentions that clients feel in a coaching session are insufficient to counter the consequences of loosely defined goals. Imagine the following statements as being expressed with great passion: "I am definitely going to act more like a leader." "I promise I will take time for myself." "For sure, I'm going to talk to my boss about this!" Now, imagine meeting these clients in the next session. What do you think their stories might be?

Frame the Timing of Goals and Subgoals

Imagine a client who states as her goal the desire to live a balanced life. The literature on goal setting distinguishes between distal and proximal goals (Locke & Latham, 2006)—or what Miller and Brickman (2004) describe as immediate and future goals. Grant (2012) also sees this temporal dimension of goals as reflecting degrees of abstraction. Someone who wants to live a more balanced life must first identify what the components of this ideal state might be. If one element of life balance might involve managing screen time on devices outside of work, setting a performance goal of under 100 minutes per workday is both more concrete than living in balance and more likely to be achieved in the short run. Usually, clients enter coaching with some future vision (distal goal) that the coach helps to detail as much as possible. From this future vision, several proximal or immediate goals can be crafted. In general, the farther away in time a goal is, the more abstract it is likely to be. As mentioned earlier, it is mostly true that clients' objectives for coaching are more abstract than the subgoals they are likely to generate in ongoing coaching sessions.

Understand Which Goal Type to Target

Let's use Weinberg and Gould's (2019) typology of goals to illustrate this. Often, what a client wants from coaching will reflect all three goal types—performance, outcome, and process—yet the client's criteria for success may be more heavily focused on one of the three goal types. Imagine someone who wants to develop a practice of daily meditation as a way of managing stress and feeling centered. An outcome goal of feeling centered can be assessed at the end of each meditation experience; a performance goal might be that the person sat on the cushion for 10 minutes with no allowance for distractions; and a process goal could be that, throughout the 10 minutes, he was able to stay in the present moment and come back to his breath without self-judgment. In other words, there is one action goal (meditating) with three faces. However, the client may be most concerned about only one facet or goal type—and that's where the coach's attention needs to be. Even so, I would suggest that when you are working with clients, you put yourself to the task of articulating to yourself what the three faces of your clients' goals might be. Whether you share these with your clients will, of course, depend on the clients' agendas and their openness to this kind of input.

Incorporate Interim Feedback About Progress

Coaching involves an ongoing dialogue about clients' desires, the steps clients will take to reach their goals, and assessments of progress along the way. In all likelihood, clients working on big goals will be moving forward simultaneously on a number of action plans created at various points in the coaching relationship. Coaches help clients implement, monitor, and modify action plans to shape desired changes (Clutterbuck, 2013; Grant, 2012; Ives & Cox, 2012; Schwarzer, 2006). Ideally, feedback about progress will be jointly designed so that clients take responsibility for evaluating their efforts and sharing information with their coaches. This implies that objective standards or assessments need to be detailed to the degree possible. Benchmarks of progress are made explicit as a way of motivating behavior and estimating time frames for completion. Referring to our discussion of outcome, performance, and process goals, specific standards might exist for each type. For instance, a client's report might sound like this: "Over the past two weeks, I lost two and a half pounds (outcome) by sticking to my eating plan at least six out of seven days each week (performance), and the interesting thing is that I actually enjoyed eating this way (process)."

State Goals in Clients' Own Words

A fundamental premise in coaching is that clients need to define their goals (Coach U, 2005; Skibbins, 2007; Steele, 2011). Though coaches contribute to dialogue wherein clients articulate their goals, it's not their role to tell clients what to do. Some schools of coaching are more explicit about how coaches can add perspectives not yet appreciated by clients

(Divine, 2009a; Frost, 2009; Hunt, 2009a). Even so, the client's metagoal or coaching objective needs to derive entirely from the client. Although coaches may play a big part in clarifying objectives, their efforts have more to do with drawing out meaning and dimensionality of these objectives than cocrafting the objectives themselves.

Encourage Clients to Share Goals Publicly

What constitutes *public acknowledgment* is key to understanding this idea. People who self-direct their own change processes are more likely to succeed if they make their commitments known to others (Locke & Latham, 2006). This principle is central to the structure of self-help groups, where participants state openly to others what they are struggling with and what they intend to do to change (Etter et al., 2000). Within the coaching sphere, clients inform coaches of their intentions. This represents public acknowledgment and is often enough to make a difference in behavior change. Each of us has ruminations about what we want, what we hope for, or what we imagine. Such wishes and hopes have more potency at certain moments than at others. As long as they remain inside our heads, however, they largely represent ideas or speculations. Saying them out loud to another person increases the probability of action and consequently the likelihood of success. It may well be that as social animals, our internal realities are validated when we announce to others our intentions in a context of acceptance and compassion. When we just say things to ourselves internally, there may be too many dissenting voices in our heads.

Strategize With Awareness of Clients' Uniqueness

Each coaching process is coconstructed with intimate knowledge of clients' personal qualities, background, needs, style, motivations, and timing. Whatever actions are codetermined in coaching are unlikely to represent off-the-shelf solutions. Even when generic guidelines are followed, such as those that might be part of a leadership development plan, personalized adaptations must be considered. The multiple dimensions of each client's patterns in approaching matters related to their coaching agendas need to be appreciated (see Flow Model of Coaching in chapter 5). Coaching methods are shaped to align closely with what works for a particular client.

A useful example of how personality influences the design of actions involves the much-discussed difference between the habits of introverts and those of extroverts (Cain, 2013). We know that the social context of a given action plan can support or sink it depending on whether your client prefers introversion or extraversion. For instance, engaging in a solitary learning activity on a regular basis could be seen as cruel punishment for an extrovert, whereas an introvert may relish this space for reflection and replenishment.

A SuPeRSMART STRUCTURE FOR SETTING GOALS

Your coaching practice can benefit from having a framework for identifying elements of what you and your client are coconstructing in a goal-setting process. If you consider all that I have presented thus far, you might be able to cobble together a reasonable set of criteria against which to measure the robustness of the action plans envisioned by your clients. To facilitate matters, let me suggest the model for goal setting known as **SuPeRSMART** (self-controllable, public, reward, specific, measurable, adjustable, realistic, time specific; Donatelle & Kolen Thompson, 2011; Powers et al., 2005). It will help you assess the detailing of client goal setting. The more commonly known representation of this framework is **SMART** (see chapter 3), which was originally proposed by Anthony Raia (1965) and George Doran (1981) in the context of management planning. The SuPeRSMART model has, in my opinion, significant advantages over the simpler SMART formulation; here's a brief review of the elements of a SuPeRSMART goal-setting process (see table 14.1 for examples of each element).

SuPeRSMART: Self-Controllable

Both short- and long-term goals need to be under the person's control. You can't aim to change something that is out of your control. For example, a client may wish to lose 10 pounds (4.5 kg) in the next month. That goal might be realistic for some, but it could prove beyond reach for others even with their best efforts. People cannot fully manage all the factors (e.g., genetic, physiological, historical, environmental) that regulate the rate at which they lose weight. A self-controllable weight-loss goal for a client could be to consume a fixed number of calories while expending a target amount of energy on a daily basis until he has lost the weight.

SuPeRSMART: Public

Even before clients announce their goals to others, they need to make them public to themselves. That is, they need to express to themselves their intention to engage in a specific process of goal pursuit. Because visions of a desired future propel us toward achievements (Senge, 2006), those who maintain attention to their goals are more likely to succeed. Reminders that focus clients' attention on their planned actions and toward tracking progress can be most beneficial. For example, a client might need to add coaching commitments to their agendas just as they would other appointments.

Public support might take the form of clients sharing goals with their coaches or enlisting the support of family and friends. In determining the robustness of an action plan, coaches normally inquire about ways to share the goal and how to get support from others in one's network.

SuPeRSMART: Reward

When clients have **intrinsic motivation** to achieve their goals, it's more likely that they will succeed than when they rely on **extrinsic motivation.** Nonetheless, an effective form of extrinsic motivation can be one that is linked to the client's goals (e.g., buying a new meditation app after meditating regularly for three weeks or going on a weekend retreat at a meditation center when the practice has been fully adopted and maintained for six months). Remember that rewards need to promote goal attainment rather than detract from it (e.g., in the example of a client trying to reduce screen time, rewarding oneself with a new app might be counterproductive).

SuPeRSMART: Specific

Bearing in mind whether the goal type is outcome, performance, process, or some other form of goal, specific details will vary. For instance, details of outcome goals may be stated in objective results, performance goals are likely to be stated in terms of standards of behavior, and process goals will most likely be presented in the framework of how actions would be engaged or experienced.

SuPeRSMART: Measurable

This element of goals requires that clients be able to articulate their progress in a quantifiable fashion. When objective data are difficult to define or unavailable, subjective information, such as self-

Table 14.1   Illustration of a SuPeRSMART Goal Statement for Managing Usage of a Cell Phone

SuPeRSMART	Example
S = self-controllable	My goal is to manage my usage of my cellphone during nonworking hours. I am largely in control of whether and how often I choose to access information on my cell phone. Except for emergency situations, I typically do not have to check for updates or new messages throughout the evening hours.
P = public	I will tell my partner and close friends that I plan to limit accessing my cell phone to under 100 minutes during nonworking hours. Likewise, I will post my commitment in a prominent note on the fridge so my family can help remind me.
R = reward	For every week where I meet my goal, I will reward myself with a 20–30-minute sauna at my health club.
S = specific	My goal is to contain screen time on my cell phone during workweek days to 100 minutes or less.
M = measurable	My cell allows a display of usage in a 24-hr graph. I will keep a record of usage during non-work hours and review it on a weekly basis.
A = adjustable	I will note in my calendar the days when I have required work commitments during off hours and make appropriate time adjustments. When exceptional personal planning or social commitments occur during nonwork hours, I will make a note in my records and estimate the exceptional amounts of time. I will also be mindful of what I consider to be exceptional.
R = realistic	I have been aware of a kind of reflexive checking of my cell in off hours, as well as a self-imposed need to respond to messages that don't have to be dealt with immediately. Also, at this point, I have verified that my current nonwork usage is around three hours per day. In reflecting on my pattern, I think this reduction is quite reasonable.
T = time specific	I will begin my program on January 7 and continue until March 1—for a total of eight weeks. At that point, I will reevaluate based on experiences and results. In the interim, I will review progress biweekly with my family and as part of my biweekly coaching sessions.

ratings, can be used. Clients engaged in meditation programs could measure heart rate and blood pressure before and after each sitting as well as subjectively assessing emotional tone and body tension.

SuPeRSMART: Adjustable

Gollwitzer (1999) described the value of implementation intentions to help people engage in the behavior to which they commit. Implementation intentions are formulated as if–then statements: "If situation x happens, then I will do y." A practical illustration might be "When I get up in the morning, then I will meditate for 20 minutes." What is even more important about Gollwitzer's theory is his addition of the even-if clause, such as "When I get up, then I will meditate for 20 minutes, even if I feel rushed to get out of the house." According

to Gollwitzer, the addition of an even-if condition solidifies clients' resolve to perform the intended behavior even if they are distracted from doing what they had originally planned.

Of course, even with well-thought-out plans, the unexpected can happen. A child might get sick, and the parent must stay home instead of going to work. The dog might need to be taken to the vet, whose only available appointment is when one's scheduled language class is taking place. Life happens! To safeguard clients from an avoidable sense of failure or incompletion, goals need to be flexible; clients need a plan B. When something arises that alters plans, implementation intentions might unfold as follows: "When situation x happens, then I will do y even if z occurs. If I am unable to do y as planned, then I will do y^1." This could be translated into the following scenario: "When I get up (x), then I will meditate (y) even if I feel rushed to get out of the house (z). If I inadvertently get up too late, then I will meditate at night (y^1).

SuPeRSMART: Realistic

This aspect of goals is often a prelude to a commitment check. Coaches might ask questions concerning possible obstacles to engagement in planned activities. Where there are challenges to implementation, similar to the emergent situations just addressed, strategies would be discussed for dealing with them. In coaching relationships, clients are likely to be working on a number of interconnected action plans at the same time. Sometimes, a session will conclude with a client committing to two or more new action plans. You need to remain mindful of all the balls your clients are juggling at the same time, which will be part of the assessment of how realistic the goal is.

SuPeRSMART: Time Specific

When is this going to happen? Virtually all coaching sessions end with an action plan—or, at the very least, a commitment to continuing an ongoing action. Normally in coaching, the expectation is that actions designed in the session will commence shortly after the session and continue until the next one. At that point, progress may be reviewed and action strategies revised as needed.

By persistently referencing all action plans to the SuPeRSMART template, clients quickly learn how to frame their proposals for commitments. They move away from loose formulations of action plans. "I'm going to get on this soon" morphs into phrases such as "Beginning tomorrow morning and for each morning thereafter until we meet again in 2 weeks, as soon as I wake up, I will spend a minimum of 5 minutes (maximum 10) mentally focusing on my main priority for the day. I will sit quietly in my bedroom with no distractions and let the one thing I most want to achieve this day come to mind."

It's important to bear in mind that this SuPeRSMART model represents the coach's internalized framework for hearing what is emerging in clients' descriptions of what they are committed to doing in the interim between sessions. You typically won't lead your client letter by letter through the SuPeRSMART elements; rather you will notice whether the client has indicated the behavior in sufficient detail to reflect elements. You may ask a question when an element like making the goal public might be missing. This might sound like, "Who in your network

might you let in on your plan so they can support you through this process?" Likewise, awareness of time factors in engagement can be important to bring to mind. Often clients sound as if they are going to leave the session and start immediately. Making dates and times explicit in coaching can be significant in helping clients shape a clear image in their minds of the *when* of their commitments.

LEARNING AGENDAS

Coaching wholeheartedly embraces learning as either the primary objective of a coaching relationship or as a derivative of pursuing a more concrete outcome. Learning incorporates insights, new awareness, increased understanding, developing competencies, knowledge gains, perspective change, and so much more. When I reflect on my clients' agendas, no matter how narrowly targeted some of them may be there is always an accompanying learning process with ramifications for other issues and areas of their lives. They may not have intended to learn how to be better parents while working on a leadership skill, but they comment about how that has happened in parallel with their shifting patterns at work. Sometimes they see reflections of their habits in earlier periods of their lives, and they are stunned by the pervasiveness of these behaviors over the course of years. Other times, they connect the dots to form a new insight about something they want to pursue or learn.

So much happens in coaching that is not on the original list of expected outcomes that clients describe. In this respect, many learning outcomes from coaching may not have been anticipated. On the other hand, as noted in chapter 3, two factors greatly influence the nature of goals that clients might identify for coaching. Clutterbuck and Spence (2017) thought that the complexity of a goal combined with the relative stability of the environment influenced whether goals would best be formulated according to SMART structures or as learning objectives. In this sense, sometimes a learning process describes the kind of outcome that clients are directly pursuing in their coaching work.

You already know that coaching takes form in a structured conversation moving from the identification of a focus for the session to the framing of mental or behavioral activities that clients will pursue in the period following the session. Even so, the process isn't necessarily linear. No matter what the client is discussing in the moment, there exists an opportunity for insight and learning. Coaches are attuned to the possibility of light bulb moments at any time and in relation to any issue within the session. Sometimes these learnings relate to practical matters, such as how to do things better or what's needed to navigate particular dynamics; and other times, they pertain to more personal learnings about how clients understand themselves, patterns of thought, feeling, or action, or perhaps how they seem to be reframing their identity in the process of change.

If different helping processes were arranged along a continuum representing the degree to which a process focuses on fostering insight or on promoting behavioral changes, where do you think coaching would be located (see figure 14.1)? The question here is not what do clients experience, but rather, what is the intention of the work within different helping processes?

Considering the approach of depth psychology, historically the focus of this work has been on developing insight. By extreme contrast, some of the harsher illustrations of behavioral psychology demonstrate a unwavering interest in behavior control as manifested in actions. Clearly, coaching is somewhere between the two ends of the continuum. But where exactly? While it is true that many of the newer forms of psychotherapy such as acceptance and commitment therapy (Hayes et al., 2011), solution-focused therapy (Kim, 2014) and cognitive behavior therapy (Beck & Beck, 2011) mirror coaching in their focus on actions and even homework assignments between sessions, it's unlikely that many therapists will have such a steadfast focus as coaches on forwarding action and creating action plans within their sessions. Of course, as you will remember from chapter 1, there are lots and lots of styles and approaches to coaching.

At different points, I have made brief references to the challenges facing the field of coaching in the future. It is likely that, using Clutterbuck and Spence's (2017) terms, you will increasingly experience complex problems that clients are addressing within unstable environments. These are not the kinds of coaching agendas that are best suited to SMART goal formulations, but rather they require different strategies emphasizing insight, learning, and sense making. Awareness of this emerging shift in coaching work has stimulated writers to propose new forms of coaching conversations, including what Richard Stelter (2013, 2014, 2018) has defined as third-generation coaching. He defines this way of coaching as

a form of dialogue where coach and coachee are focused on creating space for reflection through collaborative practices and less concerned with fabricating quick solutions. Aspiring to achieve moments of symmetry between coach and coachee, where their dialogue is driven by a strong emphasis on meaning-making, values, aspirations and identity issues, coach and coachee meet as fellow-humans in a genuine dialogue. (2013, p. 23)

Even in this emerging trend the dual emphases on learning and action continue to be represented. As Stelter (2013) further identified his understanding of coaching, he described it as a cocreative process involving developmental dialogue where clients can immerse themselves in reflections that "should enable new possible ways of acting in the contexts that are the topic of the conversation" (p. 8). As clients address increasingly complex agendas in ever more unstable environments, coaching

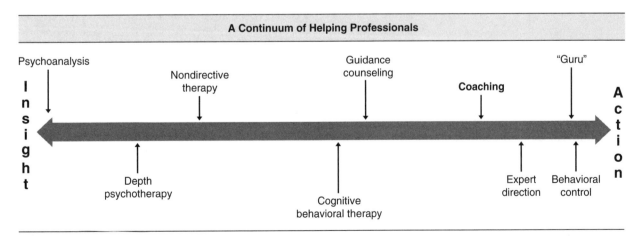

Figure 14.1 Coaching compared to other helping professions on a continuum of developing insight to promoting action.

conversations may likely represent dialogues where learnings and actions are continually harvested throughout each session. This differs from a singularly focused process where a coaching conversation identifies a specific target, gathers information and perspectives, and then drives toward a grand finale where learnings and actions are solidified and celebrated. No matter what the coaching agenda, in a goal-centric approach to coaching you will remain attuned to the action needs related to the client's agenda as well as the learnings that are either directly or indirectly correlated with the work. In all of your work, there is an open invitation for your clients to express insights and learnings as they arise.

PRACTICALITIES IN COACHING ACTION AND LEARNING

Irrespective of whether actions and learnings are shaped during the session and then articulated clearly toward the end or whether they drop out in different moments throughout, there are some fundamental tasks that coaches need to attend to within each session. These include the following: (1) a process of harvesting and confirming what has been cocreated within the session in terms of learnings, actions, and implications for the future; (2) a consideration of supportive processes needed to ensure continued engagement with learnings and actions surfaced in the present and previous sessions; (3) a determination of processes for accountability to commitments; (4) acknowledgment and celebration of clients' engagement and experiences, including progress and learning; and, (5) agreement on closing and identification of next steps, including meeting schedules.

Harvesting and Confirming

With awareness of all that has been said and done within a session, you will sense whether learnings and actions need to be reinforced toward the session's close, whether particular aspects of the cocreated results of the dialogue need further exploration, and whether current work needs to be framed in the context of the entirety of clients' coaching work. Coaching sessions are time bound, and dialogues need to be crafted so that threads of conversation are woven together through exploration and review as the session progresses. These threads pertain to what your clients might have learned about them-

selves, what actions they have structured for the upcoming period, and how these will have bearing on their lives in the immediate future.

Movement toward a session's end has a kind of choreography where coach and client partner to bring the discussion to a fruitful closure rather than an abrupt stop. A process of reflecting, summarizing, imagining, and concluding is mutually facilitated, particularly as clients learn the rhythms of a coaching process. As a coach, you are more likely to inquire of your client about their learnings, actions, and implications than offering a summary from your perspective.

Supportive Processes

What will your clients need as they contemplate moving forward from this session? What else might they have to consider to ensure that their intentions are well formed? Are there particular resources within themselves or elsewhere in their worlds that they want to draw upon to support their efforts? These kinds of questions arise throughout the session, yet they may also represent checkpoints as sessions are ending.

Sometimes there are people in the clients' worlds who need to know about their change intentions, and sometimes you as coach may represent an important source of support. How will clients continue to think about and reflect on their experiences in the session to feed momentum? Might they be best to journal each day or to devote a brief, scheduled period to contemplate where they are, what they are doing, how things are going, and what might be needed? Support needs to be framed as widely as possible to include the material and immaterial, the personal and the practical. It's hard to identify all the faces of support pertinent to different intentions, but as a coach you want to be mindful of who your clients are and what might represent strong and appropriate support for their efforts.

Commitments and Accountability

Throughout your history of working with particular clients, you will learn how commitment is manifested in their words and actions. The need to ask whether clients are committed to their learning and change agendas will depend on the unique nature of your clients and the agendas that they are confronting in the moment. Sometimes you check for commitment in a very intentional way, while at other points you can simply reflect the confirmation that is evident from clients' own words.

Commitment isn't like signing a document or shaking hands on a deal. It's a process, and that process morphs into ways in which clients monitor their ongoing engagements or keep track of themselves. At times, it's critical to explore ways of gauging the client's accountability to their commitments. This isn't about the coach keeping tabs on the client but rather encouraging clients to generate their own ways of knowing whether they are following through and identifying strategies to correct their course if they aren't. The focus on accountability is one of supporting clients' self-responsibility. Coaches help clients design reflections or benchmarks for knowing how well they are living their commitments.

Once again, it isn't the coach's responsibility to monitor client engagement. As you can imagine, unhelpful power dynamics are signified when clients see coaches in the role of judge and always feel they have to report on their actions. Moreover, clients may develop a certain reliance on the coach for the evaluation of progress instead of becoming more self-directed and autonomous. A third consideration is that when coaches become the accountability monitor for client commitments, they may become overly invested in the outcomes clients report such that they assume greater responsibility for client actions than would be appropriate.

Acknowledgment and Celebration

A client who was trying to manage a demanding personal and professional life told me the following: "What I need is acknowledgment! I'm trying to make changes and sometimes I succeed; other times I don't. I just want to be seen wherever I am and acknowledged for being where I am, how I am in the moment. Just let me know you see me." In this expression, she was imagining speaking directly to her boss, her colleagues, her spouse, and her kids. She had all the commitment in the world but sometimes it wasn't enough. What she said she needed was to be seen, to be acknowledged. That, she believed, would be an incredible boost to her energy.

Reflecting on this, you want to become more aware of how hard clients are working in their sessions and how some form of acknowledgment of who they are, how they are, what they are doing, and even how things that don't work out can be of

inestimable value. Opportunities to acknowledge clients are likely to arise numerous times in any session. This isn't a matter of jumping on every instance and saying "Wow! Good for you!" or, alternatively, "That must have been so challenging!" Rather, you want to have a kind of intention or mindset to attune yourself to moments where celebration might be welcomed or where acknowledgment of effort, achievement, or challenge might allow the client to feel more visible and understood. As Rachel Naomi Remen (1996) wisely reflected, "The places where we are seen and heard are holy places" (p. 65).

Just as I cautioned against becoming the accountability monitor for your clients, so too I would suggest awareness about your own style of acknowledging and celebrating your clients. You certainly don't want to sound like a cheerleader, nor do you want to allow experiences that you might normally applaud to pass without notice. Maybe a good question to ask yourself is to what degree do you take time to celebrate your own achievements or your courage or your efforts to change? If you rarely miss an opportunity to acknowledge and celebrate yourself, it's likely you will do so for your clients as well.

Closing and Scheduling

Given the dynamics of modern life, I find it difficult at times to schedule my clients at the same time weeks in advance. My schedule has fluctuations and so do theirs. So, I find myself confirming the next session as my sessions close and accommodating as best possible emergent changes. Beyond this task, I also want to be sure that clients aren't left hanging with some last words on their lips.

When possible, signaling to clients that the session is drawing to a close allows space for last-minute thoughts. As a coach you might note that closure is approaching and inquire whether there are any pertinent issues that can be expressed in the remaining time. This, of course, isn't a kind of reopening of the session. It's unlikely you would say with two to three minutes remaining, "Is there anything else you want to talk about?" More likely, you might say, "In these last few minutes, is there anything else you would like to express that might make you feel more complete in our work today?"

As I say this, I am aware of clients who watch the clock and let me know that we are coming to the end of our time. I am appreciative of their comanagement of the time; it helps me raise the question of how we can best end the session and whether the client has thoughts or feelings that they would like to express as we close. Given that this is a shared experience, it's often true that there are things that I want to say in these final moments, perhaps as acknowledgments of my personal experience.

There are other things that may need to happen to create a sense of wholeness and completion related to the work of a particular session, but these are likely to be unique to the circumstances, content, and relationship between coach and client. For the most part, attending to the five areas previously identified will provide ample shape to the learnings, actions, implications, and future engagements relevant to the present dialogue.

ENDINGS AND NEW BEGINNINGS

Much of what we have just looked at concerns the process of a single coaching session that moves toward the harvest at session's end. But how do coaching relationships end? Some coaching agreements have a preset number of sessions; others do not. In either instance, there is an important dialogue that needs to take place to understand, affirm, and reinforce learnings and to proactively explore the transition occurring as the relationship ends.

Endings are often referred to as *closure*, signifying a kind of relationship agenda rather than a static event. **Closure** implies that the client and coach engage in a process of reviewing experiences and extracting potential meanings for future relationships as the current work concludes. If you consider the range of agendas in coaching, you can imagine relationships lasting years. Similarly, it makes sense that some contractual coaching agreements would be shorter—that is, measured in weeks or months. Whether the agreement is short or long term, client and coach will have formed a relationship whose ending can have significant meaning.

Agendas and Opportunities in Endings

What needs to happen when coaching relationships are drawing to a close? As a coach, what might you want to bring forward as your relationships are ending? Some thoughts provided by Walsh (2007) offer guidance for identifying tasks and processes relevant to closure; here are key elements:

- Ensuring your client understands without ambiguity that the relationship is ending

- Creating opportunities for reflection on the work
- Identifying what was learned
- Acknowledging thoughts and feelings about the relationship
- Considering implications of this relationship for future engagements

To achieve objectives such as these, what kinds of conversations might be implied? Building on Walsh's (2007) work, I would like to propose a set of eight tasks for you to consider as being more or less relevant to particular coaching relationships that you have:

1. Reviewing and highlighting significant learnings and changes.
2. Celebrating learning, growth, and changes.
3. Codesigning processes to sustain learnings and changes.
4. Identifying other paths to learning and change as well as resources for emerging directions.
5. Exploring how to reconnect should another cycle of development emerge.
6. Facilitating the transfer of learning to new situations or other agendas through discussions linking what has occurred to future opportunities.
7. Reviewing boundaries and guidelines pertaining to future contact.
8. Acknowledging and addressing thoughts and feelings about this ending.

The ideal scenario is one where coach and client explore their experiences together, though this may not always be possible. Pertinent to this matter, let's consider a variety of types of endings in coaching relationships.

Types of Endings

How do you know when it's time for you and your client to consider the closure of the relationship? Based on work in the helping professions, here are some considerations to help you clarify questions around closure (Gabbard, 1995, 2016; Hepworth et al., 2010; Herlihy & Corey, 2006; Walsh, 2007):

- When you have mutually determined clear objectives through explicit contracting, client progress toward these goals will inform your decisions about ending.

- Since a significant aspect of your work is enhancing clients' autonomous functioning, monitoring the degree to which they are capable of continuing independently will help you sense when you might initiate conversations about ending.

- Self-reflective practices and working under supervision can be invaluable in appreciating when you might be prolonging or hastening the ending of relationships out of personal needs.

- Personal histories as well as culturally related expectations regarding ending processes need to be considered in appreciating when and how closure is brought about.

Even when there is a convenient structure such as a predetermined number of sessions, clients may end sooner or choose to stay longer. There are also times when you as a coach decide the relationship needs to end. Borrowing from Walsh's (2007) analysis, three categories of endings can be outlined: unplanned endings initiated by the client, unplanned endings initiated by the coach, and planned endings.

Unplanned Endings Initiated by the Client

In unplanned endings, the client terminates the relationship unexpectedly. Such endings may surprise the coach, and often clients never share with the coach their reasons for ending. The ambiguity surrounding these endings leaves matters open to interpretation. The following are possible scenarios occasioning unexpected endings.

The Client Is Unable or Unwilling to Discuss the Ending Clients may believe they have made enough progress and are either unable or unwilling to talk with the coach about ending. Studies show that this scenario occurs in 20% to 50% of premature endings in various types of helping interventions (Sweet & Noones, 1989). An interesting dynamic addressing this matter emerged from a study showing that helpers seemed to anticipate that their clients would remain in the process two to three times longer than did the clients (Pekarik & Finney-Owen, 1987). A caveat to keep in mind is that just because a client ends the relationship without warning doesn't mean the work was unsuccessful (Kazdin & Wassell, 1998).

Based on research in psychotherapy, what helpers believed to be the most significant moments in the relationship were often different from those clients believed to be most important (Stalikas & Fitzpatrick, 1995, 1996). In coaching, even when coaches see a need for continuing, clients ultimately decide whether the process is serving their needs. When clients believe they have received what they came for, they may just presume the coach will understand without an explanation of why they are ending the relationship.

The Client Is Dissatisfied With the Rate of Progress Some clients expect immediate results. If they don't get them, they may quit. Clients take varying amounts of time to reach a point of quitting because of disappointment with results. In some cases, they stay too long; in others, not long enough. Based on Strean's (1986) analysis, we can extract some hints about why coaching clients precipitously end the relationship. Clients may think their coaches don't listen well or that they are too directive. Likewise, clients may never develop sufficient trust and safety in the coaching relationship. Perhaps they believe the coach holds negative opinions of them or that the coach is identifying too strongly with their issues. Clients may experience their coaches as emotionally insensitive or, conversely, too focused on emotional agendas. As a coach, getting regular feedback from your clients may reduce the likelihood of these kinds of endings.

The Client Is Uncomfortable With Some Characteristic of the Coach This might arise from differences in cultural backgrounds, age, gender, style, or other matters; however, discomfort can also result from something entirely peculiar to the client's personal history and experiences (Reis & Brown, 1999; Walsh, 2007). Certainly, there are times when the lack of chemistry between coach and client is unclear at the beginning of the relationship but becomes more evident as time goes on. Clients may be more inclined to abruptly end the relationship when they experience difficulty in confronting their discomfort with the coach. Of course, even if such matters are confronted, the conclusion to end may be the same.

The Client Leaves During a Hiatus in the Coaching Relationship Absences, vacations, or unexpected life events can break the rhythm of a coaching relationship. During times like these, clients may consolidate lessons they have gained from the work, or they may come to realize they are not as motivated to continue as they thought. At a deeper level, it is also possible that if there is a hiatus in meetings, clients may become aware of a disquieting sense of dependency they feel and not want to perpetuate it. In most helping relations, vacations or lengthy breaks in contact increase the probability of clients' ending.

The Client Is Uncomfortable With the Coach's Style

No matter how you articulate what coaching is, clients may hang on to their own expectations of how you should approach issues. Many clients expect helpers to tell them what to do (Shebib, 2020) or believe helpers should be able to resolve their issues in a few meetings. Coaches may need to go to great lengths in describing their style and the processes of coaching. The more the client knows about the possible evolution of the work, the more positive outcomes are likely to be (Frank & Frank, 1993). Asking for feedback and clarifying role expectations on a regular basis can improve the alignment between your coaching behaviors and your clients' expectations.

Unplanned Endings Initiated by the Coach

Coaches also unilaterally decide to end their relationships with clients. Reasons may derive from issues in the relationship or specific concerns. Some possibilities identified in helping relationships (Walsh, 2007) are framed here as they might play out in coaching.

The Client Seems to Lack Commitment

Clients typically begin with good intentions. Then, reality sets in. Changing is hard. It doesn't occur automatically by hiring a coach. Clients need to engage, and these engagements may require effort they are unwilling to expend. Following a pattern of client disengagement, coaches may sensitively raise the question about clients' expectations and the appropriateness of this type of work. An important ethical issue may arise in this scenario. Some clients might be willing to continue coaching as long as they don't have to change. Since coaching is based on clear agreements to pursue agreed-upon objectives, you might need to initiate discussions regarding closure when clients consistently fail to live up to their commitments.

The Client Crosses a Professional Boundary

Boundaries have to do with limits. Bruhn and colleagues (1993) outlined five aspects of boundaries that seem relevant to coaching: (1) contact time, which is the amount of time coaches and clients agree to spend working together, including time spent in phone and email correspondence; (2) types of information shared, which include the range of topics and discussions agreed to by coach and client; (3) physical closeness, which concerns issues of touch and physical closeness permitted in the relationship; (4) territory, which refers to the range of physical settings in which the client and coach will work together; and (5) emotional space, which deals with the level and range of emotions appropriate to the goals and purposes of the relationship. Some boundary violations may have to occur only once to justify a coach's decision to end the relationship.

The Client Engages in Behaviors Unacceptable to the Coach

Clients may use language that is racist, sexist, or foul. They may show up for appointments after drinking or show indications of other offensive behaviors. Clients may repeatedly come unprepared or multitask during sessions (e.g., answering phone calls, eating). You may decide the client's behavior is unacceptable based on personal values or professional standards.

The Coach Has Negative Feelings About the Client

As Walsh (2007) suggests, helpers don't like to admit they may have negative feelings toward certain clients. Just as a client may discontinue the relationship based on the coach's personal characteristics, a coach may not want to work with certain people. When coaches can identify this attitude at the beginning of the relationship, they may readily suggest that the person work with another coach. More problematic are cases in which increasing dislike develops over time. This kind of situation may require that the coach review matters with a supervisor or mentor coach.

The Client Continues to Show Poor Progress

Despite a client's best intentions and a coach's best efforts, a client simply may not be able to successfully engage the process of coaching or implement agreed-upon steps to reach goals. This instance is different than the issue described earlier; here, the problem may arise from clients' capacities rather than their motivation. Clients may have other hurdles to contend with before they are able to take on the challenges that they have set for themselves in this coaching relationship. Although referring the client to another professional may be in order, the coaching relationship does not necessarily have to end. You might suggest a hiatus in coaching while clients work on identified impediments to progress.

The Coach Becomes Overwhelmed

Life happens, and coaches, like all humans, are vulnerable to disease, disability, stress, and strain. Though they might be expected to manage their personal and work lives well enough that conditions such as burnout do not occur, they sometimes take on more than they can handle, or the unexpected happens. It makes sense to plan for contingencies and perhaps work in concert with other coaches who have compatible styles so appropriate referrals can be made when situations of this nature might occur.

Planned Endings

Progress in coaching may mirror phases of the flow model (see chapter 5) in a relatively seamless manner. This doesn't always mean that clients achieve the fullness of their goals; rather, some other mutually determined criterion may be the determining factor in ending. The following represent a few possible scenarios.

The Client Achieves Desired Goals   Clients may progress toward their objectives until they feel they have achieved a satisfactory point. Sometimes, clients may set consecutive goals with the same coach and recycle through the phases of coaching until they feel satisfied. In these instances, the end may come after a number of successes.

Coaching Ends After a Specified Period or Number of Sessions   Clients may agree to meet for a certain number of sessions to advance a particular agenda. They may not have concrete outcome goals as much as they have process goals of working in new ways or experiencing things differently with the assistance of a coach. For practical reasons, some clients may have budgeted a particular amount of money for coaching and scheduled a specific number of sessions to work on an agenda.

A Client's Objectives Suggest Other Approaches   A coach and client may discover a host of concerns clients need to address. For instance, some clients may have serious health issues that jeopardize their capacities. Through dialogue, a coach and client may create a plan of action for the client to address these matters with other processes or other people. Contact with the coach could continue for an agreed-upon time during which strategies are planned for addressing clients' emergent issues.

Reactions to Endings

Feelings are likely to vary when coaching relationships end. Ideally, clients feel a strong sense of achievement from the goals they have pursued and attained. Through coaching, clients may also have gained an enhanced sense of autonomy and personal efficacy. Beyond achieving specific goals, they may have learned how to learn, plan, and strategize for success. Potentially, they will feel more accomplished and express greater confidence in themselves by virtue of having successfully committed to their goals.

At a process level, clients have reason to rejoice in their ability to work collaboratively with another person and to be transparent in relationship with another person. Transferring this learning to other relationships holds the potential for generating yet other sources of satisfaction. Although clients may experience such emotions as sadness regarding the ending of a significant coaching relationship, they may integrate these experiences as normal and appropriate. If they allow these emotions to be legitimate and without judgment, this can also afford a meaningful benefit from the coaching process.

More problematically, clients may react with a significant sense of loss when the coaching relationship ends. This is more likely to occur when coaching has continued over a long time or clients have been unsuccessful in achieving process goals of increased autonomy and self-efficacy. In some instances, clients may react with disappointment at the ending of a coaching relationship. They may feel the coach wasn't helpful or skilled enough to support sustainable change.

As a coach, you want to maintain perspective about what might seem like reasonable requests by clients for continuing contact through a new relationship, such as friendship or social connection. This is often an individual matter of choice, yet there are times when clients are reluctant to end yet cannot justify the continuation of coaching. In reaction, they may try to transform the coaching relationship into a form of connection they can more easily justify (e.g., social media exchanges, personal friendship, mentorship, student–teacher).

Clients are not the only ones affected by endings. Coaches also experience enhanced feelings of self-efficacy and take appropriate satisfaction in their work and clients' accomplishments. Just as clients who end long-term coaching relationships may feel some emotionality, coaches may experience similar reactions. Through those feelings, coaches will hopefully deepen their capacity for compassion.

Having considered a wide range of potential endings and recognizing that endings are ideally construed as processes rather than events, one important implication is that coaches who have robust practices are likely to be navigating multiple endings—as well as new beginnings—in the same period of time. As a coach, you might need to take time to process experiences in your practice, especially when relationships veer off in directions not intended or desired.

COACHING ACTION AND LEARNING IN THE ICF CORE COMPETENCIES

The material of this chapter seems to align well with the learning and action focus of the eighth and final ICF core competency, facilitating client growth. In Passmore and Sinclair's (2020) writing about the eight ICF core competencies, they identify four elements of this competency: (1) facilitating learning into action, (2) respecting client autonomy, (3) celebrating progress, and (4) partnering to close the session (see sidebar, ICF Core Coaching Competency 8: Facilitates Client Growth).

There may be a tendency in this final competency to imagine many of the indicated coach behaviors as occurring largely towards session's end. The fact is insights and learning may arise at any moment, and actions as well may naturally emerge throughout discussions. Especially when you consider that what occurs in each session is part of a longer, somewhat continuous conversation over the duration of the entire coaching relationship, a harvesting of ideas, learning opportunities and actionable elements may surface almost anywhere in a session, depending on developments in the current and longer conversation.

What is perhaps most interesting about this competency is the growing emphasis in the coaching field on augmenting clients' knowledge base through coaching. Such knowledge development incorporates greater self-awareness, awareness of others, perspective shifts, and an ever-broadening worldview. While the cocreation of actionable agendas remains central to the work of coaches, there seems to be a more integrated relationship between concrete and tangible outcomes and ones that occur in the inner lives of clients. Learning as it might occur in coaching relationships may largely center around the coaching objective, but it may as well have relevance to the wider realm of clients' lives. Coaches can never know what will awaken in their dialogues with clients.

Of course, this competency addresses the robustness of clients' action planning and accountability to actions to which they commit. In this chapter the SuPeRSMART model was articulated in fine detail, not as a formulaic process that coaches employ but rather as an internal template that guides sensitive and appropriate inquiry about what clients may need to augment their probabilities of engagement and success.

Celebration is an important part of this competency. At various points in this chapter, the coach's need to acknowledge and celebrate client experiences and efforts was underscored. Again, this is not seen as an end-of-the-session effort, but rather it represents a mindset where coaches inherently know the centrality of honoring clients wherever that is possible and appropriate in their work. Coaches celebrate and they acknowledge; indeed they rejoice with their clients as both unfold into this creative effort.

The theme of partnering seems deeply embedded in all aspects of this competency. The coach is never the wise one, the director, or the expert. Both parties are fully leaning into the work. This speaks to the coach's way of fostering client autonomy in all facets of the work. Finally, what surfaces once again in the ICF's description of this competency is the life-affirming and positive way of being that shows up in coaches' relationships with their clients.

ICF Core Coaching Competency 8: Facilitates Client Growth

Definition: Partners with the client to transform learning and insight into action. Promotes client autonomy in the coaching process.

1. Works with the client to integrate new awareness, insight or learning into their worldview and behaviors

2. Partners with the client to design goals, actions and accountability measures that integrate and expand new learning

3. Acknowledges and supports client autonomy in the design of goals, actions and methods of accountability

4. Supports the client in identifying potential results or learning from identified action steps

5. Invites the client to consider how to move forward, including resources, support and potential barriers

6. Partners with the client to summarize learning and insight within or between sessions

7. Celebrates the client's progress and successes

8. Partners with the client to close the session

REFLECTIONS

I remember as a session was ending one day, my client telling me, "Well, that was another hard session—but a good one." He went on to say that the last three sessions had also been hard, though only in this session could he begin to see the light. He also expressed how after some sessions, his head hurt. That's not typical feedback in my experience, but I know I sat with his remarks for a while. I have often thought that the hard part is more likely to be the engagement in action than the discovery and planning processes of sessions themselves. Even though the more common messages I get toward the ends of sessions are ones of relief, happiness, connection, or progress, I am glad this client awakened me to the challenges, if not struggles, that clients may experience in coaching dialogues.

This client's feedback reminds me that the creative processes in coaching bear at least a metaphorical resemblance to the birthing experience. A coaching process is unlikely to have anywhere near the intensity of physical and emotional experiences occurring in childbirth, yet when clients are trying to shift big pieces of their lives, their identity, their ingrained habits and patterns, there may well be monumental effort and significant discomfort.

When coaches talk about celebrating their clients, it's not a pro forma act. It derives from a deep awareness of the potential intensity in a coaching process—the moments of ecstasy and the various collisions and confrontations with our humanity, the humanity of others, and the realities of our lives. We celebrate because learning and growing represent hard-earned achievements, and pursuing our personal evolution may involve elements of mourning along with profound realizations.

CHAPTER 15

COACHING AS A WAY OF BEING

What you are to be, you are now becoming.

Carl R. Rogers

I have wondered at times what clients would think if in particular moments they could hear my interior dialogue and sense my rapidly beating heart. Early on, it comforted me to read in professional texts that too much self-disclosure in professional helping relationships is not a good thing, even though a strong part of me really wanted to be more visible. With the advent of coaching, I was drawn to the fact that coaching represents a partnership where I might bring in more of me than in other helping contexts. I have often thought my clients could see right through me anyway; I don't strive for a mask-like demeanor in my practice. Yet, for many years I experienced an ambivalence about being more transparent. In my scared moments when a client might be staring at me for a long time without words, I would practice counting as a way of remaining calm. I also kept composure by reminding myself that it's the client's job to talk so the pressure to speak first in these disquieting silences should be felt more strongly by the client.

You may have a sense of where I'm going. Why couldn't I just be transparent? What was I so afraid of clients knowing about my interior experiences in sessions? I think we are all works in progress, and at different moments in my progression, I have felt shame, embarrassment, incompetence, and a host of other things that I believed more capable professionals simply didn't feel. I know now that I'm wrong about that—that most of us feel any number of uncomfortable and even disabling things about ourselves in this very intimate work we do. Besides, I thought I had an added challenge in that I have for most of my life seen myself as being very sensitive—read that as being *too sensitive* at times. So, my journey wasn't always easy, yet I persisted for lots of really good reasons. I loved the work, I loved the people I worked with, and I loved the growth it continually provoked in me. There's no way I will ever say that I'm done growing, though at times I admit to feeling reticent to confronting yet another growth opportunity. That's kind of the nature of this path, as I see it. I don't really envision a rocking chair on a porch somewhere in my future, and I'm pretty delighted about that.

Coaching is more than skill development. Every aspect of your work with clients is impacted by the humanity you bring to your work. In this chapter, the agenda for learning is articulated as a way of being that characterizes not only your professional life but the broader scope of your thoughts, feelings, and actions as well. The concept of a way of being connects to many streams of philosophy and life endeavor, but here I will emphasize its roots in the work of Carl Rogers. I will take his framing and build onto it some further reflections on humility. These perspectives about humility have been voiced in many helping professions as a proposed way of being for practitioners. Near the end of this chapter, I will blend an advocacy for humility in coaching with considerations of inclusion and diversity in our global reality. The concluding piece will address a profoundly important conceptualization—namely, that of cultural humility. Here are some guiding questions as you read:

- What are the elements of a way of being?
- How does a way of being relate to coaching?
- Where does partnership fit into a way of being?
- What does humility mean in a professional context?
- What's the difference between cultural competence and cultural humility?
- How does one cultivate cultural humility?

A WAY OF BEING

The brilliance of coaching derives not only from the mastery of skills and methods, but perhaps more centrally from the authentic way in which coaches show up in life. This way of being is not inherent in those who become coaches but rather a cultivated presence that requires sustained commitment to one's personal evolution. Much of this book has been about understanding who clients are, how change evolves, and what you need to do in a coaching relationship. This chapter is more solidly about you and the learning agenda that extends beyond skill and competency development.

You may be aware that there are innumerable short courses on how to become a coach, and unfortunately many of them misrepresent the field by implying you can become a coach through skill development. It's my view that you can't become a coach by taking a course, no matter how long. On the other hand, you can certainly learn critical skills that will make you a better listener and communicator. Building on this argument, organizations around the globe often sponsor training sessions entitled something akin to coaching for leaders (Kouzes & Posner, 2017), and these kinds of programs can be invaluable in enhancing the communication skills of leaders within their spheres of influence. They hold the potential for shifting conversations in these environments toward more equitable and humane ways of addressing important issues. Yet we both know that if you only master the techniques of communication without manifesting, in Otto Scharmer's (2016) words, an open mind, open heart, and open will, your positive influence on others may be limited in meaning and value.

Of course, I don't know what your personal intentions are for studying coaching, but even if you are reading this book solely for skill enhancement, you might want to know that to be perceived as authentic in any relationship, your words need to fully match your actions. Your words and actions also need to be congruent across the domains of your life. It's hard to maintain multiple personalities or modes of communication in your different life settings. So, this brings us to the concept of a way of being. Let's take a bit of time here to explore this concept as presented through three different lenses: humanistic psychology, integral coaching, and a general coaching perspective.

A Humanistic Perspective

In 1980, Carl Rogers wrote a book entitled, *A Way of Being*. He was in his late 70s when the book was published, and it was largely a philosophical perspective about all that he had experienced in his life and work. He deeply believed that genuine caring and help must derive from the deepest source of our beings. We can't play act. We can't follow a set of instructions or other recipes for effective communication.

In his 1980 work, Rogers detailed the changes and forces in society that seemed to portend for him a positive evolution in our collective ways of being in the world. When he sketched some of the core characteristics of this evolving person of tomorrow (see sidebar, Carl Rogers' *Person of Tomorrow*), he prophetically identified many of the visions we have for ourselves in the present day.

It would be misleading to suggest that all coaches need to embrace such values or perspectives. However, I do think it likely that many coaches subscribe to a similar portrait of a way of being as a guidepost to their own evolution. As you can imagine, this

Carl Rogers' *Person of Tomorrow*

Writing in the late 1970s, Carl Rogers (1980) forecast a vision for humanity that many in the coaching world would readily embrace today. Borrowing from his work, here are highlights of a way of being that he believed was emerging in the late 20th century:

1. *Openness.* This way of being is characterized by an "openness to the world—both inner and outer" (p. 350). Living this way represents an openness to experience, to new ways of knowing and seeing—and a deep curiosity about all things and all people.

2. *Desire for authenticity.* This way embraces honesty and rejects "the hypocrisy, deceit, and double talk of our culture" (p. 350).

3. *Skepticism regarding science and technology.* Rogers spoke not so much of a rejection of science and technology but rather a scrutiny of how they might affect the natural world and serve to diminish human freedom (artificial intelligence, genetic engineering, and psychotropic medication). In another sense, he strongly supported ways in which science and technology might enhance the quality of our lives and our self-awareness.

4. *Desire for wholeness.* This way of being represents a yearning for integration of mind, body, and spirit in all domains of our lives—work, play, and relationships.

5. *The wish for intimacy.* Here we find a desire for new forms of "closeness, of intimacy, of shared purpose" (p. 351). For Rogers, this also implied a search for new ways of living and communicating within communities.

6. *Process persons.* In this way of being, individuals appreciate the ever-changing nature of reality and experience themselves as "always in process, always changing" (p. 351). It implies a welcoming of risk-taking as an inherent aspect of living.

7. *Caring.* This way of being shows up in a "gentle, subtle, non-moralistic, nonjudgmental caring" (p. 351).

8. *Attitude toward nature.* There is a closeness to and a nurturing attitude toward nature that shows up in this way of being. As Rogers puts it, individuals "get their pleasure from an alliance with the forces of nature, rather than in the conquest of nature" (p. 351).

9. *Anti-institutional.* While there is an acceptance of the importance of organizational structures, this way of being is averse to inflexible, highly bureaucratic, and inhumane institutions. Organizations are thought to exist in service of humanity rather than for their own perpetuation.

10. *Authority within.* Trust in one's own experience rather than a reliance on external authority characterizes this way of being. Morality is more personal, even to the extent of civil disobedience when laws are deemed unjust.

11. *The unimportance of material things.* In this way of being, one is "fundamentally indifferent to material comforts and rewards" (p. 352). Money and material status symbols are not the end goals of living. One may be affluent, but this is in no way a necessary condition for life.

12. *A yearning for the spiritual.* A yearning for meaning and purpose in life is core to this way of being. One explores the different "ways by which humankind has found values and forces that extend beyond the individual. They wish to live a life of inner peace" (p. 352). Individuals seek "the unity and harmony of the universe" (p. 352).

moves far beyond the mastery of skills and speaks about who and how you are in the world—personally and professionally. One cannot easily turn empathy on and off, nor can one show up genuinely in one context and inauthentically in another. There is bound to be a kind of leakage between such separate identities. All of this seems to beg the question, "What can I do to show up as caring, compassionate, and genuine in all the domains of my life?"

An Integral Coaching Perspective

Integral coaching represents a vibrant branch of the field. Although originally articulated in the works of James Flaherty (1998), founder of New Ventures West, the perspectives of integral coaching were further developed and expanded by Joanne Hunt (2009a) and Laura Divine (2009a) of Integral Coaching Canada. Both perspectives build from the works of Ken Wilber (Wilber, 2000a, 2000b) who presented models for the evolution of human consciousness, among other important contributions. My overview will derive largely from the work of Hunt and Divine and how they have articulated ideas about ways of being in the world.

In their model of the coaching process, Hunt and Divine rely heavily on a transformational perspective of coaching. For them, coaching represents a process wherein clients are attempting to shift their way of being in the world, rather than attempting to accomplish a singular outcome such as changing jobs. Even though an end result of an integral coaching experience could include a change of jobs, it will encompass so much more. One might say that they direct attention to the infrastructure of a client's being that would support such objectives as job changes, relationship shifts, or other more concrete goal-centric objectives. In a sense, this perspective can be expressed as the difference between writing a book and becoming a writer—or in our case, coaching a client as contrasted with being or becoming a coach.

Whether as client or coach, each of us has patterns of thinking, feeling, acting, and evaluating that are characteristic of how we go about our lives. To a large extent, these are transsituational patterns that tend to apply almost irrespective of what we are doing. This notion of consistency in human behavior can be traced to solid research in the social sciences, including that of Fritz Heider's (1946) perspective of balance theory, Leon Festinger's (1957) theory of cognitive dissonance, Osgood and Tannenbaum's (1955) congruity theory, and Abraham Korman's (1970) consistency model. If you think about your own behaviors long enough, you will likely identify the underlying patterns that essentially describe your way of being in the world.

Let's take this from a slightly different angle. You probably know the adage, "If all you have is a hammer, you treat everything as a nail." For better or worse, this may pertain to your way of being. So many wonderful expressions of your way of being have brought you delight and success over the course of your life, yet there may also be areas where your way doesn't work very well. In the language of Hunt and Divine, there are possibilities that your way of being opens up or makes available—and there are those that it closes down or prevents.

Since this chapter is about you (though its principles apply to clients as well), I want to consider the shift that might be required as you become a coach and develop your practice. Coaching represents far more than the application of tools and models—it

comprises a way of showing up in the world, a way of understanding and thinking, an openness of mind, heart, and will. While it's likely that other helping professions have a similar emphasis, I think there is something unique and special about a coach's way of being.

Let me take a moment to illustrate this last point. I trained in psychology and practiced for many years before embracing the coaching world. Sure, I wanted to help, and I studied lots of ways of being helpful, but my mindset was different. Even though I was reluctant to label clients with different diagnoses, the practice of psychology often required that I find some sort of diagnostic category for the clients with whom I worked. That alone made a big difference in how I was positioned in relationship to my clients. I could go further in identifying other reinforced patterns in my thoughts and actions that characterized me as psychologist, but hopefully you get the point.

Let's get back to the integral model. Building on Wilber's ideas, Divine and Hunt viewed the coaching process as a cycle of development wherein clients work to shift their current way of being so as to generate a new way of being (Divine, 2009a; Hunt, 2009a). If you think of the current way as being somewhat limiting for an individual's present life, then the new approach would hopefully make available so much more that would be deemed desirable. Beyond just being better and opening more possibilities, the process of transition from current to new way creates a kind of inching-along growth in consciousness. The idea of consciousness development is inherent in integral coaching, even though it is not necessarily a primary objective of the process. As always, the client's goal-attainment is primary, while consciousness development is a wonderful benefit that tends to accompany a series of cycles of development described in the integral framework.

As you transition from your current reality to one more centered in your emerging practice of coaching, you are likely to encounter moments where your current way of being feels a bit like the proverbial hammer in its limitations. In moments like these, you will be confronted with the need to change, not just at a skill level but more at the core of your being. This transformational shift offers you the potential for opening so many new ways of appreciating your world and engaging in more impactful action.

How does this happen? In an integral perspective, places where you will be called upon to change have been for the most part located in three categories: How you see the world, how you behave, and where you look to appraise how aligned you are with your intentions.

Seeing the world is about worldview; it's about your perspectives about self, others, the world, and all that these encompass. One of the core tenets of coaching is a belief that clients hold within themselves the answers to their own questions and the necessary resources for change. As a coach, you aren't trying to fix your clients because you don't really believe they are broken—and you believe that with some guidance they can find their own solutions. Sit with this for a moment and ask yourself whether you think this is true—and if you are feeling doubtful, imagine what it might require of you to shift your perspective. Hopefully, in doing so you get some sense of the magnitude of the shift being called for in how you see the world and what it means to inhabit the way of being of a coach.

Behaving in the world is about what you do. Remember the hammer. Each of us has a habitual way of behaving. It's like a default system—we fall reflexively into a pattern often without even recognizing it. Here's a simple observation arising from my years of training coaches. A lot of novice coaches have a default of being the helper or the rescuer when they are first working with clients. Sure, they read all the required texts about how clients hold the answers they need in themselves, yet in action these well-intended coaches are like the 911 response team. Again, what do you imagine it might take to shift that pattern?

Additionally, Hunt and Divine consider how we check with ourselves to know whether we are living our lives according to our intentions and values. You might think of this in relation to individuals climbing the corporate ladder. Did they get promoted on schedule? Were they slotted into various advancement programs offered to the rising stars of the organization? If they discover that they are falling short of the mark, how do they respond? What strategies do they employ to get back on track? Is it a try-harder approach or one filled with blame? In your own life, how do you measure whether you are living up to your own expectations and intentions for your life?

As a coach, what might you look for in understanding whether your work was effective? That your client was happy? That you offered great advice? Or that your client had at least one aha moment? What is your way of appraising your alignment with your purpose and intention? As I ask myself these questions, I have a number of answers, including whether I felt whole and present throughout much of the session and whether I allowed myself to connect as much as possible with my client's meanings and intentions. I know that when I am able to meet these intentions, my clients may leave sessions joyfully or reflectively, but I am likely to believe that the requisite work has taken place.

Having a sense of the three areas of shift—seeing, behaving, and appraising—you might want to know how to foster such changes. In the integral perspective, it's largely about practice—not practicing what you already know and do but rather stretching into new ways of perceiving and behaving. The point arising from this idea of practice is that change doesn't typically come from thinking or reading alone. Change needs to be embodied in our actions. We need to engage the world differently and, in consequence, we will experience ourselves and our worlds differently.

In capturing the essence of an integral view of ways of being, there are a few summary points I would like to make: First, transforming yourself into a coach's way of being will likely represent a significant and lifelong enterprise; it won't happen quickly, nor will the transformation ever be complete because as you change, the world changes, and that evokes new learning and change agendas for your journey. Second, this shift in ways of being may incorporate various kinds of skill development, yet it is so much more than that. Consider what might need to go into changing some of your fundamental ways of thinking or some of your habitual ways of behaving. This is not always easy work. Third, the process of change necessitates the incorporation of new patterns through the inclusion of well-designed practices that serve to foster the new habits you want to form. Finally, it is reasonable to anticipate that through all of these transformational efforts, you will evolve in your awareness; in your understanding of self, others, and the world; and indeed in your level of consciousness.

A General Coaching Perspective

The integral coaching approach just reviewed represents a methodology for working with clients, as well as one that is pertinent to coach transformation. It doesn't articulate any particular directions for the development of individuals or coaches, other than by suggesting that engaging this form of coaching may lead to more evolved and conscious ways of being. In contrast, the work of Chris van Nieuwerburgh (2017) advocates another model for the way of being of a coach. Similar to Rogers, van

Nieuwerburgh acknowledges that embodying this way of being represents a lifelong process of learning and development.

A core element that van Nieuwerburgh (2017) connects to Rogers' work is that of partnership, which for him "denotes a relationship between equals" (p. 165). He references the writing of Knight (2011) in exploring principles of partnership that he considers necessary conditions for coaching conversations. These principles include equality, choice, dialogue, voice, reciprocity, and reflection (see sidebar, Principles of Partnership). You have already been introduced to a number of these principles throughout this book, so they will hopefully make sense to you as keys to effective coaching practice.

As van Nieuwerburgh (2017, p. 174) describes his ideal attributes for a coach's way of being, he once again builds upon the seminal ideas of Rogers. He reasons that coaches have

---

Principles of Partnership

In describing a way of being for coaches, Chris van Nieuwerburgh (2017) articulates a set of partnership principles he believes underlie effective coaching practice. These principles originate in the work of Jim Knight's (2011) work on instructional design but are summarized from a coaching perspective.

- *Equality.* A relationship between equals that fully acknowledges and respects individual differences
- *Choice.* A requirement of freedom of choice regarding various elements pertaining to coaching, including the right to make choices that may be deemed as being bad (p.166)
- *Dialogue.* Conversations where both parties are positioned as explorers and learners, though coaches occupy far less of the conversational space than their clients
- *Praxis.* An emphasis on real-world application in the ongoing processes of coaching
- *Voice.* An honest expression of perspectives by both parties that is held and valued by each
- *Reciprocity.* As a learning experience, both parties are viewed as beneficiaries
- *Reflection.* An encouragement and engagement in reflective moments for each

---

- a deeply imbued sense of humility,
- strong confidence in their coaching talents,
- a caring quality to their work,
- a belief in clients' potential to realize their goals,
- respect for others,
- integrity, and
- intercultural sensitivity.

While there is likely to be nothing surprising in this list, it's important to acknowledge that each of us may subscribe to such a list of attributes, though our behavior may vary to some degree from our ideal way of being. In this light, you might reflect on the ideas raised with the integral perspective about the importance of engaging in transformative practices to better align ourselves with our intentions.

Van Nieuwerburgh's final attribute, intercultural sensitivity, provides a segue to our next section. He notes the increasing cultural diversity in our world and the need for coaches to manifest cultural sensitivity. Moreover, he adds that, "This should not be limited to situations in which there is a perceived difference, but should apply to every coaching conversation" (p. 174).

A HUMBLE WAY

As we move toward the close of this book, I want to suggest that much of what we have been addressing in these last sections about the coach's way of being can be incorporated in an emerging understanding of how all practitioners in our global village might need to orient themselves toward their work with clients. Anne Matthews (2014, p. 130), writing in the *American Scholar*, cites a passage from Benjamin Franklin's autobiography as follows:

> In reality, there is perhaps, no one of our natural passions so hard to subdue as pride. Disguise it, struggle with it, beat it down, stifle it, mortify it as much as one pleases, it is still alive, and will every now and then peep out and show itself.

This quotation sets the stage for our discussion of humility.

Humility

In their scholarly review of humility, Bhattacharya and colleagues (2017) remark how humility is appreciated in most indigenous traditions as an integral part of human nature, rather than as an abstract property that we either do or do not possess. In traditional Indian wisdom, humility is understood as a foundational element in healthy social functioning that facilitates individual happiness.

The meaning of humility can be traced to its Latin roots in the word *humilis*, which translates as *from the earth* (or *humus*). The word connotes a sense of modesty, although sometimes it may imply a feeling of insignificance (Bhattacharya et al., 2017). In the psychological literature, humility has been viewed as a character strength (Exline et al., 2004) that is likely to encompass such elements as an unembellished appreciation of your capacities, an acceptance of your limitations, an openness to new ideas, a valuing of all people and ways of being, and a kind of forgetting of yourself through awareness of the wider universe (Tangney, 2000, pp. 73-74). As framed by other scholars, humility is also thought to incorporate a secure and accepting identity, freedom from distortion, a focus on others, and egalitarian beliefs (Chancellor & Lyubomirsky, 2013).

As well as understanding humility as a character strength (Chancellor & Lyubomirsky, 2013), it has been viewed as a personality trait, a way in which you might see yourself intellectually, and a quality embedded in how you relate to others. Moreover, humility bears clear relationships to such other concepts as modesty, spirituality, forgiveness, self-worth, and generosity (Bhattacharya et al., 2017). As well, organizational theorists have fostered the notion of humility as an essential quality for leaders (Nielsen et al., 2010; Schein & Schein, 2018) and consultants (Schein, 2016).

Integrating the diverse writings and perspectives of humility, Bhattacharya and colleagues (2017, p. 7) suggest that common elements in humility seem to include

- focusing away from self,
- knowing and accepting oneself,
- acknowledging the minuteness of self,
- maintaining an open mind,
- allowing praise without self-exaggeration,
- appreciating others, and
- being gentle though not self-deprecating in manner.

In our increasing awareness and valuing of diversity and inclusion in our world, the theme of humility resonates strongly. It speaks to a way of being with yourself, with others, and in the world. Yet, each of us is likely to feel challenged in living

up to the bar set by the criteria for humility identified previously.

Cultural Humility

The revised ethical code (ICF, 2020b) and coaching core competencies (ICF, 2020c) offered by the International Coaching Federation (ICF) underscore the necessity for coaches to embody a capacity to appreciate and sensitively attune to the unique natures of their clients. The ethical code references the centrality of systemic equality, which includes "gender equality, race equality and other forms of equality that are institutionalized in the ethics, core values, policies, structures, and cultures of communities, organizations, nations and society." It speaks to the necessity of managing power and status differences that may be brought about by cultural, relational, psychological, or contextual issues. It requires that coaches maintain fairness and equality in all activities, avoiding discrimination that may be based on "age, race, gender expression, ethnicity, sexual orientation, religion, national origin, disability, or military status" along with other ways in which individuals may self-identify. Other professions have equally strong emphasis on what might be called cultural orientation and competencies. The question arising in this context is how does this relate to the theme of humility? I will try to answer this after first discussing a couple preliminary matters.

Individual Differences

Psychology represents a prominent root discipline of coaching. This field was founded on the importance of individual differences (Shiraev, 2014). Even so, the assumption of most theoretical approaches was that people are more similar than different. Historically, psychological issues were thought to emerge on the basis of various universal principles, and, consequently, treatment approaches were applied in a one-size-fits-all manner (Hook et al., 2017, p. 4). Whether the approach was based on Freud or some other theorist, cultural identities were minimized in their impact on underlying universal dynamics.

By the late 20th century, sufficient awareness of diversity had surfaced to provoke a revolution in thinking about all kinds of psychological premises. Gender, race, ethnic, religious, socioeconomic, and other differences were increasingly acknowledged as having major implications for treatment and client–helper relationships. With an ever-expanding appreciation of differences, the term *culture* itself was broadened to encompass every aspect of one's life, including values, beliefs, attitudes, and worldviews, along with more manifest or visible differences. More critically, individuals' multicultural identities were not thought to be simple. Each person has a rich intersection of cultural identities that create unique worldviews that can't just be associated with one or another class or group (Cole, 2009). Thus, the question arises as to what cultural identities are most salient to each individual. Unlike earlier understandings of culture, the emerging perspective has been that it is entirely up to the individual, rather than to any practitioner, what cultural identities they deem to be most significant (Hook et al., 2017). With ever-increasing awareness of the profound relevance of multicultural identities, there remained a huge question about what to do. The obvious strategy from a Western mindset was to emphasize multicultural competency training for practitioners.

A Fundamental Problem With Competency

In the psychological field, the first model of multicultural competencies for helping professionals was developed in the early 1980s (Sue et al., 1982). Sue and colleagues offered a three-part process to assist helpers in (1) developing self-awareness of their own cultural backgrounds and experiences, (2) developing knowledge for working with various cultural groups, and (3) developing specific skills for working with culturally diverse clients (Hook et al., 2017). A parallel emphasis was also evident within medical professions where programs were initiated to provide nurses, doctors, and other practitioners with practical tools for working with patients having diverse cultural identities (Tervalon & Murray-García, 1998).

By the early 21st century, cultural competency training was reasonably well embedded in professional training. In their summary of different definitions, Whaley and Davis (2007) offered a description of cultural competence

> as a set of problem-solving skills that includes (a) the ability to recognize and understand the dynamic interplay between the heritage and adaptation dimensions of culture in shaping human behavior; (b) the ability to use the knowledge acquired about an individual's heritage and adaptational challenges to maximize the effectiveness of assessment, diagnosis, and treatment; and (c) internalization (i.e., incorporation into one's clinical

problem-solving repertoire) of this process of recognition, acquisition, and use of cultural dynamics so that it can be routinely applied to diverse groups. (p. 565)

A fundamental flaw in this conceptualization can be found in its underlying premise that competency is essentially a skill set that you can learn (Hook et al., 2017; Tervalon & Murray-García, 1998). There was an implied curriculum and end point to this kind of training, at which moment you would have all that you needed. Once you had obtained a certain level of skill or knowledge for your work with culturally diverse clients, you would have checked the box on your capacity to be culturally competent!

If you are wondering where I'm going with this, let's go back to the beginning of this chapter where we considered the difference between having skills versus being coach-like in all your engagements. A number of coaching competencies, while requiring sensitivity to individual and cultural differences principally delineate communication methods for effective coaching. What you have been reading in this chapter offers the idea that coaching is far more than the accumulation of various skill sets. So, too, when you reflect on the concept of multicultural competence, there is a clear message that this isn't something you can fully embody by reading about it or learning techniques of communication.

The Emergence of Cultural Humility

In their seminal work in the medical field, Tervalon and Murray-Garcia (1998) distinguished cultural competence from cultural humility by describing the latter as "a lifelong commitment to self-evaluation and critique, to redressing the power imbalances in the physician–patient dynamic, and to developing mutually beneficial and non-paternalistic partnerships with communities on behalf of individuals and defined populations" (p. 123). Cultivating cultural humility was thought of as a lifelong process of self-reflection and self-critique to learn about others' cultures and to examine your own cultural identity and belief systems (Yeager & Bauer-Wu, 2013). Since this initial work, the meaning and implications of cultural humility for professional practices have blossomed.

Cultural humility pertains to the inside and outside spaces. It references your interior and your exterior selves—who you are and what you do. It pertains to how you engage in your coaching sessions as well as how you are in the broader world (Hook et al., 2017; Jackson & Tervalon, 2020; Owen, 2013; Owen et al., 2014). Some coaches may function in a way that implies a one-person model where the focus is largely on the client and the coach is present only through orchestrating the coaching process. Here, the person of the coach is deemed to be far less relevant than the techniques applied. Others operate more by a two-person model based on the assumption that the coach has power and meaning in the coaching process. Cultural humility certainly ascribes to a two-person perspective, but likely in a deeper way than might normally be understood (Hook et al., 2017; Wachtel, 1993). Both coach and client have multidimensional cultural identities that mutually influence one another throughout the process. In this respect, standard methods and techniques take on diverse meanings in the mix of coach–client identities.

When Cynthia Foronda and colleagues (2016) examined over 200 articles pertaining to cultural humility, they came up with a powerful definition that points to the work that each of us has to undertake in this lifelong agenda. They wrote the following:

> In a multicultural world where power imbalances exist, cultural humility is a process of openness, self-awareness, being egoless, and incorporating self-reflection and critique after willingly interacting with diverse individuals. The results of achieving cultural humility are mutual empowerment, respect, partnerships, optimal care, and lifelong learning. (p. 213)

They asserted that such an undertaking to embody cultural humility represents a transformative process (Mezirow, 1994) involving learning at the deepest levels and leading to "a change in overall perspective and way of life" (p. 214). Indeed, this path represented to them a way of being that encourages a core level interest in "kindness, civility, and respect" (p. 214) in all interactions. Other thought leaders in this area concur with the view that cultural humility refers to a way of being far more than to a mastery of knowledge and skills (Hook et al., 2017; Jackson & Tervalon, 2020; Owen et al., 2014). Culturally humble practitioners have a valid sense of their own cultural values and maintain "an other-oriented perspective that involves respect, lack of superiority, and attunement regarding their own cultural beliefs and values" (Hook et al., 2017, p. 29).

Cultivating Cultural Humility

So how do you get from here to there? Wherever you are, the mandate for cultivating cultural humil-

ity necessitates certain kinds of engagements. I was intrigued with the developmental challenges that Hook and colleagues (2017) presented in their work on the topic, and so I have reframed them so they speak more to our world of coaching. They offer each of us ideas for how to incorporate this way of being in our journeys.

1. Create a learning network with colearners in quest of greater multicultural appreciation.
2. Inhabit settings that challenge your cultural worldview.
3. Integrate your developing cultural humility into your coaching practice.
4. Explore your cultural identities, reflecting on their impacts in your life's expressions.
5. Confront how you might undervalue multicultural perspectives of your clients.
6. Connect with people who stretch your zone of toleration by their cultural differences.
7. Face your cultural limitations.

These are demanding challenges made more so by the fact that multiculturalism speaks to our identities. When I reconsider the topic of individual differences addressed before, I recognize from these challenges far more than a responsibility for knowing or understanding. The humble way in this context references a deep honoring of differences to a degree that I open myself to exploring how I might reshape myself.

BECOMING A COACH

As mentioned earlier, this chapter is about you and your learning agenda that extends beyond skill and competency development. I hope it's clear from all that you have read in this book that coaching relies on knowledge and skill but also on ways of thinking, feeling, and acting that are aligned with a humble way of being of service in the world. Just now in your reading, humility was the main theme and when reflected in the current emphasis on cultural humility, there appears to be great overlap between points made by Rogers (1980), van Nieuwerburgh (2017), Bhattacharya (2017), and the voices of those advocating cultural humility as a way of being (Foronda et al., 2016; Hook et al., 2017; Jackson & Tervalon, 2020). The consistency of thinking found in these works points out directions you may want to consider as you align your life with your understanding of a coach's way of being.

The Courage to Coach

It takes great courage to choose coaching as a path of change. This path abounds with transformations of comfortable habits into unfamiliar patterns. It requires sustained effort and doing lots of things perhaps for the first time. Though it's likely to be exhilarating, this path may also be fraught with doubts, confusion, and even fear. As a professional entering the coaching field, you may encounter calls to action in virtually every corner of your existence as you deepen your involvement in this realm. The good news is that this doesn't all happen at once. At different moments, inner voices will gain volume as you discover yet another place where you are holding on to self-limiting beliefs or living in comfort zones that no longer serve you.

Coaching as Spiritual Practice

From a certain perspective, coaching can be thought of as a spiritual practice. You may find yourself reflecting on questions about your higher purpose in the work you do. Coaching is a career that asks you to examine your deepest beliefs in order to know where you are positioned in judgment or habit. Over time, you are likely to get better at noticing when you are listening with your own agendas in mind rather than those of your clients. You may see more clearly how you sometimes subtly advance your own convictions because they have worked so well for you and others, though they may be a questionable fit for your client. In moments when you might trip over biases you never imagined you had, you will hopefully begin to smile in acknowledgment of how right this choice is for you.

A Reflective Stance

As a coach, you are likely to become more reflective about your ways. You may notice how intractable some of your habits are or how deeply ingrained certain attitudes and beliefs may be—even though they are no longer aligned with your intentions. You may see how tightly you hold on to your success formulas for doing things, not fully realizing that there is an expiration date on most of your attachments. Over time, your tried-and-true ways may lose their potency, and old habits will decreasingly bring rewards. Beliefs that allowed you to have a sense of belonging may now run counter to ones in a wider multicultural society. You may often feel the ground shifting beneath your feet. Rather than living with a gnawing sense that something is off, a reflective stance will allow you to acknowledge what works, what doesn't, and what might need changing.

Embracing the Butterfly Effect

Realities in the 21st century will continually confront you with the need to adapt, change, adjust, shift, or move. Do you live in the same home where you grew up? The same town? The same country? Do you still speak your mother tongue at work and at home? Have you held the same job for more than five years? Has your view of the world changed through the years? Change is likely a prevalent feature of your life, and as you have seen repeatedly throughout this book, one thing affects another. No change occurs in isolation—the butterfly effect! Knowing this at a deeply personal level allows you to connect more genuinely with all the change your clients bring to their work.

Nurturing Your Best Effort

How you want your career to develop and how much emphasis you give to coaching will be informed partly by your desires and partly by your personal evolution. Becoming an outstanding coach is about nurturing the best of you. There's a great quote from Maya Angelou that says, "Do the best you can until you know better. Then when you know better, do better." By its nature, a coaching career will stimulate your growth as surely as it does that of your clients. Yet this will not happen without clearly defined intentions and actions. There is a curriculum, and it is uniquely yours.

Scoping the Curriculum

So, what's your curriculum? It's challenging to offer any kind of generic template of a curriculum since each of us is so unique and comes to this work with significant amounts of understanding and skill. Yet, we might scope out three domains where relevant personal and professional learning and growth opportunities may be found. The first pertains to the kinds of experiences you may personally choose to embrace in fostering an open mind, open heart, and open will (Scharmer, 2016). The second describes activities with others as a way of learning and receiving feedback. The third references a wide range of professional development opportunities.

Personal Development

I think we covered some of this ground at an abstract level in this chapter. What you may need to do personally is very much a function of your current strengths, understandings, and emerging needs. What do you need to do in order to embody a greater sense of comfort, acceptance, wisdom, power, and fullness in who you are? It makes no sense for me to suggest meditation to you if you are already meditating. Likewise, any other suggestion for you personally would need to derive from coaching conversations related to your current way of being vis-à-vis the new way of being you want to cultivate. Perhaps some of your answers to this agenda are evident to you, or maybe it would be advisable to invest in personal coaching to create your action plan.

Getting Feedback

Each of us has blind spots, and beyond these blind spots, we have preferred ways of doing things that may preclude consideration of other paths. Feedback is invaluable and can be derived from conversations with friends, family, peers, supervisors, and mentors. I generally believe that we all need to have at least one source of reliable feedback for our work. In your early practice, it might be wise for you to find a mentor coach to consult on a regular basis. As you advance in years of practice, you may find additional sources of support with a particular supervisor or in a supervisory group. Peer supervision or codevelopment groups can also be powerful aids to learning. Though your need for mentoring and supervision may taper after a number of years, I don't believe it ever disappears completely.

Lifelong Learning

The third domain contributing to your way of being as a coach can be found in continuing professional education and development. Depending on your present professional and educational background, you may have more or less of what you might need. With the changing realities of today's world, all of us will probably remain on a steep learning curve to remain proficient in our work as coaches. Beyond courses and programs in coaching, you may want to enroll in other forms of learning in the years to come. Given the multidisciplinary roots of coaching, continued learning may take divergent paths based largely on what you already know and the directions in your career that you wish to pursue.

Choices in Your Curriculum

Over your years of practice, you will surely accumulate a wealth of understanding about the coaching field and the intriguing and variable nature of human beings. There may be times when you come across great teachers or inspired authors. You may be enthralled by their methodologies and come to believe in a specific method of coaching. Or you may sample a variety of coaching approaches and find that each approach offers a useful angle to apply to your work. In time, you will discover your own process for being the best coach you can be. It may not come easily or quickly, although hopefully you will be patient and not think you have arrived long before you have. Each experience has something to offer, even when what you learn is something you never plan to do again. Each course of study you undertake holds the capacity to stimulate deeper reflections about yourself and your clients.

Your good intentions, capacity to listen, compassionate stance with clients, and knowledge gained through various sources of learning will serve you well. They will help you know when you are in over your head so you can graciously bow out of coaching encounters that are beyond your current capacities. Perhaps it may be helpful to envision your coaching career on a scale of multiple decades. Can you imagine doing this work for the next 30 to 40 years? Perhaps your answer is an enthusiastic and unequivocal yes. If you are less certain, then taking things one step at a time is sensible. Allow your learning and experiences to inform you about where you want to go and whether this work is deeply in your heart.

COACHING AS A WAY OF BEING IN THE ICF CORE COMPETENCIES

Though this competency is listed second in the list of eight ICF core competencies, I have saved it for last. It seems to correspond to the material in this chapter on a coaching way of being. The definition and critical elements of this competency speak about self-awareness, emotional intelligence, a particular worldview, reflective practice, cultural humility, ongoing learning, and professional responsibility (see sidebar, ICF Core Coaching Competency 2: Embodies a Coaching Mindset). It is noteworthy that the previous version of ICF's core competencies did not reference these matters as clearly as they now appear.

ICF Core Coaching Competency 2: Embodies a Coaching Mindset

Definition: Develops and maintains a mindset that is open, curious, flexible and client-centered.

1. Acknowledges that clients are responsible for their own choices

2. Engages in ongoing learning and development as a coach

3. Develops an ongoing reflective practice to enhance one's coaching

4. Remains aware of and open to the influence of context and culture on self and others

5. Uses awareness of self and one's intuition to benefit clients

6. Develops and maintains the ability to regulate one's emotions

7. Mentally and emotionally prepares for sessions

8. Seeks help from outside sources when necessary.

It's unlikely that the ordering of the ICF's eight core competencies is random. While each has foundational importance, ethical behavior is listed first, followed immediately by reference to the coach's mindset. For me, these competencies have a sine qua non nature, for without ethical behavior and a coaching mindset, it would indeed be near impossible to manifest the remaining six.

When thinking about this competency, it may be evident to you how little it references a particular skill set, like listening actively, but rather it denotes a lifelong agenda of learning and development coupled with the nurturance of certain perspectives and capacities. In this respect, when observing coaching sessions, you would largely know the degree to which coaches are fully representing this mindset by the way they show up. You might think of this as being evident in the 55:38:7 formula proposed by Mehrabian (1972, 1981), which suggests that only 7 percent of your communication comes from your words, with 55 percent reflected in body language and the remaining 38 percent in vocal qualities. Someone may say the right words, but there's 93 percent of the communication that may or may not suggest congruity, compassion, authenticity,

emotional wisdom, respect, equality, and so many other facets of a coach's being.

This competency references several matters that have been covered in previous chapters. For instance, emotional self-regulation as indicated here clearly ties back to our discussions of emotional intelligence, and the theme of supporting client autonomy and self-direction has woven its way through various discussions presented earlier. Furthermore, the capacity to recognize when other sources of assistance might be pertinent to a client's needs was referenced repeatedly in our discussions. Perhaps one emphasis in this competency on mentally and emotionally preparing for sessions merits greater emphasis. Though competency-based discussions in this book have largely dwelled on in-session matters, what coaches do before meeting their clients can be pivotal. You might remember this point from the discussion of preparation for presence in Geller and Greenberg's (2012) work (see chapter 9). This might imply certain practices whereby you clear your mind and open your heart as you enter your sessions, or it might mean reviewing notes and bringing thoughts of your client to mind as you prepare. More practically, it could come down to ensuring that you have ample space between prior engagements and your sessions with clients.

In considering ongoing learning, as an ICF certified coach, you will need to periodically document continuing coach education. This requirement is relatively recent and will likely become more detailed and extensive as the learning agenda of coaches grows. In my experience, coaches seem to be highly committed to ongoing learning, often filling in gaps in their prior learning history or accessing new methodologies pertinent to their domain of practice. Beyond mastering new knowledge, coaches also seem highly committed to practicing what they preach. The ICF offers its members opportunities to be matched up with another coach in a reciprocal coaching arrangement. Here, they sign up to coach and to be coached—both for personal and professional development. Beyond these learning processes, the ICF also sponsors continuing education events, conferences, and communities of practice where coaches can further develop themselves and their coaching expertise. I mention these things partly for your general information, but also to further clarify the meaning of this competency on embodying a coaching mindset.

Coming back to the alignment of material in this chapter with this core competency, I don't believe that the ICF intends in any way to promote a univocal model for a coach's way of being. To embrace a diverse world, there has to be ample space for different ways of arriving at similar outcomes. Yet, in my view, there is sufficient resonance between the standards that the ICF has set for professional conduct and the perspectives offered in this chapter pertaining to a coach's way of being, especially as seen through the lens of cultural humility. As you saw in its definition, cultural humility calls for such qualities as openness, respect, self-awareness, self-reflection, and a degree of egolessness. Moreover, it refers to a stance of minimizing wherever possible power differences and being part of the solution rather than being a bystander in matters of systemic bias and inequality (Foronda et al., 2016; Hook et al., 2017; Jackson & Tervalon, 2020). These qualities correlate well with elements of the ICF's definition of embodying a coaching mindset.

REFLECTIONS

We have come to the end of this work, and so I will simply say, *in the end is our beginning*. Reflections on this last chapter's material can spark deep and prolonged conversations about human nature. In the ending of chapter 1, I referenced Yuval Harari's (2014, 2016, 2018) anticipations of humanity's future, and will do so once again here in my own liberal interpretation of his writings.

Harari chronicled the rise of sapiens throughout the centuries and noted that wherever we went there was death and destruction, which is a rather grim ancestry. Ironically, he notes that in terms of the three major threats to humanity—war, famine, and disease, we seem to be doing pretty well at this time with less war, less famine, and less disease (Harari, 2014). Yet, there is our nature, and in this consideration, he turns to the future where, with the advance of artificial intelligence and genetic engineering, we will be able to deprogram or genetically modify some of these problematic qualities of our inherent nature (Harari, 2016).

These innovations may offer some hope, but as Rogers pointed out, they are likely to represent a double-edged sword. In our time on this planet, however, our work is more likely to be centered in embracing our nature and moving ourselves along on the evolutionary scale as best as we can do. There are probably people in your world whom you consider to be enlightened beings. Maybe your list won't correlate 100% with mine, but there's likely to be a degree of overlap especially in the qualities we attribute to enlightened beings. We have touched upon some of this material in our discussions of transformational changes in this book, and in this regard, we can look toward the works of people like Wilber (2000a), Cook-Greuter (2006), Beck and Cowan (1996), and others to provide guidance not only for qualities representing more evolved human ways but also processes to help us move in these directions. All this to say that there is an abundance of information about what each of us might do to become better human beings—with the word better referencing the human portrait that dominates Harari's (2014) descriptions in *Sapiens: A History of Humankind*.

If you work on that kind of betterment agenda, I think you will be developing qualities that align well with what has been referred to in this chapter's discussions of ways of being and the humble way of the coach. So far so good for our humanness—but what if you do intend to become a coach? Then, there's at least one more big agenda. All the previous chapters in this book built a story of what the work of coaching entails and what kinds of skill sets you will be asked to nurture as you move ever deeper into the domain of coaching as your professional métier. There is knowing and doing—and beyond that there is knowing and doing well or mastery. Frankly, I believe that mastery is a lifelong pursuit, yet the more we learn, practice, and reflect, the more likely we are to become.

The scope of your work in becoming a coach may seem considerable, and any trepidation regarding the magnitude of this undertaking will be easily offset by the profound rewards of this work. Move at the pace appropriate to your readiness and savor your moments of deep connection and learning.

APPENDIX A

TRANSTHEORETICAL MODEL DECISIONAL BALANCE

Pros and Cons of Behavior Change

Use decisional balance to help clients take action and bring about the change they want.

1. List the pros (left side of the table) and cons (right side of the table) of performing the behavior.
2. Establish the strength or importance of each entry on a scale of 1 to 10 (see the following example).
3. Add up the pros and cons separately. Subtract the cons from the pros.

If the behavior is something positive that clients want to adopt (e.g., take work breaks, connect more with friends, start exercising, adopt a healthy diet), the pros should progressively outweigh the cons as they move from precontemplation to action. As a coach, you might help clients identify new benefits of performing the behavior (pros) to strengthen their resolve to remain in action.

If the behavior is something problematic that clients want to stop (e.g., interrupting others, procrastinating, excessive screen time, smoking), the cons should progressively outweigh the pros as the clients move from precontemplation to action. As a coach, you might help clients identify negative effects of continuing to engage in the problematic behavior (cons) to strengthen their resolve to remain in action.

Pros and Cons of Behavior Change Example

Target behavior: Walking outside 30 minutes per day

Pros	Strength	Cons	Strength
1. Burn calories	8	1. Takes time from other things	9
2. Clear my mind of the day's issues	6	2. Inconvenience in getting to nice walking area	7
3. Get some fresh air	5	3. Dressing and undressing in messy or cold weather	8
4. Take time for myself	4	4. Not really exciting	7
5. Take the dog for a much-needed walk	6		
Total pros	29	Total cons	31
Pros (29) − Cons (31) = −2			

The decisional balance is slightly negative (cons outweigh the pros), so this client needs to see further benefits of walking to adopt and maintain the new behavior. What would you do as a coach to help your client move forward?

Pros and Cons of Behavior Change

Target behavior: _____

Pros	Strength	Cons	Strength
1.		1.	
2.		2.	
3.		3.	
4.		4.	
5.		5.	
Total pros		Total cons	
Pros (_____) − Cons (_____) = _____			

From J. Gavin, *Foundations of Professional Coaching*. (Champaign, IL: Human Kinetics, 2022).

APPENDIX B
SAMPLE COACHING AGREEMENT

Coach's Name

Contact information

Website

Email and telephone

Section 1. Parties to the Agreement

Client's name: _____

Address: _____ City _____ State _____ Zip _____

Phone: (work or home) _____ (Cell) _____ Email: _____

Coach's name: _____

Address: _____ City _____ State _____ Zip _____

Phone: (work or home) _____ (Cell) _____ Email: _____

Section 2. Terms and Conditions

Meetings: Coaching sessions will normally occur on a biweekly basis for a period of 60 minutes. If we meet in person, we will agree on the location and conditions of the place where we meet. If sessions take place virtually on a web platform, I will send you a link to the session meeting, and we will both be available at the agreed-upon time. If we are meeting by phone, please call me at (phone number). You may also email me in between sessions at (email) and I will respond within 24 hours (except weekends and holidays).

In case of cancellation or rescheduling: Communication of cancellation or a need to reschedule must be made at least 48 hours in advance of sessions. All makeup sessions must be completed within the current month. There may be a time when I also need to reschedule. I commit to letting you know at least 48 hours in advance except in cases of emergency.

If I do not receive notification of cancellation or rescheduling at least 48 hours in advance, you will be responsible for 50% of the fee for that session. If you fail to show for a session without notice, you will be responsible for 100% of the fee. In case of emergency, this matter may be discussed.

Challenges: If I, as your coach, ever say or do something that upsets you or doesn't feel right, please let me know. I value truth and I genuinely invite you to discuss the situation with me right away.

Ethics code and confidentiality: The information you share is *strictly confidential*. I will not divulge the content of our sessions, nor will I disclose that you are in a coaching relationship with me without your permission. Conditions under which I cannot guarantee confidentiality are indicated in the civic and legal statutes of the jurisdiction in which I reside. Please ask me for further information in case you are not clear on the legal limits to confidentiality. Moreover, I abide by the ethical code of the (name of association) and am bound by its principles in my conduct as a coach.

Nature of relationship: A coaching relationship is not psychological counseling, psychotherapy, mentoring, teaching, or expert consulting. You are entering into this coaching relationship with the understanding of my coaching credentials, which I have described and which are explicitly listed on my website. I will work collaboratively with you and support you in identifying and achieving personal and business goals; however, you are responsible for your behavior and your personal accountability to the goals that you set for yourself in this coaching relationship. If at any time, either you or I have questions about our work together and the degree to which it reflects a coaching approach, it will be our individual responsibility to raise these questions with each other.

Fees and payments: Fees will be billed on a monthly basis. Payment may be made via etransfer, (name of credit card), or check made payable in my name. Payment is due within 30 days of receipt of billing.

Section 3. Agreement

Coach	Client
As your coach, I agree to do the following: 1. Meet with you in six biweekly 60-minute sessions at a time that is mutually agreeable. 2. Be available by phone or email for agreed-upon check-ins. You may call me twice between sessions if needed (short calls lasting no more than 10 minutes); I will respond to emails within 24 hours (except weekends and holidays). Meetings beyond these terms will be charged at an appropriate rate based on the normal session fee. 3. Work with you through inquiry and dialogue to clarify your goals and design your action plans. I will also provide ongoing support for your goal-directed activities. 4. Give you feedback about issues that impede your progress. 5. Inform you about matters that I believe are affecting our working relationship. 6. Notify you at least 48 hours in advance if I need to cancel a meeting, except in case of dire emergency. 7. Respect the (association) code of ethics and keep all our sessions confidential.	As your client, I agree to do the following: 1. Show up for scheduled meetings on time for six biweekly 60-minute sessions, starting on (date). 2. Commit myself to the coaching process, its roles and responsibilities, and the goals we agree upon. 3. Call or email you about issues that come up, within the limits we have set. 4. Communicate with you if I require additional time or meetings to arrange for those meetings under the same terms as for other sessions. 5. Be willing to talk with you about any issues that pertain to my progress or how we are working together. I will also let you know if anything you do or say does not feel right to me. 6. Pay the agreed-upon fee for all sessions in a timely manner, including those I cancel less than 48 hours in advance, except in case of dire emergency.

If you have read and agree to the above please print a copy, please sign it and bring it with you to our first session. You may also email me the document with your signature and "I approve" as the subject of your email.

Client signature: _____   **Date:** _____

Coach signature: _____   **Date:** _____

From J. Gavin, *Foundations of Professional Coaching*. (Champaign, IL: Human Kinetics, 2022).

APPENDIX C
THE FIRST SESSION

Whether it is in an initial interview or discussion with your client prior to commencement of coaching or a lengthy review of issues in an opening session, some essential issues must be understood and addressed before you and your client can fully move into a goal-centric coaching process. The following schematic offers a sense of what needs to be addressed:

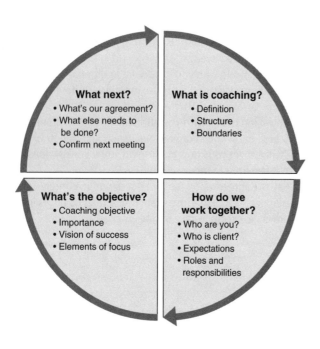

WHAT IS COACHING?

Here you would ensure that your client fully understands what coaching is, what it isn't, what the boundaries of the relationship are, and relevant structures for the work. Structures would include issues pertaining to the who, what, when, where, how, and other details. This essentially outlines the coaching plan.

HOW DO WE WORK TOGETHER?

Roles and responsibilities in coaching are critical to review. In this area of discussion, you would need to ensure coverage of expectations that you have as well as those of your client. Moreover, at some point in this contact you would try to understand relevant aspects of who your client is. In turn, you would share relevant aspects of your own identity.

WHAT'S THE OBJECTIVE?

At some point in your discussion, you will cover the coaching plan. However, this conversation needs to be closely related to one concerning the coaching objective. Here, your focus will be on clarification of the objective, including exploration of its importance, a vision of success, and some detailing of the elements of this objective that will need to be addressed in the coaching process.

WHAT NEXT?

This discussion may end with the confirmation and signing of an agreement, assuming there aren't other matters that need to be dealt with—for instance, arrangements with sponsors, coordination with stakeholders, and so on. There may be tasks that the client needs to undertake, which could involve further exploration of the coaching objective before the next session. Finally, there would be a confirmation of the next meeting.

There may be other matters peculiar to the contracting with a client that might need to be addressed. However, the aforementioned areas represent the major areas requiring discussion, understanding, and commitment.

APPENDIX D

ICF *CODE OF ETHICS*

The ICF Code of Ethics is composed of five Main Parts:

1. INTRODUCTION
2. KEY DEFINITIONS
3. ICF CORE VALUES AND ETHICAL PRINCIPLES
4. ETHICAL STANDARDS
5. PLEDGE

INTRODUCTION

The ICF Code of Ethics describes the core values of the International Coach Federation (ICF Core Values), and ethical principles and ethical standards of behavior for all ICF Professionals (see definitions). Meeting these ICF ethical standards of behavior is the first of the ICF core coaching competencies (ICF Core Competencies). That is *"Demonstrates ethical practice: understands and consistently applies coaching ethics and standards."*

The ICF Code of Ethics serves to uphold the integrity of ICF and the global coaching profession by:

- Setting standards of conduct consistent with ICF core values and ethical principles.
- Guiding ethical reflection, education, and decision-making
- Adjudicating and preserving ICF coach standards through the ICF Ethical Conduct Review (ECR) process
- Providing the basis for ICF ethics training in ICF-accredited programs

The ICF Code of Ethics applies when ICF Professionals represent themselves as such, in any kind of coaching-related interaction. This is regardless of whether a coaching Relationship (see definitions) has been established. This Code articulates the ethical obligations of ICF Professionals who are acting in their different roles as coach, coach supervisor, mentor coach, trainer or student coach-in-training, or serving in an ICF Leadership role, as well as Support Personnel (see definitions).

Although the Ethical Conduct Review (ECR) process is only applicable to ICF Professionals, as is the Pledge, the ICF Staff are also committed to ethical conduct and the Core Values and Ethical Principles that underpin this ICF code of ethics.

The challenge of working ethically means that members will inevitably encounter situations that require responses to unexpected issues, resolution of dilemmas and solutions to problems. This Code of Ethics is intended to assist those persons subject to the Code by directing them to the variety of ethical factors that may need to be taken into consideration and helping to identify alternative ways of approaching ethical behavior.

ICF Professionals who accept the Code of Ethics strive to be ethical, even when doing so involves making difficult decisions or acting courageously.

KEY DEFINITIONS

- "Client"—the individual or team/group being coached, the coach being mentored or supervised, or the coach or the student coach being trained.
- "Coaching"—partnering with Clients in a thought-provoking and creative process that inspires them to maximize their personal and professional potential.
- "Coaching Relationship"—a relationship that is established by the ICF Professional and the Client(s)/Sponsor(s) under an agreement or a contract that defines the responsibilities and expectations of each party.
- "Code"—ICF Code of Ethics.
- "Confidentiality"—protection of any information obtained around the coaching engagement unless consent to release is given.

- "Conflict of Interest"—a situation in which an ICF Professional is involved in multiple interests where serving one interest could work against or be in conflict with another. This could be financial, personal or otherwise.

- "Equality"—a situation in which all people experience inclusion, access to resources and opportunity, regardless of their race, ethnicity, national origin, color, gender, sexual orientation, gender identity, age, religion, immigration status, mental or physical disability, and other areas of human difference.

- "ICF Professional"—individuals who represent themselves as an ICF Member or ICF Credential-holder, in roles including but not limited to Coach, Coach Supervisor, Mentor Coach, Coach Trainer, and Student of Coaching.

- "ICF Staff"—the ICF support personnel who are contracted by the managing company that provides professional management and administrative services on behalf of ICF.

- "Internal Coach"—an individual who is employed within an organization and coaches either part-time or full-time the employees of that organization.

- "Sponsor"—the entity (including its representatives) paying for and/or arranging or defining the coaching services to be provided.

- "Support Personnel"—the people who work for ICF Professionals in support of their Clients.

- "Systemic equality"—gender equality, race equality and other forms of equality that are institutionalized in the ethics, core values, policies, structures, and cultures of communities, organizations, nations and society.

ICF CORE VALUES AND ETHICAL PRINCIPLES

The ICF Code of Ethics is based on the ICF Core Values [https://coachfederation.org/about] and the actions that flow from them. All values are equally important and support one another. These values are aspirational and should be used as a way to understand and interpret the standards. All ICF Professionals are expected to showcase and propagate these Values in all their interactions.

ETHICAL STANDARDS

The following ethical standards are applied to the professional activities of ICF Professionals:

Section I—Responsibility to clients

As an ICF Professional, I:

1. Explain and ensure that, prior to or at the initial meeting, my coaching Client(s) and Sponsor(s) understand the nature and potential value of coaching, the nature and limits of confidentiality, financial arrangements, and any other terms of the coaching agreement.

2. Create an agreement/contract regarding the roles, responsibilities and rights of all parties involved with my Client(s) and Sponsor(s) prior to the commencement of services.

3. Maintain the strictest levels of confidentiality with all parties as agreed upon. I am aware of and agree to comply with all applicable laws that pertain to personal data and communications.

4. Have a clear understanding about how information is exchanged among all parties involved during all coaching interactions.

5. Have a clear understanding with both Clients and Sponsors or interested parties about the conditions under which information will not be kept confidential (e.g., illegal activity, if required by law, pursuant to valid court order or subpoena; imminent or likely risk of danger to self or to others; etc.). Where I reasonably believe one of the above circumstances is applicable, I may need to inform appropriate authorities.

6. When working as an Internal Coach, manage conflicts of interest or potential conflicts of interest with my coaching Clients and Sponsor(s) through coaching agreement(s) and ongoing dialogue. This should include addressing organizational roles, responsibilities, relationships, records, confidentiality and other reporting requirements.

7. Maintain, store and dispose of any records, including electronic files and communications, created during my professional interactions in a manner that promotes confidentiality, security and privacy and complies with any applicable laws and

agreements. Furthermore, I seek to make proper use of emerging and growing technological developments that are being used in coaching services (technology-assisted coaching services) and be aware how various ethical standards apply to them.

8. Remain alert to indications that there might be a shift in the value received from the coaching relationship. If so, make a change in the relationship or encourage the Client(s)/Sponsor(s) to seek another coach, seek another professional or use a different resource.

9. Respect all parties' right to terminate the coaching relationship at any point for any reason during the coaching process subject to the provisions of the agreement.

10. Am sensitive to the implications of having multiple contracts and relationships with the same Client(s) and Sponsor(s) at the same time in order to avoid conflict of interest situations.

11. Am aware of and actively manage any power or status difference between the Client and me that may be caused by cultural, relational, psychological or contextual issues.

12. Disclose to my Clients the potential receipt of compensation, and other benefits I may receive for referring my Clients to third parties.

13. Assure consistent quality of coaching regardless of the amount or form of agreed compensation in any relationship.

Section II—Responsibility to practice and performance
As an ICF Professional, I:

14. Adhere to the ICF Code of Ethics in all my interactions. When I become aware of a possible breach of the Code by myself or I recognize unethical behavior in another ICF Professional, I respectfully raise the matter with those involved. If this does not resolve the matter, I refer it to a formal authority (e.g., ICF Global) for resolution.

15. Require adherence to the ICF Code of Ethics by all Support Personnel.

16. Commit to excellence through continued personal, professional and ethical development.

17. Recognize my personal limitations or circumstances that may impair, conflict with or interfere with my coaching performance or my professional coaching relationships. I will reach out for support to determine the action to be taken and, if necessary, promptly seek relevant professional guidance. This may include suspending or terminating my coaching relationship(s).

18. Resolve any conflict of interest or potential conflict of interest by working through the issue with relevant parties, seeking professional assistance, or suspending temporarily or ending the professional relationship.

19. Maintain the privacy of ICF Members and use the ICF Member contact information (email addresses, telephone numbers, and so on) only as authorized by ICF or the ICF Member.

Section III—Responsibility to professionalism
As an ICF Professional, I:

20. Identify accurately my coaching qualifications, my level of coaching competency, expertise, experience, training, certifications and ICF Credentials.

21. Make verbal and written statements that are true and accurate about what I offer as an ICF Professional, what is offered by ICF, the coaching profession, and the potential value of coaching.

22. Communicate and create awareness with those who need to be informed of the ethical responsibilities established by this Code.

23. Hold responsibility for being aware of and setting clear, appropriate and culturally sensitive boundaries that govern interactions, physical or otherwise.

24. Do not participate in any sexual or romantic engagement with Client(s) or Sponsor(s). I will be ever mindful of the level of intimacy appropriate for the relationship. I take the appropriate action to address the issue or cancel the engagement.

Section IV—Responsibility to society
As an ICF Professional, I:

25. Avoid discrimination by maintaining fairness and equality in all activities and

operations, while respecting local rules and cultural practices. This includes, but is not limited to, discrimination on the basis of age, race, gender expression, ethnicity, sexual orientation, religion, national origin, disability or military status.

26. Recognize and honor the contributions and intellectual property of others, only claiming ownership of my own material. I understand that a breach of this standard may subject me to legal remedy by a third party.

27. Am honest and work within recognized scientific standards, applicable subject guidelines and boundaries of my competence when conducting and reporting research.

28. Am aware of my and my clients' impact on society. I adhere to the philosophy of "doing good," versus "avoiding bad."

THE PLEDGE OF ETHICS OF THE ICF PROFESSIONAL:

As an ICF Professional, in accordance with the Standards of the ICF Code of Ethics, I acknowledge and agree to fulfill my ethical and legal obligations to my coaching Client(s), Sponsor(s), colleagues and to the public at large.

If I breach any part of the ICF Code of Ethics, I agree that the ICF in its sole discretion may hold me accountable for so doing. I further agree that my accountability to the ICF for any breach may include sanctions, such as mandatory additional coach training or other education or loss of my ICF Membership and/or my ICF Credentials.

For more information on the Ethical Conduct Review Process, please follow this link: [https://coachingfederation.org/app/uploads/2020/01/ICF-Code-of-Ethics_final_Nov12.pdf].

Adapted by the ICF Global Board of Directors. © 2020 International Coaching Federation. https://coachingfederation.org/app/uploads/2020/01/ICF-Code-of-Ethics_final_Nov12.pdf.

GLOSSARY

accommodating—A learning style described in Kolb and Fry's taxonomy such that individuals with this style learn best by feeling and doing.

amotivation—An absence of motivation or a lack of desire to act.

andragogy—Theory or model of adult learning, often contrasted with pedagogy, which tends to be concerned with the education and learning of children and teens.

assimilating—A learning style described in Kolb and Fry's taxonomy such that individuals with this style learn best by thinking and observing.

balance goal—The intent to find sufficient degrees of satisfaction with various areas of one's life. This includes achieving equilibrium in managing competing demands such as maintaining physical wellness, healthy relationships, and optimal professional engagement.

beneficence—The need to do good and promote human welfare. Typically embedded in ethical codes.

boundary crossing—An ethical matter in which a coach engages in a behavior with the client that holds the potential for jeopardizing the integrity of the relationship (e.g., attending a social event at the client's home).

boundary violation—An ethical matter in which a coach engages in a behavior with the client that jeopardizes or potentially breaches the integrity of the relationship (e.g., going on a date with the client).

butterfly effect—A hypothetical possibility described in a question to suggest the systemic relationships among people and things; it relates to the question of whether the flap of a butterfly's wings in Brazil can set off a tornado in Texas.

challenge—Coaching skill whereby the coach presents clients with evidence of their discrepant, conflicting, or inconsistent thoughts, feelings, or actions in service of their intentions in coaching.

closed question—A type of question that limits the requested response from the client and thereby enables the coach to gather specific information and control the communication flow.

closure—A process or experience of planned or unplanned ending or termination of the coaching relationship with the client. Closure ideally involves a dialogue and may evolve over a number of sessions.

coachability—The degree to which a potential client is able and willing to adequately address the structures and processes of a formal coaching relationship.

coaching conversation—Either a professional coaching dialogue or an impromptu conversation between two people addressing a particular issue or problem wherein one person is positioned to help the other.

coaching niche—A form of specialization in a coach's practice represented by a documentable record of training, work experience, reading, skill development, and knowledge acquisition that allows a coach to claim a verifiable expertise in coaching within a specific area.

coaching objective—The overarching purpose or intention for which clients engage in a coaching process. Sometimes referred to as the coaching agenda or metatopic. Coaching objectives typically comprise a number of subobjectives that are addressed in individual coaching sessions. The client's coaching objective forms the basis of the contractual agreement between coach and client.

coaching plan—The overall strategy and structure that coach and client adhere to in working toward the client's coaching objective.

coaching presence—Both a coaching skill and manner of being that is represented by the coach's full availability to the client—in mind, body, and spirit—without attachment to the coach's own agenda within a session.

coaching the person—A way of coaching that takes into account not only the client's topic(s) of focus, but also on the client's world and their place in it.

coaching the topic—A way of coaching that solely focuses on the client's topic or agenda and largely ignores the client's world and their place in it.

constructivist theory of knowing—Knowledge generated by the learner's meaning-making process through personal interactions with the world rather than by virtue of scientifically determined forms of objective data. Also known as constructivism.

content reflection—A type of reflection derived from Mezirow's work on transformational learning indicating an attentional focus on the content of an issue as you try to come to some resolution to your concern or problem.

converging—A learning style described in Kolb and Fry's taxonomy such that individuals with this style learn best by thinking and doing.

core relationship conditions—Qualities, often including trustworthiness, expertise, genuineness, and empathy, that coaches need to demonstrate in their relationships with clients so they can effectively engage the process of coaching.

countertransference—Projection onto the client by the coach of feelings, attitudes, or behaviors originating in the coach's relationship with one or more significant individuals in the coach's personal history. Also described as an unreal aspect of the relationship.

decisional balance—List of pros and cons for performing a desired behavior. The likelihood of adopting a new health-related behavior increases when the pros outweigh the cons.

direct communication—A wide range of coach interventions where the content, ideas, and feelings represent the coach's personal ideas, thoughts, and perspectives. Included are such interventions as providing feedback, challenge or confrontation, reframing, interpretation, instructing, and offering information, opinions, or advice.

direct input—Feedback, challenge or confrontation, reframing, interpretation, instructing, and offering information, opinions, or advice that a coach offers to clients in service of their goal attainment.

diverging—A learning style described in Kolb and Fry's taxonomy such that individuals with this style learn best by feeling and observing.

ethics—Moral principles adopted by an individual or a group to provide rules for conduct.

experiential learning—A concept most often associated with David A. Kolb, who proposed that learning from experience entails a cycle of experimenting; reflecting on our experience; reframing our theories of action; and applying our new learning, or doing.

external regulation—Source of motivation that occurs when your reasons or motives for action come from outside of you, for example, from external factors or people.

extrinsic motivation—A type of motivation occurring in situations where people pursue action to achieve some valued outcome or result (e.g., a prize, weight loss) rather than for the experience of the activity itself.

flow model of coaching—A model highlighting two phases within the coaching process: (1) engagement, which entails working with clients to create insight, identify patterns, and explore resources, and (2) goal pursuit, which includes a focus on action planning, committing to proceed, and staying the course until the goal is achieved.

focusing—A coaching skill whereby the coach directs the client's attention toward a specific theme, behavioral or communication pattern, or experience. Might also apply to biases for types of information that a coach chooses to pay attention to.

fulfillment goal—Type of goal in which the hoped-for outcome of a client's goal pursuit centers around finding happiness and meaning. Fulfillment goals often involve alignment of one's actions, life purpose, and core values to maximize potential.

holding environment—The safety and trustworthiness of the relationship created by the coach for the client. The term has been borrowed from counseling and psychotherapy.

identified regulation—Source of motivation that is in place when you have come to value certain actions or behaviors and you act accordingly to reach an important goal.

immediacy—Combining such processes as feedback, confrontation, and self-disclosure, this coaching skill focuses on the expression of what is happening precisely in the current moment of the coaching experience with the client, within the coach, or in their relationship.

indirect question—A coaching skill whereby the coach requests information from the client in a declarative sentence that implies to the client that certain information is needed in the dialogue. For example, "I wonder what that might do for you."

International Coaching Federation (ICF)—A not-for-profit organization formed in 1995 by individual coaches with a mission to advance the coaching profession worldwide. The ICF seeks to set high professional standards, provide independent certification, and build a network of credentialed coaches. More information can be found at www.coachingfederation.org. Formerly known as the International Coach Federation.

intrinsic motivation—Motivation seen in situations where people pursue action for pleasure, learning, mastery, or aesthetic enjoyment. Motivation of this nature derives from engagement in the activity itself rather than from outcomes of the activity.

introjected regulation—Source of motivation that develops over time and where values conveyed by others are accepted and internalized as your own.

Johari window—Model designed by Joseph Luft and Harry Ingham to demonstrate the interrelationships of self-disclosure, feedback, and self-awareness pertaining to a person's self-knowledge.

kinesics—The formal study of body motions, including all forms of nonverbal communication.

learning style—Personal preference for specific ways to process information and acquire knowledge.

learning-through-change (LTC) model—Model created by Marilyn Taylor suggesting that people involved in a change process will experience a cycle of learning where certain agendas must be addressed at certain times to successfully cope with and adapt to disconfirming events in life.

minimal encourager—An aspect of coaching communication whereby coaches acknowledge clients' verbalizations or behaviors with brief verbal references or audible expressions, such as "Mm-hmm," to reinforce client expression and openness.

monomyth—A template or structure representing the flow of experience as a hero or heroine embarks on an adventure, experiences various dilemmas and crises, and eventually returns home victorious.

morality—Determination of what is right or wrong on the basis of some broader cultural context or religious standard.

negative trigger—Negative internal or external events that may serve to become more vulnerable to lapses in self-management and behavior control.

neurolinguistic programming (NLP)—A multidisciplinary and eclectic methodology for understanding human behavior and interpersonal communications serving the purpose of identifying individual patterns to promote specific behavioral changes.

nonmaleficence—The need to avoid doing harm. It is typically embedded in ethical codes and is usually expressed in tandem with the term *beneficence*, referring to the need to do good.

normative challenges—Difficult or problematic life experiences arising within an individual or in the context of life that are commonly encountered in the course of life and that call for some form of adaptation or adjustment.

open question—A type of question in which the coach invites the client to expand on a theme or subject so that salient issues can be explored in depth.

outcome goals—Goals that typically focus on the result or end result of some activity, such as physical training or specified nutrition regimens. Outcome goals may include weight loss or winning a contest.

paralinguistics—The study of nonverbal aspects of speech, including tone, volume, speed, and pauses.

paraphrasing—A restating of clients' words in your own words, hopefully without using the exact language or distorting clients' intended messages. It resembles the skill of reflection of content.

pedagogy—The study of how we learn, how different skills and knowledge are communicated to learners, given the various social, emotional, developmental, and other factors that influence these learners.

performance goals—Goals of behavior or performance that are independent of others' actions. Examples include learning how to swim or running a distance in a specified time.

positive trigger—Positive internal or external events that may serve to decrease an individual's resilience in the face of urges to relax self-management and behavior control.

premise reflection—A type of reflection derived from Mezirow's work on transformational learning indicating an attentional emphasis on how you first defined your concern or problem and exploring the values, beliefs, and assumptions that happened to give rise to your concern at the outset.

process goals—Goals that emphasize the qualities that one wishes to experience in carrying out certain behaviors or actions, such as enjoyment or pleasure.

process reflection—A type of reflection derived from Mezirow's work on transformational learning indicating an attentional emphasis on the process by which you are considering and trying to resolve some concern or problem.

proxemics—The study of physical distances of individuals in social settings and their effects on these individuals.

psychological contract—A set of assumptions about working together that coaches and clients independently bring to the relationship without verification from one another.

reflection of content—A coaching skill involving the coach's sensitive mirroring of information provided in a client's communication to the coach; often referred to as *paraphrasing*.

reflection of feeling—A coaching skill involving the coach's sensitive mirroring of the emotional or feeling elements of a client's communications to the coach.

reflection of meaning—A coaching skill that relies on such skills as questioning, challenge, feedback, reflection of content, and reflection of feeling to help the client uncover a deeper appreciation and awareness of issues.

relapse—Behavioral incidents in which a person reverts to a previous pattern of action that he had deliberately altered, usually in the pursuit of some health or wellness goal. For instance, relapse would be seen in a person smoking a cigarette after having stopped for a number of months.

relapse prevention—Strategies for identifying high-risk situations and preventing a return to behavior previously abandoned in the pursuit of some health and wellness goal.

self-concordant goal—A goal that is highly aligned with an individual's intrinsic values, purposes, or overarching interests.

self-disclosure—A coaching skill whereby the coach strategically reveals personal information or tells personal stories to support the client's progress and goal attainment.

self-efficacy—Confidence in one's abilities to engage in goal pursuit in a specific area or domain and achieve a desired objective regardless of obstacles that might stand in the way. Most often associated with the psychologist Albert Bandura.

self-limiting beliefs—Negative thought patterns that hold us back from pursuing desired goals. Examples of self-limiting beliefs would be "I'm

too old," "I'm not smart enough," "I'm not disciplined enough," or "I'm too shy."

self-regulation—The ability to control one's thoughts, emotions, urges, and actions to reach a desired goal.

SMART—An acronym for elements of a goal-setting structure, where the letters represent the words **s**pecific, **m**easurable, **a**djustable, **r**ealistic, and **t**ime specific.

social support—All those in clients' immediate and extended networks, including the coach, who can help them achieve their desired goals.

summarizing—A coaching skill whereby the coach mirrors to the client key elements of a lengthy segment of communication or similar themes in client communication across a series of sessions.

SuPeRSMART goals—Goals that are **s**elf-controllable (under one's control); are **p**ublic to self and others; have a **r**eward attached to their achievement; and are **s**pecific, **m**easurable, **a**djustable, **r**ealistic, and **t**ime specific.

theory of action—A set of values, beliefs, attitudes, norms, and so on that inform the way people plan to act and actually behave.

transference—Projection of feelings, attitudes, or behaviors originating in the client's relationship with other significant people in the client's history onto the coach. Also described as an unreal aspect of the relationship.

transformative learning—Theory of education suggesting that adult learners play an active role in a kind of learning process that ultimately alters their worldviews and belief systems.

transtheoretical model (TTM)—Model of individual behavior change composed of six phases: precontemplation, contemplation, preparation, action, maintenance, and termination.

trigger—Internal and external events that may serve to increase an individual's vulnerability to lapses in self-management or behavior control.

values—Beliefs and attitudes that provide direction to everyday life.

virtues—Standards of moral excellence. Akin to values.

working alliance—The agreement and collaboration of coach and client in engaging in necessary tasks and patterns of relationship toward the attainment of desired outcomes. Popular in counseling and psychotherapy.

REFERENCES

Abravanel, M. (2018). *Coaching presence: A grounded theory from the coach's perspective.* [Unpublished doctoral dissertation. Concordia University]. Retrieved from https://spectrum.library.concordia.ca/984432/

Abravanel, M., & Gavin, J. (2017). Exploring the evolution of coaching through the lens of innovation. *International Journal of Evidence Based Coaching and Mentoring, 15*(1), 24-41.

Ackerman, S. J., & Hilsenroth, M. J. (2003). A review of therapist characteristics and techniques positively impacting the therapeutic alliance. *Clinical Psychology Review, 23,* 1-33.

Adler, A. (1927). *Understanding human nature.* Greenberg.

Adler, G., & Myerson, P. G. (Eds.). (1991). *Confrontation in psychotherapy.* Aronson.

Adler, R. B., Rosenfeld, L. B., & Proctor, R. F., II. (2004). *Interplay: The process of interpersonal communication* (9th ed.). Oxford University Press.

Albarracín, D., & Wyer, R. S. (2000). The cognitive impact of past behavior: Influences on beliefs, attitudes, and future behavioral decisions. *Journal of Personality and Social Psychology, 79*(1), 5-22.

Albee, G. W. (1970). The uncertain future of clinical psychology. *American Psychologist, 25*(12), 1071-1080.

Albrecht, K. (2006). *Social intelligence: The new science of success.* Jossey-Bass.

Allen, K. (2012). What is an ethical dilemma? *The New Social Worker, 19*(2), 4-5.

Allison, M. J., & Keller, C. (2004). Self-efficacy intervention effect on physical activity in older adults. *Western Journal of Nursing Research, 26*(1), 31-46.

American Psychological Association. (2012). *Our health at risk.* www.apa.org/monitor/2012/03/stress

American Psychiatric Association. (2013). *Diagnostic and statistical manual of mental disorders* (5th ed.). American Psychiatric Association.

Anderson, R., & Killenberg, G. M. (2009). *Interviewing: Speaking, listening, and learning for professional life* (2nd ed.). Oxford University Press.

Andersson, G., Cuijpers, P., Carlbring, P., Riper, H., & Hedman, E. (2014). Guided Internet-based vs. Face-to-face cognitive behavior therapy for psychiatric and somatic disorders: A systematic review and meta-analysis. *World Psychiatry, 13*(3), 288-295.

Andreas, S., & Faulkner, C. (Eds.). (1996). *NLP comprehensive training team.* Nicholas Brealey Publishing.

Andreychik, M. R., & Lewis, E. (2017). Will you help me to suffer less? How about to feel more joy? Positive and negative empathy are associated with different other-oriented motivations. *Personality and Individual Differences, 105,* 139-149.

Appiah, K. W. (2008). *Experiments in ethics.* Harvard University Press.

Argyris, C. (1970). *Intervention theory and method: A behavioral science view.* Addison-Wesley.

Argyris, C., & Schön, D. A. (1974). *Theory in practice.* Jossey-Bass.

Argyris, C., & Schön, D. A. (1978). *Organizational learning: A theory of action perspective.* Addison-Wesley.

Argyris, C., & Schön, D. A. (1995). *Organizational learning II: Theory, method, and practice.* Addison-Wesley.

Armstrong, T. (2003). *You're smarter than you think: A kid's guide to multiple intelligences.* Free Spirit.

Assagioli, R. (1965). *Psychosynthesis: A manual of principles and techniques.* Hobbs, Dorman.

Atkinson, P. M. (2014). *Creating transformational metaphors.* Exalon Publishing.

Auerbach, J. E. (2003). *Personal and executive coaching: The complete guide for mental health professionals.* Executive College Press.

Austin, J. T., & Vancouver, J. B. (1996). Goal constructs in psychology: Structure, process, and content. *Psychological Bulletin, 120*(3), 338-375.

Bachkirova, T. (2007). Role of coaching psychology in defining boundaries between counselling and coaching. In S. Palmer & A. Whybrow (Eds.), *Handbook of coaching psychology: A guide for practitioners* (pp. 351-366). Routledge.

Bachkirova, T., Cox, E., & Clutterbuck, D. (2010). Conclusion. In E. Cox, T. Bachkirova, & D. Clutterbuck (Eds.), *The complete handbook of coaching* (pp. 417-421). Sage Publications.

Bachkirova, T., Cox, E., & Clutterbuck, D. (2018). Introduction. In T. Bachkirova, E. Cox, & D. Clutterbuck (Eds.), *The complete handbook of coaching* (3rd ed., p. xxix-xlviii). Sage Publications.

Baker Miller, J. (1991). The development of women's sense of self. In J. Jodan, A. Kaplan, J. Miller, I. Stiver, & J. Surrey (Eds.), *Women's growth in connection: Writings from the Stone Center* (pp. 11-34). Guilford Press.

Baker Miller, J., & Stiver, I. (Eds.). (1997). *The healing connection: How women form relationships in therapy and in life.* Beacon Press.

Baldwin, M. (2000). Interview with Carl Rogers: On the use of the self in therapy. In M. Baldwin (Ed.), *The use of self in therapy* (2nd ed., pp. 29-38). Routledge.

Bandler, R., & Grinder, J. (1979). *Frogs into princes: Neuro linguistic programming*. Real People Press.

Bandler, R., & Grinder, J. (2005). *The structure of magic: A book about language and therapy*. Hushion House.

Bandura, A. (1977). *Social learning theory*. Prentice-Hall.

Bandura, A. (1986). *Social foundations of thought and action: A social cognitive theory*. Prentice Hall.

Bandura, A. (1995). *Self-efficacy in changing societies*. Cambridge University Press.

Bandura, A. (1997). *Self-efficacy: The exercise of control*. W.H. Freeman.

Bandura, A. (1998). Personal and collective efficacy in human adaptation and change. In J. G. Adair, D. Belanger, & K. L. Dion (Eds.), *Advances in psychological science: Personal, social and cultural aspects* (Vol. 1, pp. 51-71). Psychology Press.

Bandura, A. (2001). Social cognitive theory: An agentic perspective. *Annual Review of Psychology, 52*, 1-26.

Banks, T. (2014). *Journaling as a spiritual practice: Record your life, set your emotions free and get clarity by writing down your thoughts and experiences*. Talent Writers.

Bano, N., Ansari, M., & Ganai, M. Y. (2016). *A study of personality characteristics and values of secondary school teachers in relation to their classroom performance and students*. Anchor Academic Publishing.

Baron, L., & Morin, L. (2009). The coach–coachee relationship in executive coaching: A field study. *Human Resource Development Quarterly, 20*(1), 85-106.

Barrett, L. F., & Fischer, S. (2017). Be the architect of your emotions. *New Scientist, 233*(3116), 40-43.

Bartlett, R. C., & Collins, S. D. (2011). *Nicomachean ethics*. University of Chicago Press.

Basso, J. C., McHale, A., Ende, V., Oberlin, D. J., & Suzuki, W. A. (2019). Brief, daily meditation enhances attention, memory, mood, and emotional regulation in non-experienced meditators. *Behavioural Brain Research, 356*, 208-220.

Bateson, G. (1979). *Mind and nature: A necessary unity*. Dutton.

Baumeister, R. F., & Bushman, B. J. (2017). *Social psychology and human nature*. Cengage Learning.

Baumeister, R. F., & Heatherton, T. F. (1996). Self-regulation failure: An overview. *Psychological Inquiry, 7*(1), 1-15.

Baumeister, R. F., Heatherton, T. F., & Tice, D. M. (1994). *Losing control: How and why people fail at self-regulation*. Academic Press.

Baumeister, R. F., & Vohs, K. D. (2007). Self-regulation, ego depletion, and motivation. *Social and Personality Psychology Compass, 1*(1), 115-128.

Beck, D. E., & Cowan, C. (1996). *Spiral dynamics: Mastering values, leadership, and change*. Blackwell.

Beck, J. S., & Beck, A. T. (2011). *Cognitive behavior therapy: Basics and beyond* (2nd ed.). The Guilford Press.

Belf, T. (2002). *Coaching with spirit: Allowing success to emerge*. Pfeiffer.

Belsten, L. (2013). *What is S+EI?* From SEI Overview for Certification Class (v11.2) slide 14. http://the-isei.com/home.aspx

Bennett, J. L., & Campone, F. (2017). Coaching and theories of learning. In T. Bachkirova, G. Spence, & D. Drake (Eds.), *The SAGE handbook of coaching* (pp. 102-120). SAGE Publications.

Berger, W. (2018). *The book of beautiful questions: The powerful questions that will help you decide, create, connect, and lead*. Bloomsbury Publishing.

Bhattacharya, O., Chatterjee, A., & Basu, J. (2017). Humility: An emerging construct in moral psychology. *Psychological Studies, 62*(1), 1-11.

Binswanger, L. (1963). *Being-in-the-world: Selected papers of Ludwig Binswanger*. Basic Books.

Birdwhistell, R. L. (1970). *Kinetics and context: Essays on body motion communication*. University of Pennsylvania Press.

Biswas-Diener, R. (2009). Personal coaching as a positive intervention. *Journal of Clinical Psychology, 65*(5), 544-553.

Biswas-Diener, R. (2010). *Practicing positive psychology coaching: Assessment, activities and strategies for success* (illustrated ed.). Wiley.

Biswas-Diener, R., & Dean, B. (2007). *Positive psychology coaching: Putting the science of happiness to work for your clients*. Wiley & Sons.

Bluckert, P. (2005). Critical factors in executive coaching: The coaching relationship. *Industrial and Commercial Training, 37*(7), 336-340.

Bly, R. (1990). *Iron John: A book about men*. Da Capo Press.

Bohm, D. (2004). *On dialogue*. Psychology Press.

Bordin, E. S. (1979). The generalizability of the psychoanalytic concept of the working alliance. *Psychotherapy: Theory, Research & Practice, 16*(3), 252-260.

Boston Consulting Group. (2018). *Towards a reskilling revolution: A future of jobs for all*.

Boyce, L. A., Jackson, R. J., & Neal, L. J. (2010). Building successful leadership coaching relationships: Examining impact of matching criteria in a leadership coaching program. *Journal of Management Development, 29*, 914-931.

Brach, T. (2016). *True refuge: Finding freedom and peace in your own awakened heart*. Bantam Books.

Brammer, L. M., & MacDonald, G. (2003). *The helping relationship: Process and skills* (8th ed.). Allyn & Bacon.

Brann, A. (2017). *Neuroscience for coaches* (2nd ed.). Kogan Page.

Brems, C. (2001). *Basic skills in psychotherapy and counseling*. Brooks/Cole.

Brew, L., & Kottler, J. A. (2008). *Applied helping skills: Transforming lives*. SAGE Publications.

Briggs Myers, I., McCaulley, M. H., Quenk, N. L., & Hammer, A. L. (2009). *MBTI manual: A guide to the development and use of the Myers-Briggs Type Indicator instrument* (3rd ed.). CPP, Inc.

Briñol, P., Petty, R., & Wagner, B. (2009). Body posture effects on self-evaluation: A self-validation approach. *European Journal of Social Psychology* [Serial online], *39*(6), 1053-1064.

Britton, J. J. (2010). *Effective group coaching*. Jossey Bass.

Brock, V. G. (2006). *Who's who in coaching: Who shaped it, who's shaping it. Proceedings of the ICF Research Symposium.* http://coachinghistory.com/wp-content/uploads/2012/05/Whos-Who-In-Coaching-ICF-Research-Symposium-Paper-7-24-2006.pdf

Brock, V. G. (2008). *Grounded theory of the roots and emergence of coaching.* http://vikkibrock.com/wp-content/uploads/2008/11/brock-grounded-theory-roots-emergence-coaching-appendices-k-t-06-05-2008-v1.pdfcontent/uploads/2011/10/dissertation.pdf

Brock, V. G. (2012). *Sourcebook of coaching history*. V.G. Brock.

Brock, V. G. (2015). Celebrate: The past, present and future of coaching. *Choice, 15*(4), 20-23.

Brock, V. G. (2016). *Professional challenges facing the coaching field from an historical perspective. Library of Professional Coaching.* Posted March 11. https://libraryofprofessionalcoaching.com/research/history-of-coaching/professional-challenges-facing-the-coaching-field-from-an-historical-perspective/3/

Brown, C., & Augusta-Scott, T. (2006). *Narrative therapy: Making meaning, making lives*. SAGE Publications.

Brown, L. S. (2007). Empathy, genuineness—And the dynamics of power: A feminist responds to Rogers. *Psychotherapy: Theory, Research, Practice, Training, 44*(3), 257-259.

Brown, M. (2010). *The presence process—A journey into present moment awareness* (2nd ed.). Namaste Publishing Inc.

Bruhn, J. G., Levine, H. G., & Levine, P. L. (Eds.). (1993). *Managing boundaries in the health professions*. C.C. Thomas.

Buber, M. (2004). *I and thou* (G. S. Ronald, Trans.; 2nd ed.). Charles Scribner.

Bugental, J. F. T. (1965). *The search for authenticity*. Holt, Rinehart & Winston.

Burgess, A. (1962). *A clockwork orange*. Heinemann.

Cabana, S., Emery, F., & Emery, M. (1995). The search for effective strategic planning is over. *Journal for Quality and Participation, 18*(4), 10-19.

Cain, S. (2013). *Quiet: The power of introverts in a world that can't stop talking*. Puffin.

Cameron, J. (2002). *The artist's way* (25th anniversary ed.). TarcherPerigee.

Campbell, J. (1949). *The hero with a thousand faces*. Princeton University Press.

Campbell, J. (1991). *The power of myth*. Anchor Books.

Capra, F. (1997). *The web of life: A new scientific understanding of living systems*. Anchor Books.

Capuzzi, D., & Gross, D. R. (Eds.). (2017). *Introduction to the counseling profession* (7th ed.). Routledge.

Carkhuff, R. R. (1969). *Helping and human relations* (Vols. I and II). Holt, Rinehart & Winston.

Carpetto, G. (2008). *Interviewing and brief therapy strategies: An integrative approach*. Pearson Learning.

Carré, A., Stefaniak, N., D'Ambrosio, F., Bensalah, L., & Besche-Richard, C. (2013). The basic empathy scale in adults (BES-A): Factor structure of a revised form. *Psychological Assessment, 25*(3), 679-691.

Carver, C. S., & Scheier, M. F. (1998). *On the self-regulation of behaviour*. Cambridge University Press.

Carver, C. S., & Scheier, M. F. (2001). *On the self-regulation of behaviour*. Cambridge University Press.

Carver, C. S., & Scheier, M. F. (2002). Control processes and self-organization as complementary principles underlying behavior. *Personality and Social Psychology Review, 6*(4), 304-315.

Catmur, C., Press, C., & Heyes, C. M. (2016). Mirror neurons from associative learning. In *The Wiley handbook on the cognitive neuroscience of learning* (pp. 515-537). Wiley.

Cavanagh, M. (2006). Coaching from a systemic perspective: A complex adaptive approach. In D. Stober & A. M. Grant (Eds.), *Evidence-based coaching handbook: Putting best practices to work for your clients* (pp. 313-354). Wiley.

Cavanagh, M. (2013). The coaching engagement in the twenty-first century: New paradigms for complex times. In S. David, D. Clutterbuck, & D. Megginson (Eds.), *Beyond goals: Effective strategies for coaching and mentoring* (pp. 161-184). Routledge, Centers for Disease Control and Prevention.

Chaiklin, S., & Wengrower, H. (Eds.). (2015). *The art and science of dance/movement therapy: Life is dance* (2nd ed.). Routledge.

Chalmers, S. V. (2018*). Mindfulness coaching: Have transformational coaching conversations and cultivate coaching skills mastery*. BookBaby.

Chamine, S. (2012). *Positive intelligence*. Greenleaf Book Group Press.

Chancellor, J., & Lyubomirsky, S. (2013). Humble beginnings: Current trends, state perspectives, and hallmarks of humility. *Social and Personality Psychology Compass, 7*, 819-833.

Chang, V., Scott, S., & Decker, C. (2013). *Developing helping skills: A step-by-step approach to competency* (2nd ed.). Brooks/Cole.

Chodorow, N. J. (1991). *Feminism and psychoanalytic theory.* Yale University Press.

Chodron, P. (2019). *Welcoming the unwelcome: Wholehearted living in a brokenhearted world.* Shambhala.

Ciuchta, M. P., Letwin, C., Stevenson, R. M., & McMahon, S. (2014). Coachability: Development of a new construct and scale. *Frontiers of Entrepreneurship Research, 34*(1), 1-1.

Clark, D. M. (1995). Cognitive therapy in the treatment of anxiety disorders. *Clinical Neuropharmacology, 18*, 27-37.

Clarkson, P. (1997). On I and thou. *Gestalt Review, 1*, 56-70.

Clutterbuck, D. (2010). Team coaching. In E. Cox, T. Bachirova, & D. Clutterbuck (Eds.), *The complete handbook of coaching* (pp. 271-283). SAGE Publications.

Clutterbuck, D. (2013). Working with emergent goals: A pragmatic approach. In S. David, D. Clutterbuck, & D. Megginson (Eds.), *Beyond goals: Effective strategies for coaching and mentoring* (pp. 311-326). Routledge.

Clutterbuck, D. (2020). *Coaching the team at work 2: The definitive guide to team coaching.* Nicholas Brealey.

Clutterbuck, D., & Spence, G. (2017). Working with goals in coaching. In T. Bachkirova, G. Spence, & D. Drake (Eds.), *The SAGE handbook of coaching* (pp. 292-322). SAGE Publications.

Coach U. (2005). *The Coach U personal and corporate coaching training handbook.* Wiley.

Cohn, J. F., & Ekman, P. (2008). Measuring facial action. In J. A. Harrigan, R. Rosenthal, & K. R. Scherer (Eds.), *The new handbook of methods in nonverbal behavior research* (pp. 9-64). Oxford University Press.

Cole, E. R. (2009). Intersectionality and research in psychology. *American Psychologist, 64*, 170-180.

Collard, P., & Walsh, J. (2008). Sensory awareness mindfulness training in coaching: Accepting life's challenges. *Journal of Rational-Emotive & Cognitive-Behavior Therapy, 26*(1), 30-37.

Cook-Greuter, S. R. (2000). Mature ego development: A gateway to ego transcendence? *Journal of Adult Development, 7*, 227-240.

Cook-Greuter, S. R. (2006). *Ego development: Nine levels of increasing embrace.* www.cook-greuter.com/Cook-Greuter%209%20levels%20paper%20new%201.1'14%2097p%5B1%5D.pdf

Cooper, M. (2018). The psychology of goals: A practice-friendly review. In M. Cooper & D. Law (Eds.), *Working with goals in counselling and psychotherapy* (pp. 35-71). Oxford University.

Corey, G. (2017). *Theory and practice of counseling and psychotherapy* (10th ed.). Cengage Learning.

Corey, G., Corey, M. S., & Callanan, P. (2014). *Issues and ethics in the helping professions* (9th ed.). Brooks/Cole.

Cormier, S., Nurius, P. S., & Osborn, C. J. (2017). *Interviewing and change strategies for helpers* (8th ed.). Cengage Learning.

Covey, S. R. (1989). *The 7 habits of highly effective people.* Free Press.

Cox, E. (2013). *Coaching understood: A pragmatic inquiry into the coaching process.* Sage.

Cox, E., Bachkirova, T., & Clutterbuck, D. (Eds.). (2014). *The complete handbook of coaching* (2nd ed.). SAGE Publications.

Cox, E., Bachkirova, T., & Clutterbuck, D. (2018). *The complete handbook of coaching.* Sage.

Cozolino, L. (2017). *The neuroscience of psychotherapy* (3rd ed.). W. W. Norton & Company.

Critchley, H. D., & Garfinkel, S. N. (2017). Interoception and emotion. *Current Opinions in Psychology, 17*, 7-14.

Csikszentmihalyi, M. (2008). *Flow: The psychology of optimal experience.* Harper Perennial Classics.

Cyr, A. V. (1999). *Overview of theories and principles relating to characteristics of adult learners: 1970s-1999.* ERIC Clearinghouse on Adult, Career, and Vocational Education.

Dallow, C. B., & Anderson, J. (2003). Using self-efficacy and a transtheoretical model to develop a physical activity intervention for obese women. *American Journal of Health Promotion, 17*(6), 373-381.

Damasio, A. (2000). *The feeling of what happens: Body and emotion in the making of consciousness.* Harcourt Publishing Co.

Davis, J. (2003). An overview of transpersonal psychology. *Humanistic Psychologist, 31*(2-3), 6-21.

de Haan, E., Duckworth, A., Birch, D., & Jones, C. (2013). Executive coaching outcomes research: The contribution of common factors such as relationship, personality match, and self-efficacy. *Consulting Psychology Journal: Practice & Research, 65*(1), 40-57.

De Jong, A. (2016). Coaching ethics: Integrity in the moment of choice. In J. Passmore (Ed.), *Excellence in coaching: The industry guide* (2nd ed., pp. 209-225). Kogan Page Ltd.

De Jong, P., & Berg, I. K. (2013). *Interviewing for solutions* (4th ed.). Thomson Higher Education.

De Llosa, P. (2011). The neurobiology of "we." *Parabola,* Summer, 69-75.

De Saint-Exupéry, A. (1943). *Le petit prince.* Reynal & Hitchcock.

De Shazer, S. (1988). *Clues: Investigating solutions in brief therapy.* Norton.

De Waal, F. B., & Preston, S. D. (2017). Mammalian empathy: Behavioural manifestations and neural basis. *Nature Reviews Neuroscience, 18*(8), 498-509.

Deci, E. L., & Ryan, R. M. (1985). *Intrinsic motivation and self-determination in human behavior.* Plenum Press.

Deci, E. L., & Ryan, R. M. (2000). The "what" and "why" of goal pursuits: Human needs and the self-determination of behavior. *Psychological Inquiry, 11*(4), 227-268.

Deci, E. L., & Ryan, R. M. (2017). *Self-determination theory: Basic psychological needs in motivation, development, and wellness.* Guilford Press.

DeForest, H., Largent, P., & Steinberg, M. (2005). *Mastering the art of feedback: Tips, tools and intelligence for trainers.* ASTD Press.

Dembkouski, S., & Eldridge, F. (2008). Achieving tangible results: The development of a coaching model. In D. Drake, D. Brennan, & K. Gortz (Eds.), *The philosophy and practice of coaching: Insights and issues for a new era* (pp. 195-211). John Wiley & Sons, Ltd.

Descartes, R. (1998). *Discourse on method* (3rd ed.). Hackett Publishing Company, Inc.

DeVaris, J. (1994). The dynamics of power in psychotherapy. *Psychotherapy, 31,* 588-593.

Dilts, R., & DeLozier, J. (2000). *Encyclopedia of systemic NLP and NLP new coding.* Meta.

Ding, X., Tang, Y. Y., Cao, C., Deng, Y., Wang, Y., Xin, X., & Posner, M. I. (2015). Short-term meditation modulates brain activity of insight evoked with solution cue. *Social Cognitive and Affective Neuroscience, 10*(1), 43-49.

Divine, L. (2009a). A unique view into you: Working with a client's AQAL constellation. *Journal of Integral Theory and Practice, 4*(1), 41-67.

Divine, L. (2009b). Looking at and looking as the client: The quadrants as a type structure lens. *Journal of Integral Theory and Practice, 4*(1), 21-40.

Docety, J., & Howard, L. H. (2014). A neurodevelopmental perspective on morality. In M. Killen (Ed.), *Handbook of moral development* (2nd ed., pp. 454-474). Psychology Press.

Donatelle, R., & Kolen Thompson, A. M. (2011). *Health: The basics* (4th Canadian Edition). Pearson Education.

Doran, G. T. (1981). There's a S.M.A.R.T. way to write management's goals and objectives. *Management Review, 70*(11), 35-36.

Drake, D. B. (2018). *Narrative coaching: Bringing our new stories to life* (2nd ed.). CNC Press.

Du Toit, A. (2014). *Making sense of coaching.* Sage.

Duffy, M., & Passmore, J. (2010). Ethics in coaching: An ethical decision making framework for coaching psychologists. *International Coaching Psychology Review, 9*(2), 140-151.

Dum, R. P., Levinthal, D. J., & Strick, P. L. (2019). The mind–body problem: Circuits that link the cerebral cortex to the adrenal medulla. *Proceedings of the National Academy of Sciences, 116*(52), 26321-26328.

Dumoulin, H. (2005). *Zen Buddhism: A history India and China* (J. W. Heisig & P. Knitter, Trans.). World Wisdom.

Dunbar, A. (2017). *Clean coaching: The insider guide to making change happen.* Routledge.

Dychtwald, K. (1977). *Bodymind.* Pantheon.

Dyer, W. W. (2010). The power of intention. Hay House.

Egan, G. (2014). *The skilled helper: A problem-management and opportunity-development approach to helping* (10th ed.). Brooks/Cole.

Einzig, H. (2017). *The future of coaching: Vision, leadership and responsibility in a transforming world.* Routledge.

Eisenberg, N., & Miller, P. (1987). The relation of empathy to prosocial and related behaviors. *Psychological Bulletin, 101*(1), 91-119.

Ekman, P. (1993). Facial expression and emotion. *American Psychologist, 48,* 384-392.

Ekman, P. (2003). *Emotions revealed: Recognizing faces and feelings to improve communication and emotional life.* Holt, Rinehart & Winston.

Ekman, P., & Rosenberg, E. L. (2005). *What the face reveals: Basic and applied studies of spontaneous expression using the facial action coding system (FACS).* Oxford University Press.

Ellison, L. (2001). *The personal intelligences.* Corwin.

Engel, G. L. (1977). The need for a new medical model: A challenge for biomedicine. *Science, 196,* 129-136.

Erikson, E. H. (1959). *Identity and the life cycle.* International Universities Press.

Erikson, E. H. (1963). *Childhood and society* (2nd ed.). Norton.

Erikson, E. H. (1968). *Identity, youth and crisis.* Norton.

Erskine, R. G. (2015). *Relational patterns, therapeutic presence: Concepts and practice of integrative psychotherapy.* Karnac Books.

Esquer, K. Y. (2014). *Spirituality in coaching: Exploring the link between leadership, morality and spirituality* (Doctoral dissertation, Widener University). Retrieved from https://lib-ezproxy.concordia.ca/login?qurl=https%3A%2F%2Fwww.proquest.com%2Fdissertations-theses%2Fspirituality-coaching-exploring-link-between%2Fdocview%2F1696736635%2Fse-2%3Faccountid%3D10246

Etter, J. F., Bergman, M. M., & Perneger, T. V. (2000). On quitting smoking: Development of two scales measuring the use of self-change strategies in current and former smokers (SCS-CS and SCS-FS). *Addictive Behaviors, 25*(4), 523-538.

Evans, D. R., Hearn, M. T., Uhlemann, M. R., & Ivey, A. E. (2017). *Essential interviewing: A programmed approach to effective communication* (9th ed.). Cengage Learning.

Exline, J. J., Campbell, W. K., Baumeister, R. F., Joiner, T., & Krueger, J. (2004). Humility and modesty. In C. Peterson & M. Seligman (Eds.), *The values in action (VIA) classification of strengths* (pp. 461-475). Values in Action Institute.

Fallon, N., Roberts, C., & Stancak, A. (2020). Shared and distinct functional networks for empathy and pain processing: A systematic review and meta-analysis of fMRI studies. *Social Cognitve and Affective Neuroscience.* Online ahead of print. https://doi.org/10.1093/scan/nsaa090

Farb, N. A., Segal, Z. V., Mayberg, H., Bean, J., McKeon, D., Fatima, Z., & Anderson, A. K. (2007). Attending to the present: Mindfulness meditation reveals distinct neural modes of self-reference. *Social Cognitive and Affective Neuroscience, 2*(4), 313-322.

Fast, J. (2002). *Body language* (Revised ed.). Evans.

Fazel, P. (2013). Learning theories within coaching process. *International Journal of Psychological and Behavioral Sciences, 7*(8), 2343-2349.

Feldenkrais, M. (2009). *Awareness through movement: Easy-to-do health exercises to improve your posture, vision, imagination, and personal awareness* (Reprint ed.). HarperOne.

Ferriss, T. (2009). *The 4 hour workweek.* Crown.

Festinger, L. (1957). *A theory of cognitive dissonance.* Stanford University Press.

Flaherty, J. (1998). *Coaching: Evoking excellence in others.* Butterworth-Heinemann.

Flaherty, J. (2010). *Coaching: Evoking excellence in others* (3rd ed.). Elsevier Butterworth-Heinemann.

Fogel, A. (2013). *Body sense: The science and practice of embodied self-awareness* (Reprint ed.). WW Norton.

Forbes Coaches Council. (2018). 15 *Trends that will redefine executive coaching in the next decade.* www.forbes.com/sites/forbescoachescouncil/2018/04/09/15-trends-that-will-redefine-executive-coaching-in-the-next-decade/#18c42d396fc9

Foronda, C., Baptiste, D. L., Reinholdt, M. M., & Ousman, K. (2016). Cultural humility: A concept analysis. *Journal of Transcultural Nursing, 27*(3), 210-217.

Fradkov, A. L. (2007). *Cybernetical physics: From control of chaos to quantum control.* Springer-Verlag.

Frank, J. D., & Frank, J. B. (1993). *Persuasion and healing: A comparative study of psychotherapy* (3rd ed.). Johns Hopkins University Press.

Frankl, V. (1969). *The will to meaning: Foundations and applications of logotherapy.* New American Library.

Frankl, V. E. (1988). *Man's search for meaning* (6th ed.). Washington Square Press.

Freud, S. (1949). *An outline of psycho-analysis* (J. Strachey, Ed.). Hogarth Press.

Freud, S. (1964). An outline of psychoanalysis. In J. Strachey, F. Freud, & C. L. Rothgeb (Eds.), *The standard edition of the complete psychological works of Sigmund Freud* (Vol. 23, pp. 141-2018). Hogarth Press.

Frost, L. (2009). Integral perspectives on coaching: An analysis of Integral Coaching Canada across eight zones and five methodologies. *Journal of Integral Theory and Practice, 4*(1), 93-120.

Füstös, J., Gramann, K., Herbert, B. M., & Pollatos, O. (2013). On the embodiment of emotion regulation: Interoceptive awareness facilitates reappraisal. *Social Cognitive and Affective Neuroscience, 8*(8), 911-917.

Gabbard, G. O. (1995). Countertransference: The emerging common ground. *International Journal of Psychoanalysis, 76,* 475-485.

Gabbard, G. O. (2016). *Boundaries and boundary violations in psychoanalysis.* American Psychiatric Association.

Gallese, V., Fadiga, L., Fogassi, L., & Rizzolatti, G. R. (1996). Action recognition in the premotor cortex. *Brain, 119*(2), 593-609.

Gardner, H. (1983). *Frames of mind: The theory of multiple intelligences.* Basic Books.

Gardner, H. (2006). *Multiple intelligences: New horizons.* Basic Books.

Gavin, J. (1988). *Body moves: The psychology of exercise.* Stackpole Books.

Gavin, J., & Mcbrearty, M. (2018). *Lifestyle wellness coaching* (3rd ed.). Human Kinetics.

Gavin, J., Thomas, E., & Chacra, J. (2021). *A dynamic anatomy of professional coaches' interventions over time.* World Congress on Positive Psychology Conference Proceedings.

Geldard, K., & Geldard, D. (2008). *Counselling children: A practical introduction* (3rd ed.). SAGE Publications.

Geller, S. M. (2013). Therapeutic presence: An essential way of being. In M. Cooper, P. F. Schmid, M. O'Hara, & A. C. Bohart (Eds.), *The handbook of person-centered psychotherapy and counselling* (2nd ed., pp. 209-222). Palgrave.

Geller, S. M., & Greenberg, L. S. (2002). Therapeutic presence: Therapists' experience of presence in the psychotherapy encounter. *Person-Centered & Experiential Psychotherapies, 1,* 71-86.

Geller, S. M., & Greenberg, L. S. (2012). *Therapeutic presence: A mindful approach to effective therapy.* APA.

Gelso, C. J., & Hayes, J. A. (2007). *Countertransference and the therapist's inner experience: Perils and possibilities.* Erlbaum.

Gendlin, E. (1981). *Focusing.* Bantam Books.

Gergen, K. (1985). The social constructionist movement in modern psychology. *American Psychologist, 40,* 266-275.

Gergen, K. (1991). *The saturated self.* Basic Books.

Gergen, K. (1999). An invitation to social construction. SAGE Publications.

Gergen, K. (2009). *Relational being: Beyond self and community.* Oxford University Press.

Gert, B., & Gert, J. (2017). The definition of morality. In E. N. Zalta (Ed.), *The Stanford Encyclopedia of Philosophy* (pp. 2017-236). Stanford University

Gessnitzer, S., & Kauffeld, S. (2015). The working alliance in coaching: Why behavior is the key to success. *Journal of Applied Behavioral Science, 51*(2), 177-197.

Gielen, U. P., Draguns, J. G., & Fish, J. M. (Eds.). (2008). *Principles of multicultural counseling and therapy*. Routledge.

Gilligan, C. (1982). *In a different voice: Psychological theory and women's development*. Harvard University Press.

Gilligan, C., & Richards, D. (2008). *The deepening darkness: Patriarchy, resistance, and democracy's future*. Cambridge University Press.

Gilligan, S., & Dilts, R. (2009). *The hero's journey: A voyage of self-discovery*. Crowne House Publishers.

Gladding, S. T. (2013). *Counseling: A comprehensive profession* (7th ed.). Pearson.

Goldstein, J. (2016). *Mindfulness: A practical guide to awakening* (reprint ed.). Sounds True.

Goleman, D. (1995). *Emotional intelligence*. Bantam Books.

Goleman, D. (2006). *Social intelligence: The new science of human relationships*. Bantam.

Goleman, D., & Davidson, R. J. (2017). *Altered traits: Science reveals how meditation changes your mind, brain, and body*. Penguin.

Gollwitzer, P. M. (1999). Implementation intentions: Strong effects of simple plans. *American Psychologist, 54*(7), 493-503.

Gollwitzer, P. M., & Brandstätter, V. (1997). Implementation intentions and effective goal pursuit. *Journal of Personality and Social Psychology, 73*, 186-199.

Grant, A. M. (2003). The impact of life coaching on goal attainment, metacognition and mental health. *Social Behavior and Personality, 31*(3), 253-264.

Grant, A. M. (2006). An integrative goal-focused approach to executive coaching. In D. R. Stober & A. M. Grant (Eds.), *Evidence-based coaching handbook: Putting best practices to work for your client* (pp. 153-192). Wiley.

Grant, A. M. (2007). Past, present and future: The evolution of professional coaching and coaching psychology. In S. Palmer & A. Whybrow (Eds.), *Handbook of coaching psychology: A guide for practitioners* (pp. 23-39). Routledge.

Grant, A. M. (2012). An integrated model of goal-focused coaching: An evidence-based framework for teaching and practice. *International Coaching Psychology Review, 7*(2), 146-165.

Grant, A. M., & Cavanagh, M. J. (2007). Evidence-based coaching: Flourishing or languishing. *Australian Psychologist, 42*(4), 239-254.

Grant, A. M., & Green, R. M. (2018). Developing clarity on the coaching–counselling conundrum: Implications for counsellors and psychotherapists. *Counselling and Psychotherapy Research, 18*(4), 347-355.

Grant, A. M., & Greene, J. (2003). *Solution-focused coaching: Managing people in a complex world*. Pearson International.

Grant, A. M., & Zackon, R. (2004). Executive, workplace and life coaching: Findings from a large-scale survey of International Coach Federation Members. *International Journal of Evidence Based Coaching and Mentoring, 2*(2), 1-15.

Green, S., & Palmer, S. (Eds.). (2018). *Positive psychology coaching in practice*. Routledge.

Gregory, J. B., Beck, J. W., & Carr, A. E. (2011). Goals, feedback, and self-regulation: Control theory as a natural framework for executive coaching. *Consulting Psychology Journal: Practice and Research, 63*(1), 26-38.

Grinder, J., & Bandler, R. (1976). *Patterns of the hypnotic techniques of Milton H. Erickson, M. D.* (Vol. I). Metapublications.

Grof, S. (1988). *The adventure of self-discovery: Dimensions of consciousness and new perspectives in psychotherapy*. State University of New York Press.

Grove, D., & Panzer, B. (1989). *Resolving traumatic memories: Metaphors and symbols in psychotherapy*. Irvington.

Guttman, H. M. (2007). Coachability. *Leadership Excellence, 24*(6), 14.

Hackman, J. R., & Wageman, R. (2005). A theory of team coaching. *Academy of Management Review, 30*(2), 269-287.

Hall, E. T. (1966). *The hidden dimension*. Doubleday.

Hall, E. T. (1976). *Beyond culture*. Anchor Press.

Hanh, T. N. (2017). *The art of living: Peace and freedom in the here and now*. Harper One.

Harari, Y. N. (2014). *Sapiens: A brief history of humankind*. Penguin Random House.

Harari, Y. N. (2016). *Homo deus: A brief history of tomorrow*. Penguin Random House.

Harari, Y. N. (2018). *21 lessons for the 21st century*. Penguin Random House.

Hargie, O. (2017). *Skilled interpersonal communication* (6th ed.). Routledge.

Hargrove, R. (2008). *Masterful coaching* (3rd ed.). Jossey-Bass.

Hart, W. (2011). *The art of living: Vipassana meditation as taught by S. N. Goenka*. Pariyatti.

Hawkins, P. (2014). *Leadership team coaching: Developing collective transformational leadership*. Kogan Page.

Hawkins, P., & Schwenk, G. (2010). The interpersonal relationship in the training and supervision of coaches. In S. Palmer & A. McDowall (Eds.), *The coaching relationship: Putting people first* (pp. 203-221). Routledge.

Hayes, S. C., Strosahl, K. D., & Wilson, K. G. (2011). *Acceptance and commitment therapy* (2nd ed.). Guilford Press.

Heatherton, T. F., & Wagner, D. D. (2011). Cognitive neuroscience of self-regulation failure. *Trends in Cognitive Science, 15*(3), 132-139.

Hefferon, K., & Boniwell, I. (2011). *Positive psychology: Theory, research and applications*. Open University Press.

Heidegger, M. (1962). *Being and time* (J. Macquarrier & E. Robinson, Eds.; Trans.). Harper & Row.

Heider, F. (1946). Attitudes and cognitive organization. *Journal of Psychology, 21,* 107-112.

Hendrix, H. (2008). *Getting the love you want: A guide for couples* (20th anniversary revised). H. Holt.

Henretty, J. R., & Levitt, H. M. (2010). The role of therapist self-disclosure in psychotherapy: A qualitative review. *Clinical Psychology Review, 30*(1), 63-77.

Hepworth, D. H., Rooney, R. H., Rooney, G. D., Strom-Gottfried, K., & Larsen, J. (2010). *Direct social work practice: Theory and skills* (8th ed.). Brooks/Cole.

Herlihy, B., & Corey, G. (2006). *Boundary issues in counseling: Multiple roles and responsibilities* (2nd ed.). American Counseling Association.

Heyman, E., Gamelin, F. X., Goekint, M., Piscitelli, F., Roelands, B., Leclair, E., & Meeusen, R. (2012). Intense exercise increases circulating endocannabinoid and BDNF levels in humans—possible implications for reward and depression. *Psychoneuroendocrinology, 37*(6), 844-851.

Hickok, G. (2014). *The myth of mirror neurons: The real neuroscience of communication and cognition.* WW Norton & Company.

Hildebrandt, M.J., Fletcher, L.B ., & Hayes, S.C. (2007) Climbing anxiety mountain: Generating metaphors in acceptance and commitment therapy. In G.W. Burns, *Your casebook collection for using therapeutic metaphors* (pp. 55-64). John Wiley & Sons.

Hill, J., & Oliver, J. (2019). *Acceptance and commitment coaching: Distinctive features.* Routledge.

Hofstede, G. (2001). *Culture's consequences: Comparing values, behaviors, institutions and organizations across nations.* SAGE Publications.

Hook, J. N., Davis, D. D., Owen, J., & DeBlaere, C. (2017). *Cultural humility: Engaging diverse identities in therapy.* American Psychological Association.

Horney, K. (1939). *New ways in psychoanalysis.* Norton.

Horton, I. (1996). Towards the construction of a model of counseling: Some issues. In R. Bayne, I. Horton, & J. Bimrose (Eds.), *New directions in counselling* (pp. 281-296). Routledge.

Horvath, A., & Greenberg, L. (1994). Introduction. In A. Horvath & L. Greenberg (Eds.), *The working alliance: Theory, research, and practice* (pp. 1-9). Wiley.

Hunt, J. (2009a). Building Integral Coaching Canada: A practice journey. *Journal of Integral Theory and Practice, 4*(1), 121-149.

Hunt, J. (2009b). Transcending and including our current way of being: An introduction to integral coaching. *Journal of Integral Theory and Practice, 4*(1), 1-20.

Hutchins, D. E., & Vaught, C. C. (1997). *Helping relationships and strategies* (3rd ed.). Brooks/Cole.

Huxley, A. (1932). *Brave new world.* Chatto and Windus.

Hycner, R. (1993). *Between person and person: Toward a dialogical psychotherapy.* Gestalt Journal Press.

Hyde, R. (1994). Listening authentically: A Heideggerian perspective on interpersonal communication. In K. Carter & M. Presnell (Eds.), *Interpretive approaches to interpersonal communication* (pp. 179-196). State University of New York Press.

ICF (2012). *2012 ICF global coaching study final report.* ICF. Lexington, KY: ICF.

ICF. (2016). *2016 ICF global coaching study final report.* ICF. Lexington, KY: ICF.

ICF. (2020a). *2020 ICF global coaching study final report.* Lexington, KY: ICF.

ICF. (2020b). *Code of ethics.* International Coaching Federation. https://coachfederation.org/code-of-ethics

ICF. (2020c). *ICF core competencies.* International Coaching Federation. https://coachfederation.org/core-competencies

ICF. (2020d). *ICF membership fact list.* International Coaching Federation. https://carlyanderson.com/wp-content/uploads/ICF-Credential-Fact-Sheet.pdf

ICF. (2020e). *ICF, the gold standard in coaching: Read about ICF.* International Coaching Federation. https://coachfederation.org/about

Iliffe-Wood, M. (2014). *Coaching presence: Building consciousness and awareness in coaching interventions.* Kogan Page Limited.

Illeris, K. (2016). *How we learn: Learning and non-learning in school and beyond.* Routledge.

Illeris, K. (Ed.). (2018). *Contemporary theories of learning: Learning theorists . . . in their own words.* Routledge.

Isaacs, W. (1999). *Dialogue: The art of thinking together.* Currency.

Ives, Y. (2008). What is "coaching"? An exploration of conflicting paradigms. *International Journal of Evidence Based Coaching and Mentoring, 6*(2), 100-113.

Ives, Y., & Cox, E. (2012). *Goal-focused coaching: Theory and practice.* Routledge.

Ivey, A. E., Ivey, M. B., & Zalaquett, C. P. (2018). *Intentional interviewing and counseling: Facilitating client development in a multicultural society* (9th ed.). Cengage Learning.

Ivtzan, I., Lomas, T., Hefferon, K., & Worth, P. (2016). *Second wave positive psychology.* Routledge.

Jackson, L., & Tervalon, M. (2020). *Cultural humility in art therapy: Applications for practice, research, social justice, self-care, and pedagogy.* Jessica Kingsley Publishers.

James, R. K., & Gilliland, B. E. (2003). *Theories and strategies in counseling and psychotherapy* (5th ed.). Allyn & Bacon.

Jarosz, J. (2016). What is life coaching? An integrative review of the evidence-based literature. *International Journal of Evidence Based Coaching and Mentoring, 14*(1), 34-56.

Johns, C. (Ed.). (2017). *Becoming a reflective practitioner.* John Wiley and Sons Ltd.

Johnson, B. W. (2013). Mixed-agency dilemmas in military psychology. In B. A. Moore & J. E. Barnett (Eds.), *Military psychologists' desk reference* (pp. 107-112). Oxford University Press.

Johnson, D. W. (2014). *Reaching out: Interpersonal effectiveness and self-actualization* (11th ed.). Pearson Education.

Jordan, M., & Livingstone, J. (2013). Coaching vs. psychotherapy in health and wellness: Overlap, dissimilarities, and the potential for collaboration. *Global Advances in Health and Medicine, 2*(4), 20-27.

Jung, C. G. (1969). *The psychology of the transference.* Princeton University Press.

Jung, C. G. (1971). *Psychological types.* Princeton University Press.

Kabat-Zinn, J. (1994). *Wherever you go there you are: Mindfulness meditation in everyday life.* Hyperion.

Kabat-Zinn, J. (2005). *Coming to our senses.* Piatkus.

Kabat-Zinn, J. (2018). *Falling awake: How to practice mindfulness in everyday life.* Hachette Books.

Kahn, W. A. (2005). *Holding fast: The struggle to create resilient caregiving organizations.* Brunner-Routledge.

Kavedzija, I., & Walker, H. (2017). *Values of happiness: Toward an anthropology of purpose in life.* University of Chicago Press.

Kazdin, A. E., & Wassell, G. (1998). Treatment completion and therapeutic change among children referred for outpatient therapy. *Professional Psychology: Research and Practice, 29*(4), 332-340.

Kegan, R. (1982). *The evolving self: Problem and process in human development.* Harvard University Press.

Kegan, R. (1994). *In over our heads: Mental demands of modern life.* Harvard University Press.

Kegan, R., & Lahey, L. (2001). *How the way we talk can change the way we work: Seven languages for transformation.* Jossey-Bass.

Kegan, R., & Lahey, L. L. (2009). *Immunity to change: How to overcome it and unlock the potential in yourself and your organization.* Harvard University Press.

Kellogg, V., Lasley, M., Michaels, R., & Brown, S. (2015). *Coaching for transformation: Pathways to ignite personal and social change.* Discover Press.

Kennedy, D. L. (2013). *The impact of development on coaches' use of self as instrument* [Doctoral dissertation, Fielding Graduate University].

Kennedy, D. O., Jackson, P. A., Forster, J., Khan, J., Grothe, T., Perrinjaquet-Moccetti, T., & Haskell-Ramsay, C. F. (2017). Acute effects of a wild green-oat (*Avena sativa*) extract on cognitive function in middle-aged adults: A double-blind, placebo controlled, within-subject trial. *Nutritional Neuroscience, 20*(2), 135-151.

Kernis, M. H., & Goldman, B. M. (2005). Authenticity, social motivation and psychological adjustment. In J. P. Forgas, K. D. Williams, & S. M. Laham (Eds.), *Social motivation: Conscious and unconscious processes* (pp. 210-227). Cambridge University Press.

Kerr, C. E., Sacchet, M. D., Lazar, S. W., Moore, C. I., & Jones, S. R. (2013). Mindfulness starts with the body: Somatosensory attention and top-down modulation of cortical alpha rhythms in mindfulness meditation. *Frontiers in Human Neuroscience, 7,* 12.

Khalsa, S. S., Adolphs, R., Cameron, O. G., Critchley, H. D., Davenport, P. W., Feinstein, J. S., & Meuret, A. E. (2018). Interoception and mental health: A roadmap. *Biological Psychiatry: Cognitive Neuroscience and Neuroimaging, 3*(6), 501-513.

Killgore, W. D. (2010). Effects of sleep deprivation on cognition. *Progress in Brain Research, 185,* 105-129.

Killingsworth, M. A., & Gilbert, D. T. (2010). A wandering mind is an unhappy mind. *Science, 330*(6006), 932.

Kim, J. S. (2014). *Solution-focused brief therapy: A multicultural approach.* SAGE Publications.

Kimsey-House, H., Kimsey-House, K., Sandhal, P., & Whitworth, L. (2018). *Co-active coaching: The proven framework for transformative conversations at work and in life* (4th ed.). Quercus.

Kirschenbaum, H. (2013). *Values clarification in counseling and psychotherapy.* Oxford University Press.

Kleinke, C. L. (1994). *Common principles of psychotherapy.* Brooks/Cole.

Knapp, M. L., & Daly, J. A. (Eds.).(2002). *Handbook of interpersonal communication* (3rd ed.). SAGE Publications.

Knapp, M. L., Hall, J. A., & Horgan, T. (2014). *Nonverbal communication in human interaction* (8th ed.). Wadsworth, Cengage Learning.

Knight, J. (2011). *Unmistakable impact: A partnership approach for dramatically improving instruction.* Corwin.

Knowles, M.S. (1980). *The modern practice of adult education: From pedagogy to andragogy.* Prentice Hall/Cambridge.

Koestner, R., Lekes, N., Powers, T. A., & Chicoine, E. (2002). Attaining personal goals: Self-concordance plus implementation intentions equals success. *Journal of Personality and Social Psychology, 83*(1), 231-244.

Kohanski, A. S. (1975). *An analytic interpretation of Martin Buber's I and thou.* Barron's Educational Series.

Kohlberg, L. (1981). *Essays on moral development.* HarperCollins.

Kohut, H. (1984). *How does analysis cure?* University of Chicago Press.

Kolb, D. A. (1984). *Experiential learning: Experience as the source of learning and development.* Prentice Hall.

Kolb, D. A., & Fry, R. (1975). Toward an applied theory of experiential learning. In C. Cooper (Ed.), *Theories of group process* (pp. 33-58). Wiley.

Korman, A. K. (1970). Toward a hypothesis of work behavior. *Journal of Applied Psychology, 54*(1, Pt. 1), 31-41.

Kornfield, J. (2008). *The wise heart: A guide to the universal teachings of Buddhist psychology.* Bantam Books.

REFERENCES

...field, J. (2017). *No time like the present: Finding freedom, love, and joy right where you are*. Simon and Schuster.

Kottler, J. A. (2008). *A brief primer of helping skills* (2nd ed.). SAGE Publications.

Kottler, J. A., & Shepard, D. S. (2015). *Introduction to counseling: Voices from the field* (8th ed.). Cengage Learning.

Kounios, J., & Beeman, M. (2014). The cognitive neuroscience of insight. *Annual Review of Psychology, 65*, 71-93.

Kouzes, J. M., & Posner, B. Z. (2017). *The leadership challenge workbook*. The Leadership Challenge.

Kratcoski, P. C. (2004). *Correctional counseling and treatment* (5th ed.). Waveland Press.

Kraus, M. W. (2017). Voice-only communication enhances empathic accuracy. *American Psychologist, 72* (7), 644-654.

Kretzschmar, I. (2010). Exploring clients' readiness for coaching. *International Journal of Evidence Based Coaching and Mentoring, S4*, 1-20.

Kurz, R., & Prestera, H. (1976). *The body reveals: An illustrated guide to the psychology of the body*. Harper & Row.

Ladany, N., Walker, J. A., Pate-Carolan, L. M., & Evans, L. G. (2008). *Practicing counseling and psychotherapy: Insights from trainees, supervisors and clients*. Routledge.

Lakoff, G., & Johnson, M. (1980). *Metaphors we live by*. University of Chicago Press.

Lambert, M. J., & Barley, D. E. (2001). Research summary on the therapeutic relationship and psychotherapy outcome. *Psychotherapy: Theory, Research, Practice, Training, 38*(4), 357-361.

Lapsley, D. K. (2006). Moral stage theory. In M. Killen & J. G. Smetana (Eds.), *Handbook of moral development* (pp. 37-66). Psychology Press.

Larimer, M. E., Palmer, R. S., & Marlatt, G. A. (1999). Relapse prevention: An overview of Marlatt's cognitive-behavioral model. *Alcohol Research and Health, 23*(2), 151-160.

Latham, G. P., Ganegoda, D. B., & Locke, E. A. (2011). Goal setting: A state theory but related to traits. In T. Chamorro-Premuzic, S. Strumm, & A. Furham (Eds.), *Wiley-Blackwell handbook of individual differences* (pp. 579-588). Wiley-Blackwell.

Latham, G. P., & Locke, E. A. (2002). Building a practically useful theory of goal setting and task motivation. *American Psychologist, 57*(9), 707-709.

Lawrence, P. (2017). Coaching and adult development. In T. Bachkirova, G. Spence, & D. Drake (Eds.), *The SAGE handbook of coaching* (pp. 121-138). SAGE Publications.

Lazarus, R. S., & Lazarus, B. N. (1994). *Passion and reason: Making sense of our emotions*. Oxford University Press.

Levinson, H. (1976). *Psychological man*. Levinson Institute.

Levinthal, D. J., & Strick, P. L. (2020). Multiple areas of the cerebral cortex influence the stomach. *Proceedings of the National Academy of Sciences, 117*(23), 13078-13083.

Levitt, H. M., Minami, T., Greenspan, S. B., Puckett, J. A., Henretty, J. R., Reich, C. M., & Berman, J. S. (2016). How therapist self-disclosure relates to alliance and outcomes: A naturalistic study. *Counselling Psychology Quarterly, 29*(1), 7-28.

Lewin, K. (1935). *A dynamic theory of personality*. McGraw-Hill.

Linger, R. A. (2016). *A qualitative study of a mindfulness-based coaching intervention for perception shifts and emotional regulation around workplace stressors and quality of worklife*. Unpublished Dissertation. Saybrook University, California.

Locke, E. A., & Latham, G. P. (1985). The application of goal setting to sports. *Journal of Sport Psychology, 7*, 205-222.

Locke, E. A., & Latham, G. P. (1990). *A theory of goal setting and task performance*. Prentice Hall.

Locke, E. A., & Latham, G. P. (2002). Building a practically useful theory of goal setting and task motivation: A 35-year odyssey. *American Psychologist, 57*(9), 705-717.

Locke, E. A., & Latham, G. P. (2006). New directions in goal-setting theory. *Current Directions in Psychological Science, 15*(5), 265-268.

Locke, E. A., & Latham, G. P. (2009). Has goal setting gone wild or have its attackers abandoned good scholarship? *Academy of Management Perspectives, 23*(1), 17-23.

Locke, E. A., Shaw, K. N., Saari, L. M., & Latham, G. P. (1981). Goal setting and task performance: 1969-1980. *Psychological Bulletin, 90*, 125-152.

Lorenz, E. N. (1972). *Predictability: Does the flap of a butterfly's wings in Brazil set off a tornado in Texas?* American Association for the Advancement of Science, 139th Meeting, December 29. Washington, DC.

Luborsky, L., & Barrett, M. S. (2006). The history and empirical status of key psychoanalytic concepts. *Annual Review of Clinical Psychology, 2*, 1-19.

Luft, J. (1969). *Of human interaction*. National Press.

Luoma, J. B., Hayes, S. C., & Waiser, J. D. (2017). *Learning ACT: An acceptance and commitment therapy skills training manual for therapists* (2nd ed.). New Harbinger Publications.

Luszczynska, A., Gutiérrez-Doña, B., & Schwarzer, R. (2005). General self-efficacy in various domains of human functioning: Evidence from five countries. *International Journal of Psychology, 40*(2), 80-89.

Ma, X., Yue, Z. Q., Gong, Z. Q., Zhang, H., Duan, N. Y., Shi, Y. T., & Li, Y. F. (2017). The effect of diaphragmatic breathing on attention, negative affect and stress in healthy adults. *Frontiers in Psychology, 8*, 874.

Mackey, R. A., & Diemer, M. (2000). Psychological intimacy in the lasting relationships of heterosexual and same-gender couples. *Sex Roles, 43*(3/4), 201-227.

Maio, G. R. (2017). *The psychology of human values*. Routledge.

Marlatt, G. A., & Donovan, D. M. (2008). *Relapse prevention: Maintenance strategies in the treatment of addictive behaviors* (2nd ed.). Guilford Press.

Marlatt, G. A., & Gordon, J. R. (1985). *Relapse prevention: Maintenance strategies in the treatment of addictive behaviors*. Guilford Press.

Marshall, S., & Biddle, S. (2001). The transtheoretical model of behavior change: A meta-analysis of applications to physical activity and exercise. *Annals of Behavioral Medicine, 23,* 229-246.

Martin, C. (2001). *The life coaching handbook: Everything you need to be an effective life coach.* Crown House.

Martinez-Marti, M. L., & Ruch, W. (2014). Character strengths and well-being across the life span: Data from a representative sample of German-speaking adults living in Switzerland. *Frontiers in Psychology, 5,* 1253.

Martinez-Marti, M. L., & Ruch, W. (2017). Character strengths predict resilience over and above positive affect, self-efficacy, optimism, social support, self-esteem, and life satisfaction. *The Journal of Positive Psychology, 12*(2), 110-119.

Maslow, A. H. (1962). *Toward a psychology of being.* Van Nostrand.

Masters, K. S., & Ogles, B. M. (1998). Associative and dissociative cognitive strategies in exercise and running: 20 years later, what do we know? *The Sport Psychologist, 12*(3), 253-270.

Matthews, A. (2014). Humility. *The American Scholar, 83*(1), 130-131.

May, R. (1996). *The meaning of anxiety* (revised). Norton.

Mcbrearty, M. (2010). *Women, obesity, and weight loss: Bridging the intention–behaviour gap* [Unpublished doctoral dissertation]. Concordia University, Quebec.

McBride, B. W. (2014). *Coaching, clients, and competencies: How coaches experience the flow state* [Unpublished doctoral dissertation]. Fielding Graduate University, California.

McCrae, R. R., & Allik, J. (2002). *The five-factor model of personality across cultures.* Springer Science + Business.

McLaren, K. (2010). *The language of emotions: What your feelings are trying to tell you* (unabridged ed.). Sounds True.

McLean, P. (2012). *The completely revised handbook of coaching: A developmental approach* (2nd ed.). John Wiley & Sons.

Meadows, D. (2008). *Thinking in systems: A primer.* Chelsea Green Publishing.

Mehr, J. J., & Kanwischer, R. (2011). *Human services: Concepts and intervention strategies* (11th ed.). Allyn & Bacon.

Mehrabian, A. (1972). *Nonverbal communication.* Aldine-Atherton.

Mehrabian, A. (1981). *Silent messages: Implicit communication of emotions and attitudes* (2nd ed.). Wadsworth.

Merriam, S. B. (2004). The role of cognitive development in Mezirow's transformational learning theory. *Adult Education Quarterly, 55*(1), 60-68.

Mezirow, J. (1994). Understanding transformation theory. *Adult Education Quarterly, 44*(4), 222-232.

Mezirow, J. (2000). Learning to think like an adult: Core concepts of transformation theory. In J. Mezirow (Ed.), *Learning as transformation: Critical perspectives on a theory in progress* (pp. 3-34). Jossey-Bass.

Miller, R. B., & Brickman, S. J. (2004). A model of future oriented motivation and self-regulation. *Educational Psychology Review, 16,* 9-33.

Moriarty, O., McGuire, B. E., & Finn, D. P. (2011). The effect of pain on cognitive function: A review of clinical and preclinical research. *Progress in Neurobiology, 93*(3), 385-404.

Murdock, M. (1990). *The Heroine's Journey.* Shambhala.

Nagy, T. F. (2011). *Essential ethics for psychologists: A primer for understanding and mastering core issues.* American Psychological Association.

Neenan, M. (2018). *Cognitive behavioural coaching: Distinctive features.* Routledge.

Neenan, M., & Dryden, W. (2002). *Life coaching: A cognitive-behavioural approach.* Brunner-Routledge.

Neff, K., & Germer, C. (2018). *The mindful self-compassion workbook: A proven way to accept yourself, build inner strength, and thrive* (workbook ed.). The Guilford Press.

Nichols, P. (2002). *A voyage for madmen* (reprint ed.). Harper Perennial.

Niedenthal, P. M. (2007). Embodying emotions. *Science, 316*(5827), 1002-1005.

Nielsen, R., Marrone, J. A., & Slay, H. S. (2010). A new look at humility: Exploring the humility concept and its role in socialized charismatic leadership. *Journal of Leadership and Organisational Studies, 17*(1), 33-43.

Noddings, N. (1984). *Caring: A feminine approach to ethics and moral education.* University of California Press.

Norcross, J. (2002). *Psychotherapy relationships that work: Therapist relational contributions to effective psychotherapy.* Oxford University Press.

Novak, J. D. (1993). Human constructivism: A unification of psychological and epistemological phenomena in meaning making. *International Journal of Personal Construct Psychology, 6*(2), 167-193.

O'Connor, J., & Lages, A. (2019). *Coaching the brain: Practical applications of neuroscience to coaching.* Routledge.

O'Connor, S., & Cavanagh, M. (2017). Group and team coaching. In T. Bachkirova, G. Spence, & D. Drake (Eds.), *The SAGE handbook of coaching* (pp. 486-504). SAGE Publications.

Ogden, J., & Hills, L. (2008). Understanding sustained changes in behaviour: The role of life events and the process of reinvention. *Health: An International Journal, 12,* 419-437.

Osgood, C. E., & Tannenbaum, P. H. (1955). The principle of congruity in the prediction of attitude change. *Psychological Review, 62*(1), 42–55. https://doi.org/10.1037/h0048153.

Oshry, B. (2009). *Seeing systems: Unlocking the mysteries of organizational life.* ReadHowYouWant.com.

Ottaviani, C., Shapiro, D., & Couyoumdjian, A. (2013). Flexibility as the key for somatic health: From mind wandering to perseverative cognition. *Biological Psychology, 94*(1), 38-43.

Owen, J. (2013). Early career perspectives on psychotherapy research and practice: Psychotherapist effects, multicultural orientation, and couple interventions. *Psychotherapy, 50,* 496-502.

Owen, J., Jordan, T. A., II, Turner, D., Davis, D. E., Hook, J. N., & Leach, M. M. (2014). Therapists' multicultural orientation: Cultural humility, spiritual/religious identity, and therapy outcomes. *Journal of Psychology and Theology, 42,* 91-99.

Painter, J. E., Borba, C. P., Hynes, M., Mays, D., & Glanz, K. (2008). The use of theory in health behavior research from 2000 to 2005: A systematic review. *Annals of Behavioral Medicine, 35*(3), 358-362.

Palmer, P. J. (2000). *Let your life speak: Listening for the voice of vocation.* Jossey-Bass.

Palmer, S., & Whybrow, A. (Eds.). (2007). *Handbook of coaching psychology: A guide for practitioners.* Routledge.

Pappas, J. P., & Jerman, J. (2015). *Transforming adults through coaching: New directions for adult and continuing education, number 148.* John Wiley & Sons.

Parsloe, E. (1995). *Coaching, mentoring and assessing: A practical guide to developing competence.* Kogan.

Passmore, J. (2011). Supervision and continuous professional development in coaching. In J. Passmore (Ed.), *Supervision in coaching: Supervision, ethics and continuous professional development* (pp. 3-10). Kogan Page.

Passmore, J. (Ed.). (2013). *Diversity in coaching: Working with gender, culture, race and age.* Kogan Page.

Passmore, J., & Fillery-Travis, A. (2011). A critical review of executive coaching research: A decade of progress and what's to come. *Coaching: An International Journal of Theory, Practice & Research, 4*(2), 70-88.

Passmore, J., & Sinclair, T. (2020). *Becoming a coach: The essential ICF guide.* Springer.

Passmore, J., Underhill, B., & Goldsmith, M. (Eds.). (2019). Mastering ethics. In *Mastering executive coaching* (pp. 21-35). Routledge.

Pedersen, P., Crethar, H. C., & Carlson, J. (2008). *Inclusive cultural empathy: Making relationships central in counseling and psychotherapy.* American Psychological Association.

Pekarik, G., & Finney-Owen, K. (1987). Outpatient clinic therapist attitudes and beliefs relevant to client dropout. *Community Mental Health Journal, 23*(2), 120-130.

Peterson, C., & Seligman, M. (2004). *Character strengths and virtues: A handbook and classification.* Oxford University Press.

Peterson, D. (2018). *Embracing the future of leadership and coaching.* www.forbes.com/sites/alisacohn/2018/06/21/embracing-the-future-of-leadership-and-coaching/#1643185e2795

Piaget, J. (1952). *The origins of intelligence in children.* International University Press.

Powers, S. K., Dodd, S. L., Thompson, A. M., & Condon, C. C. (2005). *Total fitness and wellness (Canadian).* Pearson Education Canada.

Price, T. (2009). The coaching/therapy boundary in organizational coaching. *Coaching: An International Journal of Theory, Research and Practice, 2*(2), 135.

Prochaska, J., & Norcross, J. C. (2018). *Systems of psychotherapy: A transtheoretical analysis* (9th ed.). Oxford University Press.

Prochaska, J., Norcross, J. C., & DiClemente, C. C. (1994). *Changing for good.* Avon Books.

Prochaska, J., Norcross, J. C., & DiClemente, C. C. (2002). *Changing for good: The revolutionary program that explains the six stages of change and teaches you how to free yourself from bad habits.* Quill.

Prochaska, J., & Velicer, W. (1997). The transtheoretical model of health behavior change. *American Journal of Health Promotion, 12*(1), 38-48.

Prochaska, J., Wright, J. A., & Velicer, W. F. (2008). Hierarchy of criteria applied to the transtheoretical model. *Applied Psychology, 57*(4), 561-588.

Prochazkova, E., & Kret, M. E. (2017). Connecting minds and sharing emotions through mimicry: A neurocognitive model of emotional contagion. *Neuroscience & Biobehavioral Reviews, 80,* 99-114.

Pryor, R. G. L., & Bright, J. E. H. (2011). *The chaos theory of careers: A new perspective on working in the twenty-first century.* Routledge.

Puglisi, B., & Ackerman, A. (2019). *The emotion thesaurus: A writer's guide to character expression* (2nd ed.). JADD Publishing.

Quenck, N. L. (2009). *Essentials of Myers-Briggs type indicator assessment* (2nd ed.). Wiley.

Raia, A. P. (1965). Goal setting and self-control: An empirical study. *Journal of Management Studies, 2*(1), 34-53.

Raines, J. C. (1996). Self-disclosure in clinical social work. *Clinical Social Work Journal, 24*(4), 357-375.

Rainie, L., & Anderson, J. (2008). *Mirroring people: The new science of how we connect with others.* Farrar, Straus and Giroux.

Rainie, L., & Anderson, J. (2017). *Experts on the future of work, jobs training and skills.* Pew Research Center: Internet, Science & Tech. www.pewresearch.org/internet/2017/05/03/the-future-of-jobs-and-jobs-training/

Rank, O. (1958). *Beyond psychology*. Dover Publications.

Reding, P., & Collins, M. (2008). Coaching the human spirit. In D. B. Drake, D. Brennan, & K. Gortz (Eds.), *The philosophy and practice of coaching: Insights and issues for a new era* (pp. 1187-1194). Wiley.

Reis, B., & Brown, L. (1999). Reducing psychotherapy dropouts: Maximizing perspective convergence in psychotherapy dyad. *Psychotherapy, 36*, 123-136.

Remen, R.N. (1996). *Kitchen table wisdom: Stories that heal.* Riverhead Books.

Remley, T. P., & Herlihy, B. P. (2015). *Ethical, legal, and professional issues in counseling* (5th ed.). Pearson.

Ricard, M. (2016). *Altruism: The power of compassion to change yourself and the world.* Back Bay Books.

Riso, D. R., & Hudson, R. (1999). *The wisdom of the enneagram: The complete guide to psychological and spiritual growth for the nine personality types* (11th ed.). Bantam.

Ritacco, A., & McGowan, H. (2017). *Preparing students to lose their jobs (and faculty to keep theirs).* Academic Impressions. www.academicimpressions.com/blog/preparing-students-to-lose-their-jobs-and-faculty-to-keep-theirs/

Rock, D. (2020). *Your brain at work, revised and updated: Strategies for overcoming distraction, regaining focus, and working smarter all day long.* Harper Business.

Rogers, C. R. (1951). *Client-centered therapy: Its current practice, implications and theory.* Houghton Mifflin.

Rogers, C. R. (1957). The necessary and sufficient conditions of therapeutic personality change. *Journal of Consulting Psychology, 21*(2), 95-103.

Rogers, C. R. (1961). *On becoming a person.* Houghton Mifflin.

Rogers, C. R. (1975). Empathic: An unappreciated way of being. *Counseling Psychologist, 5*(2), 2.

Rogers, C. R. (1980). *A way of being.* Houghton Mifflin.

Rogers, C. R. (1986). Client-centered therapy. In I. L. Kutash & A. Wolf (Eds.), *Psychotherapist's casebook: Theory and technique in the practice of modern therapies.* Jossey-Bass.

Rogers, C. R. (2007). The necessary and sufficient conditions of therapeutic personality change. *Psychotherapy, 44*(3), 240-248.

Rogers, C. R., & Farson, R. E. (1995). Active listening. In D. A. Kolb, J. S. Osland, & I. M. Rubin (Eds.), *The organizational behavior reader* (6th ed., pp. 203-214). Wiley.

Rosinski, P., & Abbott, G. (2016). Intercultural coaching. In J. Passmore (Ed.), *Excellence in coaching: The industry guide* (2nd ed., pp. 175-188). Kogan Page Ltd.

Ruddle, A., & Dilks, S. (2015). Opening up to disclosure. *The Psychologist, 28*, 458-461.

Ruiz, M. A. (2001). *The four agreements: A practical guide to personal freedom* (special). Amber-Allen.

Rutherford, A. (2019). *The systems thinker: Essential thinking skills for solving problems, managing chaos, and creating lasting solutions in a complex world.* VDZ.

Salvi, C., Beeman, M., Bikson, M., McKinley, R., & Grafman, J. (2020). TDCS to the right anterior temporal lobe facilitates insight problem-solving. *Scientific Reports, 10*(1), 1-10.

Scharmer, O. (2007). *Theory U: Leading from the future as it emerges.* SOL Press.

Scharmer, O. (2016). *Theory U: Leading from the future as it emerges* (2nd ed.). Berrett-Kohler.

Scharmer, O. (2018). *The essentials of theory U.* Berrett-Koehler.

Schein, E. H. (2016). *Humble consulting: How to provide real help faster.* Berrett-Koehler Publishers.

Schein, E. H. & Schein, P.A. (2018). *Humble leadership: The power of relationships, openness, and trust.* Berrett-Koehler Publishers.

Schloegl, I. (1976). *The wisdom of the Zen masters.* New Directions Books.

Schneider, K. (2015). Presence: The core contextual factor of effective psychotherapy. *Existential Analysis, 26*(2), 304.

Schön, D. A. (2003). *The reflective practitioner: How professionals think in action.* Ashgate.

Schreckhise, R. (2015). *Spiritual coaching guidebook.* CreateSpace Independent Publishing Platform.

Schumann, A., Meyer, C., Rumpf, H. J., Hannover, W., Hapke, U., & John, U. (2005). Stage of change transitions and processes of change, decisional balance, and self-efficacy in smokers: A transtheoretical model validation using longitudinal data. *Psychology of Addictive Behaviors: Journal of the Society of Psychologists in Addictive Behaviors, 19*, 3-9.

Schwartz, S. H. (2012). An overview of the Schwartz theory of basic values. *Online Readings in Psychology and Culture, 2*(1), 1-20.

Schwarzer, R. (1992). Self-efficacy in the adoption and maintenance of health behaviors: Theoretical approaches and a new model. In R. Schwarzer (Ed.), *Self-efficacy: Thought control of action* (pp. 217-243). Hemisphere.

Schwarzer, R. (2006). *Health action process approach.* http://userpage.fu-berlin.de/health

Seale, S. (2011). *Create a world that works: Tools for personal and global transformation.* Red Wheel/Weiser.

Seligman, M. E. P. (1975). *Helplessness: On depression, development, and death.* Freeman.

Seligman, M. E. P. (2002). *Authentic happiness: Using the new positive psychology to realize your potential for lasting fulfillment.* Simon & Schuster.

Seligman, M. E. P. (2006). *Learned optimism: How to change your mind and your life.* Vintage Press.

Seligman, M. E. P. (2012). *Flourish: A visionary new understanding of happiness and well-being*. Free Press.

Seligman, M. E. P., & Csikszentmihalyi, M. (2000). Positive psychology: An introduction. *American Psychologist, 55*, 5-14.

Selye, H. (1956). *The stress of life*. McGraw-Hill.

Senge, P. M. (2006). *The fifth discipline: The art and practice of the learning organization* (revised). Doubleday/Currency.

Shannahan, K., Shannahan, R., & Bush, A. (2013). Are your salespeople coachable? How salesperson coachability, trait competitiveness, and transformational leadership enhance sales performance. *Journal of the Academy of Marketing Science, 41*(1), 40-54.

Sharpley, C. F., Fairnie, E., Tabary-Collins, E., Bates, R., & Lee, P. (2000). The use of counselor verbal response modes and client-perceived rapport. *Counselling Psychology Quarterly, 13*(1), 99-116.

Shebib, B. (2020). *Choices: Interviewing and counselling skills for Canadians* (7th ed.). Pearson Canada.

Sheehy, G. (1976). *Passages: Predictable crises of adult life*. Dutton.

Sheldon, K. M., Cummins, R., & Kamble, S. (2010). Life balance and well-being: Testing a novel conceptual and measurement approach. *Journal of Personality, 78*(4), 1093-1134.

Sheldon, K. M., & Elliot, A. J. (1998). Not all personal goals are personal: Comparing autonomous and controlled reasons for goals as predictors of effort and attainment. *Personality and Social Psychology, 24*, 546-557.

Sheldon, K. M., & Elliot, A. J. (1999). Goal striving, need satisfaction, and longitudinal well-being: The self-concordance model. *Journal of Personality and Social Psychology, 76*, 482-497.

Sheldon, K. M., & Kasser, T. (1995). Coherence and congruence: Two aspects of personality and integration. *Journal of Personality and Social Psychology, 68*, 531-543.

Shiraev, E. (2014). *A history of psychology: A global perspective*. Sage Publications.

Siegel, D. J. (1999). *The developing mind: Toward a neurobiology of interpersonal experience*. Guilford Press.

Siegel, D. J. (2007). *The mindful brain: Reflection and attunement in the cultivation of well-being* (Norton series on interpersonal neurobiology). W. W. Norton & Company.

Siegel, D. J. (2010). *Mindsight: The new science of personal transformation*. Bantam.

Siegel, D. J. (2012). *The developing mind: How relationships and the brain interact to shape who we are* (2nd ed.). Guilford Press.

Siegel, D. J. (2018). *Aware: The science and practice of presence—The groundbreaking meditation practice*. TarcherPerigee.

Silsbee, D. (2008). *Presence-based coaching: Cultivating self-generative leaders through mind, body, and heart*. Jossey-Bass.

Silsbee, D. (2010). *The mindful coach: Seven roles for facilitating leader development* (2nd ed.). Jossey-Bass.

Sime, C., & Jacob, Y. (2018). Crossing the line? A qualitative exploration of ICF master certified: Coaches' perception of roles, borders and boundaries. *International Coaching Psychology Review, 13*(2), 46-61.

Simone, D. H., McCarthy, P., & Skay, C. L. (1998). An investigation of client and counselor variables that influence likelihood of counselor self-disclosure. *Journal of Counseling and Development, 76*, 174-182.

Singer, T., & Klimecki, O. M. (2014). Empathy and compassion. *Current Biology, 24*(18), 875-878.

Skibbins, D. (2007). *Becoming a life coach: A complete workbook for therapists*. New Harbinger.

Skinner, B. F. (1938). *The behavior of organisms: An experimental analysis*. Appleton-Century-Crofts.

Skinner, B. F. (1953). *Science and human behavior*. Macmillan.

Smith, B. W. (2018). *Positive psychology for your hero's journey: Discovering true and lasting happiness*. CreateSpace Independent Publishing Platform.

Smith, H. (1991). *The world's religions: Our great wisdom traditions*. HarperCollins.

Smith, J. V. (2007). *Therapist into coach*. Open University Press.

Sommer, R., & Iachini, T. (2017). Personal space. *Reference module in neuroscience and biobehavioral psychology*, 1-3.

Sommers-Flanagan, J., & Sommers-Flanagan, R. (2015). *Clinical interviewing* (5th ed.). Wiley.

Sonesh, S. C., Coultas, C. W., Lacerenza, C. N., Marlow, S. L., Benishek, L. E., & Salas, E. (2015). The power of coaching: A meta-analytic investigation. *Coaching: An International Journal of Theory, Research and Practice, 8*(2), 73-95.

Spence, G. B., Cavanagh, M. J., & Grant, A. M. (2008). The integration of mindfulness training and health coaching: An exploratory study. *Coaching: An International Journal of Theory, Research and Practice, 1*(2), 145-163.

Stalikas, A., & Fitzpatrick, M. (1995). Client good moments: An intensive analysis of a single session. *Canadian Journal of Counseling, 29*(2), 160-175.

Stalikas, A., & Fitzpatrick, M. (1996). Relationships between counselor interventions, client experiencing, and emotional expressiveness: An exploratory study. *Canadian Journal of Counselling, 30*(4), 262-271.

Steel, P. (2011). *The procrastination equation: How to stop putting things off and start getting stuff done*. Vintage Canada.

Steele, D. (2011). *From therapist to coach: How to leverage your clinical expertise to build a thriving coaching practice*. Wiley.

Stelter, R. (2013). *A guide to third generation coaching: Narrative-collaborative theory and practice.* Springer Science & Business Media.

Stelter, R. (2014). Third generation coaching: Reconstructing dialogues through collaborative practice and a focus on values. *International Coaching Psychology Review, 9*(1), 51-66.

Stelter, R. (2018). *The art of dialogue in coaching: Towards transformative exchange.* Routledge.

Stiles-Shields, C., Kwasny, M. J., Cai, X., & Mohr, D. C. (2014). Therapeutic alliance in face-to-face and telephone-administered cognitive behavioral therapy. *Journal of Consulting and Clinical Psychology, 82*(2), 349-354.

Stober, D. R. (2006). Coaching from the humanistic perspective. In D. R. Stober & A. M. Grant (Eds.), *Evidence-based coaching handbook: Putting best practices to work for your client* (pp. 17-50). Wiley.

Stober, D. R., & Grant, A. M. (2006). *Evidence-based coaching handbook: Putting best practices to work for your client.* John Wiley & Sons, Inc.

Stoddard, J., Afari, N., & Hayes, S. (2014). *The big book of ACT metaphors: A practitioner's guide to experiential exercises and metaphors in acceptance and commitment therapy.* New Harbinger Publications.

Stoltzfus, T. (2008). *Coaching questions: A coach's guide to powerful asking skills.* Coach22 Bookstore LLC.

Strachan, D. (2007). *Making questions work: A guide to how and what to ask for facilitators, consultants, managers, coaches, and educators.* Jossey-Bass.

Strean, H. (1986). Countertransference. Haworth Press.

Stringer, E. T. (2007). *Action research* (3rd ed.). SAGE Publications.

Stroh, D. P. (2015). *Systems thinking for social change: A practical guide to solving complex problems, avoiding unintended consequences, and achieving lasting results.* Chelsea Green Publishing.

Strozzi-Heckler, R. (2014). *The art of somatic coaching: Embodying skillful action, wisdom, and compassion.* North American Books.

Subirana, M. (2016). *Flourishing together: Guide to appreciative inquiry coaching.* John Hunt Publishing.

Sue, D. W., Bernier, J. E., Durran, A., Feinberg, L., Pedersen, P., Smith, E. J., & Vasquez-Nuttall, E. (1982). Position paper: Cross-cultural counseling competencies. *The Counseling Psychologist, 10*, 45-52.

Sue, D. W., Sue, D., Neville, H. A., & Smith, L. (2019). *Counseling the culturally diverse: Theory and practice* (8th ed.). Wiley.

Suinn, R. M. (1986). *Seven steps to peak performance: The mental training manual for athletes.* Huber.

Surya Das, L. *Awakening the Buddha within: Tibetan wisdom for the Western world.* Broadway Books.

Sweet, C., & Noones, J. (1989). Factors associated with premature termination from outpatient treatments. *Hospital and Community Psychiatry, 40*(9), 947-951.

Talley, L., & Temple, S. (2015). How leaders influence followers through the use of nonverbal communication. *Leadership and Organization Development Journal, 36*(1), 69-80.

Tamietto, M., & Gelder, B. (2010). Neural bases of the non-conscious perception of emotional signals. *Nature Reviews Neuroscience, 11*(10), 697-709.

Tamminen, A. W., & Smaby, M. H. (1981). Helping counselors learn to confront. *Personnel and Guidance Journal, 60*, 41-45.

Tang, Y. Y., Ma, Y., Wang, J., Fan, Y., Feng, S., Lu, Q., & Posner, M. I. (2007). Short-term meditation training improves attention and self-regulation. *Proceedings of the National Academy of Sciences, 104*(43), 17152-17156.

Tangney, J. P. (2000). Humility: Theoretical perspectives, empirical findings and directions for future research. *Journal of Social and Clinical Psychology, 19*, 70-82.

Taylor, M. (1986). Learning for self-direction in the classroom: The pattern of a transition process. *Studies in Higher Education, 11*(1), 55-72.

Telle, N. T., & Pfister, H. R. (2016). Positive empathy and prosocial behavior: A neglected link. *Emotion Review, 8*(2), 154-163.

Tervalon, M., & Murray-García, J. (1998). Cultural humility versus cultural competence: A critical distinction in defining physician training outcomes in multicultural education. *Journal of Health Care for the Poor and Underserved, 9*(2), 117-125.

Thompson, E. L., Bird, G., & Catmur, C. (2019). Conceptualizing and testing action understanding. *Neuroscience and Biobehavioral Reviews, 105*, 106-114.

Tolle, E. (2003). *Stillness speaks.* New World Library.

Tonkov, G. (2019). *Feel to heal: Releasing trauma through body awareness and breathwork practice* (K. Donnan, Ed.).

Toogood, K. (2012). Strengthening coaching: An exploration of the mindset of executive coaches using strengths-based coaching. *International Journal of Evidence Based Coaching and Mentoring 6* (Special Issue), 72-87.

Topp, E. M. (2006). *Presence-based coaching: The practice of presence in relation to goal-directed activity* (Unpublished doctoral dissertation). Institute of Transpersonal Psychology.

Torneke, N., & Hayes, S. (2017). *Metaphor in practice: A professional's guide to using the science of language in psychotherapy.* Context Press.

Trautwein, F. M., Kanske, P., Böckler, A., & Singer, T. (2020). Differential benefits of mental training types for attention, compassion, and theory of mind. *Cognition, 194*, 104039.

Treace, B. M. (2019). *Wake up: How to practice Zen Buddhism.* Rockridge Press.

Trenholm, S., Jensen, A., & Hambly, H. (2010). *Interpersonal communication: A guided tour for Canadians.* Oxford University Press.

Truax, C. B., & Carkhuff, R. R. (1967). *Toward effective counseling and psychotherapy: Training and practice.* Aldine.

Turock, A. (1980). Immediacy in counseling: Recognizing clients' unspoken messages. *Personnel and Guidance Journal, 59,* 168-172.

Vainio, O. P. (2016). *Virtue: An introduction to theory and practice.* Cascade Books.

Vallerand, R. J., & Losier, G. F. (1999). An integrative analysis of intrinsic and extrinsic motivation in sport. *Journal of Applied Sport Psychology, 11,* 142-169.

van Nieuwerburgh, C. (2017). *An introduction to coaching skills: A practical guide* (2nd ed.). SAGE Publications.

VanderPol, L. (2019). *A shift in being: The art and practices of deep transformational coaching.* Imaginal Light Publishing.

Varela, F. J., Thompson, E., & Rosch, E. (1992). *The embodied mind: Cognitive science and human experience.* MIT Press.

Velandia, C. (2019). *Wake up! How to get out of your mind, stop living on autopilot, and start choosing your best life.* Claudia Velandia, Canada.

Virgili, M. (2013). Mindfulness-based coaching: Conceptualization, supporting evidence and emerging applications. *International Coaching Psychology Review, 8*(2), 40-57.

Vogler, C. (2007). *The writer's journey: Mythic structure for writers* (3rd ed.). Michael Wiese Productions.

Vohs, K. D., & Baumeister, R. F. (2011). *Handbook of self-regulation: Research, theory, and applications* (2nd ed.). Guilford Press.

Vohs, K. D., & Baumeister, R. F. (2016). *Handbook of self-regulation: Research, theory, and applications* (3rd ed.). Guilford Press.

Vohs, K. D., Baumeister, R. F., Schmeichel, B. J., Twenge, J. M., Nelson, N. M., & Tice, D. M. (2014). Making choices impairs subsequent self-control: A limited-resource account of decision making, self-regulation, and active initiative. *Journal of Personality and Social Psychology, 94,* 883-898.

Von Bertalanffy, L. (1968). *General system theory: Foundations, development applications* (revised). Braziller.

Vozzola, E. C. (2014). *Moral development: Theory and applications.* Routledge.

Wachtel, P. L. (1993). *Therapeutic communication: Principles and effective practice.* Guilford Press.

Walker, L. E. (1979). *The battered woman.* Harper Collins.

Wallis, G. (2004). *The Dhammapada: Verses on the way.* The Modern Library.

Walsh, J. F. (2007). *Endings in clinical practice: Effective closure in diverse settings* (2nd ed.). Lyceum Books.

Wampold, B. (2015). How important are the common factors in psychotherapy? An update. *World Psychiatry, 14*(3), 270-277.

Watkins, C. E., Jr. (1986). Transference phenomena in the counseling situation. *The Personnel and Guidance Journal, 62*(4), 206-210.

Weger, H., Jr., Castle, G. R., & Emmett, M. C. (2010). Active listening in peer interviews: The influence of message paraphrasing on perceptions of listening skill. *International Journal of Listening, 24*(1), 34-49.

Weinberg, R. S., & Gould, D. (2019). *Foundations of sport and exercise psychology* (7th ed.). Human Kinetics.

Weiner, I. B., & Bornstein, R. F. (2009). *Principles of psychotherapy: Promoting evidence-based psychodynamic practice* (3rd ed.). Wiley.

Welfel, E. R. (2012). *Ethics in counseling and psychotherapy: Standards, research, and emerging issues* (5th ed.). Wadsworth/Cengage.

Whaley, A. L., & Davis, K. E. (2007). Cultural competence and evidence-based practice in mental health services: A complementary perspective. *American Psychologist, 62,* 563-574.

White, M. (2007). *Maps of narrative practice.* W.W. Norton & Company.

Whitmore, J. (1992). *Coaching for performance: A practical guide to growing your own skills.* Brealey.

Whitmore, J. (2017). *Coaching for performance: The principles and practice of coaching and leadership* (5th ed.). Quercus.

Whitworth, L., Kimsey-House, H., Kimsey-House, K., & Sandahl, P. (2007). *Co-active coaching* (2nd ed.). Davies-Black.

Widiger, T. A. (Ed.). (2017). *The Oxford handbook of the five factor model.* Oxford University Press.

Wilber, K. (2000a). *A brief theory of everything: An integral vision for business, politics, science and spirituality.* Shambhala.

Wilber, K. (2000b). *Integral psychology: Consciousness, spirit, psychology, therapy.* Shambhala.

Wilber, K. (2006). *Integral spirituality: A startling new role for religion in the modern and postmodern world.* Integral Books.

Wilber, K., Patten, T., Leonard, A., & Morelli, M. (2008). *Integral life practice: A 21st-century blueprint for physical health, emotional balance, mental clarity, and spiritual awakening.* Integral Books.

Williams, P. (2012). Looking back to see the future: The influence of humanistic and transpersonal psychology on coaching psychology today. *International Coaching Psychology Review, 7*(2), 223-236.

Williams, P., & Davis, D. C. (2007). *Therapist as life coach: An introduction for counselors and other helping professionals.* W. W. Norton & Company.

Williams, R. M. (1979). Change and stability in values and value systems: A sociological perspective. In M. Rokeach (Ed.), *Understanding human values*. The Free Press.

Wilson, C. (2007). *Best practice in performance coaching: A handbook for leaders, coaches, HR professionals and organizations*. Kogan Page Ltd.

Winnicott, D. W. (1958). The capacity to be alone. *International Journal of Psychoanalysis, 39*, 416-420.

Wise, W., & Littlefield, C. (2017). *Ask powerful questions: Create conversations that matter* (2nd ed.). CreateSpace Independent Publishing Platform.

Woods, D. W., Miltenberger, R. G., & Flach, A. D. (1996). Habits, tics, and stuttering: Prevalence and relation to anxiety and somatic awareness. *Behavior Modification, 20*(2), 216-225.

Xing, Y., & Sims, D. (2011). *Leadership, Daoist wu wei and reflexivity: Flow, self-protection and excuse in Chinese bank managers' leadership practice: Management learning*. https://doi.org/10.1177/1350507611409659

Yalom, I. D. (1980). *Existential psychotherapy*. Basic Books.

Yeager, K. A., & Bauer-Wu, S. (2013). Cultural humility: Essential foundation for clinical researchers. *Applied Nursing Research: ANR, 26*(4). https://doi.org/10.1016/j.apnr.2013.06.008

Young, M. E. (2017). *Learning the art of helping: Building blocks and techniques* (6th ed.). Pearson.

Zeidan, F., Johnson, S. K., Diamond, B. J., David, Z., & Goolkasian, P. (2010). Mindfulness meditation improves cognition: Evidence of brief mental training. *Consciousness and Cognition. 19(2)*, 597-605.

Zilcha-Mano, S. (2017). Is the alliance really therapeutic? Revisiting this question in light of recent methodological advances. *American Psychologist, 72*(4), 311-325.

Zur, O. (2009). Therapeutic boundaries and effective therapy: Exploring the relationships. In W. O'Donahue & S. R. Graybar (Eds.), *Handbook of contemporary psychotherapy: Towards an improved understanding of effective psychotherapy* (pp. 341-355). SAGE Publications.

INDEX

Note: The italicized *f* and *t* following page numbers refer to figures and tables, respectively.

ABOUT THE AUTHOR

James Gavin was trained as a psychologist, receiving his doctoral degree in psychology from New York University. He taught psychology at Colorado State University and eventually moved to Montreal, where he presently serves as full professor in the Department of Applied Human Sciences and Director of the Centre for Human Relations and Community Studies at Concordia University. Within Concordia's John Molson School of Business, he directs and instructs in an ICF-ACTP coach certification program, as well as directing the LEAD Coaching Program for the Executive MBA program. He has been recognized as a master certified coach (MCC) by the International Coaching Federation and an integral master coach (IMC) by Integral Coaching Canada. He is strongly interested in the somatic aspects of human development and personal change, with emphasis on the somatic awareness and practices of coaches. Dr. Gavin teaches coaching and group dynamics in the master's program in Human Systems Intervention. Additionally, he is engaged in research on coaching issues, and enjoys rich practice experiences with individual and organizational clients. His long-term interests in the practices of Aikido, Iaido, meditation, and yoga inform his life's work.